Lecture Notes in Computer Science

Edited by G. Goos and J. Hartmanis

Advisory Board: W. Brauer   D. Gries   J. Stoer

Gerard Wijers   Sjaak Brinkkemper
Tony Wasserman (Eds.)

Advanced Information Systems Engineering

6th International Conference, CAiSE '94
Utrecht, The Netherlands, June 6-10, 1994
Proceedings

Springer-Verlag

Berlin Heidelberg New York
London Paris Tokyo
Hong Kong Barcelona
Budapest

Series Editors

Gerhard Goos
Universität Karlsruhe
Postfach 69 80
Vincenz-Priessnitz-Straße 1
D-76131 Karlsruhe, Germany

Juris Hartmanis
Cornell University
Department of Computer Science
4130 Upson Hall
Ithaca, NY 14853, USA

Volume Editors

Gerard Wijers
ID Research B. V.
Kastanjelaan 4, 3833 AN Leusden, The Netherlands

Sjaak Brinkkemper
Department of Computer Science, University of Twente
P. O. Box 217, 7500 AE Enschede, The Netherlands

Tony Wasserman
Interactive Development Environments Inc.
595 Market Street, 10th Floor, San Francisco, CA 94105, USA

CR Subject Classification (1991): H.2, D.2

ISBN 3-540-58113-8 Springer-Verlag Berlin Heidelberg New York
ISBN 0-387-58113-8 Springer-Verlag New York Berlin Heidelberg

CIP data applied for

© Springer-Verlag Berlin Heidelberg 1994
Printed in Germany

Typesetting: Camera-ready by author
SPIN: 10131251   45/3140-543210 - Printed on acid-free paper

Preface

CAiSE•94 is the sixth International Conference on Advanced Information Systems Engineering. It is hosted in Utrecht, the Netherlands, and extends the tradition of previous years, when CAiSE was held in Stockholm (Sweden), Trondheim (Norway), Manchester (England) and Paris (France). The CAiSE conferences are a platform for researchers and practitioners from academia and industry to discuss and exchange new developments in methods, techniques and tools to realize advanced information systems.

These proceedings present 30 papers that were selected by the programme committee. The programme committee was chosen among well reputed international researchers and from key professionals in Dutch industrial and consultancy companies. The programme committee reviewed 130 papers, each paper being reviewed by four referees who were specialists in the relevant topics. The papers were selected on originality, technical quality, relevance and quality of presentation. The authors of the 30 papers selected come from 15 different countries. We would like to acknowledge the efforts of the authors in making an excellent scientific contribution to the field and of the programme committee members and additional referees who carried out the reviewing process in a most thorough manner.

The papers presented show an increasing interest in changing, improving and supporting the management of IS development organisations. We have sessions on 'development process support', 'management and quality', 'reuse', and 'method engineering'. In the area of developments in conceptual modelling, three main streams are covered in the three sessions: 'object oriented requirements engineering', 'behaviour modelling', and 'formal IS modelling'. A third key area for the CAiSE•94 conference is advanced technology; we have sessions on 'workflow management', 'advanced development tools', and 'advanced database engineering'.

The conference programme not only includes sessions presenting the papers in these proceedings. It is complemented with keynote speakers, panels, workshops, tutorials, an exhibition, product presentations, poster sessions and demonstrations. Therefore the CAiSE•94 conference offers a complete set of activities for both practitioners and researchers. The CAiSE series has established itself as a truly international event on advanced information systems engineering.

April 1994

Gerard Wijers (Programme Chair)
Sjaak Brinkkemper (Organising Chair)
Tony Wasserman (General Chair)

Programme Committee

Additonal referees

S. Even	E. Lindenerona	F. Semnek
C. Francalanci	O.I. Lindland	C. Sernadas
M. Freeman	Liu	K.L. Siau
J.J. de Graaff	P. Löhr-Richter	S. Sisoid
L. Groenewegen	N. Loukopoulos	L. Somers
G. Grosz	N. Maiden	W.W. Song
N. Habra	M. Moreno	I.G. Sprinkhuizen
J.L. Hainaut	J.L.H. Oei	C.N. Taylor
F. Harmsen	O. Parchet	O. de Troyer
P. Hartel	I. Petrounias	A. Vailly
D. Heddehi	V. Plihon	A. Verbraeck
A. Heuer	N. Prat	E.M. Verharen
A.H.M. ter Hofstede	R. Prins	T.F. Verhoef
G.J. Houben	N. van der Rijst	S. Vhlund
P. Johannesson	D. Roelants	M. Voorhoeve
S. Joosten	P. Rosengren	Th.P. van der Weide
P. Katalagarianos	H.D. Ruys	Weigand
T. Khammaci	M. Sakkinen	C. Woo
Y. Kokou	K. Schewe	P. Wodon
S. Laurent	J. Schmitt	M. Yang
Lautemann	P.Y. Schobbens	X. Ye
A. Le Grand	A.H. Seltveit	

Organisation Committee

Sjaak Brinkkemper	Frank Harmsen	Han Oei
Eugene Boogaart	Arnold van Ittersum	Mirjam Knoll
Rolf Engmann	Stef Joosten	Rob van de Weg
Paul Grefen	Sandor Kloos	

Table of Contents

Method Engineering

Advanced Database Engineering

Information Systems Modernization

Anthony I. Wasserman

Interactive Development Environments, Inc. (IDE)
San Francisco, CA 94105 USA

Abstract

There is a huge investment in existing software systems, with organizations spending huge sums of money on the maintenance of old systems. As organizations transform the way that they do business, they must also transform their "legacy systems" to take advantage of these fundamental changes in technology. Lowering costs by moving applications to modern platforms and development approaches is a critical need for most organizations.

The need for modernization is driven by fundamental changes in the computing industry, including the movement from proprietary systems to open systems, the movement of applications from mainframes to client-server environments, and the resulting change from alphanumeric to graphical user interfaces. The transition to open client-server computing environments is occurring very rapidly, and has led to widespread adoption of standards for cross-platform networking and database access.

Modernization of systems is a complex process, with a bewildering set of possible options. Information systems managers often have essential applications running on their mainframes, and must therefore decide how to support their existing systems. There are many technical and non-technical ideas that address software modernization. These include, but are not limited to:

1) reverse engineering of source code, file, and database structures;
2) source to source translations (e.g., COBOL to C++);
3) rehosting the application by recompiling the source code on another machine, and;
4) redevelopment of the application, taking advantage of new hardware and software technology to create object-oriented client-server systems.

Modernization of application development often involves use of a different process for system development, as well as a new set of tools. This presentation provides an overview of issues in information systems modernization, beginning with the underlying technology trends and then describing various approaches to modernization.

Planning Support for Cooperating Transactions in EPOS

Reidar Conradi* Marianne Hagaseth
Norwegian Institute of Technology (NTH), Trondheim, Norway

Chunnian Liu
Beijing Polytechnic University, Beijing, P.R. China

Abstract

This paper describes a way to reduce the number of conflicts that may arise when several users cooperate to solve a task using a common database. The manual interaction between the users are made easier by supporting the project managers in planning of activities. Based on some interaction and an initial project division, we can analyse the connections between the activities, given as the result of impact analysis. Based on this, the project manager can choose to adjust the initial partitioning to reduce the dependencies between activities.

The impact analysis can also be used as a help for the project manager to schedule the activities. By doing this, more of the conflicts can be avoided.

However, conflicts cannot be completely avoided if some degree of concurrency should be achieved. The cooperation between users must be handled by allowing close interaction during the activities.

1 Introduction

The paper reports work on automatic planning of cooperating transactions in the EPOS Process Support Environment. Such assistance can be used by project managers to help organise software production (development, maintenance), according to incoming change-requests and according to the product/version space[1] of the software and related resources (tools, humans). It is a formidable task to manually "navigate" in the space of possible actions here.

The goal is to have powerful, low-level database mechanisms, e.g. propagation rules and locking. These can be driven by more high-level policies, e.g. communication protocols. These again are instrumented and/or generated from domain knowledge (Section 5). All this will be incorporated by an enlarged EPOS transaction model. The current paper reports work on a Transaction Planning Assistant to help organizing breakdown, scheduling and cooperation of subtransactions based on domain-specific information. An analogy to our transaction planner is AI-based program generators for (concurrent) programs. More classic project-planning to manage budgets, timing, and human resources are not considered.

2 Related work

Traditional DBMSes have a strict consistency concept, coupled to serializable (short and system-executed) transactions. For distributed and network-connected DBMSes, there is a two-phase commit protocol.

Software engineering involves many concurrent actors and long update times. Since updates may involve hard-to-predict and partly overlapping versions or subsystems, traditional locking procedures will cause intolerable delays. Software Engineering (like CAD/CAM and related fields) therefore needs non-serializable (long and user-executed) transactions (often called design transactions). This may lead to update conflicts, which later must be reconciled by version *merging*. But sometimes *no* merge is needed, because of independent development paths.

---

*Dept. of Computer Systems and Telematics, Norwegian Institute of Technology (NTH), N-7034 Trondheim, Norway. Phone: +47 73 593444, Fax: +47 73 594466, Email: conradi@idt.unit.no.
[1]The product space of the software is the actual software objects, and the relations between such objects. Version space of the software is the actual versions selected of the software product.

Many newer transaction models (e.g. in Gandalf, Marvel, COO from Nancy), use nested transactions, and these must handle both inter- and intra-transaction coordination. Description of other transaction models for cooperation is found in [1, 2, 3, 4].

Digression: When *all* transactions in an unversioned DBMS commit, there is *one* canonical and consistent version of the database (DB). In contrast, a versioned database maintains and controls *permanently* and *mutually inconsistent* (sub-)databases!

Algorithms to ensure consistency in multi-layer storage systems (cache coherence, synchrony between local and global databases) resemble those used for data exchange between long transactions. Work on crowd control and groupware (CSCW) is also related, but with focus on team organization and communication, and often not considering product/version structures (except graphic group-editors). There is often a globally persistent and shared blackboard, although there may be local and temporary workspaces. We can mention NSE from Sun [5], SPICE at CMU, and Lotus Notes, all with a central server and local database copies, but where the policies for broadcasting updates are rather strict. Experience from NSE indicates that there are few Write-Write conflicts (less that 1 per mill).

There has been much interest in database *triggers* [6]. That is, to have an *active* DBMS, which automatically performs consistency checks and side-effect propagation according to explicit event-condition-action rules. We must also consider "inter-version" propagation included. negotiation about propagation rules, and that side-effect propagation can be very time-consuming and presume unobtainable access rights. Classic DBMS triggers inside short transactions are therefore insufficient. A possible but not satisfactory solution is to use *notifiers* to handle free-standing or delayed actions.

Simple versioning systems, like SCCS [7] and Make [8], offer no help for cooperating transactions. Adele [9] has high-level configuration descriptions and some workspace control, but only triggers to start rebuilds. PCMS [10] has document-flow templates, and Mercury [11] uses attribute grammars to guide simple change propagation. ISTAR [12] has subcontracts, but little formal cooperation. NSE is strong on workspace control, and DSEE [13] has some support for handling change requests. Few DBMS systems for software engineering can adequately treat cooperating transactions, or can handle configurations as conceptual entities both inside a database and in an external workspace.

Typical domain-independent, non-linear planning algorithms can be found in IPEM [14] and TWEAK [15]. TWEAK gives a formal treatment to the subject of non-linear planning. IPEM tries to integrate planning, execution and monitoring in fine granularity, mainly for exception handling. Both TWEAK and IPEM address the non-linear planning problem in a domain-independent way, with examples mainly from the Block World domain (robot applications).

Most AI planning rules have no formal Input/Output specifications, which are essential for software development tasks. Project customisation can be done by simple rule grouping and substitution, even if the rule space is rather flat. Process evolution can generally be supported by replanning and re-execution.

In the rest of this paper, we will first summarize the EPOS background, and then present the planning extensions for cooperating transactions.

3 The EPOS context

EPOS is a Software Process Environment [16]. Internal process models are represented as object-oriented and typed networks, being automatically (re)built. The task networks and all associated model information reside in a sub-database under the versioned EPOS–DB [17] [18]. Database accesses executed by above tasks are regulated by the embedding sub-transaction/sub-project [19]. The process model is expressed by an object-oriented and reflective process modeling language, called SPELL [20].

3.1 Consistency Model

The underlying consistency model for impact analysis is that consistency must be related to the whole product structure, not only to single objects. In the EPOS–DB, consistency of single objects is easily achieved since each EPOS–transaction maintains its own copy of the object. At the commit time, either the whole object or none of it, is reflected in the database, ensuring that each single object always is consistent as viewed by the database. However, when the relations between objects are taken into account, the definition and maintenance of consistency becomes much more complicated. The problem is caused by the following:

- Overlaps in the set of objects that are accessed:

  There may be overlaps between the set of objects accessed by two different, concurrent[2] EPOS–transactions. This means that two objects accessed by two concurrent EPOS–transactions may be consistent when viewed separate, but inconsistent, when the relationship between the objects is taken into account.

- Different semantics on the relations:

  Maintenance of consistency in the database is difficult because of the semantics of the relations between objects. This problem is more difficult than just having referential integrity in a relational database. By referential integrity, the database can ensure that all tuples referenced in a foreign key field exists in some other tables. However, relations in an object–oriented model can have different semantics, thus, such simple rules cannot be used to maintain consistency. The best we can do is to follow the relations, and notify the users about possible inconsistencies that may have arisen due to changes to some of the objects. Then, it is up to the application to decide what actions must be taken to maintain the consistency.

The result of this is the following definition of consistency, viewed from the database:

1. A single, isolated object is always consistent viewed from the database, since every transaction maintains its own copy of the object.

2. Several, related objects are consistent if the database ensures that every changes are notified to the affected transactions, and if each owner of a transaction has had the the possibility to compensate for the updates.

4 Cooperating transactions in EPOS

EPOS–DB offers nested and long (non-serializable) transactions in a client-server architecture. Each internal database transaction is associated to a `Project` task and to an external file-based workspace. A transaction operates on a given database *version* "slice" (the visible sub-database), selected by a *version-choice* serving as a read filter. The transaction also specifies the scope of local changes, selected by a *version-ambition*, i.e. which other database versions might be impacted. The version-choice and the version-ambition describe a part of the *version space*, and are intentionally expressed as sets of "option" bindings. An ambition implies a *write lock* on the associated version subspaces (sub-DBs), and with access only to product subspaces (sub-products) within these versions. However, we are not constraining access to whole instances, only to versions of these instances.

The relevant part of the *product space* is described through an intentional *readset* (a set of root components and a set of directed relation types for transitive closures) and an extensional *writeset* (enumeration). Components may have normal read/write locks.

The above version- and product space descriptions are part of the *workorder* for the associated project task. In addition comes process-related information (tools, humans, time-constraints) and given cooperation protocols.

A child transaction overlaps and constrains that of its parent, and possibly overlaps that of its siblings. Transaction *overlap* is primarily defined in the version space by overlapping ambitions. In case of version overlap (no version overlap means classic variants), it is interesting also to consider product overlap.

After child commit, changes are propagated to the parent, which must handle possible update conflicts between the children, using e.g. policies like Rollback (intolerable), Priority (the last one wins?), Access locks (classic access locks), Optimistic (soft locks with notifiers), followed by Integration/reconciliation

---

[2]Concurrent means that the transactions are overlapping in time.

(negotiation, merging) etc. Clearly, such update conflicts will disappear, if strict serialization and locking are globally enforced. However, this will cause excessive waiting among developers. Thus, pre-commit cooperation is a pragmatic way to prevent, regulate and clarify update conflicts in case of overlaps.

Change propagation occurs in two steps:

1. First, we have to decide mutual version visibility or overlap, and set up (low-level) and pairwise **inter-transaction** protocols for pre-commit negotiation and propagation. That is, to *whom* should inter-transaction cooperation be established, *what* components are involved (granularity, type), *how* (automatic or manual) and *when* (eager or lazy) should it be carried out etc.? The presented planning work aims at giving more high-level support for such coordination.

2. Then, there is conventional **intra-transaction** change propagation regulated by normal task networks, regardless of the source and nature of the change. The existing Planner is used to (re)generate such networks, using domain knowledge in form of task types, product structures etc. [21].

5   High-level Transaction Planning in EPOS

`Project` is the EPOS term for execution environment, from a full scale project to a simple task performed by a single user in his own work environment.

Good planning can reduce the need for manual cooperation between the developers. A Project Manager meta-tool uses its local **Transaction Planning Assistant (TRAPLAS)** to advice the human project manager on this. TRAPLAS tries to minimize dependencies between proposed subprojects, or to minimize the cost of such dependencies, by attempting to:
1) partition an update job into "natural" subprojects,
2) schedule such subprojects, and ·
3) suggest communication patterns, that can be expanded into cooperation protocols.

The planning depends on the readsets and writesets associated with each project. An *impactset* is computed for each pair of transactions to describe their inter-connection. That is, if a component is in the writeset of one transaction and directly or transitively in the readset of another, it belongs to the impactset of the former. Typical relations used to generate the readset and impactset are `FamilyOf` (subsystem hierarchy), `ImplementedBy` (between interface and body), and `DependsOn` with subtypes (general dependencies). Each component and relationship has an associated *weight* and each relationship also a *direction*.

The *domain* knowledge used by TRAPLAS consists of global and local consistency constraints stored in types and meta-types, intentional project goals (e.g. ambitions, writesets), added semantics specially on relations, existing product/task structures, product ownerships, and possibly personnel allocation. This knowledge can be manipulated and versioned on a project basis.

5.1   Project Partitioning

This section describes how impact analysis can be used to support the project manager in the partitioning of a project into subprojects. This project partitioning is done before the actual work starts.

The `Project` type in EPOS–PM has two subtypes, `CompositeProject` and `AtomicProject`. `CompositeProjects` have subprojects, while `AtomicProjects` have not. The projects in EPOS–PM are organised in a hierarchy which follows the transaction hierarchy in EPOS–DB. This is because one EPOS–PM–project is connected to one EPOS–DB–transaction. We assume that the project partitioning continues until the leaf node projects are all atomic. The relation between project and transaction is that each project has one transaction associated with it. Both projects and transactions are organised in a hierarchy so that a project can contain several subprojects and a transaction several subtransactions.

5.1.1   Initial Project Partitioning

In the initial project partitioning, a composite project is divided into *n* subprojects. These subprojects may be either composite projects or atomic projects.

1. How the initial partitioning is determined:

An important question is *how* the initial partitioning of the composite project is determined. This question includes:

(a) Which criteria are used to do the initial partitioning?

If impact analysis is used to reduce the interconnections between the subprojects before the result is presented to the project manager, the initial clustering is not important. However, the project manager may want to use some special strategies for the initial partitioning, even if this may be changed later.

  i. One possibility is to describe the partition in terms of data that is to be accessed by each subproject.

  If each object already has an ownership associated with it, this can be used to define the partitioning. This means that every object must have an owner associated with it, and that each object can have only one owner.

  Another way to partition the data between the subprojects is to follow the subsystem structure. In this case, the ownerships information is not used in the initial project partitioning. However, it can still be used in the impact analysis, for instance included as weights on objects or relationships. This can then be used to compute the interconnection between two projects, and in the next step be used to adjust the initial project division.

  ii. The initial project partitioning could be done based on the tasks that the project consists of. In this case, we would need a way to specify the tasks, and also a way to relate these definitions to the actual data, since the impact analysis needs predefined access sets as input.

(b) How many subsets are created?

If ownership is used, initial project partitioning leads to the same number of subprojects as the number of owners. If the ownerships information is not used, but projects are defined based on substructures, the project manager may define as many subprojects as he wants. If subprojects

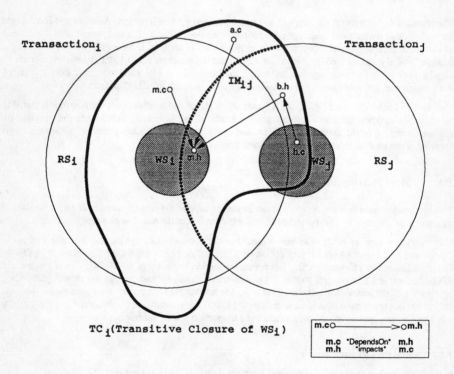

Figure 1: The Result of Impact Analysis.

follows the specified tasks, it is natural to have as many subprojects as tasks, or possibly less if some tasks are executed in the same project.

2. **How the partitioning is described:**

   The projects are described by its readset (RS) and writeset (WS). This means that the project partitioning is described by dividing the readset and writeset into n readsets and writesets. Thus, if a composite project is described by $[RS, WS]$, its subprojects are described by $[RS_i, WS_i]$, for all n subprojects. The readsets of the subprojects may possibly be overlapping. The same is true for the writesets of the subprojects. Also, the writeset of one project may overlap with the readset of another project. Further, we always have that $WS_i \subseteq RS_i$.

   The readset is specified by first listing the objects that the subproject can read. Then, relations from these objects are followed to include all objects that relates to these objects. This step is repeated until no more objects can be added to the readset. The dependency relations we are following are DependsOn, and its subtypes TextIncludes and SourceImports, and the relation ImplementedBy. For instance, if a module x is in RS and x DependsOn module y, or y is ImplementedBy x, then y is added to RS. In addition, relations in the product structure are followed, for instance, FamilyOf and ComponentOf.

   The writeset is specified by just listing the actual objects that are accessible for writing.

3. **How the interconnection between subprojects is described:**

   The following kinds of overlaps can arise due to the partitioning of the readset and writeset of the composite project:

   (a) $RS_i \cap RS_j \neq \emptyset$:

   Overlaps in the two readsets causes no problems as long as none of the common objects are updated.

   (b) $RS_i \cap WS_j \neq \emptyset$:

   The transactions can still execute in isolation, even if their readsets and writesets overlap. However, certain sequences of reads and writes to the common objects will lead to inconsistencies. By inconsistency, we mean that the transactions are interleaved in a non–isolated way, and that a transaction are allowed to read data changed by another transaction before it is committed. One sequence of accesses that leads to inconsistency is a read by $Transaction_i$, followed by a write by $Transaction_j$, followed by a read by $Transaction_i$. Another sequence is a write done by $Transaction_i$, followed by a read by $Transaction_j$, followed by a write by $Transaction_i$[3]. Since we allow these sequences to happen, every overlap of readsets and writesets are handled as possible conflicts when impact analysis is done in the project partitioning.

   (c) $WS_i \cap WS_j \neq \emptyset$:

   Overlaps between the two writesets may cause inconsistencies for certain sequences of access. This sequence is basically a write by $Transaction_i$, followed by a write by $Transaction_j$, followed by a write by $Transaction_i$[4]. When doing the project partitioning, we do not consider the sequences of operations that can be issued by the transactions. We only consider the overlaps, that is, if there is an overlap between the writesets, we assume that the projects will be interconnected in some way.

5.1.2 Impact Analysis to Improve the Project Partitioning

After the initial project partitioning is done, an improvement in the partitioning is presented to the project manager by doing *Impact Analysis*. The impact analysis computes the interconnection between every pair of subprojects, based on the initial partitioning, and based on *weights* that are put on the relations. The result of Impact Analysis is shown in Figure 1. It shows how $Transaction_i$ is interconnected to $Transaction_j$, that is, how the conflicts between the two transactions impacts $Transaction_j$.

The *interconnection* between two transactions is a way to describe how severe the conflicts are that may arise if the two transactions are executed in parallel, that is, if they are overlapping in time. By adding weights

---

[3] Several reads and writes can be added to these sequences. However, it is still the same two problems.

[4] Several reads and writes can be added to this sequence.

on objects and relations, the possible conflicts can be described as a number. This means that the conflict that may arise by executing these transactions in parallel can be compared with other conflicts. Then, we can present to the project manager which two transactions may lead to most conflicts. *Weights* on relations and object types are used to compute the weight of an impactset. We have that WT_{ij} is the weight of the impactset IM_{ij}.

- The big circles represent the readsets (RS) of the two transactions, with the enclosed writesets (WS) being shaded circles. This is the input to the impact analysis, together with the relations that are to be traversed.

- TC_i is the transitive closure of WS_i. It denotes the objects which may be influenced by updates made to objects in the writeset WS_i of $Transaction_i$. We call this the full impact of WS_i to the rest of the database, since it includes every object that is related to some object in the writeset. Both the product structure and other relations are traversed to obtain every object that in some way relates to objects in the writeset of $Transaction_i$.

  In Figure 1, TC_i is the area inside the fat lines, which here extends outside the two transactions displayed.

- $IM_{ij} = TC_i \cap RS_j$ is the impact of WS_i on RS_j. It is indicated in Figure 1 as the area between the dotted line and the fat line. We take the intersection between the transitive closure and the readset RS_j to be able to describe the impact of the writeset of $Transaction_i$ on the readset of $Transaction_j$.

  The weight of IM_{ij} is WT_{ij}. This can be presented to the project manager as a measurement of the impact of WS_i on RS_j. Based on this information, he can choose to move one or more of the objects in WS_i to another writeset. Then, impact analysis must be performed once more to compute the new impactsets.

- $IM_i = \cup_{j=1}^n IM_{ij}$, where $i \neq j$ is the total impact of the writeset of $Transaction_i$ on the readset of all other transactions. The impact of WS_i on its own readset is deleted because it is irrelevant for describing the interconnection between $Transaction_i$ and the other transactions. The weight of IM_i is WT_i.

The project manager can use the result of Impact Analysis to manually adjust the initial partitioning by reducing inter-project dependency since one transaction is associated with one project.

The project manager prepares N sub-workorders (sub-WOs) based on the final partitioning of [RS,WS]. A WorkOrder includes a change-request and a configuration description. For each sub-WO, a subtask of $PROJ$ is automatically generated. As the result, a network of subprojects (plus other subtasks such as SchemaManager task etc.) of the project is generated.

5.1.3 Example

An example of the usage of impact analysis is shown in Figures 2 and 3. The notation is the same as in Figure 1. The impactsets are indicated by dotted lines. Figure 2 shows the initial transaction division. $Transaction_1$ has the writeset WS_1 containing a.c, a.h and d.h. The readset RS_1 contains b.h in addition to the objects in the writeset. $Transaction_2$ has the writeset WS_2 containing p.c and b.c, and the readset RS_2 containing b.h and p.h in addition to the objects in the writeset. Further, the figure shows the impactsets IM_{12} and IM_{21}. The impactsets contain the following objects:

- IM_{12}: p.c, p.h, b.c, and b.h.

- IM_{21}: a.c.

The impactset IM_{12} is found by taking the intersection between TC_1 and RS_2. When the transitive closure TC_1 is computed, the edges are follwed in the reverse direction.

The project manager can choose to change the writesets to try to reduce the impact between the transactions. In Figure 3, the object d.h has been moved from WS_1 to WS_2. The new impactsets contain the following objects:

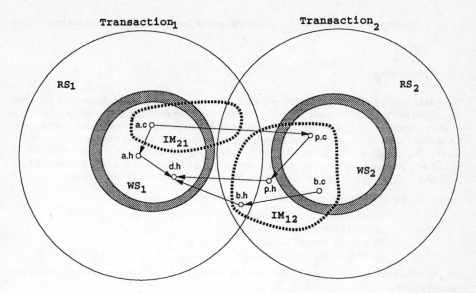

Figure 2: Example: Initial Transaction Division.

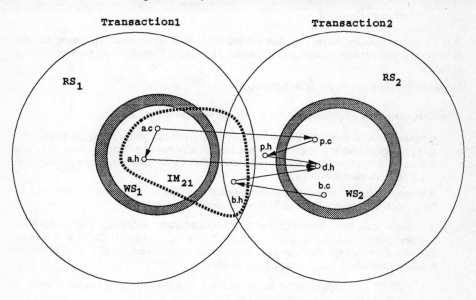

Figure 3: Example: Refined Transaction Division.

- IM_{12}: $\emptyset$

- IM_{21}: a.c, a.h and b.h.

This means that the reorganizing of the writesets has reduced the dependencies between the two transactions. What the impact analysis does, is to compute the actual impactsets, which are then used by the project manager to find a better transaction division.

The effect of changing the writesets of the transactions is that the definition of the associated projects is changed. This changing is done to find the projects that leads to as few conflicts between the projects as possible. In this way, we can use the product structure to construct a project structure with fewer inter–project conflicts.

5.2 Scheduling

The $PROJECT$ owner does further scheduling of the subprojects, using advice from Impact Analysis. Note that optimal scheduling of serial or cooperative transactions, based on more detailed read/write patterns, is a NP-complete problem [22]. Also note that the partitioning decided above, is not independent of scheduling, if optimal solutions are sought, see below examples. For instance, we can commit small and more important changes first (serialization!). We can also run "well-balanced" and mutually dependent transactions in parallel with proper coordination. Alternatively, we can run "tricky" updates in a strict sequence (if both WT_{ij} and WT_{ji} are big), or apply temporary separation (as variants) followed by later merge jobs.

For instance, consider subtransactions T1 and T2, scheduled as:

T1; T2;	(serial: T2 is based on T1's work)
T2; T1;	(serial: T1 is based on T2's work)
T1 ‖ T2;	(later merge: merge(T1,T2))
T1 ⇔ T2;	(cooperative, thus no later merge)

The previous impact analysis is used for such planning, although we foresee a strong interaction with the human project manager.

5.3 Cooperation Protocol

Here we have to negotiate, maintain and later interpret rather low-level protocols, P_{ij}, among each pair of cooperating (overlapping) transactions (subprojects). Only atomic transactions need to have exchange protocols.

The protocol contains information on the following items:

- **Granularity**: e.g. simple instances of selected types vs. entire subproducts.

- **Coupling**[5], or when to receive. This may be: Eager where all changes are propagated immediately; Lazy (recommended) to propagate or promote changes after manual confirmation from the causing transaction; or Delay-other to delay propagation till after *other's* check-in/commit, or delay them to just before *own* commit (Delay-own).

  It is important to be able to delay the effect of other's (pre-committed) updates to a later time, cf. "copy-on-read", although we eventually have to incorporate such changes.

- **Acceptance Rule**, being either AUTO-ACK or MANUAL-ACK. AUTO-ACK requires that a notification always is sent, but no answer expected. This is followed by AUTO-COPY, if there are no conflicting textual updates (otherwise a merging must be performed). MANUAL-ACK requires explicit acknowledge after notification, followed either by:

  1. REJECT: either DELAY as we are not-yet-ready, VETO with proposed changes returned, or CONSTRAIN to limit mutual version visibility.
  2. ACCEPT, with request to AUTO- or MANUAL-COPY, see below.

- **How To Receive**, or workspace connectivity: AUTO-COPY implies a shared file, an indirect file link, or a manipulated search path. MANUAL-COPY means explicit copying and possibly merging.

The protocol may have to be adjusted when new sibling transactions start and commit. Changes in version- or product-overlap may change the network of cooperating transactions, but we will initially assume stability here. The protocol can also be dynamically supplemented, and even re-negotiated in simple cases. Some policies are not independent, e.g. MANUAL-ACK excludes AUTO-COPY.

---

[5]Adapted after Adele's proposed design for workspace coordination [23].

For inter-transaction transfer we partly use an internal database "tunnel" mechanism to do pre-commit propagation of general instances, partly an external mailbox mechanism for simple notifications. Neither of these are described here. In addition comes implicit communication between external workspaces with partly shared files (e.g. through symlinks), also not dealt with here. Reconciliation with merging is not dealt with either.

The idea is to have TRAPLAS in cooperation with the human manager/developer to set up general communication patterns, that can be translated into the above low-level protocols.

To recapitulate: When $Transaction_i$ makes a change, it should eventually propagate or notify the update to all overlapping transactions $Transaction_j$ (i.e. IM_{ij} indicates connections). The idea is to have TRAPLAS, in cooperation with the human manager/developer, to set up general communication patterns, mainly based on the previous impact analysis. These patterns can later be translated into the above, low-level protocols.

Thus, we will apply some heuristics on what seems like reasonable communication patterns. For instance, changes to shared libraries may be propagated rather unconditionally (Eager, AUTO-COPY), changes to project libraries may be propagated when the receiver is ready (Delay-own, MANUAL-COPY), while changes to mutually dependent modules may require much negotiation as indicated above (Lazy, MANUAL-ACK).

5.4 Further decomposition

The previous partition-scheduling-cooperation protocol steps can be repeated during execution of composite projects, until we reach atomic ones doing the real update work.

We have chosen to gradually decompose, not make the full decomposition in one step, even if the latter may give a more optimal plan.

As mentioned in the introduction, we should also consider possible time constraints and available resources, e.g. tools, persons and their availability.

6 Conclusion and Future Work

TRAPLAS serves as a translator between more goal-oriented domain knowledge and the underlying database support. Without such a link, either more rigid update policies have to be enforced, or more flexible cooperation patterns may become unwieldy. Some issues to pursue are the following:

- **Formal transaction modeling:** a more unifying transaction model to formally express domain-knowledge, and considering consistency and user roles. We also need to formalize workspace environments and manage incremental evaluation of configurations.

- **A Transaction Description Language,** integrated or harmonized with SPELL.

- **Version space planning** to manage version-ambitions.

- **Dynamic** writesets, ambitions, protocols etc.

- **Validation** by realistic industrial scenarios.

Acknowledgments

Thanks to the entire EPOS team.

References

[1] Gail E. Kaiser and Calton Pu. Dynamic Restructuring of Transactions. In *[24]*, pages 265–295. Morgan Kaufmann, 1991.

[2] H. Korth, W. Kim, and F. Bancilhon. A Model of CAD Transactions. In *Proceedings of the 11th International Conference on Very Large Databases*, pages 25–33, 1985.

[3] Mary F. Fernandez and Stanley B. Zdonik. Transaction groups: A Model for Controlling Cooperative Work. In *3rd International Workshop on Persistent Object Systems, Their Design, Implementation and Use.*, pages 341–350, january 1989.

[4] Andrea Skarra. Concurrency control for cooperating transactions in an object–oriented database. *SIGPLAN Notices*, 24(4):466–473, february 1989.

[5] Sun Microsystems, Inc., 2550 Garcia Avenue, Mountain View, CA 94043, USA. *Network Software Environment: Reference Manual*, part no: 800-2095 (draft) edition, March 1988.

[6] Michael Stonebraker. Triggers and inference in database systems. In Michael Brodie and John Mylopoulus, editors, *On Knowledge Base Management Systems: Integrating Artifical intelligence and Database Technologies*, pages 297–314. Springer Verlag, 1986.

[7] Mark J. Rochkind. The Source Code Control System. *IEEE Trans. on Software Engineering*, SE-1(4):364–370, 1975.

[8] Stuart I. Feldman. Make — a Program for Maintaining Computer Programs. *Software — Practice and Experience*, 9(3):255–265, March 1979.

[9] Noureddine Belkhatir and Jacky Estublier. Software management constraints and action triggering in the ADELE program database. In *[25]*, pages 44–54, 1987.

[10] Tani Haque and Juan Montes. A Configuration Management System and More (on Alcatel's PCMS). In *[26]*, pages 217–227, January 1988.

[11] Josephine Micallef and Gail E. Kaiser. Version and configuration control in distributed language-based environments. In *[26]*, pages 119–143, 1988.

[12] Mark Dowson. ISTAR — an integrated project support environment. In *[27]*, pages 27–33, 1986.

[13] David B. Leblang and G. McLean. DSEE: Overview and Configuration Management. In J. McDermid, editor, *Integrated Project Support Environments*, pages 10–31. Peter Peregrinus Ltd., London, 1985.

[14] José A. Ambros-Ingerson and Sam Steel. Integrating planning, execution and monitoring. In *Proc. of AAAI'88*, pages 83–88, 1988.

[15] David Chapman. Planning for conjunctive goals. *Artificial Intelligence*, 32:333–377, 1987.

[16] Reidar Conradi, Espen Osjord, Per H. Westby, and Chunnian Liu. Initial Software Process Management in EPOS. *Software Engineering Journal (Special Issue on Software process and its support)*, 6(5):275–284, September 1991.

[17] Anund Lie et al. Change Oriented Versioning in a Software Engineering Database. In *Walter F. Tichy (Ed.): Proc. 2nd International Workshop on Software Configuration Management, Princeton, USA, 25-27 Oct. 1989, 178 p. In ACM SIGSOFT Software Engineering Notes, 14 (7)*, pages 56–65, November 1989.

[18] Bjørn P. Munch, Jens-Otto Larsen, Bjørn Gulla, Reidar Conradi, and Even-André Karlsson. Uniform versioning: The change-oriented model. In *[28]*, pages 188–196, 1993.

[19] Reidar Conradi and Carl Chr. Malm. Cooperating Transactions against the EPOS Database. In *Peter H. Feiler (Ed.): "Proceedings of the 3rd International Workshop on Software Configuration Management" (SCM3), Trondheim, 12–14 June 1991, 166 p. ACM Press Order no. 594910.*, pages 98–101, June 1991.

[20] Reidar Conradi et al. Design, use, and implementation of SPELL, a language for software process modeling and evolution. In *[29]*, pages 167–177, 1992.

[21] Chunnian Liu and Reidar Conradi. Automatic Replanning of Task Networks for Process Model Evolution in EPOS. In *[30]*, pages 434–450, 1993.

[22] Claude Godart. COO: A transaction model to support COOperating software developers COOrdination. In *[30]*, pages 361–379, 1993.

[23] N. Belkhatir, J. Estublier, and W. L. Melo. Adele2: A Support to Large Software Development Process. In *Proc. 1st Conference on Software Process (ICSP1), Redondo Beach, CA*, pages 159–170, October 1991.

[24] Ahmed K. Elmagarmid, editor. *Database Transaction Models For Advanced Applications*. Morgan Kaufmann, 611 p., 1991.

[25] Howard K. Nichols and Dan Simpson, editors. *Proc. 1st European Software Engineering Conference (Strasbourg, Sept. 1987), Springer Verlag* LNCS 289, *404 p.*, 1987.

[26] Jürgen F. H. Winkler, editor. *Proc. ACM Workshop on Software Version and Configuration Control, Grassau, FRG, Berichte des German Chapter of the ACM, Band 30, 466 p.*, Stuttgart, January 1988. B. G. Teubner Verlag.

[27] Peter B. Henderson, editor. *Proc. 2nd ACM SIGSOFT/SIGPLAN Software Engineering Symposium on Practical Software Development Environments (Palo Alto), 227 p.*, December 1986. In ACM SIGPLAN Notices 22(1), Jan 1987.

[28] Stuart Feldman, editor. *Proceedings of the Fourth International Workshop on Software Configuration Management (SCM-4)*, Baltimore, Maryland, May 21–22, 1993.

[29] Jean-Claude Derniame, editor. *Proc. Second European Workshop on Software Process Technology (EWSPT'92), Trondheim, Norway. 253 p.* Springer Verlag LNCS 635, September 1992.

[30] Ian Sommerville and Manfred Paul, editors. *Proc. 4th European Software Engineering Conference (Garmisch-Partenkirchen, FRG), Springer Verlag* LNCS 717., September 1993.

Towards Flexible Process Support with a CASE Shell

Pentti Marttiin

e-mail: ptma@jyu.fi

Department of Computer Science and Information Systems

University of Jyväskylä

Finland

Abstract. CASE technology for improving information systems development (ISD) is mostly based on the creation and verification of IS models using a fixed set of techniques. However, ISD is a complex activity, which requires well selected and suited methodologies and development practices for different situations. This calls for CASE shells (metaCASE environments) in which the methodologies can be tailored. Further, the quality of produced deliverables (e.g. specifications and models) is dependent on the development process. The focus of this paper is on integrating a flexible process support into a CASE shell. The ISD process is specified using a graphical process model, the purposes of which are the guidance and coordination of various activities, and the management of the IS deliverables produced during the development. In this paper process modeling requirements are discussed, and the methodology engineering — especially the process modeling — process using a CASE shell is described.

Keywords:

information systems development, methodology engineering, metaCASE, process modeling

1. Introduction

Many organizations invest heavily in CASE (Computer Aided Systems Engineering) technology. One reason for this is continuous problems in the fields of software engineering (SE) and information systems development (ISD)[1], which has been called the software crisis [7, 9]. The promises of CASE are often summarized as improving productivity in development processes and quality in development

---

[1] Software Engineering is systematic approach to design, implement, maintain and, re-engineering software [18]. It includes engineering a software for IS field. IS development is a process of systems improvement, where a system is transformed from its current state to new improved one [25]. It is less systematic because IS projects are often more user driven and the requirements are less concrete and change during ISD.

products as in [9, 31]. However, new technological innovations themselves can not remove those problems. As pointed out by Jeffery [23] although new technology has potential for improving productivity, without the correct form of management those improvements can not be realized. Also, it is noticed in [34, 43] that the success in the adaptation and use of CASE technology requires different contingencies to be satisfied. These include management processes, learning courses in tools and methodologies, and technical staff for maintenance as examples.

Huff [16] has examined the cost of CASE and noted that it is considerable. Therefore, there should be some return value — productivity and/or quality — for the investments in CASE. Current CASE environments are used mainly for verification of IS specification and documentation [49]. Other benefits are capability to integrate various representation techniques, automate routine tasks such as consistency checking of a diagram and automatically generate new specifications and code. The productivity problems are mostly considered as time delays and cost overruns[2]. The surveys made some years ago [2, 49] show that there is no clear evidence (either theoretical or empirical) that CASE leads to better productivity. Quality of IS/SW models can be described as a sum of various quality aspects including correctness, verifiability, validity, understandability, propriety, reusability, reliability, and robustness. CASE functionality is focused on improving and satisfying only some of these.

Two aspects having potential impacts on an ISD/SE product's validity are discussed. First, every methodology and technique takes a different viewpoint on the problem domain. The selected techniques affect what information is captured during the ISD process. Current CASE environments provide too fixed a variety of techniques. This calls for a metaCASE environment (i.e. a CASE shell) in which we can freely specify techniques and integrate them. CASE shells are described in detail in [29, 44]. Second, the problems of ISD/SE have been said to be due to undisciplined development processes and practices [7, 17]. The SE community has a wide consensus that the quality of products depends on the process through these are produced [1, 17]. Current CASE environments only provide practices to create IS models in normative, encouraging, or free ways [47]. Most of the process supporting tools are integrated to programming environments such as *IStar* [13] and *Marvel* [24]. Only a few tools provide process support for IS analysis and design, such as *HyperCASE* [12] and decision oriented *ConceptBase* [22]. Process supporting tools are discussed more detail in [1, 11].

The goal of this paper is to find a way to integrate a flexible process management environment into the flexible CASE environment. Two basic principles need to be satisfied here. First, the CASE environment should provide a variety of integrated techniques. In this paper we focus on an existing CASE shell — *MetaEdit* [41]. Because it is a graphical tool, the interest is on graphical modeling techniques. Second, the methodology support in CASE environments needs to expanded to facilitate different kind of development and management activities. Therefore, the focus is on flexible modeling of the ISD/SE process.

---

[2] In [43] the productivity effects are further divided to individual productivity to produce specifications, life-cycle effects speeding up single activities and reducing error rates, and down-stream effects that are realized in the long term.

The paper is structured as follows. Section 2 introduces the process modeling requirements. Section 3 describes the MetaEdit+ environment, and its methodology engineering principles. An example of how flexible process support is designed within MetaEdit+ is shown in Section 4. Finally, Section 5 summarizes the results and outlines future directions.

2. Process modeling requirements for flexible CASE environments

CASE environments provide computer support for ISD/SE. ISD can be seen as a composition of various engineering, dialogue, and learning aspects [26], whereas SE is mostly based on engineering. As an engineering process, ISD can be described as complex and ill-structured problem solving activity [42, 45, 25]. It is complex because of its abstract nature and large variety of system components and their relationships [45]. It is ill-structured because design problems contain a great number — sometimes an infinite set — of alternatives and solutions. Further, there is no definite criteria for testing solutions and mechanize process to apply those solutions [37]. As a dialogue process, cooperation among humans plays the fundamental role. Design problems are often called "wicked" problems [35] i.e. design involves compromises between parties with different views and conflicting objectives. As a learning process, ISD is based on the incremental outgrowth of knowledge. Due to new experiences and accumulated knowledge, solutions, views and objectives may change.

The software process is defined by Humphrey [17, pp. 249] to be "the set of activities, method(ologie)s, practices, that are used in the production and evaluation of software". Further, these are fitted to varying organizational and project based practices. A successful CASE environment needs to be powerful enough to manage these diversified needs. Several life cycle strategies, process standards and maturity models, and development methodologies have been introduced to improve ISD/SE.

Life cycle strategies for ISD/SE describe the idealized structure of development activities. These include the waterfall model [4], prototyping [8], spiral models [5, 19], and object-oriented strategies [14, 20]. Earlier waterfall models focus heavily on the engineering aspects and describe a process as a set of sequential development activities such as analysis, design and implementation. The current trend is to describe a process as a complex aggregate of activities including a set of iterative, overlapped, and interlinked activities. Also, alternative approaches based on contracts [13] and decisions [22] instead of activities are introduced.

Software development standards (e.g. *ISO9001* [21]) and maturity models (e.g. SEI's *CMM* [17]) focus on managerial and organizational issues for repeated production. The goal is improve practices by process measurements, monitoring and assessments. CMM maturity levels also take into consideration the learning effects due to the improved SE process. In contrast to the disciplined approaches above, chaos theories indicate that predictive modeling of the ISD process is impossible [3].

There exist a great number of methodologies[3] for improving ISD/SE. The core of methodologies is in the collection of techniques and guidelines to use these techniques based on the underlying life cycle strategy. The proposed process is often illustrated as a list of activities. Although methodologies is said to "standardize development rituals" c.f. [25], they focus on what techniques are used and how these are used rather than how to actually carry out work.

Finding a single best methodology suitable for all development situations seems to be a hopeless task [42]: no one methodology is superior to others if it is compared without taking into consideration the system to be created or changed. The alternative approach is situational methodology engineering. This means that every time the project starts the experience and wisdom about earlier successful and unsuccessful projects are accumulated [25]. Methodologies are contingent upon different development situations, tools available, skill levels of developers and users, complexity of systems to be built, and values of stakeholders.

As noticed above, designing process support for ISD/SE is overall a problematic issue. It needs a process model, which is an abstract description of an actual or proposed process. If we want to build computer support for ISD/SE process at least the following questions arise: what is the purpose of the process model, and what kind of process model would one like to follow.

The purposes of process models is discussed by Curtis et al. [11]. These include facilitating human understanding and communication, improving project and process management, facilitating automatic guidance in performing processes, and supporting automatic execution. In our approach, which is discussed in Section 3, the main purposes of process model are understanding by providing the guidance for the activities, and the management of the evolution and changes of ISD deliverables produced.

Because we demand *flexibility* in process models the following requirements for the ideal process model and the supporting CASE environment can be categorized based on the earlier discussion.

- *Support for life cycle strategies.* ISD process should not be forced to follow only one life cycle strategy. The basic elements (e.g. activities, decisions, or contracts) and the structure (e.g. waterfall or cyclic) of process model needs to be in some degree tailorable.

- *Support for varied methodology processes.* The need of computer support for situation specific methodologies includes techniques as well as processes. One possible strategy for a CASE environment is to provide process models described in methodology handbooks as templates. Projects can then modify them to suit their needs.

- *Management of products evolution.* We can assume that due to the complexity of ISD, user requirements, solution candidates and chosen models may change all the time. According to Baker [3, p. 260] "the CASE environment must be able to store all the alternative branches, [and] provide intuitive navigation mechanisms through alternatives". Tools for handling versions and variants of products, and for navigating between them, are needed in CASE environments.

---

[3] We use the term *methodology* as in CRIS literature [32] to denote e.g. Yourdon's SA [51].

Technically the problem of product management is closely related to problem of version control in the repository.

- *Support for managerial activities.* Methodologies and standards provides variety of managerial metrics. Information about design rationale [10] for clarifying the changes in product evolution sounds tempting. Also, information about project failures and successes is important for laying the foundation for further methodology engineering [25]. We are not always aware of what information we need to gather during the development process.
- *Process unpredictability.* We can not predict all future activities. Further, we do not know the precise *order* of activities (if there is such a feature). The process model structure and activities should be modifiable during the actual process.

3. Overview of the research environment

During the years 1989–93 the SYTI project (and further the MCC company) developed a CASE shell called *MetaEdit*™ . The principles of the tool are reported in [41]. Methodology support in MetaEdit™ means using only one technique at a time. These were specified using the *OPRR* data model (acronym of object, property, relationship and role) [39, 48]. As a further development for supporting methodologies, we are adding the ability to integrate several techniques [40] and support for ISD process [27]. We call the new design prototype *MetaEdit+*.

The three following features outline MetaEdit+.

- MetaEdit+ (and also MetaEdit™) is based on three levels of abstraction: the *ISD level* is the level where ISD takes place i.e. IS descriptions are developed by a development group; the *ME level (methodology engineering level)* is the level where a ME group specifies methodologies using a MetaEdit+; and the *ISD meta-metalevel*, which contains a set of primitive types (GOPRR, activity types and agent types) which are needed as a language to specify methodologies. The levels are shown in Figure 1.
- The division between products, activities, and agents are discussed in [11, 27]. The specifiable aspects of a methodology are shown in the model level containing the IS models, the ISD process, and the development group. These can be specified using three integrated models: *the meta-datamodel*, *the activity model* and *the agent model*. These models are further based on GOPRR, *the meta-activity model* and *the meta-agent model*. All models are shown in Figure 1.
- For all parts of the meta-metamodel and methodology specification we have separated a *conceptual* and a *representational* part. The details of this division are described in [41]. The benefit is that mere representational modifications can be done without touching any concepts. Also, one concept can appear in different representations for different techniques of the methodology. An example is a *data flow* concept represented as a line in *DFD*-model and as a cross in certain matrices.

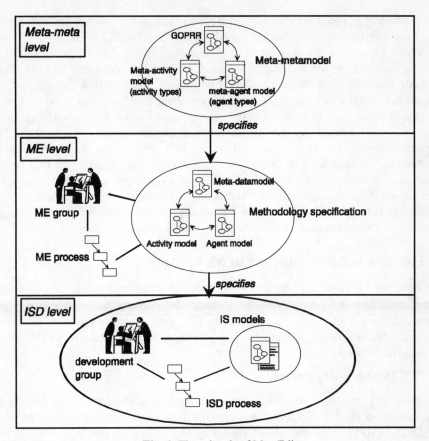

Fig. 1. Three levels of MetaEdit+.

Methodology engineering in MetaEdit+ means creation of a *methodology specification*, which MetaEdit+ uses for specifying ISD techniques, process and group/tool environment. A methodology specification consists of *a meta-datamodel*, *an activity model*, and *an agent model*.

The meta-datamodel specifies techniques and integration of these. It is modelled using the GOPRR types: graph, object, relationship, role and property types. The issues of the meta-datamodel are described in more detail in [40].

An activity model specifies the ISD process. The basic elements of the activity model are activity and deliverable types (Figure 2). The two main purposes of the activity model are:

- to manage different kinds of deliverables (e.g. IS models, specifications, documents), and tools to produce them (e.g. checking tools)
- to provide guidance for the ISD process using on-line helps and pre-defined descriptions.

Agent models define various human agents (e.g. user, project) and user roles (e.g. designer, programmer). These act as electronic notebooks where the information of agent profiles, policies, and strategies is collected. Users get their rights to use the CASE environment through the user roles. Also, technical agents (e.g. checking tool) are defined and linked to techniques through activity types.

Methodology specifications are available as "templates", which are constructed from the information taken from the methodology handbooks. A ME group (Figure 1) selects the techniques, transformations and checkings and links them to the ISD process (activity model template). A similar approach is described in [38] where suitable fragments and route maps based on project characteristics are selected and integrated. Afterwards, an ISD project may want to change or modify the IS techniques and ISD process to better fit its needs[4]. The ME group can make modifications based on the incremental learning and situational changes of the ISD project cf. [25, 38] as follows. When an ISD project has learned to use a methodology it may want to change some parts of it. For example, an ISD project may want to change the life cycle structure of an activity model or improve the techniques. Also, during the life-cycle they may learn how to improve the process by collecting measurement information for specific assessments. Situational changes may happen when the project changes and new user roles are created.

4. Flexible process support in MetaEdit+

Here we focus on one aspect of methodology engineering: process modeling. First, in Section 4.1., we look at the language for creating activity models — the meta-activity model. After that, in Section 4.2., the process of *Yourdon Structured Analysis (SA)* is used as an example of an activity model and potential modifications to it are introduced.

4.1. Meta-activity model

The most covered discussions of process languages and formalisms for SE are represented in [1, 11]. These include systems analysis and design techniques (such as DFD, SADT); data and object modeling (e.g. ER-diagrams, class structures), automata approaches including Petri-nets, AI techniques (rules, pre/post conditions), programming languages, and grammars. We base our work on the object modeling using the concept *activity*, which is the basic concept in most of the life cycle models [1, 4, 14], process modeling approaches [11, 17], and methodology processes [51]. Various types of activities creates a class structure (Figure 2). An activity is any ISD development or managerial task: it uses or produces a deliverable (including checkings and measurements), or acts as a composition of other ISD tasks (e.g. life cycle phases), or a managerial event (e.g. decision or milestone tasks, starting and finishing of phases).

Activities hold a set of user roles for defining the reading and editing rights for the deliverables the activity produces or the rules the activity holds. Activities are managed by starting date. We pay attention only to the starting point so that preceding activities need not be finished before their successors start. In some cases an activity may require a deliverable (i.e. a deliverable is used by an activity) before it can be started.

Basic activity types are a compositional activity *Phase* (Stage), and *Task* (Step) referring to a single task. A *Phase* can contain any number of sub-activities. In

---

[4] MetaEdit 1.0™ contains a method upgrade, which means that techniques can be extended conceptually or changed representationally during the CASE work.

Figure 2 *Tasks* are further specified into *Transformation, Checking, Review, Decision, Milestone,* and other "managerial tasks" *Start* and *Finish*. Most of these types are found in the reference model for ISD [15]. Here the following meanings and extra properties are given. *Transformation* means producing a report, or another deliverable from a deliverable. It includes a transformation model, which contains a set of transformation rules. *Transformation* calls a transformation tool to create and maintain these rules. *Checking* provides correctness and consistency checking for IS specifications by calling the rules attached to GOPRR primitives (e.g. constraint and verification rules in [33]), and/or offers product metrics (e.g. size metrics of the deliverables [36]). Further, it calls a checking tool. *Review* is an adjustment activity directed at deliverables and performed by human agents. *Decision* is used when we have to decide between alternatives and want a solution to be produced. *Milestone* is used when we want to coordinate or (using a technical word) synchronize work, and finish earlier tasks. It can contain a decision to release the "completed" deliverables. Further, every phase can contain informative, managerial *Start*, and *Finish* activities, which act as triggers, and record the starting and finishing of the phase.

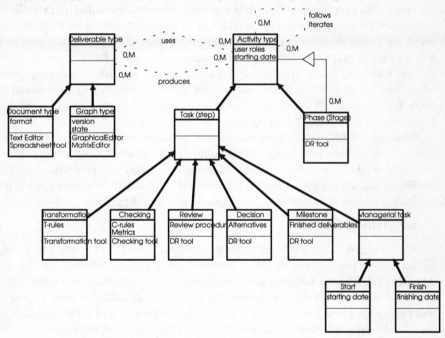

Fig. 2. Basic activity and deliverable types.

The argumentation during the *Review, Decision* and *Milestone* can be maintained using the Design rationale tool (DR tool)[5]. *Transformation rules, checking rules* and *metrics* are attached to menus of the development tools

---

[5] The information is structured as *questions* and responding personal *answers* with pro and con *arguments*. The finished discussion results can be taken up to a property of an activity such as *result*, and *goal*.

(Graphical Editor, Matrix Editor). How are these automatically attached to menus? The sphere of influence according to rules and metrics can be set to a phase like *Analysis* and *Design*, which is added as a property to the transformation or the checking tasks. The necessary rules and metrics are available when opening a tool from a deliverable node in the activity model. In the other case, a phase need be selected when opening a development tool. The user roles can affect the use of the rules and metrics.

How are the activities linked together? We place demands on simplicity in the structure of the activity model. Our approach is motivated by the simplicity of *Task structures* [6, 50], which focus on ordering the activities and decisions. Various activities are connected together using the *follows* relationship, which in pre-defined templates can contain conditions and alternative paths to be followed. Activities may also be connected using the *iteration* relationship. This shows the critical path of the changes: if we want to change an deliverable released earlier we must also adjust other related deliverables.

Because our approach is product centered, various deliverables are attached to activities with *uses* and *produces* relationships. Deliverables collect information for initializing the development tools, which can be opened straight from the deliverable node. An initial division is made between graph types and document types. In the activity model, graph type handles *version names* (e.g. initial DFD or checked DFD) and the following *states*: transient (private and locked for owner), working (public, which can be modified by the owner and copied by someone else), or released (the final "frozen" form). A document is a link to any other document, made using e.g. a text editor, in a form like *Checking report* or *Data dictionary format*.

Changes in the meta-activity model can be made by generalizing/specializing activity and deliverable types. These allows the possibility of using different graphical symbols, or collect specific information by attaching properties to various activity types. Examples of the properties might be actual or planned start/finish time, duration, entry/exit criteria, participants, goals, or arguments.

4.2. Activity models

We selected Yourdon's Structured Analysis (SA) [51] as an example methodology. The process of SA is modeled using the meta-activity model more detail in [27]. The main difference to the *Task structure* approach by Verhoef [46] is explicit deliverables in activity models. All the high level activities such as *Analysis* and *Design* are modelled as phases. These act as compositions of other activities, and are used to store the guidance information, i.e. descriptions of the phases (similarly to *HyperSRM tool* [30]), and history of argumentation related to phases.

Figure 3 shows the more detailed description of the task of *Constructing the environmental model*. It contains activities of types task, review, milestone, and transformation. During the task *Construct the event list* one produces a document *Event list*, and in the task *Construct the context diagram* a DFD specification *Initial context diagram*, which is in a working state. The project can select whether it will start with the event list or context diagram. The initial deliverables above (*Event list* and *Initial context diagram*) are used in the reviewing activity *Interrelate event list and context diagram*, which reviews both deliverables and produces the checked ones. *Release context diagram* is a managerial activity added to Yourdon's example. In this milestone decisions can be made to release the final deliverables. It describes an iteration using two iteration lines to get deliverables completed. As a result, the released *Context diagrams* are collected behind their own specification node. *Produce an initial data dictionary* is a transformation. It implies the use of a transformation model to produce the data dictionary syntax (DD form) described in Yourdon's book. Finally, one can produce an ER model of external stores.

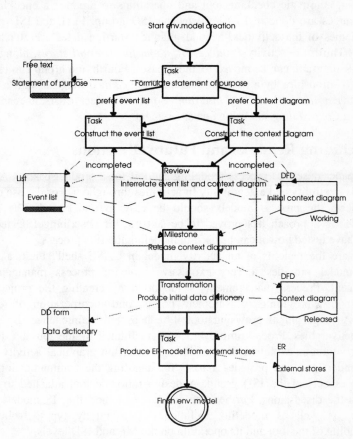

Fig. 3. 'Constructing the environmental model' in Yourdon's SA.

We could continue further to detailed activity diagrams to show how to construct the event list or context diagram. On this level graphical diagrams are powerful tools for guidance. Verhoef [46] describe tasks on the level of *Add Object Type* and *Add Relationship*, and attach operations create_concept(Object) and create_concept (Relationship) to tasks. In MetaEdit GOPRR already handles the semantics of creations, updates and removals. Our aim is to provide better notes and guidelines on how to use the technique: in what order different elements (e.g. object types) can be created, and what information stores (e.g. manuals, reports) can be used to aid methods' use.

SA process is described first as a template, which is the level a metaCASE tool vendor can offer for organizations. The ME group needs to analyze the suitability of templates for the ISD group and change them. The possible changes to the template on the level of *Construction of the Environmental model* can be the following ones. The ME group can first change in the ME level the graphical representations e.g. change the milestone representation to a circle. Also, it can replace the *review* activity with the *checking* activity, giving a second change where the checking contains an automatic checking tool and operations to produce a checking report. Other changes are done in ISD level by the ISD group. First, the ISD group can modify names of the activities. Second, planned starting dates are attached to all activities. Third, the activity *Produce ER-model for external stores*, along with the related ER-diagram, can be moved to later phases. Fourth, the group can replace the *iteration* relationships by a new milestone *Assess context diagram* and a new task *Change event list and context diagram*. So, this project trusts its capability to complete a *Context diagram* using one assessment.

5. Concluding Remarks and Future Directions

This paper describes process modeling support for a product based CASE shell. ISD needs flexibility and extendibility in activities throughout. For the use of various ISD projects the process models should be easy to understand. The graphical metamodeling approach has proved to be suitable for describing ISD techniques. Here we have tested how it can be used in modeling the ISD process.

What are the benefits of an activity model in CASE shell? First, a graphical activity model provides a very expressive tool for process management and improvement. Process management is supported by creating the project-tailored activity model, providing measurement points, and incorporation of tools to a process. As a graphical browsing tool it reduces the maintenance difficulties of various deliverables. Process improvement is facilitated by the reusable templates, and the continuous evolution of a process. Second, the graphical activity model is easy to understand and provides a basis for handling the communication and co-operation aspects of the ISD group. A design rationale tool attached to activities maintains the discussions. Further, the similarity of modeling IS models and ISD processes, as well as modeling techniques and activity types, facilitates the understanding of the tool and its operation on the ME and ISD levels.

The following aspects will be studied in the future. First, the definition of meta-activity models, and the use of activity models have been tested using MetaEdit's capabilities to model techniques. We will implement the designed process support into MetaEdit+. According to this, a version control system to support the versions and states of deliverables will be build into the repository. Second, structuring the design rationale during ISD is one of the ongoing studies. Third, this paper does not address the rule language and mechanism by which the rules are attached to IS models through the activity model. Fourth, possible viewing mechanisms of the activity model filtered by human agents and user roles are not introduced here. These allow developers to use their own subset of the activity model. Fifth, hypertext links empowering the navigation capabilities between deliverables need to be studied.

Acknowledgements

I would like to thank the other members of the MetaPHOR project for fruitful discussions. Special thanks are given to Kalle Lyytinen, Sjaak Brinkkemper, Mauri Leppänen, and Steven Kelly for the improvements of this paper.

References:

1. Armenise, P., Bandinelli, S., Ghezzi, C., Morzenti, A., "A survey and assessment of software process representation formalisms", *International Journal of Software Engineering And Knowledge Engineering*, 3, 3, 1993, pp. 410-426.
2. Aaen, I., Siltanen, A., Sørensen, C., Tahvanainen, V.-P., "A Tale of Two Countries - CASE Experiences and Expectations", *The Impact of Computer Supported Technologies on Information Systems Development* (Eds. K.E. Kendall, K. Lyytinen and J.I. DeGross), Amsterdam, North-Holland, 1992, pp. 61-93.
3. Baker, J.M., "Project Management Utilizing an Advanced CASE Environment", *International Journal of Software Engineering and Knowledge Engineering,* 2, 2, 1992, pp. 251-261.
4. Boehm, B.W., "Software Engineering", *IEEE Transactions on Computers*, 25, 12, 1976, pp. 1226-1241.
5. Boehm, B.W., "A spiral model of software development and enhancement", *IEEE Computer*, 21, 5, 1988, pp. 61-72.
6. Bots, P.W.G., *An environment to Support Problem Solving,* PhD thesis, Delft University of Technology, Delft, The Netherlands, 1989.
7. Brooks, F.P. Jr., *The Mythical Man-Month.* Addison-Wesley, Reading, Mass., 1975.
8. Budde R., Kautz, K., Kuhlenkamp, K., Züllighoven, H., *Prototyping - An approach to Evolutionary Systems Development*, Springer-Verlag, Berlin, 1992.
9. Charette, R.N., *Software Engineering Environments: Concepts and Technology*, McGraw-Hill, New York, 1986.
10. Conclin, J., Begeman, M. L., "gIBIS: A Hypertext Tool for Explanatory Policy Discussion", *ACM Transactions on Office Information Systems*, 6, 4, 1988, pp. 303-331.
11. Curtis, B., Kellner, M.I., Over, J., "Process modeling", *Communications of the ACM*, 35, 9, September 1992, pp. 75-90.
12. Cybulski, J.L., Reed, K., "A Hypertext Based Software Engineering Environment", *IEEE Software*, March 1992, pp 62-68.
13. Dowson, M., "Integrated Project Support with IStar", *IEEE Software*, November 1987, pp. 6-15.
14. Henderson-Sellers, B., Edwards, J.M., "The Object-oriented Systems Life Cycle", *Communications of the ACM,* 33, 9, 1990.
15. Heym, M., Österle, H., "A reference model of information systems development", *The Impact of Computer Supported Technologies on Information Systems Development* (Eds. K.E. Kendall, K. Lyytinen and J.I. DeGross), Amsterdam, North-Holland, 1992, pp. 215-240.
16. Huff, C.C., "Elements of a Realistic CASE Tool Adoption Budget", *Communications of the ACM*, 35, 4, 1992, pp. 45-53.
17. Humphrey, W.S., *Managing the Software Process*, Addison-Wesley, Reading, MA, 1989.

18. IEEE Glossary of Software Engineering Terminology. IEEE Std. 720, IEEE, New York, 1983.

19. Iivari, J., "Hierarchical Spiral Model for Information System and Software Development", *Information and Software Technology*, 32, 6, 1990, pp.386-399.

20. Iivari, J., "Object-oriented Design of Information Systems: The design process", *Object Oriented Approach in Information Systems*, (Eds. F. Van Assche, B. Moulin and C. Rolland), Elsevier Science Publishers, North-Holland, IFIP, 1991, pp. 61-87.

21. Hall, T.J., "The quality manual — The applications of BS5750 ISO9001 EN29001". John Wiley and Sons, Chichester, 1992.

22. Jarke, M., "Strategies for Integrating CASE Environments", *IEEE Software*, March 1992, pp. 54-61.

23. Ross Jeffery, D., "Software Engineering Productivity Models for Management Information Systems Development", *Critical Issues in Information Systems Research* (Eds. Boland R.J. jr. and Hirschheim R. A.), John Wiley and Sons Ltd. 1987, pp. 113-134.

24. Kaiser, G.E., Feiler, P.H., Popovich, S.S., "Intelligence Assistant for Software Development and Maintenance", *IEEE Software*, May 1988, pp.40-49.

25. Kumar, K., Welke, R.J., "Methodology Engineering$_R$: A proposal for Situation-specific Methodology Engineering", *Challenges and Strategies for Research in Systems Development*, (Eds. W.W Cotterman. and J.A. Senn), John Wiley and Sons Ltd., 1992, pp. 257- 269.

26. Lyytinen, K., "Different Perspectives on Information Systems: Problems and Solutions", *ACM Computing Surveys*, 19, 1, March 1987, pp. 5-46.

27. Marttiin, P., "Methodology Engineering in CASE Shells: Design Issues and Current Practice", Licentiate Thesis, Computer Science and Information Systems Reports, Technical Reports TR-4, University of Jyväskylä, 1994.

28. Marttiin, P., Lyytinen, K., Rossi, M., Smolander, K, Tahvanainen, V.-P., Tolvanen J.-P, "Modeling requirements for future CASE: issues and implementation considerations", *Proceedings of the 13th ICIS*, (Eds. J.I. DeGross, J.D. Becker and J.J. Elam), Dallas, USA, 1992, pp. 9-20.

29. Marttiin, P., Rossi, M., Tahvanainen, V.-P., Lyytinen, K., "A comparative review of CASE Shells: a preliminary framework and research outcomes", *Information and Management*, 25, 1993, pp. 11-31.

30. Oinas-Kukkonen, H., "Intermediary hypertext systems in CASE environments", Licentiate thesis, Research papers SERIES A16, Department of Information Processing Science, University of Oulu, 1993.

31. Osterweil, L.J., "Software processes are software too", *Procs. of the 9th International Conference on Software Engineering*, Monterey, California, 1987, pp. 2-13.

32. Olle, T.W., Sol, H.G., Verrijn-Stuart, A.A. (Eds.), *Information Systems Design Methodologies: A comparative review*, North-Holland, 1982.

33. Persson, U., and Wangler, B., "A Specification of Requirements for an Advanced Information Systems Development Tool.", *Procs. of the workshop on the Next Generation of CASE Tools,* (Eds. S. Brinkkemper and G. Wijers), SERC, Netherlands, 1990.

34. Rai, A., Howard, G.S., "An Organizational Context for CASE Innovation", *Information Resources Management Journal*, 6, 3, 1993, pp. 21-35.

35. Rittel, H.W.J., Webber, M.M., "Planning Problems are Wicked Problems", *Policy Sciences*, 4, 1973, 155-169.

36. Rask, R., Laamanen, P., Lyytinen, K., "A comparison of Abrecht's Function Points and Symons' Mark II Metrics", *Proceedings of the 13th ICIS*, (Eds. DeGross J.I., Becker J.D. and Elam J.J.), Dallas, USA, 1992, pp. 207-221.

37. Simon, H., "The Structure of Ill-structured Problems", *Artificial Intelligence*, 4, 1973, pp. 181-200.

38. van Slooten, K., Brinkkemper, B., "A Method Engineering Approach to Information Systems Development", *Information Systems Development Process*, (Eds. N. Prakash, C.Rolland, B. Pernici), Elsevier Science Publishers, North-Holland, 1993, pp. 167-186.

39. Smolander, K., "OPRR - A Model for Methodology Modeling", *Next Generation of CASE Tools*, (Eds. K. Lyytinen and V.-P. Tahvanainen), Studies in Computer and Communication Systems, IOS press, 1992, pp. 224-239.

40. Smolander, K., "GOPRR - a proposal for a meta level model", MetaPHOR internal technical document, Dept. of Computer Science and Information Systems, University of Jyväskylä, 1993.

41. Smolander, K., Lyytinen, K., Tahvanainen, V.-P., Marttiin P., "MetaEdit - A flexible graphical environment for methodology modelling", *Advanced Information Systems Engineering*, (Eds. R. Andersen, J. Bubenko and A. Sølvberg), LNCS #498, Springer-Verlag, 1991, pp. 168-193.

42. Sol, H.G., "A Feature Analysis of Information Systems Design Methodologies: Methodological Considerations", *Information Systems Design Methodologies: A Feature Analysis*, (Eds. T. W. Olle, H. G. Sol and C. J. Tully), Elsevier Science Publishers, North-Holland, Amsterdam, 1983.

43. Sørensen, C., *Introducing CASE Tools into Software Organizations*, Ph.D. Thesis, Dept. of Mathematics and Computer Science, Institute of Electronic Systems, Aalborg University, Denmark, 1993.

44. Sorenson, P. G., Tremblay, J-P., McAllister, A. J., "The Metaview system for many specification environments." *IEEE Software*, 30, 3, 1988, pp. 30-38.

45. Turner, J.A., "Understanding the Elements of System Design", *Critical Issues in Information Systems Research* (Eds. R.J. Boland jr. and R. A. Hirschheim), John Wiley and Sons Ltd. 1987, pp. 97-112.

46. Verhoef, T.F., "Structuring Yourdon's Modern Structured Analysis", *Proceedings of the Second Workshop on The Next Generations of CASE Tools*, (Eds. V.-P. Tahvanainen and K. Lyytinen), Technical Reports TR-1, Jyväskylä, 1991.

47. Vessey, I., Jarvenpaa, S., Tractinsky, N., "Evaluation of Vendor Products: CASE Tools as Methodology Companions", *Communications of the ACM*, 35, 4, 1992, pp. 90-105.

48. Welke, R.J., "The CASE Repository: More Than Another Database Application", Meta Systems Ltd., Ann Arbor, Michigan, 1988.

49. Wijers, G., van Dort, H., "Experiences with the use of CASE tools in the Netherlands", *Advanced Information Systems Engineering*, (Eds. Steinholz, Sølvberg, Bergman), LNCS#436, Springer-Verlag, 1990, pp. 5-20.

50. Wijers, G., *Modeling Support in Information Systems Development*, Ph.D. Thesis, Thesis publishers, Amsterdam, 1991.

51. Yourdon, E., *Modern Structured Analysis*, Yourdon Press, 1989.

A Collaborative Process-Centered Environment Kernel

Jacques Lonchamp

C.R.I.Nancy - Campus scientifique, BP n. 239,
54506 Vandoeuvre les Nancy Cedex, France (jloncham@loria.fr)

Abstract. The Collaborative Process-Centered Environment project (CPCE) aims at applying process modeling approach and technology to a given class of collaborative applications. The challenge is to deal with fine grain entities and interactions, and to provide the high level of adaptability and controlled flexibility required by real world collaborative situations. The concept of a collaborative meta process model which drives the evolution of the executing collaborative process model, and the underlying object-oriented technology are two important aspects discussed in the paper.

1 Introduction

Most software systems only support interaction between a single user and a computer. Even so-called 'multi-user' operating systems and applications basically provide support for isolated work, hiding the activities of other users. In contrast, the general aim of collaborative computing is to suppress the 'protective walls' between users [29], to encourage collaboration, and to directly support and assist the work of groups. Over the past ten years, collaborative computing has established itself as a research field in its own right. Collaborative computing is a complex area because many different shared work styles exist. A fist classification is related to the degree of engagement of participants: for instance, 'division of labour', where several component tasks address separately sub-goals of a common goal, or 'focussed collaboration', where people work closely together. Another taxonomy is the time/location matrix: applications are either local (same place) or distributed (different places) and their interactions occur synchronously (same time) or asynchronously (different times). Other important parameters are the degree of 'repeatability' and 'structuredness' of the collaboration process: from completely unstructured and unpredictable interactions (e.g. a real-time collaborative free-hand sketching tool [11]) to collaborative routines which can be 'programmed' [25].

Early collaborative systems, for instance in the office automation field, have failed because they implicitly assumed a rigid procedural conception of work which is inadequate for representing many real world cooperative work arrangements [30]. They were developed using available computer techniques, especially the dominant procedural programming style. More flexible and customizable approaches have been recently proposed, for instance in the field of software process modeling [14, 15]. Executable software process models are interpreted within so-called 'process-centered environments' (PCEs), to provide control, coordination, assistance, and guidance to the developers. Automation is no longer the central focus, but just one possible effect of process model interpretation. Flexible programming paradigms (logic, functional, object oriented, rule-based, hybrids) are extensively used [7]. However, most PCEs are devoted to large grain entities management (e.g. design documents, code files), finer granularity being managed by classical tools integrated into the environments. Therefore, PCEs often restrict cooperation to consistent sharing of large grain entities between long transactions. Other styles of collaboration are generally not considered.

The project described in this paper, CPCE (standing for 'Collaborative Process-Centered Environment'), *aims at applying process modeling approach and technology to a given class of collaborative applications.* The challenge is to deal with fine grain entities and interactions, and to provide the high level of adaptability and flexibility required by real world collaborative situations. Not all collaborative applications can take advantage of a process modeling orientation. Asynchronous applications are more likely to be process model driven. They are long term activities, requiring various policies enforcement, and sophisticated assistance: for instance, to 'resynchronize' people working intermittently to the current state of the work through process history and decision rationale. In contrast, synchronous applications are generally short lived, and rely more on spontaneous reactions of the participants sharing a common view of the ongoing work, than on predefined policies and processes enforcement. CPCE project *aims at supporting asynchronous 'focussed' collaborative applications, having a sufficient amount of structure* (see section 2). The environment kernel prototype can be customized for applications belonging to this class (sections 3 to 6 discuss the requirements, design, and implementation).

2 Application Domain

In the class of applications currently supported by CPCE, several participants (local or remote), bring their ideas and opinions in order to build consensually a given artifact. They participate to the work when they wish and freely join and quit. The overall process is long lived, but the elementary activities to obtain consensus or to evolve a specific aspect of the artifact are short lived. The main emphasis is on consensus [23]: most of the decisions about the artifact being designed must be consensually taken all along the artifact construction through issue resolution processes. Issues are solved, either individually by their author or, more often, collectively by the participants through positions (i.e. statements or assertions which resolve the issue), arguments (which either support or object a position), and a resolution protocol implying the selection of a position (e.g. unanimous choice, choice by a majority of participants). In general, all kinds of issue cannot be raised from the beginning: a process including several steps is defined, every step encompassing a subset of the issue type set. Often, the termination of a step is itself an issue to be collectively solved. Parallelism between issues of the same step, and between steps is possible. An issue resolution contributes to (or triggers) a subsequent step which generally evolve the artifact, raising new issues. Every participant plays a given role: a role defines which issues he can raise, which deliberations he can participate in (by giving positions and arguments), which steps he can invoke.

In this paper, the customized environment which exemplifies the approach, supports the collaborative design of a document. Main ideas about the process are taken from Cognoter [31]. The document design process encompasses several phases.

A brain-storming phase. Participants propose ideas. These ideas are made visible to all participants as soon as they are proposed. As usually during brain-storming, discussion and deletion of ideas by other participants are forbidden during this initial phase "to not interfere with or inhibit the flow of ideas"[31]. Adding a new idea is an issue solved individually by its author, who must provide an argument as the rationale for his proposal.

A structuring phase. Participants propose directed links asserting that an idea should come before another in the document. New ideas can also be proposed during this second phase. The process for proposing links is similar to the process for proposing ideas.

An evaluation phase. Participants evaluate collectively the network of ideas resulting from the two first phases. They eliminate peripheral and irrelevant elements, and fill in missing elements. All issues are solved consensually (e.g. with a majority protocol).

A clustering proposal phase. One participant proposes a set of clusters, and for every cluster, the set of ideas it encompasses. The system computes intra and inter cluster links, on the basis of existing links between ideas.

A clustering evaluation phase. Participants evaluate collectively the proposed clustering. They can evolve it through consensual issue resolutions (e.g. with a majority protocol).

Starting the 'Cognoter-like' design process for a given topic, and finishing every process phase are other collectively solved issues (e.g. with an unanimity protocol).

CPCE team is currently studying a second application in the field of technical review/inspection of software development products [34]. This second application is more complex because it requires various shared work styles: parallel isolated work, for the individual preparation phase, followed by the merging of all individual findings into a common workspace, for the collaborative phase of the inspection. The customized environment will be functionally similar to some recent dedicated environments [12, 18, 22], with a review process not hard coded in the tool but explicitly modeled and tailorable to specific needs and contexts.

3 Main Requirements and Design Decisions

The basic 'process model orientation' of the project means that a set of classical requirements has to be satisfied by the supporting environment, such as: model-based control of user initiatives, model-based automation of some parts of the process, model-based assistance and guidance for users. These aspects have been often discussed for process-centered software engineering environments. For instance, within the ALF project, initiated by the same research team as CPCE [9]. More specific requirements under consideration here are *fine grain interaction modeling, adaptability, and flexibility*.

Fine grain interactions shall be explicitly modeled besides classical process entities such as tasks, artifacts, roles, actors, and their relationships. In the target application domain, it means entities for the description of consensual decisions. Issues, positions, and arguments are frequently used for modeling such deliberations

[16]. More generally, a 'decision-oriented' process modeling is appropriate [13, 17]. A detailed description of the internal structure and semantics of the artifact, which is the topic of most of the deliberations, is also required. CPCE generic model, which is an extension of Potts' model for representing design methods [26], will be described in the next section. Process models and process histories include many objects of various granularities. As persistency of models, histories and rationale is mandatory to ensure model interpretation and retrospective assistance, object oriented repositories are good candidates for founding the supporting environment.

Adaptability has been extensively studied for process-centered software engineering environments. A software process model is built by customizing a generic model, and instantiating it before its execution [6]. The large variety of asynchronous collaborative tasks, sharing an important set of common features, requires a similar approach: the supporting environment shall be a kernel which can interpret every process model customizing a given generic model. The specialization concept, with inheritance for both statical and dynamical aspects, reinforce the interest for an object orientation: generic entity types can capture the common structure and behavior associated to all their instances. For example, what happens when a user gives an argument, whatever its type is. The specific behavior of every customized type is specified at the sub-type level.

Statical customization is not sufficient. Dynamical change to the running process model has been recognized as a major issue by the process modeling community [10]. For collaborative environments two main reasons can be stated: first, groups often evolve and adapt their way of working to their evolutive contexts. Secondly, describing in advance all aspects of a given model is difficult, especially for argumentative entity types such as issues, positions, and arguments. CPCE distinguishes two aspects: (1) the technical aspect of implementing dynamic evolution of the running model, (2) the organizational and decisional aspects of managing evolutive environments. Aspect (2) is one of the main originality of CPCE. The requirement is that the dynamic evolution of a collaborative environment shall be controlled, assisted, and consensual. CPCE solution is to drive process model evolution thanks to another dedicated collaborative process model, called the 'meta-process model'. To avoid meta circularity, changing the meta process model is not required to be itself model driven: the meta process model is statically customized for every application and cannot evolve on the fly. The meta process model is obtained by customizing the same generic model which is used to produce the process model. Both processes are very similar, and participants work in a similar consensual way either to evolve the artifact or to evolve the model which defines how they work. This mirrors usual meetings, where people discuss in the same way of the job and of its organization (see Fig.1). It is worth noting that effective meta process modeling implies fine grain modeling to be able to describe and control the evolution of every fine grained process model component. For aspect (1), the 'full object' orientation of languages such as Smalltalk [4], where all entities, including classes and methods, are dynamically modifiable objects, in conjunction with the interpretative, reflective, and dynamic nature of these languages, make more easy the implementation of the meta level.

Therefore, a persistent object repository extending such a 'full object' language-based environment, and supporting multi-user concurrent access (local or remote), constitutes the core of the CPCE prototype. The object base is used to store the

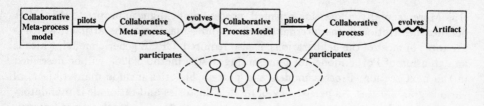

Fig. 1. CPCE logical architecture

artifact, the customized process model, the customized meta process model, the process history and rationale, and the meta process history and rationale. Models are expressed at the schema level, histories and rationales are expressed at the instance level. Users invoke class methods (i.e. methods of metaclasses), either to work (modify the artifact and create new process history instances), or to evolve the process model (modify the process classes and create new meta process history instances).

Dynamic schema evolution, which support dynamic model evolution, has been studied through different perspectives: taxonomy of meaningful changes, semantics of schema changes, and cost. 'Soft changes', which do not require database updates, have been distinguished from more costly 'hard changes' [3, 19]. Here, the meta process specifies which dynamic schema evolutions (i.e. dynamic process model evolutions) are supported and how, on the basis of their significance for the process being modeled, and their practical feasibility in a collaborative setting. Low cost changes are those which can be defined by manipulating menus and typing values, without complex programming. In contrast, changing the code of a method is a costly soft change. The meta process should also enforces integrity rules of the meta model. For instance, adding a new issue class requires at least adding one position class responding to it, and one supporting or objecting argument class.

4 Process Modeling in CPCE

Every customized process model is built by refining the set of predefined generic classes and methods, belonging to the generic model.

From the statical point of view, the generic model depicted in Fig.2 is an extension of Potts' model [26]. New generic classes with regard to Potts' model are written in italics and new link classes are depicted with bold lines. The 'Artifact' class is the root of an application specific hierarchy with application specific semantic links. Every other generic class (e.g. 'Argument') is specialized into generic process model classes ('ProcessArgument') and generic meta process model classes ('MetaArgument'). Then, each of them is further customized according to the needs of a given application. Links between specialized classes and attributes of specialized classes express specific static aspects of the customized model. The set of attributes is richer in the prescriptive model of CPCE than in the descriptive model of Potts. There are both class variables for expressing various model properties (e.g. 'IssueType' specifying the resolution protocol used to solve issues of a given type) and for implementing the relationships of Fig.2 (e.g. argument class X 'ToSupport' position class Y), and

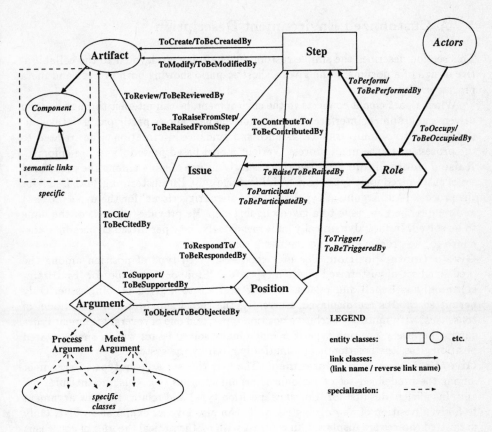

Fig. 2. The generic process model

instance variables for expressing history values (e.g. the text of argument x) and relationships (e.g. argument instance x 'hasSupported' position instance y).

From the dynamical point of view, class methods of generic classes embody the basic behavior of all collaborative environments. They are extended within customized sub-classes. Class variables are extensively used to describe model properties in a declarative way. Many dynamic changes to the customized running model are made just by changing the value of such variables. Class methods of generic classes are written to cope with all the anticipated values of these variables. For instance, the 'SolveIssue' class method of every customized issue class uses a 'SolveIssueFixed-Part' class method inherited from the generic 'Issue' class, which can cope with all the anticipated consensus protocols. For every customized issue class, a class variable 'IssueType' gives the kind of protocol which is used to solve it. Therefore, one can change the protocol, under the control of the meta process model, just by changing the value of 'IssueType'. It's a good example of 'low cost' change. Conversely, creating a new unanticipated resolution method is much more costly: a non trivial piece of code has to be included within the kernel part.

5   A Customized Environment Description

This section describes the simple customized environment devoted to the collaborative design of a document and gives a short scenario showing both process and meta process activities.

When a participant connects to the environment, he can interact through a menu driven and graphical interface. The menu driven part allows participants to take initiatives and to obtain various assistance and guidance information either related to the process or to the meta process. Various model-based prescriptions are enforced.
Raise a (meta-)issue. The user chooses a given type of issue among the predefined set of customized issue types (e.g. 'AddIdeaIssue', 'EndBrainstormingPhaseIssue' for the process, 'AddArgumentTypeIssue', 'SuppressTriggerIssue' for the meta process) and relates the new issue to a given ongoing step. He provides the text of the issue to be solved. In fact, dynamically built menus only show permitted choices in accordance to the process state and the user's role.
Give a (meta-)position. The user chooses a given type of position among the predefined set of customized position types (e.g. 'Stop' or 'Continue' for 'EndBrainstormingPhaseIssue') and relates the new position to a given ongoing issue. Only permitted choices are displayed. Currently, the kernel supports a simple model of consensus, with mutually exclusive position types, and one or several argument types supporting every position type. For individually solved issues with a single related position class, the position is automatically given by the system.
Give/Remove a (meta-)argument. The user chooses a given type of argument among the predefined set of customized argument types (e.g. 'InsufficientDuration' and 'InsufficientResults' for 'Continue' position type) and relates the new argument to a given position of an ongoing issue. He can also give an explanation text. Only permitted choices are displayed. In contrast with mathematical theories of consensus described in [23], interactions between participants are possible: a participant may give several consistent arguments for the same position in order to react to other participants' arguments. He can also remove his own arguments, if he changes his mind.
Solve a (meta-)issue. Every customized issue type is characterized by a resolution protocol. If the issue cannot be solved, i.e. no position can be selected by the protocol according to the process state, the request is rejected. The current kernel provides three protocols: individual resolution, collective unanimous resolution, collective resolution by a majority of participants. Others could be supported, such as resolution by the author of the issue after obtaining an authorization.
Perform a (meta-)step. Within every process model there are two kinds of steps: process phases (e.g. 'BrainstormingPhase', 'StructuringPhase') defining which issue types can be raised at which moment, and activity steps (e.g. 'CreateDocument', 'AddIdea', 'DeleteLink') evolving the artifact. Apart from the initial step, every step is either automatically triggered or made ready for invocation by an issue resolution. The user interface is used in the latter case, when a participant takes the initiative to perform a step.
Query about ongoing (meta-)steps and (meta-)issues.
Display historical data: the set of existing (meta-)steps, (meta-)issues, (meta-)positions, (meta-)arguments.

Obtain guidance information: about 'raisable' (meta-)issues and 'performable' (meta-) steps in the current process state and according to the participant's role.

The following snapshots exemplify the interleaving of process and meta process activities. As these activities take place asynchronously on several user workstations we show their effects mainly through graphical representations of process and meta process histories. In Fig.3 the 'Step view model' window gives the overall organization of the document design process with a sequence of phases. It is worth noting that non sequential structures are also possible. Links between phases in the graph are just abstractions of links between some positions inside the phases and subsequent phases (steps) they 'ContributesTo' or 'Trigger' (see Fig2). The 'Step graph' window details the 'BrainstormingPhase' model when participants individually propose their ideas for the document. The 'Issue view model' window gives the position and the argument classes related to the 'AddIdeaIssue' (there is only one position type because this kind of issue is individually solved).

The purpose of the scenario is to exemplify the dynamical and consensual creation of a second argument class ('RelevantIdea') supporting 'AddIdeaPosition'. Extending argumentative capabilities is expected to be a rather frequent kind of dynamic change. The 'Step view history' window displays the current history of the process: two ideas have been proposed. 'Issue view history' windows detail the corresponding individual issue resolutions. 'Idea graph' window displays the resulting document design state.

In Fig.4 we have similar windows showing the meta process model with only one phase ('ChangeProcessModel') and several meta issue types within it for evolving the process model. The 'AddArgumentTypeIssue' model is detailed in the 'Meta issue view model' window. The meta process history shows the dynamical creation of the new meta argument type. The meta issue has been solved consensually by the two model performers each giving a 'UsefulType' meta argument. The 'inspect' windows displays the textual definition of the meta issue. In the TEXT field, the three parameters for creating the argument class appear. No other data is needed. This exemplifies what we have called a 'low cost' unanticipated change.

Fig.5 demonstrates the use of this new consensually agreed argument class for creating, through the menu based interface of one participant, the third idea in the document. The central window shows the interaction trace with an example of a system initiative (trigger). The pop-up menus for process execution and process assistance are pinned up on the low part of the picture. The graphical representation of the new 'AddIdeaIssue' resolution and the new document design state are depicted on the right part of the screen.

6 Some Implementation Issues

CPCE prototype is built on top of the GemStone multi-user object-oriented database management system which offer a distributed client-server architecture[4].

For the control aspect, both controls related to the semantics of generic classes, which are coded in their class methods, and specific controls, through the test of predefined class variables of the customized sub-classes, are supported. For instance, every customized step class has a 'Precond' class variable with a conditional block

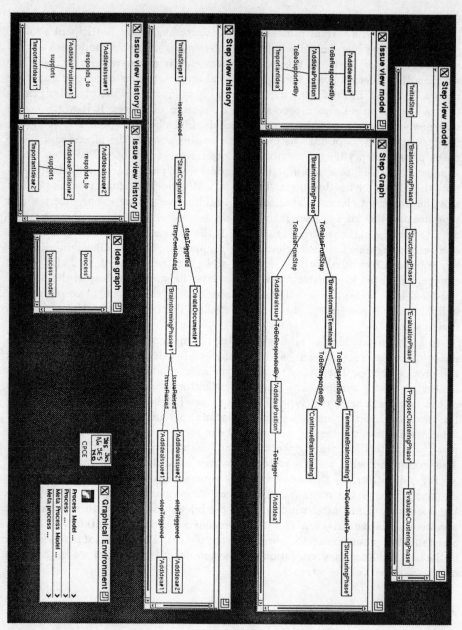

Fig. 3. The process model and process history.

37

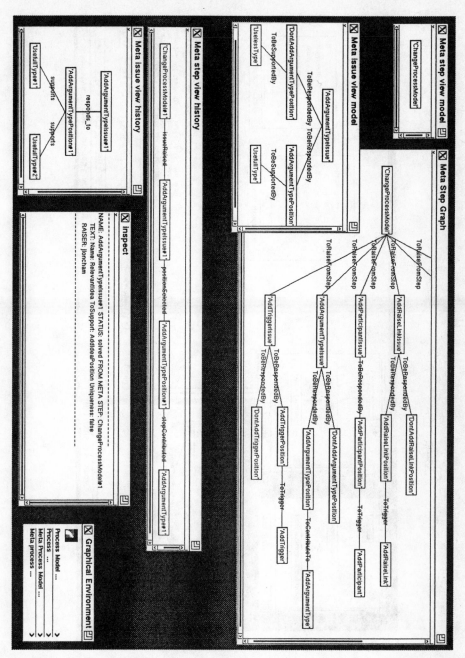

Fig. 4. The meta process model and meta process history.

38

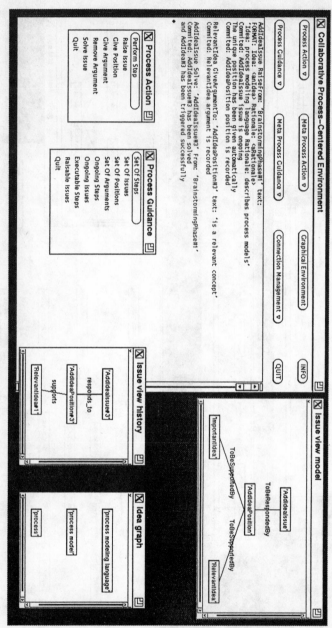

Fig. 5. A participant menu based interface.

(i.e. a parameterized logical expression) as its value. When a 'Perform' message is sent, the method is executed only if the 'Precond' block is evaluated to true.

For the automation aspect, only one kind of process-related 'trigger' is currently implemented. Methods are used to implement triggers [20]. When an issue is solved through a position selection, the generic 'SolveIssueFixedPart' class method tests if a 'ToTrigger' link exists between the customized issue class and a step class. If a link exists, a step of the corresponding class is automatically performed by the system. This implements a simple event(-condition)-action rule. Different events could be considered for other trigger types (e.g. raising automatically a given issue at every beginning of a given step).

For the assistance aspect, the main focus is on 'retrospective assistance' relying on the history and design rationale. Guidance based on the current process state and user's role is also available (see 'raisable issues', and 'performable steps' queries). 'Prospective assistance', for instance through planning and impact analysis capabilities, is not currently considered.

For the evolution aspect, dynamic 'hard changes' rely mainly on class versioning and instances migration as provided by GemStone.

In the document design application, all activities, such as participating to issue resolutions or modifying a given aspect of the document, are short lived. These activities can proceed in parallel and their results are committed into the repository when they finish if no read/write or write/write conflict has occurred between them. In the case of a conflict, a rollback is performed. Obviously this optimistic scheme is not sufficient for all applications. In the next future we plan to enrich the kernel with other schemes. In the technical review application, a new requirement for the kernel is to support parallel isolated work before the merging of all individual contributions into a common workspace for the collaborative phase of the inspection. Sub-schema and sub-database mechanisms are required. Other working modes with semi-isolated work and conflicts resolution should also be supported. It implies to mix asynchronous and synchronous work, for instance for negotiating how conflicts have to be solved. We plan to rely mainly on user consensus to solve conflicts, and to assist them by tracking all dependencies and commitments resulting from their interactions.

The current prototype has shown that simple programming techniques were available for implementing basic control, automation, assistance, evolution, and multi-user support. They will be used more extensively and enhanced in next versions of CPCE.

7   Related Works

Most of process-centered software engineering environment prototypes provide to a certain extent control, assistance, and automation. For instance, the ALF project [9] has put a strong emphasis on assistance and guidance for its users, mainly through planning techniques Object oriented process model formalisms have been studied, among many other paradigms. The IPSE 2.5 project [33] is a well known example of an object oriented process modeling approach. Model customization through class specialization is one of its basic mechanism [28].

Groupware tools for collaborative document design [24, 2] and for collaborative technical review [18, 22] are available. Their processes are hard coded into the tools. Other less specialized groupware tools are partially process model oriented: the Conversation Builder (CB) system [21] is a representative example of such customizable active groupware tools. CB protocols are roughly similar to process model fragments. No concept can be related to the meta process level. A customized environment for technical review built on top of CB has been developed [12].

The general concept of meta process, is discussed in several papers ('the process of development and evolution of a process model' [6]). A few projects have started to study issues for implementing model driven meta process support: reflective high level Petri nets in [1], schema updating controlled by meta-level operations and incremental replanning of task networks when task types dynamically evolve in [8], model construction from a single base role to a set of dedicated roles driven by a meta process model written in a reflective process modeling language in [32]. But modeling and implementation issues for assisted consensual process model evolutions were unexplored so far.

Future work will improve incrementally the kernel. The second version is under development and a customized environment will be devoted to collaborative review/inspection. The main effort will be to make concrete ideas of 'open' (or 'reflective') object-oriented implementations as described in [27]. Implementation aspects that could evolve will be clearly localized ('reified') within specific distinct meta-objects, with their access and change under the control of the meta-process, playing the role of an active meta-interface [27]. [1]

References

1. S. Bandinelli, A. Fuggetta: Computational Reflection in Software Process modeling: the SLANG Approach. Proc. 15th ICSE, Baltimore, 144–154, 1993, IEEE Press.

2. S. Baydere, T. Casey, S. Chuang, M. Handley, N. Ismail, A. Sasse: Multimedia Conferencing as a Tool for Collaborative Writing-A Case Study. Research Note RN/91/77, University College London, 1991.

3. J. Banerjee, W. Kim, H.J. Kim, H.F. Korth: Semantics and Implementation of Schema Evolution in Object-Oriented Databases. Proc. ACM SIGMOD Int. Conf. on Management of Data, San Francisco, 1987.

4. R. Bretl, D. Maier, A. Otis, J. Perrey, B. Schuchardt, J.Stein, E.H. Williams, M. Williams: The GemStone Data Management System. in W. Kim, F.H. Lochovsky, ed., Object-Oriented Concepts, Databases and Applications, 283–308, Addison-Wesley, 1989.

5. J. Conklin, M.L. Begeman: gIBIS-A Hypertext Tool for Exploratory Policy Discussion. ACM Trans. on Office Inf. Systems, 4, 303–331, 1988.

6. R. Conradi, C. Fernstrom, A. Fuggetta, R. Snowdon: Towards a Reference Framework for Process Concepts. Proc. 2nd European Workshop on Software Process Technology, Trondheim, Norway, LNCS 635, Springer-Verlag, 1992.

7. PROMOTER: Software Process Modeling and Technology. Research Studies Press, 1994.

8. R. Conradi, M.L. Jaccheri: Customization and Evolution of Process Models in EPOS. Inform. System Development Process, IFIP Transact. A-30, Elsevier Pub., 3–20, 1993.

[1] I would like to acknowledge all the members of the Software Engineering Team in CRIN and all the partners of 'PROMOTER' ESPRIT Working Group for fruitful discussions, and Coumba Diouf Ndiaye for participating to the prototype development.

9. G. Canals, N. Boudjlida, J.C. Derniame, C. Godart, J. Lonchamp: ALF, a Framework for Building Process-Centered Software Engineering Environments, in [7].

10. M. Dowson: Software Process Themes and Issues. in [14].

11. S. Greenberg, R. Bohnet: GroupSketch-A multi-user Sketchpad for Geographically Distributed Small Groups. Proc. Graphics Interface'91, Calgary, Alberta, 207–215, 1991.

12. J. Gintell, M. Houde, J. Kruszelnicki, R. McKenney, G. Memmi: Scutiny-A Collaborative Inspection and review System. Proc. CASE'93, Singapore, 1993.

13. U. Hahn, M. Jarke, T. Rose: Teamwork Support in a Knowledge-Based Information Systems Environment. IEEE Trans. on Software Engineering, Vol 17, 5, 467–481, 1991.

14. Proc. of 2nd Int. Conf. on The Software Process, Berlin, Germany, IEEE Press, 1993.

15. Proc. of First Int. Conf. on The Software Process, Redondo Beach, IEEE Press, 1991.

16. A. Jarczyk, P. Loffler, F. Shipman: Design Rationale for Software Engineering-A Survey. Proc. 25th Hawaii Int. Conf. on System Sciences, 577–586, 1992.

17. M. Jarke, K. Pohl: Vision Driven System Engineering. Information Systems Development Process, IFIP Transact. A-30, Elsevier Pub., 3–20, 1993.

18. P. Johnson, D. Tjahjono: Improving Software Quality through Computer Supported Collaborative Review. Proc. Third European Conference on CSCW, Milan, Italy, 1993.

19. W. Kim: Introduction to Object-Oriented Databases. Computer Systems Series, The MIT Press, 1990.

20. W. Kim, Y.J. Lee, J. Seo: A Framework for Supporting Triggers in Object-oriented Database Systems. Int. Journal of Intelligent and Cooperative Information Systems, 1, 1, 127–143, 1992.

21. S. Kaplan, W.J. Tolone, D.P. Bogia, C. Bignoli: Flexible, Active support for Collaborative Work with Conversation Builder. Proc. CSCW'92, Toronto, 1992, ACM Press.

22. V. Mashayekhi, J. Drake, W. Tsai, J. Riedl: Distributed, Collaborative Software Inspection. IEEE Software, 66–75, 9/1993.

23. K. Ng, B. Abramson: Consensus Diagnosis - A Simulation Study. IEEE Trans. on Systems, Man, and Cybernetics, 22, 5, 916–928, 1992.

24. C.M. Neuwirth, D.S. Kaufer, R. Chandhok, J.H. Morris: Issues in the Design of Computer Support for Co-authoring and Commenting. Proc. CSCW'90, Los Angeles, 1990.

25. L. Osterweil: Software Processes are Software Too. Proc. 9th ICSE, Monterey, CA, IEEE Press, 3–12, 1987.

26. C. Potts: A Generic Model for Representing Design Methods. Proc. 11th ICSE, 217–220, 1989.

27. R. Rao: Implementational Reflection in Silica, Proc. ECOOP91, Geneva, 251–267, 1991.

28. C. Roberts: Describing and Acting Process Models with PML. ISPW4, Moretonhampstead, 1988.

29. T. Rodden, J.A. Mariani, G. Blair: Supporting Cooperative Applications. CSCW Int. Journal, 1, 41–67, 1992

30. K. Schmidt, L. Bannon: Taking CSCW Seriously. CSCW Int. Journal, 1, 7–40, 1992.

31. M. Stefik, G. Foster, D. Bobrow, K. Kahn, S. Lanning, L. Suchman: Beyond the Chalkboard-Computer Support for Collaboration and Problem Solving in Meetings. CACM, 1, 32–47, 1987.

32. R. Snowdon: An Example of Process Change. Proc. 2nd European Workshop on Software Process Technology, Trondheim, Norway, LNCS 635, Springer-Verlag, 1992.

33. R.A. Snowdon: An Introduction to the IPSE 2.5 Project. ICL Tech. Journal, 6, 3, 467–478, 1989.

34. G. Weinberg, D. Freedman: Reviews, Walkthroughs, and Inspections. IEEE Trans. on Software Engineering, Vol 10, 1, 68–72, 1983.

Building Workflow Applications on Top of WooRKS[*]

Gang Lu and Martin Ader

Bull S.A.
7, rue Ampère, 91343 Massy Cedex, France
M.Ader@frmy.bull.fr

Abstract: On top of an object-oriented database management system, we have developed WooRKS, a workflow system used to synchronize a group of users working together based on the circulation of documents. Thanks to the object-oriented development methodology and the generic reusable object class library of WooRKS, we can quickly build a concrete workflow application for a specific customer. In this paper, we will describe how we can obtain this high productivity through a concrete application. This workflow application is used now in Bull's Imaging and Office Solution department. As such, we will present also the initial reactions of WooRKS users.

Key Words: CSCW, workflow, object-oriented application, object-oriented database, object reusability, user interface, object-oriented development methodology and office automation

1 Introduction

A lot of routine office task can be described as structured recurring tasks (called **procedures**) whose basic work items (called **activities**) must be performed by various persons and computer systems (called **actors**) in a certain order (sequential or parallel). Inside a procedure, the coordination between the actors in different places (e.g., the synchronization of activities in a procedure) is characterized by the circulation of a folder, forms or papers. The examples of such routine office tasks include dealing with a customer order requirement in a sales department and preparing a business trip in a big company. The examples of the activities inside the above order processing procedure include "order entry", "inventory check", "shipping", "eval order", etc. A **workflow system** is used to assist people in defining, executing, coordinating and monitoring such routine office procedures based on a shared environment. Unlike other CSCW systems[Grudin 91], such as electronic conferencing [Applegate 86] and real time shared editors [Ellis 90], a workflow system, in general, interacts asynchronously with its actors (e.g., end users) working in different places [Johansen 91], and a workflow procedure can spread over several weeks.

In this paper, we will describe the designs and the first experience of WooRKS, an object-oriented workflow system which is developed as a demonstration of a 4 year

---

[*] The research was founded by the Commission of the European Communities through ITHACA, Esprit project No. 2705.

Esprit project ITHACA (Integrated Toolkits for Highly Advanced Computer Applications [Proefrock 89]). The objectives of ITHACA are to build an object-oriented database management system [Elsholtz 90], to develop the tools ([Bellinzona 91], [De Mey 91] and [Vassiliou 90]) to support a complete object-oriented methodology [De Antonellis 91], and to validate the database, the tools and the methodology by applications like office automation, financial management and chemical process control.

The goal of the ITHACA methodology is to reduce the long-term costs of application development and maintenance for standard applications in selected application domains [De Antonellis 91]. The key assumption here is that one must be able to adequately characterize the selected application domains so that individual applications can be constructed largely from a reusable object class library. On the one hand, we have to build different workflow applications for different customers because a workflow procedure in one company is rarely the same as that in another company. On the other hand, different workflow applications for different customers do have many common features. As such, workflow applications meet our assumption to reach a good reusability.

In the ITHACA development life cycle, as shown in Figure 1, we clearly separate two roles: application engineers and application developers. The application engineers build and maintain a generic reusable object class library; based on this object class library, the application developers build and maintain a concrete application application package according to the requirements of a customer.

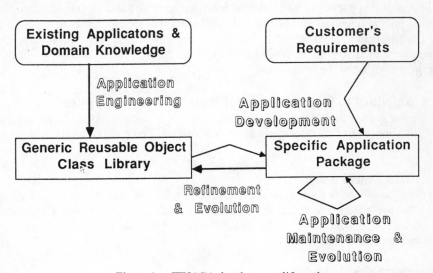

Figure 1.   ITHACA development life cycle

WooRKS is implemented on top of an object-oriented database management system (e.g., NooDLE [Elsholtz 90]). WooRKS now consists of nearly four hundred reusable object classes belonging to five modules. The five modules are: **Organization** (e.g., line unit, manager and project), **Information** (e.g., folder, document and letter),

Time (e.g., time point, event and calendar), **Operator** (e.g., mail, print and revise), and **Coordination** (e.g., procedure and workflow basket). The Organization module describes who will work in workflow procedures and which roles they will play. The Information module describes the semantic attributes and contents of the information circulated inside workflow procedures. The Time module provides the basic to define timing constraints for procedures and activities. The Operator module describes the atomic actions of each actor, while the Coordination module describes how a group of actors work together to carry out a procedure. If we compare building a procedure in the Coordination module to writing a sentence, the Organization module, the Information module, the Time module and the Operator module provide respectively four lexical modules: who will work, what will be dealt with, when the work will be done and how the work will be done.

WooRKS is a generic workflow system, instead of one workflow application developed for a specific customer. WooRKS defines an architecture (i.e., client-server communication, sharing information based on an object-oriented database management system, and a method for structuring object classes), imposes a development methodology, and provides a reusable object class library. Based on this generic workflow system, we can develop a workflow application for a specific customer in one month. The short building time of a workflow application is one of the most important features compared with the workflow systems based on a relational database management system, such as FlowPATH of Bull, ProcessIT of NCR and Workflo of Filenet.

In the rest of this paper, we will describe how we can obtain this high productivity in our first pilot application. In Section 2, we will present some guidelines to choose our first pilot workflow application. In Section 3, we will present how we practise the development methodology of WooRKS through the application. In Section 4, we will give an evaluation of the application.

2   Guidelines to Choose the First Pilot Workflow Application

In Chinese, we say that a good beginning is half way to success. As such, we need to carefully choose our first pilot application of WooRKS. Some of our guidelines are as follows:

- Overhead-Benefit Relation

The question of who is paying for the overhead of a CSCW system and who is going to receive the benefits is crucial for its success [Grudin 89]. We should ensure that the persons who benefits from WooRKS can persuade the persons who pay the overhead to use the system.

- Minimum Critical Mass

A CSCW system serves a group of persons. Every person working on the same procedure should use WooRKS in order to maximize the benefit of WooRKS and to minimize the overhead to exchange information between different persons [Francik 91]. This requires that our pilot application should support enough users to cover a critical mass [Markus 87]. In order to simplify our work, we should choose an application having a small critical mass.

- Integration with Existing System
Groupware is based on the computerization of individual's work. This requires the compatibility and interoperability between WooRKS and existing tools. In our pilot application, we have tried to minimize the work to integrate WooRKS with other existing tools without dissatisfying the users. The integration is not limited to technical issues. Other points to consider include existing company procedures and organizational constraints.

- Typical Workflow Problem
We need to design an attractive demonstration to get end users interested in WooRKS. Attractive demonstrations, however, may mislead users as described by [Francik 91] about Wang's Freestyle system. The customers of Freestyle were strongly drawn to the power and ease of use of annotation tools per se. particularly the synchronized playback of their handwriting and voice. As a result, they initially paid less attention to group communication: that is, how the annotated documents would enter and leave their PCs. Therefore, our pilot application should focus on the true workflow problem, i.e.. the asynchronous coordination between a group of users in different places.

- Minimum Testing Cost
We could spend at most two man-months to develop the first pilot application and to train the users to use it.

3   Development Methodology
The main steps to build a concrete workflow application using WooRKS include identification of the problem. identification of the objects in the different modules of WooRKS. prototype of the user interface. development of new object classes, and modifications according to the end-users' comments. In this section, we will briefly describe the first three steps.

3.1. Identification of the Problem
Keeping the above guidelines in mind, we start to look for our pilot application. Our secretary is heavily overloaded. As such, we think that she will be interested in WooRKS. She described several routine tasks, and we choose the leave management problem. The way to manage leave in our department of Bull is as follows:

- The employee fills in a specific form and passes it to his* manager;
- The manager approves the request and passes the form to his secretary;
- The secretary checks the leave balance of the employee; and
- If the employee has enough leave remaining. the secretary modifies the leave records; Otherwise, the secretary will notify the employee to modify his request.

At the end of every week, the secretary sends a summary to the payment department.

---

* Through this paper, the pronoun "he" is used in the neuter sense.

3.2. Identification of the Objects in the Different Modules

For the leave management problem, we identify four kinds of persons: the employee, the secretary, the manager and the persons in the payment department. The manager only signs the request, and the communication with the persons in the payment department is only through the secretary on papers. As such, we decide that WooRKS supports only the employee and the secretary at the first stage.

After browsing the reusable object class library, we identify the existing objects which can be reused and the new objects to be created. In the Organization module, we create **bullActor**, a sub-class of actor, where the new attributes include birthday, service duration, leave entitlement, home address and home telephone. In the Information module, **leave request**, a sub-class of information, where the new attributes include leave applicant (bullActor), leave starting date, leave ending date, leave reason, the number of leave days and leave approval status. In the Operator module, we introduce **weeklyReport**, a sub-class of command, to generate weekly leave reports based on agenda objects in the Time module. In the Coordination module, **leaveRequest** where the employee executes the first activity to fill in a request form; the secretary executes the second activity to check the leave balance; WooRKS executes automatically the third activity to print the leave request form; and when the secretary receives the signed leave request form, he executes the forth activity to archive the leave request and to send the employee a notice if his request is not approved.

3.3. Prototype of the User Interface

WooRKS allows the application developers to rapidly build the end-user's working scenario without creating the object classes in various modules (e.g., Organization, Information and Coordination). As such, we can ask the end users to evaluate a WooRKS application before the application is built.

The introduction of workflow will change the way people work. For the employee, the way to require leave using WooRKS will be modified as follows:

- The employee (e.g., Mr. Ader) logs in to WooRKS and sees the top-level menu as shown in Figure 2;
- The employee selects "otherOps", then "leave request" from a pull-down menu. A "leave request" procedure is created and Figure 2 will be modified as Figure 3 to ask the employee to work on the "request" activity of the procedure. The activity is started automatically so that Figure 4 is shown also;
- The employee fills in Figure 4 (e.g., "from", "to" and "Leave reason"). WooRKS has an agenda for each actor (i.e., employee). The agenda of the employee will be modified automatically after the employee confirms his request by selecting "OK" in Figure 4; and
- Figure 3 becomes Figure 2, and the employee can select "OK" to quit WooRKS.

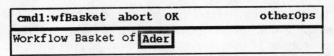

```
cmd1:wfBasket  abort  OK                    otherOps
Workflow Basket of Ader
```

Figure 2.   Employee's top-level menu

```
cmd1:wfBasket  abort  OK                         otherOps
Workflow Basket of Ader
Activities:
     Activity            Procedure               Responsible
     request        leave request 00010          Souriau
```

Figure 3.   Update of Figure 2

```
cmd2:create  abort  OK                           otherOps
Leave Request Form
Last name          Ader
First name         Martin
Employee Id        62639 AR
Department Id      28460
Leave entitlement (91):        29 days
Duration of leave:
from
to                        included
Leave reason:
Leave balance:                 17 days
Date: 20/02/92
```

Figure 4.   Leave request form for the "request" activity

For the secretary, the way to deal with a leave request will be as follows:

> - The secretary (e.g., Mrs. Souriau) logs in to WooRKS and sees the top-level menu as shown in Figure 5. Figure 5 consists of three parts: an indication line (Workflow Basket of Souriau), a list of activities (e.g., all activities which the secretary is asked to work on) and a list of procedures (e.g., all procedures under the responsible of the secretary);
> - The secretary selects "otherOps", then "start activity" from a pull-down menu, and finally selects the activity to be started (e.g., "verification" in Figure 5). Then Figure 6 will be shown;
> - The secretary fills in Figure 6 (e.g., "Number of leave days"). After he selects "OK", a complete form will be printed; Then Figure 7 will be shown. The secretary puts the printed form in the employee's mail box; and

48

- When the secretary receives the form signed by both the employee and his manager, he initiates the "archive" activity in Figure 7. If the leave request is not approved by the manager, a notice will be printed and the employee's agenda will be modified to cancel the leave mark.

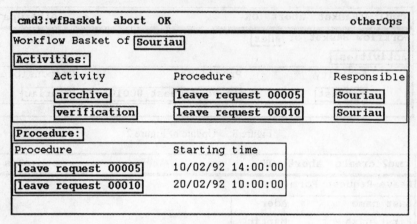

Figure 5.   Secretary's top-level menu

```
cmd4:revise  abort  OK                              otherOps
Leave Request Form
Last Name          Ader
First name         Martin
Employee Id        62639 AR
Department Id      28460

Leave entitlement (91):          29 days

Duration of leave:
from 12/03/92
to 18/03/92        included
Number of leave days:

Leave reason: CP 91

Leave balance:                   17              days
```

Figure 6   Leave request form for the "verification" activity

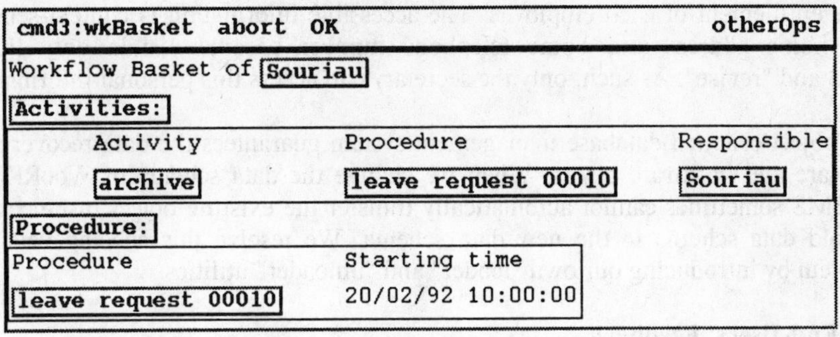

```
cmd3:wkBasket  abort  OK                                    otherOps
Workflow Basket of Souriau
Activities:
      Activity              Procedure              Responsible
        archive         leave request 00010         Souriau
 Procedure:
Procedure                    Starting time
 leave request 00010        20/02/92 10:00:00
```

Figure 7.   Archive activity

The weekly reports will be printed automatically thanks to the periodic event mechanism of WooRKS.

4. Evaluation

The leave management is a typical workflow problem. The critical mass is small after we limit WooRKS to support only the employees and the secretary. Because we can try our pilot application within our own department, this significantly reduces the testing cost. One of main reasons to choose leave management as our pilot application is that the leave management is not yet computerized. As such, we are quite free to choose systems and information formats. After we resolve the signature control problem as described in the section above, the integration problem is resolved.

4.1. Overhead-Benefit Balance
The employee need to fill in only 3 fields in Figure 4, instead of 16 before WooRKS is used. He need not remember his Bull employee Id and his Bull internal department Id. He need not refer to the calendar to calculate the number of working days during his vacations. He need not worry about mistake of leave balance calculation. The overhead of the employee is that the creation of the leave request form is separated from the signature of the form.

The secretary gets the most benefit from WooRKS. The weekly reports will be generated automatically. The verification of leave request is also simplified because a large part of "leave request form" (Figure 6) is filled in by WooRKS. Because the agenda is modified automatically to take into account the absence of the employees, other persons can retrieve the absence information from WooRKS without interrupting the secretary. The overhead of the secretary is that he has to involve twice for each leave request (i.e., leave balance calculation and archive).

4.2. Security Control
Data security is one of the key issues to decide whether WooRKS can really be used. Each user has to give his password when he logs in to WooRKS. The user can only access the authorized commands according to his roles defined in the Organization module. For instance, only the secretary can access command "revise" to modify the

leave entitlement of each employee. The accessible information is context-sensitive. The home address and home telephone number become visible only through command "revise". As such, only the secretary can access this personal information.

The object-oriented database management system guarantees the data recovery from software and hardware errors. When we change the data schema of WooRKS, the ODBMS sometimes cannot automatically transfer the existing object instances from the old data schema to the new data schema. We resolve this schema versioning problem by introducing our own "loader" and "unloader" utilities.

4.3. End-Users' Feedback

We officially introduced WooRKS in our department in February 1992. The users, in general, like WooRKS. WooRKS really simplifies their work. So, they use WooRKS.

People apply for leave only several times per year so that they are always occasional users of WooRKS. Occasional users require the user interface to be simple, flexible and informative. The main criticism about WooRKS comes from the users of Microsoft Windows. The user interface style is not the same as what they use to be.

Using WooRKS, the secretary now spends about 2 minutes to deal with one leave request. This is much shorter than when she deals with leave request without WooRKS. However, the secretary has to frequently wait for WooRKS to deal with his inputs during these two minutes. As such, he requires a better response time of WooRKS.

5 Conclusions

This pilot application proves our idea of generic application framework based on the object-oriented technologies. Less than 10% of the object classes used in this first pilot application were newly developed. Other objects were reused from WooRKS generic object class library. To build this application, we spent:

- a half-day to identify the problem,
- a half-day to identify the reusable object classes and the object classes to be developed,
- four days to prototype user interfaces and to edit the end-user manual,
- ten days to develop new objects and perform integration, and
- two days to make modifications according to user's initial comments.

This well meets our basic objective to **build a concrete workflow application using WooRKS in one month**. This first experience show that the object-oriented technologies increase the productivity of CSCW software development and maintenance. We live in a world changing rapidly. Companies are jointed and reorganized all the times. Their workflow procedures have to follow the changes.

To the best of our knowledge, few papers describe a workflow system built on top of an object-oriented database management system. Our experience shows that the performance and the functionalities of an object-oriented database management system can satisfy the requirements to build a usable workflow product. Our first pilot application of WooRKS is successful. WooRKS simplifies the work of everybody. **It is really used by our department**.

We have ported a part of WooRKS on top of commercial object-oriented database management systems: Versant and Ontos in order to show that WooRKS does not depend on a specific object-oriented database management system. We need to enrich the development and maintenance tools of WooRKS.

6. Acknowledgement

We gratefully acknowledge Mr. Najah Naffah for his support of this research. Frequent discussions with Mr. Clarence Ellis when he worked in our department helped greatly in the design of WooRKS. Mr. Patrick Pons was one of the key members of WooRKS and made many suggestions for the first WooRKS pilot application. Thanks are also due to Mr. Srinivas Raghunandan. Mr. Kabada Srivaths. Mr. Kumar Venkataraman and Mr. Sudarshan Murthy who helped to undertake a large portion of WooRKS implementation.

References

[Ang 91] J.Ang. G.Lu and M.Ader. The Active Office Object Model: its Conceptual Basis and its Implementation. Proc. of the IFIP Conference on the Object Oriented Approach in Information Systems, Quebec City. Canada. Oct. 1991. pp. 419-431.

[Applegate 86] L.Applegate. B.Konsynski and J.Nunamaker. A Group Decision Support System for Idea Generation and Issue Analysis in Organization Planning. Proc. of the First Conference on Computer-Supported Cooperative Work. New York, 1986. pp. 16-34.

[Bellinzona 91] R.Bellinzona and M.Fugini, RECAST Prototype Description. ITHACA.POLIMI.91.E.2.8.#1, Politecnico di Milano, 1991.

[De Antonellis 91] V.De Antonellis and B.Pernici, ITHACA Object-Oriented Methodology Manual: Introduction and Application Developer Manual. ITHACA.POLIMI-UDUNIV.E.8.#1, Politecnico di Milano and Univ. of Udine. 1991.

[De Mey 91] V.De Mey. VISTA Implementation. ITHACA.CUI.90.E4.#1, University of Geneva. 1991.

[Deux 91] O.Deux. The O2 System. Communication of the ACM. vol. 34. no. 12. October 1991. pp. 35-48.

[Elsholtz 90] A.Elsholtz. The NooDLE Database Kernel. Technical Report ITHACA.Nixdorf.90.X.4.#4. Siemens Nixdorf Informationssysteme A.G.. Germany. 1990.

[Ellis 90] C.Ellis. S.Gibbs and G.Rein. Design and Use of a Group Editor. Engineering for Human-Computer Interaction. North-Holland. Amsterdam. 1990. pp. 13-25.

[Ellis 91] C.Ellis and S.Gibbs. Groupware Implementation: Issues and Examples. Tutorial Presented at CHI'91, New Orleans, U.S.A., 1991.

[Francik 91] E.Francik, et al, Putting Innovation to Work: Adoption Strategies for Multimedia Communication Systems. The Communications of the ACM, vol. 34, no. 12, December 1991, pp. 53-63.

[Gerson 86] E.Gerson and S.Star. Analyzing Due Process in the Workplace. ACM Trans. on Office Information Systems, vol. 4, no. 3, July 1986, pp. 257-270.

[Grudin 89] J.Grudin, why groupware applications fail: problems in design and evaluation. Office: Technology and People, vol. 4, no. 3, 1989, pp. 245-64.

[Grudin 91] J.Grudin, CSCW Introduction. The Communications of the ACM, vol. 34, no. 12, December 1991, pp. 30-34.

[Johansen 91] R.Johansen. Leading Business Teams. Addison-Wesley, 1991.

[Lu 90] G.Lu, A Task-Oriented Architecture of Man-Machine Interaction for Office Automation Systems, Ph.D dissertation, Ecole Nationale Superieure des T\o'e\"l\o'e\"communications, Dec. 1990.

[Markus 87] M.Markus, Toward a "Critical Mass" Theory of interactive Media: Universal Access, Interdependence and diffusion. Commun. Res., vol. 14, no. 5, 1987, pp. 491-511.

[Proefrock 89] A.Proefrock, D.Tsichritzis, G.Muller, and M.Ader, ITHACA: An Integrated Toolkit for Highly Advanced Computer Applications, Object-Oriented Development, Univ. of Geneva, July 1989, pp. 321-344.

[Vassiliou 90] Y.Vassiliou, et al, Technical Description of the SIB. ITHACA.FORTH.90.E2.#2. FORTH, Greece, 1990.

Modeling Cooperative Work for Workflow Management

Jon Atle Gulla and Odd Ivar Lindland

Faculty of Electrical Engineering and Computer Science
The Norwegian Institute of Technology
N-7034 TRONDHEIM, NORWAY

Abstract. Characteristic to workflow management is modeling of workflow of manual coordination activities and automated production activities. Conceptual models are used to analyze and describe workflow, though most of these models are not very suitable for representing and relating both coordination activities and production activities. In the Input-Process-Output paradigm, workflow is modeled in terms of processes and data flow, whereas the Customer-Supplier paradigm defines conversation patterns between the actors. The rather intimate relationship between actor interactions and processual structures is recorded in neither of them. In this paper, we suggest to extend the IPO paradigm with concepts for coordination activities. We introduce actors and services as a separate model, and show how two-way flows, ports and rules help us model cooperative and manual aspects in data flow diagrams.

1 Introduction

Workflows describe the coordination and performance of work undertaken in businesses. Workflow management provides mechanisms for planning and controlling workflow, and has received a lot of attention the last few years. Workflow management should allow the analysis of current workflow in order to detect potential bottlenecks and the design of new workflow patterns so that shortcomings can be eliminated. Typically, this includes reorganizing, automating, and/or supporting activities in the current workflow. Business process re-engineering is an approach to organizational and technological change that has drawn on the achievements of this field [5].

In order to investigate and manipulate workflow in a business, a model of the current workflow is used for documenting, understanding, and communicating the coordinating business activities. Furthermore, the model is a natural basis for experimenting with and evaluating the consequence of introducing changes in the model prior to realization.

When doing so, it is important to recognize that workflow is linked to processes that business are performing. Two types of processes exist: *production processes* and *coordination processes* [10]. In production processes the business produces a result (information or material) to a customer. Since the result is expected to be of a certain value for the customer, the processes involves *value-adding* activities. The work in production processes can be manually and automatically performed. Gerrits denotes this process type business processes for either material production or information production [3]. Coordination processes controls the performance of the value-adding activities without directly adding value to the product. Typically, this process type the administrative layer of the production processes and involves manual coordination of people in order to carry out certain actions. Coordination processes are denoted information processes by Gerrits.

These definitions differ from the process definition of Medina Mora et al. [8]. They distinguish between material, information, and business processes. Material processes describe activities which involve physical and mechanical work to move, transform, manipulate, consume or combine materials. Information processes reflect electronic transfer, manipulation, etc. of information. Business processes coordinate actions carried out by people. In Flores and Winograds definition information and material processes are low-level and well-defined, whereas business processes are high-level, ad-hoc and involve a certain degree of uncertainty. They manifest themselves in communication between people and may trigger material and information processes.

Although different process terminology exists in literature, it is important to recognize that workflow involves and affects both production activities and coordination activities. In order to model the workflow in organizations two dominating "paradigms" exists [2]: The *Input-Process-Output (IPO)* paradigm and the *Customer-Supplier (CS)* paradigm. The paradigms are complementing in that the IPO paradigm is particularly suited for modeling the chain of production activities, whereas the CS paradigm is appropriate for modeling the coordinating structure within a business and between the business and its customers.

This paper further elaborates on integrating the IPO and CS paradigms. Section 2 briefly describes the characteristics of these paradigms. In Section 3 the shortcomings of the IPO paradigm with respect to workflow modeling is discussed. As such the section provides the rationale for the new concepts that are introduced in Section 4. In Section 5 a concluding discussion is offered. Directions for further work are also indicated.

2   The IPO and CS paradigms

The Input-Process-Output (IPO) Paradigm is used to model the workflow production processes. The structure of the IPO paradigm is shown in Figure 1(a). The workflow is regarded as a chain of activities that takes information and material as input and produces information or material as output. Complex activities can be decomposed into simpler and more structured activities. The management of the workflow chain is realized by control to and feedback from the process. In an IPO model it is expected that inputs, transformations, and outputs are well-defined. The IPO paradigm is suitable for modeling workflows in repeatable procedure-based processes. The commitments among the workers and in particular between the business and its customers in order to carry out the work is is not explicitly described in IPO models.

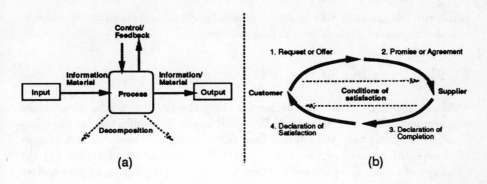

Fig. 1. (a) The IPO paradigm and (b) the CS paradigm to workflow modeling.

Whereas the IPO paradigm views the workflow as a chain of production activities the CS paradigm focuses on coordination among people. The paradigm has been established by Flores and Winograd [14] and is founded on Searle's *Speech Act* [15]. The basic structure is shown in Figure 1(b). Two major roles, *customer* and *supplier*, are modeled. Workflow is defined as coordination between these roles, and is represented by a conversation pattern with four phases [14]. In the first phase the customer makes a request for work, or the supplier makes an offer to the customer. In the second phase the customer and supplier aims at reaching a mutual agreement about what is to be accomplished. This is reflected in the contract *Conditions of Satisfaction*. In the third phase, after the performer has performed what has been agreed upon and completed his work, completion is *declared* for the customer. In the fourth and final phase the customer assesses the work according to the conditions of satisfaction and declares satisfaction or dissatisfaction The ultimate goal of this paradigm is *customer satisfaction*. This implies that workflow loops have to be *closed* and that the customer must acknowledge that the work has been satisfactory completed. As such, the paradigm is appropriate for explicitly modeling the chain of commitments that exists between people in order to satisfy the customer. The specific activities carried out in order meet the contract is not modeled. Also, the information and material needed in each production activity is not described.

In order to manage the workflow properly, we would like to a comprehensive overview of the workflow both in the coordination activities and in the production activities. Furthermore, we would to model the interdependencies between the coordination and the production processes. When doing so, the shortcomings in the coordination process might be explained by an insufficient production process. A comprehensive workflow modeling technique encompassing these interdependencies can be obtained in several ways. In this paper, we show how the IPO paradigm can be extended to capture customer-supplier relationships. We add new concepts for modeling actors and their cooperation within the IPO paradigm. We are then able to model manual parts of coordination processes as well as automated parts of production processes.

3 Shortcomings of the IPO Paradigm

Although there are good reasons for adopting the IPO paradigm in workflow management, there are aspects of IPO that make it insufficient for modeling coordination activities. We address here three issues that concerns the cooperative aspects of workflow management: (1) the involvement of actors, (2) the exchange of information between actors, and (3) the structuring of cooperative work processes.

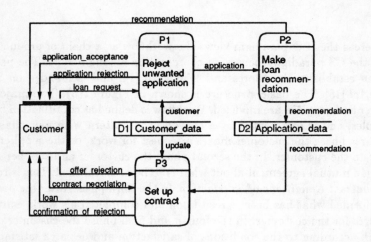

Fig. 2. Data flow diagram for loan processing.

3.1 Involvement of Actors

Consider the DFD model shown in Figure 2, which describes a rather simple processing of loan applications. A clerk checks that the customer is eligible for a loan, and either rejects the application or sends it to a loan consultant for further processing (process P1). The consultant suggests an appropriate amount to the customer, and if the customer accepts the offer, a loan contract is set up in cooperation between these two. In case of a rejection of the offered loan, the consultant just returns a confirmation that ends the whole process. However, neither the clerk nor the consultant is explicitly represented in the model, and we just have to know who is responsible for doing the tasks. For a simple model like this, that might not be a problem, but in a more general setting it can be difficult to decide who the actors are. And looking at the characteristics of workflow management systems, we wee that this lack of information is rather problematic. Both manual and automated tasks are relevant in workflow management. Automated parts can — at least in theory — be specified all the way down to algorithms, and these can then be analyzed with respect to correctness, efficiency, and effectiveness. What manual parts are concerned, an analysis must also take into account who is designated to do the various tasks. Bottlenecks due to overloaded employees, for example, cannot be detected if there is no information about actors in the model.

3.2 Exchange of Information

Exchange of information is common both in production activities and in coordination activities. Consider for example process P3 in Figure 2, where the customer and the loan consultant are to work out a loan contract. Both actors contribute to the final contract, and the whole work is organized as a negotiation process where new ideas and suggestions are exchanged. However, the flow contract_negotiation, which should represent the costumer's contribution, only model the sending of one single piece of information and is unable to capture the responsive nature of negotiations like that.

What is needed here, is the ability to specify that the input flow's values at time t, for any t within the receiving process's active period, depend on the output flow's values at $t' < t$, and vice versa. As long as the flows are modeled as independent, this relationship cannot be made explicit in the model.

3.3 Structuring of Activities

Traditionally, process logic has been specified as algorithms [4], state transition diagrams [11, 13], Petri nets [7], and decision tables/trees [12]. These may work fine for automated processes, but in manual ones one cannot specify the process as a complete calculation — if that was possible, it would not have to be a manual process. Instead, notations for structuring the work itself is needed, in particular for coordinating the efforts of the actors involved. Looking back at process P3 in Figure 2, we see that there is little information represented that can be used to guide the manual execution of the process. The customer should either reject the offer or start negotiating the contract, but this is not clear from the model. Similarly, the result is either a loan or a confirmation that the offer is rejected, but the model just states that there are a number of possible input flows and a number of possible output flows. It is not feasible to specify that a flow depends on or excludes another one, or that the work has to be carried out in accordance to certain rules or constraints.

4 Concepts for Modeling Cooperative Work

Our objective is to extend the IPO paradigm with some basic concepts for modeling coordination activities and cooperative work. The concepts can be worked out at different levels of formalization for integration with other formalized extensions of DFD, but we will here assume the traditional DFD notation (as described in [9]) as a basis.

A coordination activity involves actors and describe how these interact and cooperate with each other. They can be described on the basis of conversation theories like Speech Act though there is a great deal of variation among the activities. In some coordination activities, the actors are negotiating as independent customers and suppliers; in others, the cooperation is manifested more as a command or dependency relationship. In [1], the relationships between actors are classified as power relationships, peer relationships, and service relationships. Each is characterized by its own pattern of cooperation, and there is no general conversation theory that can easily account for them all. Still, there are some fundamental principles that underpin all these relationships, and these have to a large extent been neglected in the IPO paradigm used today. We define an additional model, the *Actor Service* model, that provides a cooperative point of view and is linked to the DFD model as part of the modeling process.

The DFD model itself is also supplemented with some extra concepts. These enable modeling of cooperative work processes and routing decisions.

4.1 Actor Service Model

The *Actor Service* model is a supplement to the DFD model, intended for the modeling of actor relationships in coordination activities. It describes how actors interact and cooperates in accordance to intentions and goals, but there is no control flow or data flow represented. The main concepts are — not surprisingly — *actor* and *service*, and these are briefly explained below.

- An *actor a* is any entity that has the ability to provide a service to another actor. A hardware or software component can be classified as actors, though in this exposition the focus is rather on human actors. These can be external to the workflow management system, like external entities in DFD, but can also be employees working as part of it. Furthermore, an actor can be formed by grouping other actors, in which case it is more like a role played by these actors. Formally, the role actors are defined as sets of other actors a_i, $a = \{a_i\}$. An actor is assumed to have some kind of intention $i(a, s)$ that motivates her action; that is, $i(a, s)$ is a's reason for taking the responsibility for bringing about s.
- A *service* is defined in terms of a *task*, a *result*, or both. Its boundaries relate it to actors, so that there are actors responsible for performing it as well as actors requesting or benefiting from its result. Formally, the service itself is represented as the tuple $s = \langle t, r \rangle$, where t is a task and r is a result specification. A service with its associated actors is called a *service constellation*. This constellation may also contain the intentions of the performing actors and the means for realizing the service, and is specified as a 4-tuple $c = \langle p, b, s, m \rangle$. Variable p is the set of performing actors $p = \{\langle i(a_i, s), a_i \rangle\}$, where a_i is an actor, s is the service, and $i(a_i, s)$ is a_i's intention of doing

s. Variable *b* is the set of actors $\{a_j\}$ benefiting from or requesting service *s*, and *m* is a set of subordinate service constellations $\{s_i\}$, DFD processes $\{p_i\}$, or DFD flows $\{f_i\}$. At the level of elementary services, thus, a service is realized as a number of elements in the DFD model.

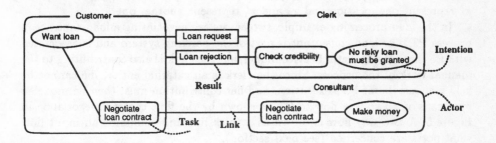

Fig. 3. Actors and services.

Graphically, we use the symbols shown in Figure 3. This figure is the Actor Service model for our loan processing system from Figure 2. The customer is responsible for sending the loan request to the clerk and is also negotiating with the consultant about the contract. The clerk rejects loan applications when the applicants do not have the necessary credibility.

At last, the Actor Service model can be worked out at different levels of detail. In our model in Figure 3, for example, we could decompose the contract negotiation constellation, introducing the consultant's offer as well as customer's rejection and acceptance as new services. Alternatively, we could specify the realization of the constellation as the set of DFD processes $\{P2, P3\}$. The constellation containing the task Check credibility is given a reference to DFD process P1 in its specification.

4.2 A Two-Way Flow

An ordinary one-way flow transports information from one location to another. A *two-way flow* denotes the exchange of information between two parties, such that information floating in one direction is followed by a response in the other direction. Conceptually, this corresponds to a conversation pattern where two or more actors work together and contribute to a common task.

Following the formalization of DFD indicated in [9], we assume flows to carry *items*, where each item is defined as a set of attributes. A flow transports an item from one location to another in zero time, without changing the values of the item's attributes[1]. It is defined as the tuple $f = \langle \pi_1, \pi_2 \rangle$, where item place

---

[1] Actually, this type of flow is referred to as an *ideal flow* in [9].

π_i specifies a location of a chosen type of item, which means that an item at a location represented by π_1 is consumed and an item with exactly the same attributes is immediately produced at a location represented by π_2. Item places π_1 and π_2 represent locations for the same type of item, and the locations must be different from each other. Let us also define $\langle f, t \rangle$ to mean that a particular item is transported along flow f at time t. Now, a two-way flow can be defined as the tuple $\phi = \langle f_1, f_2 \rangle$, where $f_1 = \langle \pi_1, \pi_2 \rangle$ and $f_2 = \langle \pi_2', \pi_1' \rangle$, where π_1 and π_1' represent one location and π_2 and π_2' represent another one.

In the loan processing example, two actors are negotiating a loan contract in process P3. The loan consultant is part of the banking system and is associated with P3 through the Actor Service model, but the clerk is also contributing to the manual work of the process. Since the clerk is an external entity, she cannot be held responsible for P3's execution, and her contribution must then be modeled by means of a two-way flow to P3, as shown by the flow contract_negotiation in Figure 5. A two-way flow is drawn as a thick line and counts as an input flow what ports are concerned (see next section).

4.3 Ports and Rule Modeling

An automated completely specified process can be described by its input flows, its output flows, and the functions determining the attribute values of the output flows' items on the basis of the input flows' items. Being a little more precise, we say that a process can consume items from a set of item places, Π_I, and produces items to another set of item places, Π_O, where all $\pi \in \Pi_I \cup \Pi_O$ represent the same location.

For manual processes, and incompletely automated ones, the functions may not be available, and one must use other means for describing their contents and internal structures. Rather than formulating functional relationships between inputs and outputs, we then specify constraints on the flows consumed and produced during process executions. These constraints serve as a structure for the work to be carried out and provide guidelines for the actors in cooperative work processes. We introduce *input port expressions*, *output port expressions*, and *constraint rules* for the specification of the constraints:

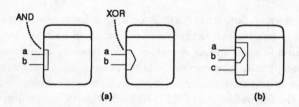

(a)   (b)

Fig. 4. (a) AND port and XOR port. (b) Nested ports.

- An *input port expression* lists all possible combinations of input flow items that can be consumed during one process execution. Formally, it is specified as the tuple $\langle \Pi_I, \Pi_{IC} \rangle$, where set Π_I is as above and Π_{IC} is a subset of Π_I's powerset, $\Pi_{IC} \subseteq \mathcal{P}(\Pi_I)^2$. Π_{IC} identifies combinations of item places, from which items are consumed during a single process execution.

  In the DFD model, we add input port expressions using XOR ports and AND ports on input flows to processes. The AND port in Figure 4(a), which includes two flows with destination places π_a and π_b, means that the process must consume both item a from π_a and b from π_b. Correspondingly, the XOR port means that the process must consume either a from π_a or b from π_b, but not both. Of course, ports may be nested, so that the port expression in Figure 4(b) specifies that the process consumes either $\{a, b\}$ or $\{b, c\}$ during each execution.

- An *output port expression* lists all possible combinations of output flow items that can be produced during one process execution. Formally, it is specified as the tuple $\langle \Pi_O, \Pi_{OC} \rangle$, where set Π_O is as above and Π_{OC} is a subset of Π_O's powerset, $\Pi_{OC} \subseteq \mathcal{P}(\Pi_O)$. Π_{OC} identifies combinations of item places, to which items are produced during a single process execution.

  Similarly to input port expressions, XOR ports and AND ports are used in the DFD model for the specification of the constraints.

- A *constraint rule* specifies the existence relationship between consumed items and produced items; that is, given that a process consumes a specific combination of input flow items, the rule determines which output flow items are produced. The values of the items' attributes are not involved in these rules, just their existence. Formally, we can describe the relationship R as a subset of the Cartesian product of the sets Π_{IC} and Π_{OC}, $R \subseteq \Pi_{IC} \times \Pi_{OC}$, where Π_{IC} and Π_{OC} are as described above.

  In the model, the constraint is specified as a number of constraint rules associated with a process. Each rule is of the form

$$\text{IF} \quad < input\ flows >$$
$$\text{THEN} < output\ flows >,$$

and specifies how the production of items to specific output flows depends on the consumption of items from specific input flows. Note that this notation is consistent with the rule notation in TEMPORA [6], so that our additions can easily be integrated with rule-based approaches to information systems development.

We can now describe the internal structure of manual processes more precisely. In process P3 in Figure 2, the process must either receive offer_rejection, or contract_negotiation and recommendation, and this is easily shown as an XOR port with an subordinate AND port in Figure 5. The output port expression says that an update is always produced, though only one of loan and confirmation_of_rejection can be produced during a particular process execution. The

---

² $\mathcal{P}(\Pi_I)$ is the collection of all subsets of Π_I.

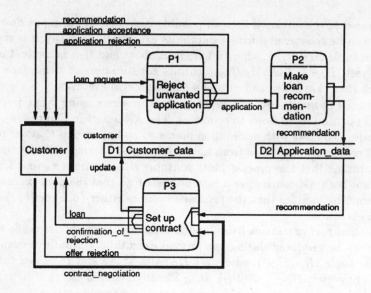

Fig. 5. Extended data flow diagram.

relationship between input flows and output flows is specified by means of the two constraint rules in Table 1. An offer_rejection is followed by the sending of confirmation_of_rejection, whereas an contract_negotiation leads to the generation of a loan. With these constraints specified, one can define tools and methods that structure the cooperative work of P3.

> IF   contract_negotiation AND recommendation
> THEN update AND loan
>
> IF   offer_rejection
> THEN update AND confirmation_of_rejection

Table 1. Rules associating input flows and output flows for process P3.

Additionally, we can restrict the values of the items carried by the flows. This is done by extending the constraint rule notation with a special WHERE field, which specifies the arithmetic or logical relationships between items consumed and produced during a process execution. For example, the flows recommendation, update and loan in Figure 5 all carry an item applicant, and the value of this item must be the same for all flows. Similarly, the amount item carried by loan and update must have the same value. Assuming that the value of this amount has to be less or equal to recommendation's amount, we can now replace the first rule in Table 1 with the following extended rule:

```
IF        contract_negotiation AND recommendation
THEN      update AND loan
WHERE     recommendation.applicant = update.applicant = loan.applicant AND
          recommendation.amount ≥ loan.amount AND
          loan.amount = update.amount
```

Finally, the rule can contain an initial WHEN field that specifies what flow — or combination of flows — triggers the execution of the rule. Looking at the rule above, we notice that the rule is triggered by the arrival of flow contract_negotiation: WHEN contract_negotiation. In the diagram, this information can be made explicit by marking that particular flow with a T.

5 Concluding Discussion

Our work relies on the distinction between workflows manifested in coordination and production processes. As indicated in Figure 5, the IPO paradigm is appropriate for modeling production processes, but lacks concepts for modeling coordination processes. For the CS paradigm the situation is the other way round. It is suitable for modeling coordination processes, but lacks direct links to production activities. Although both paradigms are flexible and can be extended with new concepts, it seems problematic to combine them as they are today. We find a focus on *control flow* in both paradigms — though differently modeled — and if these models are just combined, this redundancy of information would clutter the model and complicate consistency checks. Other problems are related to the cyclic and linear nature of these paradigms, and their different interpretation of flow content.

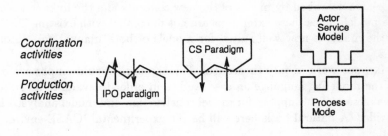

Fig. 6. Towards an integrated workflow modeling approach.

Our main contribution has been to provide a comprehensive framework for workflow modeling, where coordination activities and the production activities are integrated. The IPO paradigm forms the basis, but we have now added concepts for the modeling of coordination and cooperative work. First, we introduced the Actor Service language which enable us to explicitly model the services provided by the actors, their intentions, and the relationships among the actors. Secondly, a two-way flow makes it possible to model exchange of information between two parties. Finally, ports and rules give us the opportunity to model the routing of work and the constraints imposed on it. In that sense, we have extended the modeling language to the realm of coordination activities and also established well-founded links between these too kinds of activities.

The Actor Service model records coordination patterns among people involved or affected by the organization. It captures many facets of the CS paradigm, though the following properties of our model should also be noted:

- A model like this does not represent a fixed conversation pattern, since such a pattern would include both a number of fixed types of interactions and a control flow specifying their sequencing. As the model is, we have the freedom to specify simplified interaction patterns when that is appropriate, whereas control aspects can be completely left out of the model.
- Contrary to the CS paradigm, we can here associate tasks and results with intentions of the actors, which in turn provides a mechanism for recording the rationale of DFD elements. Actors may cooperate in doing a task, but the model does not require them to have the same intentions.

In our current model, intentions are modeled in a rather simplistic way, but the basis idea now is to extend the notion of *intention* and relate it to other parts of the enterprise model. Intentions provide background information that can help us analyze communication breakdowns and predict both desirable and undesirable situations in organizations. More specifically, we are working on the relationship between intentions and constraint rules, letting the intentions influence on the organization of work among people.

The data flow model itself now includes concepts that enable a more precise specification of manual working procedures. Actor responsibilities and collaborative work are described by means of the new concepts and the links to the Actor Service model. Since these extensions are not in conflict with existing DFD concepts, the model is now well suited for models of both manual and automatic systems.

So far, our work is only theoretical. Further work should emphasize on applying the modeling language on case studies in order to evaluate its strengths and weaknesses. Tool support for model construction and model analysis should be provided. A natural basis here will be the experimental ICASE-environment PPP [4].

References

1. A. J. C. Blyth, J. Chudge, J. E. Dobson, and M. R. Strens. ORDIT: A new methodology to assist in the process of eliciting and modelling organisational re-

quirements. In *Proceedings on the Conference on Organisational Computing Systems*, San Jose, November 1993.

2. P. J. Denning. Work Is a Closed-Loop Process. *American Scientist*, 80:314–317, July-August 1992.

3. H. Gerrits. Business Process Redesign and Information Systems Design: A Happy Couple? In N. Prakash, C. Rolland, and B. Pernici, editors, *IFIP WG 8.1 Working Conference on Information System Development Process*, pages 325–336, Como, September 1993. Elsevier Science Publishers B. V. (North-Holland).

4. J. A. Gulla, O. I. Lindland, and G. Willumsen. PPP: An Integrated CASE Environment. In R. Andersen, J. A. Bubenko jr., and A. Sølvberg, editors, *Proceedings of the Third International Conference on Advanced Information Systems Engineering (CAiSE'91)*, pages 194–221, Trondheim, May 1991. Springer-Verlag.

5. M. Hammer. Reengineering Work: Don't Automate, Obliterate. *Harvard Business Review*, pages 104–112, July-August 1990.

6. J. Krogstie, P. McBrien, R. Owens, and A. H. Seltveit. Information Systems Development Using a Combination of Process and Rule Based Approaches. In R. Andersen, J. A. Bubenko jr., and A. Sølvberg, editors, *Proceedings of the Third International Conference on Advanced Information Systems Engineering (CAiSE'91)*, pages 319–335, Trondheim, May 1991. Springer-Verlag.

7. D. C. H. Kung. The Behavior Network Model for Conceptual Information Modeling. *Information Systems*, 18(1):1–21, 1993.

8. R. Medina-Mora, T. Winograd, R. Flores, and F. Flores. The Action Workflow Approach to Workflow Management Technology. In *Proceedings of CSCW'92*, 1992.

9. A. L. Opdahl and G. Sindre. Concepts for Real-World Modelling. In C. Rolland, F. Bodart, and C. Cauvet, editors, *Proceedings of the Fifth International Conference on Advanced Information Systems Engineering (CAiSE'93)*, pages 309–327, Paris, June 1993. Springer-Verlag.

10. M. E. Porter and V. E. Millar. How Information Gives You Competitive Advantage. In *Revolution in Real Time: Managing Information Technology in the 1990s*, chapter II-1, pages 59–82. Harvard Business Review, Boston, 1984.

11. G. Richter and B. Maffeo. Toward a Rigorous Interpretation of ESML — Extended Systems Modeling Language. *IEEE Transactions on Software Engineering*, 19(2):165–180, February 1993.

12. A. Sølvberg and D. C. H. Kung. *Information Systems Engineering*. Springer-Verlag, 1993.

13. P. T. Ward. The Transformation Schema: An Extension of the Data Flow Diagram to Represent Control and Timing. *IEEE Transactions on Software Engineering*, 12(2):198–210, February 1986.

14. T. Winograd. A Language/Action Perspective on the Design of Cooperative Work. *Human-Computer Interaction*, 3(1):3–30, 1987-88.

15. T. Winograd and F. Flores. *Understanding Computers and Cognition: A New Foundation for Design*. Ablex Publishing Corporation, New Jersey, 1986.

IKUMI: A Groupware Development Support System with Visual Environment

Hiroyuki Tarumi, Atsushi Tabuchi, Kenji Yoshifu *

Kansai C&C Research Labs., NEC Corporation

Abstract. IKUMI is a groupware development support system, which is based on MEGUMI, the e-mail platform, developed by the authors. IKUMI provides the workflow feature, including body-less mail for synchronizing activities (beacon messages), visually defining of branching conditions, and cooperation between e-mail and realtime groupware. With IKUMI, end-users can easily and dynamically define relatively simple cooperative work with workflow, and system engineers are able to embed groupware functions into applications at low cost.

1 Introduction

Recent CSCW technologies have produced many kinds of groupware systems — *general communication tools*, including teleconference systems like MERMAID[1], e-mail, and bulletin board systems, and *task-oriented applications*, including co-authoring systems like Quilt[2] and decision support systems like gIBIS[3].

Task-oriented groupware applications are specifically designed only for particular tasks, e.g. co-authoring or decision making. Application developers, however, may want to build groupware applications for other unsupported group tasks by using general communication tools. If a groupware toolkit and a groupware development support system (GwDvSS) are provided to the application developers, these applications would be developed at lower cost.

GwDvSS should be able to be used not only for developing groupware applications, but also for customizing groupware configuration. In case of cooperative writing systems, for example, comments and corrections are transmitted with e-mail. If the system user wants to change the number of commentators or co-authors, e-mail routing must be customized. Such customization are sometimes prepared as built-in features of the cooperative writing system. If such customizations can be implemented without changing any application code, groupware applications would be more flexible.

For the above reasons, GwDvSS is very important and promising. GwDvSS should provide the following features:

1. Workflow design:
   (a) Information structure design, including multimedia data.
   (b) Information processing program design.

---

* {tarumi,tabuchi,yoshifu}@obp.cl.nec.co.jp

(c) Information routing design among people, designed programs, and existing tools.

(d) Hierarchical workflow structure design.

(e) Teleconferencing system usage design in the groupwork context.

(f) Bulletin board usage design in the groupwork context.

(g) Organizational structure design for the groupwork participants.

2. Generating executable rules and/or codes from the workflow.

3. Allowing ad-hoc design and customization of the groupwork by end users.

For this purpose, many *workflow* management systems[4] were developed and are in the marketplace now. The authors appreciate them as innovative systems, but they are still insufficient as GwDvSS. First, their application area is mostly focused on business applications. To support other areas, e.g. software development management or co-authoring, GwDvSS should support ad-hoc workflow definition, coordination between realtime and non-realtime groupware tools, multimedia data handling, etc. Second, application development assistance should be enhanced, e.g. by means of workflow libraries.

The GwDvSS described in this paper, IKUMI, generates rules from visually defined workflow, which consists of information structure, processing, and flow design. IKUMI also supports a realtime and non-realtime groupware connection model and parameterized workflow library model. The generated rules are passed to an e-mail platform "MEGUMI," which can handle multimedia data, developed by the authors.

Thus, IKUMI is designed to support all above requirements, while existing workflow systems do not or weakly support 1(a), 1(e), 1(f), 1(g), 2, and 3.

After describing MEGUMI in Section 2, IKUMI profile is given in Section 3. Special IKUMI workflow features will be described in Section 4. Comparison and discussion will be given in Section 5.

2 MEGUMI: the E-mail platform

2.1 Features

MEGUMI is an e-mail system developed by the authors. It has the following pertinent features:

- Semi-formal message structure, like OVAL[5], with form oriented user interface, developed on Canae[6] and OSF/Motif UI toolkit.
- Multimedia data: figures, images including handwritten image and fax image.
- Form definition based on an expansion of the MIME[7].
- Flow management features: circular mail, express mail, and deadline management.
- File attachment on mail, as an external-body defined in MIME standard.
- Mail tracking.

- Mail processing rules in the HyperScheme language [8]. [2]
- Application Program Interface (API) as C and HyperScheme functions.

2.2 Configuration

Each MEGUMI user has one's own daemon process, megumi-d (Fig. 1). It receives all mail for the user, applies rules every time mail is received, opened, accepted, or sent, reminds the user of a deadline, invokes application programs for the user and passes them the mail, and manages the mail traffic history. Because a megumi-d can ask other megumi-d about the traffic history, mail tracking is possible.

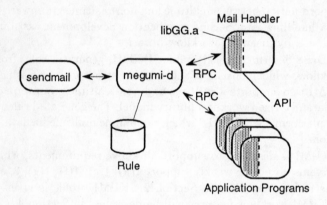

Fig. 1. MEGUMI Configuration

Application programs and mail handler (i.e. mail reader/composer program) are connected to megumi-d, via RPC protocol. Precisely, the mail handler is an application, too. The RPC protocol routines for applications are prepared as a library: libGG.a. The functional specification for libGG.a is the API for MEGUMI.

A megumi-d can communicate with two or more applications with RPC. According to the rule, megumi-d dispatches mail to their corresponding application programs. There are two groupware application architectures with this mechanism. On one architecture, all mail traffic belonging to the application is exclusively handled by an application-oriented tool. On another architecture, application mail traffic is put into one's inbox and handled with the standard mail handler, with special rules pertinent to the application.

---

[2] HyperScheme is a Scheme language expansion, providing object oriented features and an easy way to accomplish mutual calling with the C language.

3 IKUMI: the GwDvSS

3.1 Configuration

The IKUMI configuration is shown in Fig. 2.

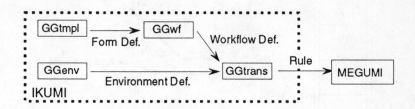

Fig. 2. IKUMI configuration

IKUMI is a set of tools, whose names all begin with the prefix GG[3]. The final tool for IKUMI, GGtrans, generates rules for the MEGUMI mail system. Other tools are all prepared for the definition of workflow or groupwork environment, with graphical user interfaces. Their main tool is GGwf (Fig. 3)[4], for defining the workflow based on the visual workflow chart.

In this subsection, we will describe each tool.

GGtmpl — Form Definition Tool With GGtmpl, the user can define the e-mail format with a visual user interface. Fig. 4 is a hardcopy showing GGtmpl's user interface.

The upper window is a palette of form components. They are form sheet, label, choice field, number field, text field, figure field, and image field, from left to right. The lower big window is the form editor. The user can pick up a form component from the palette, put it on the form editor, and resize individual components to fill the sheet.

Individual component attribute can be specified by double-clicking the component to open the attribute editor, as shown at top of the form editor window in Fig. 4. In this example, the attributes for a choice field — candidate choices, allowed choice number, etc. — are being edited.

After creating a form definition (in the authors' special language), it is passed to GGwf. Since the definition can also be directly referred to by MEGUMI mail to specify the mail's format, GGtmpl can be used separately from other IKUMI tools.

---

[3] GG stands for Groupware Generator

[4] All screen dumps are taken from IKUMI English version, which is converted from the original Japanese version.

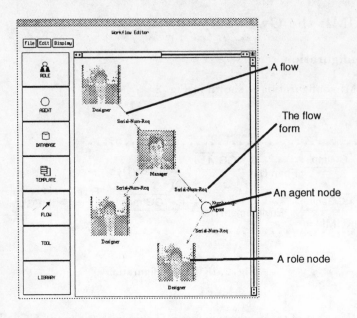

Fig. 3. GGwf

GGwf — Workflow Definition Tool The following explains the GGwf outline with rather simple workflow examples. Enhanced workflow features will be
described in Section 4.

As already shown in Fig. 3, the user defines a workflow as a visual workflow
chart — a directed graph — in GGwf. Each node may be a *role* or an *agent*.
Each arc of the graph is an e-mail transfer. In this paper, individual arc is called
a *flow*.

Role Role is a task unit in the workflow, which is performed by a single person.
The role definition is given as the one responsible for receiving a form as an e-
mail, filling or editing particular fields of a form, invoking a program and putting
a form to the program, creating a new form, or sending a form; or a combination
of these responsibilities.

These responsibilities are defined in the detailed definition window shown in
Fig. 5, which appears when the user double-clicks the role node. In this window,
the workflow designer can specify the program that processes the incoming mail,
fields that should be filled by the role, conditions for branch, and the processing
deadline at this node.

To specify fields that should be filled, the user pops up another window, like
Fig. 6, and clicks the target field on the window. This visual definition method
is simple and acceptable by end users.

More description regarding condition specifications are given in Section 4.2.

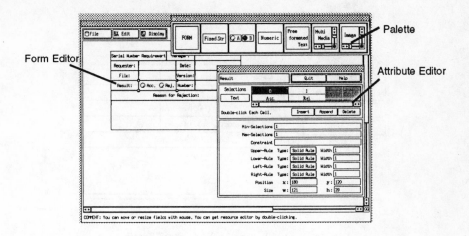

Fig. 4. GGtmpl

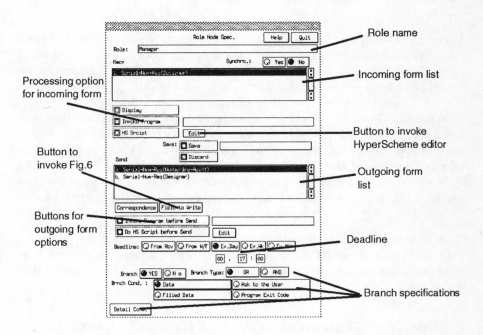

Fig. 5. Node Specification in GGwf

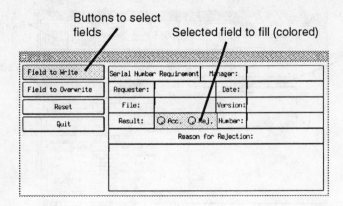

Fig. 6. Field Selection in Node Specification

The user can also define the name for each role, the icon for each role, and constraints among roles. An constraint example is a rule to prohibit a person from concurrently engaging in two particular roles.

Agent In IKUMI, agent means a computer program which receives and sends e-mail traffic, without interacting with any user. For example, a program which automatically fills in the serial number field for a form can be an agent, if the form is given from and sent to another node as e-mail. Each agent is represented as a circle icon in the visual workflow chart.

When the GGwf user double-clicks an agent node, the detail definition window similar to Fig. 5 appears. In this window, the user can specify the program name that processes the incoming mail, or directly write a program in Hyper-Scheme language. If the agent function is simple, e.g. copying fields or filling fields with constant values, the user can specify this visually in almost the same way as in Fig. 6. Hence, even end users can define agents without writing codes.

Flow A flow basically represents an e-mail transfer from one node to another node. The user can specify the mail form by attaching a form name to the flow. More discussion on a special flow type (beacon message) will be presented later in this paper.

Total GGwf Usage Description The GGwf usage outline is as follows:

1. Click the ROLE button and select the role subwindow; create new roles on the subwindow and insert them on the workflow editor.
2. In the same way, click the AGENT button and select the agent subwindow; create agents on the subwindow and insert them on the workflow editor.

3. Connect nodes by flows.
4. Click the FORM button and select a list of forms defined in GGtmpl. For each information flow, a form name must be selected and attached.
5. Double-click each node, and select a detail definition window for the role or agent, and give the detailed definition.
6. Save the workflow and quit.

The GGwf output is given as a set of S-expressions.

GGenv — Environment Definition Tool With GGenv, the user defines the environment for executing the groupware application. For example, the name of person who fulfills each role, machine type which each person uses, and people's organizational structure are environmental parameters. These definition will be reflected onto the rule generation phase at GGtrans.

Currently, GGenv only supports the definition of the name of the person who fulfills each role. To achieve workflow portability, it is necessary to separate this definition from the workflow.

GGtrans — Rule Generation Tool GGtrans is the only tool which has no graphical interaction with the user. It receives the definitions from other IKUMI tools, and generates rules for each user's megumi-d.

For each person engaging in any role in the workflow, GGtrans generates rules, i.e. compile workflow and environment definition into rules, that will be invoked at the event of creating, receiving, and sending a form, and originating a workflow. It also generates metarules, which are used to select the rule file at each event. These rules and metarules are distributed by control mail to the megumi-d for each groupwork member.

If a person engages in two or more roles in a workflow, rules for all these roles are merged for the user with metarules. The user's megumi-d selects the proper role rule, when it receives or sends e-mail traffic, by evaluating the metarules.

An metarule example is:

```
( gg-eval-rule "receive"
  ( "ex1" 1.0  1.0  "FL001" ) ( "FormA" 1.0 1.0 ) "ex1-1.0-C-1.scm" )
```

This metarule means that, if the megumi-d receives mail, whose workflow-name is "ex1," whose workflow-version is 1.0, whose flow-id in the workflow is "FL001," whose form is named "FormA," and whose form-version is 1.0, then it executes a rule file "ex1-1.0-C-1.scm." Flow-id is a unique ID in a workflow, which is appended on every e-mail, by the sender node's rule at the sending event.

For each agent, rules are given to the agent program. The agent program is a UNIX program, invoked from /usr/lib/sendmail on receiving mail traffic.

3.2 Target Users

IKUMI's target users are groupware application developers and groupware end users. This subsection describes the applications for these target users.

Groupware Application Developers Application developers develop groupware application, in the following way:

1. Designs the workflow, and defines it on IKUMI tools.
2. Installs the generated rules and agents.
3. If necessary, develops programs which are called from the rules or agents, using MEGUMI's API (libGG.a).
4. Installs the programs.

Groupware End-Users End users can use IKUMI in almost the same way as the developer's. However, because they cannot develop programs in C or HyperScheme language, function of agents and roles are restricted.

Even with this restriction, end users can develop form handling groupware applications. They can define forms, each role's responsibility for filling form fields, and flows. They can even define agents for copying or filling form fields. MEGUMI's standard mail handling program is used for such an application. It supports sufficient features for such simple groupware applications, i.e. form-like user interface and interface for reminding the user of a deadline for making a response.

Thus, the end-user can create and install ad-hoc workflow definitions. This is important for supporting real office work.

4 Workflow Features

This section describes special IKUMI workflow features. These features are given by expansion or additional attributes for flows (Section 4.1) or nodes (other). These features enhance the workflow expressive power in the visual environment.

4.1 Beacon Message

A beacon message is a special flow category, which is implemented as e-mail with no body and is invisible to the end users. A beacon message is represented as a broken line arrow in GGwf.

It is useful to synchronize group members' activities. For example, assume such a workflow as that shown in Fig. 7. Role A, the originator of this workflow, creates a progress report and sends it to Role C. At the same time, Role C requires the newest financial report, which is made by Role B, in reading the progress report. In this case, Role A sends a beacon message to Role B, when Role A sends the progress report to Role C. Role B's megumi-d prepares (i.e. invokes or creates a GUI icon for) an editor for the financial report, when it receives the beacon message. The beacon message is, of course, automatically sent by the rule. With this mechanism, Role A and Role C do not need to write a message to Role B, like "Please prepare the newest financial report." Role B does not need to read such routine-work mail, either.

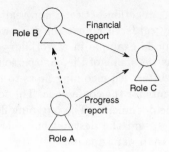

Fig. 7. A Workflow with Beacon Message

4.2 Branch in Workflow

Some workflows have flow branches. IKUMI provides two branch categories: *AND-branches* and *OR-branches*.

The OR-branch specification is visually defined in the detailed definition for the branching node, with a window such as shown in Fig. 8. The user defines the specification by clicking the focused field on the form, specifies the value and operator for comparison, and gives the selection for each comparison result.

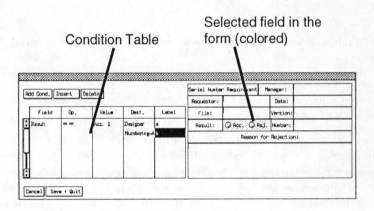

Fig. 8. Window for branch specification

4.3 Realtime Conference Node

Realtime communication and non-realtime communication are both necessary for groupwork. Most existing groupware tools support only one of them. The authors support seamless connection between non-realtime communication and realtime communication by *conference nodes* in groupwork workflow.

Fig. 9 is a conference node example in a workflow definition. A conference node has attributes such as the name of the chairperson, names of participants, and the name of minutes writer. All incoming flows to the conference node represent the required documents for the conference. The sources for these flows are the roles responsible for the documents. The outgoing flows from the conference node represent the minutes, and the destination nodes of these flows are the receivers of minutes other than participants.

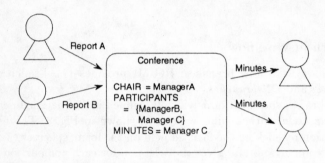

Fig. 9. A Conference Node Example

From such a workflow, GGtrans will generate the following rules for the chairperson's megumi-d .

1. Rules to wait for all incoming documents.
2. Rules to prepare a GUI icon for the conference, which can invoke a conference program with specified parameter file.

GGtrans also generates a parameter file for the conference. The parameter includes the names of required documents, the conference participants, the chairperson's and minutes writer names. When the conference is started, an editor for the minutes appears on the minutes writer's display. The editor sends the minutes to all destinations by e-mail, when the conference is finished and minutes are completed.

This type of workflow is still effective for a non-electronic, traditional style meeting. In such a case, GGtrans can generate rules for the chairperson, like:

1. Rules to wait for all incoming documents
2. Rules to send these documents to all participants by e-mail
3. Rules to show a message to the chairperson indicating that the chairperson can call the meeting.
4. Rules to send a beacon message to the minutes writer, which let the minutes writer's megumi-d prepare the editor for minutes.

4.4 Workflow Library

Frequently used workflow patterns should be collected and prepared as a work-flow library set. For example, a *comment-and-rewrite* pattern should be prepared as a parameterized skeleton for the workflow in Fig. 10(a). It will be used as a node in a concrete workflow in the same way as macro expansion, as shown in Fig. 10(b).

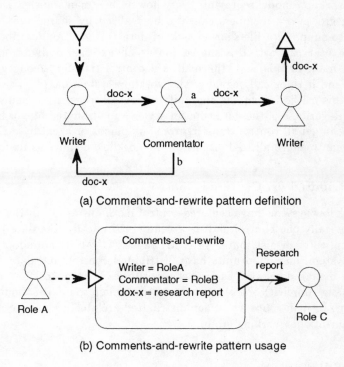

(a) Comments-and-rewrite pattern definition

(b) Comments-and-rewrite pattern usage

Fig. 10. An Workflow Skeleton Example

Note that the role "writer" in Fig. 10(a) is replaced by "Role A" in (b). This causes the source and destination nodes for the beacon message to be identical. In such cases, no beacon message is made when this workflow is executed, but a state transition from the previous mode to the comment-and-rewrite mode is caused in Role A's megumi-d .

5 Comparison and Discussion

5.1 Comparison with Other Workflow Systems

The closest systems to IKUMI would be WorkMAN [9][10] and Regatta[11]. WorkMAN provides Forms Designer and Forms Router tools, corresponding to

GGtmpl and GGwf. Regatta[11] also provides a visual environment for group-work design. IKUMI's most notable differences from them are visual programming environment with direct manipulation on forms (Fig. 6 and Fig. 8) and connection to realtime conference.

5.2   Mail vs. Shared File

IKUMI's workflow model represents every flow as an e-mail transfer. Data transfer among groupwork members can also be realized by shared files. However, IKUMI also supports a file sharing type of data transfer. As described in Section 2, the user can attach a shared file as an external-body component to MEGUMI mail. In this case, the mail is a control transfer among groupwork members, and it is logically equal to the workflow system based on shared files.

Using this method, a simple and uniform control transfer mechanism can be obtained. Regardless of the data transfer style — mail, shared file, or hybrid —, megumi-d can get all control transfers from any person or agent by mail, so that megumi-d can manage all to-do items for all workflow definitions uniformly.

5.3   Distributed vs. Centered Control

Some workflow systems have centered control mechanisms [9]. In this category, there is logically one control and data center. (Physically, the data repository may be duplicated or distributed.) IKUMI and MEGUMI do not adopt it. In the author's system, megumi-d units have distributed control, and data stores are personally managed or given as project repositories in each workflow. Megumi-d units exchange implicit control messages to track mail, to inform about dynamic alternations to mail route, etc. Such distributed architecture can be applied to cross-organizational working group.

6   Conclusion

This paper has described a Groupware Development Support System IKUMI, especially its function and the workflow model. IKUMI supports multimedia mail (requirement 1(a) in Section 1), agents(1(b)), mail routing (1(c)), workflow libraries (1(d)), conference node (1(e)), rule generation (2), and visual environment which gives easy interfaces even to end users (3).

Groupwork support is expected in not only business applications, but also in CASE and CAD applications. In these areas, questions and answers on product specifications, bug reports, progress reports, etc. are e-mail items. Tracking these documents is helpful for manager's work, and also an effective way to satisfy ISO-9000 standards. Of course MEGUMI's multimedia mail feature is indispensable to these application areas.

The authors believe that the workflow system is an important unit in the groupware toolkit, but it is not the entire thing. Other important factors are co-producing and sharing. As for co-producing, multimedia document review and decision support would be important functions in a groupware toolkit. For sharing, bulletin boards must be in the toolkit. Co-producing and sharing toolkit are now being developed.

IKUMI and MEGUMI are implemented on SVR4 UNIX system. Client program library, libGG.a, is also implemented on personal computers running MS-Windows 3.1 operating system. IKUMI and MEGUMI are applied to CASE and CAD products.

Acknowledgements

The authors would like to thank Masao Managaki, Hitoshi Miyai, and other laboratory members for helpful comments on this research, and thank Hiroyuki Yagyu for the implemention of IKUMI and MEGUMI. Finally the authors wish to acknowledge the support of several divisions in NEC.

References

1. Watabe, K., et al. : Distributed Multiparty Desktop Conferencing System: MERMAID. Proc. of ACM 1990 Conf. on CSCW (1990) 27–38
2. Leland, M. D. P., et al. : Collaborative Document Production Using Quilt. Proc. of ACM 1988 Conf. on CSCW (1988) 206–215
3. Conklin, J., and Begeman, M. L. : gIBIS: A Hypertext Tool for Exploratory Policy Discussion. Proc. of ACM 1988 Conf. on CSCW (1988) 140–152
4. Marshak, R.T.: Requirements for Workflow Products. Groupware '92 Proceedings, Coleman, D.D. Ed. (1992) 281–285
5. Malone, T.W. and Fry, Ch. : Experiments with Oval: A Radically Tailorable Tool for Cooperative Work. Proc. of ACM 1992 Conf. on CSCW (1992) 298–205
6. Tarumi, H., Rekimoto, J., Sugai, M., et al.: Canae — A User Interface Construction Environment with Editors as Software Parts. NEC Research and Development. **98** (1990) 89–98
7. Borenstein, N. and Freed, N.: MIME (Multipurpose Internet Mail Extensions) Part One: Mechanisms for Specifying and Describing the Format of Internet Message Bodies. RFC1521 (1993)
8. Saji, K. and Kageyama, T.: HyperStation: Concept of Distributed Object-Oriented Dynamic Language HyperScheme. Proc. 45th Annual Conf. of IPSJ. (1992) 2Q-1 (in Japanese)
9. Reinhardt, A.: Smarter E-mail is Coming. Byte. **18-3** (1993) 90–108
10. Udell, J.: Workman Needs Work. Byte. **18-9** (1993) 167–170
11. Swenson, K.D.: A Visual Language to Describe Collaborative Work. Proc. of 1993 IEEE Symp. on Visual Languages. (1993) 298–303

Consistent Development

**Results of a First Empirical Study on the Relation Between
Project Scenario and Success**

Victor van Swede+ & Hans van Vliet++

+ Cap Volmac, Utrecht, The Netherlands
++ Vrije Universiteit, Amsterdam, The Netherlands

Abstract. Different project characteristics call for different project scenarios. It follows that, for a project to be successful, the scenario should fit project characteristics. In this study, we investigate statistical relations between different measures for project success and factors that characterize project situations. The study is based on a survey of project managers. The results provide valuable insight into factors that impact success.

1. Introduction

Each project should be developed according to a *project scenario,* a specific plan at the start of the project for the subsequent development of the information system. A project scenario is an organization of people, resources, products, activities, techniques and regulations called in to solve some information supply problem. Inventing a good scenario is difficult and takes a lot of time. Although there is considerable agreement nowadays that different situations demand different project approaches [1, 2], few quantative data are available on the relationship between a project's contingency factors, scenario chosen and success. Related studies include those concerned with failure factors e.g. [3], specific systems [4], system aspects [5] or process models [6]. Although their findings contribute to the insight in information engineering, they have not led to a theory that allows us to select a successful approach from given project characteristics. Such a theory is currently being developed by the authors. It is discussed in section 2. Then a research model is presented to study the effect of system development factors on project success (section 3). Based on this model, a survey was sent to a large group of project managers. The results were analyzed statistically. The results are presented and discussed in section 4. It follows that specific factors are related to specific kinds of success. These relationships may help a project leader in composing a scenario.

2. A Consistency Theory for Information Systems Engineering

In order to get insight into which scenarios are successful in a particular situation, we use an analogy between succesfully running a business and succesfully running a project. This allows us to profit from the extensive research done in this area. Much of this research is reflected in the consistency model of Broekstra [7] that models an enterprise in its environment. The term 'consistency' refers to the harmony that must exist between the different factors involved. Broekstra describes how a company, in order to reach a successful performance in terms of effectiveness, efficiency and quality, must react to changes in its environment by making decisions about four variables:

1. the products and markets to service;
2. the (primary) processes and means necessary to manufacture and deliver products;
3. the way these processes and means will be controlled;
4. the behaviour of employees in relation to the first three choices.

Attention to only one of these variables is not enough. Both contingency variables (from environment and decisions made in the past) and design variables (the four choices) must be tuned to each other. E.g. if a new product is made, the right people and processes must be present and the product must comply with market and social developments in the environment. A decision to educate employees for their new task leads to changes in other variables such as hiring teachers. So the consequences of decisions must be taken into account. The consistency model names, groups and describes the various contingency variables and design parameters and their interaction. Therefore, it is useful for describing the current situation of an enterprise, the situation to be, the changes that must be abridged and the situation at times in between.

A project may be seen as a temporary business, established to deliver one main product, the information system (including all relevant organizational changes) to a customer. The primary process consists of modelling, realizing, testing and other activities to develop the system. The type of control is determined by the project management choices made. The employees are the project staff that carry out development or control activities. This enables us to introduce a consistency model for development, the Consistent Development-, or CD-model. The CD-model, an adapted version of the consistency model, is depicted in figure 1. It is a socio-technical interaction model (in line with e.g. [8]) that effectively deals with the drawbacks of a contingency approach [9, 10]. A more extensive discussion of the CD-model can be found in [11].

Six dimensions are distinguished. The *results* dimension pertains to statements about the system products to deliver, and accompanying delivery terms. These statements may be formal (as in the case of a software house and its customers) or more informal (often found when a company has its own system development department).

The *environment* dimension contains influence forces in the environment of the project organization which are not under control of the project organization. These factors include organizational structure and experience of parties in the environment of the project organization such as clients and users, along with available infra-structure and tools. They also include factors originating in developments in business, technology, society, or politics.

The *system development* dimension pertains to the particular development approach of the project. It includes factors used in constructing the system such as development method, analysis and design techniques, tools and other resources.

The project management dimension refers to managing the primary development process and the resources involved. Factors in this dimension are concerned with

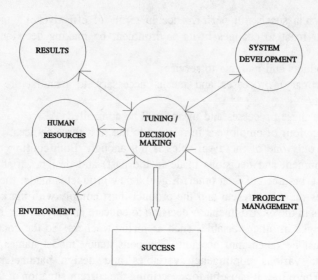

Figure 1. The CD-model.

operational control activities of defining, planning, organizing, staffing, directing, measuring, analyzing and evaluating of resources or aspects such as time, money, materials, developers, information and environment.

The *human resources* dimension is included to reflect the importance of socio-psychological influence factors in system development. Many studies neglect the influence of political power, motivation, skills and satisfaction of individuals and groups. Note that this dimension refers to properties of project members.

The *tuning or decision making* dimension is the one most crucial. In this dimension strategic and tactical decisions with respect to the project are made, concerning the definition of required results, the development and operational control approach and resources used in the development process, taking into account different influence factors and participants' goals. This dimension thus has to ensure that the other dimensions are mutually attuned. Decisions are often made in a steering committee in which various parties are involved.

The results and environment dimensions may be seen as the problem that must be solved in development and the other four as the solution chosen. It should be understood however that the dimensions interact and must be in harmony for successful development. It may be unclear however when a project is considered a success. In a company, success is associated with attaining certain performance levels of effectivity, efficiency, continuity, stability, flexibility or innovative power. In a project, success may e.g. be seen as satisfaction to all parties involved (win-win situation, see [12]), as delivery conform agreements, as staying within budget or time or as the degree of maintenance that is needed after the project is finished. In section 3 we offer a research model based on the CD-model to investigate the relationships between the various consistency factors and different measures of success.

3. Research Model

In this section we describe the current study (which may be considered a first step towards a more general study) in terms of hypotheses and methods. The CD-model does not directly lend itself to statistical research. It must first be translated into a causal model which shows the types of effects of variables on success. Such a model would include both direct effects (such as the effect of staff quality on success), indirect effects (such as the effect of the combination of a particular development method and a particular environment on success), and feedback effects (such as plan revision due to changes in the environment). In this first study we only investigate the direct effects of the variables in the 6 dimensions on success. In order to do so we need measures of project success. 10 potential success measures were chosen:

- *Success to User Organ*: the degree of success as experienced by the User Organization, i.e. the group of people for which the system development project is carried out.
- *Success to Client Organ*: the satisfaction of the Client Organization that controls the user organization, commissions the project and pays the bill. Most often, the user organization is a subset of the client organization.
- *Success to Project Organ*: the degree of success as experienced by the Project Organization. This temporary organization is the group of people and resources brought into being to develop the information system and to offer services to the user organization.
- *Success to Devel Organ*: the degree of success as experienced by the Development Organization. This organization controls several project organizations. It offers services, people and resources to project organizations.
- *Success to Project Manager*: the degree of success as experienced by the Project Manager.
- *Success to All Parties*: the degree to which all parties involved are satisfied with the results of the project. It is the average of the five aforementioned success measures.
- *Conformance to Budget*: the extent to which the project budget was exceeded, varying from 0% (highest success) to more than 100% (no success).
- *Conformance Time Sched*: the extent to which the project schedule was overrun, varying from 0% (highest success) to more than 100% (no success).
- *Absence of Result Change*: the extent to which changes to the agreement were needed during the project, varying from numerous changes (low success) to no changes (high success).
- *Succ Meet Qual Specs*: the degree in which the quality requirements posed in the agreement were met, varying from full (high success) to not at all (low success).

We hypothesize that consistency variables would exert different effects on different success factors. If this is true, it would be possible for a project manager to aim at special kinds of success by influencing the appropriate variables. Of course the research model may easily be extended with other interest groups, and/or other success measures. In order to study the direct effects relationship between consistency variables and success, we chose variables for each consistency construct (dimension in CD-model):

- *EnvirCooper*   : environmental cooperativeness; environment dimension.
- *ResultComplx* : complexity of result; results dimension.
- *WinwinSituat* : considering interests of all parties on results; results dimension.
- *QualContract* : quality of contract; results dimension.
- *QualProjOrg*   : quality of project organization; human resources dimension.
- *QualDevelop*   : quality of development; system development dimension.
- *QualProjMngt* : project management quality; project management dimension.
- *QualDecis*   : quality of decision making; tuning dimension.

For all variables we expect more success for a higher value of the variable, except for results complexity, in which case more complexity would lead to less success. For each variable, a number of indicators were defined, which are listed in the Appendix. Selection of indicators was based on theoretical methods, techniques and models of system development [11, 13].

In order to test our hypothesis that project characteristics impact project success in various ways, we conducted a survey amongst project managers. A questionnaire was developed which addresses the issues above. The questions mostly used a 7-point pseudo-interval scale whose endpoints were labelled (e.g. 1 very low satisfaction - 7 very high satisfaction). Sometimes 7-point ordinal scales were used (say, 1: 0-10%, 2: 10-20%,..., 7: > 100%). Because of this ambivalent character, we used both Pearson's (interval) correlations (P) and Spearman's rank (ordinal) product moment correlations (SP) to test the various hypotheses. The latter is more proof against deviations from normality, but may give trouble because of ties. The effect of missing cases was investigated by comparing Pearson correlations obtained by mean substitution (PMS) with Pearson correlations obtained by pairwise deletion of missing values (PMV). For each variable defined above a number of indicators (one question per indicator) was defined that was thought to contribute to the value of the variable. The resulting value of a variable was obtained by taking the average of all its contributing indicators. We describe the indicators shortly in the Appendix. Internal consistency of indicators in a variable was tested by inspecting the correlation between (corrected) item and total, and by Cronbach's alpha. An alpha greater than .50 suffices for earlier stages of basic research [14]. Content validity was looked at by the researchers and by a survey methodology specialist. Two project managers filled in the survey to test for clarity and comprehensibility. Although the questionnaire provided some help in clarifying conceptions, misunderstandings could not be ruled out. No other independent measurement instrument was used to assess criterium validity. A likely cause of bias is that project managers tend to rate their success higher than it is in reality. Real correlations may therefore be somewhat higher than those observed. This effect may be stronger because the survey sample was not entirely random. About two thirds of the project managers were selected by their managers, who perhaps chose more successful projects. Construct validity [15] was considered premature for a first survey.

4. Discussion of Results

The questionnaire was sent to 105 project managers of Cap Volmac, the largest information system supplier in the Netherlands; 63 responses were received. From those that did not respond, most appeared to be no project manager any more or did their last project more than two years ago. Some did not have real project manager experience and two persons did not want to answer the questions. Some global characteristics of the projects assessed (always the project manager's latest project) are: the average project manager has a fair amount of expertise (5 years), a variety of application domains was involved, and the average staffing of these projects is substantial (more than 20 people). In addition, about 35% of the projects was estimated to take more than 100 manmonths of effort, and to take more than 1 year to complete. For more information on these projects, see [16].

Table 1 shows the PMS-results of the effect of our variables on the various success measures. Only effects significant at the 5%, 2-tailed level (for 63 cases: corr. > .25) are shown. Some variables had a considerable number of missing cases due to one or two indicators (questions) that were not relevant for a number of projects, e.g. 'contract price' when there was no formal contract. These indicators were removed from the variable. Logically, for the variable 'QualContract' this was not possible and results for this variable are based on only about 30 cases. PMV-results were generally the same as PMS-results, both for significance and values of the correlation coefficient. As indicated in the table, values just around the significance level may pass this boundary with change of method. SP-values tended to be somewhat lower; extreme differences (> .07) are indicated in the table. Alphas varied from .51 (QualDevelop) to .91 (Success to All Parties). Deleted indicators, alphas, number of missing cases, mean, standard deviation and skewness of variables and indicators are listed in the Appendix.

	Success to All Parties	Success to Client Organ	Success to User Organ	Success to Devel Organ	Success to Project Organ	Success to Project Manager	Conformance to Budget	Conformance Time Sched.	Absence of Result Change	Succ Meet Qual Specs
EnvirCooper	.41	.47⁻⁻	.44		.29	.35	.32*	.47⁻⁻	.40	
ResultComplx			-.32				-.38	-.33	-.48	
WinwinSituat	.44	.41	.55	X	.38	.38			.27*	
QualContract							.25	.28		
QualProjOrg	.46	.50⁻⁻	.29	.32	.39	.44		.42		.26
QualDecis					.25					
QualDevelop					.29				.26*	
QualProjMngt	.36	.29*		.25*	.35	.35				

Table 1. Significant (> .25) PMS Pearson product moment correlations between consistency variables and success measures. *: disappears with PMV; X: appears with PMV; --: SP much lower (difference > .07).

The results do not contradict our hypothesis that success measures differ per consistency variable. Furthermore, all variables behaved like we expected, i.e., except for 'result complexity' they were positively correlated with success, albeit only for a limited number of success measures. Looking at the columns, we notice that

- the main contributants to success in the sense of satisfaction of all parties, as advocated in [12], are (re the first column) cooperation of environment, presency of a win-win starting-point, quality of project staff and quality of project management;
- each party involved (clients, users, development organization, project organization and project manager) has its own set of variables correlated with success; the same applies to project results often associated with success such as staying within budget and time, no need for result change during the ride and meeting quality specifications. This suggests that it is possible for a project manager to influence the kind of success he is after by paying more attention to variables positively correlated with that kind of success.
- success in meeting quality specifications is correlated with only one variable.

Looking at the rows we find that

- two variables, environmental cooperativeness and quality of project staff, are correlated with almost all success measures. This suggests that concentrating on these factors pays off. This is in line with findings of e.g. Boehm [17] that personnel quality is the most important factor.
- each variable is correlated with some success measures, showing the relevance of all dimensions of the CD model.
- quality of decision making is, surprisingly, only correlated with one success measure, the success as felt by the project organization. There are a number of possible reasons for this result; correlations could be non-linear, or weak, the questions may have been interpreted wrongly or the wrong set of indicators may have been chosen. Alternatively, quality of decision making could have almost no effect on success measures. Further study should reveal whether such is the case.

To be able to look at influences on success in more detail, the effects on success of the individual indicators are presented in table 2. Only indicators that show significant correlation with at least one success measure are listed. Some SP-values were much higher than the corresponding P-values for the correlation coefficient. This effect is stronger for correlations between indicators that were considerably skewed and success indicators (all highly skewed). Since Pearson correlation values are decreased by skewness and Spearman correlations do not require normality of distribution, the higher SP-values are probably more reliable. For the variables of table 1, based on additive scales that better approximate normality, this effect is absent.

For every success measure (column) specific indicators are found that correlate with that type of success. This suggests that it is possible to aim at certain kinds of success by paying more attention to these indicators.

Per variable we discuss salient features of some indicators:

- indicators for environmental cooperativeness 'internal agreement on project within client organization' and 'quality of communication between users and project organization' show correlations with almost all success measures; 'simplicity and stability of organizational environment', 'internal agreement within the user

	Success to All Parties	Success to Client Organ	Success to User Organ	Success to Devel Organ	Success to Project Organ	Success to Project Manager	Conformance to Budget	Conformance Time Sched.	Absence of Result Change	Succ Meet Qual Specs
ENVIRONMENTAL COOPERATIVENESS										
Organ. Stability							.30	X	.27	
Organ. Simplicity	.26	.34	.33++					.30	.33	
Absence Organ. Hostility		.29*	.37					.41		
Users Experience	.27	X		.29		.25				
Internal Agreement Client	.40	.44	.32		.33	.39	.27	.32	X	.26
Internal Agreement Users	X	X	X				.31	.32	.31	
User Motivation		.	.33							
QualCommun Users/ProjOrg	.53	.52	.50	.33++	.42	.45	X	.43	.40	
Availability DevelMethods								.28		.32
Change Capability Client								.30		
Rational Decisions Client			.35	X					.31	
COMPLEXITY OF REQUIRED RESULTS										
Project price (item deleted)			-.32						-.34++	
Project Size Estimate									-.32	
ProjDurationAgreed (deleted)			-.28							X
Organizational Complexity	-.26	-.29*	-.42						-.27	
Diversity of Results							-.28		-.33	
Innovativeness of Results							-.32	-.35	-.26	
Uncertainty User Results			-.28++					-.32		
Changes in Results	-.31	-.36	-.31++			-.30	-.51	-.51	-.61	
WIN-WIN SITUATION										
ResultAgreemntClient/ProjOrg	.51	.47	.57	X	.40	.49	X	.26	.32	X
Attention User Expectations	.27++	X	.35			X	X			
Attention Client Expectations			X							
ResultAgreement Client/Users	.31	.31	.41		.31				.26	
QUALITY OF CONTRACT										
Contract Clarity	.36	.35	.29	X	.26*	.36	.35	.42		
Absence Vague Agreements	.42++	.42	.31	.26	.35	.42	.31	.43		
ContractDefinitionsClear								.35		
AbsenceMeaningDifferences	.36++	.33	.37++		.29++	.34	.28	.37		
Documentation Specification			-.26							
Milestone Specification							.26			
Implementation Specification	.26++		.30++							.25
QUALITY OF PROJECT ORGANIZATION										
Absence Political Games								.30		
Motivation Project Staff	.41++	.45	.38		.39	.38				.34
Experience Project Staff	.56++	.57	.29	.48++	.52	.47		.33		.29
InternalCommunicProjStaff	.43++	.36	.35++	.32++	.35	.44		.34		

Table 2. Significant correlations (> .25) of indicators with success measures. Continued with explanation of notes on next page.

	Success to All Parties	Success to Client Organ	Success to User Organ	Success to Devel Organ	Success to Project Organ	Success to Project Manager	Conformance to Budget	Conformance Time Sched.	Absence of Result Change	Succ Meet Qual Spec
QUALITY OF TUNING AND DECISION MAKING										
Feasibility of Agreements	.29*		.26		.29	.34			.29	
Tasks Staff Indicated		-.26*					X	-.26++	-.32	
Decion Making ProcedureSpecified					.27					
Activity List Agreed	.27*			.28	.37	.31	.25			
InfluenceProjManager onAgreemnts						.27*				
QUALITY OF DEVELOPMENT										
Quality of Used Methods					.32					
Quality of Used Tools	.36	.37	.29*		.38	.26				
Attention to Testing					.26					
Precisely Followed Procedures										.39
QUALITY OF PROJECT MANAGEMENT										
Poject Plan Surveyable	.25++			X	.32++	.35				
Attention to Client Goals	X		X							
Attention to User Goals	X	.30*	.43		X			X	.32	
Attention to Goals Developm Organ	X				X					.30
Attention to Goals Project Organ	.29			.26	.30	X				
MeasurementPossibilityProjManager	.34	.32		.34++	.31	.35	.36	.40		
Control Possibility ProjManager	.40	.38	X	.31	.30	.42	.30	.32		.34
Advantage of Measurement	.27++	.33		.28	X	.28	.27	.33		.26++
AttentionInfogatheringProjManager			.25*		.28					
AttentionMeasurementProjManager	.27			.27	.27					

Table 2 (continued). Significant correlations ($>.25$) of indicators with success measures. *: disappears with PMV; X: appears with PMV and/or SP; ++: SP much higher (difference $>.07$). Indicators without any significant correlation are left out (see Appendix).

organization', 'better communication between users and project organization' and 'rational decision making within client organization' are related with absence of result changes during the project; 'hostility of organizational environment' is correlated with staying within time, but not with staying within budget;

- almost all indicators of result complexity show that more complexity is associated with (re column) more changes during the project; the correlation coefficient of .61 between Changes in Results and Absence of ResultChange is not surprising, since these were based on equivalent, but slightly different phrased questions at the beginning and end of the questionnaire, respectively; no result complexity indicator is correlated with less success to development and project organization; an agreed longer project is probably correlated with better meeting quality specifications;
- agreement on results beween client and users as well between client and project organization are correlated with satisfaction of most of the parties involved;
- clearer contracts, represented by three of the first four indicators of the Quality of Contract variable, are associated with more success, whereas better definitions only

help in staying within time, and more elaborate documentation guidelines are even associated with less success (to the users!).
- motivation, experience and good communication of developers are strongly related to success, but do not help in staying within budget or in reducing changes during the project.
- more specification of the tasks of developers is associated only with less success (for four success measures).
- better tools are related to more satisfaction to almost all parties, while strictly following procedures leads to better meeting of quality specifications, but not to other types of success.
- better measurement and control possibilities are associated with most types of success but not with reducing the number of changes during the project.

No significant correlation with any success measure was found for a number of indicators, such as 'project necessity for client'. These are not included in table 2, mut may be derived by comparing table 2 with the Appendix. Absence of correlations offers some interesting information too. E.g., in general, more specifications in the contract are not associated with more success, in contrast to clearer specifications (see above). As noted before in the discussion of the results for the variable Quality of Decision Making, absence of significant correlation does not have to mean that correlations in reality do not exist.

Although a lot of significant correlations between consistency variables (or indicators) and success are found, this does not automatically mean that they cause the success. For this to be true there should at least be a good explanation of why the factor leads to more success. For most correlations this is the case, although we have no space here to discuss all these explanations. By doing this reasoning for themselves, and taking measures to influence the success factors found, project leaders may improve the success of their projects.

5. Conclusions

Although the effect of interaction has not yet been investigated in this study, the results show that the CD-model is a useful model for investigating the relationship between situational variables and success. A number of hypotheses were confirmed: both situation and approach chosen influence the success of a project. There is considerable difference in influences of the variables involved, depending on the kind of success that is considered. This makes it possible for project leaders to aim at different success objectives by influencing the right variables. This study already identified a large number of variables that may be used for that purpose, although the rate of success improvement per variable was not yet studied. The two tables contain a lot of valuable material for those who are interested in finding factors that determine the right kind of project scenario in a specific situation.

Like most of these kinds of surveys, a number of weaknesses in the research method (and thus possibly in the validity of the results) are present:
- All estimates of satisfaction of clients, users etc. were made by the project leader. These estimates may differ from the real values, resulting e.g. in a higher mean success. For correlations however, ranking projects as more succesful than they really are, results in lower values than in reality.

- Estimates of success may vary over time. E.g. it is possible that users consider a project a failure just after the end of the project, but are satisfied a year later, when they have become more familiar with the system. The present study has not taken these effects into account.
- The procedure for selecting project managers in the survey was not strictly aselect. However, a large part (63) of the population of project managers (some 200) were interviewed.
- Project managers may have interpreted the questions wrongly. This is a serious drawback of the automatic survey procedure. Although help texts were available, we don't know to what extent they were studied and whether this was necessary.
- The variables chosen within the dimensions may not be coherent enough. A factor analysis could be used to find logically formed clusters of indicators.
- Results may vary for different types of projects. To investigate this, we need more cases for each type of project.

We did not yet look at how much a variable or indicator contributed to a specific success type e.g. by means of causal analysis and modelling. Merely the presence or absence and value of a correlation between them was noted. In order to do the former, to look for indirect and feedback effects, and to overcome weaknesses mentioned; we will extend the study with qualitative and quantitative data on more variables by interviewing clients, users and project managers, as well as by using more advanced statistical methods to analyze available and new data.

6. Acknowledgements

We would like to thank Eric van Heck and Gerrit van der Veer for their advise with respect to the questionnaire, statistical processing and interpretation of data. We also thank Jochem Schulenklopper, Jeroen Mickers and Arjen de Jong for their help with the questionnaire. Lastly we thank numerous colleagues at Cap Volmac for their contributions to the CD-model and for help with the survey.

7. References

1. K. Lyytinen: New challenges of system development: a vision of the 90's. Data Base 20, fall 1-12 (1989)
2. M.A. Ould: Strategies for software engineering: the management of risk and quality. Chicester: John Wiley & Sons 1990
3. K. Lyytinen, R. Hirschheim: Information system failures- a survey and classification of the empirical literature. In: Oxford Surveys in Information Technology 4, 257-309 (1987)
4. E. van Heck. Design management of EDI systems. Alphen aan den Rijn: Samsom 1993
5. D.E. Kieras, S. Bovair: The role of a mental model in learning to operate a device. In: J. Preece, L. Keller (eds.): Human-computer interaction. Hemel Hempstead: Prentice Hall 1990
6. M.J. Kellner: Experience with enactable software process models. In: D.E.

Perry: Proceedings of the 5th international software process workshop. IEEE 1989

7. G. Broekstra: Organizational humanity and architecture. Cybernetics and Systems 17, 13-41 (1986)
8. P. Checkland: Systems thinking, systems practice. Cicester: Wiley 1981
9. J. Child: Organization guide to problems and practice. London 1977
10 C.B. Schoonhoven: Problems with contingency theory: testing assumptions hidden within the language of contingency theory. Administrative Science Quarterly 26, 348-377 (1981)
11. V. van Swede, J.C. van Vliet: A flexible framework for contingent information systems modelling. Information and Software Technology 35, 530-548 (1993)
12. B.W. Boehm, R. Ross: Theory-W software project management: a case study. In: Proceedings of the 10th international conference on software engineering. IEEE, 30-40 (1988)
13. W. van Zijp, J.J.M. van der Pol. Project management: models in practice (in Dutch). Rijswijk: Cap Gemini Publishing 1992
14. J.C. Nunnally: Psychometric theory. New York: McGraw Hill 1967
15. R.P. Bagozzi, Y. Yi, L.W. Phillips: Assessing construct validity in organizational research. Administrative Science Quarterly 36, 421-458 (1991)
16. J. Schulenklopper, V. van Swede, J.C. van Vliet. Situational metrics. In: Proceedings of the international workshop on quality assurance and software metrics, Amsterdam, 1993. Centre for Software Reliability, City university, London (to be published)
17. B.W. Boehm, P.N. Papaccio: Understanding and controlling software costs. IEEE Transactions on Software Engineering 14, 1462-1478 (1988)

Appendix: description of indicators for consistency variables

Precise meaning success variables / indicators: see above	Missing cases	Mean	Standard deviation	Skewness
Success to All Parties Alpha: .91	17	5.2	1.2	-.38
Success to Client Organization	6	5.6	1.1	-1.0
Success to User Organization	9	5.3	1.2	-.93
Success to Development Organization	13	5.2	1.5	-.81
Success to Project Organization	5	5.3	1.4	-.83
Success to Project Manager	4	5.1	1.5	-.79
Conformance to Budget	1	5.4	1.7	.98
Conformance to Time Schedule	2	5.5	1.5	1.1
Absence of Result Change	5	4.0	1.7	.12
Success in Meeting Quality Specifications	7	5.0	1.0	-.74

Meaning variables / indicators	Missing cases	Mean	Standard deviation	Skewness
EnvirCooper: COOPERATIVENESS OF ENVIRONMENT Alpha: .81	13	4.0	.80	.17
Organ. Stability: stability of the organization	0	4.1	1.7	.17
Organ. Simplicity: simplicity of organizational environment	0	3.2	1.7	-.44
Absence Organ. Hostility: absence of hostility in organizational environment	0	4.2	1.5	-.1
Users Experience: user experience with automation	0	3.7	1.8	.15
Internal Agreement Client (on project)	0	4.5	1.5	-.16
Internal Agreement Users (on project)	0	3.8	1.6	.07
User Motivation (at project start)	9	3.4	1.7	.48
QualCommun Client/ProjOrg: Quality of communication between client and PO	2	4.1	1.5	-.04
Quality of communication between users and project organization	0	4.5	1.4	-.05
Availability DevelMethods: Availability of Development Methods	0	4.6	1.4	-.32
Availability of Resources (such as tools, means, time, money, staff)	0	4.8	1.2	-.31
Change Capability Client	7	3.4	1.1	.10
Project Necessity for Client	1	5.7	1.2	-1.0
Rational Decisions Client: degree of rational decision making of client organization	3	4.7	1.7	-.42
ResultComplx: COMPLEXITY OF REQUIRED RESULTS Alpha: .67	6	4.5	.95	-.21
Project price (indicator deleted): agreed price	11	6.1	1.0	-.84
Project Size Estimate: project size as estimated by project manager	6	4.9	1.7	-.43
ProjDurationAgreed (deleted): Proj. duration in manmonths according to contract	11	5.1	1.4	-.12
Complexity of automated part of system	0	5.1	1.2	-.21
Organizational Complexity: complexity of organizational change	0	4.2	1.7	-.09
Diversity of Results	0	4.5	1.4	-.19
Innovativeness of Results	0	4.5	1.6	-.35
Uncertainty User Results: uncertainty of users with respect to automation	0	4.3	1.9	.19
Changes in Results: degree of changes in result during project	0	4.4	1.7	-.07
QualProjMngt QUALITY OF PROJECT MANAGEMENT Alpha: .74	5	4.9	.63	-.19
project plan communicated to staff	1	3.7	1.7	-.75
Poject Plan Surveyable	2	5.2	1.4	-.41
Attention to Client Goals attention of PM to goals of CO	3	5.4	1.4	-.88
Attention to User Goals attention of PM to goals of UO	0	4.7	1.7	-.55
Attention to Goals Developm Organattention of PM to goals of DO	0	4.8	1.5	-.50
Attention to Goals Project Organattention of PM to goals of PO	0	5.2	1.2	-.62
attention of PM to strategic decisions	0	4.5	1.5	-.35
attention of PM to tactical decisions	0	5.0	1.3	-.65
attention of PM to operational decisions	0	5.3	1.3	-.53
MeasurementPossibilityProjManager (to measure aspects such as time and money)	0	4.1	1.1	.17
Control Possibility ProjManager (to control aspects such as time and money)	0	4.5	1.1	-.69
Advantage of Measurement (accoring to the project manager's expectation)	0	4.6	1.3	.17
AttentionInfogatheringProjManager (information on behalf of the project)	0	4.3	.84	-.25
AttentionMeasurementProjManager (attention paid by PM to measuring)	6	4.5	.98	-.17

Meaning variables / indicators	Missing cases	Mean	Standard deviation	Skewness
WIN-WIN SITUATION: considering interests of all parties　　　　Alpha: .72	7	4.6	1.1	-.68
ResultAgreemntClient/ProjOrg: results agreement between Client and PO	0	5.0	1.5	-.74
Attention User Expectations: attention paid to self-evident user expectations	6	4.6 ·	1.6	-.84
Attention Client Expectations: attention paid to self-evident client expectations	6	4.5	1.6	-.70
ResultAgreement Client/Users: agreement between client and users on results	0	4.4	1.6	-.16
QualProjOrg: QUALITY OF PROJECT ORGANIZATION (PO)　　　Alpha: .57	0	4.9	.94	-.84
Absence Political Games: absence of behaviour of PO driven by political reasons	0	4.7	1.9	.30
Motivation Project Staff: motivation of PO	0	5.3	1.1	-.77
Experience Project Staff: skills/experience of staff PO	0	4.7	1.2	-.49
InternalCommunicProjStaff: quality of internal communication PO	0	4.7	1.3	-.47
QualContract: QUALITY OF CONTRACT　　　　Alpha: .75	34	4.0	.90	-.55
Contract Clarity: clarity of contract	7	4.7	1.8	-.69
Absence Vague Agreements: absence of problems with vague agreements	8	4.9	1.9	.65
ContractDefinitionsClear: clear definitions in contract	11	4.7	1.5	-.44
AbsenceMeaningDifferences: absence of meaning interpretation problems	3	5.0	1.8	.99
quality requirements precisely defined	10	3.1	1.6	.37
Documentation Specification: agreements on documentation specified in contract	4	5.0	1.6	-.60
Milestone Specification: agreements on milestones specified in contract	5	4.7	1.7	-.56
agreements on education specified in contract	9	2.7	2.0	.78
Implementation Specification: agreements on implementation specified in contract	13	3.3	1.9	.06
agreements on warranty specified in contract	12	3.7	2.4	.05
agreements on maintenance specified in contract	1	3.1	2.6	1.0
agreements on acceptance specified in contract	7	4.4	1.9	-.30
QualDecis: QUALITY OF TUNING AND DECISION MAKING　　　Alpha: .75	14	4.8	.87	.38
Feasibility of Agreements	7	5.4	1.5	-1.0
attention to general project plan	3	5.3	1.4	-.45
attention to project phase plans	6	4.8	1.8	-.74
authorizations and responsibilities PO specified	1	4.9	1.6	-.75
way of communication in PO specified	1	4.7	1.7	-.67
way of attaining adequate staff specified	6	2.7	1.8	.86
required facilities specified	1	5.7	1.5	-1.2
Decion Making Procedure Specified	4	4.5	2.0	-.54
Tasks Staff Indicated: function descriptions PO specified	2	3.4	1.9	.08
need for personnell specified	2	5.1	1.6	-.67
Activity List Agreed: survey of activities made	1	5.6	1.2	-.70
InfluenceProjManager onAgreemnts (deleted): effort estimates of PM used	25	3.8	2.5	.00
QualDevelop QUALITY OF DEVELOPMENT　　　　Alpha: .51	6	4.8	.84	-.15
Quality of Used Methods (and techniques)	0	4.7	1.1	-.35
Quality of Used Tools (for development)	0	4.5	1.4	-.47
Attention to Testing	0	5.4	1.3	-.47
use of automated support	0	4.4	2.0	-.38
Precisely Followed Procedures (PO working strictly conform procedures)	6	4.6	1.4	-.09

Goal Decomposition and Scenario Analysis in Business Process Reengineering

Annie I. Antón, W. Michael McCracken, Colin Potts[1]

Center for Information Management Research
College of Computing
Georgia Institute of Technology
Atlanta, GA 30332-0280, USA

Abstract This paper presents experiences in applying the goal decomposition and scenario analysis model in the context of Business Process Reengineering (BPR). The relationships of goals, scenarios, as well as the understanding and description of business processes are discussed. Different methods of goal refinement, and the application of scenarios to support this process of refining goals and roles are reviewed. A case study is presented which serves to exemplify and validate the process of using scenarios in refining business process descriptions. We tried deriving full scenarios for business processes, but obtaining them from the organization's prescriptive goals was difficult. Explanatory scenarios that justify descriptive goals are easier to obtain but are fragmentary. We conclude that both types of scenario and goal analysis are necessary for effective BPR. The need for technology support for this process is discussed and attention is given to future anticipated research in this area.

1   Introduction

Business Process Reengineering (BPR) attempts to avoid the penchant of automating existing processes or tasks in organizations in order to achieve efficiencies, and it attempts to question the reasons why specific processes and activities are linked together in support of a particular business entity [Smith93]. BPR models an organization's behavior so that we may better understand how to modify that behavior, and then develop the requirements for the needed automation to support that changed behavior. Hammer and Champy [Hammer93] suggest that BPR requires "discontinuous thinking" (abandoning outdated rules and business operations) or starting from a "clean slate" in order to achieve dramatic improvements in performance. BPR usually involves the automation of some activities in the overall process, or the redistribution of process-related responsibilities from people to software systems (or even physical devices). The requirements for a software system that support a reengineered process therefore, must be understood in the context of the goals of the BPR project.

A less radical approach than Hammer and Champy's [Hammer93] 'clean slate' philosophy is to identify local inefficiencies in business processes, and recommend interventions to remove or mitigate them. In such cases of incremental automation, the requirements for systems still arise out of a process analysis and can only be understood as a response to an organizational need. Most system development falls somewhere on a spectrum between 'clean slate' and 'incremental improvement.' Smith and McKeen [Smith93] use the term *business re-engineering* to refer to the 'clean slate' philosophy, and the term *process re-engineering* refers to incremental automation. We will use these two terms in the remainder of this paper.

A critical factor in successful projects appears to be that developers not only understand what they are developing, but *why* [Conklin90, Potts94a]. In the context of business

---

[1] Email: {anton,mike,potts}@cc.gatech.edu

reengineering and process reengineering, the issues of 'why' are critical to understanding current processes and identifying inefficiencies in those processes so that they may be improved. Our approach centers on describing the activities of an organization so that needs for improvement may be identified. This approach suggests the need for a mechanism to describe the organization's behavior (not the organization's structure), as a precursor to the specification of the software to automate some of the behavior of the organization.

To describe this behavior, we are using operational concept definitions, not specifications. A specification is a description of behavior that should be able to generate all possible or valid behaviors. Specification languages are very valuable for describing software systems because they describe in detail and with minimal ambiguity the behavior of a mechanistic system. Researchers in the 1970's explored the use of special purpose specification languages for describing business processes as formally as possible [Hammer77], but businesses are not mechanistic systems and current opinion about the usefulness of business process specifications is divided. Another shortcoming of the specification approach is that a specification language provides a means of expression but does not tell the user what to say. The successful use of a specification language therefore depends on the application of an analysis method.

Operational concept definitions (OCD) are an alternative to specifications. An OCD describes business processes in terms of scenarios, critical incidents, or examples of the problems an organization must solve. Whereas, specifications abstract away from the concrete, OCDs describe the organization through a collection of concrete examples. Although this makes them easy to understand, and a good source of information system requirements [Benner92], there is the danger that a random collection of scenarios may not actively represent what the organization does or needs. It is essential, therefore, to populate OCDs with representative cases and relate them to goals of the organization.

In the rest of this paper, we discuss the relationships between goals and scenarios, as well as the understanding and description of business processes. We review different methods of goal refinement, and the application of scenarios to support this process of refining goals and roles. A recently conducted case study is presented. The case study serves to exemplify and validate the process of using scenarios in refining business process descriptions. Additionally, the case study will aid in determining the requirements for a suite of tools we are developing to support goal decomposition and scenario refinement. The last section of the paper explores the needs for technology to support our process and discusses further research we anticipate conducting in this area.

2　Goals

Business processes and the operations that roles perform are *operationalizations* of goals. While the processes, organizational structures, and operations of a system will evolve continually, goals remain more stable. An efficient enterprise and an effective use of information technology depends on a close correspondence between goal structure and role responsibilities; if the goal structure of the enterprise is incompatible with its physical structure (including the automated components) there will be much inefficient and unnecessary communication of information across subsystem boundaries.

2.1　Semantic Classification of Goals

Goals may be classified in several ways. Dardenne et. al. [Dardenne93] present a goal refinement method which offers a way of modeling concepts acquired during requirements elicitation. Their goal classification scheme differentiates among types of goals according to the conditions that are the target of the goals. In this scheme, goals are of three types: achievement, maintenance and avoidance goals. An achievement goal is satisfied when a target condition is attained. A maintenance goal is satisfied as long as its target condition remains true. An avoidance goal is satisfied for as long as its target condition remains false. This classification is useful when it comes to operationalizing the goals as actions the system must perform [Dardenne93].

Sutcliffe and Maiden [Sutcliffe93] present a model in which goals are classified according to the desired system states. Goals are classified into six classes: positive state, negative state, alternative state, exception-repair, feedback, and mixed state. These six classes are expressed in terms of a policy-goal model which consists of three levels: policy level, functional goal level and domain goal level. Policy goals describe what should be done. At the functional goal level, goals express information about what may be done to achieve policy level goals. At the domain goal level, goal descriptions are refined in order to give consideration to management implications, operational implications, and opportunities for automated support. The decomposition model facilitates the structuring of the problem space by refining policies to identify the functions necessary for achievement [Sutcliffe93].

Yu and Mylopoulous [Yu94] present a modeling framework composed of goals, rules, and methods to support the systematic analysis and design of business processes. The two main components of their framework are an Actor Dependency model and an Issue Argumentation model. These two models allow one to distinguish between process goals and design goals. The Actor Dependency model provides a representation of an organization as a network of interdependencies among actors. The Issue Argumentation model serves to support reasoning during the design process. It captures the design argumentation and the relative merits of each alternative with regard to relevant issues of concern [Yu94].

2.2 Pragmatic Classification of Goals

While semantic classification schemes are valuable for elucidating the formal relationships among goals, once they are identified, they do not suggest strategies for identifying goals during business reengineering and process reengineering. A pragmatic classification of goals differentiates *prescriptive* and *descriptive* goals. A prescriptive goal is offered by a stakeholder to account for organizational structures and processes that *should* be observed. These goals typically come from strategic management or are codified in the organization's written procedures. A descriptive goal, in contrast, emerges from an analysis of actual processes. These goals are most often found in the transcripts of interviews with operational staff or observational records. Descriptive goals usually lie buried in the current operational processes of the organization. Without prompting, stakeholders seldom reflect on these goals, being aware only of the operationalizations of the goals in the form of actions they regularly perform. Our observations lead us to believe that management stakeholders lean towards expressing goals as prescriptive, while stakeholders in support positions tend to describe goals in a descriptive fashion.

Another distinction among classes of goals, glossed over by research into the semantics of goals, is that between *objective* goals and *adverbial* goals. Objective goals refer to the object of the business. For example, a university parking space allocation system may need to satisfy the goal of assigning all requests for parking before the start of the year. The object of the goal is parking space allocation - precisely what the stakeholders think the purpose of the system to be. Elucidating objective goals is the aim of much recent research in requirements engineering. An adverbial goal, on the other hand, is a meta-level goal that refers to the manner of achieving an objective goal. For example, the parking allocation department may have the goal of responding to all customer queries courteously. Adverbial goals are an important part of all businesses, and in some service industries the boundary between objective and adverbial goals is not clear-cut. We find the distinction useful, however, because it translates directly into different strategies for elucidating goals and using them in the requirements specification process. For example, adverbial goals are seldom refined into system requirements, but they affect how the requirements themselves are evaluated and refined. Adverbial goals often serve as the rationale for the non-functional requirements (e.g. performance, reliability, and usability requirements). In this paper, we concentrate on objective goals and functional requirements.

2.3 Goal Structure

Goals are high-level objectives that require refinement before they give rise to system requirements or constraints. The two refinement processes that accomplish this are operationalization and responsibility assignment. Operationalization is the process of refining goals so that the resulting subgoals have an operational definition. This means that the goals are defined in sufficient detail for their achievement to be a matter of objective measurement. It is not generally possible to refine a goal into a set of operationalized subgoals in one step. Not only are many goals sufficiently abstract that they must be decomposed through several levels of subgoals before they can be operationalized, but many goals potentially conflict with other goals. In cases of goal conflict, the refinement process involves providing more detailed and qualified definitions of the goals that reflect exceptions and priorities.

Responsibility assignment allocates some operationalized goals to organization components (including automated systems). Information system requirements therefore emerge from an analysis of operationalized goals.

2.4 Goal Refinement

The literature on goal refinement assumes a relatively orderly or rational organization of goals [Benner92, Dardenne93] provided that the analyst knows enough about the domain. It should always be straightforward to decompose a goal into its subgoals. While this is true of prescriptive goals, in part because they have usually been written down and organized in advance, descriptive goals present more problems to the analyst. There are often large gaps in the descriptive goal structure that emerges from an analysis of stakeholder input.

Because a rational organization of goals cannot be taken for granted, we regard the refinement of goals as a type of discovery or inquiry process throughout which the analyst repeatedly asks questions of certain types. For example, to refine an achievement goal [Dardenne93] the analyst asks what constituent conditions must be attained for the target condition to become true. By resolving these questions it becomes possible to refine, operationalize and reorganize the goals. The goal refinement strategy depends most of all on asking 'what if' questions and using *scenarios* to explain the rationale for goals (especially the operationalization of goals).

3   Scenarios

From our studies of existing projects [Lubars93] we have concluded that concrete scenarios are essential to an understanding of the operational concept of a system, and that scenarios therefore play a major role in deriving goals and thus, the requirements for the system. There are at least two types of scenarios which may affect the derivation of requirements, which we call *process* scenarios and *explanatory* scenarios. Both types are closely related to the goal structure of the organization.

3.1 Process scenarios

In process scenarios, the analyst and user walk through a detailed process from beginning to end to investigate the opportunities for improvements or to investigate the impacts of a proposed system on their current processes. In a process scenario, the analyst asks the question: "what do we actually do?" or, alternatively: "how would the proposed system handle the following case?"

Goals and process scenarios are closely related. Process scenarios result from the aggregation of phases, or *episodes*, each of which is a short sequence of goal-related activities to achieve or thwart a goal [Potts94b]. We are investigating the identification of episodes (and therefore scenario discovery) through the analysis of maintenance goals (which are usually refined into activities that periodically, or sporadically, check the state of some system state variables) and avoidance goals (which are usually refined into tests that are performed before or after potentially goal-violating actions). Process scenarios require a thorough understanding of the organization's goals or global understanding of the operations in a process. They are therefore most useful for business reengineering.

Because scenarios usually explicate the interactions among several organization components (including existing or proposed systems) it is important to highlight which actors perform the constituent actions in the scenario. We refer to these actors as *roles*. Ideally, the actions performed by the role in a scenario should reflect a rational assignment of responsibilities for the achievement of operationalized goals.

Table 1 shows a process scenario from a group meeting scheduling system [Potts94b]. This scenario represents an end-to-end sequence of activities performed by several roles to achieve the goal of scheduling a meeting.

3.2 Explanatory scenarios

In explanatory scenarios, the analyst and users may describe current operations or desired features of the system by referring to concrete incidents. Unlike process scenarios, which refer to end-to-end, purposive transactions in the organization, explanatory scenarios are fragmentary illustrations of details. We find that they are particularly illuminating when an organizational member has to explain an inefficiency to an analyst who is not familiar with the business process.

3.3 Scenarios in BPR

In moving from systems requirements analysis to business process reengineering, the question arises: do the types of scenarios that we have described occur when stakeholders describe current processes? And how are the scenarios related to the goal structure of the organization and its operationalization in role responsibilities and actions?

No.	Role	Action
1	Initiator	Request meeting of a specific type, with meeting info. (e.g. agenda/ purpose and date range)
2	Scheduler	Add default (active/ important) participants, etc.
3	Initiator	Determine 3 participants
4	Initiator	Identify 1 presenter as active participant
5	Initiator	Identify initiator's boss as important participant
6	Initiator	Send request for preferences
7	Scheduler	Send appropriate e-mail messages to participants (incl.. additional requests to boss and presenter)
8	Ordinary Participant	Respond with exclusion and preference set
9	Active Participant	Respond with exclusion and preference sets and equipment requirements
10	Scheduler	Request required equipment
11	Important Participant	Respond with exclusion and preference sets and possibly location preference
12	Scheduler	Schedule meeting based on responses, policies and room availability
13	Scheduler	Send confirmation message to all participants and meeting initiator

Table 1: Process scenario script for No Conflicts scenario in Meeting Scheduling System.

Dardenne [Dardenne93] has found that scenarios are not common in users' dialogues with analysts in the case of a library information system. Looking at Dardenne's data, it appears that when scenarios do occur, they tend to be explanatory scenarios. This agrees with our experience [Lubars93b] that process scenarios must be investigated by means of a deliberate, inquiry process. Whereas, explanatory scenarios are offered more spontaneously.

Often the scenarios whose exploration yields the best insights into the proposed system are those that revolve around the operational definition of roles and their responsibilities [Potts94b]. This conclusion, taken together with our interpretation of Dardenne's results, suggests that explanatory scenarios are more likely to be useful when analyzing descriptive goals, and process scenarios are more likely to be useful when analyzing prescriptive goals. We must be careful, therefore, in moving our ideas about goals and scenarios to practical BPR interventions, because the rational approaches that work best on artificial laboratory exercises may not be the ones that are amenable to the data gathered from real stakeholders.

4 Case Study

We now describe a case study involving a College Financial Services Office (FSO) which employs four full time employees, two part time student assistants, and requires the integral involvement of three College administrators. The FSO is responsible for all of the College's finances. Six stakeholders participated in initial interviews (two College administrators and four FSO employees), and these information gathering sessions provided us with an understanding of the organizational structure, the lines of communication within the organization, and the business processes that the FSO is responsible for.

4.1 Goal Structures

The FSO administration provided a set of very high-level goals which were prescriptive in nature and emphasized deliverables. Upon speaking with the actual FSO employees, it was obvious that no one outside the administration was aware of the existence of these prescriptive organizational goals and objectives. This led us to believe that these goals were not representative of the perceived goals of all stakeholders. The prescriptive goals were analyzed using a top-down approach in order to develop a goal hierarchy. This goal hierarchy was then compared to the goal hierarchy which resulted from a bottom-up analysis of the goals from the perspective of the FSO employees. These goals, from the bottom-up analysis were much more concrete, process/task oriented, and *descriptive* in nature.

4.2 Initial Goal Identification

By analyzing the list of process inefficiencies which we identified in our initial analysis of the FSO business processes, we were able to identify some of the organizational goals using the bottom-up approach. We examined each process inefficiency, asking *"What goal is prevented from being satisfied by this inefficiency?"* We initially chose this approach, because it was structured, methodical, and would enable us to identify scenarios that satisfy the system goals. It is important to recognize, however, that this approach in no way provides a 'complete' set of goals. The goals identified in this manner proved to be very high level and did not offer a direct correspondence to our set of prescriptive goals. Thus, the results of this analysis were not extremely useful for the consideration of information system requirements. For purposes of our BPR effort which concentrated on the *current* business processes, we chose to focus our analysis on the descriptive goals.

Bottom-up Approach to Goal Identification. In order to identify a more concrete set of 'process' goals, we reviewed the scenario fragments elicited from the stakeholders. For each scenario we asked, *"What goal does this scenario fragment either support or* *satisfy?"* and/or *"What goal does this scenario fragment prevent the achievement of?"* We then constructed a goal hierarchy using the representation scheme presented in [Benner92]. This is a bottom-up approach to goal identification. As such, it is less structured and by no means offers a complete set of goals. It does, however, raise exceptional cases which may not have been apparent in the prescriptive goal set. This goal hierarchy is shown in Figure 1. Goals identified in this fashion are defined primarily by the current organizational procedures. The goal Avoid AccountsUndesignated (see '2' in Figure 1) was derived upon examination of the following natural language scenario:

> **Scenario 1: Accounts Undesignated.** *Professor salaries are not always paid completely by State funds. When we do not know which account or contracts will be used to pay a Professor's entire salary, we put the professor on a dummy number (undesignated account). We are not supposed to use dummy numbers so we try to move them off of undesignated accounts as soon as possible.*

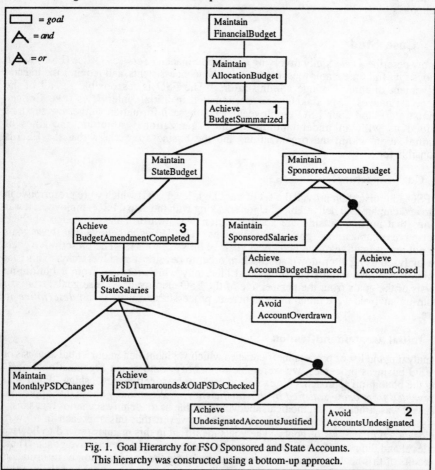

Fig. 1. Goal Hierarchy for FSO Sponsored and State Accounts.
This hierarchy was constructed using a bottom-up approach.

Top-down Approach to Goal Identification. The goal hierarchy in Figure 2 is based on the given set of prescriptive goals. These goals were systematically decomposed into subgoals. The scenario transcripts were then reviewed in an effort to identify supporting and/or non-supporting scenario fragments as in the bottom-up approach. Scenarios were identified for three of the prescriptive goals (1. Achieve ConsolidatedReport, 2.

Maintain UndesignatedSalaryExpenditures, and 3. Achieve BudgetSummarized). These scenarios/goals correspond to goals 1, 2, and 3 in Figure 1. The top-down approach requires an initial set of prescriptive goals. In our case study, these goals displayed a definite emphasis on deliverables. The following scenario was identified for the goal Avoid UndesignatedSalaryExpenditures:

> *Scenario 2: Undesignated Salary Expenditures. Often times, when Winter quarter rolls around, a lot of professors still have their research assistants on a dummy number (undesignated account). That is not supposed to be the case. You are supposed to know which accounts will be used to support all employees all year long.*

4.3   Analysis

Our analysis exhibits that employing solely a bottom-up approach to goal identification fails to provide a sufficiently high-level view in order to reorganize/restructure the organization. Similarly, simply employing a top-down approach, limits one's understanding of the actual current processes in an organization. However, a top-down approach coupled with a bottom-up approach offers a more complete view of an organization and its processes. Both views augment each other and result in the identification of multiple viewpoints which can then be resolved. It is interesting to note in conventional systems analysis, one speaks with the *real* users in order to get a *descriptive* view of the system and one speaks with people at a more elevated level (in our case the administration) in order to get a *prescriptive* view of the system. Both views are desired and this case study further illustrates that.

Viewpoint Resolution. Our analysis did not yield conflicting viewpoints which leads us to believe that in cases where there exists a well defined task differentiation, and roles do not overlap, there is less opportunity for viewpoint conflict. Further study may allow for examination of whether or not the existence of multiple viewpoints is affected by how structured the organization is. Every goal shown in Figure 1 has at least one supporting scenario. For example, Scenario 1 which was presented in the previous section. In contrast, only four of the goals shown in Figure 2 have supporting scenarios. This is partly due to the fact that the goals in Figure 1 were identified by examining the entire set of available scenario fragments. Thus, intuitively, we know that every goal in Figure 1 should indeed have at least one supporting scenario.

Contrasting both of the goal hierarchies gives rise to the issues of synonym identification and goal relationships. What is referred to as the "Allocation Budget" by the FSO employees (shown in Figure 1), is referred to as the "Monthly Consolidated Report" by the administration. If we were to resolve this 'viewpoint conflict', it is apparent that we would be able to identify a few more supporting scenarios for the prescriptive goals in Figure 2. Some of the scenarios which support the Maintain AllocationBudget goal in Figure 1 would also support the Achieve MonthlyConsolidatedReport goal in Figure 2. Thus, synonym identification may be useful in facilitating viewpoint resolution. In comparing the goal relationships for both of the goal hierarchies, we see that only the 3 to 2 relationship between goals is maintained.

Our analysis has shown that prescriptive and descriptive goal hierarchies are lacking in levels of correspondence. In our experience, it is difficult to obtain a factual goal hierarchy due to the large gap between goals and actual operations. Viewpoint contradictions do not occur because the roles are highly compartmentalized. However, gaps do occur due to different viewpoints (as noted in the synonym example). This gives rise to the need to consider schema integration and the merging of different viewpoints. Similar findings have been uncovered by operations management researchers. Their investigations have focused on the relationships of organizational goals and operational strategies. The findings have shown that organizational goals are often not reflected in operational strategies. An example that has been found is that the organizational goal of improving quality is not operationalized since the reward system at the operations level remains focused at productivity without regard to quality [McCracken90].

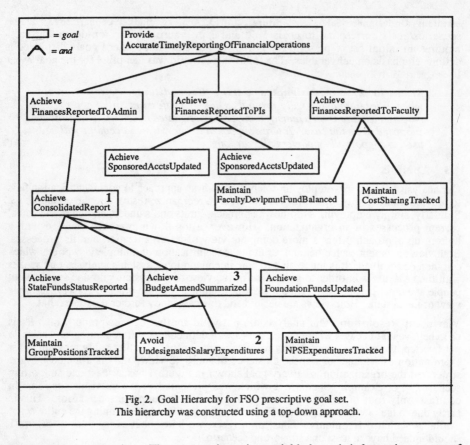

Fig. 2. Goal Hierarchy for FSO prescriptive goal set.
This hierarchy was constructed using a top-down approach.

Explanatory scenarios. The context interviews yielded much information, some of which was expressed as scenario fragments or subscenarios. The initial elicitation of scenarios was unguided. Each stakeholder was asked to explain the business processes that he/she is currently responsible for. Often times, they voluntarily expressed their processes as scenarios to illustrate a process goal or to demonstrate exceptional cases. As previously described, we used these scenario fragments for the identification of goals. Each of the goals identified in this fashion had at least one corresponding scenario (either supporting or non-supporting). The scenarios were also used to try to identify similarities and relationships between the goals in both of the goal hierarchies (as described above). Scenarios were beneficial in terms of identifying ways of redesigning the system as well as for the identification of exceptional cases.

Scenarios As Design Rationale Artifacts. Although our analysis has mainly provided requirements for a new system, the scenarios and goals provide an explanation of why we need the new system. Our goals and scenarios constitute part of the rationale for the new system.

5   Conclusions

Our initial premise of conducting the case study was based on the evaluation of scenarios to support identification of requirements and improvements of the business processes of the organization we studied. We anticipated using methods and techniques to identify *process* scenarios that describe the end to end business processes. As the case study progressed, though, we found that the initial efforts of defining the organization's goals, both prescriptive and descriptive, focused our work on understanding the relationships between these two sets of objectives. We found that when we identified our initial *prescriptive* goals, and then tried to identify the supporting scenarios that the goal refinement process broke down. We had to revert to *descriptive* goals related to the activities at the operations level. We were able to identify explanatory scenarios which supported those operations, but we were unable to elicit process scenarios that described complete sequences that supported the prescriptive goals, and their subgoals.

The above findings have prompted us to rethink the goal refinement process and to try to understand the relationships between refinement of goals and scenarios. Our future work will concentrate in part on this question, and in particular these results will influence our plans for building tools to support this process. We are developing tools that will allow us to support the process of goal refinement, scenario depiction, and the discussion and resolution of issues, and in particular we will support the process with "synchrony weakening" technologies that will support the continuous dialogue we have found necessary to support the process of identification of goals (both prescriptive and descriptive), and the determination of scenarios that describe the activities supporting the attainment of those goals.

Acknowledgments

The case study and research presented in this paper is partially supported by the United States Army Research Lab TRANSOPEN project under grant DAKF1191-D-004-0019.

References

[Antón93] Antón, A.I., Gale, T.A., McCracken, W.M., Shilling, J.J., "Object-Based Requirements Modeling for Process Continuity," in *Proceedings of the Twenty-Sixth Hawaii International Conference on System Sciences*, Vol. 3, pp. 191-202, 1993.

[Bauer81] Bauer, F.L. "Programming as Fulfillment of a Contract" in P. Henderson (ed.) *System Design* Infotech State of the Art Report 9:6, Pergamon Infotech Ltd., 1981, pp. 165-174.

[Benner92] Benner, K., Feather, M.S., Johnson, W.L., Zorman, L. "Utilizing Scenarios in the Software Development Process," *IFIP WG 8.1 Working Conference on Information Systems Development Process*, 9 December 1992.

[Conklin90] Conklin, E. J., Burgess Yakemovic, K. C., "Report on a Development Project Use of an Issue-Based Information System," *Proceedings of the Conference on Computer-Supported Cooperative Work*, Los Angeles, CA, October, 1990.

[Dardenne93] Dardenne, A., van Lamsweerde, A., Fickas, S., "Goal-directed Requirements Acquisition", *Science of Computer Programming*, Vol. 20(1-2), pp. 3-50, April 1993.

[Hammer93] Hammer, M., Champy, J., *Reengineering The Corporation: A Manifesto for Business Revolution*, HarperCollins Books, 1993.

[Hammer77] Hammer, M., Howe, W.G., Kruskal, V.J., Wladawsky, B., "A Very High Level Programming Language for Data Processing Applications," *Communications of the ACM*, 20(11): 832-840, November 1977.

[Lubars93a] Lubars, M., Potts, C., Richter, C., "A Review of the State of the Practice in Requirements Modeling," *Proceedings of the IEEE International Symposium on Requirements Engineering*, San Diego, CA, January, 1993.

[Lubars93b] Lubars, M., Potts, C., Richter, C., "Developing Initial OOA Models," *Proceedings of the 15th International Conference on Software Engineering*, Baltimore, MD, May, 1993.

[Potts94a] Potts, C. "Supporting Software Design: Integrating Design Methods and Design Rationale," in Moran, T.P. and Carroll, J.M. (eds.) *Design Rationale: Concepts, Techniques and Use*, Lawrence Erlbaum Associates, to be published 1994.

[Potts94b] Potts, C., Takahashi, K., Antón, A.I., "Inquiry-Based Scenario Analysis of System Requirements," to appear in *Proceedings of the International Conference on Requirements Engineering (ICRE '94)*, Colorado Springs, March, and *IEEE Software*, March 1994.

[Smith93] Smith, H.A., McKeen, J.D. "Re-engineering the Corporation: Where Does I.S. Fit In?," *Proceedings of the Twenty-Sixth Hawaii International Conference on System Sciences*, 1993.

[Sutcliffe93] Sutcliffe, A.G. and N.A.M. Maiden. "Bridging the Requirements Gap: Policies, Goals and Domains," *Proceedings of the Seventh International Workshop on Software Specification and Design*, Redondo Beach, California, December 1993.

[Swartout82] Swartout, W. and Balzer, B. "On the Inevitable Intertwining of Specification and Implementation," *Communications of the ACM*, 25(7): 438-440, July 1982.

[Yu94] Yu, E.S.K. and Mylopoulos, J. "Using Goals, Rules, and Methods to Support Reasoning in Business Process Reengineering," *Proceedings of the Twenty-Seventh Hawaii International Conference on System Sciences*, 1994.

Reaching out for Quality: Considering Security Requirements in the Design of Information Systems

Hubert F. Hofmann and Ralph Holbein
Institute for Informatics, University of Zurich
Winterthurerstr. 190, CH-8057 Zurich, Switzerland
email: {hofmann, holbein}@ifi.unizh.ch

Abstract. Security requirements are a fundamental ingredient for an information system's quality. Despite their importance, security requirements play the role of a "stepchild" in software engineering. If considered at all they cover the technical dimension of information systems, i.e. the electronic part of information processing. This view is insufficient to deal with the requirements of the "real world", i.e. the organisational practice. It is not just the technical criteria which are decisive in specifying security requirements. We have extended these criteria to incorporate the social *and* the economic dimension of information exchange in organisations. We will illustrate this extension of traditional approaches in a comprehensive security framework and we will demonstrate the interaction of the additional security criteria with traditional approaches.

1 Introduction

Quality is a multi-faceted concept. Depending on the experiences and expectations of the people involved, the quality of information systems is defined by various characteristics. The characteristics making up the quality of an information system depend both on its technical implementation and on its working environment. In other words, when defining characteristics like security, efficiency, usability, and portability for an information system, we also have to consider its organisational context. Defining these characteristics, often called non-functional requirements, is part of the requirements analysis (RA) process; not an "add-on" when the system is already in productive use [15]

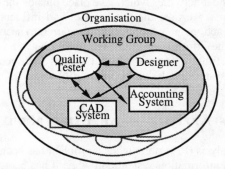

Fig. 1: Information system quality: schematic representation of the different aspects of information system quality. There are three levels: product, individual, and organisation. Details: See text.

Quality Aspects. The various aspects of quality are depicted in Figure 1. The most prominent quality measures concern the technical information system (e.g. CAD system, accounting system). The term *verification* denotes those measures that are available at this level. Verification is the proof of consistency between two formal descriptions, typically the consistency of the programs with its specification, or the internal consistency of the specification against the demands of the specification language. Various standard verification techniques exist, e.g. [33] While verification operates between two formal domains, *validation* operates between an informal domain and a formal one. Validation focuses on the questions such as: Does the information system fulfil its quality goals? To be valid a system's specification has to describe the desired system appropriately, i.e. the specification has to be "correct" concerning the requirements. If the validation process is inadequate, misunderstandings and errors are propagated throughout the development process, and expensive modifications of the information system are later required to correct them.

Less prominent quality measures concern areas where non-functional requirements must be validated. First, at the individual and group level, there are quality measures of system-user interaction. Quality measures taken at this level relate to the field of HCI (Human-Computer Interaction). Also work psychological aspects, e.g. motivational factors or user satisfaction with the system must be considered. Second, we have to consider the information system in the larger context of the whole organisation. Measures taken at this level to ensure quality are derived from organisational theory [6, 18]. It should be noted that an assessment at the organisational level is normally not considered part of a particular project, but the result of strategic business and information management.

In this paper, we will focus on one particular quality characteristic: security requirements. They address threats considered as relevant and directed to valuable objects. Their goal is to define appropriate security measures, so that the resulting risks are deemed acceptable [17]. Despite their importance, security requirements play the role of a "stepchild" in software engineering. Traditionally, they exclusively cover the technical part of information processing. In the traditional view, loss of confidentiality, integrity and availability are the basic threats. However, they do not deal with those threats that result from the IS's productive use and its working environment. Hence, we will extend the "basic" threats to achieve a more comprehensive view of information processing. We encompass the system's environment and consider activities which take place outside the technical information system. In other words, we take the use, impact and influence of information on decisions and human actions in an application domain into account. We will identify security criteria for the information exchange in and between organisations. These security criteria constitute a framework that guides the specification of security requirements and the systematic derivation of security measures.

2 Requirements Analysis — An Exploration Cycle

Requirements Analysis (RA) starts when a problem has been perceived that offers some potential for an information system and when it has been decided to tackle the problem this way. In our case, the use of computer systems for the exchange of information in and between organisations. It is difficult to specify the correct and complete specification at the beginning of RA. The "right first time" principle will only work, if at all, for simple problems. Complete knowledge about a problem

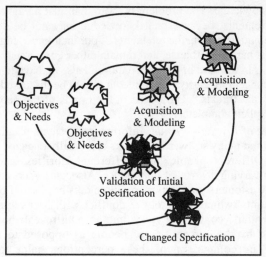

Fig. 2. Requirements Engineering Process

situation occurs in "artificial" situations only. In reality there are some doubts what the actual problem is, which solutions are available, and which solution should be selected (Fig. 2).

We understand RA as a cyclic process of exploring the perceived problem (objectives & needs), proposing alternative solutions (acquisition & modeling), and validating them (validation). This cyclic process comprises functional and quality (non-functional) requirements and allows the client to receive feedback on the analyst's interpretation of requirements and to correct misunderstandings as early as possible.

RA defines the boundaries of the proposed system by *elaborating needs and objectives* [26; 7]. The objectives for the information system are usually defined by (strategic) management, whereas the needs or the "wishes" of the client for the system are subject to debate. Quality requirements are usually formulated as goals and security requirements are an important component of quality goals, considering both organisational and individual needs. Elaborating objectives and needs and *requirements acquisition and modeling* are interrelated. The purpose of acquisition and modeling is to describe the requirements using informal, semiformal and formal notations. By acquisition and modeling we mean that individual(s) or group(s) identify or create requirements specifications together. Specifications are developed with the help of whatever sources are available, e.g. repositories, experts, textbooks, existing implementations. Candidate specifications must then be *validated*.

Analysing this process, several key issues can be identified [14]. In what follows, we will explain these issues and illustrate them from the viewpoint of security requirements.

Communication Barriers and Tacit Knowledge. Formal communication barriers among project teams and their members often hinder the understanding of requirements. Such barriers create a need for individuals to span team boundaries and to set up informal communication networks. While organisational changes can solve these problems, we are facing more fundamental communication barriers in RE: People know more than they can ever tell (learning by doing). When this "tacit knowledge" concerns a proposed information system, we are often at a loss as how to bring forth this knowledge. The problem is more than just a vagueness of the client concerning requirements, because tacit knowledge may not be describable by the client. It is an open question whether elements of our tacit knowledge are inaccessible in principle, or just hard to verbalise, and remain either consciously or unconsciously suppressed [19,18]. In the case of security requirements, we have to deal with a multi-faceted, abstract concept. Security requirements cannot be discussed by "putting one's hands on the relevant threats." They exist in the minds of the people and therefore cannot be made explicit completely.

Multiple Views of Involved People. Information systems usually have a diverse client community and many software engineers are usually engaged in an information system project. Different people have different priorities, and view different requirements with varying degrees of importance. Also, customers and users are rarely the same people. Customers may impose requirements because of organisational and budgetary constraints, which are likely to conflict with user requirements. Taking different and potentially conflicting views into account reveals how the application domain is framed by the perceptions of people as opposed to being defined as objective facts. The comparison of these perceptions helps to investigate the advantages and limitations of each viewpoint. It shows, for instance, in what kind of situations users are performing and the way practice is distributed among them. Moreover, the use of multiple views prevents each party from monopolising the decisions on what to represent and what not to represent in the system [13, 9]. In specifying security requirements multiple views are absolutely necessary, because security is a concept, which is subjective in nature. Its subjectivity refers to the relevant threats, valuable goods and to the risks deemed acceptable.

Specification Integration. The emphasis shifts from designing and implementing a system from scratch to choosing and combining existing software components. Few information systems are built from scratch. In practice many projects extend an existing information system. Thus, the requirements analysts must understand these systems and the underlying requirements, which are often implemented by an integration of components from multiple vendors. Because existing components impose constraints, it is even more important to map between their formal specification and the requirements of the information system under consideration. Note that an immediate mapping from requirements to system implementation would lead to changes in the implementation, but not in the specification. This would cause the information system to diverge from the specification and the implementation would no longer reflect the requirements as stated by the client.

Specification Evolution. The introduction of information system will not only change the environment in which users work, but also their perceptions of it. As developers we have to be aware that this will happen and should observe and discuss the changes that information system has brought. Change does not only occur when an information system is introduced and put into practical use, but also when the environment changes (new insights into problems, new machines being installed, etc.). The need for change is exemplified by the countless adaptations an information system undergoes during its productive use. Although there are many reasons for the difficulty of maintaining information systems, lack of thorough attention to requirements analysis is a major problem, e.g. [23]. One reason for inadequate information systems is that the initial specification often is also the final one, thus hindering the communication and learning process of the stakeholders which might lead to more suitable information systems. Concerning security requirements, we protect the information system against threats which are explicitly considered in the specification. As the environment and the information system changes we have to adapt the specification to changing security requirements. To keep track of this process, we validate security requirements by "spot-tests" over extended periods of time.

In what follows, we will show the technical, individual and organisational dimensions that must be considered within a high-quality RA process, when dealing with *security requirements for information exchange in and between organisations*. Thus, we encompasses the exchange of information about the organisation itself, the business and know-how between members of organisation(s) or technological systems for the purpose of co-operation and division of labour, and the establishment of legal binding contracts or the co-ordination of semi-automated processes in the working environment. We describe these aspects as the components of a security framework (security criteria) which forms the basis for our ongoing research: the development of a comprehensive management of IT-security.

3 Security of Information Exchange in Organisations: Relevant Dimensions

In analysing the exchange of information in commercial areas, we have identified three basic dimensions: social interaction, economic potential, and technical data exchange. While the technical dimension and the social dimension are established in interpersonal communication [32], we will introduce the economic dimension as the third dimension of information exchange in organisations.

Characteristic properties of the *social dimension* (social interaction) are the creation of obligations and assertions between communication partners (Figure 3). Considering security requirements, relevant threats are: Loss of "Authenticity of the communication partners" and Loss of "Obligation to the content of the interaction." The *economic dimension* concerns the economic potential given by information and depends on its relevance to fulfil a particular task. In this case, security requirements

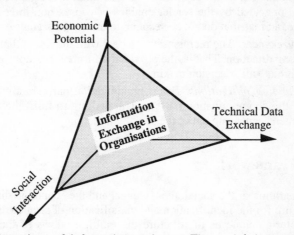

Fig. 3: Dimensions of information exchange. The *social interaction* comprises, for example, assertions and legally binding obligations. The *economic dimension* denotes the potential for the generation of economic benefits and the *technical dimension* focuses on the transmission of data.

are only concerned that the information will be used for the intended goals of the organisation and that it builds a valid basis for the activities of the recipient. Relevant threats are: Loss of "Authenticity of the content" and "Misuse of information bound to intended goals." The *technical dimension* for secure information exchange in organisations covers the transmission of data between communication partners. Relevant threats are: Loss of "Confidentiality," Loss of "Integrity" and Loss of "Availability of the data and services" and also Loss of "Authenticity of the communication partners."

Traditional IT-security primarily covers the technical dimension described above. In the case of information exchange, security requirements for confidentiality are reduced to the question of data security, i.e. to prevent against unauthorised data access or disclosure and the misuse of organisational resources for data processing. These criteria allow the specification of an appropriate level of *confidentiality concerning a third-party* (Security for the OSI Reference Model: ISO 7498-2, ECMA, Bell/La Padula, etc.) [7, 8, 19, 20].

While the social dimension has been considered to some extent (e.g. non-reputation of communicative acts, legal aspects of electronic data interchange), the economic dimension, i.e. preventing the misuse of information in the case of conflicting goals, has not been considered up to now. Hence, this dimension must be considered also to ensure the confidentiality of communication partners. That is, one must differentiate between the issue of access control to data and the possibilities for the use and misuse of information which can be acquired. While the first one ensures authorised data access, the second one considers its intended use when granting authorisation. The important questions for identifying security requirements in this area are: What possible uses of the information exist? Which overall goals does the information support? What kind of misuse is possible?

Thus, we integrate three dimensions to specify security requirements. We consider the misuse and "incorrectness" of information, and the neglecting of obligations:

(1) *Misuse of information*: The sender has to deal with threats resulting from an inadequate behaviour of the recipient. We talk about inadequate behaviour when the information provided by the sender enables or causes non-intended actions of the recipient, i.e. actions that do not correspond to the sender's goals or interests.

(2) *Incorrectness:* The recipient has to deal with the threat that he will be guided into the wrong direction. That is, the provided information is not trustworthy (correct) and thus inhibits valid decision making.

(3) *Neglecting obligations:* For communication partners always exists the risk that one of the communication partners is unwilling to fulfil the obligations (e.g. a legal agreement) emerging out of the social interaction.

4 The Framework

The integration of the social, the technical and the economic dimension provide a basic structure for the identification and classification of security criteria [16]. These security criteria enable us to structure the multiple views of the involved parties, therefore reducing communication barriers and also supporting the integration of the multiple views.

The technical dimension of this framework considers the security criteria that result from the technical realisation of the information system. The technical

Fig. 4: Security levels of information processing

dimension alone is insufficient to cover the security requirements of information systems, because technical data exchange does not cover the essential phenomena of information processing. While information processing can be based on technical data exchange, it also takes place in the system's environment, i.e. in the "real world." Consequently, we also have to consider the social and the economic dimension of information processing to achieve the goal of a correct and complete specification of security requirements for information exchange.

Thus, our framework includes both of the following areas [17]: (1) Security of the technical communication processes realised by IT-systems (hardware, software and data). (2) Security of subsequent IT-external processing, i.e. the acquisition of content and information by individuals. Here we are concerned with (2a) relationships between the communication partners, e.g. emerging obligations, (2b) physical and cognitive activities which are enabled by the acquisition of information and by the extension of knowledge.

Figure 4 depicts the security levels of information exchange: (1) communication security including data security, (2a) the security of content exchange and (2b) information security form the generic levels for secure information exchange. Information systems are grounded in the workplace through the data and information they maintain. They represent the knowledge of one or more persons in the application domain. These persons are involved in a continuous interaction with a changing environment, make sense of this environment, and take action in it. When acting humans interpret and use the current situation as perceived. They are situated agents [3, 15], humans act in the "real world" and can communicate with each other using technical information systems. The technical information system provides data processing and transmission (*data and communication security*). The data exchanged by the technical information system and their sense-making, i.e. the content ascribed to the data, forms the cross point between the technical information system and the "real world." The interpretation process necessary for this last step normally takes place outside the scope of the technical system. *Securing the content exchange* ensures that the social interaction, which has been established between the communication partners by acquiring the data's content, is conform to a set of rules (e.g. law, group norms, organisational roles). *Information security* finally covers the

Fig. 5: Components of a comprehensive information exchange security framework: (1) goal conformity; (2) obligation; (3) authenticity of content; (4) authenticity of communication partners; (5) confidentiality; (6) integrity; and (7) availability are the security criteria that have to be considered when specifying the requirements for secure information systems. For more details, see text below.

economic dimension of information exchange, i.e. the goal-oriented behaviour made possible as a result of the communication.

Considering security requirements on all these levels of information exchange, we can define seven security criteria that are essential for specifying secure information systems [17]. All these security criteria describe basic threats regarding information exchange and hence their consideration is absolutely necessary when specifying secure information systems.

To explain the seven security criteria, we will use the following example: The design information for high-tech engines is one of the most valuable resources in the motor industry. We assume that designers develop and maintain engines with the help of CAD systems. Designers are responsible for design information, i.e. they are the "owners" of the resource. To ensure the quality of the design process, the information concerning intermediary design artifacts (e.g. plans, prototype engines) has to be exchanged between organisational units. We will select the exchange of design information between a drawing office and a quality assurance department in a motor company to illustrate the seven criteria that constitute our security framework. In doing so, we consider the technical, social and economic dimension introduced in the previous section (Figure 5).

(1) Goal Conformity. Goal conformity prevents the misuse of information, i.e. it ensures that the use of information is bound to the intended goals of the owner/sender. It considers the influence of information on the relationship between what humans think and their resulting goal-oriented actions (what they decide and/or do). To guarantee goal conformity, damage caused by the misuse of information must be prevented. Misuse of information damages the organisation when information enables an individual to act in a way that contradicts with the organisation's goals. Threats

arising from the possible uses of information depend on the questions: What could anyone do with specific information? What could a specific recipient do given their individual competencies? That means the recipient's interpretation of information is very important, especially when he or she has specific competence. Goal conformity extends the traditional IT-security criteria to meet the requirements of the application domain. It considers the economic relevance of information arising from human interactions.

In terms of our example, goal conformity means that the quality assurance department does not misuse the received design information, e.g. they only use it to perform quality tests. So goal conformity ensures that the members of the quality department may only act according to organisational goals, when receiving design information. In other words, the boundaries of acceptable behaviours are given by the "spotlight" of organisational goals (Figure 5).

(2) Obligation. The exchange of information between communication partners includes social interaction. From the security point of view, we require that the obligations emerging from this interaction are binding to the communication partners, i.e. they accept the obligations. Their binding character is based on the kind of interaction, the legal systems, organisational policies, commitments or guidelines. For example, if a social interaction is documented as a legally binding contract, then obligations are provable and therefore enforceable in a social context [11, 12]. Like goal conformity, binding obligations are independent of the realisation of technical information systems and are an extension of traditional IT-security criteria.

In our example, the primary reason for communication is to ensure the quality standard during motor manufacturing. Hence, communication establishes the following obligations: The designers have to provide the "right" information, i.e. necessary information which enables performance of quality testing, and members of the quality department have to perform the quality test adequately as negotiated.

(3+4) Authenticity. Authenticity of communication partners is a widely accepted security criterion for information systems. It stems from the nature of interpersonal communication. Authenticity requirements encompass the authenticity of communication partners (as is the case of KERBEROS [26]) as well as the authenticity of a message's content, i.e. correspondence between representation and reality. Often the latter is not considered[1] or discussed in the context of integrity. Authenticity of the content means that the representations can be validated according to the organisational "reality". In this sense, authenticity guarantees that valid decisions can be made based on the content of the system model.

In our example, the authenticity of content ensures that the design information adequately maps "reality," i.e. the design information precisely describes the "real" engine. The authenticity of communication partners ensures that the designer's communication partner is really the one who is intended to receive the design information and in turn this communication partner can be sure that the received information has been sent by the designer.

(5) Confidentiality. Confidentiality of data is a traditional IT-security criterion. It describes the state of being private or secret, i.e. only accessible by authorised people [25, 5, 1]. Unauthorised disclosure of data is a violation of confidentiality. Confidentiality is ensured by data access controls or encryptions in technical systems. Access controls are classified as either mandatory access controls that specify user

---

[1] An exception is the Clark/Wilson model [4].

privileges and object classifications (e.g. top-secret, private, public) or discretionary access controls that define discrete relationships between an active and a passive component [5, 1]. The more flexible techniques to access control are based on user-role descriptions [21, 30, 22]. To formally specify the underlying authorisations, various approaches are proposed in the literature [31, 27, 28]. Steinke, for example, uses a group security model which describes access rights through a teamwork-oriented organisational model [27]. Another way to ensure confidentiality is data encryption which uses cryptographic methods to preserve against the unauthorised interpretation of data. There are two major methods for data encryption: (a) symmetric encryption, i.e. encryption and decryption using the same key; and (b) asymmetric encryption, i.e. public and private keys for encryption and decryption respectively.

Considering confidentiality in our example, the technical information system has to guarantee that the data representing the design information is not accessible by unauthorised persons.

(6) Integrity. Integrity, like confidentiality, is a traditional IT-security criteria [2]. The distinction between the integrity of the data and the correspondence between representation and reality is rarely considered when specifying security requirements. We call the correspondence between representation and reality the authenticity of content (3). Integrity, as we define it, relates to the internal state of data and depends on the technical realisation of the system in use, but not on the system's representation.

Integrity, for example, prevents unauthorised and accidental modification of the data representing design information as stored or while transmitted.

(7) Availability. Availability is a state of existence or readiness for the resources and services (infrastructure, data, services) belonging to a technical information system. Availability is a basic requirement that is barely considered in existing security models [25].

In our example this security criterion guarantees that the data representing the design information is available when needed by authorised persons.

The criteria (1) goal conformity, (2) obligation, and (3) authenticity of content correspond to informal phenomena. Thus, these criteria specify quality requirements that must be *validated* in the first place. The security criteria (4) authenticity of communication partners, (5) confidentiality, (6) integrity, and (7) availability can be formally specified and thus are under the reign of *verification*.

5 Managing Secure Information Exchange

Corresponding to the suggested framework, we briefly describe those requirements an information system in productive use has to fulfil to achieve secure information exchange.

- *Classification of the economic potential of information to be exchanged* within a communication context, i.e. which activities of the communication partners are intended and which are possible? etc. Additionally, a classification of the communication partners is necessary: What organisational roles do they have? Which roles are possible based on their individual competence? etc.

- *Classification of the type of interpersonal interaction.* The type of interpersonal interaction refers to the obligations which arise out of this interaction.

- *Classification of the overall sensitivity of the data* for loss of confidentiality, integrity, and availability.

- *Anticipation of threats based on the previous classifications.* Example threats are misuse of information, neglecting obligations, and disclosure of data. The probability of misuse can be anticipated, for instance, by using a model of goal-based human behaviour [24]. Although the risk of opportunistic behaviour is quite common in organisations, behaviour is not completely arbitrary, but governed by norms and rules. Acting depends on the situation, the individual's competence and on the available information to be exchanged. Usually the goals of the communication partners overlap but are not congruent. Their differences must be anticipated to discover the conflicts of interests arising from the exchange of the information.

- *Selection of measures appropriate for preventing anticipated threats.* That is, the selection of security measures to be used for data access and transmission, e.g. document exchange; and the selection of security measures to prevent the misuse of information, to establish obligations and to guarantee the correctness of the content.

6 Conclusion

A comprehensive security framework must consider the interdisciplinary aspects of socio-technical systems (e.g. the technical information system within an organisation). Thus, our security framework for information exchange within and between organisations considers the social, the technical and the economic dimension of an information system, i.e. (a) the security requirements specific to the basic threats concerning valuable objects of the application domain, and (b) the security requirements arising from the use of technical systems which have to be dealt with in general. The primary focus of this paper has been to illustrate the implications of this point of view when specifying security requirements.

We discussed the subjectivity of security (valuable objects, relevant threats and acceptable risks) and proceeded to explain the security relevant dimensions of information exchange. Then we described the components (security criteria) of a framework for information exchange. This security framework constitutes the basis for a systematic analysis of security requirements. According to its structure the framework guides the formal specification of requirements. That is, the framework shows the contribution of existing approaches to the overall security of information exchange [31, 27, 28]. Up to now existing approaches for secure information systems do not consider the economic dimension appropriately.

Moreover, economic, social and technical security criteria form a basis for the flexible application of security measures to achieve overall security. For that, contextual properties have to be defined to allow the anticipation of the mutual threats concerning communication partners (economic potential of information, intended interpersonal relationships, etc.). Then we can select a set of security measures which are completed by measures for preventing unauthorised data access and modification. Finally, the security levels of our framework and their structured set of security criteria support the quantitative specification of the risks underlying information processing in the application domain.

Further work will be done in this area by the OBS project [29] and the Requirements Engineering project [10]. The goal of the OBS project is to realise security management that is flexible and enables the economic use of security measures. That is, we are developing a method for bridging the gap between the security requirements for information exchange and their formal representation.

Acknowledgements. We would like to thank Johannes Geiger, Andrew Hutchison, and Volker Stadler for discussing this article and suggesting improvements. Further thanks for the support of this work in general go to Norbert E. Fuchs and Steffi Teufel. We also gratefully acknowledge the support of the Swiss National Science Foundation. The work of Hubert F. Hofmann is partially supported by grant SNF 21-32746.91. Ralph Holbein's work is supported by grant NFP/SPP 5003-34271.

7 References

[1]   D.E. Bell, L.J. La Padula, *Secure Computer Systems: Unified Exposition and Multics Interpretation.* EDS-TR-75-30, The MITRE Corp., Bedford, March 1976.

[2]   K.J. Biba, *Integrity Considerations for Secure Computer Systems.* TR-3153, The MITRE Corp., Bedford, 1977.

[3]   W.J. Clancey, Situated Action: A Neuropsychological Interpretation. *Cognitive Science*, vol. 17, no. 1, 1993.

[4]   D. Clark, D. Wilson, A Comparision of Commercial and Military Security Policies. *Proceedings of the IEEE Symposium on Security and Privacy*, 1987.

[5]   Department of Defense, *TCSEC — Trusted Computer System Evaluation Criteria.* DoD 5200.28-STD, Department of Defense, USA, December 1985.

[6]   W.E. Deming, *Out of the Crisis.* Cambridge, MIT Center for Advanced Engineering, 1986.

[7]   ECMA, *Security in Open Systems – A Security Framework.* 46, European Computer Manufacturers Association (ECMA), 1988.

[8]   ECMA, *Standard ECMA-138 – Security in Open Systems – Data Elements and Service Definitions.* Standard ECMA-138, European Computer Manufacturers Association (ECMA), 1989.

[9]   A. Finkelstein, J. Kramer, B. Nuseibeh et al., Viewpoints: A Framework for Integration Multiple Perspectives in System Development. *International Journal of Software Engineering and Knowledge Engineering*, vol. 1, no. 2, 1992, pp. 31-58.

[10]   N.E. Fuchs, *Software Development Based on Executable Specifications.* SNF 21-32746.91, Institute for Informatics, University of Zurich, 1993.

[11]   R. Grimm, A Model of Security in Open Telecooperation. In: G.Neufeld, B. Plattner (eds.). *Proceedings of the IFIP TC6/WG 6.5 International Conference on Upper Layer Protocols, Architectures and Applications*, Vancouver, Canada, 27-29 May, 1992.

[12] R. Grimm, A. Steinacker, Das Kooperations- und das Gleichgewichtsmodell – Theorie und Praxis. *VIS 93: Verlässliche Informationssysteme – GI-Fachtagung*, München, Springer, 1993.

[13] R. Hirschheim, H.K. Klein, M. Newman, Information Systems Development as Social Action: Theoretical Perspective and Practice. *OMEGA International Journal of Management Science*, vol. 19, no. 6, 1991, pp. 587-608.

[14] H.F. Hofmann, *Requirements Engineering: A Survey of Methods and Tools.* TR 93.05, Institute for Informatics, University of Zurich, 1993.

[15] H.F. Hofmann, R. Pfeifer, E. Vinkhuyzen, Situated Software Design. In: *Proceedings of the Fifth International Conference on Software Engineering and Knowledge Engineering* San Francisco, Knowledge Systems Institute, 1993, pp. 622-628.

[16] R. Holbein, Informationssicherheit — Ein Blick über den Tellerrand der (Informations-) Technologie. *European Conference on Computer Science, Communication and Society: A Technical and Cultural Challenge*, Neuchatel, Schweiz, 1993, pp. 161-172.

[17] R. Holbein, *Secure Information Exchange in Organisations.* OBS-Report, University of Zurich, 1994.

[18] M. Imai, *Kaizen: The Key to Japan's Competitive Success.* New York, Random House, 1986.

[19] ISO, *ISO: Security Frameworks Overview.* International Organisation for Standardization, 1991.

[20] ISO, *WD 10746-1: Reference Model for Open Distributed Processing ODP Part 1: Overview.* WD 10746-1, International Organisation for Standardization ISO, 1992.

[21] J.I. Jones, M. Sergot, Formal Specification of Security Requirements using the Theory of Normative Positions. *Computer Security – ESORICS 92*, Toulouse, France, 1992, pp. 103-121.

[22] D. Jonscher, K.R. Dittrich, *A Formal Security Model Based on an Object-Oriented Data Model.* TR 93.41, University of Zurich, Institute for Informatics, 1993.

[23] F. Lehner, H.F. Hofmann, R. Setzer et al., Maintenance of Knowledge Bases. *Fourth International Conference on Database and Expert Systems Applications*, Prag, Springer, 1993, pp. 436-447.

[24] A. Newell, The Knowledge Level. *AI Magazine*, vol. 2, no. 2, 1981, pp. 1-20.

[25] D.B. Parker, Neuformulierung der Grundlagen der Informationssicherheit. *Datenschutz und Datensicherung*, no. 11, 1991.

[26] J.G. Steiner, C. Newman, J.I. Schiller, Kerberos, An Authentication Service for Open Network Systems. *Winter USENIX Conference*, Dallas, 1988.

[27] G. Steinke, M. Jarke, Support for Security Modeling in Information Systems Design. *Database Security, VI: Status and Prospects (A-21)*, Elsevier Science Publisher, 1993, pp. 125-141.

[28]   R. Strens, J. Dobson, *How Responsiblity Modeling Leads To Security Requirements*. Department of Computer Science, University of Newcastle, 1993.

[29]   S. Teufel, *Offene Bürokommunikation — Sicherheitsmanagement im inner- und zwischenbetrieblichen Informationsaustausch (OBS)*. NFP/SPP 5003-34271, Institute for Informatics, University of Zurich, 1993.

[30]   T.C. Ting, S. Demurjian, M.-Y. Hu, Requirements, Capabilities, and Functionalities of User-Role Based Security for an Object-Oriented Design Model. *Database Security*, vol. 5, 1992.

[31]   T.C. Ting, S.A. Demurjian, M.-Y. Hu, A Specification Methodology for User-Role Based Security in an Object-Oriented Design Model. *Sixth Working Conference on Database Security*, Burnaby, IFIP WG 11.3, 1992, pp. 351-378.

[32]   T. Winograd, F. Flores, *Understanding Computers and Cognition*. New York, Ablex, 1986.

[33]   John A. Wise, V. David Hopkin, Paul Stager (eds.), *Verification and Validation of Complex Systems: Human Factors Issues*. Berlin, Springer, 1993.

Capturing Semantics by Object Relativity

William Wei Song
SYSLAB, Department of Computer and Systems Sciences
Royal Inst. of Technology and Stockholm University
and
Swedish Institute of Systems Development (SISU)
Electrum 212, 164 40, Kista, Sweden
E-mail: william@sisu.se

Abstract. To acquire the semantics of objects in schemata and hence to identify the objects is becoming a crucial research problem in schema integration. It is an effective and feasible way to make use of a group of schemata (schema family) to capture the meaning/concept of objects. In this paper we analyze the various relations between a given object and its related objects in the existing schemata and construct a characteristic set for the object. The relations include attributes, relationships and mapping constraints, contexts, and some specific inter-object relations like generalization, etc. The characteristic set so generated for an object can uniquely identify the object. We also attempt to apply the obtained characteristic set for the semantic conflict detection and resolution.

Keywords. view integration, schema integration, semantics, entity-relationship model, conceptual schema design, data dictionary

1 Introduction

Schemata are the products of an activity, called conceptual database design, which uses the semantic model to describe data in an abstract and understandable manner. Schema integration is the activity of integrating the schemata of existing or proposed databases into a global, unified schema [2]. Nowadays, the research on schema integration, has gained increasing attentions because of its significant effect on methods for conceptual information modelling. The aim of schema integration is either to create a global schema, which takes in all the possible user's views, and makes these views consistent; or to provide a common access or interface to local schemata in which the user's diverse requests (or views) are represented.

Usually, the process of schema integration consists of the following five iterating steps, canonization (pre-integration), comparison, conciliation, merging (integration), and restructuring. 1) In the canonizing step the intra-schema conflicts and inconsistencies are detected against some pre-defined criteria or requirements, such as "an entity type is not allowed to connect to an attribute by a relationship". 2) The comparison step performs a pairwise comparison of objects of the schemata to be integrated and finds possible object pairs which may be semantically similar. The object pair set so generated is called the semantic similarity relation with respect to some properties, such as synonym, equal key attributes and equal contexts. 3) In the conciliation step, a variety of user assisted techniques are used to resolve conflicts and mismatched objects. 4) The merging step generates an integrated schema from two component schemata. 5) In the last step, restructuring, the objective is to check the consistency of the integrated schema and build correspondences between the component schemata and the integrated schema [13].

One of the main tasks of schema integration is to detect semantic conflicts among objects from schemata or find out semantic similarities between objects. Due to the differences between the user and designer perceptions of the reality, semantic conflicts arise from time to time in the schema evolution and integration. These conflicts must be solved with specific methods, which are not considered in ordinary information system and database design methodologies.

It is apparent that a common problem both to the processes of schema design and integration is that of acquiring and applying semantic knowledge. In the process of schema design, the designer chooses some words to symbolize the concepts in the reality of interest. He also chooses suitable words to reflect the associations between the concepts. He has still to choose some words to display the attributes of entities. Therefore, so generated schemata contain three basic components, entities, which represent the conceptual meaning of the objects in the real world, relationships, which describe the association between the entities, and attributes, which give the possible features of the entities. These schemata, which represent some portions of the reality of interest, are usually intersected and interrelated.

In the process of schema integration, the components of schemata are contrasted to and compared with each other. The aim of such contrasts and comparisons is to find the semantic similarity between schema objects for the subsequent object integration or to detect the semantic conflicts among schema objects for the schema semantic integrity. At present, these contrasts and comparisons are mainly fulfilled by human (such as DBA). He uses his experiences and knowledge (including both syntactic and semantic) to interpret the schemata to be integrated and further perform integration on schemata. In addition to the user's subjective understanding of the schemata to be integrated, he also uses the semantic relations which exists between the object types in the previous schemata and his previous integration assertions.

1.1 Problems to be addressed

One of the major problems of schema integration is the semantic knowledge acquisition from the existing schemata and the representation of such acquired knowledge in some way. It is difficult to precisely and exactly acquire the semantics of the objects in schemata, since it involves the correct interpretation of people's perceptions (views) of the reality, the correct representation of these perceptions (views) by using schemata, and the correct re-appearance of these perceptions after schema integration [12].

Key problems, addressed in this paper, are how to obtain and apply the semantic knowledge which exists in the previous schema design for the use of subsequent schema integration and semantic integrity checking. In schemata, entities are assigned certain conceptual meanings. Such meanings stipulate that an object is different from the other objects. Similarly, the conceptual meanings of relationships stipulate that what entities can be the domain and what entities can be the range of the relationships. Still as the like, the attributes of an entity may tell the distinction of this entity from the other entities. Besides, many schemata are modelled by an extended ER modelling tool. This extension will give some additional semantics. For instance, generalization offers a new association (supertype) between entities.

Consequently, the capture of the schema object semantics should focus on the existing schemata and make use of the semantic relationships among the schema objects for establishing the characteristic set of the objects. In the paper we analyze the various relations between a given object and its related objects in the existing schemata and construct a characteristic set for the object. The relations include attributes, relationships and mapping constraints, contexts, and some specific inter-object relations like generalization, etc. The characteristic set so generated for an object can uniquely identify the object. We also attempt to apply the obtained characteristic set for the semantic conflict detection and resolution. To our knowledge, little research work has been focused on this aspect of schema integration issues.

1.2 Related work

Since the mid eighties, the research direction in schema integration has been gradually changed. It can be featurized as 1) the entity relationship model or some extension of it is considered as the major schema design model [10, 13]; 2) the in-depth structure (the role of attributes, mapping constraints, etc.) of schemata is focused on [8, 9, 13, 15]; and 3) the semantics of schema objects is emphasized [13]. Recently, the research on data or semantic dictionary is emerging [1, 4, 11]. In our opinion, research on semantic of schema object types consists in the basis of the semantic dictionary while the development of semantic dictionary is undoubtedly the result of the semantic analysis on schemata. A comprehensive survey of early view integration research results can be found in [2].

An incisive analysis of schema integration semantics is made in [6], where some of the methods are analyzed for the database syntax and semantics which populate and can differ among the resources of an enterprise information system. These distinctions are caused by a number of factors, including the different perspectives of the schema designers, the different representations of the reality concepts by the users, etc. The author emphasizes that the database semantics should be taken into account at the early stages of the database design process.

It is stated in [3, 5] that the view integration is a semantic unification which takes into account the domains of atomic objects. Semantic relations are based on the name relation, domain relation, and structure relation of objects. The result of the semantic unification of two concepts is represented by a multiple information called similarity vector whose interpretation of the different components will vary from the semantic equivalence, the semantic similarity, to the semantic dissimilarity.

A deep analysis of the semantic similarity relations between schema objects is presented in [13]. Based on such semantic similarity relations, the user is supposed to have more decision information (suggestions) for the assertion makings during the schema integration. The similarity relation between two objects is obtained through the examination of their names, their attributes, their relationships, and their contexts. Such similarity relations are further categorized into 4 groups: weak semantic relation, compatible semantic relation, equivalence semantic relation, and mergeable semantic relation.

A methodology for data dictionary design is proposed in [1, 11]. The methodology is based on the concept of local area schema, a data description realized with a given model, at different levels of abstraction. Data abstraction is realized through the introduction of refinement, which is a mechanism allowing for modelling the same portion of reality in terms of several schemata at different levels of abstraction. Refinements are formally defined through the introduction of transformations from a source schema to target one. The methodology for data dictionary design performs a multilevel integration starting from the chain of refinements of local schemata and the sequence of transformations representing them, and generates an integrated schema.

Consequently, it is widely accepted that semantic relations in schemata play an important role in the schema integration. Even more important is the use of such semantics already-existing in the schemata. However, current research is restricted to obtaining such semantic knowledge from the current, isolated schemata to be integrated and to temporarily applying the semantic knowledge obtained only for the current integration work. To our knowledge, little attention has been paid to the capture of semantic knowledge existing in a group of schemata which are designed for a certain application domain and closely related to one another. We name such a group of schemata a schema family. In this paper, we attempt to take into account the semantic knowledge which exists in a schema family and to present an approach to expand the knowledge during the process of schema design and integration for an application domain.

1.3 An overview of the paper

The acquisition of the semantics from the existing schemata is a key problem of correct understanding of the current schemata to be integrated. In this paper, we are going to propose an approach to schema semantics capture for schema integration, which makes use of various relations existing between different schema objects, such as attributes, relationships and mapping constraints, object contexts, generalization, etc., to extract the semantic knowledge (i.e., characteristic set) for objects. we also extend this concept to the semantic capture of objects from a group of schemata, we call it **schema family**. In the next section, we present some assumptions as the basis on which object semantics is expressed. We will discuss the relations among a concepts, its name (or word), and its physical occurrences. We define entity types, relationship types and attribute types in schemata as concepts which are represented by names. In the section 3, we analyze the functions of various relationships and contexts of a given entity type and investigate their contribution to the characteristic set of the given entity type, as well as the contribution from a schema family, and hence form some characteristic set expansions. The detection of possible semantic conflicts in terms of the entity characteristic set is observed in section 4, where three typical semantic conflicts are taken into account, i.e., synonym, homonym and cyclic generalization. We conclude the paper in the last section, the section 5, and discuss future work in this area.

2 Some Basic Concepts

2.1 Motivation

Two major steps of the database design process are: conceptual schema design and physical database design. The corresponding products are respectively conceptual schémata and databases which contain instances (the facts in the reality). For example, let us consider modelling Department and Employee, and the relationship works-at between them. Two possible schemata can be designed to model the case (see Fig.1), and the result database is shown in Table 1.

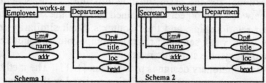

Fig.1 The schemata for employee, secretary and department.

Employee

Em#	name	addr
600102	John	addr1
600202	Mary	addr2

Department

Dp#	title	loc	head
1111	CS	loc1	John
2222	Ph	loc2	Mary

Table 1 An example of instances of the schema 1.

Comparing the two schemata, 1 and 2, one may possibly jump to the conclusion that the entity 'Secretary' could be identical to the entity 'Employee', which is hint by the facts that both the entities have the same attribute 'Em#', 'name' and 'addr', and the same context 'works-at-Department'. In other words, by attributes, relationships, and contexts of entities, we can capture the semantic of the entities of interest and identify them. Database design involves two aspects of matters: the concepts appearing in the database schema and the instances or the facts in the concrete database. Table 1 gives a part of instances of the proposed schema in Fig.1. The concepts reflect the understanding of the users or the designers to the reality and are used to describe the reality. The instances are the physical occurrences of the concepts in the real world. As a matter of fact, we have a third component, words (or names), which symbolize the concepts. In other words, an object in schema corresponds to three components: its name (word), a concept the word represents, and a set of instances the concept refers to. The relationships between them are illustrated in Fig.2. In the database schema design and integration, concept capture and representation are the main problems to be attacked. In the rest of this section we give some assumptions, based on which we can discuss the semantic properties of objects.

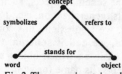

Fig.2 The meaning triangle

2.2 Words and concepts

Schemata are designed to describe a portion of the real world, its perceived concepts and the associations among the concepts. This portion of the real world is called the universe of discourse, denoted U. We assume that the universe of discourse U is monolithic, i.e., no association existing between U and outside U. All the elements contained in U are concrete objects[1] (in contrast to abstract, conceptual objects) for a certain application domain in the reality. We still assume that the schemata defined on U are homogeneous, i.e., designed for a certain particular area of interest and by the same modelling tool. To make such assumptions is to better investigate the contribution of schema family to the schema semantic capture. These concrete objects are grouped into classes. Each class corresponds to a concept in the concept set C. A class in U can be further divided into sub-classes, which also correspond to sub-concepts in C. A concept is symbolized by a word (or name) in the word set W. In the following, we will define these relations between them.

Definition 2.1 Let W and C be the word set and the concept set respectively. We define that symbolize is a mapping from W to C,

$$symbolize : W \rightarrow C,$$

so that **symbolize**(w) = c, c $\in$ C and w $\in$ W.

When the mapping **symbolize** maps two different words to one concept, the two words are considered *synonymous*. When it maps one word to two different concepts, the word is considered *homonymous*.

Definition 2.2 Given that C is the concept set and U the universe of discourse, which contains the concrete objects, we define that **extension** is a mapping,

$$extension : C \rightarrow 2^U,$$

so that **extension**(c) = {o1, o2, ..., on}, c $\in$ C and oi $\in$ U.

The concept of a word is also called the intension of the word. The *intension* of a word is that part of meaning that accords with general principles in semantic memory. The *extension* of a word is the set of all existing things (instances) to which the word applies [14]. In the other words, the intension of a word is a set of properties, a set of characteristics which uniquely identify a concept represented by the word. During the comparison step in schema integration process, one of the main tasks is to identify words. Because the difficulties of capturing the intension of words, this work is mainly carried out by the user. Our aim is to acquire the intension of words through investigating the interrelations of schema objects.

2.3 The characteristics of a word (or a concept)

There are three approaches discussed in [14] to capture the semantics (concept) of a word: 1) using the type definition, 2) using a prototype and 3) using schemata. *Type definition* of a word (concept), in general, is to give its genus and differentia. In a simpler way, we may explain it as that to define a word is to find out its super-concept (of course symbolized by a word) and one or several properties which differ the word to be defined from the words which represent the rest concepts within the super-concept. However, it is rather difficult to find a suitable super-concept and the properties which exactly identify the word to be defined[2]. *Prototype* approach is to recognize a word (concept) against an existing set of properties. When the word resemble all the properties, it is considered to be identified. However, the problem here is how to obtain the needed properties and according to what criteria to group the properties. *Concept schemata* are considered as a kind of means to acquire the properties of a word (or a concept). For each concept symbolized by a word, schemata describe the conventional, normally occurring, or default roles that it plays with respect to other concepts. Comparing to the type definition method, where for example, the definition of Employee will present the primary (identically, uniquely) defining characteristic, a schema would include the

---

[1]We use the 'concrete object' to indicate an individual instance (or fact) in the real world, e.g., Mr. Smith, in contrast to the 'abstract object' , e.g., person. We adopt the term object for the latter.

[2]In addition, normally the definitions are in natural languages, therefore difficult to deal with by computer.

neighbouring information about Employee such as having an employee number, earning salary, reporting to a manager, working in a department, and so forth, all of which together form the properties of Employee and may uniquely identify it.

Definition 2.3 (Characteristic function and characteristic set[3]) For each concept c in C, there is a function $\lambda: C \rightarrow 2^{\Sigma}$ (Σ is a set of all properties for all the concrete objects in U), that $\lambda(c) = \sigma$, σ can uniquely identify the concept c. We call λ the *characteristic function*, σ the *characteristic set*. This set is assumed to contains all the characteristics (or properties) of the concept c.

The intension of a word indicates the nature of the word and therefore indicates the common nature of all the objects in the word extension, i.e., the object type. Therefore, we may conclude that if two words have the same intension, their corresponding object types in the schemata can be integrated. In the section 3, we will discuss in detail how to form the characteristic set of a word from the schemata to be considered and the users' assertions given during the schema integration.

2.4 Schema and its components

As known to us, schemata are designed by some semantic models (for example, the ER model). Semantic models attempt to provide more powerful abstractions for the specification of database schemata. They allow the designers to think of data in ways that correlate more directly to how data arise in the real world and to model data at a higher, conceptual level [7]. ER model is one of such semantic models. The schemata created by this model support the representation of abstract sets of entities, relationships which establish some conceptual associations between entities, and attributes to describe the features of entities. In this paper, we apply an extended ER model, called ER+, which has been defined in [13]. However, for the aim of capturing semantics of the objects (i.e., entities, relationships, and attributes) we only focus on the parts of an object, which are dedicated to semantics, and rule out the other information attached to the object. Fundamentally, we consider the name and the characteristic set of an object.

Definition 2.4 (Object type) An object type O is a triple:
$$\langle name(O), \lambda(O), extension(O)\rangle,$$
where
1) name(O) is the name of the object type O,
2) $\lambda(O)$ is the characteristic set of O, which uniquely identifies O, and
3) **extension(O)** is all possible instances of O.

Definition 2.5 (Entity type) An entity type e is an object type. We assume that no entity type in a schema is isolated. That is, any entity type in a schema must be related to at least one other entity type by a relationship type.

Definition 2.6 (Relationship type) A relationship type r is an object type, which, expressed by an arrow, connects an entity type, the domain of the relationship, with one or more entity types, the ranges of the relationship. Each relationship type has a *mapping constraint*, described by the predicate
$$rel\_map(r, [(M1:N1), (M2:N2)]),$$
where r is the relationship type, $(M_1:N_1)$ represents that the domain entity must participate in at least M_1 and at most N_1 instances of the relationship type r, and $(M_2:N_2)$ indicates that the range entity must participate in at least M_2 and at most N_2 instances of the relationship.

For example, the mapping constraint of the relationship type 'owns' in the schema

---

[3]We use characteristic set and semantic set as synonym.

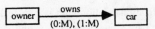

indicates that an owner may have zero up to many cars and a car must be owned by at least one owner.

Definition 2.7 (Attribute type) An attribute type A is a an object type. An attribute type must be associated to an entity type and an entity type must have at least one attribute. The entity type is called the domain of its attributes. Each attribute type has also a *mapping constraint*, denoted by a predicate as

attr_map(A, [(M1:N1), (M2:N2)]),

where A is the attribute, and the mapping constraint [(M1:N1), (M2:N2)] shares the same explanation as in the definition of relationship type.

Definition 2.8 (Key Attribute) Let **extension**(A) and **extension**(E) be the extensions of an attribute A and an entity type E respectively. If there is one-to-one mapping between **extension**(E) and **extension**(A), and the element number of **extension**(E) is the same as that of **extension**(A), it is said that A is the key attribute of E.

This definition implies that some attribute (i.e. key attribute) can uniquely determine an entity type.

Definition 2.9 (Schema) A schema is a meaningful conceptual structure (or graph), which has four components:

S = <S_name, **E'**, **R'**, **A'**>,

where S_name ∈ W, **E'** ⊆ **E**, **R'** ⊆ **R**, and **A'** ⊆ **A**.

Assumption The entity type set **E**, the relationship type set **R**, and the attribute type set **A** together partition the object type set and are pairwisely disjoint.

This assumption intentionally excludes the structural conflicts, such as a word is used for an entity type in one schema and an attribute type in another.

These definitions are graphically illustrated by the following meta-schema (Fig.3).

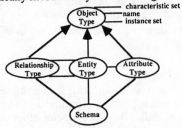

Fig.3 A meta-schema for the interrelations of schema components.

In addition to the general relationships described above, there are three relationships which are the elements of the above stated relationship types and play a special semantic role in the schema design and integration. They are generalization, coverage, and aggregation. Thus, it is necessary to define them separately.

Definition 2.10 (Generalization) Let c1 and c2 be two concepts. The concept c1 is a generalization of c2, denoted <c1, c2> ∈ **Gen** if **extension**(c2) ⊂ **extension**(c1). **Gen** is a binary relation[4].

In terms of this definition, we can directly jump to the theorem as follows:

---

[4]The generalization relation sometimes is represented as **is-a**(c2, c1), which indicates c1 a generalization of c2. The reverse relation of **Gen** is specialization, denoted **Spec**.

Theorem 1 The generalization relation Gen is non-reflexive and transitive. That is, suppose that c1, c2, and c3 are three concepts in C and $<c1, c2> \in$ **Gen**, and $<c2, c3> \in$ **Gen**, then $<c1, c3> \in$ **Gen**.

Definition 2.11 (Coverage) Suppose that c1, c2, ..., cn, are n concepts, and **extension**(ci) are the extensions of ci, i=1, 2, ..., n, the relation coverage can be defined as a binary relation,

Cov: $C \rightarrow 2^C$, C is the concept set, so that

$<c1, \{c2, ..., cn\}> \in$ **Cov** if

extension(c1) = extension(c2)$\cup$ extension(c3)$\cup$ ...$\cup$extension(cn),

and extension(ci) $\cap$ extension(cj) = $\emptyset$, i, j = 2, ..., n, i$\neq$j.

3 The capture of characteristic set

The existing schemata provide us with a list of entity types, a list of relationship types which associate the entity types, and a list of attributes which describe the entity types. The integration activities provide us with the assertions which are formalized into a so called knowledge base. All these inter-object type relations provide us the semantic interpretation of the object types in schemata. In other words, we can build the characteristic set of an object type and then expand the characteristic set with the help of such inter-object type relations. Although the characteristic set so obtained may not contain all the features and may not be sufficient to identify an object type, they will lead to at least a correct and exact interpretation of the object type. The integration activities could be built on such solid basis -- a relatively full, correct, and exact interpretation of the meaning of the object type. In this section, we propose a set of methods for the obtainment and expansion of the characteristic set of a given entity type. Let us first consider to capture the characteristic set of an object type within **one** schema. Without loss of the generality, we consider just entity types in the schema. Suppose that e is an entity type in schema S. We denote the characteristic set of e $\lambda_S(e)$, which are obtained only from the schema S.

Then, a broader context, schema family, is taken into account for capturing the characteristic set of an entity type. Suppose that an entity type e occurs in a group of schemata S1, S2, ..., **Sn** (schema family **F**). We denote the characteristic set of e $\lambda_F(e)$, which are obtained only from the schema family **F**.

3.1 Capture $\lambda_S(e)$ from attributes

The attributes of an entity type play an important role in understanding the meaning of the entity. Any pair of object types whose identifying attributes can be integrated can themselves be integrated [9]. This statement claims that the attributes of an entity can in some way give the intension of the entity. In one place, an attribute (say, key attribute) or a group of attributes can determine its entity, for example, security number vs. person while in the other place, a group of attributes can partly determine an entity. That is, the group of attributes may at least constitute a part of the intension of the entity. For example, the attribute 'name' gives an intension of a concept. All the objects which have 'name' will be the extension of the concept.

Definition 3.1 (Key semantic expansion) Let $\lambda_S(e)$ be the characteristic set of entity type e in a schema S. If **k** is the key attribute of e, then $k \in \lambda_S(e)$.

Definition 3.2 (Attribute semantic expansion) Let $\lambda_S(e)$ be the characteristic set of entity type e in a schema S. If a set of attributes $\{a1, a2, ..., an\}$ of e can uniquely determine e, then $\{a1, a2, ..., an\} \in \lambda_S(e)$.

In fact, the definition 3.2 indicates that a set of attribute types may play a role of key which can uniquely identify the entity type they are attached to. For instance (see Fig.4), the entity type 'Book' can be certainly uniquely identified by its key attribute 'B#' (book number), so B# is an element of λ_S('Book'). Assuming that B# is missing from the schema S (This happens more often than not during the schema design), the other three attributes, 'authors', 'edition', and 'publisher' may together uniquely determine 'Book'. In this case, these three attributes as a whole will be an element of λ_S('Book').

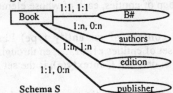

Fig.4 capture semantics of the entity 'Lecturer' from its attributes

3.2 Capture $\lambda_S(e)$ from relationships and their mapping constraints

Relationship types play an important role in stipulating the semantics of the entity types it relates, since a relationship type not only associates two entity types but also dominates them. In other words, a relationship needs a subject which carries out the action represented by the relationship and an object which accepts the action. Therefore the relationship, or the action, demands that its subject should possess some particular features which stipulate a semantic category (the category here means a set, each of whose elements can be a subject of this relationship) of which the subject is an element. Similarly, the object is also an element of a semantic category. The semantic category is intensionally a set of features, and extensionally, a group of things which possess these features. For instance, the relationship type 'attends' in the statements 'author attends a conference' and 'submitter attends a conference' imply that 'author' and 'submitter' as subjects should belong to the same semantic category, which has the feature 'can attend', on one hand. On the other hand, 'attends' stipulates that 'conference' should be an element of the semantic category having the feature 'can be attended'. Inversely, relationships are of course affected by their subjects and objects.

Definition 3.3 (Mapping constraint) Let **r** be a relationship type which has a domain e1 and a range e2, both being entity types. The mapping constraint of r with respect to e1 and e2, denoted [m1:m2, n1:n2], indicates that
1) for each element in **extension**(e1), there are at least m1 and at most m2 elements in **extension**(e2) participating in the relationship r; and
2) for each element in **extension**(e2), there are at least n1 and at most n2 elements in **extension**(e1) participating in the relationship r.

Definition 3.4 (Relationship semantic expansion) Let $\lambda_S(e)$ be the characteristic set of entity type e in a schema S. If the entity type e is related to another entity type e' with a relationship type **r** and the mapping constraint is [1:1, 1:1], then {name(r), $\lambda_S(e')$} $\in \lambda_S(e)$, where name(r) is the name of the relationship type **r** and $\lambda_S(e')$ is the characteristic set of entity type e'.

This definition states a fact that an entity type can be uniquely identified by a given relationship and a known entity type which participates in the relationship when there is a one-to-one mapping between the extensions of two entity types with respect to the relationship. For example, a schema contains such components as 'Dean administrates Department'. The mapping constraint of this particular 'administrates' is [1:1, 1:1]. Suppose that we have already known the key of the entity type 'Department' to be 'Dept#', according to the definition, we can uniquely identify the entity type 'Dean' by 'administrates' and 'Department'.

3.3 Capture $\lambda_S(e)$ from contexts

As we discussed above, the relationships of an entity can give some characteristics (or part of intension) of the entity, whereas the contexts of the entity can give more refined characteristics of the entity set which the entity is contained. A context of an entity e' is a set, whose element is an ordered pair, $<r, e>$, where r is a relationship and e is an entity. Obviously, a context of e', $<r, e>$, specifies a set of entities, while e' is an element of the entity set. Consider the example 'Driver drives a Car'. The relationship 'drives' and the entity 'Car' together determine a group of entities, each of whose elements has the property 'able to drive a car'.

> **Definition 3.5 (The context of an entity type)** Let e be an entity in schema S and e is related to a set of entities e1, e2, ..., en through a set of relationships r1, r2, ..., rn. The context of e, denoted **Context$_S$(e)**, is the set $\{<ri, ei> \mid i = 1, ..., n\}$.

> **Definition 3.6 (Context semantic expansion)** Let $\lambda_S(e)$ be the characteristic set of entity type e in schema S and the context of e be **Context$_S$(e)**. If **Context$_S$(e)** can uniquely identify the entity type e, then the set $\{<name(ri), \lambda_S(ei)>$ $\mid i = 1, ..., n\} \in \lambda_S(e)$, where name(ri) is the name of the relationship ri and $\lambda_S(ei)$ is the characteristic set of entity type ei, for i = 1, 2, ..., n.

For instance (see Fig.5), schema S contains three entities 'Lecturer', 'Department' and 'Course'. The entity 'Lecturer' has the context **context$_S$('Lecturer')** = {<'works-at', 'Department'>, <'gives', 'Course'>}. Then λ_S('Lecturer') includes {<'works-at', 'Department'>, <'gives', 'Course'>}.

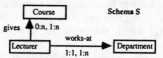

Fig.5 capture semantics of the entity 'Lecturer' from its contexts

3.4 Capture $\lambda_S(e)$ from the special relationships

3.4.1 Generalization

> **Definition 3.7 (Generalization semantic expansion)** Let e1 and e2 be two entity types in schema S and $\lambda_S(e1)$ and $\lambda_S(e2)$ the characteristic sets of e1 and e2 respectively. If $<e1, e2> \in$ **Gen**, then $\lambda_S(e1)$ is included in $\lambda_S(e2)$.

This definition indicates the fact that a sub-concept inherits all the characteristics of its super-concept. For instance (see Fig.6), in the schema S, we have the entity 'Lecturer', which is sub-concept of the entity 'Employee'. Then it inherits all the characteristics of 'Employee'. That is, λ_S('Lecturer') is expanded to include {Em#, salary, <'works-for', 'Organization'>}.

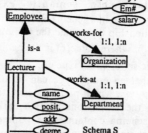

Fig.6 capture semantics from generalization

Note that during the process of this semantic expansion of λ_S('Lecturer'), a new semantic relationship between, for example, the entities 'Organization' and 'Department' may be discovered. Hence, the characteristic sets for 'Organization' and 'Department' should be formed for the identification of this new relationship. Possibly, the two entities have synonymous names, or one is the generalization of the other, etc.

3.4.2 Coverage

Definition 3.8 (Coverage semantic expansion) Let e be an entity and e1, e2, ..., en be a group of entities in schema S. $\lambda_S(e)$ is the characteristic sets of e and $\lambda_S(ei)$ the characteristic sets of ei, i = 1, 2, ..., n. If <e, {e1, e2, ..., en}> $\in$ **Cov**, then

1) $\lambda_S(e)$ is included in $\lambda_S(ei)$; and

2) $\cap\lambda_S(ei)$ is included in $\lambda_S(e)$, for i = 1, 2, ..., n.

The first conclusion of the definition indicates the fact that a sub-concept inherits all the characteristics of its super-concept. The second conclusion is that the characteristics that are possessed by all the sub-concepts should be the characteristics of the super-concept. As a matter of fact, it is still the inheritance put in another way. A schema appears in Fig.7, which model a part of a library information. In a library, we keep the publications which can be broken into three disjoint classes: books, journals, and newspaper. That is, the entity 'Publication' covers the entities 'Book', 'Journal', and 'Newspaper'.

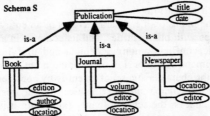

Fig.7 capture semantics from generalization

According to the definition 3.7, λ_S('Book') should be expanded to include λ_S('Publication'), and so should λ_S('Journal') and λ_S('Newspaper'). Since the attribute 'location' belongs to all the covered entities, the property {location} should be included in λ_S('Publication').

3.5 Capture $\lambda_F(e)$ from schema family

Conceptual schemata can be considered to be a very effective approach to the capturing of the characteristics of an object, where the objects related to the given object along with the relationships are taken into account for the contribution of the object characteristic set. The $\lambda_S(e)$ obtained from a single schema S for an entity is only reflecting a lopsided view of a concept, whereas the characteristic set $\lambda_F(e)$ obtained from a group of schemata F may reflect a relatively manifold views of a concept. This is rather crucial in schema integration. However, since several schemata are considered in order to obtain the $\lambda_F(e)$ for an entity, the pre-condition is necessary that these schemata should be consistent, i.e., no semantic conflicts existing between them.

The semantic conflicts include 1) synonym, where two different words represent the same concept, 2) homonym, where one word represents two different concepts, and cyclic generalization, where the concept A is a sub-concept of the concept B in one schema while in another schema B is a sub-concept of A. When a semantic conflict is detected, a semantic dictionary or the user's assertion is required to resolve the conflict. In the semantic dictionary, we maintain a list of synonyms for looking up when necessary [13]. A detailed definition and discussion for these conflicts will be given in the next section.

After all the semantic conflicts detected among the schema family are eliminated, the $\lambda_S(e)$ of the entity e can be expanded to include $\lambda_{Si}(e)$ into $\lambda_F(e)$, S_i is a schema in the schema family. The $\lambda_F(e)$ can be defined as follows.

Definition 3.9 (Collectives semantic expansion) Suppose that the entity e occurs in a group of schemata $S_1, S_2, ..., S_n$ and the characteristic sets of e in these schema are respectively $\lambda_{S1}(e), \lambda_{S2}(e), ..., \lambda_{Sn}(e)$. If $S_1, S_2, ..., S_n$ are consistent, then $\lambda_F(e) = \lambda_{S1}(e) \cup \lambda_{S2}(e) \cup ... \cup \lambda_{Sn}(e)$.

For instance, the entity Employee is common in two schema S1 and S2 in Fig 8. The characteristic set of Employee in schema 1 is λ_{S1}('Employee') = {<works-at, Department>, Em#}, and that of Employee in schema 2 is λ_{S2}('Employee') = {<works-for, Project>, Em#}. Hence, the characteristic set of Employee in the schema family (combining schema 1 and 2) is λ_F('Employee') = {<works-at, Department>, <works-for, Project>, Em#}.

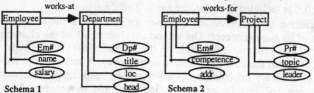

Fig. 8 Schemata of department and project

3.6 A summary of this section

We have observed that the intension, i.e., characteristics of an entity can be acquired from its attributes, its relationships with other entities, and its contexts in a single schema. Through eliminating the semantic conflicts among schemata and unifying the characteristic sets obtained from these schemata, the intension of a common entity can also be acquired. It is more significant to form the characteristic set of an entity by considering a group of schemata. In addition, by capturing the schema family semantics, we may maintain the schema design and integration history. That is, the schema family (assuming it is content after removing conflicts) can be used as a new semantic dictionary in broader sense for the detection of new schema design and integration. Therefore, the detection and resolution of the semantic conflicts become crucial in this sense. In the following section, we will discuss how to apply the characteristic sets to the conflict detection and hence the suggestions for the user's assertions when the conflicts are detected.

4 Some examples of using the semantic set

The aim of capturing the characteristic set of an entity is to support the resolution of the semantic conflicts which are found during schema integration. The semantic conflicts arise because of the diversity of the people's understanding of concepts and the diversity of their representations in names (or words) in schemata. Semantic conflicts can be seen as the incorrect or inappropriate usage of words for concepts which are established during people's percepting the reality (or part of the reality). The characteristic sets obtained by the methods discussed in the last section are mainly applied, in the schema comparison step, to detect the semantic conflicts. The semantic conflicts can break into these cases: synonym, homonym, and cyclic generalization. When the semantic conflicts are found some suggestions to indicate the causes resulting in the conflicts and the possible resolutions of the conflicts should be provided for the user's assertions.

4.1 The detection of synonym

The semantic conflict case - synonym occurs when the same concept is represented by two or more words (names).

Definition 4.1 Let w1 and w2 be two different words of the word set W respectively. If there exists the equation **symbolize**(w1) = **symbolize**(w2), the words w1 and w2 are considered to be synonymous.

An example appears in Fig.9, where two schemata are designed to describe the departments in a university.

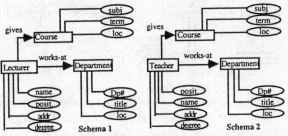

Fig.9 Example of synonym

The words 'Lecturer' and 'Teacher' are adopted to represent the same group of people who have degrees, work at a department, and advise courses, etc. (the same concept in the real world). Keeping two distinct entities in the integrated schema would result in modelling a single concept by means of two different entities.

1) Detection of synonym. Synonymous words can be detected by comparing the semantic sets of the words. Suppose that $\lambda_1(e_1)$ and $\lambda_2(e_2)$ are two characteristic sets and e_1 and e_2 are two different entity types in two different schemata 1 and 2. If $\lambda_1(e_1) = \lambda_2(e_2)$, e_1 and e_2 have the great possibility to be synonymous since they share almost all the characteristics in common. Consider again the above example, the semantic set of the entity 'Lecturer' is λ_1('Lecturer') = {<name, position, addr, degree>, <works-at, Dept>, <gives, Course>}, and the semantic set of the entity 'Teacher' is λ_2(Teacher) = {<name, position, addr, degree>, <works-at, Dept>, <gives, Course>}. Here we assume that <name, position, addr, degree> can determine 'Lecturer'.

Since for each element in λ_1('Lecturer'), there is a same element existing in λ_2('Teacher'), we may conclude that the entities 'Lecturer' and 'Teacher' are synonymous. However, It is quite often that not all elements in one semantic set can be found in another semantic set and vice versa. That is, for example, λ_1('Lecturer') and λ_2('Teacher') have majority of common elements. Then, the suggestion that 'Lecturer' is synonymous to 'Teacher' is proposed to the user for confirmation.

2) Suggestion. After the synonym conflict is detected, the suggestion that two entities be synonymous is presented, along with their characteristic sets, to the user for confirmation. When the user asserts that the two entities are same, then one preferable name is required to replace the names of the two entities and a new item is recorded in the semantic dictionary with the fact that the two entities are synonymous. At last, the two entities are integrated with the union of their characteristic sets.

4.2 The detection of homonym

The second semantic conflict case is homonym, which arises when the same name (word) is used to represent two different concepts in different schemata.

> **Definition 4.2** Let w be a word in the word set W and c1 and c2 be two concepts in the concept set C. If w is mapped into two different elements of C, i.e., **symbolize**(w) = c1 and **symbolize**(w) = c2, then w is a homonym.

Consider the example in Fig.10, where two entities 'Equipment' in schema 1 and 'Equipment' in schema 2 obviously refer to different concepts, but are represented by the same name. Merging the two entities in the integrated schema would result in producing a single entity for two distinct concepts.

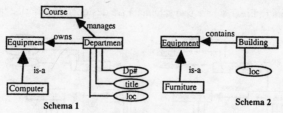

Fig.10 Example of homonym

1) Detection. By analyzing the semantic sets of the entities with the same name, we can find out whether the homonym case occurs. Suppose that $\lambda_1(e1)$ and $\lambda_2(e2)$ are two characteristic sets and e1 and e2 have the same name in two different schemata. If $\lambda_1(e1) \neq \lambda_2(e2)$, e1 and e2 can be considered to be two distinct concepts since they have no characteristics in common. Consider again the above example, the semantic set of the entity 'Equipment' in schema 1 is $\lambda_1('Equipment') = \{<Department, owns>, <has-sub-concept, Computer>\}$ and the semantic set of the entity 'Equipment' in schema 2 is $\lambda_2('Equipment') = \{<Building, contains>, <has-sub-concept, Furniture>\}$.

Since there is no element which belongs to both $\lambda_1('Equipment')$ and $\lambda_2('Equipment')$, we may conclude that 'Equipment' is homonymous and a suggestion should be given to rename one the entities.

2) Suggestion. When a homonym conflict is detected, the user is required to assert whether the two entities refer to different concepts (perhaps they refer to the same concept). The assertion making is of course supported by presenting the user with the characteristic sets of the entities. After the user's confirmation that the two entities are homonymous, a rename operation is triggered to give a more suitable name to either of the entities.

4.3 The detection of cyclic generalization

The semantic conflict, cyclic generalization, happens when in one schema $<e1, e2> \in$ **Gen** and in another schema $<e2, e1> \in$ **Gen**, and the two schemata are merged into one This case often occurs, in particular, when the schemata are designed by different designers with different perspectives and views on the reality. This conflict must be eliminated during schema integration; otherwise a cyclic generalization will appear in the integrated schema, which apparently violates the transitivity of the generalization.

> **Definition 4.3** Let e1 and e2 be two entities. When that there exist both the generalization relations $<e1, e2> \in$ **Gen**[5] and $<e2, e1> \in$ **Gen**, a cyclic generalization occurs.

1) Detection. Suppose that $\lambda_{S1}(e1)$ and $\lambda_{S1}(e2)$ are two characteristic sets and $<e1, e2> \in$ **Gen** in schema S1, and $\lambda_{S2}(e1)$ and $\lambda_{S2}(e2)$ two characteristic sets and $<e2, e1> \in$ **Gen** in schema S2. According to the Definition 3.7, $\lambda_{S1}(e1)$ should be included in $\lambda_{S1}(e2)$ and $\lambda_{S2}(e2)$ should be included in $\lambda_{S2}(e1)$. By comparing $\lambda_{S1}(e1)$ and $\lambda_{S2}(e1)$ (assuming that $\lambda_{S1}(e1) = \lambda_{S2}(e1)$ before the *generalisation expansion*), immediately, we have the contradiction that $\lambda_{S1}(e1)$ is a subset of $\lambda_{S2}(e1)$. The same contradiction happens when comparing $\lambda_{S1}(e2)$ and $\lambda_{S2}(e2)$ (assuming that $\lambda_{S1}(e2) = \lambda_{S2}(e2)$ before the generalisation expansion).

2) Suggestion. As soon as a cyclic generalization is found, this generalization chain will be presented to the user along with all the characteristic sets associated with the entities in the

---

[5]According to the theorem 1, e1 can be an indirect generalization of e2. That is, there may exist an entity e', so that $<e1, e'> \in$ Gen and $<e', e2> \in$ Gen.

generalization chain. Due to misuse of some concepts, and/or some words, the user's assertions are necessary to either re-consider more precise concepts or rename some words which will precisely represent the concepts.

In conclusion, by applying the characteristic sets of entities, not only can the semantic conflicts be detected, but some suitable suggestions can be presented to the users for confirmation as well. In particular, when such characteristic sets of entities are acquired from a family of schemata, the conflict detection proposed will be more powerful and the suggestions presented to the users will be more precise.

5 The conclusion and future work

To acquire the semantic of schemata is difficult but significant a research area both for schema design and integration. By investigating the surroundings of schema objects to capture the schema semantics is one of the approaches to the schema semantic capturing. In this paper, we have discussed some methods to acquire the semantics of schema objects in schemata in terms of their attributes, their relationships and their contexts, and hence to form the characteristic sets for the schema objects. In our opinion, this approach is feasible to explore, to a large extent, the semantic associations of objects existing in schemata.

The contributions in the paper are 1) to investigate the semantic association of schema objects; 2) to present an approach to the obtainment of the object semantics and to the expansion of the semantics; 3) to use the characteristic sets obtained for the detection of the semantic conflicts; and 4) to pave a road to the further study of the semantic knowledge acquisition for schema design and integration.

There are still a lot to do in the semantic knowledge search for schema integration. Our future work is intended to deeply explore the semantics existing in the schema objects, not only entity types but relationship types and attribute types as well, and to form a semantic dictionary based on the semantic knowledge so obtained. Such semantic knowledge acquisition, in our opinion, can be done not only from the schema families, but also from the users assertions during schema integration.

The semantic dictionary, which was discussed in [1, 13], can be considered to be a powerful tool for schema integration since it plays the role of a carrier both for semantic knowledge explored in schema design and integration, as well as for semantic knowledge obtained from the user's assertions for the schema integration. However, the forming and structure of the semantic dictionary have not yet been well studied.

In addition, little focus has been put on the quantitative analysis of the semantic similarity of the integrating schemata. This is perhaps another bottleneck problem (schema semantic knowledge acquisition is one) of the generation of semi-automatic, even automatic schema integration.

The author would like to thank Prof. Janis A. Bubenko, jr. for his valuable comments on the previous version of the paper.

Reference

1. Batini, C., G. Di Battista and G. Santucci. Representation Structures for Data Dictionaries. Dept. of Informatics and Systematics, The university of Rome. Report No. 09.91. Sept. 1991.
2. Batini, C., M. Lenzerini and S. B. Navathe. A Comparative Analysis of Methodologies for Database Schema Integration. ACM Computing Surveys. 18(4): 323-364, 1986.
3. Bouzeghoub, M. and I. Comyn-Wattiau. View Integration by Semantic Unification and Transformation of Data Structures. the 9th Int'l Conf. on Entity-Relationship Approach. Lausanne, Switzerland. 1990
4. Bubenko, J. J. Knowledge for Schema Restructuring and Integration Tools. SYSLAB, DSV. Internal Working Note. SYSLAB IWN No.1. Dec. 1985.

5. Comyn-Wattiau, I. and M. Bouzeghoub. Constraint Confrontation: An Important Step in View Integration. the 4th Int'l Conf. CAiSE. Manchester, UK. 1992

6. Howe, G. A. A Collision of Semantics. DP&D. 93(2) pp.54-61, 1993.

7. Hull, R. and R. King. Semantic Database Modelling: Survey, Applications and Research Issues. ACM Comput. Surveys. 19(3): 201-260, 1987.

8. Johansson, B.-M. and C. Sundblad. View Integration: A Knowledge Problem. Department of Computer and Systems Sciences, University of Stockholm. Working Paper. SYSLAB WP No. 115. 1987.

9. Larson, J., S. Navathe and R. Elmasri. A Theory of Attribute Equivalence in Database with Application to Schema Integration. IEEE TOSE. SE-15(4): 1989.

10. Navathe, S. and S. G. Gadgil. A Methodology for View Integration in Logical Database Design. the 8th Int'l Conf. on VLDB. Mexico City, Mexico. 1982

11. Pirri, F. and C. Pizzuti. Data Dictionary Design: A Logic Programming Approach. The 11th Int'l Conf. on the Entity Relationship Approach. Karlsruhe, Germany. 1992

12. Song, W. W. and P. Johannesson. Schema Integration: Present and Future. ICYCS'93. Beijing. 1993

13. Song, W. W., P. Johannesson and J. J. Bubenko. Semantic Similarity Relations in Schema Integration. the 11th Int'l Conf. on the Entity Relationship Approach. Karlsruhe, Germany. 1992

14. Sowa, J. F. Conceptual Structures: Information Processing in Mind and Machine. Addison-Wesley Publishing Company. 1984.

15. Spaccapietra, S. and C. Parent. View Integration: A Step Forward in Solving Structural Conflicts. Laboratoire de Bases de Donnees, Dept. d'informatique, Ecole Polutechnique de Lausanne. Research Report. Report No. 1990.

Automated Support for the Development of Formal Object-Oriented Requirements Specifications

Robert B. Jackson
David W. Embley
Scott N. Woodfield

Department of Computer Science
Brigham Young University
Provo, UT 84602 USA

Abstract. The creation of a requirements specification document for systems development has always been a difficult problem and continues to be a problem in the object-oriented software development paradigm. The problem persists because there is a paucity of formal, object-oriented specification models that are seamlessly integrated into the development cycle and that are supported by automated tools. Here, we present a formal object-oriented specification model (OSS), which is a seamless extension of an object-oriented analysis model (OSA), and which is supported by a tool (IPOST) that automatically generates a prototype from an OSA model instance, lets the user execute the prototype, and permits the user to refine the OSA model instance to generate a requirements specification. This approach leverages the benefits of a formal model, an object-oriented model, a seamless model, a graphical diagrammatic model, incremental development, and CASE tool support.

1. Introduction

Perhaps the most critical element in the development of a software system lies in properly understanding and in properly documenting the requirements for a system to be developed. A precise, formal, easily understood requirements specification is one of the most important, yet one of the most elusive components of the entire software development process. We suggest that the development of a requirements specification does not have to be elusive, and, indeed, can be a natural and integrated component of the software life cycle.

This general problem of more easily creating and integrating high quality requirements specifications into the software development process is exacerbated by the current major shift in development paradigms from structured to object-oriented. Although the object-oriented paradigm is proving to be effective, many of the current methods, models, CASE tools, prototyping languages (4th GLs), and formal specification languages still contain substantial structured technology. The end result is a development approach that tries to marry the structured paradigm with the object-oriented paradigm. Unfortunately, this marriage does not work well. Software engineering principles and tools that support prototyping and the development of requirements specifications within the object-oriented paradigm are critically needed.

Our approach to more easily developing high quality object-oriented requirements specifications is based on a formal, object-oriented model that serves all phases of the software life cycle. It is our belief that a formal model is a prerequisite for assimilation of engineering principles into software development, and that a seamless development cycle requires a pervasive model around which tools and methods can be built.

The formal, object-oriented model we use in our approach is OSM (the Object-oriented Systems Model), which is based primarily on an analysis model called OSA (Object-oriented Systems Analysis) [8]. The formal definition for OSA is formulated using set theory and first-order predicate calculus (see Appendix A of [8] and [3]). OSA is an integrated model because it can be used to describe object structure, object relationships, object behavior, and object interaction, all within the same formal context. A second component of OSM is OSS (Object-oriented Systems Specification), which is a formal model that extends OSA and is appropriate for specification. Our approach to the development of formal specifications is to generate an OSS model by executing (prototyping) and incrementally extending an OSA model through the use of a CASE tool, called IPOST (Interactive, Prototyping Object-oriented Specification Tool).

Our approach is as follows: Using OSA, a systems analyst builds an object-oriented model instance (generally a partially complete instance) of the problem domain. Next IPOST reads the OSA model instance from the data repository and automatically creates a user interface and working prototype. As the user executes and modifies the prototype, the OSA model instance is enhanced and becomes an OSS requirements specification. The end result of prototype execution and model enhancement is a precise, formal specification in a graphical notation with embedded formal textual descriptions of behavior and interactions. The details of our approach in the remainder of this paper are as follows. In Section 2 we outline some of the difficulties of current approaches to specification development, and we show how our approach builds on some of the best work of others. In Section 3 we describe OSA and the specification language extensions required for OSS. In Section 4, we describe IPOST and our methodology for developing an OSS model instance. In Section 5 we discuss the implementation of current support tools. We conclude in Section 6.

2. The Problems with Specifications

2.1 Informal Specification Techniques

Early attempts at explaining to clients the details of a proposed system were done with informal, natural-language narratives. The narratives were later enhanced to include strict guidelines, organization directives, diagrams and informal models.

Informal models, which are characterized by the lack of an all-encompassing theoretical foundation, are included in techniques such as Modern Structured Analysis [20], Data Structured System Development (DSSD) [19,15], Structured Analysis Design Technique (SADT) [16], and Object Oriented Analysis (OOA) [4]. Inclusion of more stringent directives and informal diagrammatic models have helped informal requirements specifications become more precise and understandable, but they still suffer from several problems, including problems of organization, redundancy, incompleteness and misinterpretation.

To ease the problem of misinterpretation, developers frequently build prototypes to raise the level of understanding between clients and developers. The addition of a requirements prototype to the development cycle has been beneficial. "Operational Prototyping" [5] is one of various new prototyping approaches that are increasing the benefits derived from prototyping. However, prototyping is not without its own problems. The addition of a prototype to an informal method requires two paradigm shifts during this first phase of a project. A paradigm shift occurs between the analysis model and the prototyping language. Then another paradigm shift occurs in writing the specification. Not only are these shifts time consuming, but they also raise the potential for information loss.

2.2 Formal Specification Techniques

To increase precise communication between developer and client, researchers and a small number of practitioners have begun using more formal analysis and specification techniques. These techniques usually contribute to the development process by adding principles of engineering discipline. An additional benefit is that formal languages can frequently be directly executed. These benefits usually come with a cost, however; namely, the cost of formal, mathematical constructs that are difficult to understand.

Examples of formal languages used for specification include PLEASE and SPEC [2, 18], which are algebra based languages. Z and VDM are formal models based on logic, sets, sequences, lists, relations and functions [7, 11, 17]. SXL (State Transition Language) [13] and PAISley ([21], which are more operative based, are oriented towards describing behaviors. All these formal languages provide the precision required for unambiguous interpretations for contractual needs.

There are two major problems with formal languages. First, formal languages are difficult to read and write. Second, there is frequently a major paradigm shift between analysis and specification. Analysis is done using one model or language and specification is done in another.

2.3 CASE Tool Techniques for Specification

Although the primary focus of CASE tools has not been to create specifications, they have nevertheless made a substantial contribution to producing precise specifications. CASE tools, especially I-CASE tools, are based on a central repository of information that helps integrate analysis and prototyping with specification. Information captured from analysis is stored in a central repository and can be used to generate forms and reports to assist in the development of a working prototype. As the prototype is refined, the repository is updated. This updated repository can thus serve as an information base to generate specifications for client agreement.

There has been some excellent research in the use of CASE tools for prototyping and especially in using more formal models in a CASE environment. MASCOT [9] (Modular Approach to Software Construction, Operation and Test) is a diagrammatic approach for parallel processes. Execution is effected by translating MASCOT diagrams to a formal notation. PROTOB is an object-oriented CASE tool based on high-level Petri Nets and is used to model distributed systems [1]. A method for transforming between formal languages to develop executable prototypes using PROLOG has also been developed [10].

2.4 Formal Model with CASE Tool Technique

Our approach builds on both the formal-model approach and the CASE-tool approach. The fundamental principle is that there must first exist a formal, seamless model that integrates all relevant information and that can serve all phases of the software development cycle. Given that we have a formal, integrated, seamless model, CASE tools can be built around this model to provide a tool-supported, seamless development methodology. Because the model is seamless, there are no paradigm shifts between analysis, specification, design and implementation.

Other benefits also accrue from this approach. Because the model is formal, it can be precisely interpreted for contractual purposes. Also because it is formal, it can be executed as a working prototype. Furthermore, the model is graphical which facilitates understanding. A textual form is also available for situations in which this may be more suitable.

3. OSA and OSS Model Components

3.1 OSA Model

An OSA model is comprised of three submodels: an object-relationship model (ORM), an object-behavior model (OBM), and an object-interaction model (OIM). Figure 1 parts a,b, and c depict the three submodels for a simple library application. In our brief tutorial, we have included only those parts of OSA that are germane to our discussion. For further details see [8].

ORM instances describe object classes, relationship sets, and constraints. Boxes in an ORM diagram represent object classes, such as *Book*, *Loan*, and *Librarian* in Figure 1a. *Book*, for example, represents the set of books in the library.

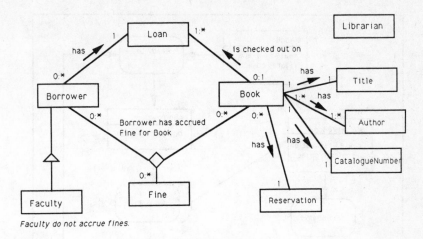

Figure 1a. Object Relationship Model of Library system classes.

We show three different types of relationship sets. *Borrower has Loan* is a binary relationship set. *Borrower has accrued Fine for Book* is a ternary relationship set. *Faculty IsA Borrower* is a Generalization/Specialization relationship set denoted by an open triangle. Participation constraints constrain the possible relationships among objects. The *Book is checked out on Loan* relationship set has a *0:1* participation on the *Book* side, indicating that a book may participate either zero or one times in the relationship set. General constraints, such as *Faculty do not accrue fines*, are shown by italics on an ORM diagram. OSA also permits more abstract constructs such as high-level object classes and relationship sets.

The behavior of objects within an object class is described by a state net. Figure 1b shows a state net for the *Book* object class. This state net serves as a template for the behavior of all book objects in the set. Each transition (represented by a box) defines both a trigger (described in the upper part of the box) and a set of actions (described in the lower part of the box). A set of state nets, one for each object class, make up the OBM, which thus describes the behavior of all objects.

Figure 1b is interpreted as follows: When the AddBook event occurs, the trigger evaluates to true, transition *[1]* fires, and a new book object is created. At the completion of the action in transition *[1]*, the newly created book goes into the *Ready to Loan* state. If a book is in the *Ready to Loan* state, and the *BorrowBook* event occurs, then the action in transition *[2]* is executed and the book goes into the *On Loan* state. The half circle and arrow going to transition *[4]* indicate the spawning of a new, concurrent thread of control. The multiple threads indicate that a book may in both states *On Loan* and *On Reserve* at the same time.

Interactions among objects are described in an OIM instance, which is comprised of various types of interactions and may be organized using various levels of abstraction. Figure 1c shows some possible interactions between a librarian and a book, and are shown as interactions between the *Librarian* class and the *Book* class.

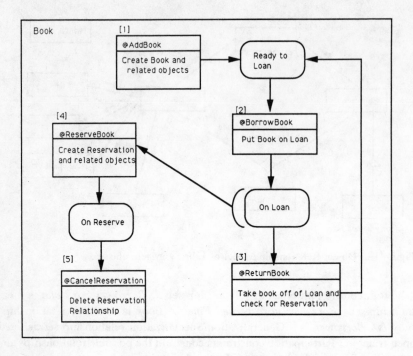

Figure 1b. State Net for Book from Object Behavior Model.

A librarian can add new books as well as check out and return books for patrons.

One feature of OSM modeling is that more detailed information can be provided by views which integrate submodels together. Figure 2 is a combination that contains elements of all three submodels in one view. In this case, the *Librarian*

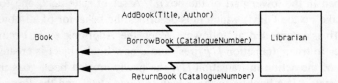

Figure 1c. Interaction with origin Librarian and destination Book.

class is still the origin of the interactions, but the interaction destinations have been integrated with the *Book* state net by denoting destination transitions for each interaction. The *AddBook* interaction has transition *[1]* as its destination, and in fact the event type trigger of transition *[1]* becomes true when the interaction is received.

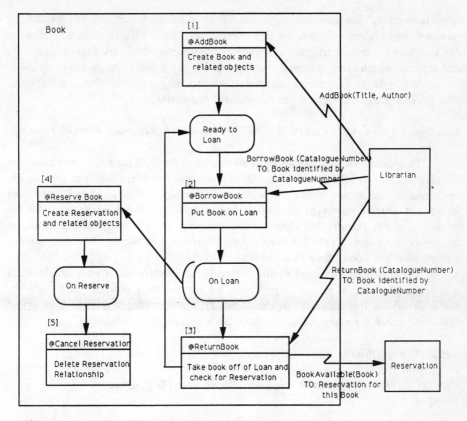

Figure 2. Interaction Diagram combined with Book State Net.

The *TO* clause on the *BorrowBook* interaction indicates that the interaction cannot go to just any book, but must go to a particular book, in this case to the *Book identified by CatalogueNumber.*

3.2 OSS Extensions

Although, both the syntax and semantics of OSA have been formally defined, an OSA model instance does allow for some constructs -- namely, triggers, actions, interaction descriptions, and general constraints -- to be written in natural language. For example, transition *[1]* in Figure 1b has an informal action: *Create Book and related objects*. Components written in an informal language may be subject to misinterpretation. Here, for example, what exactly are the related objects? A formal OSS language has been defined that can formally express these natural language statements.

Several criteria were considered in the development of the OSS language. One consideration is that this language should be easy to write and understand by non-technical clients. To satisfy this criteria, an English like syntax was chosen. Next, it had to support triggers and general constraints which are logic statements, and actions, which are procedural statements. Finally it had to be precisely defined.

In Figure 1a the general constraint, *Faculty do not accrue fines*, is informal. The OSS language expression for this general constraint is:

Faculty() IsA Borrower(x) IMPLIES NOT Borrower(x) has accrued Fine() for Book().

This statement illustrates a logic statement in the OSS language, and based on the classes and relationship sets in the OSA instance. The terms with parentheses are class names which are embedded within relationship set names from the model instance. During prototype execution, "x" is unified to those borrowers who are members of the *Faculty IsA Borrower* relationship set and then tested against the *Borrower has accrued Fine for Book* relationship set. Unspecified variables (empty parentheses) are "don't care" variables as in PROLOG.

The procedural portion of the language has control statements for decision making and looping as well as expressions for manipulating objects. In Figure 1b, the informal English statement in transition *[3]*, for example, says *Take book off of Loan and check for reservation*. In the OSS language this becomes:

DELETE Book(this) is checked out on Loan();
IF Book(this) has Reservation(w) THEN
  SEND_INTERACTION BookAvailable (Book(this)) TO Reservation(w);
ENDIF;

Here, "this" represents the book object that received the interaction. Prototype execution is done by unifying "w" based on the value bound to "this" and existing relationships, and then executing the statements. The combination of both procedural and logical constructs in the language make it suitable for specifying a wide range of constraints, triggers and functions.

4.0 Specification Development

Figure 3 illustrates our approach to the incremental development of OSA model instances and OSS specifications, using IPOST. Initially, a systems analyst develops an OSA model instance, for example the one in Figures 1 and 2. A high-level object class which identifies the system boundary is required. IPOST reads an OSA model instance, with system a boundary and creates an executable prototype. Prototype generation, including a user interface, is automatic.

There are three types of refinements that can occur. Two of these are directly supported by IPOST and are illustrated by the feedback paths in Figure 3 labeled *OSA Model Instance Refinements* and *Logical Interface Refinements*. Model-instance refinements include replacing natural-language descriptions for triggers, actions, and constraints with OSS language statements. Logical interface refinements allow a user to formalize interaction descriptions and refine the interface. When major errors or omissions are observed in the OSA model instance, the user can make appropriate changes to the OSA instance using the drawing tool. A new prototype can be automatically generated from the modified OSA model instance. This process may continue until a fully-formalized OSS model is developed or it may stop at any point deemed satisfactory to both client and developer.

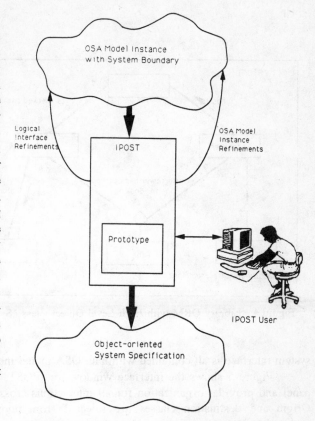

Figure 3. Specification Development using IPOST.

4.1 Automatic Generation of an Executable Prototype

Addition of a System Boundary. The system boundary encloses those components of an OSA model instance that are to be included within the system to be specified and excludes other components. Technically, in OSA, the enclosed components constitute a high-level object class that only has interactions crossing its boundary. All other components of an OSA model instance must move to one side or the other of a system boundary, or must divide into multiple components, each of which are placed on one side or the other of the system boundary. In Figure 4, for example, we define a high-level object class that includes all the ORM components except the *Librarian* object class.

Creating an Interface. The set of interactions that cross a system boundary become the components that define the logical interface. The interface is logical because it focuses on the events and the information flows, rather than on actual physical devices, the look and feel of a user interface, or a particular user interface implementation. IPOST generates a default user interface and does not require an additional user interface specification. The information necessary to develop a logical

144

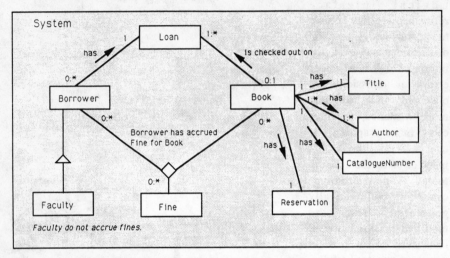

Figure 4. Library ORM with High-Level Object Class "System".

system interface is all contained within an OSA model instance.

Figure 5 shows the interface window for IPOST. The top panel is a menu panel and provides organization for all interactions crossing the system boundary. Origin and destination classes are selected from popup windows. Then the appropriate interaction for the selected origin and destination classes is selected. In Figure 5, the *AddBook* interaction has been selected. The middle panel illustrates how an interaction corresponds to a logical form. Since the *AddBook* interaction was chosen, the parameters listed in the middle panel are *Author* and *Title*, the object parameters sent by the interaction. Space is provided for the IPOST user to enter data for the object parameters and to "execute" the interaction.

4.2 Executing and Refining OSA Model Instances.

Prototype Execution Mode. Prototype execution consists of presenting to the user the set of menus and forms defined by the interface. The user initiates interactions through these forms. As prototype execution proceeds, objects are instantiated and they behave and interact according to the defined OSA model instance. Thus, prototype execution consists of creating objects, deleting objects, initiating interactions, evaluating and firing triggers, evaluating constraints, and performing actions within transitions.

Refer again to Figure 2, which shows the destinations of interactions within the *Book* object class. As these interactions are initiated by the IPOST user, the trigger on the appropriate transition is evaluated. The bottom panel of Figure 5 shows transition *[1]*, which is the destination transition for the *AddBook* interaction. When the *AddBook* interaction arrives, then the trigger *@AddBook* evaluates to true.

After the user enters the *Title* and *Author* data into the form and initiates the *AddBook* interaction, IPOST attempts to execute the action for transition *[1]*: *Create Book and related objects*. However, since the action is informal, IPOST cannot execute it, and provides an execution message to the user, as shown in Figure 6. At this point the user can select one of several possible courses of action. For triggers and general constraints, the user can act as an "oracle"

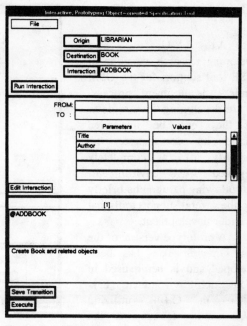

Figure 5. IPOST interface showing Menu Panel, Input Form Panel, and Execution Panel.

and provide a true or false answer. For actions, the user may skip execution of that component. Of course, just skipping execution may cause the prototype to behave incorrectly. To achieve the objective of specification development, it is preferable that the user enter edit mode and replace the informal statements with formal OSS language statements. At the end of each transition, IPOST verifies the populated model against all constraints any informs the user of any constraint violations.

Refinement (edit) Mode. Several types of changes to the OSA model instance are made through IPOST during prototype execution. Figure 7 illustrates the change of the informal action *Create Book and related objects* into formal OSS language statements. The edit mode also supports changes to the interface forms. Since each logical form is mapped to an interface interaction, changes to a form also modify the underlying interaction. Changes can be made to the TO clause, the FROM clause, the interaction description, and the object list.

For example, upon execution of the action statement for transition *[1]*, IPOST would note that a participation constraint for the *Book has CatalogueNumber* relationship set is violated. The participation constraint (see Figure 4) requires that there be a *CatalogueNumber* for every book. The user could then edit the input form by adding another parameter for catalogue number. This change would be reflected back to the OSA model instance.

5. Implementation of Tools

At BYU we are developing research versions of CASE tool support for the OSM seamless development process. We are developing these tools so that they can be integrated together to demonstrate the feasibility of a completely integrated CASE environment. The following paragraphs briefly describe several support tools that are under development.

A prototype version of the OSA Drawing Tool has been developed and is being used in our research environment. It is written in C++ utilizing X-Windows. It supports the drawing of OSA including object classes, relationship sets, state nets, and interactions. Other

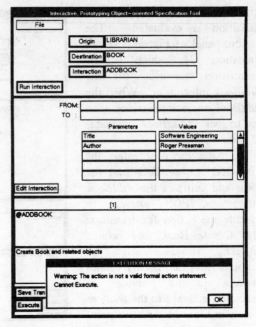

Figure 6. Execution of an *AddBook* Interaction with informal action statement.

more complex OSA constructs, such as high-level views are being developed. It is based on a graphical user interface development tool called ART, which has also been developed at BYU [14].

The OSA Storage Facility serves as the data repository for OSA and OSS model instances. This repository has also been written using C++ under X-Windows. In addition to providing standard database management facilities for storing, modifying, and querying the database, it also provides comprehensive validity checking of OSA model instances. Finally, it also generates database schemas based on OSA model instances stored under the OSA metamodel schema.

An initial prototype version of IPOST is running, and is in systems test. IPOST is written in C++ to run under X-Windows. The user interface is written using ART and the data manipulation uses the OSA Storage Facility. In Edit mode, the user can observe and modify those components of an OSA model instance that contain natural language components. Changes to these components are captured and saved back in the Storage Facility. In Execute mode, IPOST organizes and presents to the user the set of interactions that comprise the user interface for an OSA model instance. As the user "fires" these interactions, the appropriate state net paths are followed to emulate the behavior of objects moving between states via transitions. The appropriate triggers and actions within the transitions are read, parsed, interpreted and executed based on the OSS language. Any applicable constraints are also read, parsed, interpreted and executed at the appropriate time. As execution occurs, the user is able to view the results of the execution by querying the storage facility for the presence of objects, their states of behavior, and associated relationships.

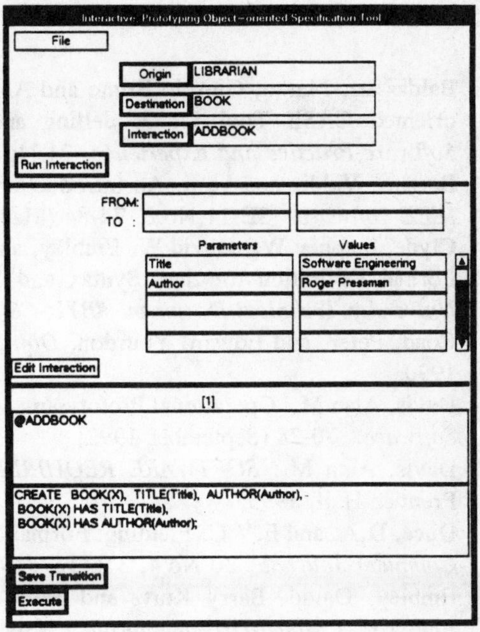

6. Conclusions and Future Research

A requirements specification has always been an elusive part of software development--not only its production, but also its definition. The objective of this research has been twofold: (1) to define a specification model that is formal, is object based, can be used to specify all parts of a proposed software system, and conceptually integrates well with the other models and phases of the software development cycle; and (2) to demonstrate a method

Figure 7. IPOST Window showing the formal action statements to create a Book.

to develop a specification that naturally integrates with accepted methods of software development (analysis and prototyping) and can be supported by automation tools.

Specifically this research is of benefit because it demonstrates improvements in software development through the addition of formalism and principles of engineering. These benefits include: (1) direct execution of analysis model instances; (2) generation and refinement of a formal specification through rapid prototyping; (3) a seamless systems development approach that requires no paradigm shifts between analysis, specification, and prototyping; and (4) the foundation of a formal specification that is based on the object-oriented systems development paradigm.

The OSM Research Group at BYU is currently engaged in long term model development and software engineering research. Although the research agenda is broad, its focused purpose is to provide a systems development paradigm that includes analysis, specification, design, implementation, evolution, re-engineering, and management, all based on a single conceptual model. Research in all areas is proceeding in parallel.

Further research in the area of specification, beyond the project described in this paper, has two major thrusts. The first is to expand the capabilities of IPOST to include expert system capabilities, enhanced model modification capabilities and user interface "look and feel". The second thrust is to integrate the OSS CASE tools with the other phases of software development, such as design and code generation.

Acknowledgements: To Steve Clyde and Jeff Pinkston who helped with this research.

References

1. Baldassari, Marco, Giorgio Bruno and Andrea Castella: PROTOB: and Object-oriented CASE Tool for Modelling and Prototyping Distributed Systems. *Software-Practice and Experience.* 21 No 8, 822-844 (August 1991)

2. Berzins, Valdix and Luqi: An Introduction to the Specification Language Spec. *IEEE Software.* SE-11 No 8, 74-84 (Mar 1990)

3. Clyde, Stephen W., David W. Embley, and Scott N. Woodfield: The Complete Formal Definition for the Syntax and Semantics of OSA. *Brigham Young University Technical Document #BYU-CS-92-2.* (February 1992)

4. Coad, Peter, and Edward Yourdon: *Object Oriented Analysis.* Yourdon Press, 1990.

5. Davis, Alan M.: Operational Prototyping: A New Development Approach. *IEEE Software.* 70-78 (September 1992)

6. Davis, Alan M.: *SOFTWARE REQUIREMENTS: Analysis and Specification.* Prentice-Hall, 1993.

7. Duce, D.A. and E.V.C. Fielding: Formal Specification of Two Techniques: *The Computer Journal.* 30 No 4, 316-327 (1987)

8. Embley, David, Barry Kurtz and Scott Woodfield: *Object-oriented Systems Analysis: A Model-Driven Approach.* Prentice-Hall, 1992.

9. Friel, G. and D. Budgen: Design Transformation and abstract design prototyping. *Information and Software Technology.* 33 No 9, 707-719 (November 1991)

10. Habra N.: Computer-aided prototyping: transformational approach. *Information and Software Technology.* 33 No 9, 685-697 (November 1991)

11. Hekmatpour, Sharam, and Darrel Ince: *Software Prototyping, Formal Methods and VDM.* Addison-Wesley, 1988.

12. Lantz, Kenneth E.: *The Prototyping Methodology*, Prentice-Hall, 1989.

13. Lee, Stanley and Suzanne Sluizer: An Executable Language For Modeling Simple Behavior. *IEEE Transactions on Software Engineering.* 17 No 6, 527-543 (June 1991)

14. Olsen, Dan R.: *The ART Users Manual*, Brigham Young University, 1992.

15. Orr, Kenneth T.: *Structured Requirements Definition*, Kenn Orr & Associates, 1981.

16. Ross, Douglas T.: Applications and Extensions of SADT. *Computer.* 18, 25-34 (April 1985)

17. Spivey, J.M.: *The Z Notation: A Reference Manual*, Prentice-Hall, (1992).

18. Terwilliger, Robert B. and Roy H. Campbell: PLEASE: Executable Specifications for Incremental Software Development. *The Journal of Systems and Software.* 10, 97-112 (Oct 1989)

19. Warnier, Jean Dominique: *Logical Design of Systems*, Van Norstrand Reinhold, 1981.

20. Yourdon, Edward: *Modern Structured Analysis*, Prentice-Hall, 1989.

21. Zave, P.: An Operational Approach to Requirements Specification for Embedded Systems. *IEEE Transactions on Software Engineering.* SE-8 No 8, 250-269 (1982)

Abstraction Forms in Object-Oriented Conceptual Modeling: Localization, Aggregation and Generalization Extensions

Corine Cauvet*, Farida Semmak**
* University of Paris I - IAE,   ** University of Paris I - CRI
alecsi@masi.ibp.fr,   semmak@masi.ibp.fr

ABSTRACT. This paper proposes abstraction mechanisms in the field of object-oriented conceptual modeling. It introduces new abstraction form of localization principle and extends existing ones - aggregation and generalization - to make them suitable to recent advances in object-oriented approaches.

Localization is a principle for encouraging the design of object properties in isolation from other objects. Currently a large variety of object-oriented models support the localization principle by means of object structure and object behavior. Typically the *object structure* consists of a set of attributes. The *object behavior* is defined as a set of events. The object life cycle construct is introduced as an abstract representation of all possible event sequences on the object.

Aggregation is used to put objects together in order to build larger objects and to control the resulting behavior of these complex objects. Usually aggregation is used as an *object structuring* mechanism, we propose to apply aggregation to events as well. *Event aggregation* is a useful mechanism for relating the behavior of complex objects with the behavior of their constituent objects.

Generalization is introduced to organize both *object classes* and *object states* into hierarchies. Classes and class hierarchies allow the stepwise organisation of similarities and differences between objects. States and state hierarchies allow to organize the similarities and differences of an object at various points of time in its life cycle in a controlled manner.

1 Introduction

This paper proposes abstraction mechanisms in the field of object-oriented conceptual modeling. Aggregation and generalization abstractions are typically treated as structuring mechanisms for building a conceptual schema. Recent emergence of the object-oriented paradigm in conceptual modeling results in a need to reconsider these abstraction forms.

In the past, a large number of authors have widely proven the usefulness of abstraction in systems design. The major benefits of all abstraction forms in systems design [20, 21] are: the stability of models (data independence), the support of highly structured models, the contribution in managing the system's complexity and a more systematic approach to the design process. The so-called semantic models [2, 11, 14] converge on the idea that classification, aggregation and generalization are fundamental abstraction forms in the field of conceptual modeling. By using a semantic model, a designer focuses on classes and structures them both in the aggregation plane and the generalization plane. The lack of support for the specification of operations in systems design in current semantic models might be due to the fact that these models have evolved from the relational database models.

On the other hand, a large number of authors are currently taking advantage of the object-oriented paradigm in the task of conceptual modeling by developing object-oriented conceptual models [16, 7, 19, 9]. A major contribution of the object-oriented approach to conceptual modeling is the localization principle that encourages the modeling of individual objects in isolation from others [10]. From a dynamic point of view, objects evolve concurrently in this approach. They have the capability to recognize events occurring within their life cycle and to react to such events by changing their states [17, 18].

By using aggregation mechanism to build complex objects, the designer only need to concern about with the problem of event propagation from an initial aggregate object to its component objects. Moreover, event concurrence within an aggregate object is possible because of the parallel evolution of its components. We believe that the object-oriented paradigm lacks conceptual tools to conceptualize these situations in a natural way. It is argued that the behavior of complex objects can be designed in a systematic way by using the aggregation mechanism to structure events.

In the same way, classification is usually based upon similar inherent features of objects. However due to the fact that objects evolves within their life cycles, they may have temporary differences that the class construct cannot capture. We propose to combine the class approach with a state approach to capture some time-dependent differences between objects of the same class. By using the generalization mechanism, both classes and states can be organized into hierarchies. The combination of class hierarchies and state hierarchies provides a suitable approach to introduce both inherent and temporary relevant features of objects.

We consider an object-oriented approach that combines three object modeling planes. The *inner plane* relates to local features of objects. The *aggregation plane* is used to put objects together in order to build larger objects and to control their evolution. The *generalization plane* deals with hierarchies by introducing relevant object features in a controlled manner. *Section II* emphasizes the localization principle through modeling of attributes and events that characterize individual objects. It also defines the object life cycle construct as an abstract representation of the states and the behavior of an object. *Section III* focuses on the aggregation mechanism. At first, this section presents aggregation as an object structuring mechanism. Then, aggregation is applied to events in order to control the behavior of complex objects. *Section IV* addresses on the generalization abstraction. It introduces the "is_a_class" link and the "is_a_state" link, the former is used to define class hierarchies and the latter to define state hierarchies.

This paper employs the graphical notations and the terminology of an object-oriented conceptual model called Modway[1] [4].

2 Localization and Behavior Abstractions

In the past, classification, aggregation and generalization have received most attention in conceptual modeling. It is argued that both the object construct and the construct of object life cycle provide new abstraction mechanisms. Each of these supports the principle of localization and emphasizes object behavior modeling.

2.1 Localization through Attributes and Events

The localization principle was motivated by the principles of programming such as modularity [12], which is a major goal of abstraction in conceptualizing complex systems. In this section, we consider localization as a principle for encouraging the design of object properties in isolation from others. Currently a large variety of object-oriented models support the localization principle by means of the concept of object structure and the concept of object life cycle. Typically the object structure consists of a set of attributes and the object life cycle is defined as a set of events.

---

[1] This research is supported by the French Association for Research Development (ANVAR) under the MODWAY project. The MODWAY project is a collaborative project between University of Paris I and ALCATEL ISR company.

Attributes define structural properties of an object; they exist at any time in the life span of an object, although the values of these attributes may change in time. E.g., "title", "authors" and "editor" define attributes for a book in a library. An attribute value can be a data or an object.

Events correspond to temporal properties of an object; they occur at certain points of time in the life span of an object, once they have occurred, they do not undergo changes; for instance, "purchase", "loan", and "reservation" correspond to the events that may occur in the life cycle of a "book" object. An event changes an object state, it may modify attributes values or it may change the behavior of an object by making it migrate from a state to another state.

The state of an object at a given time t is defined as the set of its attribute values and the sequence of events that have influenced the object up to time t. We call *t_state*, the state of an object at a given time t. An event which occurs at a given time on an object triggers a change in the t_state of the object at that time. A t_state of an object o is denoted as follows:

$$S_t(o) = [Id; \{at_i(o)\}_{i \in [0,m]} ; \{ev_j(o, t_k, p_{j1}, ..., p_{jl})\}_{j \in [0,n], tj \leq t}]$$

where:
- $at_i(o)$ is the value of the attribute at_i,
- $ev_j(t_j, p_{j1}, ..., p_{jl})$ is the occurrence of the event ev_j occurred at the time t_j with the parameters $p_{j1}, ...p_{jl}$,
- k, m and n are the natural numbers.

For example, the t_state of the book B1 is denoted as follows:

[B1;
{title ("An introduction to Database Systems"),
 authors (C.J. Date),
 editor (Addison-Wesley)};
{purchase (t_0, "An introduction to Database Systems", C.J. Date,

Addison-Wesley),
loan (t_1, S1),

return (t_2, S1),

reservation (t_3, S5),

reservation_cancellation (t4, S5),

withdraw (t5)}];

The events, *loan* and *return,* have the parameter "S1"; "S1" is the identifier of a subscriber. In the same way, "reservation" and "reservation cancellation" have the identifier "S5" of a subscriber as their parameter.

The set of events that may occur on an object provide a complete view of what can affect it, while the set of attributes define its characteristics in the domain space. Attributes and events enable to consider objects as having a distinct spatial and temporal existence. This principle is a major improvement over classical models in that the latter offers little support for spatial independence and no support at all for temporal independence. Furthermore, localization supports integration of static and dynamic properties which can both be modeled through abstractions.

2.2 Behavior Modeling through States

Object-oriented models emphasize the design of the behavioral features of objects. So, they should provide powerful abstraction mechanisms to support the description of object changes. In traditional object-oriented models, the design of object changes is reduced to its simplest terms: an object change simply corresponds to a change of state variables through an operation execution. Furthermore, the possible sequences of changes on an object are often hidden in the implementation of the operations.
We propose an object-oriented approach in which *event* remains the only means to trigger an object change. Furthermore, the change may represent a simple change of its attribute values or it may represent changes in its behavior. Indeed, the set of events applicable to an object as well as attribute values vary in time. The concept of *object state* will be introduced for supporting changes in the object behavior.

A state can be viewed as a set of t_states, all the t_states of an object receive the same set of events. For instance, "available", "reserved" and "loaned" are relevant states for a "Book" object. By defining several states for an object, we modeled individual time-dependent differences of this object. Two distinct states of an object differ on the set of applicable events to the object at a given time. An object change of one state to another captures the change in the behavior of the object.

By relating a state to a set of applicable events, we restrict event occurrences to particular t_states of an object. States improve the definition of events by restricting the event occurrences to particular t_states of the objects. A state can be viewed as a necessary condition on the t_states of the object which allows an event to occur on the object.

Thus, this approach makes a clear distinction between the t_states of an object at different points of its life cycle and its states. An event occurring on an object always changes the t_state of the object, whereas it does not necessarily change its state. For instance, a "price_modification" event changes the t_state of an object "product" (this changes not only the "price" attribute value, but also its past sequence of events) without changing the state of this product. Contrary to the "stock_breaking" event that changes both the t_state and the state of a "Product" object, the new state (so-called "in_breaking") is relevant because it may imply a "replenishment" event.

It must be noticed that the states are not necessary values of attributes stored in the object memory. They may be derived from the t_state of the object. This makes the difference between the traditional O.O. view in which the object behavior is reduced to methods performed on or suffered by objects.

Events and object states allow to model the possible evolution of the object by describing an entire, possibly infinite range of sequences of event occurrence. Events and object states facilitate the design of the behavior of an object, furthermore they make the behavioral rules of an object explicit and localized.

2.3 Integrating States and Classes for Describing Objects

Classification is well known and widely used in systems design as an abstraction form in which an object class defines a set of object instances. An object class describes a group of objects with similar properties and a common behavior. Each object belongs to a class and its attributes and operations are described in its class. Inherent differences among objects can properly be modeled as different classes. Although this approach is satisfactory for some applications, there are many applications where the strict uniformity of objects in a class is unreasonable. There must be a way to extend the modeling capability of the class construct so that certain differences between objects can be specified.

In this section we investigate the combination of the *class approach* (each object is assigned permanently to a class and acquires the attributes and behavior of that class) with a *state approach* (each object is assigned temporarily to a state that restricts its behavior at a certain time). By using both the class approach and a state approach the distinction between inherent structural features of objects and their temporal features can be emphasized.

A class describes a set of similar objects. All the objects of the class have the same attributes and the same behavior. According to the behavior modeling approach previously introduced, objects within a class have the same set of possible states. Formally, *a class definition* consists of an extension (C_EXT) and a schema (C_SCH). The extension of a class is the set of objects belonging to that class at a certain time. A class schema defines all the common attributes ({A}) and the common states ({S}) to all the objects belonging to the class. A class is denoted as follows :

$$C = (class\_name, C\_EXT, C\_SCH)$$
$$where \ C\_SCH = (\{A\}, \{S\})$$

Each object has a state and its possible event occurrences at a time result from its state. Formally, *a state definition* consists of an extension (S_EXT) and a schema (S_SCH). The state extension is a set of t_states object of a single object. A state schema defines both the condition describing the state and all the possible events which can occur when an object of the class is in that state. A state is denoted as follows :

$$S = (state\_name, S\_EXT, S\_SCH)$$
$$where \ S\_SCH = (state\_condition, \{event\})$$

A class defines common events on the objects of the class, while a state within a class captures those of the events which can occur when an object has that state. For instance, the "Book" class defines a "loan" event, while the "available" state within the "Book" class restricts a "loan" event occurrence to a book which is neither borrowed nor reserved. Two different states of an object model different possible evolutions of that object.

By combining a class approach with a state approach, we make a clear distinction between two abstraction mechanisms: the class and the state. All the objects of a class have a common possible set of states, however, at a certain time, all the objects of a class are not in the same state. Thus, time-dependent differences among objects of a certain class are properly modeled as different states within the class, whereas inherent differences among objects are modeled by different classes.

A single object can have different states at different time - preserving its identity- but it belongs to one and the same class during its existence.

It is the authors' belief that object class and object state are two useful abstraction forms, the former captures the common features of several objects in an unique place (the class), the latter emphasizes the common events applicable at different points of time in the life cycle of the object.

2.4 Object Representation through Diagrams

The local view of an object given by its *attributes* and *events* can be graphically represented in an *object class diagram.*

The behavior description of an object is a *life cycle graph* whose nodes are *states* and whose directed arcs are transitions labelled by *event* names. Each transition is caused by an event: if an object is in a state and an event labelling one of its transition occurs, the object enters the state on the target end of the transition. However an object may have several independent life cycle graphs, each corresponding to a particular finite state machine. At a given time, for one life cycle graph, an object can be in one and only one state of the life cycle graph.

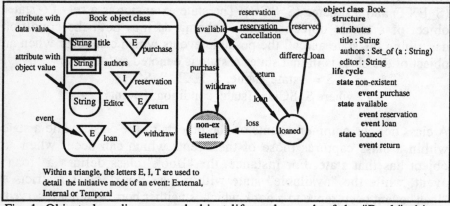

Fig. 1. Object class diagram and object life cycle graph of the "Book" object.

Locally an *attribute definition* consists of a name and a domain. An attribute value can be a data or an object. An attribute can be mono-valued (simple symbol) or multi-valued (double symbol).

Locally a *state definition* consists of a name, a condition and the set of applicable events on an object in that state. The applicable events on a state appear on the life cycle graph as outcoming arrows from the node representing that state.

Locally an *event definition* consists of a name, a context (event parameters), an initiative mode (external, internal, temporal), an occurrence condition (this condition is related to the attribute values and to the past sequence of events that the object received) and a text which describes how an event occurrence affects the object. An event occurrence can trigger several kinds of operations:

* An event which triggers the *creation of the object* appears on a transition with the "non-existent" node as origin,

* An event which triggers the *destroying of the object* appears on a transition with the "non-existent" node as target,
* An event which triggers an *update of object attribute* values appears as a loop on one or several nodes of the life cycle graph,
* An event which triggers an *object state change* appears on a transition defined between two distinct nodes and none of these nodes is the "non-existent" node. (In figure 1, we have omitted the detailed description of events for the sake of simplicity; for more details about concept and specifications of event, see [4]).

This section has proposed conceptual tools to design objects according to the "inner plane". An object is defined by a set of attributes and a life cycle. The life cycle provides a shortened view of the infinite range of the sequences of event occurrence on an object. Each object belongs to a class and its attributes and life cycle result from its class. Each object has a state and the set of applicable events at a given time results from its state. In the next section we consider that objects can be composed in the "aggregate plane", that is objects can be put together in order to build larger objects. Consequently the control of the behavior of the resulting complex objects requires some extensions of the event construct.

3. Aggregation of Objects and its result on Object Behavior

It is well known that the real-world can be usefully modeled in terms of two types of phenomena: entities and relationships [6]. Object-oriented models have proposed a more powerful method for real-world modeling based on only one concept: the object. This approach makes use of aggregation by modeling a real-world entity with all its constituents as a unique complex object. Complementarily, this approach enlightens the need to use additionnal mechanisms for capturing more semantics in the description of the object constituents [13, 16, 3]. Furthermore, using aggregation to build complex objects requires new mechanisms for taking into account the behavioral aspects of these complex objects. This section proposes to exploit the aggregation mechanism for both structuring complex objects and designing their behavior.

3.1 Applying Aggregation to Structure Objects

We propose to use aggregation for defining an object as a composition of properties, component objects and references to other objects. It is argued that aggregation carries three kinds of semantics which can be exploited to enrich conceptual models and to facilitate the design of complex object behavior. In the following we outline the three kinds of aggregation semantics proposed to use in object-oriented conceptual modeling.

Object as an aggregate of its properties.

This form of aggregation is used to define local characteristics of objects, for instance, the size, the location and the category for representing an "hotel" object. This kind of aggregation associates some atribute values to an object.

Object as an aggregate of component objects.

This form of aggregation (so-called composition) is used to define "part-of" relationships between a composite object and each of its component objects. The underlying semantics of the composition is that a component object cannot be shared and that its life cycle is totally embedded in the life cycle of the composite object. For instance, rooms are parts of an "hotel" object.

Object as an aggregate of references to constituent objects.

Semantically an object with references to other objects may be viewed both coupled with its constituents and independently from them; for instance if we consider that an hotel has a reference to a manager, the manager is an important constituent of the hotel but he is in no way a part of the hotel. The hotel and its manager have independent life cycles, however certain events on the hotel may infer an event in the life cycle of the manager.

Properties, component objects and reference to constituent objects can be combined to define some objects with a complex structure. Notice that the representation of object structure consists of attributes that are classified in three classes: property attributes, composition attributes and reference attributes.

We now discuss a refinement of the attribute part within an object class diagram. In Figure 2, properties and composition attributes are placed within the object class diagram, they are respectively related to data type names and component object class diagrams. Referenced objects appear on the border of the object class diagram.

We call an elementary object, an object with only property attributes in its structure, whereas a complex object involves reference and / or composition attributes in its structure. An object with a composition attribute in its structure is called a composite object.

As an object can encapsulate component objects and references to other objects, its evolution design requires mechanisms relating its events and those of the objects forming its structure.

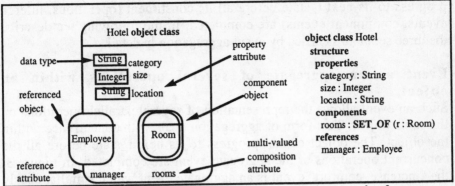

Fig. 2. Object as an aggregate of properties, components and references.

3.2 Applying Aggregation to Structure Events

Because the localization principle suggests to design objects locally, we consider that the design of complex objects with their resulting behavior becomes crucial. One of the major results of the localization principle is that objects in a system are inherently concurrent and can change state independently. On the other hand, objects can be put together to form complex objects; so an event may imply several objects. Applying both localization and aggregation on objects requires event synchronization mechanisms to control the interactions of dependent objects.

This section explores the coupling of the *event construct* previously introduced to design inner behavioral features of an object, with the *aggregation mechanism* for dealing with concurrence and interaction between objects. According to the localization principle, an event which involves several objects must be modeled and reduced to elementary events defined in the life cycle of the involved objects. Furthermore, the elementary events have to be synchronized. The aggregation mechanism is applied to events in order to build such complex events.

We propose to exploit event aggregation to be able to systematically design three types of complex events:
- an event occurring on an object may be complex if it triggers several operations on this object,
- an event occurring on a complex object can be complex if it infers events defined on related objects,
- an event can be complex if it consists of several elementary events (so-called component events).

In each of these situations, aggregation is considered as a behavior abstraction form in which an object processing a complex event cannot progress to its next t_state before all its constituent (operations, infered events, component events) are completed. In the following we describe the three semantics carried by event aggregation in detail.

Event as an aggregate of several operations within an object.

Such an event allows the representation of several parallel operations on the same object. This form of aggregation deals with concurrence within the object. The object cannot progress to its next t_state before all the concurrent operations of the aggregate event are completed. In Figure 3, the "increase_comfort" event is an aggregate event which simultaneously triggers an increase of the room price and a change of the room category.

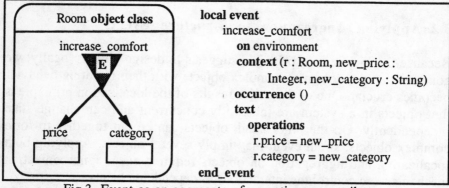

Fig.3. Event as an aggregate of operations on attributes

Parallel operations may occur on an object if the object has several life cycle graphs and if changes occur simultaneously on the different graphs. For instance, in Figure 4 the "subscription" event simultaneously triggers two state changes on the object : from state "non-existent" to state "valid" in the upper life cycle graph and from state "non-existent" to state "up_to_date" in the lower life cycle graph.

Local to an object, an event can be used to synchronize several operations on that object. Such an event is viewed as an aggregate of operations within a single object.

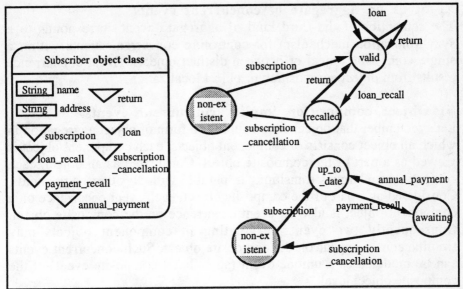

Fig. 4. Event as an aggregate of simultaneous state changes

Event as an aggregate of event inferences to related objects.

This form of aggregation corresponds to the propagation of an event occurrence from an initial object to some related objects linked through part_of relationships and reference links. The initial object cannot progress to its next state before all its inferences are completed. The semantics of such an event corresponds to a triggering mechanism. Notice that the events infered by an event may be aggregates of events too. In Figure 5 the event "new_hotel" is an aggregate event which invokes two events: the first one affects the manager of the hotel, the second one corresponds to the creation of new rooms. The infered event can only occur if its occurrence condition is true.

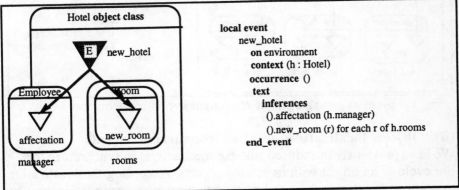

Fig. 5. Event as an aggregate of event inferences

Event as an aggregate of concurrent events.

The semantics of the third kind of aggregate event corresponds to a synchronization mechanism for controling concurrent events within a single composite object or between distinct objects. Event concurrence results from object composition or object localization.

(i) Object composition implies concurrent events.

Let's remember that object composition is a form of object aggregation in which an object consists of component objects; each component object is viewed as a part of the composite object. Considered as an object, each component undergoes transitions in parallel with all other components. Considered as a part of the composite object, each event occurrence on a component object is also an event occurrence on the composite object. Consequently two events originating in component objects may simultaneously appear on the composite object. Such concurrent events can be modeled as a unique event (so-called a composite event) at the composite object level.

A composite event defined on a composite object can only occur if each of its component events occurs at the same time. The semantics of this kind of event corresponds to a synchronization point for several events defined on the component objects within a composite object.

For instance let's consider a composite object "Traffic_light" with three components "red_light", "yellow_light" and "green_light"; event concurrence exists for the "Traffic light" object because its "red_light" lights up at the same time its "green_light" goes out.

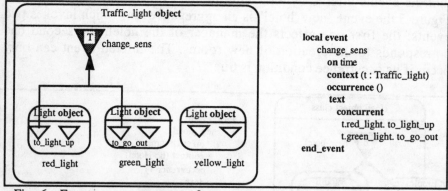

Fig. 6. Event as an aggregate of concurrent events on a composite object.

(ii) Object localization implies concurrent events

We have previously introduced suitable mechanisms to synchronize the life cycle of an object with its related objects. According the localization principle, objects are designed as autonomous processors, so it may be useful to schedule the life cycles of indirectly related objects. Concurrent events between independent objects require an event sharing mechanism. For instance a certain relationship between a person, a hotel and a room may be abstracted as a shared event which simultaneously occurs on the three objects. In the same way a transfer between two banking accounts is viewed as a shared event occurring at the same time on the life cycles of the two accounts.

Being an event, a shared event may be an aggregate of events defined on objects sharing that event. Such an event supports event synchronization on unrelated objects. For instance, let's assume that the two events "borrow_agreement" and "to_take_off" have been locally introduced in the objects "Books" and "Subscriber". The "loan" event is an aggregate event which only occurs when its components "borrow_agreement" and "take_off" occur in parallel.

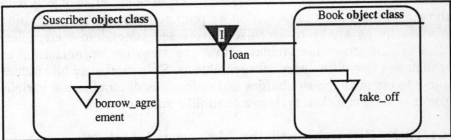

Fig. 7. Event as an aggregate of concurrent events between unrelated objects.

An aggregate event with concurrent component events may be used to synchronize either events in a composite object or events of unrelated objects. In addition, event aggregation is a suitable tool to make event specification modular. Indeed, each concurrent event of a shared aggregate event can be used to gather the dependencies of each single object sharing the aggregate event. In the same way, each concurrent event of a complex event defined on a composite object can be used to gather the relations with each component object.

These three semantics of aggregation may be combined to capture the complexity of an event that belongs to the life cycle of an object. Event aggregation is a suitable behavior abstraction form for dealing with situations of concurrency between related or autonomous objects.

An event which affects a single object (through operations) is called an elementary event, whereas a complex event involves several objects. A composite event is an event with concurrent events.

In summary, the proposed object-oriented approach suggests to:

- (i) use aggregation to consider all characteristics of an object as a whole. The properties, the components and the references to other objects are parts of the object structure,

- (ii) use aggregation to construct complex events for dealing with situations of concurrency. Such situations result from the application of both the localization principle and the aggregation mechanism in designing objects.

From an object point of view, (i) relates to object structuring whereas (ii) deals with object interaction. Thus, aggregation is both a structure abstraction form and a behavior abstraction form.

4 Applying Generalization on Classes and States

Section II introduced class and state constructs to characterize objects with the same properties. In this section we propose to use the generalization mechanism as a way to organize classes and states into hierarchies. Classes and class hierarchies allow the stepwise organization of similarities and differences between objects. States and state hierarchies allow to organize the similarities and differences of an object at various points of time in its life cycle in a controlled manner.

4.1 Class Hierarchy and the "Is_a_class" Link

Generalization is a powerful abstraction for sharing similarities among classes while preserving their differences. Generalization involves a relationship between a class (generic class) and one or more refined versions of the class (specialized classes). In conceptual modeling, generalization is usually used as a construct for structuring classes. Generalization is related to an inheritance mechanism of sharing attributes and operations defined on classes: all attributes and operations of the generic class apply to the specialized classes.

According to the class definition introduced in section II, a class consists of a set of attributes and a set of states; each state provides a set of applicable events. If we consider G as a generic class and S as a specialized class, the semantics of the "is_a_class" link from S to G is carried out by the following definition:

(i) $EXT\_C(S) \subseteq EXT\_C(G)$ (inclusion of the class extensions; the specialized class extension is a restriction of the extension of the generic class),

(ii) SCH_C (G) $\subseteq$ SCH_C(S) (inclusion of the class schemas; the specialized class schema is an extension of the schema of the generic class).

Considering this definition, let's remark that:
    - an object belongs to several classes of the same class hierarchy. It is modeled by features defined in several classes; for instance, an employee might be modeled by attributes and states of the "Employee" and "Person" classes,
    - a specialized class schema can have specific features, however because an object belongs to a class and its superclasses, it is not possible for a specialized class to violate superclass features, thus attributes and states can only be refined according an augmentation principle. This principle is a major difference from overriding in the traditional object-oriented approach in which a generic feature may be bypassed by the refined one.

The definition of generalization is illustrated in Figure 8. "Book" is the generic class. "Consulting_only" and "For_loan" correspond to specialized classes of the "Book" class. Bold arrows between class symbols represent the "is_a_class" links.

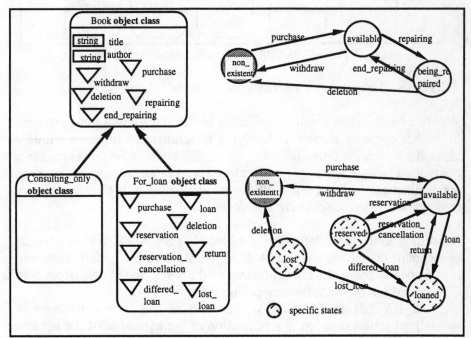

Fig. 8. A class hierarchy with inherited, refined and specific states.

* The states "reserved", "loaned" and "lost" are specific states to a book which can be borrowed by subscribers. This states are defined in the specialized "For_loan" class.
* The state "available" is refined with additional events such as "reservation" and "loan".
* Finally, "being_repaired" is a generic state which is simply inherited.

A class may be the root of several class hierarchies; each hierarchy can be thought of as a different perspective on the object modeled in the hierarchy; in Figure 9 the "Book" class is the root of two hierarchies, one related to the category of books (Novel, Proceeding, Publication) and the other one related to the use of the book (books which can be loaned, books which can only be consulted).

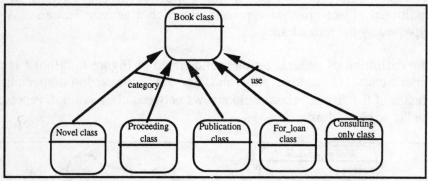

Fig.9. A class as root of several class hierarchies.

4.2 State Hierarchy and the "Is_a_state" Link

Within a class, states capture applicable events at different points of time in the life cycle of an object. Applying generalization to states within a class allows relevant details on the object life cycle to be introduced in a controlled way. State generalization is related to an inheritance mechanism of sharing events: all events applicable to a generic state are also applicable to the specialized states.

According to the state definition introduced in Section II, a state consists of a condition and a set of events. If we consider G as a generic state and S as a specialized state, the semantics of the "is_a_state" link from S to G is carried out by the following definition:

$S\_EXT(S) \subseteq S\_EXT(G)$ (inclusion of the state extensions, a specialized state extension is a restriction of the extension of the generic state),

$S\_SCH(G) \subseteq S\_SCH(S)$ (inclusion of the state schemas, a specialized state schema is an extension of the schema of the generic state).

Considering this definition, let's remark that:

- An object belongs to several states of the same state hierarchy. The set of applicable events on an object is modeled in several states; for instance a "book" object might be modeled by events defined in the state "existing" and events in the state "available",

- it is not possible for a specialized state to violate the generic state features, thus events defined on a generic state can only be refined according to the augmentation principle.

The definition of the "is_a_state" link is illustrated in Figure 10.

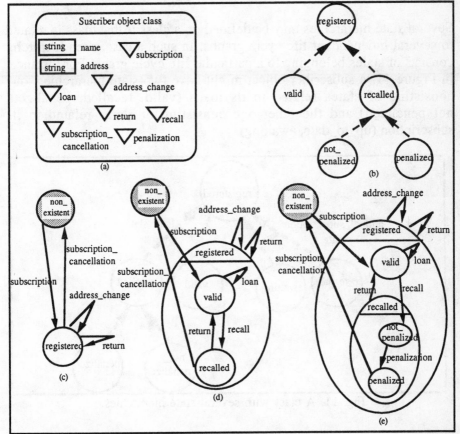

Fig.10. A state hierarchy for a suscriber object.

Graphically we represent a state hierarchy within a class with circles for the states and dotted arrows for the "is_a_state" links. In Figure 10, (b) provides a state hierarchy for the "Subscriber" object class; (c), (d), (e) represent the life cycle graph of the "Subscriber" object class at different levels of detail. Graphically, in the object life cycle graph, substates appear as circles inside the circle corresponding to the generic state. By considering the substate "valid":

* the "subscription" event is refined; such an event makes "valid" subscriber,
* the "loan" event is specific. A loan can only occur on a subscriber being in the "valid" state,
* the "change_address" event is simply inherited.

State hierarchies permit a simplification of life cycle graphs through the inheritance of events among states. For instance, an event which appears as a loop on each state of an object life cycle graph can migrate to the superstate "Existing" and it is inherited by all its substates.

Several state hierarchies may be defined on a class if that class is related to several independent life cycle graphs. In such a case, each hierarchy consists of states belonging to a particular life cycle graph. For instance, in Figure 11, a subscriber object might have two state hierarchies, one consisting of states related to its loans (valid, recalled, penalized, not_penalized) and the other one consisting of states related to its subscription (up_to_date, awaiting).

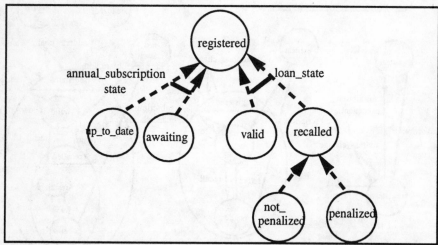

Fig. 11. A class with several state hierarchies.

5 Conclusion

The paper presented an object-oriented modeling approach that emphasizes three modeling dimensions:

- the inner dimension concerning object structure and object behavior. The proposed approach provides major improvements on object behavior modeling. Events defined in the object life cycle are the only means of changing objects. The change of an object may represent a simple change of attributes values or it may represent a change in the set of events which are applicable to the object. Object states are introduced to capture the set of applicable events to an object.

- the aggregation plane is used to put objects together in order to build larger objects, we propose to apply aggregation to events as well. Event aggregation is a useful mechanism for relating the behavior of complex objects with the behavior of their constituent objects. Event aggregation can be also used to schedule life cycles of unrelated objects.

- The generalization plane allows to organize both object classes and object states into hierarchies. Such hierarchies emphasize both the inherent differences between objects and the temporary differences of an object at various points of time on its life cycle.

Future research should address the problem of combining the three modeling dimensions in a methodological framework. The objective will be to show how localization, aggregation and generalization can be efficiently used for developing a systematic way of working in designing conceptual schemas. This work should result in process discipline patterns which provide guidelines to drive the object-oriented conceptual modeling process.

6 References

[1] G. Booch, "Object-Oriented Design with Applications", Benjamin Cumming Ed., 1991
[2] A. Borgida, J. Mylopoulos, H. Wong, "Generalization/Specialization as a Basis for Software Specification", in "Conceptual Modelling: Perspectives from Artificial , Database and Programming Languages", M.L. Brodie, J. Mylopoulos and J. W. Schmidt (eds), Springer-Verlag(pub), Harrisonburg, Virginia, 1986
[3] J. Brunet, "Modeling the World with Semantic Objects", in Proc. of the IFIP TC8/WG8.1 Working Conference on the Object-Oriented Approach in Information Systems, F. Van Assche, B. Moulin, C. Rolland (eds) North-Holland (pub) Quebec, Canada, Octobre 1991
[4] J. Brunet, C. Cauvet, D. Meddahi, F. Semmak, "Object-Oriented Analysis in Practise", the Proc. of the Fifth Conference on Advanced Information Systems Engineering, C. Rolland, F. Bodart and C. Cauvet (eds), Springer-Verlag (pub), Paris, France, 1993

[5] C. Cauvet, C. Rolland, "An event-driven Approach to the Dynamic Modelling of Objects", 3rd Int. Working Conference on Dynamic Modelling of Informations Systems, Delft, 1992

[6] P.P.S. Chen, "The Entity-Relationship Model: Towards a unified view of data", ACM Transactions on Database Systems, Vol 1, No 1, March 1976

[7] P. Coad, E, Yourdon, "Object-Oriented Analysis", Second Edition, Yourdon Press, 1990

[8] A.M. Davis, "A Comparaison of Techniques for the Specifications of External System Behavior", in Com. of the ACM, Vol 31, No 9, September 1988

[9] L.J.B. Essink, W.J. Erhart, "Object Modelling and System Dynamic in the Conceptualization Stages of Information Systems Development", IFIP TC8/WG8.1 Working Conference on the Object-Oriented Approach in Information Systems, F. Van Assche, B. Moulin, C. Rolland (eds) North-Holland (pub) Quebec, Canada, October 1991

[10] B. Henderson-Sellers, J.M. Edwards, "The Object-Oriented Systems Life Cycle", Com. of the ACM, Vol 33, No 9,September 1990

[11] R. Hull, R. King, "Semantic Database Modeling: Survey, Applications and Research Issues", ACM Computing Surveys, Vol 19, No 3, 1987

[12] B. Meyer, "Object-Oriented Software Construction", Prentice Hall, Hemel Hemstead, 1988

[13] R. Motschnig-Pitrik, "The Semantics of Parts Versus Aggregate in Data/Knowledge Modeling" in the Proc. of the Fifth Conference on Advanced Information Systems Engineering, C. Rolland, F. Bodart and C. Cauvet (eds), Springer-Verlag (pub), Paris, France, 1993

[14] J. Peckham, F. Maryansky, "Semantics Data Models" ACM Computing Surveys, Vol 20, No 3 September 1988

[15] B. Pernici, "Objects with Roles", ACM/IEEE Conf. on Office Information Systems, Boston, MA, April 1990

[16] J. Rumbaugh, M. Blaha, W Premerlani, F. Eddy, W. Lorensen, "Object-Oriented Modeling and Design", Prentice Hall, Englewood Cliffs, NJ, 1991

[17] A. Sernadas, J. Fiadero, C. Sernadas, H.D. Ehrich, "The Basic Building Block of Information Systems, Information Systems Concept", North Holland, Namur, 1989

[18] C. Sernadas, P. Resende, P. Gouveia, A. Sernadas, "In-the-Large Object-Oriented Design of Information Systems", IFIP TC8/WG8.1 Working Conference on the Object-Oriented Approach in Information Systems, F. Van Assche, B. Moulin, C. Rolland (eds) North-Holland (pub) Quebec, Canada, October 1991

[19] S. Shlaer, S. J. L. Mellor, "An Object-Oriented Approach to Domains Analysis", Software Engineering Notes, Vol 14, No 5, 1989

[20] J.M. Smith, D.C.P. Smith, "Database Abstractions: Aggregation", Com. of the ACM, Vol 20, No 6 June 1977

[21] J.M. Smith, D.C.P. Smith, "Database Abstractions: Aggregation and Generalization", ACM Trans. Database Systems 2, 2, 1977

Capturing Information Systems Requirements Through Enterprise and Speech Act Modelling

Christer Nellborn[†] and Peter Holm[†,‡]

[†]SISU - Swedish Institute for Systems Development, Electrum 212; S-164 40 Kista; Sweden; E-mail: chn@sisu.se, pholm@sisu.se
[‡]Department of Computer and Systems Science, Stockholm University, Electrum 230, S-164 40 Kista, Sweden

Enterprise modelling is a technique for capturing and validating information systems requirements. The validity depends on how well the requirements reflect the real needs of the enterprise and how well they are understood by both requirements holder and requirements engineer. In the F^3 project[1], enterprise models are designed for modelling goals, activities, concepts and actors and linking them to information system requirements.

Speech act modelling can improve traditional process and activity models, since it introduces a richer terminology in how people use information. The speech act modelling method, developed within the NATURE project[2], also introduces a classification of the organisational use of software.

In this paper we illustrate how these two methods developed within the F^3 and the NATURE project can be combined for improving the capture and validation of business process related information system requirements. We show this by applying the methods to a common example.[3]

1 Introduction

Understanding the enterprise is important for requirements engineering. An information system that is going to be well received and beneficial to the enterprise must be based on requirements that reflect the real needs of the enterprise [8, 1, 5]. Based on a field study, Curtis and Krasner [9] described the three worst problems of system development as being:
- the lack or scarcity of application domain knowledge
- fluctuating and conflicting requirements
- communication and co-ordination breakdowns between the participants in the projects.

This first was manifested by the fact that few people really understood the problem and the application domain well enough. On a project level this led to substantial design effort being spent on co-ordinating a common understanding among the staff of

---

[1]ESPRIT III project 6612. See [7] for details about project purpose and scope.

[2]ESPRIT III project 6353. See [14] for details about project purpose and scope.

[3]The F^3 Enterprise Model is described in more detail in [6,16], and the speech act modelling method is described formally in [11] and is presented in [12].

both the application domain and of how the system should perform within it. The conclusion indicates that the management of learning, especially of the application domain, is a major factor in productivity, quality and costs.

Fluctuating and conflicting requirements were usually the result of market factors such as differing needs among customers, changing needs of a single customer, changes in underlying technologies of competitors' products and misunderstanding the application domain. Other sources were company-internal, such as marketing and corporate politics. The requirements were not the stable reference for implementation that they were intended to be.

The communication and co-ordination processes within a project were crucial for managing the fluctuating and conflicting requirements. Organisational boundaries hindered understanding of the requirements and temporal boundaries buried the design rationale. Complex customer interface with many varying contacts hindered the establishment of stable requirements and increased the communication and negotiation costs.

In the report on the field study, three ways of improving software productivity and quality were proposed:
- Increase the amount of application domain knowledge across the entire software development staff.
- Software development tools and methods must accommodate change as an ordinary process and support the representation of uncertain design decisions. Change management and propagation is crucial throughout the design and development process.
- The software development environment must become a medium of communication to integrate people, tools and information.

In order to achieve these goals we need to develop methods that can be used for describing relevant aspects of an enterprise in such a way that they become useful for requirements engineering, models that can express and explain business objectives, processes, and organisational structure. It is also important to develop flexible and adaptive software development methods, where the set of models used is integrated. The F^3 and NATURE projects address these issues in various ways. In this article we will focus on describing and analysing the business processes. We will also show how this can improve the capture of information systems requirements.

2 Enterprise Modelling

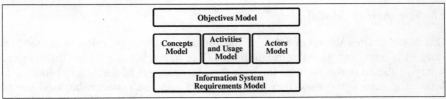

Figure 2-1. The F^3 Enterprise Model set

The purpose of Enterprise Modelling is to describe the application domain in such a way that is useful for the capture, analysis and validation of information system requirements. Willars [19] and others have described the importance of modelling the enterprises for the purpose of understanding its rationale. Within the F^3 project, a set of models is being developed for modelling the enterprise. The set contains five interlinked models as shown in figure 2-1.

2.1 The Objectives Model

This model contains components describing goals, problems, causes, business rules, opportunities, et cetera, interrelated through directed binary links. The components describe states of the application domain and the links describe how these states are related. The Objectives Model is used for analysing the rationale of the enterprise and the information system to be developed and to provide a framework where application domain processes described in the Activities and Usage Model, and information system requirements and goals described in the Information System Requirements Model can be motivated. An example of a simple Objectives Model is shown in figure 2-2.

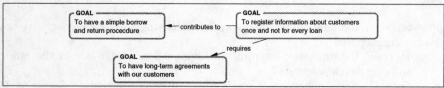

Figure 2-2. Part of an Objectives Model for a library

2.2 The Concepts Model

The Concepts Model is used for defining the concepts, relationships, and concept properties of the application domain. As in the Objectives Model, the Concepts Model components are interrelated through directed binary links. In the Concepts Model, the important concepts of the application domain and how they are interrelated are defined. It has as a subset the concepts that will be used within the automated information system. Figure 2-3 shows an example of a Concepts Model. Concepts are defined by actors.

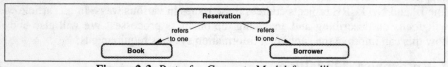

Figure 2-3. Part of a Concepts Model for a library

2.3 The Actors Model

This model defines the set of actors of the domain, (individuals, roles, organisational units, et cetera), and their interrelationships. The interrelationships are directed and binary as shown in the example in figure 2-4. The purpose of the Actors Model is to define the actors and how they are related. It can for instance be used in the information system development project to describe a complex customer organisation with many roles, groups and chains of command. Actors are responsible for requirements and goals and perform activities.

Figure 2-4. Example of part of an Actors Model for a library

2.4 The Activities and Usage Model

Activities and processes in the application domain are described in the Activities and Usage Model. The structure of this model is similar to that of traditional data-flow models. It contains activities, information sets and material sets. The information sets and the material sets go from and to activities. The purpose of modelling the activities of an enterprise is to describe the dynamic behaviour of the enterprise. In figure 2-5, the right hand side shows the traditional DFD type of modelling. The left hand side makes use of a graphical technique for describing how information can be made available without knowing in advance where that information is going to be used. This technique has been described by Janning and Sundblad in [13]. Processes are performed by actors and are motivated by the goals of the enterprise.

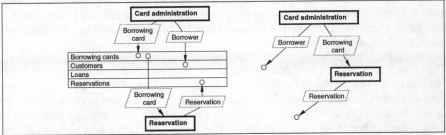

Figure 2-5. Example of an Activities and Usage Model for a library, two slightly different ways of modelling. Note: The horizontal layers in the middle of the left hand side of the figure indicate that information is made available for other activities.

2.5 The Information System Requirements Model

The Information System Requirements Model contains components such as information system goals, information system requirements et cetera. Requirements are semantically similar to goals. Both express states of affairs that should be achieved, although the word requirement is often regarded as a stronger word than goal. In the Information System Requirements Model, the word requirement is used to refer to details of the information system. Requirements should be measurable quantitatively or qualitatively. Requirements are motivated by information system goals which in turn are motivated by processes and activities or by the goals of the enterprise. Actors have the responsibility for defining requirements. Figure 2-6 illustrates a simple example.

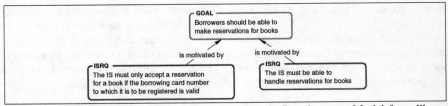

Figure 2-6. Example of part of an Information System Requirements Model for a library

2.6 The Requirements Engineering Responsibility

The requirements engineer and the requirements holder share the responsibility for the requirements. The requirements engineer for understanding and analysing the requirements well enough to understand how to design and develop the system, and the requirements holder for validating the requirements, i.e. that the requirements reflect the real need of the enterprise. In short, they share the responsibility for getting the *right requirements*, and for getting the *requirements right*.

3 Speech Act Modelling

The speech act modelling method proposed in the NATURE project is called the COMMODIOUS method. This is an acronym for *Com*munication *mod*elling as an aid to *i*llustrate the *o*rganisational *u*se of *s*oftware. In this paper we will show how it can be combined with the F^3 Enterprise Model. In order to do this, we will interpret the F^3 Concepts Model as a specification of statements that are made in the organisation. We will then classify some of the activities in the F^3 Activities and Usage model, as speech acts of various types, whose propositional content is described in the Concepts Model. Other activities, performed by computers, will be classified with respect to how they support the users.

The speech act theory formulated by Austin and later on developed by Searle [17, 18] has been very influential in the field of philosophy and linguistics. One of the major points for Austin, when he introduced the speech act concept, was to criticise what he called the *descriptive fallacy,* i.e. to suppose that people use language primarily to inform each other about certain states of affairs. An alternative approach is to view the use of language as consisting of different types of "speech acts". By saying things we act in different ways. Only one special kind of action is concerned with the assertions of facts. Searle has developed a taxonomy with five basic types of speech acts (illocutionary acts) [17]. Lyytinen et al. have developed a method for speech act modelling, based on Searle's theory, called the SAMPO method [2,3,4]. The method is intended to be used as a means for requirements capture in information systems development. It also aims at supporting business communication re-engineering in general. However, the SAMPO method has not focused on how we can analyse the role played by software systems. This is one of the objectives behind the COMMODIOUS method. In general the COMMODIOUS method tries to improve requirements engineering by using concepts from the speech act theory. People are viewed as performing different types of actions with the information in a database. Consider the act of making a work order. This act may be performed by storing information in a database. In this case the *information is the instrument of the action. It does not describe an action* performed somewhere else in the organisation.

In this paper we shall use a taxonomy of speech acts for so called contracting discourses. We will show how a development team may use this taxonomy to classify actions that are already described in a F^3 Activities and Usage Model. This is an attempt to improve the understanding and evaluation of the model. It will also help them to check both the Activities and Usage Model and the Concepts Model for completeness, and to identify new information needs for specific activities.

3.1 Contracting Discourses

A contracting discourse is, according to the COMMODIOUS method, a communication session between an organisation or a department and its customer. These discourses typically have two sub-discourses, one that administers long term agreements and one that administers the ordering procedure each time a service is provided. Figure 3–2 shows how this is represented graphically. Each arrow illustrates a customer-supplier relation, i.e. where one task or external agent is providing service to another task or external agent. Each symbol (or pair of symbols) of two shaking hands illustrates a contracting discourse. The large symbol represents an ordering procedure and the small symbol represents a sub-discourse for administrating long term agreements.

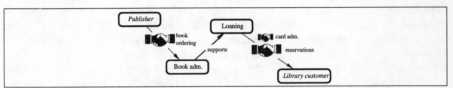

Figure 3–1. Identification of contracting discourses in a library

Each sub-discourse contains a set of speech acts of certain types, see figure 3-2. Some of them typically occur in a strictly defined sequence (group 1), others are loosely related to this sequence. The basic taxonomy for speech acts in contracting discourses as proposed in the NATURE project is based on Winograd and Flores' generic schema for "conversation for action" see, e.g. [10,15].

Taxonomy for speech acts in a contracting discourse:

Group 1 (fully sequenced): make invitation, make request, decline request, inhibit request, create commitment, describe fulfilment of service, register claim, describe fulfilment of customer obligations, report completion of service, debit customer, send invoice, report completion of customer obligations, complaint against supplier, complaint against customer, accept completion of service, accept completion of customer obligation, cancel commitment

Group 2 (partially sequenced): declare regulations, describe customer, describe supplier, describe the services

Group 3: User defined type of speech acts (specific to the company or application)

Figure 3–2. Taxonomy for speech acts in a contracting discourse

Once a user of the COMMODIOUS method has identified which types of speech acts that exists in a contracting discourse, the sequence in which they occur is relatively predictable. In a sequence diagram, like the one in figure 3-3, each arrow specifies that one speech act may follow upon another. (In the Nature project we are developing a tool that can generate such diagrams as suggestions to the user.)

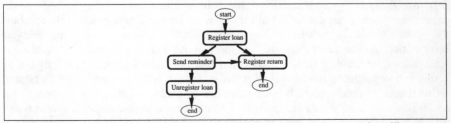

Figure 3–3. Part of a sequence diagram for a contracting discourse in a library

3.2 Classification of Software Support Functions

An essential part of the COMMODIOUS method is the classification of the organisational use of software. We propose a classification of software functions into six categories, with respect to how they are supposed to support the users.

Type of support function in the system	Type of activity supported
Resource supplying function	ordinary action
Product storage function	ordinary action
Performance function	ordinary action/ speech act
Instrumental function	ordinary action/ speech act
Action guidance function (active or passive)	ordinary action/ speech act

Table 3–1. A classification of software components, based on a characterisation of its relation to the action or task in the organisation that it is intended to support

Here follow some examples and comments to table 3-1. *Resource supplying function*: Consider the task of selling electronic books. The system stores the books and makes them available to the salesman whenever he wants to deliver them to a customer. *Product storage function*: Consider a research organisation that sells reports. Whenever the task of writing a report is finished, this report is stored in a database, together with all the other reports produced by the organisation. *Performance function* (for ordinary actions): The system performs a whole task. All robots can be considered to be agents performing tasks. Performance function (for speech acts): e.g. a system that automatically orders new material, when the company's store is below a certain level. *Instrumental function* (for ordinary actions): A support function (or subsystem) that is used as a tool, when performing a task, e.g. a word processor or a painting tool. (An alternative term might be "performance support function"). Instrumental function (for speech acts): All situations where the system mediates the communicative action, i.e. when the speech act is performed by using the system, e.g. an e-mail system or a system where a customer can make an order by directly inserting information in a database that is accessible by the supplier. (An alternative term might be "media function"). *Action guidance function*: The system instructs the user how to perform a task. In a passive action guidance function, the system simply presents information that is relevant to the task, so that the user can decide how to perform the task. We will focus on software functions that support speech acts.

The classification of support functions is meant to enhance the understanding and evaluation of a software requirements specification. It is also a way to illustrate the relevance of the enterprise model for the task of developing a software system. This can be illustrated with a simple example: Consider a library where there exists a task of lending books. There are many things we can say about this task. But, should we? How is our knowledge about the task relevant for requirements engineering and software design? By characterising the role of the future software system, the development team can get an initial idea of what knowledge is needed. How should the system guide the task of lending books? Should it passively monitor relevant information to the users, e.g. information about existing borrowing cards and reservations, or should it actively advice, instruct, or control the user? A design of an active action guidance function is (directly or indirectly) also a design of an organisational control mechanism. It must therefore be evaluated also with respect to the social institutions it creates or confirms. There is a need to discuss and analyse issues like: What are the rules for lending books? Can a book be lend to a customer, even if it is reserved for another customer? Who is allowed to change such rules?

3.3 The COMMODIOUS Method as a Complement to the F^3 Enterprise Model

In the next chapter, we shall show how we can use a part of the COMMODIOUS method as an auxiliary method in order to evaluate a partially specified F^3 Enterprise Model. We will also show how the development team will be guided in their further analysis, and how they obtain concrete guidelines for extending the models. We will apply the method according to the following schema:

- Identify the contracting discourses that exist in the enterprise
- Identify what speech acts there are in these discourses
- Create a sequence diagram (see figure 3-3) for each sub-discourse
- Identify which actions in the F^3 Activities and Usage Model corresponds to these speech acts
- Identify what parts of the F^3 Concepts Model constitute (a description of) the propositional content of these speech acts

4 An Example

In this chapter we will illustrate the basic ideas of the F^3 Enterprise Model and the COMMODIOUS method, and how they can complement each other. We will do this by using part of a library example.

4.1 Modelling a Library with the Enterprise Model Set

Populating the Objectives Model: The analysis may begin with any of the five submodels described in chapter 2. We choose the Objectives Model and focus on the goals and problems of the library example. In the example, we assume a dialogue between the requirements engineer (RE) and the requirements holder (RH) both being members of the development team.

All borrowers should be able to borrow the book they want is found to be an important goal for the library. The following question "why is it a goal?" is answered with "because it contributes to our goal to have satisfied borrowers". From this the RE concludes that there is a goal satisfied borrowers and that the first goal contributes to the second, see figure 4-1.

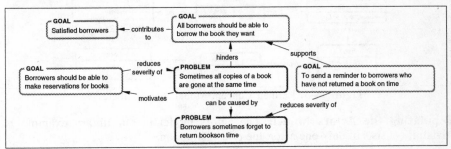

Figure 4-1. Objectives Model for the library example

Next the RE analyses potential problems in the first goal. The RE finds that sometimes all copies of a book are gone at the same time. The RE notes that this hinders the achievement of the first goal. The next question is what the cause of this problem is.

The answer that borrowers sometimes forget to return books on time is given and the RE makes a note of this in the model. Asked the question "how can the problem that borrowers do not return the books on time be solved?" the RH answers that sending reminders to borrowers who have not returned a book on time reduces the problem, which is noted in the model. The rest of the model is developed in the same way.

Populating the Activities and Usage Model: The next focus is the library processes and activities and the submodel is the Activities and Usage Model. From the Objectives Model it is found that the core of the library business is lending books and a core activity is loaning. Further analysis of the library processes reveals that the library also issues and cancels borrowing cards. Information about loans, borrowers and borrowing cards is available for, and may be used by other activities. In the Activities and Usage Model we introduce two activities: Loaning and Card Administration. Through analysis of the objectives of the library, the need for two additional activities, reservation and send reminder, are detected and the Activities and Usage Model is updated accordingly, see figure 4–2. The layer in the centre of the picture is a graphical way of indicating that the information is commonly available.

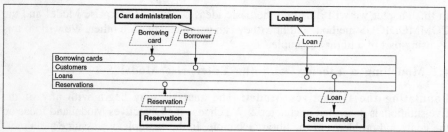

Figure 4–2. Activities and Usage Model for the library example

Populating the Concepts Model: Using the information we have gained so far, the Concepts Model may now be populated. From the Activities and Usage Model, the concepts Borrowing card, Borrower, Reservation and Loan are derived, and from the Objectives Model, the concepts Book and Copy of book, figure 4–3. The links between the concepts show how the concepts are semantically related.

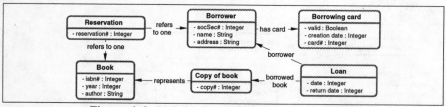

Figure 4–3. Refined Concept Model with attributes

Populating the Actors Model: The actors model in our library example is trivial: it consists of only one actor, the role of librarian.

Linking the Enterprise Submodels together: Using inter-model links between the enterprise submodels we are able to express the motivation for activities, the responsibilities for activities and for the achievement of goals, see figure 4-4.

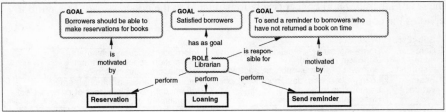

Figure 4–4. Responsibilities and motivations in the library example

The activities are motivated by goals. The role of librarian is needed to describe the responsibilities for the goals and to describe who actually performs the activities. In a more complex enterprise this becomes more complicated and requires a more thorough analysis of the actors.

4.2 Further Guidance Through Speech Act Modelling

So far we have produced a partial F^3 Enterprise Model for the library. We will now focus on how we can make the model more detailed, by using the COMMODIOUS method as a vehicle to detect incompleteness, e.g. with respect to the specification of sub-activities, information needs, and rules for activities.

The first step when applying the COMMODIOUS method is to identify customer-supplier relations in the library and to detect contracting discourses. We have already illustrated, in figure 3-1, the discourses that exist in this library. The core business task, Loaning, is providing service to the library customers (i.e. to let them borrow books). The Activities and Usage Model produced so far is obviously concerned with parts of the contracting discourse for loaning, i.e. to administer long term agreements with the customers (borrowing cards) and to administer the ordering procedure for a specific service occasion (reservations and registrations of loans). We may use the generic taxonomy of speech acts in contracting discourses to identify what speech acts need to be performed in this particular library. We can then map these to the partially specified Activities and Usage Model. This is illustrated in table 4-1. (The speech act Report to customer about available book is viewed as a speech act specific for libraries. It is therefore not an instance of a speech act type in the predefined taxonomy.)

Sub-disc.	Speech act	Speech act type	Perf. in activity
Card administ-ration	Register new customer	Describe customer	Card administration
	Give borrowing card	Make agreement	Card administration
	Invalidate card	Cancel commitment	Card administration
Reservation	Make reservation	Create commitment	Reservation
	Cancel reservation	Cancel commitment	Reservation
	Report to customer about available book	User defined type of speech act	Reservation
	Register loan	Describe fulfilment of service	Loaning
	Send reminder	Complaint against customer	Send reminder
	Register return	Describe fulfilment of customer obl.	Loaning
		Cancel commitment	
	Unregister loan		Send reminder

Table 4-1. The identification of speech acts performed in the contracting discourse regarding loaning

We can also classify the concepts, attributes, and concept relations in the Concepts Model directly, by linking each one of them to the speech act that is producing the information. This is illustrated in table 4-2. (The notation Loan.{date, borrower,-} denotes the set of attributes and concepts relations related to the concept Loan. The symbol "–" denotes the concept itself.)

Sub-disc.	Predicate	Type
Card admi- nistration	Borrowing card.{ -, creation date, card#} Borrower.{has card} Borrower.{ -, name, address, socSec#}	Information about commitment Information about commitment Information about customer
Reser- vation	Loan.{ -, borrower, date, borrowed book} Loan.{return date} Reservation.{all attributes}	Information about fulfilment if service Information about fulfilment of customer obl. Commitment information

Table 4-2. Classification of the concepts, concept relations, and attributes in the Concepts Model

This classification of speech acts can be used to guide the interpretation and evaluation of the activities in the Activities and Usage Model. There is a big difference between making an agreement, making a promise, and describing a state of affairs. The different types of speech acts should be understood and validated in different ways, e.g. for promises and agreements we may ask if it is clear to all partners how to interpret the commitments that are created, i.e. check commitment ambiguity. For cancellations of commitments, we may ask who is allowed to do it and under what conditions, i.e. check role ambiguity, confer Auramäki et al. [1]. As the information flows and activities were described earlier, they were all treated in the same way.

The COMMODIOUS method can also help us to give the Activities and Usage Model and the Concepts Model a rationale. If there is a customer-supplier relation, there is often a need for a contracting discourse. There are general social conventions in our society as to how such communications should be performed. This can motivate the existence of specific activities, information flows, and rules. In this way we can use the notion of a contracting discourse and the speech act taxonomy as a complement to the Objectives Model.

The next step is to specify sequence conditions for the speech acts in the discourses. Figure 4-5 describes what speech acts may follow upon each other in each sub-discourse. Such a diagram should include all speech acts in group 1 (see figure 3-2). Figure 4-6 illustrates additional sequence conditions, i.e. between the two sub-discourses and between speech acts in group 1 (the fully sequenced speech acts) and others.

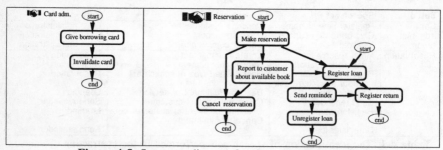

Figure 4-5. Sequence diagram for the two sub-discourses

After producing the sequence diagram, we can test the discourse for completeness by checking that each branch ends in an appropriate way and that the discourse model covers all possible moves after each speech act. It is easy to forget the speech act Unregister loan. This speech act has to be performed if a book is not returned. It is, however, easily discovered when checking that the diagram covers all things that may happen after sending a reminder. By examining the information produced by each speech act, we may also check the Concepts Model for completeness. For instance, the current Concepts Model does not contain any reminders.

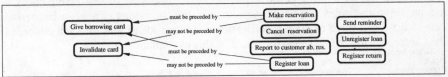

Figure 4-6. Graphical illustration of sequence conditions between the two sub-discourses

When each speech act in a sub-discourse is performed, the actors need information that is produced earlier in the discourse. There are two reasons for this. They must identify the chain of information produced in the discourse of concern and they must check that the precedence conditions are fulfilled, i.e. that a speech act that must precede the current speech act actually has occurred. They do not need to access all parts of the information produced in a specific sub-discourse, but a good heuristic rule is that they need to access the information produced by the latest speech act in the discourse, that must have been performed. For example, when Register return is performed, people need to access the information produced by the speech act Register loan, in order to identify the discourse (about a particular loan) that Register return is a part of. From this simple rule we can detect a set of missing information flows in the Activities and Usage Model. Here are some examples, which are illustrated in figure 4-7: Loaning needs the information Loan (when register returns). Send reminder needs to access the information Loan. Reservation needs to access the (public) information Reservation. Loaning needs to access the information Reservation. Some of the information flows will not be made public, though, but are local within one activity. In the activity Send Reminder, for example, they need to store information about the reminders sent to customers. This information is, however, only needed locally in this activity.

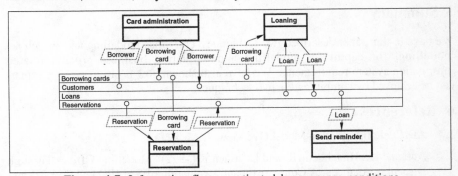

Figure 4-7. Information flows, motivated by sequence conditions

Another rule is that all speech acts that must (or may not) be preceded by a specific speech act, as specified in figure 4-6, need to access the information produced by the latter speech act. Register loan must be preceded by a Give borrowing card. It may not be preceded by the speech act Invalidate card. Hence the activity of loaning needs information about the borrowing cards. More precisely it needs the information Borrowing card.{all attributes} and Borrower.{has card}. The same holds for the speech act reservation. Analogously, Card administration needs to access (the public information) Borrower (when giving borrowing cards).

The COMMODIOUS method also supports the capturing of rules regarding certain speech acts, e.g. by looking at the sequence conditions. A set of reasonable checking mechanisms and rules for active action guidance functions can even be derived automatically, if there exists a specification of unique identifiers for each concept in the Concepts Model. Consider, for instance, this example:

Software function: active action guidance function for registration of loans
Input: aCardNr
Preconditions: "The information produced by the speech act 'Give borrowing card' must exist"
$\exists x,y(borrowing\_card(x) \& card\#(x, y) \& y = aCardNr)$

Finally, we can use the classification of software support proposed by the COMMODIOUS method, and characterise the type of software support that each speech act should have. This classification will guide us in the further analysis. Consider the speech act Send reminder. Should it be supported by an active or a passive action guidance function? If we decide to design an active action guidance function, then the enterprise model must be made more detailed regarding this task. The system will probably contain rules that implement the customer policy on this point. Should, for instance, all customers be treated the same? If the team, on the other hand, should decide to have a passive action guidance function, such aspects may still be important to describe. However, in this case the rules are probably not as important and essential for the task of designing a software system.

By classifying support functions in this way we gain important information on how functions in the system should behave towards, and be perceived by, the user. This information is valuable input when analysing non-functional-, functional- and human-computer interface requirements, and when designing system functions. But perhaps more important as a tool for validation of the behavioural consistency of the system and as a trigger for further requirements analysis.

5 Summary

We have in this paper described two techniques, enterprise modelling and speech act modelling, for capturing, modelling and validating business process related information system requirements. We have also shown how positive synergy effects can be achieved by combining the two techniques.

6 References

1. AD/Cycle Information Model Overview, IBM, 1992

2. Auramäki E, Hirschheim R, and Lyytinen K (1992) "Modelling Offices Through Discourse Analysis: A Comparison and Evaluation of SAMPO and OSSAD and ICN", In *The Computer Journal*, 35, No 5 1992, (pp. 492 -500)

3. Auramäki E, Hirschheim R, and Lyytinen K (1992) "Modelling Offices Through Discourse Analysis: The SAMPO Approach", In: *The Computer Journal*, 35, No 4 1992, (pp. 342 - 352)

4. Auramäki E, Lehtinen E, and Lyytinen K (1988) "A Speech-Act-Based Office Modeling Approach", In: *ACM Transactions on Office Information Systems*, 6(2), (pp. 126-152)

5.   Avison, D E, Fitzgerald, G, *Information Systems Development, Methodologies, Techniques and Tools*, Blackwell Scientific Publications, 1988

6.   Bubenko J A jr, Gustafsson M R, Nellborn C, and Song W *Computer Support for Enterprise Modelling and Requirements Acquisition,* E6612/SISU/3-1-3-R1.B, 1992, SISU, Electrum 212, S-164 40, Kista, Sweden

7.   Bubenko J A jr, Rolland C, Loucopoulos P, and DeAntonellis V (1994) *Facilitating "Fuzzy to Formal" Requirements Modelling,* In conference proceedings: IEEE International Conference on Requirements Engineering, Colorado Springs, Colorado, USA and Taipei, Taiwan, ROC, IEEE

8.   Bubenko, J A, jr, *Next Generation Information Systems: an Organisational Perspective* SYSLAB Report, DSV, University of Stockholm, Sweden, ISSN 1101-8526, 1991

9.   Curtis, B, Krasner, H, *A Field Study of the Software Design Process for Large Systems*, Communications of the ACM 1988 31(11): 1268 ff.

10. Flores F, Graves M, Hartfield B, and Winograd T (1988) "Computer Systems and the Design of Organizational Interaction", In *ACM Transactions on Office Information Systems*, 6 (2), (pp. 87-108)

11. Holm P (1994) *A Formal Description of the COMMODIOUS Method,* Technical Report, Manuscript

12. Holm P (1994) *The COMMODIOUS Method - Communication Modelling as an Aid to Illustrate the Organisational Use of Software*, In conference proceedings: Sixth International Conference on Software Engineering and Knowledge Engineering, Jurmala, Latvia

13. Janning, M, Sundblad, C, *Key Charts - a visualisation technique for business analysis*, Technical note, Swedish Institute for Systems Development, 1991

14. Jarke M, Bubenko J A jr, Rolland C, Sutcliffe A, and Vassiliou Y (1993) *Theories Underlying Requirements Engineering: An Overview of NATURE at Genesis* In conference proceedings: IEEE Symposium on Requirements Engineering, RE'93, San Diego, CA, Jan. 4-6, 1993

15. Medina-Mora R, Winograd T, Flores R, and Flores F (1993) *The Action Workflow Approach to Workflow Management Technology*, In conference proceedings: Third European Conference on Computer Supported Cooperative Work, (pp. 281-288), Milano, Italy

16. Nellborn C, Gustafsson M R, and Bubenko J A jr *Enterprise Modelling - an Approach to Capture Requirements,* E6612/SISU/3-1-3-R1A, 1992, SISU, Electrum 212, S-164 40 Kista, Sweden

17. Searle J R (1979) *Expression and Meaning*, Cambridge, 1979, Cambridge U P

18. Searle J R and Vanderveken D (1985) *Foundations of Illocutionary Logic*, Cambridge, 1985, Cambridge University Press

19. Willars, H, *Amplification of Business Cognition Through Modelling Techniques*, 11th IEA congress in Paris 1991, In congress proceedings

Dynamic Modelling with Events

Maguelonne Teisseire[1], Pascal Poncelet[2] and Rosine Cicchetti[2]

[1] Digital Equipment
[2] IUT Aix-en-Provence
LIM - URA CNRS 1787 - Université d'Aix-Marseille II,
Faculté des Sciences de Luminy, Case 901
163 Avenue de Luminy, 13288 Marseille Cedex 9 FRANCE.
E-mail: teisseir@gia.univ-mrs.fr

Abstract. This paper focusses on the behavioural aspects of the IFO_2[3] model, an extension of the semantic model IFO defined by S. Abiteboul and R. Hull. Its originality is in the formalization of complex events and their specification, which adopts semantics and syntax indentical to those of the structural part. In addition, it offers concepts - particularly modularity and re-usability - that are unanimously recognized as useful for structural specification of applications.

1 Motivation

Recent development tools for advanced applications - mainly Extended Relational or Object-Oriented Database Management Systems [1] - introduce new concepts relevant for complex object management. In parallel, conceptual approaches [3, 5, 9, 10, 13, 14, 15, 19] strive to meet the needs of both traditional and advanced applications. Some of them give pride of place to behaviour representation and resort to OODB models for the structural modelling, while forgetting their typically implementable feature. Thus the models defined can be used for manipulation of complex objects, but they lose some of the benefits of semantic approaches [8]. Dependent upon target systems, they have shortcomings as regards the proposed constructors and only express semantic constraints (such as cardinalities) with the aid of methods (i.e. coding, which is paradoxical for conceptual approaches).

From a dynamic viewpoint, conceptual approaches are based on new concepts and mechanisms or make use of temporal logic [5, 6]. Since they aim to specify application behaviour, the problems which are studied are nearly similar to those of concurrent system design and software engineering.

In proposing the IFO_2 conceptual model [11, 12], we intend to integrate both structural and behavioural representation of applications in a consistent and uniform manner with respect to both the formalization introduced and the associated graphical representation. It is based on the IFO model of S. Abiteboul and R. Hull [2] and its aim, for the structural part, is to combine the advantages of both semantic and object-oriented approaches[4].

---

[3] This work, supported by an External European Research Project in collaboration with Digital Equipment, comes within the scope of a larger project whose aim is to provide an aided modelling and design system for advanced applications.

This paper is devoted to the dynamic aspect of the model. Its originality is in the formalization of complex events and their specification, which adopts semantics and syntax identical to those of the structural part. In addition, it offers concepts - particularly modularity and re-usability - that are unanimously recognized as useful for structural specification of applications. With IFO_2, it is possible to fully comprehend the overall behaviour of a system, by specifying it in a manner that is both "fragmented" and "optimized". These strong points are stressed in Section 2, which summarizes our contribution by drawing a parallel with the mentioned conceptual work. The various concepts introduced to represent the application behaviour are defined in Section 3. Then, to conclude, we have a brief look at the IFO_2 system that is currently being developed.

2 Related Work and Proposal

An event is the representation of a fact that participates in reactions of the modelized system. It occurs in a spontaneous random manner (in the case of external event) or is generated by the application. In both cases, it occurs instantaneously, i.e. it is of zero duration. Like in [7], we make the following assumption: no more than one event can occur at any given instant.

The structural part of IFO_2 is defined with respect to the "whole-object" philosophy. We extend its scope to the behavioural part and refer to a **"whole-event"** representation. In fact, event modelling in IFO_2 complies with a dual precept: typing and identification. As regards the latter point, we use the instant of occurrence of an event as its identifier.

The IFO_2 model proposes two basic types:

- the simple event type (TES) represents the events that trigger an operation (method) included in the IFO_2 structural description;
- the abstract event type (TEA) is used to specify external or temporal events or events that generate other events.

To modelize a system behaviour, it is necessary to express different variants of event conjunction and disjunction. To answer this need, we have chosen to represent complex events by using **constructors**: composition, sequence, grouping and union. With this approach, we provide not only the required expressive power but also the uniformity with respect to the IFO_2 structural modelling. When representing both static and dynamic parts of an application, the designer handles concepts having the same philosophy.

The types of events are interconnected by functions through the event fragment concept. Its role is to describe a subset of the modelized behaviour that can then be used as a whole by means of the represented type concept. Consequently, it is possible to manipulate another type - without knowing its description - via an IS_A event link. These concepts offer a real modularity and re-usability of specifications:

---

[4] Here we do not aim to present the structural part of IFO_2 (the interested reader may refer to [11, 12]).

the designer may defer a type description or entrust it to somebody else, while using a represented type which symbolizes it.

The fragment functions express various constraints on the event chain (obligation of occurrence, multiplicity and any possible wait). In addition, we make a distinction between triggering functions and precedence functions which loosely express the fact that an event triggers the occurrence of other ones or that it is preceded by the origination of other ones. In order to underline this, let us consider an external or temporal event. By its very nature, it cannot be triggered by another modelized event, therefore it is sometimes necessary to express that its occurrence is mandatorily preceded by other events. This makes it possible, by adopting a specific observation point (called the fragment heart) to have an overview of the behaviour in question, i.e. including not only generating events (preceding events) but also generated events (triggered events). The fragment can thus be considered as a unit of description of the system behaviour.

In order to modelize the general behaviour of the application, the partial views provided by the fragments are combined (via IS_A links) within an event schema.

With the proposed approach, an application is described by a structural specification and a behavioural specification, which are closely related but clearly distinct. Our philosophy is therefore different to that of models such as in [10, 13, 14] that choose to combine these two aspects in a single schema. Therefore the behaviour is described for each class of objects and an additional mechanism must be used to specify the interactions between classes.

Our philosophy has two advantages in relation to these approaches: a single uniform description of events, including events shared by objects of different types, but, above all, an overview of the system dynamics, which we believe to be essential for a conceptual model. However, it should be noted that, in common with the approach proposed in [10], we are mindful of the modularity of specifications: the represented type concept in IFO$_2$ has the same purpose as that of a role.

An overall dynamic vision is also proposed in [6, 17], which describes the behaviour of an object database by using temporal logic. In this model, the constraints applied to the occurrence of events are expressed with the aid of the trace concept [16] (event history) and operators applied to the traces. We make use of such a concept for specification of precedence and triggering functions and manipulate traces to translate particular conditions of the event chain.

3   IFO$_2$ Behavioural Model: Formal Presentation

3.1   Time and Event Type

The behaviour of any real system is within the "time" dimension, therefore it is firstly necessary to specify this concept. We do so, in a similar manner to [4], by defining time as a set of equidistant instants with an origin and where each point in time can be represented by a non-negative integer. The spacing of intervals corresponds to the system granularity (i.e. the smallest representable unit of time). In our approach, the events that take part in the system dynamics occur in an ordered manner in this temporal dimension.

Definition 1 *Time* is an infinite set of symbols and $<_{Time}$ the total order relation on this set.

Apart from the identifier and event domain concepts (determining the events and operations that take part in instances), the definition of an event type entails structural elements through the concept of parameter domain.

Definition 2 $\mathcal{TE}$ is an infinite set of event types such that: $\forall te \in \mathcal{TE}$, $Did(te)$ is an infinite set of symbols called the **identifier domain** of te with $Did(te) \subset time$, $Dom(te)$ is an infinite set of symbols, including the empty set, called the **event domain** of te and $Dpara(te)$, the **parameter domain** of te, is included in $\mathcal{P}(S_S)$ (where $\mathcal{P}(S_S)^5$ is the powerset of the object types of the structural schema).

Definition 3 An **event** of type Te is a triplet $(id, occ, para)$ such that: $\forall e, e'$ of type Te, $\exists (id, id') \in Did(Te)^2$, $\exists (occ, occ') \in Dom(Te)^2$, $\exists (para, para') \in Dpara(Te)^2$ such that: if $e = (id, occ, para)$, $e' = (id', occ', para')$ and $id = id'$ then $e = e'$. The infinite event set of type Te is called $Evt(Te)$.

To illustrate this paper, the modelized system is a lift. An event type involved in the description of the lift behaviour is "Up", which describes the ascending motion of the lift cage. Let us consider an event, e_{Up_1}, of this type. It could be specified as follows: $e_{Up_1} = (id_{Up_1}, up, @_1\_cage)$. This means that the event e_{Up_1} occurred at the instant id_{Up_1}, with the $@_1\_cage$ as parameter. The up component maps with an operation of the structural schema.

For each event type te of $\mathcal{TE}$, there are two functions: a bijective function Id with domain $Evt(te)$ and codomain $Did(te)$ which associates with each event of type te its identifier and an injective function $Para$ with domain $Evt(te)$ and codomain $Dpara(te)$ which associates with each event of type te its parameters.

3.2 Basic Event Types

A simple event type, TES, describes the triggering of an operation which is specified in the structural schema. Other atomic types are modelized through the abstract event type concept, TEA. It describes events which are external or temporal events or generators of other events. Figure 1 shows the graphical formalism for basic event types.

Definition 4 Let $\mathcal{TES}$ be an infinite set of **simple** event types and let $\mathcal{TEA}$ be an infinite set of **abstract** event types, two disjoint subsets of $\mathcal{TE}$, such that:

1. $\forall te \in \mathcal{TES}$:
   (a) $\exists op \in O\dot{P}(F_{Struct}) \mid Dom(te) = op$ where $OP(F_{Struct})$ is the operation set of the structural fragment $F_{Struct} \in G_s$;
   (b) $Dpara(te) \subseteq \mathcal{P}(V_S)$ where $\mathcal{P}(V_S)$ is the powerset of V_S and V_S is the object type set of the fragment F_{Struct}.
2. $\forall te \in \mathcal{TEA}$, $Dom(te) = \emptyset$.

Fig. 1. Example of Basic Event Types

Figure 1 presents the TES "Up", evoked in the previous example, and two TEAs: "Satis-Request" and "Floor-Request". The former describes events generated when the lift reaches the required floor. The latter represents external events occurring when users request a floor.

3.3 Complex Event Types

To describe the system behaviour, complex event combinations have to be expressed. They provide constraints on event occurrences. The four constructors (shown in Figure 2) proposed in the IFO$_2$ model specify the logical conditions on events: conjunction with different constraints and disjunction.

Each event may only take part in a single construction since it occurs only once. Accordingly, in the constructor definitions, this is formally expressed through an exclusivity constraint. Furthermore, a composite event stems from the occurrence of its components.

Composition and Sequence Event Types: the event composition and sequence constructors reflect the conjunction of events belonging to different types. The sequence includes a chronological order on the occurrences of the component events.

Definition 5 Let $\mathcal{TETC}$ be an infinite set of **composition** event types, and let $\mathcal{TETS}$ be an infinite set of **sequence** event types. $\mathcal{TETC}$ and $\mathcal{TETS}$ are two subsets of $\mathcal{TE}$, such that: $\forall te \in \mathcal{TETC} \cup \mathcal{TETS}$, $\exists te_1, te_2, ..., te_n \in \mathcal{TE}$, $n > 1$, such that:

1. $Dom(te) \subseteq Evt(te_1) \times Evt(te_2) \times ... \times Evt(te_n)$.
2. $Dpara(te) \subseteq Dpara(te_1) \cup Dpara(te_2) \cup ... \cup Dpara(te_n)$.
3. te is structurally defined as:
   $\forall e \in Evt(te)$, $\exists e_1 \in Evt(te_1)$, $e_2 \in Evt(te_2), ..., e_n \in Evt(te_n)$ such that:

$$e = (id, [e_1, e_2, ..., e_n], \bigcup_{i=1}^{n} Para(e_i))$$

and $\forall e' \in Evt(te)$ with $e \neq e'$, $\exists e'_1 \in Evt(te_1)$, $e'_2 \in Evt(te_2), ..., e'_n \in Evt(te_n)$ such that $e' = (id', [e'_1, e'_2, ..., e'_n], para')$ with $\forall i \in [1..n]$, $e_i \notin \{e'_1, e'_2, ..., e'_n\}$.

---

[5] A structural schema is defined as a directed acyclic graph $G_S = (S_S, L_S)$ where S_S is the set of object types and L_S the link set of the schema.

Furthermore, if $te \in \mathcal{TETS}$, we have: $Id(e_1) <_{Time} Id(e_2) <_{Time} \cdots <_{Time} Id(e_n) <_{Time} Id(e)$.

The occurrence of a composition or sequence event type is defined by the Cartesian product of the aggregated events. Its parameters are the union of its component parameters. The exclusivity constraint imposes that a composite event type cannot occur from events which are already used.

Grouping Event Types: the grouping represents an event collection, i.e. a conjunction of events belonging to the same type.

Definition 6 Let $\mathcal{TESG}$ be an infinite set of **grouping** event types, subset of $\mathcal{TE}$, such that: $\forall te \in \mathcal{TESG}, \exists! te' \in \mathcal{TE}$, such that:

1. $Dom(te) \subseteq \mathcal{P}(Evt(te'))$ where $\mathcal{P}(Evt(te'))$ is the powerset of $Evt(te')$.
2. $Dpara(te) \subseteq \mathcal{P}(Dpara(te'))$.
3. te is structurally defined as:
   $\forall e \in Evt(te), \exists e_1, e_2, ..., e_n \in Evt(te')$ such that:

$$e = (id, \{e_1, e_2, ..., e_n\}, \bigcup_{i=1}^{n} Para(e_i))$$

   with $\forall i \in [1..n], Id(e_i) <_{Time} Id(e)$ and $\forall e' = (id', [e'_1, e'_2, ..., e'_n], para') \in Evt(te)$ with $e \neq e'$ then $\forall i \in [1..n], e_i \notin \{e'_1, e'_2, ..., e'_n\}$.

Union Event Types: a disjunction of different event types is described by the union constructor.

Definition 7 Let $\mathcal{TEUT}$ be an infinite set of **union** event types, subset of $\mathcal{TE}$, such that: $\forall te \in \mathcal{TEUT}, \exists te_1, te_2, ..., te_n \in \mathcal{TE}, n > 1$, such that:

1. $Dom(te) \subseteq Dom(te_1) \cup Dom(te_2) \cup ... \cup Dom(te_n)$.
2. $Dpara(te) \subseteq Dpara(te_1) \cup Dpara(te_2) \cup ... \cup Dpara(te_n)$.
3. te is structurally defined as:
   $\forall i, j \in [1..n]$ if $i \neq j$ then $Evt(te_i) \cap Evt(te_j) = \emptyset$ and
   $Evt(te) = Evt(te_1) \cup Evt(te_2) \cup ... \cup Evt(te_n)$
   with $\forall e \in Eut(te), \exists! k \in [1..n]$ such that $e = e_k$ where $e_k \in Evt(te_k)$.

In figure 2, the union type "Up-Down" is an alternative between the two simple types "Up" and "Down". It triggers the descending or ascending lift motion. Thus an event of the union type "Up-Down" may be an event of either type "Down" or type "Up".

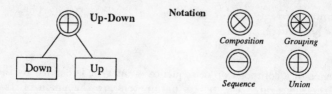

Fig. 2. The Up-Down Event Type

3.4 Represented Event Types

This type, symbolized by a circle, handles another event type through the IS_A specialization link (Cf. Definition 16). Consequently, the designer may use an event type without knowing its complete description. This concept is particularly interesting when considering modularity and re-usability goals.

Definition 8 Let TER be an infinite set of **represented** event types, subset of TE, such that:
$\forall te \in TER$, $\exists te_1, te_2, ..., te_n \in TE$, $n > 0$, called the sources of te, such that:

1. $Dom(te) \subseteq Dom(te_1) \cup Dom(te_2) \cup ... \cup Dom(te_n)$.
2. $Dpara(te) \subseteq Dpara(te_1) \cup Dpara(te_2) \cup ... \cup Dpara(te_n)$.
3. te is structurally defined as: $Evt(te) = Evt(te_1) \cup Evt(te_2) \cup ... \cup Evt(te_n)$ with $\forall e \in Evt(te)$, $\exists e_i \in Evt(te_i)$, $i \in [1..n]$, such that $e = e_i$.

The definition of represented event types takes into account the multiple inheritance since a represented event type may have several sources.

3.5 Event Types

From basic and represented types and constructors, event type may be defined. Event and parameter domains are explained as well as instance (at a given instant).

Event Type Specification: an event type is built up from simple, abstract and represented types and constructors which may be recursively applied.

Definition 9 An event type $Te \in TE$ is a directed tree (S_{Te}, E_{Te}) such that:

1. S_{Te}, the set of vertices, is included in the disjoint union of seven sets TES, TEA, TER, $TETC$, $TETS$, $TESG$ and $TEUT$.
2. E_{Te} is the set of edges called type links.

Event Set and Type Domains

Definition 10 Let Te be an event type, the infinite set of **events** of the type Te, $Evt(Te)$, the **event domain**, $Dom(Te)$, and the **parameter domain**, $Dpara(Te)$ are respectively equal to the set of events and the domains of events and parameters of its root type.

A **type instance** includes all the events of this type which already occurred.

Definition 11 Let Te be an event type, an **instance** J of Te, denoted by J_{Te}, is a finite set of events of type Te, i.e. $J_{Te} \subseteq Evt(Te)$.

The **attached events**, denoted by Evt_att, describe, for each vertex of the type, which events occurred. This concept is particularly useful to specify certain complex constraints (for instance, if an event triggering depends on some other specific events).

3.6 Event Fragment

The fragment goal is to describe a part of the system behaviour. One of its advantages is that it can be re-used and manipulated as a whole through the represented type concept. The fragment description focusses on a particular event type, called the heart, which is related to other types. These links represent the event chaining, i.e. a part of the specified behaviour. In the real world, events occur according to particular rules (temporal or not). In IFO$_2$, these rules are specified by using functions which combine the following features. They can be simple or complex (multivalued); partial or total (mandatory) and immediate or deferred. Furthermore, we have a distinction between triggering functions (whose source is the heart) and precedence functions (whose target is the heart).
There is at the most one precedence edge in a fragment.

Fragment Specification

Definition 12 An **event fragment** is a directed acyclic graph $F_e = (V_{F_e}, L_{F_e})$ with V_{F_e}, subset of $\mathcal{TE}$, the event type set of the fragment and L_{F_e}, the set of fragment links, defined such that:

1. there is only one directed tree $H_e = (V'_{F_e}, L'_{F_e})$ whose root is called fragment heart such that:
   (a) $V'_{F_e} \subseteq V_{F_e}, L'_{F_e} \subseteq L_{F_e}$.
   (b) The source of a triggering edge is either the root of the heart or the root of a target type of a complex edge whose source is the heart root (case of subfragment).
2. $(V_{F_e} - V'_{F_e})$ is either equal to the empty set - and $(L_{F_e} - L'_{F_e})$ too - or it is reduced to a singleton, source of the precedence edge belonging to $(L_{F_e} - L'_{F_e})$ whose target is the fragment heart.

The event fragment is called by its heart.

Figure 3 illustrates a fragment whose heart is an external event type "Floor-Request". In this fragment, there is no precedence function. This fragment describes the lift reactions when a user wishes to go to a floor, i.e. either he calls the lift from a floor or he pushes a button in the cage. The fragment heart is linked with a partial and deferred function to the simple type "Closure". The associated method in the structural fragment "Lift-Cage" closes the lift doors. The function[6] is partial because,

---

[6] Due to lack of space, the function specification language is not described in this paper.

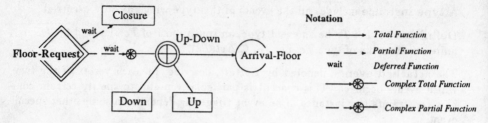

Fig. 3. The "Floor-Request" Event Fragment

in some cases, an event of "Floor-Request" would not trigger a door closure. These cases are the following: (i) the user wishes to go to the floor where he is currently located; (ii) or the door closure stems from another event, i.e. a previous request from the same floor or a previous button activation if the user is already in the lift cage. The function is deferred to take into account the case where the user requests the lift while the cage is moving up or down.

The TEA is also related to the composite type "Up-Down" through a partial, deferred and complex function. It is partial to take into account three cases: cases (i) and (ii) of the previous function and the case where the requested floor is served when satisfying previous current requests. The deferred feature of the function takes into consideration the possible delay between the user request and the resulting lift motion. In fact the methods corresponding to the TESs "Up" and "Down" perform a single floor ascent or descent for the cage. This is why the triggering function is complex. The union type "Up-Down" is heart of a subfragment. The triggering function which relates it to the represented type "Arrival-Floor" (whose consequences are described in another fragment) is total and immediate. This means that any event of the types "Up" and "Down" generates an event of "Arrival-Floor".

A fragment instance is a triplet: the generators of heart events, the heart events themselves and those triggered by heart events. It gives an historical view of the fragment behaviour with causality links between events.

The fragment generated events are those triggered from heart events, i.e. those obtained by applying the triggering functions to heart type instance.

Definition 13 Let F_e be an event fragment whose heart is T_{e0} with root r_{e0}, let $a_1 = (r_{e0}, r_{e1})$, $a_2 = (r_{e0}, r_{e2})$, ... $a_n = (r_{e0}, r_{en})$ be edges whose source is r_{e0}. For each $i \in [1..n]$, let f_{a_i} be the function associated to the a_i edge and let Z_{ei} be the subfragment obtained from the maximal subtree with root r_{ei}.
The set of events generated from an event e of the heart type of F_e, is achieved by the function Ψ_{F_e} which is such that:

$\Psi_{F_e}(e) = \emptyset$ if the F_e fragment is reduced to one type
else,

$$\Psi_{F_e}(e) = \bigcup_{i=1}^{n} (\bigcup_{k=1}^{q_i} (ei_k, \Psi_{Z_{ei}}(ei_k)))$$

where $\{ei_k ; k \in [1..q_i]\}$ is the event set obtained by applying the f_{a_i} function to the event e (q_i is equal to 1 when f_{a_i} is a simple function) and $\Psi_{Z_{ei}}(ei_k)$ is the set of events generated from the event ei_k in the subfragment Z_{ei}.

The set of events triggered from the $J_{T_{e0}}$ instance with m elements, denoted by $\Psi_{F_e}(J_{T_{e0}})$, is then defined by:

$$\Psi_{F_e}(J_{T_{e0}}) = \bigcup_{j=1}^{m} (\Psi_{F_e}(e_j)).$$

The **generator events** are those having one image by the fragment precedence function.

Definition 14 Let F_e be an event fragment whose heart is T_{e0} with root r_{e0} and let $a_b = (r_b, r_{e0})$ be the possible edge whose target is r_{e0}. The set of generator events of heart events is obtained with the function Υ_{F_e} whose domain is $J_{T_{e0}}$ - a T_{e0} instance with m elements - and codomain is either the empty set if a_b does not exist or I_{T_b} an instance of type T_b with root r_b. Υ_{F_e} is defined by:

$\forall e \in J_{T_{e0}},$ $\Upsilon_{F_e}(e) = e_b$ if $e_b \in I_{T_b}$ exists and is such that $f_{a_b}(e_b) = e$ else $\Upsilon_{F_e}(e) = \emptyset$ where f_{a_b} is the function represented by the a_b edge.

The set of generator events through the a_b edge of the $J_{T_{e0}}$ instance, denoted by $\Upsilon_{F_e}(J_{T_{e0}})$, is defined by:

$$\Upsilon_{F_e}(J_{T_{e0}}) = \bigcup_{j=1}^{m} \Upsilon_{F_e}(e_j).$$

Fragment Instance

Definition 15 Let F_e be an event fragment whose heart is a type T_{e0} and let $J_{T_{e0}}$ be an instance of T_{e0} with m elements.
An **instance** of F_e, denoted by I_{F_e}, is defined by:

$$I_{F_e} = (\Upsilon_{F_e}(J_{T_{e0}}), J_{T_{e0}}, \Psi_{F_e}(J_{T_{e0}})).$$

In the "Floor-Request" fragment, there is no precedence function. Consequently, the fragment instance is equal to the following triplet: $I_{F_r} = (\emptyset, J_{F_r}, \Psi_{F_r}(J_{F_r}))$.
Let us suppose that J_{F_r} is reduced to the event e_{Fr1}, we have: $\Psi_{F_r}(J_{F_r}) = \Psi_{F_r}(e_{Fr1})$ $= (e_{C1}, \emptyset)$ where e_{C1} is of type "Closure". This instance expresses that there is not yet a going up or down order associated to the event e_{Fr1}.

3.7 Event Schema

The overall behaviour of a system is modelized by grouping the partial views described through fragments. The resulting event schema is thus composed by fragments related by IS_A links according to two rules.

Specialization Link: the specialization link represents either the role of an event type in another fragment or the event subtyping.

Definition 16 Let Te be a type of $\mathcal{TER}$ and let $Ts \in \mathcal{TE}$ be a source of Te and heart of fragment, the link of source Ts and target Te is called an **IS_A** link and is denoted by $L_{IS\_A(Te-Ts)}$.

Schema Specification

Definition 17 An **event schema** is a directed acyclic graph $G_{Se} = (S_{Se}, L_{Se})$ such that:

1. S_{Se}, the set of schema types, is a subset of $\mathcal{TE}$.
2. L_{Se} is the disjoint union of two sets: L_{Se_A} the fragment link set and L_{Se-IS_A} the IS_A link set.
3. (S_{Se}, L_{Se-A}) is a forest of event fragments.
4. (S_{Se}, L_{Se-IS_A}) follows the two rules: there is no IS_A cycle in the graph and two directed paths of IS_A links sharing the same origin must be extended to a common vertex.

Figure 4 partly shows the IFO$_2$ event schema "Lift", involving three fragments, each one dedicated to a particular aspect of the lift reactions. "Floor-Request" describes the system behaviour when a user request occurs. "Cage-Arrival" is a particular fragment since it is reduced to its heart which is a TES re-used in other fragments. The corresponding method in the structural fragment "Lift" returns the floor reached by the cage. Finally "Satis-Request" is dedicated to the lift behaviour when the cage arrives at the requested floor. These fragments are related by IS_A links through the represented types "Go-Floor", "Arrival-Floor" and "Arrival".

Schema Instance

Definition 18 Let G_{Se} be an event schema composed by p event fragments F_{e1}, $F_{e2},...,F_{ep}$ with $p > 0$. An **instance** of G_{Se}, denoted by $I_{G_{Se}}$, is such that:

1.

$$I_{G_{Se}} = \bigcup_{i=1}^{p}(I_{F_{ei}})$$

where $I_{F_{ei}}$ is the instance of the F_{ei} fragment.

2. If $L_{IS\_A(T_e'-T_e)} \in L_{Se-IS\_A}$, $T_e \in F_{ei}$ and $T_e' \in F_{ej}$ then:
$Evt\_att_{T_e}(I_{F_{ei}}) \subseteq Evt\_att_{T_e'}(I_{F_{ej}})$.

3.8 Satisfaction Fragment

The application behaviour is represented by the event schema. It may be simulated by navigation through the graph, from the root to the leaves, from left to right. An outline of this behaviour consists in a propagation of event triggering. It stops when all the actions reflecting the goal sought by the system, are achieved. These actions

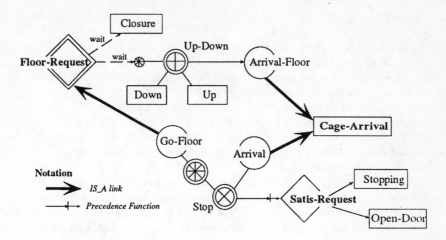

Fig. 4. Part of the IFO₂ event schema "Lift"

are described in the schema, within one or more fragments called satisfaction fragments. The latter have to include a TER. All the events belonging to the IS_A link origin would be satisfied when generated events in the satisfaction fragment occur. This vision has to be refined by taking into account iterations that would possibly be performed during the graph navigation. Iterations aroused by the satisfaction fragment are performed by considering triggering functions which are complex or deferred. The chosen iteration is the first one found along the reverse path.

Definition 19 Let G_{Se} be an event schema composed by p fragments $F_{e1}, F_{e2},...,F_{ep}$ with $p > 0$, let $I_{G_{Se}}$ be the instance of G_{Se} and let $I_{F_{ei}}$ be the F_{ei} instance. A **fragment of satisfaction** F_{ej}_sat for a represented type T_{er} is a G_{Se} fragment such that:

> $T_{er} \in V_{F_{ej}\_sat}$ and $\forall k \in [1..p]$, $k \neq j$, such that the source of T_{er}, T_s, belongs to the fragment F_{ek} with: $\forall e \in Evt\_att_{T_{er}}(I_{F_{ej}}\_sat)$, $Cause(e)^7 \in Tr_{F_{ek}}$.
> The fragment of satisfaction F_{ej}_sat is such that:

$$Evt\_att_{T_s}(J_{F_{ek}}) \subseteq Evt\_att_{T_{er}}(I_{F_{ej}}\_sat).$$

When the represented type is the target of several IS_A links, all the sources have to be taken into account. This is performed by the inclusion of attached events belonging to the types which are IS_A link origins.

In our example, the satisfaction fragment is "Satis-Request", which specifies that each user who requests a floor has to reach it, in the end. Iterations are made to trigger the complex function between "Floor-Request" and "Up-Down" until the requested floor is reached.

---

[7] For each event, the *Cause* function determines its generator event

4 Conclusion

In this paper, we have presented the behavioural part of the IFO$_2$ conceptual model. Its originalities are a "whole-event" approach, the use of constructors to express complex combination of events and the re-usability and modularity of specifications in order to optimize the designer's work. The IFO$_2$ model proposes a twofold specification, structural and behavioural, for application modelling. The advantage of this choice is the uniformity of the resulting approach. We think that such a feature is particularly important on a conceptual level. In the two frameworks, static and dynamic, the designer uses the same fundamental concepts, such as re-usability, modularity, identification, etc.

Links between the two specifications are stated as follows. First of all, basic operations are included in the associated structural schema and are used as simple types in the behavioural description. Object types on which event types operate are specified through the parameter domain concept. Finally, conditions on data may be expressed in the triggering functions.

According to us, a formal model is strongly required to avoid ambiguities particularly in a conceptual context. A rigourous approach must provide real assistance to the designer without constraining him to a tedious learning process. Consequently, it is important to offer him an aid that supports the IFO$_2$ model and guides its intuitive perception. The IFO$_2$ system is currently developped under Unix/X11R5 with the Interviews programming environment developed in C++. It is an extension of the tool presented in [18].

References

1. Directions for future database research and development. *Special Issue of Sigmod Record*, 19(4), December 1990.
2. S. Abiteboul and R. Hull. IFO: A formal semantic database model. *ACM Transactions on Database Systems*, 12(4):525–565, December 1987.
3. M. Bouzeghoub and E. Métais. Semantic modelling of object-oriented databases. In *Proceedings of the 17th International Conference on Very Large Data Bases (VLDB'91)*, pages 3–14, Barcelona, Spain, September 1991.
4. S. Chakravarthy and D. Mishra. Snoop: An expressive event specification language for active databases. Technical report, University of Florida, March 1993.
5. E. Dubois, P. Du Bois, and M. Petit. Elicitating and formalizing requirements for C. I. M. information systems. In *Proceedings of the 5th Internation Conference on Advanced Information Systems Engineering (CAiSE'93)*, Lecture Notes in Computer Science, pages 252–274, June 1993.
6. J. Fiadeiro and A. Sernadas. Specification and verification of database dynamics. *Acta Informatica*, 25:625–661, 1988.
7. N. H. Gehani, H. Jagadish, and O. Shmueli. Event specification in an active object-oriented database. In *Proceedings of the ACM Sigmod Conference*, pages 81–90, San Diego, California, June 1992.
8. R. Hull and R. King. Semantic database modelling: Survey, applications and research issues. *ACM Computer Surveys*, 19(3):201–260, September 1987.
9. P. Loucopoulos and R. Zicari. *Conceptual Modeling, Databases and CASE: An Integrated View of Information Systems Development*. Wiley Professional Computing, 1992.

10. B. Pernici. Objects with roles. In *Proceedings of the Conference on Office Information Systems*, pages 205–215, Cambridge, April 1990.

11. P. Poncelet and L. Lakhal. Consistent structural updates for object-oriented design. In *Proceedings of the 5th International Conference on Advanced Information Systems Engineering (CAiSE'93)*, volume 685 of *Lecture Notes in Computer Science*, pages 1–21, Paris, France, June 1993.

12. P. Poncelet, M. Teisseire, R. Cicchetti, and L. Lakhal. Towards a formal approach for object-oriented database design. In *Proceedings of the 19th International Conference on Very Large Data Bases (VLDB'93)*, pages 278–289, Dublin, Ireland, August 1993.

13. C. Quer and A. Olivé. Object interaction in object-oriented deductive conceptual models. In *Proceedings of the 5th International Conference on Advanced Information Systems Engineering (CAiSE'93)*, volume 685 of *Lecture Notes in Computer Science*, pages 374–396, June 1993.

14. C. Rolland and C. Cauvet. Modélisation conceptuelle orientée objet. In *Actes des 7ièmes Journées Bases de Données Avancées*, pages 299–325, Lyon, France, September 1991.

15. G. Saake. Descriptive specification of database object behaviour. *Data & Knowledge Engineering*, 6:47–73, 1991.

16. A. Sernadas, C. Sernadas, and H. D. Ehrich. Object-oriented specification of databases: An algebraic approach. In *Proceedings of the 13th International Conference on Very Large Data Bases (VLDB'87)*, pages 107–116, Brighton,UK, August 1987.

17. C. Sernadas and J. Fiadeiro. Towards object-oriented conceptual modeling. *Data & Knowledge Engineering*, 6:479–508, 1991.

18. M. Teisseire, P. Poncelet, and R. Cicchetti. A tool based on a formal approach for object-oriented database modeling and design. In *Proceedings of the 6th International Workshop on Computer-Aided (CASE'93)*, IEEE, Singapore, July 1993.

19. R. J. Wieringa. A formalization of objects using equational dynamic logic. In *Proceedings of the 2nd International Conference on Deductive and Object-Oriented Databases (DOOD'91)*, volume 566 of *Lecture Notes in Computer Science*, pages 431–452, Munich, Germany, December 1991.

Representation and Communication in Information Systems - A Speech Act Based Approach

Paul Johannesson

Department of Computer and Systems Sciences
Stockholm University
Electrum 230, S-164 40 Kista, Sweden
email: pajo@sisu.se

Abstract. One of an information system's important roles is to provide a representation of a Universe of Discourse, which reflects its structure and behaviour. An equally important function of the system is to support communication within an organisation by structuring and coordinating the actions performed by the organisation's agents. In many systems development methods, these different roles that an information system assumes are not explicitly separated. Representation techniques appropriate for one role are uncritically applied to another. In this paper, we propose a unifying framework based on speech act theory, which reconciliates the representation and communication roles of information systems. In particular, we show how communication can be modelled by means of discourses, which are viewed as sequences of events.

1 Introduction

There are several different views of the functional role of information systems. Two of the most important are the model view and the communicative action view. According to the model view, the primary purpose of an information system is to provide a model of a Universe of Discourse (UoD), thereby enabling people to obtain information about reality by studying the model. In this respect, an information system works as a passive repository of data that reflects the structure and behaviour of the UoD. In contrast, the communicative action view states that the major role of an information system is to support communication within an organisation by structuring and coordinating the actions performed by the organisation's agents. The system is seen as a medium through which people can perform social actions, such as stating facts, making promises, and giving orders. In certain cases, the system can itself take on the role of an agent and perform actions on its own initiative.

Most representation techniques used in systems development are based on the model view of information systems. For example, Entity-Relationship diagrams are used to represent the static and structural aspects of a UoD. Further examples are entity life cycle diagrams and Jackson Structure diagrams, which describe the behaviour of objects. Another technique, which focuses more on communicative aspects, is the data flow diagram technique by which the information and control flow between agents in an organisation can be represented.

The aim of this paper is to show how the model view and communicative action view of information systems can be reconciliated. For this purpose, we propose a speech act based formalism for describing the structure of communicative action. The graphical representation of this formalism is very similar to data flow diagrams, but in contrast to these it also provides a clear connection with the structural object representation of a UoD, as expressed in a conceptual schema. In the next section, we briefly review the data flow diagram technique and indicate some of its shortcomings when representing communicative action. In section 3, we give an outline of speech act theory. In section 4, we focus on the model view of information systems and present a logic based approach to conceptual modelling. The main results of the paper are given in section 5, where we introduce a formalism for representing communicative action. In the final section, we summarise the paper and suggest some possibilities for further research.

2 Data Flow Diagrams

When trying to understand the information requirements of an organisation, it becomes necessary to conceptualise the way data moves through the enterprise, the processes or transformations that the data undergoes, and what the outputs are. For these purposes, data flow diagrams are used to graphically characterise data processes and flows in an organisation. The data flow diagram is fundamental to structured systems methodologies, such as STRADIS, [Gane79], and was developed as an integrated part of these methodologies. There are four basic concepts in the data flow diagram technique: the data flow, the process, the external agent, and the data store.

One of the most important features of the data flow diagram technique is the ability to construct a variety of levels of data flow diagrams according to the level of abstraction required. An overview diagram can be consulted in order to obtain a high level understanding of a system. Any part of this overview diagram can then be exploded and examined at a more detailed level. The different levels of diagrams must be consistent with each other so that data flows present on the higher levels also exist on the lower levels. In essence it is the processes which are expanded at a greater level of detail as we move down through the levels of a diagram. This hierarchical decomposition process gives the data flow diagram technique its top-down characteristics.

The data flow diagram technique has received wide-spread acceptance and is now an important part of several systems development methodologies. However, the technique has also been heavily criticised, see for example [Buben88], [Coad90], [Auramäki88], [Opdahl93]. One line of critique argues that the basic concepts of data flow diagrams are inappropriate for describing the activities of an organisation. When using data flow diagrams, an enterprise is viewed as a collection of physical places or objects, and the work performed is accordingly analysed as physical activities such as sending and storing data. This focus on the physical transfer of data results in a computer and technology biased representation of the communication taking place in an organisation. Thus, the very starting point of the data flow diagram technique is itself flawed and should be replaced by an approach that focuses on the communicative actions of an enterprise.

Another critique pertains to the hierarchical decomposition of data flow diagrams. One problem here is that of knowing how to decompose a diagram and in particular when to stop the decomposition process. A practical rule of thumb is that the decomposition should end before the diagram becomes too cluttered. However, with the arrival of CASE tools and their ability to suppress details this answer is not especially helpful. Another objection to the hierarchical decomposition approach is that the modelling of complex interaction and behaviour cannot be carried out in a top-down fashion. In general, it is not clear at the top stages of decomposition what kinds of activities to include in a process. Instead, the analysis process has to proceed in a combined bottom-up and top-down fashion. Still another problem is that the relationship between data flow diagrams and semantic data models is not clear, although some work on this issue has appeared during the last years, [Kung89], [Batini91]. An important aim of this paper is to show how the critique outlined above can be answered. We do this by providing a bridge between semantic data models and data flow diagrams and by reinterpreting the concept of a process using speech act theory.

3 Speech Act Theory

An important feature of language is that it can serve purposes other than that of representing the states of affairs of the world. Certain statements are equivalent to actions. For example, when someone says "I apologise", "I promise...", or "I name this ship...", the utterance immediately conveys a new psychological or social reality. An apology takes place only when someone admits having been at fault, and a ship is named only when the act of naming is complete. In such cases, to speak is to perform. Statements such as those above are called *performatives* or *speech acts,* and they make it possible to use language as a means both for acting and for coordinating action. The study of speech acts has been an active research area in analytical philosophy since World War II, and the most influential approach to date is *speech act theory* as developed by John Searle, [Searle69], [Searle86]. Searle proposes a taxonomy for speech acts consisting of five classes: assertives, commissives, directives, declaratives, and expressives. These are also called the *illocutionary points* of a speech act.

An *assertive* is a speech act, the purpose of which is to convey information about some state of affairs of the world from one agent, the speaker, to another, the hearer. Examples of assertives are "It is raining" and "The cat is on the mat". A *commissive* is a speech act, the purpose of which is to commit the speaker to carry out some action or to bring about some state of affairs. Examples of commissives are "I promise to be at home before nine o'clock" and "I swear to bring it back". A *directive* is a speech act, where the speaker requests the hearer to carry out some action or to bring about some state of affairs. Examples of directives are "Please bring me the salt" and "I order you to leave the room". A *declarative* is a speech act, where the speaker brings about some state of affairs by the mere performance of the speech act. Examples of declaratives are "I hereby pronounce you man and wife" and "I hereby baptise you to Samuel". An *expressive* is a speech act, the purpose of which is to express the speaker's attitude about some state of affairs.

Searle makes a distinction between elementary and complex speech acts. An *elementary* speech act has the form F(P), where F is the illocutionary point and P is the propositional content of the act. Different speech acts may have the same propositional content but different illocutionary points. For example, the assertive "You are going to leave the room" and the directive "I order you to leave the room" both have the same propositional content, but their illocutionary points differ. There are also *complex* speech acts of which the two most important forms are the denegated speech act and the conditional speech act. A *denegated* speech act has the form ¬F(P). This expresses that the speaker is not prepared to perform the speech act F(P); for example "I do not promise to come". A *conditional* speech act has the form p → F(P). This expresses that the speaker will perform the speech act if some condition is fulfilled; for example "If it rains, I will go to the cinema with you".

Most speech acts can only be successful if certain conditions hold. For example, a promise is successfully made only if the speaker is able to carry out the promised act and this act is in the interest of the hearer. Similarly if a speaker apologises he presupposes that the thing he apologises for is bad or reprehensible. Conditions that in this way are necessary for the performance of a speech act are called *preparatory conditions.* They can be thought of as certain sorts of states of affairs that have to prevail in order for a speech act to be successful.

There are a few contributions in the literature on the application of speech act theory to information systems. Flores et. al. have developed a speech act based tool, the Coordinator, which is used to coordinate communicative action within an organisation in the context of collaborative work, [Flores88]. The Coordinator is primarily intended to support semiformal and informal communication. Auramäki, Lehtinen, and Lyytinen have proposed a modelling approach based on speech acts called SAMPO, which studies office activities as a series of speech acts creating, maintaining, modifying, reporting, and terminating commitments, [Auramäki88]. They introduce the concept of a discourse, as a sequence of speech acts, and suggest some graphical notations for representing discourse types. Dietz has proposed a novel approach to process modelling based on speech acts, called the Essential Process Model, in which essential business activities are clearly separated from non-essential, i.e., informative, activities, [Dietz92]. The approach presented in this paper is in many respects similar to that of SAMPO. One difference, however, is that we attempt to provide a clear connection between models of communicative action and conceptual schemas representing the structure and behaviour of a UoD. Further, we do not propose any completely new graphical notation for discourse types. Instead, we try to keep the notation as close as possible to ordinary data flow diagrams and show how the constructs of data flow diagrams can be reinterpreted using speech act theory.

4 Conceptual Schemas

In this section, we attempt a formalisation of some of the basic notions in conceptual modelling. We first recall some definitions concerning first order languages. Let Pr and C be two sets of symbols. A *(first order) language based on <Pr,C>*, written $L(Pr,C)$ is defined on an alphabet consisting of connectives, quantifiers, punctuation symbols, variables, constants C, and predicate symbols Pr, where each predicate symbol has an arity. A *term* is a constant or a variable. A (first order) *formula* in a language L is defined as usual. An *atom* is a formula of the form $p(t_1,...,t_n)$, where p is a predicate symbol and $t_1,...,t_n$ are terms. A *literal* is an atom or a negated atom. A *ground formula* is a formula without variables. For any language $L(Pr,C)$ we assume that Pr contains a special symbol, "=", which is interpreted as the identity.

We now introduce some notions for describing the behaviour of a UoD. These will be based on the assumption that the dynamics of an application can be modelled through events which are grouped together in event types.

Definition 4.1: An *update operation* is a formula of one of the following forms:
- insert(L), where L is a positive literal
- delete(L), where L is a positive literal
A *ground update operation* is an update operation, in which all terms are ground.
A *symbol generator* is a formula of the form "new(S)", where S is a variable.

Definition 4.2: An *event type* is a triple <P, Pre, Post>, where
P is a set of variables, called the *input variables* of the event type. Pre is a conjunction of literals. Post is a list of update operations and symbol generators, and the variables in Post constitute a subset of those in P and Pre. Pre is called the *preconditions* of the event type and Post the *post conditions*. We shall sometimes use the following notation for event types: "**if** Pre **then** Post", leaving P implicit.

A fundamental notion in conceptual modelling is that of the conceptual schema, which is usually informally defined as an implementation independent description of the contents in an information system.

Definition 4.3: A *conceptual schema* is a triple <L, IC, ET>, where L is a language, IC is a finite set of closed formulas, called *integrity constraints*, and ET is a set of event types. It is assumed that all predicate symbols in L are either unary or binary, and that for each binary predicate symbol p there is an integrity constraint in the form:

$\forall x \forall y (p(x,y) \rightarrow p1(x) \wedge p2(y))$. p1 is called the *domain* of p, and p2 the *range* of p.

The unary predicate symbols are called *object types* and the binary ones are called *attributes*.

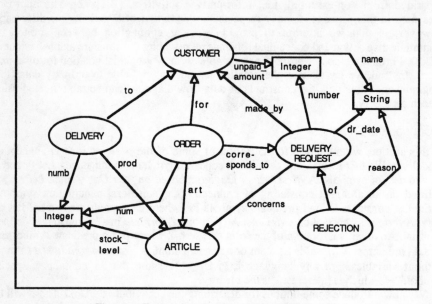

Fig. 4.1 Example of a Conceptual Schema

Example 4.1: In fig. 4.1, a graphical representation of a conceptual schema is shown. Note that the graph only depicts a part of the language of the schema and some integrity constraints. The graph shows that the schema contains eight object types {customer, delivery, delivery_request, rejection, order, article, integer, string} and sixteen attributes, displayed as labeled arcs. The graph also shows a number of integrity constraints, e.g., $\forall x \forall y (\text{made\_by}(x,y) \rightarrow \text{delivery\_request}(x) \wedge \text{customer}(y))$. Object types containing data values are shown in the graph as rectangles, in this case "String" and "Integer".

Example 4.2: Continuing example 4.1, we give three examples of event types, which will be used throughout this paper. We use the convention of beginning variables with a capital letter.

make_delivery_request:
<{Customer, Article, Number, Date},
Ø,
[new(DR), insert(delivery_request(DR)), insert(made_by(DR, Customer)),
insert(concerns(DR, Article)), insert(number(DR, Number)), insert(dr_date(DR, Date))]>

make_order:
<{Customer, Article, Number, Del_request},
{stock_level(Article, S) ∧ S > Number,
unpaid_amount(Customer,Up) ∧ Up < 50000}
[new(O), insert(order(O)), insert(corresponds_to(O, Del_request)), insert(art(O, Article)),
insert(num(O, Number)), insert(for(O, Customer))]>

rejection:
<Del_request, Reason>,
∅,
[new(R), insert(rejection(R)), insert(of(R, Del_request)), insert(reason(R, Reason)).

We now turn to the definition of an information base; informally an information base contains information about particular entities and the associations between these.

Definition 4.4: An *information base* for a Conceptual Schema <L, IC, ET> is a pair <C, F>, where C is a finite set of constants, and F is a finite set of ground atoms.

Example 4.3: An example of an information base for the schema in Fig. 4.1 is:

customer(c1)	name(c1,'Jones')	customer(c2)	name(c2,'Smith')
delivery(d1)	to(d1,c1)	numb(d1,100)	
article(a1)	prod(d1,a1)	stock_level(a1,5000)	

The role of integrity constraints is to state conditions that must hold for each information base.

Definition 4.5: Let CS = <L, IC, ET> be a conceptual schema and IB = <C, F> an information base for CS. The information base IB *violates* the schema CS if not (F |= IC).

Now we can give the semantics for event types. Intuitively, the idea is that when an event occurs in the UoD, it will be reported by submitting an event message. Based on the event message, the event type, and the present information base, a new information base will be computed. First, the preconditions are checked, and if they are satisfied in the present information base, a new information base is derived by applying the post conditions. If the preconditions are not satisfied, no updates will be performed. Informally, the semantics of the predicate symbol "new" is to generate a new constant that has not been used before.

Definition 4.6: An *event occurrence* is a pair <E, S> where E = <P, Pre, Post> is an event type and S is a ground substitution that binds each variable in P.

Definition 4.7: A *transaction* is a formula of the form
if $\alpha_1,...,\alpha_n$ then $p_1;...;p_m$,
where the α_is are ground literals and the p_is are ground update operations or symbol generators. A transaction is *expressible in a language* L if all literals in the transaction are expressed in L.

Definition 4.8: Let CS = <L, IC, ET> be a conceptual schema. We define a function μ: $IB_{CS} \times T_{CS} \to IB_{CS}$, where IB_{CS} is the set of all information bases for CS and T_{CS} is the set of all transactions expressible in L.

Let IB = <C, F>. We define μ recursively:

μ(IB, **if** $\alpha_1,...,\alpha_n$ **then** p_1) = IB if not (F $\models \alpha_1 \wedge ... \wedge \alpha_n$)

  = IB' if F $\models \alpha_1 \wedge ... \wedge \alpha_n$, where

IB' = <C $\cup$ {A_C}, F $\cup$ {A}> if p_1 = insert(A)

IB' = <C, F - {A}> if p_1 = delete(A)

IB' = IB if p_1 = new(S)

(A_C is the set of constants appearing in the formula A.)

μ(IB, **if** $\alpha_1,...,\alpha_n$ **then** $p_1;...;p_m$) = IB if not (F $\models \alpha_1 \wedge ... \wedge \alpha_n$)

  = μ(IB', **if true then** $p_2;...;p_m$)

  otherwise, where IB' is defined as above.

Definition 4.9: Let CS = <L, IC, ET> be a conceptual schema. Let IB_{CS} be the set of all information bases for CS, and EO the set of all event occurrences for event types in ET.

Define a function Perform$_{CS}$: EO $\times$ IB_{CS} $\to$ IB_{CS}, by

(<<P,Pre,Post>, Θ >, IB) $\mapsto$ μ(IB, **if** Pre[Ψ] **then** Post[Ψ]), if there exists a unique
extension Ψ of Θ such that F $\models$ Pre[Ψ], (IB = <C, F>)

  $\mapsto$ IB, otherwise

The approach to modelling dynamics that we have chosen has certain limitations compared to some of the more advanced approaches in the literature, such as that of LDL, [Naqvi89]. For example, in definition 4.9, we require the existence of a unique extension of the incoming event message, while other approaches may accept several extensions. Further, we do not attempt to formalise the behavioural aspects of a conceptual schema within the framework of a logic formalism, such as dynamic logic. However, the approach above has the advantage of capturing our intuitions about the event concept in a simple way, and it is sufficient to serve as a vehicle for analysing the relationship between semantic data models and communicative action modelling.

Example 4.4: Let CS be the conceptual schema from Fig 4.1, let IB be the information base in example 4.3, and let Eo be the event occurrence <make_delivery_request, {Customer/c1, Article/a1, Number/25, Date/930601}>.
Then, Perform$_{CS}$(Eo,IB) is the following information base:

customer(c1)	name(c1,'Jones')	customer(c2)	name(c2,'Smith')
delivery(d1)	to(d1,c1)	numb(d1,100)	article(a1)
prod(d1,a1)	stock_level(a1,5000)	delivery_request(dr1).	
made_by(dr1,c1)	concerns(dr1,a1)	number(dr1,25)	dr_date(d1,930601)

By means of the event concept it is possible to describe the dynamics of a UoD. However, describing the dynamics using only event types has the limitation that the interrelationships among various event types are not made explicit. There is no way of specifying that certain events must precede or usually precede other events, or that the occurrence of certain events excludes the occurrence of others, etc. To represent these types of interrelationships among events, we need to put an additional structure on top of the event types. In the next section, we propose such a structure for the special case of events corresponding to communicative actions.

5 Discourse Structures

We will now present a speech act based formalism for the description of control and information flow in communicative action. Our point of departure is that the event types in the conceptual schema that correspond to communicative actions should be organised by so called discourse structures. A discourse structure is a graph that displays the form of a dialogue, or discourse, between two or more agents. We make the assumption that for each type of discourse, there is a unique organisational unit (department, person etc.) responsible for that type of discourse. The basic concept of the formalism is that of a speech act, formally defined as below.

Definition 5.1: Let CS(L, IC, ET) be a conceptual schema. A *speech act* is a quintuple <IllPoint, Speaker, Hearer, PrepCond, PropCont>, where Illpoint $\in$ {assertive, commissive, directive, declarative}, Speaker and Hearer are either object types in CS or the special symbol "unit", PrepCond is a set of formulas in L, and PropCont is a formula in L. A *speech move* is a set of speech acts.

In definition 5.1, we require that the hearer and speaker of a speech act are explicitly modelled as types in the conceptual schema, except for the case where the speaker or hearer is the organizational unit responsible for the discourse in which the speech act takes place - in the latter case the symbol "unit" is used. This requirement is a deviation from current practice in conceptual modelling, where the agents in the environment of an information system are often omitted from the conceptual schema. However, including these agents in the schema is an important means of relating the conceptual schema to the modelling of communicative action.

The component PrepCond in the definition of a speech act specifies the preparatory conditions, and PropCont the propositional content. The formula PropCont is to describe some state of affairs. In the case of an assertion, the speaker asserts that this state of affairs prevails. In the case of a commissive, he commits himself to bring about this state of affairs. In the case of a directive, he requests another agent to bring it about, and in the case of a declarative, he brings it about simply by performing the speech act. In the graphical notation we are going to use, a speech act is displayed as a rounded box with six compartments, as shown in fig. 5.1. The meaning of the contents in the top compartment is explained below; the other compartments correspond to the five components of a speech act. In the example of fig. 5.1, the speaker requests the hearer to create a situation where a certain delivery to the hearer has been performed.

We also introduce the concept of a speech move. The motivation for this concept is that certain speech acts are always performed simultaneously and therefore constitute a natural unit, or move, in a discourse. An example of a speech move is the borrowing of a book at a library, where two speech acts are performed at the same time. First, the library performs a declarative, allowing the borrower to have the book at his disposal for a certain period of time. Secondly, the borrower performs a commissive, promising to return the book within a certain time limit.

We now turn to the question of how to represent the structure of discourses. An adequate representation must provide the means of expressing both the control flow and the information flow between the speech moves of a discourse. When exchanging speech acts, the agents can often choose between several alternatives at each particular point of the discourse. Consequently, it is necessary to be able to model the control flow and the rules that govern the choices being made by the agents. Further, objects introduced by one agent in a certain speech move may be referred to by the same or another agent in subsequent speech moves of the discourse. Thus, it must be possible to represent the flow of information between speech moves. In the following definition, we introduce the concept of a discourse structure.

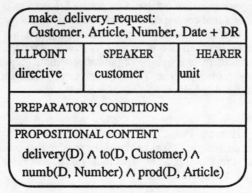

make_delivery_request: Customer, Article, Number, Date + DR		
ILLPOINT directive	SPEAKER customer	HEARER unit
PREPARATORY CONDITIONS		
PROPOSITIONAL CONTENT delivery(D) ∧ to(D, Customer) ∧ numb(D, Number) ∧ prod(D, Article)		

Fig 5.1 Example of a speech act

Definition 5.2: A *control statement* is a closed formula.

Definition 5.3: Let CS = <L, IC, E> be a conceptual schema. A *discourse structure* is a quadruple <D, V, ϕ, ψ>, where D is a directed graph <N, A>, and N = SM∪ CT is a set of speech moves and control statements, and A is a set of arcs. V: A → $(2^{Var}$ ∪ {true, false}) is a function, where Var is the set of variables in L. ϕ: SM → E is an injective function. ψ: SM → T is an injective function, where T are the types in L. A discourse structure must satisfy the following conditions:

(i) For each s in SM, ϕ(s) includes the postconditions "new(Y), insert(ψ(s)(Y))"

(ii) For each s in SM, pre(ϕ(s)) = ∪ {prep(sa) | sa ∈ s}, where prep and pre are functions returning the preparatory conditions of a speech act, and the preconditions of an event, respectively

(iii) For any arc a from n_1 to n_2, V(a) ⊂ Var(ϕ(n_1)) if n_1 ∈ SM, and V(a) ⊂ Arg(ϕ(n_2)) if n_2 ∈ SM, where Var is a function returning the set of all variables in an event type, and Arg is a function returning the input variables of an event type

(iv) For any c in CT, there is a path from c to an s in SM such that s contains an sa with c ∈ prep(sa)

(v) For each c in CT, there are exactly two arcs leaving c, one of them labelled "true", the other "false"

A *basic discourse structure* is a discourse structure, where all nodes are speech moves.

The functions ϕ and ψ specify the relationships between a conceptual schema and a discourse structure. For each speech move, there must exist a unique corresponding object type in the conceptual schema - this is given by the function ψ. Thus, all speech moves must be explicitly modelled in the schema. Similarly, for each speech move there must exist a unique corresponding event type - this is given by ϕ. Further, condition (i) states that at each occurrence of this event type, an object corresponding to the speech move must be created. In this way, a record is kept of all speech moves occurring. Note that the functions ϕ and ψ are not surjective; there may well exist event types and object types that do not correspond to any speech move. Condition (ii) requires that the preparatory conditions of a speech move be equal to the preconditions of the corresponding event type. The information flow in a discourse is expressed by means of the variables associated with the arcs, and condition (iii) states that a variable may occur on an arc only if it has been introduced in one speech move and is later to be used in another. The control flow in a discourse is represented by the control statements of a discourse structure. Condition (iv) places a restriction on which control statements may occur in a discourse structure: each control statement must be equal to a preparatory condition in a subsequent speech move. Informally, the purpose of condition (v) is to express that if a control statement is true, then the discourse is to continue along the arc labelled "true" and otherwise along the arc labelled "false". In the graphical notation, see fig. 5.1, the topmost compartment contains the name of the event type corresponding to the speech move and its input variables. Further, the new variable referred to in condition (i) is specified after the "+" sign, thereby providing a handle to the speech move.

When constructing a discourse structure, one possible starting point is to construct a basic discourse structure containing only speech moves that shows the basic and typical form of the discourse. This discourse structure can then be expanded by adding control statements corresponding to preparatory conditions in the speech moves and specifying which actions to undertake when a preparatory condition is not satisfied. In this way, a discourse structure can be systematically expanded until no more control statements can be added. In the definition below, we introduce the term "extended discourse structure" to denote a discourse structure that cannot be extended any further.

Definition 5.4: An *extended discourse structure* $<D, V, \phi, \psi>$, where $D = <SM \cup CT, A>$ is a discourse structure where for each preparatory condition P occurring in some speech act in SM, there exists a $c \in CT$ such that $P = c$, and there is a path from c to the speech move in which P occurs.

In fig. 5.2, a basic discourse structure is shown. The first speech act is the same as the one in fig. 5.1, whereas the second is a promise by the speaker to deliver an article to the hearer, thereby satisfying the request of the preceding speech act. This discourse structure is extended in fig. 5.3 by including two control statements, which check whether the stock level is sufficient and that the customer's debt is not too large. If these conditions are not satisfied, the customer's request is rejected and an assertive is performed telling the customer why.

We are now in a position to define the term "discourse" precisely as a sequence of speech move occurrences that satisfy certain conditions.

Definition 5.5: Let $DS = <D, V, \phi, \psi>$ be a discourse structure. A *discourse according to DS* is a sequence of event occurrences $<e_1,s1>,...,<e_n,s_n>$ such that there exists a path through D containing a subsequence of speech moves $m_1,...,m_n$, where $\phi(m_i) = e_i$, and if the same variable occurs in two substitutions s_i and s_j, $i \neq j$, and on some arc of the path, it must be bound to the same constant in each substitution.

Definition 5.6: Let DS be a discourse structure and $D = <e_1,s1>,...,<e_n,s_n>$ a discourse according to DS. Let I be a non-violating information base. D is *successful* in I if

(i) Perform($\langle e_i, s_i\rangle$, B_i) does not violate CS for $i = 1,...,n$, where B_i = Perform($\langle e_{i-1}, s_{i-1}\rangle$, B_{i-1}) and $B_0 = I$

(ii) The preconditions of the event type e_i are satisfied in Perform($\langle e_{i-1}, s_{i-1}\rangle$, B_{i-1}), $i = 2,...,n$, and B_i is defined as above

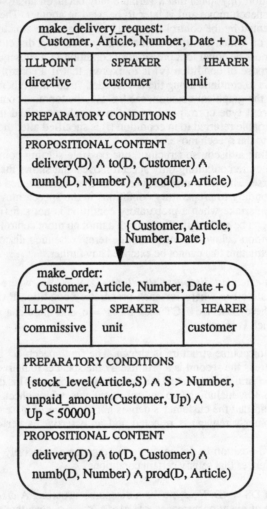

Fig. 5.2 A basic discourse structure

We will now introduce a completeness requirement that should be satisfied by each discourse structure. When an agent has performed a directive, this should be taken care of by the hearer in a subsequent step of the discourse. The directive can be handled in three different ways. First, the hearer can perform a commissive with the same propositional content as the directive, i.e., the hearer promises to do what the speaker requested. Secondly, the hearer can immediately fulfil the request of the speaker by performing a declarative with the same propositional content as the speaker's directive. Thirdly, the hearer can reject the speaker's request, and in that case he should give a reason for the rejection. Usually, the reason is that he could not perform an appropriate commissive or declarative because some preparatory condition was not satisfied.

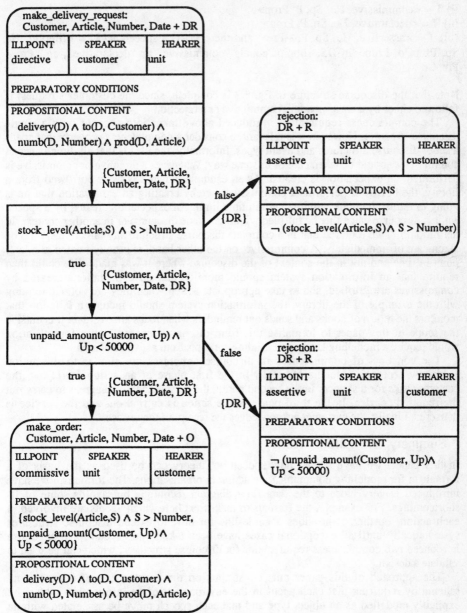

Fig. 5.3 An extended and complete discourse structure

Definition 5.7: A discourse structure DS is *complete* if for any speech act S = <directive, Sp, He, Prep, Prop> in DS there exists a speech act T in DS, there is a path from S to T, and T has one of the following forms:

(i) T = <commissive, He, Sp, P, Prop>

(ii) T = <declarative, He, Sp, P, Prop>

(iii) T = <assertive, He, Sp, P, ¬Pre>, and there exists a speech act U = <Illpoint, He, Sp, PrepCo, Prop> in DS, Illpoint equals "commissive" or "declarative", and Pre ∈ PrepCo

Note that the discourse structure in fig. 5.3 is complete, since the customer's request is followed either by a corresponding commissive or a rejection.

The completeness requirement introduced above takes into account only a single discourse structure. However, it is relevant to consider a completeness property that spans a set of discourse structures and event types. Informally, the idea is that all directives and commissives should be taken care of in some way. Whenever a directive or commissive is performed, an expectation is created. As an example, when a book is borrowed from a library, the borrower performs a commissive thereby creating an expectation that he is going to return the book within a certain time limit. An expectation created by a speech act in a discourse can either be fulfilled within the same discourse or in another context. In definition 5.7, we required that in a complete discourse structure any directive should be taken care of immediately. A commissive, on the other hand, is usually treated at a later point in time and not in the context of the discourse where it was made. We could then require that an information system should monitor that all expectations created by commissives are fulfilled, and to take appropriate action when they are not. Continuing with the example of the library, the information system should include a function that monitors the return of books and sends out reminders when loans are overdue. It is outside the scope of this paper to formalise this form of completeness. Such a formalisation would require a modelling language including concepts from active databases.

The concepts of completeness in discourse structures are similar to the action workflow protocol, [Medina-Mora92]. In the first phase of an action workflow, the customer asks for a service. In the second phase, the person addressed agrees to carry out the required service. In the third phase, some action is carried out and the service is delivered. Finally, the customer acknowledges the receipt of the service.

6 Summary and Further Work

In this paper, we have shown how speech act theory can be used as the basis of a formalism for modelling communicative action in organisations. The formalism we have introduced is very close to the data flow diagram technique but avoids some of its shortcomings. For example, the formalism makes explicit which agents are involved in each action. Further, it provides a guide-line for how to extend discourse structures systematically until all exceptional cases have been taken into account. We have also introduced two completeness requirements for discourse structures, which can be used to validate a design.

The approach of this paper puts constraints on the construction of a conceptual schema by requiring that each agent in the environment of an information system be explicitly modelled as an object type and that each speech move be associated with an object type. By following these requirements, one obtains a conceptual schema that is closely related to the model of the communicative processes. In definition 5.3, we assumed that a conceptual schema should already exist when describing a discourse structure. An interesting observation, however, is that it is possible, almost automatically, to construct a conceptual schema from an informally described discourse structure, [Holm93].

The approach presented in this paper represents only a beginning, and much work remains to be done. First, we need to consider also complex speech acts in order to model discourses more accurately. For example, in section 5 we modelled a rejection of a directive as an assertive, but it would have been more correct to represent it as a denegated commissive or declarative. As another example, a request may be answered not only by an acceptance or a rejection, but also by a counteroffer, which should be modelled as a conditional commissive.

Another issue concerns the form of the propositional content of a speech act. In this paper, we have assumed that the propositional content is a formula in the language of a conceptual schema. However, this may be unsatisfactory, since commissives and declaratives are almost invariably associated with some time restriction and this is not reflected in the propositional content. (The most typical time restriction is for some action to be performed by a specified date.) It would therefore be desirable to include a mechanism for representing time in speech acts explicitly. One possible approach here could be to use a temporal conceptual modelling language.

References

[Auramäki88] E. Auramäki, E. Lehtinen and K. Lyytinen, "A Speech-Act Based Office Modelling Approach", *ACM Transactions on Office Information Systems*, vol. 6, no. 2, pp. 126 - 152, 1988.

[Batini91] C. Batini, S. Ceri and S. Navathe, *Conceptual Database Design*, Benjamin/Cummings, 1991.'

[Buben88] J. A. Bubenko Jr., "Problems and Unclear Issues with Hierarchical Business Activity and Data Flow Modelling", SYSLAB Working Paper no. 134, The Royal Institute of Technology and the University of Stockholm, 1988.

[Coad90] E. Coad and D. Yourdon, *Object Oriented Analysis and Design*, Addison-Wesley, 1990.

[Dietz92] J. Dietz, "Modelling Communication in Organizations", in *Linguistic Instruments in Knowledge Engineering*, Ed. R. v. d. Riet, pp. 131 - 142, Elsevier Science Publishers, 1992.

[Flores88] F. Flores, M. Graves, B. Hartfield and T. Winograd, "Computer Systems and the Design of Organizational Interaction", *ACM Transactions on Office Information Systems*, vol. 6, no. 2, pp. 153-172, 1988.

[Gane79] C. Gane and T. Sarson, *Structured Systems Analysis: Tools ans Techniques*, Prentice-Hall, 1979.

[Holm93] Peter Holm, Swedish Institute of Systems Development, Personal Communication

[Kung89] C. H. Kung, "Conceptual Modeling in the Context of Software Development", *IEEE Transactions on Software Engineering*, vol. 15, no. 10, pp. 1176 ff., 1989.

[Medina-Mora92] R. Medina-Mora et.al., "The Action Workflow Approach to Workflow management Technology", *4th CSCW Conference*, Toronto, 1989.

[Naqvi89] S. Naqvi and S. Tsur, *A Logical Language for Data and Knowledge Bases*, Computer Science Press, 1989.

[Opdahl93] A. Opdahl and G. Sindre, "Concepts for Real-World Modelling, *5th International Conference on Advanced Information Systems Engineering*, Ed. C. Rolland, Paris, Springer, 1993.

[Searle69] J. Searle, *Speech Acts - An Essay in the Philosophy of Language*, Cambrudge University Press, 1969.

[Searle86] J. Searle and D. Vanderveken, *Foundations of Illocutionary Logic*, Cambridge University Press, 1986.

From Analysis to Code Generation: Experiences from an Information Engineering Project Using I-CASE Technology

Karl Kurbel

University of Muenster, Institute of Business Informatics,
Grevener Strasse 91, D-48167 Muenster, Germany

Abstract. Development of a large information system, following the Information Engineering approach by James Martin, is described. Knowledge-Ware's Application Development Workbench (ADW) was used as I-CASE (Integrated CASE) environment. The 3½-person-year project went all the way from analysis to code generation. Within the project, 160,000 lines of code were successfully generated; the final system is expected to amount to 330,000 lines. The information system is probably one of the first ones of such size that was actually generated with ADW for an OS/2 target environment. The paper gives an outline of the project and reports on experiences with I-CASE technology. The project was part of advanced business-informatics education at Muenster university.

1 Computer-aided Information Engineering

In this paper, a medium-size project following James Martin's approach to Information Engineering (IE) is described. Both Information Engineering methodology and corresponding integrated CASE tools were applied. The goal of the project was to develop an information system (IS) that supports administrative work of a fairly large university institute.

Information Engineering as introduced by James Martin looks at the organization as a whole. According to Martin, Information Engineering stands for "the application of an interlocking set of formal techniques for the planning, analysis, design, and construction of information systems on an enterprise-wide basis or across a major sector of the enterprise" ([4], p. 1). The comprehensive Information Engineering view covers all stages of IS planning and development, starting from strategic planning down to technical construction of programs and data structures. It also means that the focus is not (only) on a particular information system, but on enterprise-wide information processing as a whole. Finally, separate views of information systems are integrated: data, functions, and processes are analyzed and modelled within a unique framework.

Information Engineering consists of four main stages: *Information Strategy Planning* is the top stage where strategic goals, critical success factors, and informa-

215

tion requirements of major parts of the enterprise are determined. The result of Information Strategy Planning is a global model of the enterprise and its division into business areas. On the second level, *Business Area Analysis* is performed within one or more major sectors of the enterprise. Data models (e.g. entity-relationship diagrams), process models (e.g. decomposition diagrams) and other models are developed, and desirable information systems within the business areas are defined. *System Design* is the third level where procedures, data structures, screen layouts, windows, reports, etc. are specified. On the fourth level called *Construction*, programs and data structures are implemented, tested, and integrated. Figure 1 shows a pyramid view of the stages as presented by James Martin.

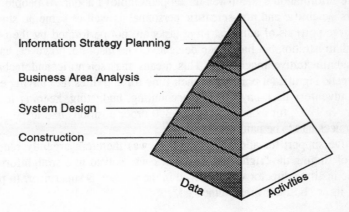

Fig. 1: Stages of Information Engineering according to Martin [4]

Information Engineering requires integrated CASE support for all stages. One of the objectives is to generate code automatically. Tool integration is to be achieved by a common repository, the so-called *encyclopedia*. All information collected during the stages of Information Engineering is transformed into a common representation format, and stored in the encyclopedia.

Although there is quite a number of integrated CASE (I-CASE) tools (see [12] for a survey, for example), only two of them support the comprehensive Information Engineering approach so far: ADW (Application Development Workbench) by KnowledgeWare [2] and IEF (Information Engineering Facility) by TI Information Engineering [13]. Both have been used to develop mainframe-oriented applications in practice [8, 10, 12]. However, little has been reported on workstation LANs as target environments yet. In this paper, we set the focus on the workstation level and describe our experiences with ADW in such an environment.

2 What are the "Business Areas" of a University Institute?

The Information Engineering approach is tailored to meet the requirements of enterprises and does not lend itself naturally to bureaucratic organizations like German universities. Information strategy planning with regard to strategic goals and critical success factors would certainly have been a challenging task, but it was beyond the scope of our project. Therefore, only some global relations were considered and modelled, and the business areas to be analyzed later were defined during this stage.

At first glance, "teaching", "research", and "administration" might be considered "business areas" of a university institute. A closer look reveals, however, that only formal aspects of research lend themselves to analysis and modelling, whereas administration is a very complex field that needs to be split up in several business areas.

The Institute of Business Informatics at Muenster university in Germany for which the information system was developed employs about 70 people (including professors, scientific and non-scientific personnel as well as some 30 student assistants). Large portions of administrative tasks are not performed by the central university administration but have been delegated. The institute, however, has no comparable administrative machinery. This means that scientific and technical staff have to spend significant portions of their time for activities like buying equipment, updating inventory lists, paying bills, accounting, budgeting, keeping leave books, and so on. In 1992, for example, about 3,300 order positions had to be booked and 1,840 invoices had to be paid.

Effective support for administrative tasks was therefore urgently required. The problem of finding the "right" tasks to attack was solved in a straightforward manner, as the institute director was involved in the project as supervisor. In pre-project planning, three "business areas" emerged:

Budgeting and Purchasing

Administration of financial means on the one hand, and preparations of purchases (hardware, software, furniture, books, etc.) on the other hand are the most time-consuming tasks, involving about 15 people throughout the institute. Different procedures apply, depending on where the funds come from (state, foundations, enterprises, etc.), whether they are assigned to the institute as a whole or to individual professors, and what their intended appropriations are. Accounts correspond to those determinants. Purchases are closely related with accounts. For example, reservations have to be made when procurement orders are placed; they have to be confirmed when goods are delivered and finally booked when invoices are paid. Therefore budgeting and purchasing are based on the same data model.

Resources Management

Resources to be administered are chairs, projects, persons, posts, hardware, software, rooms, keys, etc. A large number of connections between them - some of them rather sophisticated - have to be considered. For example, hardware configurations - which monitors, boards, disks, etc. belong to which computers? - are treated as relationships between hardware components. Some procedures depending on resources data are: updating inventory lists, leave books, and lists of official tours, assigning office rooms to persons and lecture rooms to courses or other events, etc.

Teaching

"Teaching" as a business area does not refer to contents of courses, but to operational and administrative activities: Announcements of lectures, catalogs of lectures, tables of contents, handling of admission requirements, textbook lists; distribution, collection, and marking of exercises, grades, certificates, etc. Exercises including computer-work may require assigning students to computer pools, workstations, and times.

3 Information Engineering Environment

As to computer support, KnowledgeWare's I-CASE environment ADW (Application Development Workbench), version 1.6, was employed. ADW is the OS/2 version and successor of IEW (Information Engineering Workbench). The tools of ADW are grouped into four categories corresponding to the four stages of Information Engineering:

Planning Workstation
Analysis Workstation
Design Workstation
Construction Workstation

These workstations run under OS/2, whereas target environments are primarily IBM mainframes under MVS. Since 1992, OS/2-based PCs as target environment are also supported. Major tools of ADW are:

Decomposition Diagrammer (for hierarchical structures)
Entity Relationsship Diagrammer (for data modelling)
Data Flow Diagrammer (for specification of data flows)
Association Matrix Diagrammer (to represent relationships between encyclopedia objects)
Minispec Action Diagrammer (to describe procedural logic)
GUI Layout Diagrammer (for interface design and generation of Cobol source code)
Structure Chart Diagrammer (to define module hierarchies)
Module Action Diagrammer (for detail specification of procedural logic)
Relational Database Diagrammer (for database design)
Data Structure Diagrammer (to specify data structures, records, and relations)
GUI Code Generator (to specify database access and generate Cobol source code)

These tools are highly interconnected as shown in figure 2. Unfortunately, I-CASE means here also that *all* the tools have to be employed, and that the user has to know all the connections and dependencies depicted in the figure. Tools are integrated by means of an *encyclopedia*. Objects of the information model that were generated and stored in the encyclopedia by one tool can be read by other tools. Sometimes different tools may be employed to generate objects of a certain type. Figure 2 indicates this kind of relation by double-headed arrows. In two cases, integration has to be achieved by auxiliary functions (broken lines). For example, the Relational Database Diagrammer does not process objects of an entity-relationship diagram directly, but requires transformation into a so-called "first-cut model" by means of a generating function first.

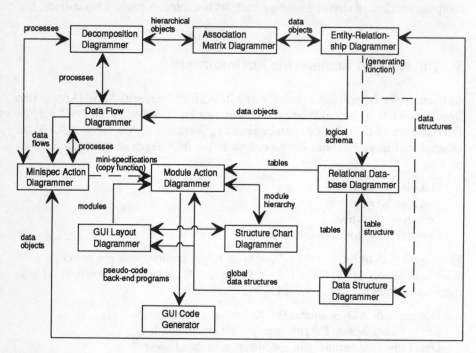

Fig. 2: Connections between ADW tools

The hardware and software environment for the project was a Novell network where ten PCs (80486, 33 MHz) had been additionally equipped with OS/2. Those PCs could be run both under MS-Windows/DOS and OS/2. Some of the tools had to be installed locally, whereas others could remain on the server.

Unfortunately, ADW does not have a LAN encyclopedia yet. As 30 people had to work simultaneously, a master encyclopedia on one computer and nine additional working encyclopedias (three per business area) on the other computers were created. They were consolidated at regular intervals. Between consolidation runs, read-only copies of the master encyclopedia and of the working encyclopedias were given to other project subteams.

User interface specifications generated by ADW were translated by the OS/2 Resource Compiler. It is part of the Developer's Toolkit for OS/2. For the other components generated by ADW (procedural logic, database access), Micro Focus Cobol Compiler (version 3.0) had to be employed. It contains a precompiler for embedded SQL generated by ADW for relational data manipulation. The target database system was the Database Manager that is part of IBM's Extended Services for OS/2. The data definition statements generated by ADW could be used directly as input for the Database Manager.

4 Project Stages

4.1 Business Area Analysis

The three business areas outlined in chapter 2 were analyzed with the help of the Analysis Workstation tools. Results were hierarchies of functions and processes on the activities' side, and entity-relationship diagrams on the data side. Data flow diagrams were used to describe data flows between processes, transformation of data by processes, access to databases, and communication between processes and the environment. Coarse procedural logic in elementary processes was outlined in so-called "mini-specifications".

4.2 System Design

User-interface design was the main concern during this stage. Elementary processes and their respective input/output interfaces had been specified during business area analysis. Now the windows of the information system were designed, and those interfaces were mapped to the windows. On the data side, a so-called first-cut database schema was generated from the data model. Following this intermediate step, attribute hierarchies and ranges from analysis were available to the design workstation tools. They only needed to be connected to the windows where respective attribute informations were required. In order to make windows appear in a unique way, guidelines developed during analysis had to be observed by all team members. Layouts of reports and forms (e.g. application for leave or official tour) were also specified.

A very important part of this stage was to design a multi-level system of access rights. Particular consideration had to be given to the fact that users are professors, scientific and technical staff, and students. On the other hand, there are user groups such as staff of a particular chair, students taking the same course, etc.; and finally, there are users that have specific tasks (such as administration of funds). Access to certain data may thus depend on several factors and furthermore, on the mode of access (create, read, write, modify). For example, read access to a student's grade is granted to professors, perhaps to other scientific personnel, and to the student himself but not to other students, whereas write access may be restricted to professors. In order to satisfy all these requirements, a rather sophisticated system of access rights had to be designed. Its basic idea is that *roles* can be defined and rights can be associated with these roles. There is a number of default roles, but new roles may also be introduced. One or more roles may be assigned to each user. Access rights are checked whenever the respective windows are to be activated or the respective data are to be addressed.

4.3 Construction

During the construction stage, procedural logic, connections between procedural logic and user interface, and database accesses were developed.

First, the logic of elementary processes was specified in detail. According to Martin's Information Engineering approach, this task actually belongs to the design stage. For several reasons including poor tool support, it was postponed until construction. The tool for detailed specification of logic is the *Module Action Diagrammer*. The language to be used on this level is *Enriched Cobol*. It contains Cobol elements as well as constructs supporting communication with the window interfaces (e.g. "get from window") and data manipulation. Embedded SQL statements lying behind those data manipulation commands may be modified by the developers.

Next, connections between procedural logic and user interface were established. The tool supporting this step is the *GUI Layout Diagrammer*. The hierarchy of modules was examined with the help of the *Structure Chart Diagrammer*. It depicts the hierarchy of calls in a graphical manner. Nodes of the calling tree are elementary processes.

Rather awkward is ADW's distinction between GUI and non-GUI programs (GUI = graphical user interface). *GUI programs* are programs containing only procedural logic, windows, and connections between those components. They determine primarily when and which windows have to be called, and how data read from the windows are to be processed. *Non-GUI programs* are programs that contain not only procedural logic but also access to files or databases. They are treated in a different manner and are much more awkward to create than GUI programs (see section 6.1).

GUI programs were developed first, by adding Enriched Cobol procedural logic to the window specifications. From the program source texts ("module actions"), the *GUI Layout Diagrammer* generates so-called "front-end programs" in Micro Focus Cobol code. The front-end programs were then compiled and tested with respect to user input. Afterwards, the non-GUI "back-end programs" were developed. They were generated by means of the *GUI Code Generator*. The necessary databases and relations were created by the *OS/2 Database Manager*.

Since reports based on user data are not supported by ADW, separate Cobol programs had to be written. The *Micro Focus Workbench* was used for this purpose. At least, Cobol programs could be called directly from inside the programs generated by ADW. Necessary call statements did not have to be put into the generated Cobol code but could be inserted into the module actions.

5   Project Conditions and Results

The information system was developed within a project that was part of advanced business-informatics education at the University of Muenster, Germany. Projects are part of the curriculum, summing up and integrating experience from other courses such as information-system development, software engineering, data modelling and database management systems. Participants were at the end of their eight semester studies. They had worked before with tools supporting the above fields; in particular, they had gained some experience solving "small" problems with ADW during a one-semester course. What was still missing was substantial experience with cooperative project work, subject to activity schedules, milestones, and delivery dates.

The project team comprised 30 people altogether, not counting the users involved into JRP and JAD sessions [3] nor technical staff (network, OS/2 administration, etc.). Since the project was embedded in a semester curriculum, its duration, beginning, and end were predetermined: The project had to be completed within a period of exactly three months. Project conditions thus were rather untypical. Whereas "ordinary" projects with comparable output might be executed by two or three persons over a period of one or two years, here a fairly *large number* of people had to be coordinated for a rather *short time*. Project planning and management had to take these circumstances into account; for example, project management was more rigorous and stricter than in normal projects. Both the project manager and the project supervisor had successfully completed projects of that type before. In a report on one of them, the expression "million-monkey approach" was used (by others) as a description [7].

	Project preparation and strategy planning	Project execution	Total hours
Project management and supervision	150 h	600 h	750 h
Technical administration	100 h	700 h	800 h
Students		4,500 h	4,500 h
Total hours	250 h	5,800 h	6,050 h

Fig. 3: Development effort

Development effort amounted to 38 person months in total. Figure 3 shows how it is distributed among management, students, and major phases. Management and administration were time-consuming (1,550 hours), partly because of inherent complexity of novel I-CASE technology, partly because of problems with the toolset.

Results of the project were not only programs and databases, but also a number of different models of the business areas. They are stored in the encyclopedia which had reached a size of 14 MB at the end. The overall system consists of 17 sub-systems - the "front ends". According to Information Engineering philosophy, we did not attempt to complete all possible subsystems identified in business area analysis in one run. Some of them will be treated later. Some went all the way to construction but could not be finished within the given project duration. Summing up the programs that were truly generated and tested, the code amounts to about 160,000 lines (excluding separate Cobol programs for reports). When the missing back-end programs will be completed, the total system will comprise some 330,000 lines of code. Figure 4 summarizes quantitative project results.

Data		Activities		Program components	
Entity types	73	Functions	64	Front-end programs	17
Relationship		Processes	242	Windows	102
types	119	Elementary		Back-end programs	116
		processes	382	Separate Cobol programs	20
				Generated lines of code	116,000
					(330,000)

Fig. 4: Quantitative project results

6 Observations and Experiences from the Project

6.1 Information Engineering Workstation Tools

The Information Engineering approach to IS development places individual information systems into an organization-wide context based on common data, function, and process models. Integration is not only conceptual, but it is also supported by interlocking tools. This means, for example, that consistency of different models can be checked by these tools. In fact, it would have hardly been possible to validate 73 entity types and 119 relationship types of the data model without tool support.

ADW's tools for the early stages - Planning, Analysis, and Design Workstation - proved to be efficient and well integrated. Our experience from this particular project primarily refers to the latter two ones, because the Planning Workstation was not employed by the students. Whenever objects were created or modified by one tool, the respective information was immediately available to other tools. Handling of the tools is mostly simple, intuitive, and easy to learn. However, this does not hold for the GUI Code Generator (see below).

Vertical tool integration across stages is satisfactory with regard to the data side. Components of the data model defined during planning or analysis can be processed directly in the design stage. They may be further transferred to construction where the relational model is generated. On the activities side, top-down refinement from business functions to processes and further on to elementary processes is intuitive and easy to carry out. However, vertical integration is less satisfactory, going only until design (see below).

Some of the tools enhance productivity significantly. By means of the GUI Layout Diagrammer, for example, it was possible to define and validate all 102 windows within one week. Since model information stored in the central encyclopedia can be used by any tool, no additional recording is necessary. For the same reason, a good deal of documentation can be derived automatically (e.g. entity-relationship diagrams, call hierarchies).

On the other hand, the list of *drawbacks* is rather long. Many of them are due to the fact that the tools (under OS/2) have not completely matured yet. Some of them contain severe errors whereas others still suffer from their mainframe origins.

The artificial distinction between GUI and non-GUI programs is particularly awkward, as these two types of programs have to be developed in completely different ways. The separation of GUI and non-GUI components is maintained all the way down to executable programs. Figure 5 illustrates how different tools have to be employed. Whereas GUI programs can be specified and generated very efficiently with the help of the GUI Layout Diagrammer, the way on the right hand side is extremely ponderous.

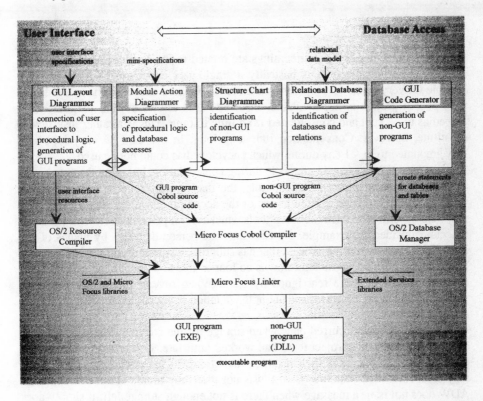

Fig. 5: Relations between construction tools

Response times are sometimes very long. The process of building up the screen took up to two minutes when a group of windows had to be loaded. *Tool documentation* proved to be incomplete and full of errors. This was particularly hampering to project progress as lengthy trial-and-error processes were necessary to find out what was wrong, what was right, and what was missing in the documentation. For example, there is no coherent description of which specifications are needed and how to proceed to generate Cobol programs. Motivation of the project team was severely damaged by the effects of documentation flaws.

As to vertical integration of *procedural-logic* components, there is a complete break between analysis and design/construction. Mini-specifications from business area analysis cannot be processed in the design stage. The only way to make use of those earlier descriptions is to copy them into program specifications where they may serve as comments. Procedural logic has to be redeveloped completely. Since the language is Enriched Cobol, the level of expression is only slightly above "ordinary" 3GL programming! Another drawback is that error messages refer to the code generated by ADW. Debugging becomes rather awkward as developers have to examine code they did not write! Unfortunately, no debugger on the specification level is available (yet).

6.2   Encyclopedia

Quite a number of ADW's shortcomings are related to the current state of the encyclopedia. The encyclopedia is basically a single-user encyclopedia and, at most, suitable for very small development teams. A LAN-based encyclopedia as needed in a 30-people project is not available. Instead, ADW allows several parallel encyclopedias to be kept and consolidated from time to time. This is a rather insufficient substitute, however. Consolidation runs take long; in our case (9 encyclopedias) they amounted to ½ - 1 day during which encyclopedias could not be used.

Some *consistency checks* are made during consolidation, but often the user has to ensure consistency himself. For example, the master encyclopedia will not notice that an element has been deleted in one of the decentral encyclopedias. Consistency may also become a problem between tools when several persons work with the same objects. Consider, for example, the case that one person deletes - by means of the Data Flow Diagrammer - a process that has subprocesses specified by other persons. The Decomposition Diagrammer now is no longer able to associate the subprocesses correctly unless they are reassigned by hand. When several people are involved, problems may arise if information about the deletion is not passed to all of them in a coordinated way.

A severe setback occurred once when storage for the encyclopedia was used up. Some members of the project team had worked until late. Before going home, they proceeded as usual to store their results. Frustration was big the next morning when they discovered that yesterday's work was not there any more. The reason was that ADW does not issue a message when there is not enough storage left; it simply does not store! To avoid this kind of problem, oversize extra storage had to be provided from then on, considering that the encyclopedias grew at a rate of 10 MB per day during that particular phase of the project.

KnowledgeWare meanwhile seems to have recognized that many ADW problems are due to the weak encyclopedia. The announcement was made that the *Rochade* repository will be supported in the future, too.

6.3 Information Engineering Methodology

To some extent, Information Engineering methodology as proposed by Martin was applied in the project. End users were involved at several stages. In particular, requirements were analyzed and specified with the help of end users, and prototyping was applied to demonstrate and revise intermediate results.

During analysis, JRP (joint requirements planning) workshops were conducted for each subarea, including both end users, designers responsible for that subarea, and the subproject leader. Some JAD (joint application design) workshops were also scheduled. For several reasons, however, workshops were not as elaborate as suggested in IE publications [3, 6]. First, sufficient experience with JRP and JAD methodology was lacking. Second, time for the project was extremely limited. Third, the persons heading the project (project/subproject managers, supervisor) knew the business areas very well themselves. Thus, JRP and JAD were not so much conducted in the form of workshops, but resembled more ordinary requirements analysis with some end-user prototyping.

Timebox methodology was not applied explicitly ([6], p. 170). However, in all phases of the project, functions and processes to be analyzed, designed, constructed, or left out, respectively, were prioritized. In this way, the basic idea of timeboxes underlay the whole project.

Consistency problems arose whenever models from design or analysis needed to be changed. Modifications at a later stage were made within the specific forms of representation of that stage (e.g. relational data structures). Models of former stages (e.g. entity-relationship model) were neither adapted automatically, by ADW, nor by the developers, because of lack of time. From this, it was inevitable that inconsistencies among analysis models, design models, data structures, and programs grew constantly.

7   Outlook

According to Ed Yourdon, it takes some 10 - 15 years for new technologies to reach widespread use ([14], p. 268). Today, dissemination of Information Engineering-based I-CASE is still at its beginning. One reason is certainly that the rather sophisticated Information Engineering approach to IS development will only work if developers have received adequate education in analyzing and modelling. In particular, they need the capability to develop *models* of the problem domain, rather than write specifications and programs as taught in software engineering.

Another reason seems to be that tools have not reached the stability needed for industry-scale application yet; this was one of the experiences from our project. Furthermore, the code generated automatically is often considered inefficient. Therefore, some users employ ADW or IEF for analysis and design only, but leave construction to their experienced Cobol programmers. Some use less comprehensive "lower CASE" tools that generate more efficient code. Better code generation following the modelling phases in a natural way are indispensable for truly *integrated* CASE.

At present, only "typical" data processing problems are supported, i.e. transaction-oriented problems where input/output by way of windows and forms, and accesses to databases dominate. Other problem types, e.g. problems including complex algorithms or active graphics, are still beyond the scope of I-CASE. Following Ed Yourdon, some 5 - 10 % of business information-processing problems can be tackled today, but 90 % might be reached by the end of the decade ([14], p. 273).

Finally, many potential users are still uncertain about the cost and benefit of I-CASE. Although tool vendors have been promising significant gains in productivity, objective investigations are still rare. In an article of May 1993 [10], three enterprises reported on their I-CASE activities. Two of them actually tried to measure costs and benefits. One company found that productivity had raised substantially. The second one recognized only moderate savings. The third company had not quantified expectations and did not perform measurements. They felt that their vague hopes were not fulfilled and hence cancelled further CASE activities.

References

[1]   Ernst & Young GmbH: Application Development Workbench; Ernst & Young CASE Services GmbH & Co.; Stuttgart o.J.

[2]   KnowledgeWare, Inc.: Application Development Workbench/Workstation Basics, Release 1.6.02; KnowledgeWare, Inc., Atlanta, GA 1991.

[3]   Lucas, M.A.: The Way of JAD; Database Programming and Design 6 (1993) 7, pp. 42-49.

[4]   Martin, J.: Information Engineering, Book I, Introduction; Englewood Cliffs, NJ 1989.

[5]   Martin, J.: Information Engineering, Book II, Planning and Analysis; Englewood Cliffs, NJ 1990.

[6]   Martin, J.: Information Engineering, Book III, Design and Construction; Englewood Cliffs, NJ 1990.

[7]   N.N.: Die Kunst der gebändigten Unordnung; Computerworld Schweiz (1987) 12, pp. 7-11.

[8]   N.N.: Modellgetriebene Anwendungsentwicklung; IBM Nachrichten 41 (1991) 306, pp. 46-49.

[10]   N.N.: The Costs and Benefits of CASE; I/S analyzer 31 (1993) 6.

[11]   Short, K., Dodd, J.: Information Engineering \with Objects, Issue 1.2; Texas Instruments Technical Paper; JMA Information Engineering Ltd., Ashford, Middlesex (England) 1992.

[12]   Snell, N.: Users Rethink Life Cycle CASE; Datamation (1993) May 15, pp. 102-105.

[13]   Texas Instruments Inc. (Eds.): IEF Information Engineering Facility, Technology Overview, Second Edition; TI Part Number 2739900-8027; Plano, Texas, November 1990.

[14]   Yourdon, E.: Decline and Fall of the American Programmer; Englewood Cliffs, NJ 1992.

A Knowledge-based Program Transformation System

P. C-Y. Sheu
Department of Electrical & Computer Engineering
University of California
Irvine, CA 92717

S. Yoo
Department of Industrial Automation
Inha University
Souel, Korea

Abstract. This paper describes a Knowledge-Based Program Transformation System (KBPTS) that has been designed on top of an object-oriented knowledge base for the purpose of automatic program transformation and optimization. In KBPTS, a program can be specified by means of a flowchart or a set of logical descriptions. Generally, given a specification of a program, it can be synthesized with a set of procedural methods. However, a simple substitution of a method for a basic computation in a specification may leave a large amount of possible optimizations unexplored. Assuming that a set of efficient algorithms for abstract problems (e.g., graph algorithms) is implemented and saved in an object-oriented knowledge base, a given program (or parts of it) can be evaluated by those algorithms efficiently with proper instantiations of variables. To identify the proper algorithms, the conventional unification algorithm has been modified into an *analogical unification* algorithm. Also, in order to control the overall search space more clearly, a set of global search strategies are encoded in meta rules.

1. Introduction

This paper describes a Knowledge-Based Program Transformation System (KBPTS) that has been designed on top of an object-oriented knowledge base for the purpose of automatic program transformation and optimization. In KBPTS, a program can be specified by means of a flowchart or a set of logical descriptions. A flowchart is a set of nodes and directed edges, where each node represents some computational actions and each edge designates a possible passage of control between nodes. In an object-oriented knowledge base, the computational actions for each node can be considered as a predefined method. A set of logical descriptions specifies the precondition and the postcondition of a program which correspond to the functionality of the program. Generally, given a specification of a program, it can be synthesized with a set of procedural methods. However, a simple substitution of a method for a basic computation in a specification may leave a large amount of possible optimizations unexplored. Assuming that a set of efficient algorithms for abstract problems (e.g., graph algorithms) is implemented and saved in an object-oriented knowledge base, a given program (or parts of it) can be evaluated by those methods efficiently with proper instantiations of variables.

This transformation system works as an assertion-based logical system [Floy67] [Hoar69]. In an object-oriented knowledge base, a set of methods is associated to each object class, and the definition of each method includes a precondition and a postcondition. If a method's precondition is true before its execution, the postcondition will be true upon its termination. These assertions do not necessarily assign particular values to each variable, but they specify some properties of the values or any relationships among them. The object-level knowledge base also includes axioms and rules of inference specified in first-order predicate calculus, which can be applied to transform a program according to the global strategies defined as meta rules. The meta rules are not domain specific; they specify a set of general control criteria which guides the overall search process [DaBu84].

The paper is organized as follows. Section 2 overviews the architecture of KBPTS. Section 3 describes the structure and the internals of the algorithm library.

Section 4 discusses an mechanism that can be applied to substitute program specifications with library algorithms. Section 5 sketches some global control strategies to reduce the search space. Section 6 compares KBPTS with some related work. Finally, Section 7 concludes the paper with some future research directions.

2. Overviews of KBPTS

In [Zani84] [Sheu88], mathematical logic has been employed to describe *objects*, *classes*, and *methods*. In the object-oriented knowledge base framework, the first-order language consists of the following [Sheu88]:

(1) *class(a)* is true if a is the name of a class of objects.

(2) *instance_of(a,b)* is true if object a is a member of class b.

(3) *subclass_of(a,b)* is true if class a is a subclass of class b.

(4) *attribute(a,b,c)* is true if every object in class a has b as one of its attributes, and the domain of b is c.

(5) *attribute_value* (a,b,c) is true if object a has the value c of its attribute b.

(6) $a(x_1,...,x_r)$ is true if a is a method which has the arguments $x_1,...,x_r$. We call $a(x_1,...,x_r)$ a *method predicate*.

(7) $f(x_1,...,x_n)$ is true if a tuple $<x_1, ... , x_n>$ is a member of user-defined relation f. In this case, we call $f(x_1,...,x_n)$ a *relational predicate*.

With this first order language, database schemata, deductive laws and integrity constraints can be defined. The key components of KBPTS can now be described in the following:

(a) *Object Schema:*

The object schema defines classes in predicate forms, where the definition of a class includes the name, the attributes, the methods, and the class hierarchy. Suppose we have a set of object classes related to graphs, i.e., *vertex*, *edge* and *weighted_graph*. Assuming the length of each edge is available, the class *weighted_graph* can have the procedure *shortest_path* as a method. The method *shortest_path* searches a given graph and returns a shortest path between two given vertices. The definition of this database in the object schema can be summarized as follows:

☐ class(vertex)

$\left\{\begin{array}{l} attribute\,(vertex,VID\,,string\,) \\ attribute\,(vertex,X\_POS\,,real\,) \\ attribute\,(vertex,Y\_POS\,,real\,) \end{array}\right.$

☐ class(edge)

$\left\{\begin{array}{l} attribute\,(edge\,,EID\,,string\,) \\ attribute\,(edge\,,V1,vertex\,) \\ attribute\,(edge\,,V2,vertex\,) \\ attribute\,(edge\,,WEIGHT\,,integer\,) \end{array}\right.$

☐ class(weighted_graph)

$\left\{\begin{array}{l} attribute\,(weighted\_graph\,,GID\,,string\,) \\ attribute\,(weighted\_graph\,,V\,,set-of-vertex\,) \\ attribute\,(weighted\_graph\,,E\,,set-of-edge\,) \end{array}\right.$

☐   method
    shortest_path(V1:vertex, V2:vertex, G:weighted_graph, P:path)

(b) *Data Base:*

Objects in a class can be stored in the form of a table, where each tuple corresponds to an object instance in the class. A class consists of a number of attributes, and the value of an attribute is an object or a set of objects which belongs to some other class. This relationship among attributes and classes forms a *class–attribute* hierarchy [BeKi89].

(c) *Rule Base:*

In the rule base, we have both deductive laws and integrity constraints in the following form without function symbols:

$$P_1 \wedge P_2 \wedge \cdots \wedge P_n \rightarrow Q_1 \vee \cdots \vee Q_m$$

which can be interpreted as " if all of P_1, P_2, ..., and P_n are true, then at least one of Q_1, Q_2, ..., or Q_m is true ".

(d) *Meta Rule Base:*

While the rules in the rule base (i.e., deductive rules and integrity constraints) describe the knowledge about the objects in the database, meta rules represent the knowledge about the object-level knowledge. For example, the meta rule base can include a set of rules of cost estimation so that a single rule can be selected to apply among several possibilities. As a result, meta rules form a set of strategies to guide the use of object-level knowledge by pruning or reordering the rules in the rule base [DaBu84].

(e) *Knowledge Base Management System:*

The main functions of the knowledge base management system are query optimization, transaction processing, and object management. In addition to queries, insert and delete operations can be included in a transaction. To process a transaction, data dependency among queries and other operations needs to be analyzed for optimization. The management system also provides other amenities such as concurrency control, integrity validation, crash recovery, and authorization.

(f) *User Interface:*

The system interacts with the user in various methodologies, such as flowcharts, logical descriptions and database programs [ShYo90]. In this paper, we assume that a program is presented as an annotated flow chart as described in [Floy67] and [Hoar69]. In [Floy67], Floyd associated an assertion with each arc in a flowchart such that if the assertion P associated with the entrance arc of an action π is true before π is executed then the assertion R associated with the exit arc of π will be true after π is executed. Using the notation in [Hoar69], this can be represented as

$$\{P\} \ \pi \ \{R\},$$

where P and R are usually mentioned as *precondition* and *postcondition*, respectively, of process π.

3. A Library of Algorithms

In an object-oriented knowledge base, for each object class, a set of methods can be associated. We assume that a large number of abstract algorithms are coded as methods in an object-oriented knowledge base. These methods usually belong to abstract object classes such as *graph* and other data structures. Clearly, it will be desirable if a programmer can reuse some of these algorithms deliberately or with some help from the system.

We consider a library of algorithms as a collection of useful methods. In order to be selected properly for substitutions, the definition of each method should include the following:

(a) method name
(b) a list of arguments, where the domain of each argument should be specified
(c) the functionality of the method in terms of its precondition and postcondition
(d) order of complexity

As an example, we can present a set of object classes related to the class *graph* and some methods which implement efficient algorithms. In the following example, we use *P*, *Q* and *O* to denote a precondition, a postcondition, and the order of complexity of a method, respectively.

object classes and methods

<class>
vertex(VID:integer)
edge(EID:integer, V1:vertex, V2:vertex)
vertex_pair(VPID:integer, V1:vertex, V2:vertex)
weighted_edge(WEID:integer, V1:vertex, V2:vertex, W:integer)
path(PID:integer, V1:vertex, V2:vertex, E:set-of-edge)
weighted_path(WPID:integer, V1:vertex, V2:vertex, E:set-of-weighted_edge)
graph(GID:integer, V:set-of-vertex, E:set-of-edge)

    <subclass>
    weighted_graph(E:set-of-weighted_edge)

        ; set all the possible paths between V1 and V2 to SP
        <method> (all_path (V1:vertex) (V2:vertex) (V:set-of-vertex)
            (E:set-of-weighted_edge) (SP:set-of-weighted_path) ...)
        P = { true }
        Q = { (∀P) [member_of(P, SP) → weighted_path(WP1, V1, V2, P.E)] }
        O = cardinality_of(V) + cardinality_of(E)

        ; return *true* if a given graph *(V,E)* is connected
        ; the returned value is denoted by *RETURN*
        ; in the following logical descriptions
        <method> (connected_graph (V:set-of-vertex) (E:set-of-weighted_edge) ...)
        P = { true }
        Q = { [(∀X) (∀Y) [member_of(X, V) ∧ member_of(Y, V)
            ∧ weighted_path(WP1, X, Y, E)] → RETURN] ∨
            [~ [(∀X) (∀Y) [member_of(X, V) ∧
            member_of(Y, V) ∧ weighted_path(WP1, X, Y, E)]] →
            ~ RETURN] }
        O = cardinality_of(V) + cardinality_of(E)

        ;return *true* if a given graph *(V,E) is a tree*
        <method> (is_tree (V:set-of-vertex) (E:set-of-weighted_edge) ...)
        P = { true }
        Q = { [(∀X) (∀Y) [member_of(X, V) ∧
            member_of(Y, V) ∧ all_path(X, Y, V, E, SP) ∧
            equal(cardinality_of(SP), 1)] → RETURN] ∨
            [~ [(∀X) (∀Y) [member_of(X, V) ∧

$member\_of(Y, V) \wedge all\_path(X, Y, V, E, SP) \wedge$
$\quad equal(cardinality\_of(SP), 1)]] \rightarrow \sim RETURN] \}$
$O = cardinality\_of(V) + cardinality\_of(E)$

;set the total weight of a weighted path to SW
<method> (sum_of_weight (WP:weighted_path, SW:integer) ...)
$P = \{ true \}$
$Q = \{ equal(SW, summation(W, WP.E)) \}$
$O = cardinality\_of(WP.E)$

;set the spanning tree with the minimum weight to MST
<method> (minimum_spanning_tree (G:weighted_graph,
$\qquad\qquad$ MST:weighted_graph) ...)
$P = \{ true \}$
$Q = \{ (\wedge X) [spanning\_tree(X,G) \wedge weight\_of\_graph(X, WX) \wedge$
$\quad weight\_of\_graph(MST, WS) \rightarrow$
$\quad lesseq(WS, WX)] \}$
$O = cardinality\_of(G.V)^2$

;set the path between given two vertices with the minimum weight to SP
<method> (shortest_path (G:weighted_graph, V1:vertex,
$\qquad\qquad$ V2:vertex, SP:weighted_path) ...)
$P = \{ true \}$
$Q = \{ (\wedge X) [weighted\_graph(G, V, E) \wedge all\_path(V1, V2, V, E, P\_SET)$
$\quad \wedge member\_of(X, P\_SET) \wedge sum\_of\_weight(SP, WSP) \wedge$
$\quad sum\_of\_weight(X, WX) \rightarrow lesseq(WSP, WX)] \}$
$O = cardinality\_of(G.V)^2$

<subclass>
directed_graph(E:set-of-vertex_pair)

;set all the vertices which can be reached from a given vertex to TC
<method> (transitive_closure (G:directed_graph, V1:vertex,
$\qquad\qquad$ TC:set-of-vertex) ...)
$P = \{ true \}$
$Q = \{ (\wedge X) [member\_of(X, TC) \wedge directed\_graph(G, V, E) \wedge$
$\quad all\_directed\_path(V1, X, V, E, P\_SET) \rightarrow$
$\quad greater(cardinality\_of(P\_SET), 0)] \}$
$O = cardinality\_of(G.V)^2$

;remove any directed cycle in a given directed graph
<method> (topological_sorting (G:directed_graph,
$\qquad\qquad$ TS:list-of-vertex) ...)
$P = \{ true \}$
$Q = \{ (\wedge X) (\wedge Y) [member\_of(X, TS) \wedge member\_of(Y,TS) \wedge$
$\quad vertex\_pair(VP, X, Y) \rightarrow precede(X, Y, TS)] \}$
$O = cardinality\_of(G.V) + cardinality\_of(G.E)$

We can classify methods according to the way in which they return their results. Some of the methods return *true* or *false* according to their evaluation; we call these *logical* methods (e.g., *is_tree* and *connected_graph*). Other methods which are not logical methods are considered as *general* methods. In the above example, the returned values from logical methods are denoted by a special variable *RETURN* in the description of postconditions. The treatment of *RETURN* during the process of program transformation will be discussed later in this paper. The meanings of some predicates which have not been defined in the above example are briefly explained in the following:

(a) *member_of(A, S)*: which is true if object A is a member of a set S.

(b) *cardinality_of(S)* : which returns the cardinality of a set S.

(c) *equal(A, B)* : which is true if A is equal to B.

(d) *summation(A, B)*: which returns the sum of A for all the member of a set B.

(e) *lesseq(A, B)*: which is true if A is less than or equal to B.

(f) *greater(A, B)*: which is true if A is greater than B.

(g) *precede(A, B, L)*: which is true if A precede B in a list L.

(h) *all_directed_path(V1,V2,V,E,DP)*: which set all the possible directed paths from $V1$ to $V2$ to DP.

(i) *set-of-A*: denotes an object domain which is a set of objects of class A.

(i) *list-of-A*: denotes an object domain which is a list of objects of class A.

(j) *A.B*: denotes an attribute B of an object A.

4. Substituting Library Algorithms For Program Specification

Substituting a library algorithm for a part of program specification can be done by comparing the assertion of the specification part with that of the pre-stored methods. The procedure of this comparison is similar to that of a unification process in predicate calculus [Nils80]. A unification process is to find a set of substitutions which can be applied to two or more expressions and make them the same substitution instances. For example, consider two expressions: $E_1 = p(X,Y,a)$ and $E_2 = p(b,Y,Z)$. A substitution s can be applied to an expression E; the result of a substitution is an *substitution instance* and it is denoted by Es. If there exists a substitution s_i such that $E_1 s_i = E_2 s_i$, then E_1 and E_2 are *unifiable* and s_i is an *unifier*. In the above example, we can identify the following substitution instances:

$$E_1 s = p(X,Y,a) \{ \ b/X, \ a/Z \} = p(b, Y, a)$$
$$E_2 s = p(b,Y,Z) \{ \ b/X, \ a/Z \} = p(b, Y, a)$$

Because $E_1 s = E_2 s$, $p(X,Y,a)$ and $p(b,Y,Z)$ are unifiable with a unifier $\{ \ b/X, \ a/Z \}$.

A unification process can be considered as a pattern matching problem with substitutions of arguments. Several unification algorithms have been proposed, and it was proved that two expressions can be determined to be unifiable or not [Robi65]. However, most of the existing algorithms only allow a matching between two predicates with the same head. For this reason, using the conventional algorithms only allows the program transformation process be performed within an object class. For example, suppose that a detailed program has been designed in order to find a shortest path between vertices a and b. The program is written in a flowchart language, and suppose that the assertion for an edge which is incident on the *Stop* node has been derived as follows:

$A = \{ \ (\forall X) \ [\ weighted\_graph(G, \ V, \ E) \ \wedge \ all\_path(a, \ b, \ V, \ E, \ P\_SET) \ \wedge$
$member\_of(X, \ P\_SET) \ \wedge \ sum\_of\_weight(SP, \ WSP) \ \wedge \ sum\_of\_weight(X, \ WX) \ \rightarrow$
$lesseq(WSP, \ WX) \ ] \ \}$

Clearly, Assertion A and the postcondition of the method *shortest_path* in class *graph* are unifiable if we substitute a for $V1$ and b for $V2$. In other words, assertion A is a special case for the postcondition of the method *shortest_path*, where *shortest_path* is a general function which finds a shortest path between any two vertices in a graph. Intuitively, the above unification is an example of instantiating variables (e.g., $V1$ and $V2$) with constants (e.g., a and b).

Now, consider a program written for an airline reservation system. The program finds the cheapest connection between two cities c_1 and c_2. Suppose that, after applying the transformation rules to the program, we have the following assertion:

$$B = \{ \ (\sim Y) \ [\ airline(F, \ CITIES, \ FLIGHTS) \ \wedge \ all\_connection(c_1, \ c_2, \ CITIES, \ FLIGHTS, \ C\_SET) \ \wedge \ member\_of(Y, \ C\_SET) \ \wedge \ sum\_of\_fare(SC, \ FSC) \ \wedge \ sum\_of\_fare(Y, \ FY) \rightarrow lesseq(FSC, \ FY) \ ] \ \}$$

If we compare this assertion with the postcondition of the method *shortest path* in class *graph*, we can find the following terms which syntactically correspond to each other:

weighted_graph(G, V, E)	*airline(F, CITIES, FLIGHTS)*
all_path(V1, V2, V, E, P_SET)	*all_connection(c_1, c_2, CITIES, FLIGH*
member_of(X, P_SET)	*member_of(Y, C_SET)*
sum_of_weight(SP, WSP)	*sum_of_fare(SC, FSC)*
sum_of_weight(X, WX)	*sum_of_fare(Y, FY)*
lesseq(WSP, WX)	*lesseq(FSC, FY)*

In conventional unification algorithms, two predicates which have different predicate heads (e.g., *weighted_graph(G, V, E)* and *airline(F, CITIES, FLIGHTS)*) cannot be unified. However, we know that the *shortest_path* algorithm in class *weighted_graph* can be used for finding the cheapest connection in the class *airline* by properly instantiating the variables in the *shortest_path* algorithm with those in the airline reservation system. This is an example of matching with analogy, and in order to perform this we need an *analogical* unification process. The term "analogical" has been used in various contexts in the artificial intelligence community (e.g., "analogical problem solving" [Carb81] and "programming by analogy" [Ders86]). While an analogical approach can include some interactive modification processes in order to use an existing program for a new problem, in this paper, the term "analogy" is strictly limited to exact correspondences between object classes or between programs. In this way, we can automate the process of program transformations.

In the above list of correspondences, each predicate is either a relational predicate or a method predicate. Here, a relational predicate represents the membership in a class, i.e., *weighted_graph(G, V, E)* is true if an instance of *G*, *V* and *E* is a member of the class *weighted_graph*. In order to compare two classes, we first identify the pairs of corresponding attributes, which should be kept consistent throughout the entire process. To be matched analogically, the domains of attributes in a pair should be the same. If an attribute is a compound object (i.e., it is a collection of other objects), the object structures (i.e., attributes and their domains) should be the same recursively. For example, the attribute *FLIGHTS* is a compound attribute and it specifies each *FLIGHT* with *FARE*, where *FLIGHT* corresponds to *EDGE* and *FARE* matches *WEIGHT*. As for method predicates, their unifiability should be determined by comparing the assertions of their functionality (i.e., their preconditions and postconditions) recursively.

During this unification process, the special variable *RETURN* which denotes the returned value from a *logical* method can match either a variable or a predicate. As an example, we consider a logical method *is_tree*. Suppose that we have a program which contains a variable *Tree* that is set to zero initially. After the main procedure is executed, *Tree* has the value one if a given graph is a tree. In this case, the assertion *C* can be given as follows:

$$C = \{ \ [\ (\sim X) \ (\sim Y) \ [\ member\_of(X, V) \ \wedge \ member\_of(Y, V) \ \wedge \ all\_path(X, Y, V, E, SP) \ \wedge \ equal(cardinality\_of(SP), \ 1) \ ] \ \rightarrow \ equal(Tree, 1) \ ] \ \vee \ [\ \sim \ [\ (\sim X) \ (\sim Y) \ [\ member\_of(X, V) \ \wedge \ member\_of(Y, V) \ \wedge \ all\_path(X, Y, V, E, SP) \ \wedge \ equal(cardinality\_of(SP), \ 1) \ ]] \rightarrow \ \sim equal(Tree, 1) \ ] \ \}$$

If we compare C with the postcondition, we can notice that the variable *RETURN* matches the predicate *equal*(*Tree*,1).

In the analogical unification process, we expand the substitutions in conventional unification algorithms (in which only variables are substituted) by including those for predicate heads (e.g., substituting *weighted_graph* for *airline*). Given two expressions to be unified, first, the numbers of predicates in them should be the same. More precisely, the number of relational predicates should be the same, and the number of method predicates should also be the same. Once the above requirements are met, for each possible pairing, the process of analogical unification can be applied. An analogical unification succeeds if we can find a set of substitutions (of predicate heads and variables) which is consistent throughout the unification process. By modifying the unification algorithm in [Nils80], we can derive a recursive algorithm which analogically unifies two expressions:

Algorithm 1. Analogical Unification Of Two Expressions
INPUT: Two expressions E_1 and E_2.
OUTPUT: A list of substitutions.

1) If E_1 and E_2 are variables, return E_1/E_2.

2) If E_1 is *RETURN* and E_2 is a constant or a predicate, return E_2/E_1.
   If E_2 is *RETURN* and E_1 is a constant or a predicate, return E_1/E_2.

3) If E_1 is a variable and E_2 is a constant, return E_2/E_1.

4) If E_2 is a variable and E_1 is a constant, return E_1/E_2.

5) If E_1 is a predicate head, a connective or a constant, do the following:

   5.1) If E_1 equals E_2, return *NIL*.

   5.2) If E_1 and E_2 are predicate heads for object classes, compare the attributes and their domains. If they are comparable, return E_1/E_2. Otherwise, return *FAIL*.

   5.3) If E_1 and E_2 are predicate heads for methods, analogically unify their preconditions and their postconditions. If the unifications succeed, return E_1/E_2. Otherwise, return *FAIL*.

   5.4) Otherwise, return *FAIL*

6) If E_2 is a predicate head, a connective or a constant, return *FAIL*.

7) Set $FIRST_1$ = the first element of E_1 and $REST_1$ = the rest of E_1.
   Set $FIRST_2$ = the first element of E_2 and $REST_2$ = the rest of E_2.
   Set S_{FIRST} = the result of analogical unification of $FIRST_1$ and $FIRST_2$.
   If S_{FIRST} is *FAIL*, return *FAIL*.

8) Set $MODIFIED_1$ = the result of applying S_{FIRST} to $REST_1$.
   Set $MODIFIED_2$ = the result of applying S_{FIRST} to $REST_2$.
   Set S_{REST} = the result of analogical unification of $MODIFIED_1$ and $MODIFIED_2$.
   If S_{REST} is *FAIL*, return *FAIL*.
   Otherwise, return the composition of S_{FIRST} and S_{REST}.
   $\square$

Once a program analogically unifies an algorithm, a method which implements the algorithm can be used for the program. In order to include a method into a program, objects used in the program should be restructured before they can be used as the arguments for the method. For example, the attribute names for all object instances in class *airline* (e.g., *CITIES* and *FLIGHTS*) should be renamed according to the attribute names in the class *weighted_graph* (e.g., V and E) in order to be used as the arguments for the method *shortest_path*. After the method is evaluated, the results need to be interpreted properly (e.g., a shortest path should be interpreted as a cheapest connection). This substitution and interpretation should be based on the *unifier* set derived from the analogical unification process. Given a unifier set, the change of attribute names and interpretations can be done mechanically.

Example 1. For the problem of finding the cheapest connection in an airline reservation system, we can find an analogical match with the method *shortest_path* in class *graph*. In the match we have two sets of substitutions as follows:

Substitutions for Variables =

  { *F/G, CITIES/V, FLIGHTS/E,* c_1/V1 c_2/V2, C_SET/P_SET, Y/X, SC/SP, FY/WX, FSC/FSP }

Substitutions for Predicate Heads =

  { *airline/weighted_graph, all_connection/all_path, sum_of_fare/sum_of_weight* }

In order to call the method *shortest_path* in the program, the attribute names in class *airline* should be changed temporarily according to the substitution set (in this example, the variable names happen to be the same as the corresponding attribute names). The change of attribute names can be listed as follows:

$$CITIES \rightarrow V$$
$$FLIGHTS \rightarrow E$$
$$FARE \rightarrow WEIGHT$$

Once a solution *SP* (which is a list of nodes) is derived, the above modification should be applied reversely and the solution should be interpreted as a list of *CITIES*
□

In the above example, because the preconditions of the program and the method are {*true*}, we only need to unify their postconditions in order to substitute the method for the program. However, if a part of a program is tried to be unified, the precondition of the part may include some assertions which are not relevant to the part but to the status of the program as a result of executing the previous portion of the program. Suppose that a program consists of two parts A and B, where part A and part B are connected serially so that the postcondition of part A and the precondition of part B are the same (i.e., $Q_A = P_B$). In this case, a method M can be substituted for part B if the following conditions are satisfied:

(a) P_B and Q_B can be decomposed into

$$P_B = C \wedge P$$
$$Q_B = D \wedge Q$$

where C implies D, i.e., $C \rightarrow D$.

(b) P can analogically unify the precondition of the method, and Q can analogically unify the postcondition of the method, i.e.,

$$P \text{ analogically unifies } P_M$$
$$Q \text{ analogically unifies } Q_M$$

As an example, consider a program which sorts a set of *flights* after it computes the sum of the cost for all the *flights* in the set. If we consider the program segment which computes the sum as part A and the other program segment as part B, we can have the following assertions (here we assume that part A assigns the result to *SUM*, and part B sorts in ascending order the *flights* from the set *F_SET* according to their *COST* and sets the result to *SORTED_LIST*):

$$P_A = \{ \text{ true } \}$$
$$Q_A = \{ \text{ } equal(SUM, summation(COST, F\_SET)) \text{ } \}$$

P_A = { $equal(SUM, summation(COST, F\_SET))$ }

P_A = { $equal(SUM, summation(COST, F\_SET)) \land [(\sim X) (\sim Y) [member\_of(X,$ $SORTED\_LIST) \land member\_of(Y, SORTED\_LIST) \land lessthan(X.COST, Y.\overline{COST})$ $\rightarrow prece\overline{d}e(X, Y, SORTED\_\overline{L}IST)]]$ }

Suppose that we have a method M, which sorts a set of *weighted_edges*, with the following precondition and postcondition:

P_M = { $true$ }

P_M = { $(\sim U) (\sim V) [member\_of(U, LIST) \land member\_of(V, LIST) \land lessthan(U.W, V.W)$ $\rightarrow precede(U, V, LIST)]$ }

Using the notations in conditions (a) and (b) above, we can derive the following:

C = { $equal(SUM, summation(COST, F\_SET))$ }

D = { $equal(SUM, \overset{\scriptscriptstyle\backprime}{s}ummation(COST, F\_SET))$ }

P = { $true$ }

Q = { $(\sim X) (\sim Y) [member\_of(X, SORTED\_LIST) \land member\_of(Y, SORTED\_LIST) \land$ $lessthan(X.COST, Y.C\overline{O}ST) \rightarrow prece\overline{d}e(X, Y, SORTED\_\overline{L}IST)]$ }

Because all the conditions in (a) and (b) are satisfied, i.e.,

$C \rightarrow D$,
P analogically unifies P_M, and
Q analogically unifies Q_M,

we can substitute the method M for part B with proper instantiations.

Once we have a successful unification between two object classes or between two methods, we can save the relationship and reuse it later. The collection of previously proved relationships can be considered as a *library of substitutions*. If two methods are saved in the library of substitutions, the unification process can be much easier because we only need to unify the arguments without unifying their preconditions and postconditions. For example, after successfully unifying a program with the method *shortest_path* in the above example, we can save the following relationship in the library of substitutions:

weighted_graph	↔airline
all_path	↔all_connection
sum_of_weight	↔sum_of_fare

The overall process of analogical unification can be described as a set of meta rules such as the following, where P_X and Q_X represent the precondition and the postcondition, respectively, of a method or a program X, and we assume that the predicates in a rule are evaluated from left to right.

If   *unifiable(A, B, S)*

Then   *compatible(A, B, S)*
where *unifiable(A, B, S):* which is true if two expressions A and B are unifiable with a unifier S by the conventional unification process.

5. Global Search Strategies

Given a program specified in a flowchart language, the best thing to do is to replace the whole program by an efficient algorithm. However, in a real situation, it is not always possible to find an algorithm which exactly matches a given program. If we fail to transform the entire program, then we can try to substitute parts of the program by good algorithms. In this section, some global search strategies are discussed, which can be encoded as meta rules. The global search strategies include the following:

(a) *The overall search method:*
By the rule of composition and the rule of iteration, in a program written in a flowchart language, two or more nodes can be composed into one. The process of successive compositions forms a tree, where a set of children is composed into their parent recursively until the whole program is represented by a root node. Each node in the tree represents a part of a program to be substituted by a proper algorithm. If no proper algorithm is found for a node, it can be composed with adjacent nodes or decomposed into details and any proper substitution is searched again. Considering this, the overall search process for finding an optimal transformation can be a top-down search, a bottom-up search, or various combinations of both.

(b) *Preference in selecting rules:*
When more than one object-level rule is applicable at a time, the most promising rule should be selected in order to optimize the overall transformation. The preferences among the rules can be determined by comparing the algorithms which are substituted by the rules. In general, algorithms can be compared by their orders of complexities. Two orders of complexity can be compared if they are expressed by means of one variable (e.g., n^2 and n^3). However, if the orders of complexity are defined in terms of multiple variables (e.g., $|E|^2$ and $|E| |V|$, where $|E|$ is the number of edges and $|V|$ is the number of vertices in a graph), we need some information about the object classes (e.g., the cardinalities of E and V) in order to compare these.

(c) *Policies to solve ambiguities:*
When a program is non-deterministic, a transformed program can produce results which are correct but different from those generated by the original program. For example, the algorithm *topological ordering* can produce different orderings according to implementations. In this situation, only with logical assertions, it is not always possible to assure that the new program generates the same results as the original program. One way to resolve this problem is to get a confirmation from the user. The program can be transformed with user's grant; otherwise, only subparts of the program will be searched for transformation.

6. Related Work

Related work to the program transformation and optimization described in this paper can be classified into three categories: program transformation, program reuse, and knowledge-based editors.

Program transformation includes predefined transformations (e.g., rewriting rules) and program constructions from a high level nonexecutable specifications to a low level executable form. Existing transformation systems can be divided into two classes: those that perform transformations automatically and those which are guided by users. The CIP project [CIP84] [BMPP89] focused on correctness-preserving and source-to-source program transformation at different levels of abstraction. The development process is guided by the programmer who has to choose appropriate transformation rules. The user guidance accomplishes the creative part in the development process. DEDALUS [MaWa79] and KBSA [PrSm88] attempted to auto-mate the transformation selection process. DEDALUS was able to create a program, a correctness proof, and a proof of termination for programs of a limited scope. DEDALUS selects candidate rules by pattern-directed invocations and applies those rules sequentially. KBSA focused on automatic algorithm design, deductive inference, finite differencing, and data structure selection. Given a problem description, KBSA generates an optimal program through correctness-preserving transformations. One of the problems for existing automatic program transformation systems is the lack of driv-ing force of a design process. Even though some search approaches such as cost func-tions and efficient search methods have been employed, global strategies have not been integrated effectively. In KBPTS, global strategies were implemented as meta rules, in which control knowledge can be more clearly represented and executed [Cavi89] [OSGR89] [Past89].

Software reuse appears in two levels of abstraction: reuse at the code level and reuse at the specification level [Dill88]. While code-level reuse involves modifying existing code [PrFr87], specification-level reuse is based on an external, often formal, program specification. Existing methodologies include program transformation [Chea84] [BoMu84] and software components catalogue [WoSo88]. Program transfor-mations are used to refine an abstract program defined in a very high level language into a program written in a target language. Software components catalogue requires the ability to match users' requests onto descriptions of software components which satisfy these requests. The main barriers to software reuse have been pointed out as follows:

(a) It is difficult to develop an enough set of generalized components for potential reuse [WoSo88].

(b) Even with a catalogue of reusable components, the matching processes are not effective enough [Dill88].

In STA, a collection of abstract algorithms replaces the software components catalo-gue, where abstract algorithms form a smaller set than reusable software components. The search method in KBPTS is an extended unification process, which is general enough to find existing solutions.

Simple program editors have been extended to be more powerful ones. Some incorporate an understanding of the syntactic structure of the program being edited [MeFe81] [TeRe81]. This makes it possible to support operations based on the parse tree of a program (e.g., inserting, deleting, and moving between nodes in the parse tree). Syntax-based editors also ensure the syntactic correctness of the program being edited. KBEmacs [Wate85] extended program editors further by including an under-standing of the algorithm structure of the program. By comparing the algorithm struc-tures with programming cliches, which are standard models of solving programming problems, KBEmacs can intelligently assist programmers. KBEmacs assists program-mers to construct programs more rapidly and more reliably by combining or modifying existing algorithmic cliches. The idea of using algorithmic cliches is similar to that of using abstract algorithms in KBPTS. One difference is that cliches are domain depen-dent reusable components while abstract algorithms are general ones which can be applied to problems in various domains.

7. Conclusion

In this paper, we have discussed a knowledge-based program transformation and optimization system. Given a program, it can be transformed into a (or a set of) well-designed abstract algorithm by comparing their preconditions and their postconditions. To compare two conditions, the conventional unification algorithm has been modified into an *analogical unification* algorithm, where two predicates with different heads can be unified if the corresponding classes or methods are compatible with each other. When we allow transformations of subparts of a program, the search space could be increased enormously. In order to control the search space more clearly, a set of glo-bal search strategies is proposed.

Parts of the transformation process have been implemented and some examples are demonstrated in [Yoo90]. From the experimentation, we have learned that a logical description of a program (by a precondition and a postcondition) can easily include errors if we do not have some rigid rules. Also, if the description of a program includes some assertions which are not relevant to the functionality of the program, it is difficult to search for an appropriate algorithm. An example of the irrelevant assertions is the description of local variables in a program. To be more practical and general, it is essential to develop a standard method which is applicable to logical descriptions of algorithms and programs.

References

[Bars87]   Barstow, D., "Artificial Intelligence and Software Engineering," *9th International Conference on Software Engineering,* 1987, pp. 200-211.

[BeKi89]   Bertino, E., and Kim, W., "Indexing Techniques for Queries on Nested Objects," *IEEE Trans. on Knowledge and Data Engineering,* Vol. 1, No.2, June, 1989, pp. 196-214.

[BoMu76]   Bondy, J., and Murty, U., *Graph Theory with Application,* Macmillan Press Ltd., Great Britain, 1976.

[BoMu84]   Boyle, J., and Muralidharan, M., "Program Reusability through Program Transformation," *IEEE Trans. on Software Engineering,* Vol. SE-10, No. 5, Sept. 1984, pp. 574-588.

[BMPP89]   Bauer, F., Moller, B., Partsch, H., and Pepper, P., "Formal Program Construction by Transformations - Computer-Aided, Intuition-Guided Programming," *IEEE Trans. on Software Engineering,* Vol. 15, No. 2, Feb. 1989, pp. 165-180.

[Carb81]   Carbonell, J., "A Computational Model of Analogical Problem Solving," *Proceedings of IJCAI,* 1981, pp. 147-152.

[Cavi89]   Caviedes, J., et al., "A Meta-Knowledge Architecture for Planning and Explanation In Repair Domains." in *Knowledge-Based System Diagnosis, Supervision, and Control,* Tzafestas, S. ed., Plenum Press, New York, 1989.

[Chea84]   Cheatham, T., " Program Reusability Through Program Transformation," *IEEE Trans. Software Engineering,* Sept. 1984.

[CIP84]   CIP Language Group, *Lecture Notes in Computer Science. Volume I: The Munich project CIP,* Spring-Verlag, 1984.

[DaBu84]   Davis, R., and Buchanan, B., "Meta-level Knowledge," in *Rule-based Expert Systems,* Buchanan, B., and Shortliffe, E. eds, Addison-Wesley, Reading, Massachusetts, 1984.

[Ders86]   Dershowitz, N., "Programming by Analogy," in *Machine Learning: An Artificial Intelligence Approach, Vol. 2,* Michalski, R., Carbonell, J., and Mitchell, T. eds, Morgan Kaufmann Publishers, Inc., 1986, pp. 395-423.

[Dill88]   Dillistone, B., "Configuration management within an IPSE and its implications for software re-use," in *Software Engineering Environments,* Pearl Brereton ed., Ellis Horwood Limited, England, 1988.

[Floy67]   Floyd, R., "Assigning meanings to programs," *Proc. Amer. Math. Soc. Symposia in Applied Mathematics,* Vol. 19, 1967, pp 19-31.

[FoSL83]   Foderaro, J., Sklower, K., and Layer, K., *The Franz Lisp Manual* University of California, 1983.

[Hoar69]   Hoare, C., " An axiomatic basis for computer programming," *Comm. ACM,* Vol. 12, No. 10, Oct. 1969, pp 576-580.

[MaWa79] Manna, Z., and Waldinger, R., "Synthesis: Dreams ⟹ Programs," *IEEE Trans. on Software Engineering,* Vol. SE-5, No. 4, July 1979, pp. 294-328.

[MeFe81] Medina-Mora, R., and Feiler, P., "An incremental programming environment," *IEEE Trans. on Software Engineering,* Vol. SE-7, Sept. 1981.

[Nils80] Nilsson, N., *Principles of Artificial Intelligence,* Springer-Verlag, 1980.

[OSGR89] Oussalah, C., Santucci, J., Giambiasi, N., and Roux, P., "Expert system based on multi-view/multi-level model approach for test pattern generation," in *Knowledge-Based System Diagnosis, Supervision, and Control,* Tzafestas, S. ed., Plenum Press, New York, 1989.

[Past89] Pastre D., "MUSCADET: An Automatic Theorem Proving System Using Knowledge and Metaknowledge in Mathematics," *Artificial Intelligence,* Vol. 38, 1989, pp 257-318.

[PrFr87] Prieto-Diaz, R., and Freeman, P., "Classifying software for reusability," *IEEE Software,* Vol. 4, No. 1, January 1987, pp 6-16.

[PrSm88] Pressburger, T., and Smith, D., "Knowledge-based software development tools," in *Software Engineering Environments,* Pearl Brereton ed., Ellis Horwood Limited, England, 1988.

[Robi65] Robinson, J., "A Machine-Oriented Logic Based on the Resolution Principle," *JACM,* Vol. 12, No. 1, January 1965, pp. 23-41.

[Sheu88] Sheu, P.C-Y., "Describing Semantic Databases in Logic," *Journal of Systems and Software,* 1988.

[Sheu90] Sheu, P.C-Y., "OASIS - An Object-oriented And Symbolic Information System," *Proc. First Int'l Conf. on System Integration,* April, 1990.

[Shoo83] Shooman, M., *Software Engineering: Design, Reliability and Management,* McGraw-Hill Book Co., 1983.

[ShYo90] Sheu, P. C-Y., and Yoo, S.B., "A Knowledge-Based Software Environment (KBSE) for Designing Concurrent Processes," *International Journal of Human-Computer Interactions,* Vol. 1, No. 2, pp. 161-185, 1990.

[TeRe81] Teitelbaum, T., and Reps, T., "The Cornell program synthesizer: A syntax-directed programming environment," *Communication of ACM,* Vol. 24, No. 9, Sept. 1981.

[Wate85] Waters, R., "The Programmer's Apprentice: A Session with KBSmacs," *IEEE Trans. on Software Engineering,* Vol. SE-11, No. 11, November 1985.

[Wile84] Wilenski, R., *LISPcraft,* W.W.Norton & Company, Inc., New York, N.Y., 1984.

[WoSo88] Wood, M., and Sommerville, I., "A knowledge-based software components catalogue," in *Software Engineering Environments,* Pearl Brereton ed., Ellis Horwood Limited, England, 1988.

[Yoo90] Yoo, S., "Integrated Process Management In A Parallel Database Programming Environment," Ph.D. Thesis, School of Electrical Engineering, Purdue University, May 1990.

[Zani84] Zanilo, C., "Object-base Logic Programming," *Symp. on Logic Programming,* 1984.

Concept Bases: A Support to Information Systems Integration

Michel Bonjour, Gilles Falquet

University of Geneva, Centre Universitaire d'Informatique
24, Rue Général Dufour
CH-1211 Geneva, Switzerland
E-mail: {bonjour, falquet}@cui.unige.ch

Abstract. In this paper, we describe a technique for integrating heterogeneous information systems using concept bases. A concept base is build on top of each system to integrate, in order to semantically enrich its description. Each concept is described at three different levels: terminological definition, formal characterization, and representation in the underlying system. The different concept bases are then used to compare the concepts represented in the different systems and to establish correspondences between them in order to facilitate communication, cooperation, or integration. Our approach relies on results of the *ConcepTerm* project, dedicated to the study of concept dictionary building methodology and process. We also show that the building of a concept base can benefit database design and high-level interface definitions.

1 Introduction

It is currently recognized as very important to be able to integrate different information resources (among others, databases) within an organization. In fact, information is required in various applications which are becoming more and more complex and need to share information, procedures and rules. This information becomes a strategic resource of the organization that has to be used in an optimal way. However, the heterogeneity of existing systems in terms of data and process models makes very hard any attempt to share information or services.

The integration of different types of information systems (in a broad sense, ranging from specialized applications, real time data feeds, spreadsheets to classical database centred systems, knowledge bases, etc.) is the actual focus of many research projects, with a view to develop "intelligent and cooperative information systems" (the IJICIS Journal[12] is dedicated to them). These systems combine the possibilities of databases, artificial intelligence and programming languages. The notions of "distributed object system"[18] and of "knowledge communication"[25] are also suggested by the "object" research community.

In the database field, numerous research works have been undertaken to facilitate the sharing of information and services in an organization. They lead to the concept of database "interoperability" or "integration". Different projects about (mainly view or schema) integration gave rise to new approaches, described by Batini in [2] and more recently by Kambayashi in [13]. Several architectures have been defined to support a set of interoperable and/or integrated databases. Among them one can mention: distributed databases [19], multidatabases [17], and federated databases [22].

We have chosen the object oriented database schema integration framework to describe our approach. Concept bases are built on top of a set of schemes to integrate; they contain an enhanced semantic description of each schema and will help to establish and control equivalencies between schema elements. The first steps of the integration process are presented and a solution using a three level concept base architecture is described.

The proposed approach is based on an enrichment process using different types of complementing reference sources. Both domain and terminological knowledge are collected, resulting in a concept base able to provide a sharable knowledge space to be used in any activity involving:

- reusability, genericity, evolution of information system components
- domain learning and documentation
- semantic understanding and compliance.

The paper is organised as follows. After an introduction to the schema integration framework, chosen as an example of concept base use (section 2), we define terminology as both a theoretical and practical subject in section 3. Our approach is described in section 4, where the concept base building process is detailed. An architecture of concept base is proposed in section 5. The problem of concept translation is mentioned in section 6. Section 7 presents methodology aspects with the *ConcepTerm* project, dedicated to the building process of "multilingual concept dictionaries". Finally, section 8 presents some other interesting applications of concept bases related to information systems, future research directions, and a conclusion.

2 Schema Integration

Most of the work done on schema integration deal only with schemes which are descriptions of data stored in a database or a file, or used by an application. Existing schema integration approaches usually decompose the integration process in several steps, the main ones being:

- *Preintegration:* translation of source schemes in a common data model
- *Comparison:* finding inter-schema correspondences
- *Integration:* creation of a new (global) schema using source schemes, inter-schema correspondences and integration rules
- *Schema Transformation:* modification of source schemes.

Our approach is best suited for both preintegration and (partially) comparison steps. Following Spaccapietra in [24], we'll gather these two steps together under the term "investigation". The next sections (2.1 to 2.4) describe these main steps.

2.1 Preintegration

The goal of this step is to translate the different schemes to be integrated into a common data model sometimes called "canonical" model [21], to extract as much information as possible concerning the schemes elements (attributes, classes, methods, etc.), and the relationships and rules existing between these elements. Generally, the data model chosen for this step is a semantic one (entity-relationship or object-oriented [15]). This preintegration step is justified, among others, by the relative semantics weakness of schemes and the heterogeneity of used data models.

Semantics of Schemes

The emergence of modern data models and their relative ease of use ("bubbles and arrows") have promoted them as the main way to model real-world situations. However, the oversimplifying effect of any modelling effort led to a loss of semantics: a large part of the domain knowledge the designer acquired during the design phase is lost because it cannot be represented in the schema [9].

Thus, a schema, when viewed as a vocabulary or a glossary, reflects only a small part of the semantic richness of the domain it is supposed to represent. Previous works on preintegration have proposed the following formalisms to enhance schema semantics:

- Word dictionaries: linguistic information (synonyms, homonyms) are added to all of the terms (labels) present in a schema
- Name mappings: the database administrator establishes mappings from existing labels (attribute and class names) to more meaningful ones in order to improve their expressiveness.

Role of the Preintegration step

Most of the integration approaches cover this step in a partial way, only quoting it as a "precondition" to the integration step itself [24] or defining it as a "manual process" [26]. In any case the preintegration step is considered the responsibility of the database administrator (DBA).

On the contrary, we think that this step should play an important role in the integration process. For instance, knowledge stored in a schema is strictly limited to the knowledge needed by the functionality the database is developed for; other concepts of the domain without a direct (and specified) utility are ignored. Thus, the preintegration step can represent an opportunity to show the actual limits of a system with respect to an application field, by enumerating the domain concepts which aren't taken into account in this system. Consequently, it should be conducted using both domain knowledge and terminological skills. Indeed, the quality of the information added to a schema will directly determine its "semantic influence" in relation to other schemes during the comparison step. (Eick, in [6], describes the "quality" of a schema depending on the classification of objects and on its power to express rules coming from the domain).

2.2 Comparison

The comparison step is dedicated to finding out correspondences between schema elements by using probability or pattern matching techniques. This task is generally computer-assisted (the DBA has to validate/invalidate the correspondences suggested by the system).

Comparison is done at two levels:

1. *Comparison of the Schema Elements* (attribute and class names, method signatures): A probability of correspondence is computed using similarity of element names and types. A threshold is then chosen to submit only the more probable correspondences to the database administrator [11].

2. *Comparison of Population*: The comparison of instances allows the discovery of logical relationships (inclusion, intersection) between data and values in the databases, indicating a generalization/specialization kind of relationship between the corresponding classes and attributes.

Some of the comparison approaches are:

- Computation of a similarity function between pairs of attributes [26]
- Computation of a semantic pertinence between elements using fuzzy logic [10].

Once established, these correspondences sometimes reveal different representations of the same concept, depending on the schema. These differences, called "inter-schema conflicts" or "semantic heterogeneity" (see[22] for a classification) are responsible for several types of problems during the integration step. Thus, the goal of the comparison step is twofold: first, to discover the inter-schema correspondences and second, to identify the conflicts and distinguish their type in order to prepare the integration step.

2.3 Integration

The integration process consists, generally in a semiautomatic way, to build an integrated schema starting with:

- source (original) schemes (eventually translated in a canonical data model)
- inter-schema correspondences (coming from the comparison step)
- integration rules (depending on the method and data models used).

2.4 Schema Transformation

This step is mainly present in case of view integration. The recent approaches (federated ones) don't allow later modifications of source schemes, to preserve the local environment (data, applications) of the databases composing the federation and to guarantee their autonomy.

3 Terminology and Concept Bases

3.1 Foundation of Terminology

Among the numerous meanings of the word *terminology*, we note the following ones (coming from [5]) which justify the usage of terminology in our work:

1. *Description of an Existing Terminology Content.* This is a systematic study of an existing terminological reality. It consists in making an inventory of the terms of a domain and to organize them as a "domain tree". Each term is defined, described, its relationships with other terms are noted. This is an analytic activity describing the lexical and conceptual aspects of a domain in order to establish a dictionary.

2. *Set of Terms Related to a Domain.* This is a coherent set of terms reflecting the conceptual system of a domain. It constitutes the vocabulary used by experts of the domain. In that sense, it represents a particular language.

Thus, the approach we propose supports the schemes preintegration task by a terminological activity (in the sense of 1) to establish one or many terminologies (in the sense of 2) of a domain. These terminologies will then constitute the core of concept bases.

Terms, Concepts, and the Domain

A *term* is the significant unit which uniquely defines a concept within a domain. The term is made up of one word (simple term) or several words (complex term).

A *concept* is a representation of a reality's aspect isolated by the mind. This is a unit of thinking based on a set of properties attributed to an object or a class of objects.

The *domain* may be an activity, a problem, a discipline in which a language called "particular language" (as opposed to the general language) exists and is used by experts of the domain.

The relationships between term, concept and domain are shown in Fig. 1:

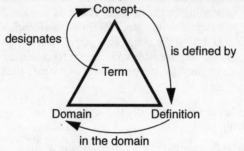

Fig. 1 Term, Concept and Domain relationships

Theoretical Aspects of Terminology

Terminology studies the designation process, the organization of concepts in classes and systems, the conceptual structuration of a domain. It also studies lexicons and nomenclatures, their structure and their use. Moreover, terminology uses results from other fields such as taxonomy, logic, linguistic, etc.

The role of the definition is very important in terminology. A concept definition must permit to distinguish it from any other. For that purpose, the existing relationships between a concept and the rest of the domain must be enumerated and its defining characteristics values specified.

3.2 Terminology Building Method

The "classical" approach of a terminologist building the terminology of a domain begins with a precise delimitation of this domain. Complementing sources of information are then collected. The goal is to collect documents acting as domain reference sources like dictionaries, regulations or any other accepted and up-to-date documents.

The domain tree materializes the generic-specific relationships existing between the concepts. It is augmented each time a new concept is found and/or when analysing its definition. An other use of the domain tree is to delimit a domain by enumerating the set of its concepts.

The main data representation tool of the terminologist is the term record. A term record represents a concept, using a set of textual fields filled with the concept corresponding values. Apart from the concept's definition, terminological, linguistic and other information concerning the making of a record are also noted (source mention, reliability degree, etc.). A set of such records can be stored in a database to form a *terminological database* (or term bank).

3.3 From Terminological Bases to Concept Bases

A concept base is a database dedicated to the storage and management of a set of concepts related to a common domain. The information stored for each concept is composed of its definition and its relationships with other concepts (in particular the generic/specific relationship).

Since the definition of a concept stored in a terminological database is expressed in a natural language form, it is not easily machine processable. If one wants to automatically manage concepts, it is necessary to express their definition in a formal way. This is usually accomplished by choosing a set of characteristics, the values of which are necessary and sufficient to distinguish each concept from the others. The formalized definition of a concept is then expressed by specifying the values it takes for each characteristics.

For example, during our study of the furniture domain (see section 7), the following defining characteristics have been collected: *accessories*, *parts*, *dimension*, *shape*, *perception*, *place*, *localization*, *material*, *main usage*, *secondary usage*. Thus, when establishing the furniture terminology, each concept has been defined and described by giving the value it takes for these common properties.

The formalization of concepts' definitions makes it possible to implement functions such as finding a concept on the basis of characteristics or comparing concepts and express what makes them different.

4 A Terminological Approach to Schema Preintegration

We focus our attention on the first step of the integration process, called "preintegration". As explained in section 2.2, this step is dedicated to the analysis of the source schemes in order to extract their semantic content. To this end we propose to create a concept base on top of each schema to integrate. Such a concept base aims at (re-)building the conceptual dictionary of the domain currently modelled by a schema.

The goal is to build a concept description as complete as possible to better inform the "integrator" on the meaning of concepts existing in the several databases to integrate. The more precise the concepts descriptions are, the more reliable will be their comparison, thus avoiding to consider as equivalent concepts which are only superficially (at the schema level) equivalent.The main advantage of a concept base over a simple terminological database is its formal representation of concepts that will ease automatic processing during the schema comparison step.

4.1 Terminology Building

To build a concept base it is necessary to first establish the terminology of the schema's domain.The first task is to identify the domain and to establish a list of all its terms. The schema may be a good starting point, its study showing the partial organization of the concepts stored in the database. Nevertheless, the schema only covers a subset of the domain (see point 2.1); it must be considered as an incomplete source, so other sources (like dictionaries or regulations) are necessary to reveal missing concepts. These sources provide precise (and accepted) definitions of the different concepts as well as the statements of rules governing relationships between concepts. Their textual orientation allows also to gather other information like synonyms, attribute domain, context, etc.

When building the domain tree (conceptual structure), concepts that were not present in the schema may appear. For example, the concept of "teacher" is not taken into account in a database containing classes Professor and Lecturer, both subclasses of Employee. However, the concept of teacher owns characteristics which are different from other employees like technicians or secretaries.

4.2 Concept Base Building

The main task involved in concept base building is to find properties that characterize the domain's concepts. These properties are sometimes ignored at the data schema level, because they seem to be implicit in the framework of a database. For example, the usage is a common property of any piece of furniture; nevertheless, it is unlikely that it will be explicitly given for each entity in a furniture database composed of classes like "seat" and "wardrobe". Indeed, each of these classes represents a set of furniture sharing an implicit value of usage ("to seat", "to arrange"). This is why the discovery of characteristics must use the definitions stored in the terminological database. Although this task cannot be fully automated, an array of computerized tools for browsing terms definitions, doing textual searches, etc. greatly enhance human capabilities.

5 Architecture and Functions of the Concept Base

The concept base we propose to build on top of each schema must not only store concepts characteristics, it must also support activities like: terminology building, formal characteristics finding, concepts comparison, and finally schema integration. For these purposes each concept is described at three levels, namely: terminological, formal characteristics, and representation in the underlying schema.

5.1 Terminological Information and Functions

The terminological description of a concept includes common terminological information such as: *term*: *definition*, *position* in the concept hierarchy, *related and dependent concepts*, *linguistic context* (the set of verbs, actions, adjectives, etc. which may be associated to the term in the domain language).

As mentioned earlier, finding out an appropriate set of characteristics for the concepts of a domain is an exploratory process that requires browsing, navigation, and search tools as well as more sophisticated tools to establish statistics and concordance. This is why we chose to represent terminological information in a hypertext structure. Each hypertext node stores textual information about a concept (term, definition, etc.), while hyperlinks represent semantic relationships between concepts (generic/specific, existential dependency, "part-of", etc.).

The navigation capabilities of hypertext systems, combined with global associative search and easy link building make it an efficient support to knowledge acquisition and exploration during the base's building phase, and a helpful tool for domain understanding and learning during both integration and exploitation.

In the *ConcepTerm* prototype this hypertext layer is implemented as a set of Hyper-Card® "stacks", with specialized exploration tools programmed in the HyperTalk® scripting language.

5.2 Formal Characteristics

In order to be automatically processed, the description of each concept must be based on a common "mould", its elements having to be as elementary as possible.

The formal characterisation of a set of concepts is based on the finding of common properties systematically present in each concept description, but with different values. Since characteristics values can themselves have a complex structure we chose to represent the formal definition of concepts as complex objects in an object-oriented data model. For instance the concept of "bergere" (in the furniture domain) can be represented by the following complex object:

```
BERGERE =
  [    generic: "easy chair"
       term: "bergere"
       parts: {    [type: "arm" number: 2]
                   [type: "seat" number: 1 dimension: [adjective: "wide"] ] }
       material: [type: "upholstered]
       particularity: [type: "style" value "18th century"] ]
```

In addition, an object-oriented data model with complex values is well adapted to the specification of operations and methods acting on a concept base. Some of these operations are:

- complex properties inheritance, which needs more complicated process than the usual duplicating of generic inherited values
- comparison of concepts based on properties values
- search of equivalent concepts in another concept base.

The formal characteristics layer of the ConcepTerm prototype is based on the F2 object-oriented database management system [7] and its F2Concept extension [8][9]. The whole system is implemented as a client/server architecture, the hypertext layer acting as a graphical user interface and the F2 DBMS as a concept management system.

5.3 Mapping to Underlying Schemes

Generally, databases aim at storing a (computer) representation of a subset of the complete extension of a concept. For example, in a College database, we'll find the subset of the "student" concept extension corresponding to the students registered in that College. Each individual student will be represented by a tuple of values expressing his(her) name, first name, degree, etc. On the other hand, some concepts will not be represented by data but by a process, an integrity constraint, a deduction rule (if available) or even by a combination of data/process/constraint/rules.

The description of a concept's representation in a database is given by a function which associates to each concept:

- its representation in terms of object-oriented schema elements, describing the form taken by an instance of the concept within the underlying database
- several instance management procedures describing the primitives operations to create or delete an instance, to search (access to) any or all instances, etc. These procedures are only specified if they are not implied by the representation schema.

The following list enumerates a set of elementary representation schemes we have identified:

a) Concept → (Virtual) Class

In this simplest case, a concept is mapped to a class; an object represents an instance of the concept. The operations defined on instances correspond to those on objects (create, update, delete).

If the class is virtual, i.e. computed using one or many other classes (like a relational view), the operations of instance creation and deletion may be more complex and have to be explicitly described.

Example: The concept of "literary works" may be represented by a virtual class derived from the *Author* and *Book* classes:

```
virtual class Works
    attributes
        author:     Author,
        novels:     set(Book),
        essays:     set(Book))
    connections
        novels = select n in Book where n.author = author and n.type = "novel"
        essays = select e in Book where e.author = author and e.type = "essay"
```

To find the works instance corresponding to the author "Hugo", we need to select an *Author* object and to join it with objects from the *Book* class. The deletion of this instance would require the deletion of all books of this author.

b) Concept → Attribute

Each instance of the concept is represented by a value of the same attribute. It should be noted that the existence of an instance depends on the existence of an object in the class owning the attribute.

Example: The concept of "mother tongue" may be represented using an attribute *mother_tongue* in the *Person* class, its set of values defined in class *Language*. To create an instance of mother tongue amounts to give a value of *mother_tongue* for an existing entity of the *Person* class.

When an attribute is calculated (not stored), the creation and suppression operations have to be explicitly defined. Note that concepts represented by attributes are always dependent on other concepts and act as links between concepts.

c) Instance → Class or Set

An instance of a concept may appear as a set of objects of the same type. In that case, the instance will be represented by a "container" which should be a class extension or a selection of objects.

Example: The market prices of stock S (the values of stock S during a period) may be represented as

class S
    attributes date, value, exchanged_volume

or as

select x.date, x.value, x.exchanged_volume **from** x **in** Exchange_daily_record
where label = "S".

d) Concept → Integrity Constraint Schema

Some concepts do not generate any data, i.e. their instances are not explicitly stored in the database, but they act upon its content either as constraints or as data transformations rules.

Example: The concept of "land occupation" may be represented by a generic constraint:

for all p **in** PieceOfLand p.surface_built / p.surface < t

An instance of this concept corresponds an instantiation of the constraint formula, i.e. a formula obtained by replacing all free variables by constants, as in

for all p **in** PieceOfLand: p.surface_built / p.surface < 0.25

e) Concept → Process Schema

When a concept is an action, its representation may be a process (method, transaction, or application). An instance of such a concept corresponds to the execution of this process.

Example: The concept of *promotion* is represented by a method:

    promote (toGrade, date)

of class Student. The creation of an instance of *promotion* corresponds to the execution of the method on an object with actual parameters, like in:

    joe.promote(G6, 1994-06-31)

The ability to delete an instance depends on the existence of an inverse process; in the same way, the access to existing instances is realized by querying the process execution history (to be recorded in a journal). The architecture of a concept base is illustrated in Fig. 2 below.

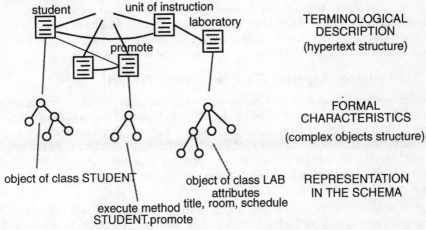

Fig. 2 A three level Architecture of a Concept Base

6 Concepts Comparison and Translation

The building of a concept base on top of each schema to integrate allows a two-levels comparison of these schemes: First, on the represented concepts and second, on the schema elements and population. Concepts comparison is necessary since the same term may designate different concepts, depending on the system. For instance, although there exists a class Student in two schemes to compare, the concept of student may be different in the two systems; it is thus necessary to exactly understand the similarities and differences between these concepts before trying to integrate or translate underlying schema elements.

The comparison of concepts is based on their characteristic values and on the existence of well established equivalencies between these values. An equivalence function is defined for each formal characteristic. Thus, an equivalence function may be "simple", consisting of value comparison according to their identity or to a value scale. On the other hand, some functions may consist of complex comparison and calculation to determine equivalence.Examples of equivalence functions:

- "Simple" function: equivalence between *dimension*s (tall, small): This function is based on an existing order between dimension values (ex: small ≤ tall)
- "Complex" function: Equivalence between the *usage* of pieces of furniture (to store books, to store clothes, to seat, to sleep). In that case, the function has to

be defined on both the action (to store, to seat, to sleep) and the objects on which the action is acting (books, clothes)

• Function with translation: equivalence between characteristics values express in different language or with synonyms, e.g., *usage.action: to sleep* (English) is equivalent to *usage.action: schlafen* (German). In that case a set of simple term equivalencies (like *to sleep* ≈ *schlafen*) between the two languages must be provided.

Once equivalencies between concept of different schemes have been discovered, inter-schema correspondences can be established using the schema representation of these concepts and validated at the population level. Generally, equivalencies will not be perfect, indicating that some extra work has to be done to find correct inter-schema correspondences. In this respect one can mention concepts which are not completely equivalent although they have the same representations in the underlying schemes. This is the kind of semantic conflict that cannot be detected at the schema level.

7 Methodology Aspects: The *ConcepTerm* Project[1]

ConcepTerm is a research project dedicated to the creation of encyclopedic and multilingual dictionaries of concepts. The building and management process of such dictionaries is studied. *ConcepTerm* is a collaboration between database specialists and terminologists from the University of Geneva. The interdisciplinary nature of the project aims at putting together database and terminological formalisms, in order to define a set of generic methods and tools to support the building of a new generation of computerized dictionaries.

The architecture defined for this project is based on concept bases describing the conceptual spaces of a particular domain in four different languages. In this case, the four languages should be seen themselves as four different *domains*, each one with its own domain tree and concept space. These concept bases are used to physically store the terminologies of the domain; they were realized with terminological techniques assisted by computer tools.

Building of the Dictionary "0"

The domain of furniture was chosen to serve as conceptual space for our first dictionary. This domain was chosen for different reasons, including the fact that everybody knows it and that documents describing the domain are abundant.

A first set of defining characteristics was drawn up by analysing the definitions found in general dictionaries and reference books of the domain. Concepts definitions, together with their characteristics were entered in a hypertext system. Using exploration and analysis tools we were able to further refine the structure of characteristic values until they were broken into sufficiently simple pieces (words or numbers). Once this structure was well established concepts descriptions were entered into an F2 database linked to the hypertext system. This resulted in the building of four separate dictionaries of furniture (in French, English, German and Italian) of approximately 250 concepts each.

The next step was to establish equivalencies between defining characteristics values for each pair of languages. Once again, an exploratory approach was taken to create equivalence relations between simple values stored in the dictionaries.

---

1. Supported by Swiss FNRS. See [4] for a description of the project

Finally an interactive tool to find concept equivalencies has been designed, that is based on a set of value equivalence relations. We are currently studying the definition and implementation of more complex equivalence functions.

Development of Computer Tools

The dictionary "0" has been used as a test platform for the data structures, tools and interfaces developed for *ConcepTerm*. It allowed us to recognize the different functionalities needed by the users during both the dictionary building process (expert users) and query process (non-expert users). These needs have also been considered for both mono- and multilingual usage.

8 Conclusion and Future Directions

We have presented a possible solution to the investigation step of the database schema integration process. This solution proposes to use terminological techniques during the preintegration step. Each schema is semantically enriched by building a concept base on top of it. These concept bases will then support the comparison of concepts and the establishment of correspondences between schema elements. The main advantages of this approach are:

- Better inter-schema correspondences based on domain knowledge instead of schema information
- Clear distinction between concepts comparison and schema comparison
- The discovery of possible semantic conflicts that do not appear at schema level (when different concepts have the same representation)
- The building of a very high level, yet computer based, description of an information system.

Moreover, other activities where a complete and precise description of a domain is necessary may gain advantages from such a concept base:

Design Dictionaries: A concept base may be used to build and manage a design dictionary, frequently called "encyclopedia" or "repository". The CASE tools success has shown the interest for that kind of dictionaries. Unfortunately, it has also shown that a simple "schema collection" support system is not sufficient to help a team of designers work together on a project. A concept base should allow the sharing of a terminology, based on precise definitions coming from accepted sources and improved with more personal information like abbreviations or synonyms used by the different designers during their activities.

High-level Interfaces: The recent World Wide Web project [16] and its growing success show that both the electronic (wide) publication of information and the access to information are becoming major concern of organizations. Consequently, databases, as potential sources of huge information volumes, have to participate to this process. A concept base seems to be a possible support to the publication of a database, by presenting to the "external" world a semantically improved schema (multi-language descriptions, definitions, synonyms). Mappings defined in the concept base should be used to access the underlying system.

The remote users have to be considered as a new type of users for a database. They ignore some aspects implicitly known by the "local" users, members of the organization. Thus, a concept base representing a complete terminology of the domain and clearly describing these implicit aspects should improve the navigation and the information search process in conventional databases.

Future Research Directions

Our future research directions include the definition and implementation of more complex equivalence functions in a semiautomatic comparison system. We have also observed that it would be valuable to include encyclopedic information (like examples, properties, pictures, etc.) within the description of concepts in order to help their understanding and comparison, in particular for abstract and complex domains. Finally, we continue to study hypertext and hypermedia interface for concept bases and to develop the tools needed to build and manage such systems.

Acknowledgments

We are deeply grateful to Prof. Michel Léonard for giving us the opportunity to work on this subject and for fruitful discussions. We also thank Bruno de Bessé for exposing us to terminology and Atika Laribi and Ian Prince for their precious comments.

References

1. T. Barsalou, G. Wiederhold, "Knowledge-directed Mediation between Application Objects and Base Data", In *Data and Knowledge Base Integration* (ed. S M Deen).

2. C. Batini, M. Lenzerini, S.B. Navathe, "A comparative analysis of methodologies for database schema integration", *ACM Computing Surveys*, 15, 1986.

3. M.W. Bright, A.R. Hurson, "Linguistic support for semantic identification and interpretation in multidatabases", In *Proceedings of First International Workshop on Interoperability in Multidatabase Systems*, Kyoto, 1991.

4. ConcepTerm: "Construction de dictionnaires encyclopédiques de concepts multilingues et informatisés", *projet FNRS no. 12-28834.90*. Common project of CUI (database) and ETI (terminology).

5. B. de Bessé, "Stage de terminologie", Ecole de Traduction et d'Interprétation, Genève, mars 1991.

6. C. F. Eick, "A Methodology for the Design and Transformation of Conceptual schemes", In *Proceedings of 17th VLDB*, Barcelona, 1991.

7. Th. Estier, G. Falquet."F2: an Evolution Oriented Database System, CUI Tech. report no. 69, Centre Universitaire d'Informatique, Genève, 1993.

8. G. Falquet, J. Sindayamaze, M. Bonjour, M. Léonard. "F2Concept, un Modèle intégrant la Description de la Compréhension et l'Extension des Classes d'Objets", Proc. VIIèmes Journées Bases de Données Avancées BD3, Lyon, 1991.

9. G. Falquet, M. Léonard, J. Sindayamaze. "F2Concept: a Database System for Managing Classes'Extensions and Intensions.", In Proc. of the 3rd European-Japanese seminar on Information Modelling and Knowledge Bases, Budapest, 1993.

10. P. Fankhauser, M. Kracher, E.J. Neuhold, "Semantic VS. Structural Resemblance of Classes", *SIGMOD RECORD*, Vol 20, No 4, Dec. 1991.

11. S. Hayne, S. Ram, "Multi-User View Integration System (MUVIS): An Expert System for View Integration", In *Proceedings of 6th Conference on Data Engineering*, 1991.

12. International Journal of Intelligent & Cooperative Information Systems, ed. M.P. Papazoglou, T.K. Sellis.

13. Y. Kambayashi, M. Rusinkiewicz, A.P. Sheth, "First International Workshop on Interoperability in Multidatabase Systems", Kyoto, 1991.

14. M. Kaul, K. Drosten, E.J. Neuhold, "ViewSystem: Integrating Heterogeneous Information Bases by Object-Oriented Views", In *Proceedings of DATA Engineering*, Los Alamitos [etc.]: IEEE, cop. 1992.

15. W. Kim, N. Ballou, J.F Garza, D. Woelk, "A Distributed Object Oriented Database System supporting Shared and Private Databases", *ACM Trans. on Information Systems*, Vol 9, No 1, 1991.

16. E. Krol, M. Loukides (eds). *The Whole Internet: user's guide and catalog*, Sebastopol: O'Reilly, 1992.

17. W. Litwin, L. Mark, N. Roussopoulos, "Interoperability of Multiple Autonomous Databases", *ACM computing surveys*, Vol 22, No 3, Sep.1990.

18. F. Manola, S. Heiler, D. Georgakopoulos, "Distributed Object Management", *International Journal of Intelligent & Cooperative Information Systems*, Vol 1, No 1, March 1992.

19. T. Ozsu, P. Valduriez, "Principles of Distributed Database Systems", Prentice Hall ed., 1989.

20. M.P. Papazoglou, S.C. Laufmann, T.K. Sellis, "An Organizational Framework for Cooperative Intelligent Information Systems", *International Journal of Intelligent & Cooperative Information Systems*, Vol 1, No 1, March 1992.

21. F. Saltor, M. Castallanos, M. Garcia-Solaco, "Suitability of data models as canonical models for federeted databases", *SIGMOD RECORD*, Vol 20, No 4, Dec. 1991.

22. A.P. Sheth, J. Larson, "Federated Database Systems for managing heterogeneous, distributed and autonomous Databases", *ACM Computing Surveys*, Vol 22, No 3, 1990.

23. A.P. Sheth, V. Kashyap, "So Far (Schematically) yet So Near (Semantically)", in *Proceedings of Interoperable Database Systems*, Lorne, Australia, 1992.

24. S. Spaccapietra, C. Parent, Y. Dupont, "Model Independant Assertions for Integration of Heterogeneous schemes", *VLDB Journal*, 1, ed. Dennis McLeod, 1992.

25. C.C. Woo, F. Lochovsky, "Knowledge Communication in Intelligent Information Systems", *International Journal of Intelligent & cooperative Information Systems*, Vol 1, No 1, March 1992.

26. C. Yu, W. Sun, S. Dao, "Determining Relationships among Names in Heterogeneous Databases", *SIGMOD RECORD*, Vol 20, No 4, Dec. 1991.

Formalisation of Data and Process Model Reuse Using Hierarchic Data Types

Dongsu Seo and Pericles Loucopoulos
Department of Computation
UMIST
POBox 88, Manchester M60 1QD, U.K.

Abstract. A need for new paradigms has emerged for the construction of IS models based on the concept of reuse. The aim of this paper is to present a methodology that adopts the type information obtained from existing software structures to the development of new data and process models. A formalism and methodology are presented that advocate model reuse in terms of both data and process modelling viewpoints. By providing entity affinity sets and synonym function, an effective way of mapping a reusable data model to its corresponding process model can be achieved. Additionally, examples are presented whose objective is to demonstrate the applicability of the proposed techniques.

1   Introduction

An early reuse of requirements and specifications may improve the productivity of new software systems [2], [3], [9], since early decisions for reuse recognise existing mappings from those concepts of design alternatives. This facilitates both effective design of new software systems and management of existing systems by addressing the reuse of requirement and conceptual models [2], [7], [8]. Such an orientation of reuse is often referred to as "wide reuse" [3]. In addition research results, such as REDO [5], GIST [1], Objectwork [13], present examples of the use of domain sensitive techniques. Significant benefits expected from an early reuse have been pointed in [14]. In line with the optimistic views in [14], this paper observes the potential of reuse on information systems from two properties: (a) the perceived benefits of reuse can be expected during requirement modelling stages so that earlier assistance can be provided in the development of lifecycle and (b) specifications tend to be more easily understood and reused than design components, since they are represented using structured development notions (e.g. data flow diagrams, entity life histories, etc.). This paper restricts research concerns on reuse within the range of information systems and their related environments. Conventional techniques used for reuse will also be revised to make them suitable for the business models where reuse activities are defined.

1.1   Problems of Reusable Component Construction

In [4] some factors were pointed out that software engineers should take into account in designing the potentially reusable systems from the following viewpoints[1]: ability to

---

[1]Cognitive aspects of the inhibiting factors have not been fully exploited in [3]. For more detail, refer to [14]

represent knowledge about software; ability to express controlled degree of abstraction; ability to create partial specifications; ability to allow flexible coupling between instances of designs. A discipline for the structuring of reusable knowledge is strongly required because development fragments obtained from various application systems tend to differ from each other. One typical problem is to name and classify the reusable components for mapping and linking to the related applications. One cannot comprehend the potential of the components by simply referring to the component's name. More relevant information such as semantic relations, that explain semantic meaning of the components would be helpful. The ability to express some degree of abstraction, i.e. genericity, is also an important factor to be considered for the reusable model. In modelling an information system, data generalisation has not been properly dealt with in the reuse of conceptual modelling. As an attempt to provide abstract representations for data models, some research [7], [13] has adopted a variety of composition and abstraction techniques including *component composition*, *component abstraction*, and *genericity*. Coupled to the demand for abstract representation of the model, generic representations have also been studied. Genericity means parameterisation of software components which serves as a specification for data types in making new components.

In this paper, we will address the first two issues, i.e. *representing reusable information* and *controlling the level of abstraction in model representation*. The last two factors that are related to partial specifications and component coupling, are much more cognitive intensive areas and are beyond the scope of this paper.

1.2   Related Works

Models and methods supporting the development of reusable components have been defined for both software components [10] and conceptual specification [7], [8]. In [8] methods and techniques for the reuse of object-oriented specifications were suggested. Behavioural components, in that approach, are described by use of two generic modules, called a generic resource and meta class and generic process class. Both generic classes are constructed from a set of similar application dependent process specifications, factoring out their common behaviour. One advantageous factor in the approach is to utilise semantic mapping functions that infers corresponding synonyms from the entity dictionary. However, because this approach deals with information defined in the entity domain of synonyms, its efficient application in process description is debatable. Furthermore, it lacks a semantic definition of abstract mapping of process classes. A similar effort has been made in developing a wide reuse support system, the IDeA [12]. In this, common representations of reusable knowledge have been provided based on a data type hierarchy. By introducing type constraint variables, selections on data types are made at the different levels of abstraction. However, the reusable components considered in [12] form a rather simple structure. The data structure the IDeA can deal with is a set of enumerative data. Complex notions of data (e.g. complex object or entity clusters) are not adequately supported.

Our aim is to show equivalence relations for data and process related models that can be easily understood, and to give a more clear view of reusing the models based on the *behaviour of hierarchical type systems*. Thus, this paper will approach both the structural and semantic representation problems that [8] and [12] have overlooked.

1.3   Basic Assumptions and Overview

The aim of this paper is to develop a methodology that adopts the type information obtained from existing software structures to the development of new data and process models. A collection of techniques and formalisms will be integrated into a uniform view of conceptual modelling. To this end, the paper identifies the factors that facilitate the use of type information for reuse. Due to the fact that information systems make use of data models and process models, we provide assumptions on the two models and the mapping function that facilitates the reuse of the data model. The main concerns of the data model presented in this paper is to examine abstract relations of data models on the semantic level from the viewpoint of reuse. Thus, reuse concerns should be of the reuse of: data model components and the process descriptions that access the data model

The conceptual modelling paradigm of TEMPORA [15] has been chosen as a target data model, since TEMPORA supports well known ER-based representation for data model with enhanced features such as complex, temporal, and hierarchical representations and its process model is closely related to the data model.

Polymorphic functions use type variables, which can be assigned particular type values, to represent relationships between different instances of data types. We assume that process descriptions with regard to the data models should be polymorphic in the sense that they can be applied to a variety of specific data types. The polymorphic descriptions need to be type-checked to be applied with the individual applications of the polymorphic descriptions later in the integration stages. Type checking and inference make it possible to propagate design information from a context that is established by the user specifications. This will reduce the burden on the user of supplying complete specifications, since the missing details can be found while performing the type checking. The main use of mapping functions considered in this paper will be the selection of reusable data models. For this purpose, we introduce a semantic relation called *affinity relation* that defines a degree of similarities between objects[2]. Two types of affinity relation are allowed between a pair of objects: an *overlap* relation and an *equivalent* relation. A component pair belongs to the overlap relation if property sets of the two components are overlapping; and a component pair belongs to the equivalent relation if property sets of the two components are identical in terms of affinity data sets. The structure of this paper is as follows. Section 2 presents the groundwork for entity types and type hierarchy that will facilitate the representation of ISA relations shown in a TEMPORA data model. In sections 3 and 4, structuring the data model and process model are discussed respectively. Finally section 5, gives a summary and discusses future research directions.

2   Types and Subtypes in Data Models

Coupled to the demands for the representational flexibility, a concise way of understanding the semantic information is also needed. As preparatory steps for the proposed paradigm this section introduces a concept of entity types and type hierarchy that can support flexible representation of the data and process models for reuse.

---

[2] In this paper information on affinity sets is obtained from the analysis of type structure from the components. This way of obtaining semantic information differes from [7],[8].

2.1 Simple Hierarchic Relation

A canonical, but rather intuitive definition for data types as advocated in [6], is that a data type is a categorisation of objects according to their usage and behaviour. In an information systems modelling paradigm, such as TEMPORA, perception of data types is rather complex. In order to define a type of entity sets with regard to their corresponding value and relationships, we take into account all properties and present the entity set as a record. Each instance of ERT is considered as a stream of data, called an *ERT record*. The ERT record is a finite association of values to labels made by composite operators. The labels belong to separate simple entity domains, i.e. the value, the relationship, the cardinality and time stamp class. To make the idea clear we introduce the following syntactic notation for the ERT record type:

```
T := BaseType|(e_1 : T_1   and ... and e_n : T_n)|BaseType:= Val;Rel;Card
V := Const | Var | ( e_1 : V_1   and ... and e_n : V_n ) | V.e
```

Type T contains base types including *Val, Rel, Card* which represent the type of three classes; the value, the relationship, the cardinality, respectively. Each element in *BaseType* consists of the following:

```
Val  := integer | real | boolean | string <length>
Rel  := characters
Card := (integer, integer)
```

Value V includes constants *Const*, variables *Var*, and constructors and selectors for ERT record types. The record constructor is $(e_1:V$ and ... and $e_n:V_n)$, while $V.e$ returns the value part of V, if its label is e and fails otherwise. As an example of record-based representation of ERT model, consider the following ERT diagram in figure 1. The ERT model shown in figure 1 has corresponding record structure as follows:

Employee = (has; Address; (1,1) and has; ProjNo; (1,1) and has; Salary; (1,1))

In its record expression, types are assigned to all subcomponents that constitute an entity. By using the subcomponent sets, an entity component can have one or more types. For this purpose, we write $e:t$ (meaning entity component e has type τ). The type of an entity is defined by the following definition.

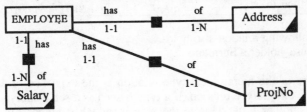

Figure 1. Example Employee ERT

Definition 1 Let an attribute v be v $\in$ {Val, Card, Rel}, and an attribute type τ be $\tau \in$ {val_type, card_type, rel_type}. If $v_1 : \tau_1 .. v_n : \tau_n$ then a ERT record $(e_1 : v_1 ;... ;e_n: v_n)$ has an ERT type $(e_1 : v_1 ;... ;e_n: v_n) : (e_1 : \tau_1 ,...., e_n : \tau_n)$

For example, definition 1 enables an ERT record to have a entity type according to the types of component sets. For example, *Employ* has a type

Employee: (Rel:char; Val:string; Card:(int,int))

A subtype relation on ERT can be viewed as follows: consider some ERT classes *Goods*, *Furniture*, and *Desk* with the following value classes:

Object	= (has;product_year)
Goods	= (has;product_year and has;price)
Furniture	= (has;product_year and has;price and has;material)
Desk	= (has;product_year and has;price and has;material and has;colour)

Intuitively, we know that the entities *Furniture* and *Desk* belong to *Object*, and *Desk* belongs to *Furniture*. Then, *Desk* is called a subtype of the entities *Furniture* and *Goods*; *Furniture* is a subtype of *Goods*, etc. This subtype relation is denoted by ≤ relations. In relation to the subtype definition above, the following rule 1 denotes the ordering relation of subtypes.

Rule 1 Given entity set $e_i \in \{E\}$ and component types $\tau_i \in \{Val, Card, Rel\}$, where $1 \leq i \leq n+m$, iff $\tau_1 \leq \tau_2, .., \tau_m \leq \tau_n$ then $(e_1:\tau_1, .., e_{n+m}:\tau_{n+m}) \leq (e_1:\tau_1, .., e_n:\tau_n)$

Based on rule 1 the following relations hold:

Desk ≤ Furniture

Furniture ≤ Object

When a schema deals with objects of many different related types, subtyping allows concise way of representing similar data objects by allowing the model only on the maximum type. The related objects then inherit structural properties from their parent (or super-) class. For example, consider the following example

Furniture	= (has;product_year and has;price and has;material)
House_holder	= (has;name, has;address; has:Furniture)

Intuitively, the relation of Furniture and House_holder indicates that *Furniture* has been used in describing the part of*House_holder* as as a subtype. A type system that allows the notion of subtyping is called *hierarchical* . The relations defined in hierarchical ordering is defined by the following definition.

Rule 2 Given entity set $e_i \in \{E\}$ and component types $\tau_i \in \{Val, Card, Rel\}$, where $1 \leq i \leq n$, iff.$\tau_i \leq \tau_i'$ then $(e_1:\tau_1 , ..e_i:\tau_i.., e_n:\tau_n) \leq (e_1:\tau_1 ,..e_i:\tau_i'.., e_n:\tau_n)$

Thus, by rule 2 the following relation also holds.

House_holder ≤ Furniture

One important feature of the hierarchical type relation is the existence of easy and intuitive semantics for the subtype relation. If a type is seen as a set, a subtype can be seen as a subset of another type. This is the way in which subtypes are usually informally explained.

2.2 The Use of Subtyping in Process Description

In TEMPORA, a process is an abstraction of a business activity. It performs some identifiable task in the information system. It is a series of steps or operations towards a desired result or product, and can denote anything from a vague activity taking place in an organisation to a simple hardware related activity. In order to facilitate reuse of process definition we need to define types for functions that include entities with types as their input and output arguments. A function is called meaningful if the function's argument are defined with regard to the type. This property of a function is represented by the following two rules:

Rule 3 Given entity types $\tau, \tau', \sigma \in$ {Val, Card, Rel}, and process f, if f: $\sigma \rightarrow \tau$ and a: σ then f(a) is meaningful, and f(a):τ

Rule 4 Given entity types $\tau, \tau', \sigma, \sigma' \in$ {Val, Card, Rel}, and process f, if f: $\sigma \rightarrow \tau$ and a:σ', where $\sigma' \leq \sigma$ then f(a) is meaningful, and f(a):τ

The conventional subclass relation is usually defined on entities in which functions take as inputs and returns as outputs. Cardelli's subtype relation also extends naturally function types. Consider for given entity relation

$$Employee \leq Person \text{ where,}$$
$$Employee \text{ (has;name and has address has;id\_number)}$$

the function *find_employee* that returns *Employee* according to its attribute *id_number*.

$$find\_employee: id\_number \rightarrow Employee$$

One may notice that *find_employee* returns entity *Employee*, as well as entity Persons, since all Employee valued functions are also Person valued function. That is,

$$\tau \rightarrow Employee \leq \tau \rightarrow Person \text{ because Employee} \leq Person$$

In general, given any function f: $\sigma \rightarrow \tau$ from domain σ to its codomain τ, we can always consider it as a function from some similar domain $\sigma' \subseteq \sigma$ to some bigger codomain $\tau' \supseteq \tau$ as shown in function *find_employee*. For this purpose, the following rule is given for the function with the parameter that has a subtyping relation.

Rule 5 Given entity types $\tau, \tau', \sigma, \sigma' \in$ {Val, Card, Rel}, and process f, if $\sigma' \leq \sigma$ and $\tau \leq \tau'$ then $\sigma \rightarrow \tau \leq \sigma' \rightarrow \tau'$

One important implication of rule 5 is the use of a polymorphic function. As mentioned earlier, the polymorphic function uses type variables. Consider the following definition of a polymorphic function *CheckMale*.

SexType = (male:object or female:object)
Person = (name:string and age:int and sex:SexType)
CheckMale : Person $\rightarrow$ Bool
CheckMale(pers:Person) ::= if (pers.Sex = male) then *True* else *False*

Although specified as operating on value of type *Person*, the function *CheckMale* could be applied, as defined, also to every entity with at least the *name:string* and *sex:SexType* fields, where *SexType* should be a union type with at most the male:object and the *female:object* fields. In a system with subtyping this can be expressed precisely associating the type:

(name:string and sex:SexType) $\rightarrow$ Bool   to this function.

The property of a polymorphic function, like CheckMale, which allows it to operate on values of many different record type is called *inclusion polymorphism* as the exact set of types of the function can be characterised in a hierarchical type system.

3   Data Model Reuse with Type Information

In this section the structure of entity objects is introduced on the basis of the ER modelling concept. The reusable object considered in this paper consists of two components: a generic entity class, and generic process class definition. A generic entity class explains characteristics of information and agents in a generic form. A generic process class defines interactions between different resources in common procedure

3.1 Generic Entity Classes

According to [15], objects can be complex, i.e. their properties can refer to other objects, or can have a complex domain, defined as a set/list of simple domain. Let C and C' be two object classes that are defined in the two domains Dom(C), Dom(C') respectively:

$$Dom(C) = d_1 \times d_2 \times ... \times d_n$$
$$Dom(C') = d'_1 \times d'_2 \times ... \times d'_n$$

Given two classes C, C', an inheritance hierarchy $\Psi = (G,E)$ is defined as a directed acyclic graph with a class set C, where C, C' $\in$ G, and a set of edges E labelled "IS-A" relation. There is a path from C to C' in , written C $\rightarrow$ C', if either C = C' or there exists a class C" $\in$ G with a path C $\rightarrow$ C' in Ψ. The degree of path D(C,C') with starting class C and ending class C" is the length of the longest path in Ψ from C to C'. The affinity set $\Delta(C)$ in the inheritance hierarchy Ψ is defined as a set of classes which satisfies the relation,

$$\Delta(C) = \{C_i \mid C \subseteq C_i\}$$

The affinity set contains all reachable data types within a single inheritance hierarchy. The affinity of data type is grouped together to form the set which includes different reachable cases from different elements. Within an affinity set, the ordering relation $\leq$ holds only between an element set and an affinity set. For example, in figure 1, the following ordering relation holds:

$$\{Lecturer\} \leq \{Academic\_Staff\}$$
$$\{CourseWork\_Student\} \leq \{Student\}$$

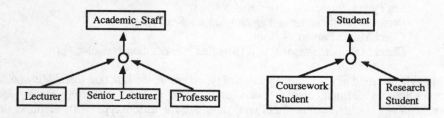

Figure 2. Hierarchy diagram for academic staff and student

However, the relation does not hold among the elements that share the same parent in the affinity set. For example, *Academic_Staff* shown in figure 1 has an element set:

$$\{Lecturer, Senior\_Lecturer, Professor\}$$

In this affinity set, the relations such as

$$\{Lecture\} \leq \{Professor\} \text{ or } \{Professor\} \leq \{Lecture\}$$

do not hold. Such relations are called incompatible. Given two entities C, C', in the inheritance hierarchy Ψ, the incompatible relation I(C,C') is defined as follows: I(C,C') returns true if C, C' are siblings, i.e. C and C' share the same parent node and the degree of path is the same, otherwise false.

Here, we present two kinds of affinity sets: a *data affinity* and *name affinity* sets. A data affinity set contains common data that are collected from two different entity affinity sets. A name affinity set provides possible synonyms that are deduced from two different entity affinity sets. Given two entities C, C', in the inheritance hierarchy Ψ, the data affinity set, DA(C,C') is defined as follows:

$$DA(C,C') = \Delta(C) \cap (C')$$

where, the subset term indicates the common entities that belong to both closure sets, thus explains commonalties for both sets.

The abstract mapping of two entity names, en, en', is the function φ defined as follows:

φ(en,en') = **if** syn(en,en') **then** en

else if Syn(en,en") $\wedge$ Syn(en',en") **then** en" **else** $\perp$

where syn(en,en') denotes a synonym function that finds corresponding synonyms from the entity dictionary in the component repository, and the symbol $\perp$ denotes "undefined".

For arbitrary domains d, d', the mapping function φ defines the abstract mapping of two domains d,d', denoted as φ(d,d'), as follows:

φ(d,d') = **if** d, d' are pre-defined scalar domains **then** d $\cap$ d'

else if GA(d,d') $\neq$ {} and I(d,d') **then** d **else** $\perp$

As an example of the affinity sets explained above, consider the ER diagram shown in figure 3 which shows the data model representing student-lecturer relations used in college admission systems. Based on it the following affinity sets can be obtained:

Δ(UCCA_Candidate)={UCCA_Candidate,Non_UCCA_Candidate,Research_ Candidate}

Δ(Student) = {CourseWork_Student, Research_Student}

The next stage is to determine a synonym set. The synonym set can be extracted from the analysis of relationship names and the overall context from the ERT diagram. For example, it is likely to happen that *Research_Candidate* contains a possibility to become *Research_Student*. Thus, we consider both to be in the same synonym set. Also, ISA relationship provides another opportunity for constructing the synonym set. For example, *Candidate* can be used as a synonym for both *Research_Student*, and *UCCA_Student* and possibly more. However, *Research_Student* can not be a synonym of *UCCA_Student* or vice versa. The followings are examples of synonym sets obtained from figure 3.

Syn_set 1 : {Candidate, Research_Candidate, Research_Student, Student}
Syn_set 2 : {Candidate, UCCA_Candidate, Student}
Syn_set 3 : {Candidate. Non_UCCA_Candidate, Student}
Syn_set 4 : {Lecturer, Supervisor, Admission_Tutor, Academic_Staff}
Syn_set 5 : {Course_Work, Student_Module}

Based on the above observation, we can obtain the following mapping function φ.

Syn(Research_Candidate, UCCA_Candidate) = {Candidate, Student}
Syn(Course_Work, Lecture) = {}
φ(Research_Candidate, UCCA_Candidate) = {Candidate}

The data affinity set and synonym set are used to build simplified ERT models that exhibits abstract mechanisms for future reuse. As a result we can obtain a generic ERT diagram shown in figure 4.

4 Process Model Reuse with Type Information

In most modelling paradigms, such as TEMPORA, behavioural aspects of an application domain are captured and represented by process models. The behavioural aspects involve representing functions or processes, external agents, events that invoke the various processes, and inputs and outputs of the process. In TEMPORA, a process model is expressed in the process description language, called PLL. It creates flows which are the means of interaction with other processes described in the process diagram, called PID, or with external agents and the ERT. Figure 5 presents an example of PID, which accesses and changes entity sets shown in figure 4.

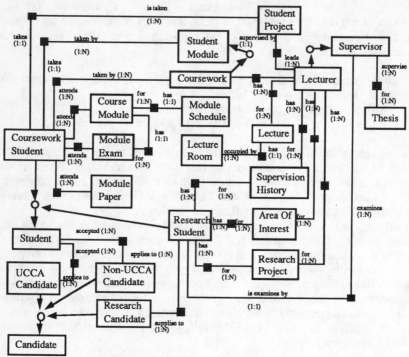

Figure 3. Student-Lecture ERT diagram

The processes appeared in the PID shown in figure 5 can be referred to by relating the process names with their corresponding input and output entities. The following is an example of processes defined in the above diagram.

P2 make_decision :   Research_Student, Supervisor →Bool
P5 report_vacances :   UCCA_Candidate → Admission_Tutor
P6 arrange_interview : UCCA_Candidate → UCCA_Candidate

4.1 Generic Process Class

In section 1 the importance of some features, i.e. abstraction, genericity, has been addresses in designing the reusable process model. A process model can form the generic process component that is extracted from a set of similar application-dependent process specifications by factoring out their common arguments. Before introducing the refinement steps for the generic process components, some definitions of a generic process class and its related functions are presented.

Let $E = \{e_1, ..., e_m\}$ and $E' = \{e'_1, ..., e'_n\}$ be the set of generic entities identified in the previous section. Then, the corresponding generic process classes, p, p', are characterised by the similarity of related entities, called data affinity set. The data affinity set $DA = \{d_1, ..., d_q\}$, is defined as follows,

$$\forall d_i \in DA, \exists e_i \in E, e'_i \in E' \mid d_i = \varphi(e_i, e'_i)$$

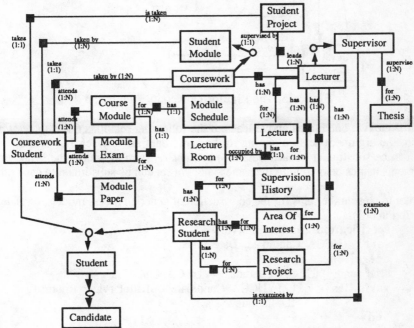

Figure 4. Generic Student-Lecture ERT diagram

For the abstract mapping of two processes p, p', defined in entity domains, Dom(E), Dom(E'), where $e \in$ Dom(E) and $e' \in$ Dom(E'), mapping function φ is defined as follows, with respect to input entities e_{in}, e'_{in} and output entities e_{out}, e'_{out}:

$\varphi(p,p') =$ **if** $(d = \varphi(e,e') \wedge \varphi(e_{in}, e'_{in}) \wedge \varphi(e_{out}, e'_{out}))$

         then   the generic function of p is definable

         else $\perp$

There may exist more than one generic function that explain subject processes p, p', according to the required abstraction level. Mapping function φ only examines the possibility of the generic function. On deciding the mapping function, two co-ordination arguments are considered compatible if: they involve compatible arguments and they are the same type.

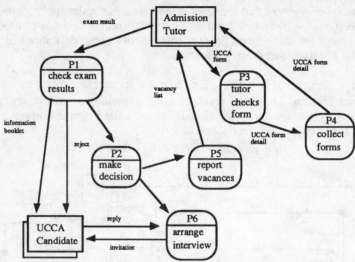

Figure 5. The PID for University Admission

Each of the two conditions above leads to the following relations.*Overlap relation* in which, the argument sets belonging to the same data affinity set, i.e. overlap entity sets, can be substituted to each other. *Equivalent relation* in which, the synonyms of arguments names belonging to the same synonym set can be substituted to each other.

In order to present the steps for the construction of generic process models, consider the description of P1.

> **specification** arrange_interview
> **sort**   UCCA_Candidate, Date, Place
> **operation**
> send_mail(_): UCCA_Candidate → UCCA_Candidate
> **variables**   UC : UCCA_Candidate;   IR: Interview_Room;
>   ID: Interview_Date
> **body**
> Send_mail:
> If UCCA_Candidate(DA) and UCCA_Candidate(DA) = "accepted"
> Then Chech_availability(Interview_Room(IR), Interview_Date(ID)) and
>   Post(DA.Address)
> **end specification**

Process P6 checks the decision status for *UCCA_Candidate* and availability of the interview room on a certain date first, then send a letter to *UCCA_Candidate*. On the basis of the process description P6, a data type for the generic description of P6, denoted as, Arrange_meeting, can be established.

> Arrange_meeting : Candidate E Candidate

Since we have identified the synonym set of *UCCA_Candidate* from the generic Student-Lecturer ERT model,

> Syn(UCCA_Candidate) = {Candidate, UCCA_Candidate, Student}

Both *UCCA_Candidate* and *Candidate* are defined in the same domain, *Candidate*, and this enables the other member entity, *Student*, to be in the overlap relation with *UCCA_CAndidate* and *Candidate*. That is, the generic function may have either

Candidate or *Student* as its argument. To facilitate this idea, we introduce separate descriptions of overlap arguments and their body, which are denoted as Attendee_type and Arrange_ meeting, respectively.

component specification Attendee_type
       sort   Person
       operations
         Student: Person; Employee: Person;
         Candidate: Person; personal_details: Person $\rightarrow$ String
       body
            personal_details(content omitted...)
       end specification
component specification Arrange_meeting
       sort   Attendee, Date, Place
       operation
       send_notice(_): Attendee $\rightarrow$ Attendee
       variables   A1 : Attendee;   Interview_Room : Place;
                     Interview_Date : Date
       body
       Send_notice: If Attendee(A1) and Attendee(A1) = "accepted"
                    Then Chech_availability(Interview_Room, Interview_Date)
       end specification

By use of the two specifications, Arrange_meeting and Attendee_type, process P6 is reconstructed as P6' that contains explicit sub-specification.

       component specification P6'
       compose Arrange_meeting **with** Attendee_type
       using Candidate for Attendee
       end specification

5   Concluding Remarks

The technical motivations presented in this paper have been from the work in [8] that addressed the behavioural specification of conceptual models. In comparison to the model shown in [8], the proposed paradigm explains in a more immediate way some property of hierarchical type systems that are oriented to specification reuse. This is achieved by pointing out the distinction between the domain of a type and the domain partitioned by the associated equivalence relations. The proposed paradigm supports the application engineer in the analysis of existing conceptual models and in the extraction of reusable components. Major contribution of this paper consists in the definition of techniques for the reuse of data and process components, and in the representation of polymorphism in the reusable repository. As addressed in [10], [14], reuse technology can take some advantages of emerging CASE technologies whose successful uptake will result in organisation-wide repository of potentially reusable specifications. Existing CASE environments have largely ignored the potential of specification- and design-level reuse. More research is needed in the area of the CASE environment and its integration into the CASE environment in order to utilise development experiences by providing the organisation-wide repository of reusable components.

References

1. Balzer, R., *A 15 year perspective on automatic programming*, IEEE Trans. on Software Engineering, Vol 11, No 11, 1985.
2. Biggerstaff, T. *Design Recovery for Maintenance and Reuse*, IEEE Computer, Vol 22, No 7, July, 1989, pp.36-49.
3. Biggerstaff, T.J., Perlis,A.J. *Software Reusability, Vol I, II*, ACM Press, 1989.
4. Biggerstaff, T. J., Ritcher, A.J., *Reusablility Framework, assessment and Directions*, IEEE Software, Vol 4, No 2, 1987, pp.41-49.
5. Brener, P.T., Lano, K. *REDO at Oxford*, Proceedings of Software Reuse Workshop, Utretcht, The Netherlands, November 1989, Springer-Verlag, 1991, pp.39-50.
6. Cardelli, L., Wegner, P., *On understanding types, data abstraction, and polymorphism*, Computing Surveys, Vol 17, No 4, December 1985, pp.471-522.
7. Castano, S., De Antonellis, V., *Classifying and Reusing Conceptual Schemas*, Entity-relationship Int. Conf. Karlsruhe, Lecture Note in Computer Science 645, Springer Verag, October 1992.
8. Castano, S., De Antonellis, V., *Reusing Process Specification*, personal contact, 1993.
10. Hodgson, R., *Reusability using object-orientation: the next challege for CASE tools*, IBM Reusable Software Conference, London, May, 1990, pp.1-25.
11. Hooper, J.W., Chester, R.O., *Software reuse: Guidelines and Methods*, Plenum Press, NY, 1991.
12. Iscoe, N., *Domain specific reuse: An object-oriented and knowledge-based approach*, Software reuse: Emerging technology (ed.) Tracz, W., Computer Society Press, 1987, pp.299-308.
13. Marrek, Y.S., Berry, D.M., Kaiser, G.E., *An Information Retrival Approach for Automatically Constructing Software Libraries*, IEEE Trans. on Software Engineering, Vol 17, No 8, August 1991, pp.800-813.
14. McGregor, j., Sykes, D., *Object-oriented software development: Engineering software for reuse*, Van Nostrand Reinhold, New York, 1992, pp.15-23.
15. Sutcliffe, A., Maiden, N., *Why cognitive aspect of software reusability are important*, Proc. of the software reuse workshop, November 1989, Utrecht, Holland, Springer-Verag, 1991, pp.109-114.
16. *TEMPORA Concept manual*, UMIST et al, 1989.

Modeling multiple views of common features in software reengineering for reuse

Stan Jarzabek and Chew Lim Tan

Department of Information Systems and Computer Science
National University of Singapore
Singapore 0511
stan@iscs.nus.sg, tancl@iscs.nus.sg

Abstract. Common objectives of software reengineering are to improve program maintainability, to port programs into new platforms or to support new functions. To meet reengineering objectives, sometimes it is necessary to substantially re-design programs; then, reengineering becomes an opportune moment to address reusability. In the "reengineering for reuse" scenario, a reusability framework is built prior to reengineering efforts. Within the framework, potentially reusable features are modeled and representation structures for capturing reusable features are built. The core of the framework is a family of domain models. Domain models are built in the course of both reverse engineering of existing programs and independent domain analysis. Domain models consist of documentation templates, organized in Object-Oriented way, that describe common (therefore reusable) features and their implementation. Often we find that, apart from similarities, there are also some variations in feature specifications and implementation from one system to another. Modeling reusable features and capturing variations in feature specification is the topic of this paper.

1. Introduction

Recent surveys [20] show that investments in Information Technology (IT) do not yield expected benefits. Many of the aging business programs are expensive to maintain, run on outdated platforms and do not meet requirements of strategic information systems companies need today. In short-term, some of those programs must be restructured for better maintainability and converted into new computers, databases, operating systems, languages, etc. In long-term, however, programs must be reengineered (or re-written) to fully exploit advantages of new technology and to be in tune with company's strategic plans [16,21]. We call this strategic reengineering [13]. Strategic reengineering may involve re-designing program architecture or even change of the implementation technique (e.g., taking programs under control of a CASE tool or re-designing procedural programs into the Object-Oriented architecture). Strategic reengineering is expensive and must be cost-justified. Addressing reusability during reengineering can increase the value of a reengineering solution [14].

To ensure consistency of reengineering efforts with company's business and IT strategies, we defined a lifecycle model whose phase and process structure is shown on figures 1-3.

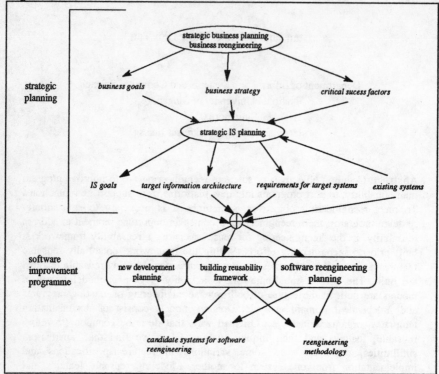

Fig. 1 Strategic reengineering: lifecycle

Fig. 1 depicts reengineering as part of an overall software improvement program determined during strategic planning [16]. During business planning, a company clarifies business goals and modifies business operations to meet new goals and to take advantage of new IT options. Information System (IS) planning leads to identifying software systems a company needs in order to follow its business plan. A stable target computer/software architecture for future software development and maintenance activities is also defined. Company's existing platforms and programs are assessed and based on this assessment future development and reengineering efforts are planned.

The logical structure of the reengineering for reusability process is depicted on fig. 2. During reengineering, we transform an old system S into a new system, S-NEW. To facilitate program transformation, we recreate program views at various levels of abstraction. The physical level is created using reverse engineering techniques. The physical layer includes abstract syntax trees and design abstractions such as control flow and data flow graphs, procedure calling trees, data structure charts, various cross-reference lists, etc.

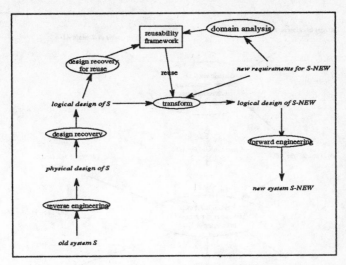

Fig. 2 Reengineering process model

The logical level provides the description of a program in terms of user-oriented, application domain concepts. The logical level may consist of Object-Oriented (OO) program descriptions[19], Entity-Relationship (ER) data models [5], Data Flow Diagrams (DFD), etc. The choice of representation for logical design depends on specific forward engineering techniques to be used as well as on programmer/user preference. Above logical program description level, there is a reusability framework that consists of a family of domain models and reusability management facilities. Each domain model describes designs and code that can be reused across systems in a given application domain such as payroll or customer service. (Application domains are also called business areas.) Domain models form OO program descriptions that are created in the course of independent domain analysis [1] and reverse engineering of systems that service a given application domain.

The technical scenario for software reengineering consists of three steps (fig. 3) that are performed at the application domain, system and system component levels, resp. The domain level step takes into account all the systems in a given application domain (AD). Objectives of this step are (1) to understand systems in AD, (2) to prepare an architectural framework for new systems (in particular, a common data model consistent with the target architecture), and (3) to do domain analysis in order to address problems of reusability.

The objective of the system level step is to produce complete logical design specifications for a selected system S in AD. Design specifications for both the original system S and target system (S-NEW) are produced. The design of S-NEW is based on a portion of a common data model relevant to S-NEW.

During the last step, a selected system is incrementally reengineered, component-by-component. Components may be individual programs or subsystems. Reusable features, accumulated within the domain model, are reused in component reengineering. As incremental reengineering of systems progresses, additional common features may be identified. They are extracted and linked into the domain model for future reuse.

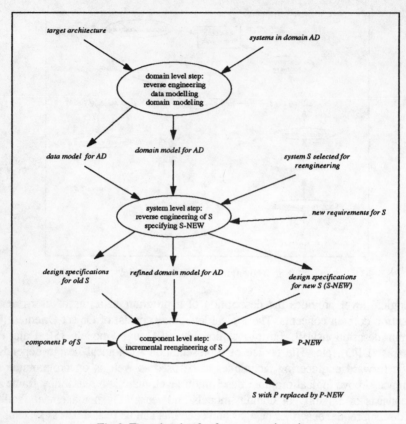

Fig 3. Three levels of software reengineering

Domain models capture specifications and implementation of features that are common to all the software systems in a given application domain. But, apart from commonalties, we often observe that there are some variations in the way features are specified and/or implemented in different systems. In the reengineering context, those variations can be quite substantial. Suppose we reengineer system S to obtain system S-NEW. Having created domain models, we need to know how various features are specified/implemented in both systems S and S-NEW. This traceability of information from domain models to code is essential in software reengineering for reuse [12]. But some of the requirements for system S may no longer hold for S-NEW. Also, system S may be implemented in COBOL while S-NEW may be designed with CASE or built around an Object-Oriented architecture. Furthermore, software houses often maintain multiple implementations of a software package for different software/computer platforms. In such cases, platform-independent, logical model of reusable features (and of software packages) and explicit transformations from logical model into multiple implementations increase reuse potential and reduce maintenance effort. Therefore, multiple views of common features should be explicitly modeled to facilitate reengineering for reuse scenario. Fig. 4 depicts the architecture of such software models.

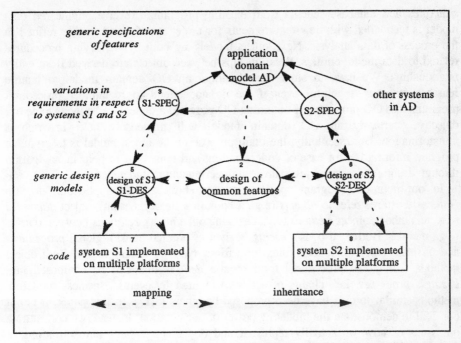

Fig. 4 An architecture of software models and mappings between models

Model 1 identifies common features in a given application domain AD and contains generic, user requirement level specifications of those features. Models 3 and 4 explicate variations in requirement specifications from the perspective of two systems in AD, S1 and S2. As we explain later in the paper, variations in requirement specifications across systems are modeled using inheritance. In the reengineering context, S1 can represent a system before reengineering and S2 - a reengineered version of that system. Models 5 and 6 contain system design specifications, expressed in terms of common features, in a platform-independent way. Finally, boxes 7 and 8 represent system implementations on multiple target platforms. In the remaining part of this paper, we concentrate on models 1, 3 and 4 in fig. 4, and describe a modeling technique of reusable features that is suitable in the reengineering context. In other papers, we described the role of domain analysis in reengineering [12], strategic reengineering lifecycle [13] and techniques involved in reengineering for reuse [14].

2. Modeling reusable features

We build domain models based on Object-Oriented approach (OO). Objects represent meaningful concepts from the application domain (e.g. an employee in a payroll system). In business programs, many of the interesting candidates for objects are naturally derived from a conceptual data model [12,19]. Objects comprise data models and procedures related to specific data groups. Modeling reusable features starts by reverse engineering of a conceptual data model based on analysis of data structures and database schema from existing programs. Reverse engineered data model is reconciled with new requirements for target systems and further refined in the process of data analysis. Next, object models are built by identifying procedures related to data model entities. Relationships between objects are derived from entity relationships. We have to stress that building an OO domain model to handle reusable features is helpful even if we do not intend to reengineer procedural programs into OO programs. If obtaining OO program architecture happens to be our objective, certainly an OO domain model will immensely help in such a transformation. But essentially, the main purpose of the object model is to organize program information for ease of understanding and reuse and to help in navigation through design/code during program reengineering and maintenance.

In our notation, program specifications are built around application domain *features*. Features refer to *objects* (e.g., a book in a library system), object *attributes* (e.g., an author), object *methods* (e.g., checking out a book), *relations* between objects (e.g., member Borrowed book), *events* (arrival of ordered books), global *procedures* and *business rules* (e.g., loan rules for various types of library users). Both object methods and global procedures form atomic *actions* that can be composed into *business processes*, i.e., chains of actions triggered by events. Business modeling methods similar to ours have been proposed by others [2,17]. In this paper, it is not our goal to demonstrate the modeling power of our notation. Instead, we concentrate on issues of how we actually represent and document features and variations in feature specifications. Features are described by *documentation templates*. A documentation template consists of *descriptors* grouped into *specification sections*. Each section has a title which is unique in a given template. Descriptors may be elements of formal specification, semi-formal or a free text. Descriptors may denote features and in such case they may refer to other documentation templates that describe those features in more detail. A descriptor consists of a *descriptor signature* (a name with optional list of arguments), followed by (an optional) descriptor body. Descriptor signatures must be unique in a specification section in which they appear. Documentation templates are organized into inheritance networks. The subject of inheritance are specification sections and descriptors.

As an example, we show how we document objects and methods. A documentation template for objects provides the following information:
- parent templates (in an inheritance network)
- a list of attributes
- for each attribute it may be specified:
  - attribute value domain and value constraints
  - whether attribute value can be changed or not
  - whether attribute is a key or not
  - whether attribute is computed or not
- a list of methods (methods are specified by separate method templates)
- object constraints (Boolean conditions)
  - invariants: characterize valid object states
  - initial: must be true for an object to be created
  - final: must be true for an object to be destroyed
- a list of rules (rules are specified by separate rule templates)

In a library system, we have library items such as books, journals, films, etc. Properties shared by all the library items might be defined in object template LIB-ITEM and templates for specific items might be derived from LIB-ITEM. Below we show documentation templates for features LIB-ITEM and BOOK:

domain object template LIB-ITEM {

informal description:

attributes:
 CatalogNo
 Title
 int #copies = <1,Max>
 Status = (Borrowed, Reserved, Available)

methods:
 RegisterNew(LIB-ITEM)
 CheckOut(LIB-ITEM,MEMB)
 CheckIn(LIB-ITEM,MEMB)
 BOOL IsReserved(LIB-ITEM)
 BOOL IsBorrowed(LIB-ITEM)
 BOOL IsOverdue(LIB-ITEM)

relations:
 Borrowed(LIB-ITEM,MEMB)

object constraints:
 IsAvail: Status = Available ↔ ~IsBorrowed(lib-item) & ~IsReserved(lib-item)

rules:
 Overdue: If a LIB-ITEM is overdue more than one week, send a reminder to a borrower
  if (IsOverdue(item)) **then** memb.Remind(item) **where** Borrowed(item,memb)
}

domain object template BOOK {

informal description:

derived from:
 LIB-ITEM

attributes:
 Author
 ISBN
 Status = (LIB-ITEM::Status, Reference)

methods:
 CheckOut(BOOK,MEMB)
 BOOL IsReference(BOOK)

rules:
 Removal: If a book has not been used for 5 years, remove a book from library
}

Comments: Documentation template BOOK inherits all descriptor sections from LIB-ITEM. Method CheckOut is re-defined which means that specifications of CheckOut for books differs from CheckOut procedure defined in LIB-ITEM. In addition to descriptors inherited from LIB-ITEM, BOOK has a rule called 'Removal' and a method BOOL IsReference(BOOK). Attribute 'Status' is re-defined to reflect the fact that books can be placed on a reference shelf. 'IsAvail' is a signature of an object constraint that relates the value of attribute 'Status' to a condition expressed in terms of methods. (Symbol ↔ means "if and only if".) The body of rule 'Overdue' contains both informal and formal specifications.

Method descriptors (in object template) may refer to method documentation templates that provide detail specifications of methods. In particular, method templates contain the following information (global procedures are documented in the same way as methods):

- method header: name, arguments and returned value
- objects involved in method; each object may be qualified as:
  - MODIFIED - if method modifies objects
  - INQUIRY - if method reads objects without changing them
  - CREATE - if method creates a new object
  - DELETE - if methods deletes objects
- pre-conditions: must be true before a method can be executed
- post-conditions: describes the effect of method execution

Here are documentation templates for methods CheckOut():

domain method template LIB-ITEM::CheckOut (LIB-ITEM item, MEMB b) {

informal description:

objects involved:
LIB-ITEM (MODIFIED), MEMB (MODIFIED)

pre-conditions:
Avail: ~IsReserved(item) & ~IsBorrowed(item) & MEMB::CanBorrow(b)

post-conditions:
NotAvail: IsBorrowed(item)
Borrowed: Borrowed(item, b)
}

Comments: The header indicates that this template refines a method descriptor CheckOut from template LIB-ITEM. The descriptors listed in LIB-ITEM can be used without qualification as long as this does not lead to ambiguous references. Descriptors from other templates must be qualified (e.g., MEMB::CanBorrow(b)).

Methods can inherit specifications one from another. In our example, method CheckIn is not re-defined in BOOK, therefore it applies to books. But specifications of documentation template for method CheckOut(BOOK,MEMB) slightly differs from method CheckOut(LIB-ITEM,MEMB), as books may remain on a reference shelf. To reflect this, we re-define pre-condition for method CheckOut(BOOK,MEMB):

domain method template BOOK::CheckOut (BOOK b, MEMB) {

informal description:

derived from:
    method template LIB-ITEM::CheckOut(LIB-ITEM, MEMB)

pre-conditions:
    Avail: LIB-ITEM::Avail & ~IsReference(b)
}

Comments: This example shows reuse of specifications across templates at low level of granularity: pre-condition 'Avail' defined in the parent template is used in definition of a stronger pre-condition in a derived template.

3. Modeling variations in feature specifications

The domain model is created not just for one system, but for all the systems in a given application domain. The domain model captures generic knowledge about an application domain, but there may be slight variations in requirements across systems. For example, a library may be located in several locations. It may happen that most sites allow users to reserve library items, but one site, say X, does not provide reservation service. Because of that BOOKs and method CheckOut will have different specifications in a system servicing site X from those that service other sites. Those variations must be traceable from the domain model down to design specifications and code in various systems under consideration. Differences between generic, domain model view and system-specific view of a given feature can be modeled by multiple inheritance.

    We use the following conventions in modeling system-specific views:
1. a derived template must resolve any ambiguities resulting from multiple inheritance,
2. a template may hide certain elements inherited from parents,
3. an element hidden in template A cannot be accessed in templates derived from A,
4. a template can add new elements or re-define any inherited elements.

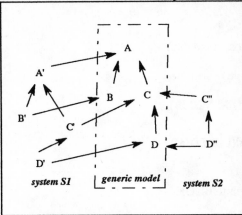

Fig. 5 Modeling system-specific views

In fig. 5, features A, B, C and D describe a generic model of application domain, say AD. S_1 and S_2 are two systems in AD. (In particular, S_1 might be a system before reengineering and S_2 - a reengineered version of that system.) System S_2 shares features A and B with its generic model. Feature C" is derived from C to show similarities and differences between system S_2 and generic model AD. As feature D" has some properties of D and some properties of C", it is derived from two parents. In system S_1, all the features are derived from the generic model.

To give a more intuitive illustration of a situation that involves modeling system-specific views, let's return to our library example. We model a view of library site X as follows:

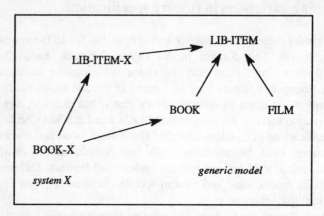

Fig. 6 System-specific views in a library system

domain object template LIB-ITEM-X {

informal description:

derived from:
  LIB-ITEM

attributes:
  Status = (Borrowed, Available)

            ...

methods:
  CheckOut(LIB-ITEM,MEMB)

hidden:
  BOOL IsReserved(LIB-ITEM)
}

domain object template BOOK-X {

informal description:

derived from:
  LIB-ITEM-X, BOOK

attributes:

Status = (LIB-ITEM-X::Status, Reference)

methods:

    CheckOut(BOOK,MEMB)

hidden:

    BOOL IsReserved(LIB-ITEM)

}

Comments: Documentation template BOOK-X re-defines attribute 'Status' in terms of attribute inherited from LIB-ITEM-X, re-defines specifications of method CheckOut and hides method IsReserved. (It is necessary to hide method IsReserved in BOOK-X as it is inherited from two parents.)

In case of method CheckOut, we could derive a system-specific view and re-define the pre-condition (by deleting ~IsReserved(item) from the condition). But we also need to modify documentation template LIB-ITEM to reflect change in requirements from the point of view of X. Documentation templates for method CheckOut are derived in the following way (with pre-conditions modified to reflect no reservation service):

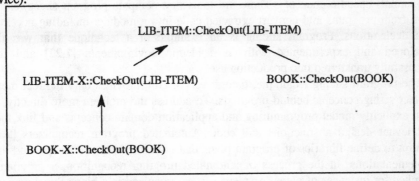

Fig. 7 Derivation of system-specific views of methods

We experiment with using a generator for language-based editors to support the above modeling notations. The generator can handle families of inter-related syntax trees. Each documentation template is represented by an attributed syntax tree and relationships between trees model inheritance. An incremental attribute propagation mechanism ensures semantic correctness of the domain model. We feel that more specialized environments should be built to support manipulation of OO domain models.

Design and implementation information is captured within the *design documentation templates*. Each domain feature may have an associated design template that explains how a given feature is implemented. A design template linked to a domain model feature provides generic implementation (stored in a library of reusable components), while a design template linked to a system-specific feature explains how a given feature is implemented in that system.

4. Related work

A number of authors identified a need for an explicit model to capture program design during reengineering and maintenance. Object-Oriented models for program understanding, based on application domain concepts, are described in [8,11,12].

During reengineering for reusability, programmer's task often is to isolate code that implements a given concept, to raise code to the logical level by removing implementation-dependent details and, eventually, to convert code into a reusable module. As it often happens in old programs, code that implements related concepts is not found in one program module, but is delocalized (i.e., spans a range of program modules). The process of finding and isolating that code can be greatly simplified with use of static program analysis tools [18]. Those tools can compress huge amount of code into a compact abstract view that is directly related to a certain aspect a programmer wants to study. Irrelevant details are filtered out of this view. Many useful program views are produced based on control and data flow relations. Particularly, program slicing views can automate the process of searching code that implements specific concepts. There are tools that compute program slices, extract them from programs and convert extracted code into a module, including necessary data declarations. Program slicing is an example of a technique that was first developed and experimented with in academic environments [7,22] and then successfully transferred into production use.

The program slicing technique, though very useful, provides only indirect means for recovering concepts behind programs. To address the problem more directly, we must explicitly model programming and application domain concepts and link them to relevant design abstractions and code. Automated program recognizers [9,10] attempt to define libraries of program plans that connect abstract concepts and their implementations. In the process of automated program recognition, a program is searched for instances of plans. As plans can be organized in a hierarchical way, the recognition process can progress from lower to higher abstract levels of program description. Today, most of the techniques for recovering reusable features are semi-automatic. If the results of research on automated program recognition scale up to real world programs, it may be possible that future tools will be able to control a bigger portion of the reengineering for reusability process.

Research on recovering object-oriented views from programs is also relevant to the reengineering for reusability. A method for identifying objects in C programs is described in [15]. Candidate objects are selected based on the analysis of type definitions; next, procedures which have arguments of a given type, or return a value of a given type, are identified as candidate methods. In [11], procedural programs are incrementally reengineered into an object-oriented architecture.

5. Conclusions

Many researchers and practitioners express opinion that software reuse has a potential to bring productivity breakthroughs and can fundamentally change the way we develop programs [3]. An important source of potentially reusable software assets are existing programs. Some of those programs, though they still contain much business value, will have to be reengineered, as they have become technically obsolete. To reengineer programs, we must understand them. Therefore, reengineering is an opportune moment to capture viable assets from existing programs and make them available for future reuse. Reengineering and reusability have potential to reinforce each other, but we need technical means to realize this potential. In work reported in this paper, we defined a mechanism for specifying common features in a given application domain and for modeling variations in feature specification/implementation across systems. Our specification method is suitable for the "reengineering for reuse" scenario.

We found it difficult to adopt one of the existing Object-Oriented systems to support the documentation resulting from domain analysis described in this paper. A system should be sensitive to the inheritance rules dealing with program specifications and should provide strong browsing capabilities. We are implementing a prototype documentation support environment using a structure editor generation system based on extended attribute grammars. Further work will also concentrate on adding more formality into specifications (based on notations proposed in [2]) and on modeling program dynamics.

References

1. Arango, G. "Domain Analysis - From Art Form to Engineering Discipline," *Proc. Fifth International Workshop on Software Specification and Design*, May 1989, Pittsburgh, pp. 152-159
2. Berztiss, A. "The Specification and Prototyping Language SF," Report No 78, SYSLAB, The Royal Institute of Technology, Sweden, 1990
3. Biggenrstaff, T. and Perlis, A. (Editors) *Software Reusability*, vol. I and II, ACM Press, 1989
4. Blum, B. "Documentation for Maintenance: A Hypertext Design," *Proc. of Conference on Software Maintenance*, 1988, 23-31
5. Chen, P. "The Entity-Relationship Model -- Toward a Unified View of Data," *ACM Transactions on Database Systems*, vol. 1, no. 1, 1976, pp. 9-36
6. Chikofsky, E. and Cross II, J. "Reverse Engineering and Design Recovery: A Taxonomy," *IEEE Software*, January 1990, pp. 13-18
7. Gallagher, K. "Using Program Slicing in Software Maintenance," TR CS-90-05, Ph.D. Thesis, University of Maryland, 1990
8. Hart, C. and Shiling, J. "An Environment for Documenting Software Features," *Proc. 4'th ACM SIGSOFT Symp. on Software Development Environments*, Irvine, USA, Dec. 1990, pp. 120-132
9. Hartman, J. "Technical Introduction to the First Workshop on Artificial Intelligence and Automated program Understanding," *Workshop Notes AAAI-92 AI & Automated Program Understanding*, July 1992, San Jose, pp. 8-31
10. Hartman, J. "Understanding Natural Programs Using Proper Decomposition," *13th International Conference on Software Engineering*, May 1991

11. Jackobson, I. and Lindstrom, F. "Re-engineering of old systems to an object-oriented architecture," *Proc. OOPSLA'91*, pp. 340-350
12. Jarzabek, S. "Domain Model-Driven Software Reengineering and Maintenance," *Journal of Systems and Software*, Jan. 1993, pp. 37-51
13. Jarzabek, S. "Strategic Reengineering of Software: Lifecycle Approach," 6th Int. Workshop on CASE, CASE'93, Singapore, July 1993, pp. 211-220
14. Jarzabek, S. "Software Reengineering for Reusability," *Proc. 17th Annual Int. Computer Software & Applications Conference, COMPSAC93*, Phoenix, November 1993, pp. 100-106
15. Liu, S. and Wilde, N. "Identifying Objects in a Conventional Procedural Language: An Example of Data Design Recovery," *Proc. Conference on Software Maintenance*, 1990, pp. 266-271
16. Martin, J. *Information Engineering*, Vol. 1, Prentice-Hall, 1986
17. McBrien, P. *et al* "A Rule Language to Apture and Model Business Policy Specifications," *Proc. 3rd Int. Conference on Advanced Information Systems Engineering CAiSE'91*, Trondheim, May 1991, Lecture Notes in Computer Science, no. 498, Springer-Verlag, pp. 307-318
18. Rock-Evans, R. and Hales, K. "Reverse Engineering: Markets, Methods and Tools," *Ovum Report* vol. 1, published by Ovum Ltd. England, 1990
19. Rumbaugh, J., Blaha, M., Premerlani, W., Eddy, F. and Lorensen, W. *Object-Oriented Modeling and Design*, Prentice-Hall, 1991
20. Strassmann, P. *The Business Value of Computers*, The Information Economics Press, 1990
21. Ulrich, W. "Re-development Engineering: Formulating an Information Blueprint for the 1990's," *CASE Outlook*, No. 2, 1990, pp. 15-21
22. Weiser M. "Program slicing," *IEEE TSE*, vol. 10, no. 4, July 1984, pp. 352-357

A Hypertext-Based Tool for Large Scale Software Reuse

Burkhard Freitag

Universität Passau
Fakultät für Mathematik und Informatik
Innstr. 33, D-94032 Passau, Germany
freitag@fmi.uni-passau.de

Abstract. A hypertext-based interactive tool supporting the management of large software libraries is presented. We claim that a simple, pragmatic approach to software reuse is best suited to aid the software engineer in solving the practical problems of software configuration from reusable components. When developing the system described in this paper emphasis has been put on the semi-automatic classification and interactive retrieval of components and their descriptions. The system has been installed at the BMW automobile manufacturing facilities in Munich. First experiences show good usability and acceptance.

Keywords: software reuse, hypertext, software configuration, reusable components, software re-engineering, taxonomic classification.

1 Introduction

Component reuse is a theme of growing importance as regards the productivity as well as the quality of software development. Reuse is of course not limited to program code but covers all levels of the software production process, such as program specifications both formal and informal, documentation, source code, object code, individual notes, to name just a few.

The configuration of complex systems from reusable software components requires the search for possible implementations in increasingly large component libraries. The success of this approach strongly depends on efficient methods for finding the appropriate reusable components, which is a very hard task in practice [9]. Thus tools are needed to support this activity.

We present a simple, practice oriented tool for software synthesis that supports the configuration of complex systems from a library of reusable software components. Our prototype system SEL[1] has been developed in a joint project with the German automobile manufacturer BMW and is currently installed and running at the BMW facilities in Munich.

---

[1] SEL - Software Engineering Library

The basic assumption underlying the system is that software modules can be described precisely enough by a set of *attributes* such as name, problem class, atomic types, i.e. a formatted description that can be scanned for matching keywords. In addition, a problem-specific *taxonomy*[2] of tasks can be defined, according to which modules can be classified. Even if an exact description is not known the user can roughly characterize the modules of interest by specifying some classes of the taxonomy in order to restrict the search space. The system also supports the user in defining *relationships* between any two modules. Using relationships, the search for a module can optionally be extended to "neighbouring" modules. This feature allows us also to relax the naming conventions that would otherwise have to be obeyed in order to guide the search for a particular "group" of modules.

Some novel approaches to the semi-automatic determination of relationships between component descriptions are incorporated into the system that increase both the precision and the efficiency of component retrieval. The determination of hidden relationships may sometimes be the only feasible approach to software re-engineering since formal descriptions are often missing in existing libraries. Practical experience shows that our approach is powerful enough for most configuration tasks.

The rest of the paper is organized as follows: In Sect. 2 we give a motivation and list some requirements that a system supporting software reuse and re-engineering should satisfy. Sect. 3 contains a detailed description of the SEL system. In Sect. 4 some facts concerning the implementation of the protoype system are collected. In Sect. 5 a comparison of the SEL to other systems supporting reuse is given. In Sect. 6 we summarize our experiences and briefly discuss future research directions.

2   Requirements for Software Reuse Support Systems

The size of component libraries, in particular in object-oriented environments, is continuously growing. While the amount of potentially reusable components increases the problem of finding appropriate components gets more and more complex. It is no longer possible to rely on simple naming conventions or a naive scan through a library database in order to retrieve a (set of) component(s) that satisfy certain constraints. Because the software industry and software departments in other industries are faced with a huge amount of existing components that have been designed in an "ad-hoc" fashion software re-engineering has become an essential problem, too. Thus it is not enough to have systems that support the development of new reusable software components. An automatic tool must also address the generation of documentation and interface descriptions

---

[2] Taxonomic classification should not be confused with classification in the sense of object-oriented programming languages. The latter can also be used to guide the search for modules, but the former normally does not induce subtype relations or code inheritance.

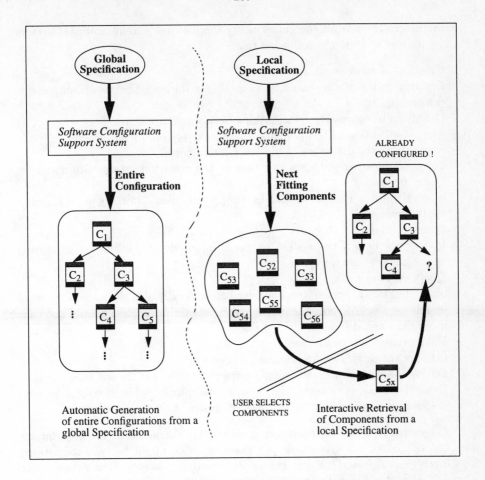

Fig. 1. Different objectives of configuration support systems

for existing modules. These modules often differ drastically in their structure. Consequently, the adaptability of the component descriptors that are handled by the system is strongly required.

Generally, a system supporting the construction of software systems from reusable components can have two different objectives (see Fig. 1):

- Automatic generation of entire configurations, i.e. sequences of components that "fit together", from a global specification, or
- Interactive search for the set of components that fit to an already established partial configuration. In this case only local specifications governing the selection of a single component are considered.

The SEL system described in this paper belongs to the second class.

The key idea of reuse support systems [1, 2, 4, 5, 10] is the separation of component descriptions from the components themselves. A reuse support system has to address at least the following issues:

- Creation of component descriptions.
  Description templates should be adaptable to the specific class of components considered.
- Definition of expressive relationships between components.
  The classification of components should not rely on a fixed scheme.
- Support for the discovery of hidden relationships.
  For re-engineering purposes this may be the most important requirement.
- Query flexibility.
  General ad-hoc queries should be supported in addition to pre-fabricated special queries.
- Query precision.
  It does not help if the system proposes hundreds of candidate components as the answer to a query.
- Query efficiency.
  Since the class of systems we consider here typically aids the user in the local search for a set of components the query answering process should not take more than about 0.5 sec.
- Concurrent multiuser access.
- Component migration and access privileges.
  During the development of a single software component the software engineer should have exclusive access rights. After the component is released, however, it should be visible by other project members or the entire company.

Theoretically, a formal specification completely characterizes the appropriate set of modules for the given task. A weaker criterion might be type correctness or, more general, interface correctness. In practice, however, it is necessary to have selection conditions beyond type or interface correctness to guide the search for modules that are suitable for the given task [3]. From the user's point of view it may sometimes be most important to find the set of modules that offer the intended functionality [9] according to an *informal* specification.

3 The SEL component library system

3.1 Overview

The SEL system presented in following sections addresses the problems described in Sect. 2. Fig. 2 shows an overview of the various tasks performed by the system.

Ideally, a SEL user specifies his or her needs and lets the system search for a component that exactly or nearly satisfies the specification. If none such component can be found the user will certainly define a new software module that should be brought into the SEL system for later reuse. It is the responsibility of the designer of a new component to add an expressive component description to

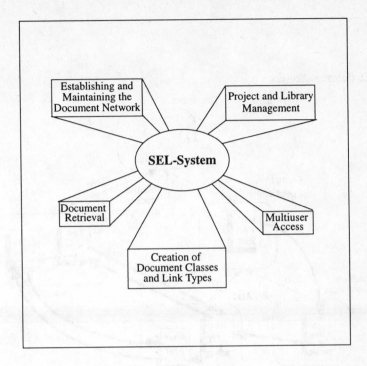

Fig. 2. Overview of the SEL system

the SEL system. To this end, the SEL system offers tools with a graphical interface that facilitate the definition of new component classes with the appropriate descriptive framework, access privileges for the new component descriptions, and links to existing component (descriptions). Initially, new component classes and (descriptions of) new components reside in the private library of the designer. Later, when a component has been tested and approved its description may migrate to the next higher library where it can be read by other users.

3.2 The SEL data model

Documents and Document Classes Component descriptions are represented as *documents* which in turn are records with a set of attribute names and attribute values. Recall that several different descriptions may be attached to a software component, e.g. specification, informal description of the component's semantics, documentation, manual entry. However, descriptions of the same sort that are attached to components that are "similar" normally have a uniform representation. Consequently, the SEL system allows to group documents having the same structure into *document classes* which are organized in an inheritance hierarchy[3]. Document subclasses inherit the structure of the superclass (i.e. all

---

[3] Only single inheritance is allowed.

288

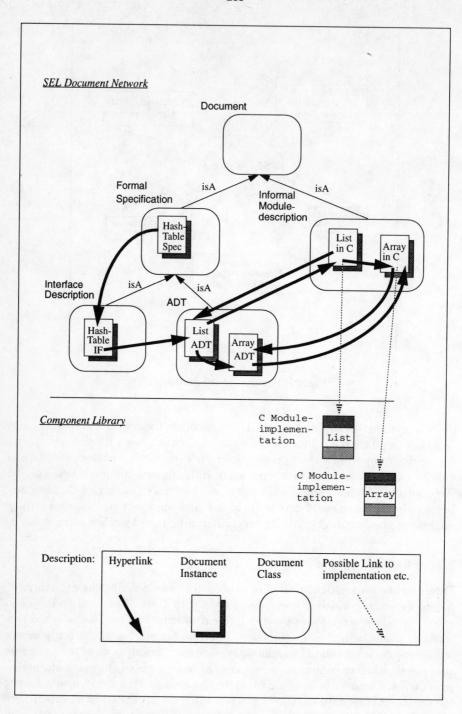

Fig. 3. A hierarchy of document descriptions

document attributes) so that documents of the subclass have a more detailed structure than those of the superclass. Note that not the software components themselves are organized in an inheritance hierarchy but rather the document classes that define the form of component descriptions. For the rest of the paper it is essential to understand that the hierarchy of document classes is to be distinguished from classes in the sense of object-oriented programming languages. Fig. 3 shows sample document classes and documents, i.e. instances of document classes. As for document classes, a document has a user-supplied name that serves as an object identifier. A document can be an instance of only one document class.

It should be mentioned that document classes can also serve as a simple means for a taxonomic classification of component descriptions according to the semantics of the components they describe. It is, for instance, possible to group all documents related to C-programs into a document class C_DOCUMENTS and similarly for LISP_DOCUMENTS.

To give an example[4] of document creation let us assume that the user intends to create a new document class MY_SIMPLE_DOCUMENTS. Let the class SIMPLE_DOCUMENTS be among the already defined document classes and let the structure of SIMPLE_DOCUMENTS be closest to the needs of the new document class. In our example SIMPLE_DOCUMENTS has the following structure[5]:

```
CLASSIFICATION:
    Name:
    Informal Description:
    Programming Language:
    SW-Engineer:
```

The user defines MY_SIMPLE_DOCUMENTS as a subclass of the document class SIMPLE_DOCUMENTS with the following additional attributes that represent relationships to other documents:

```
RELATIONS:
    uses:
    is used by:
```

The class MY_SIMPLE_DOCUMENTS is now available, and document instances may be created. Of course, attribute values have to be defined for each instance.

Relationships between documents As the example above indicates, relationships between documents can be represented by attributes that have object identifiers, i.e. document names, as their values. Documents can be retrieved by specifying some attribute values. Consequently, in the example all documents

---

[4] For the sake of clarity we choose a very simple example. Real-life examples, for instance those investigated in cooperation with BMW, are beyond the space limitations of this paper.

[5] Note, that SIMPLE_DOCUMENTS has a two-level attribute structure.

describing the components used by a given component can be retrieved via the **uses** attribute.

Using virtual document classes *views* can be defined on the set of documents.

Because scanning a large library may be prohibitively expensive tools have been developed that support an efficient search (see Sect. 3.4).

Libraries The SEL supports different user classes, i.e. users, experts, project leaders, and a system administrator, each having different access privileges for the documents stored in the system. Documents, i.e. component descriptions, are organized in libraries at the following three levels:

1. User libraries belong to single users who have exclusive read and write access to the documents stored. New documents or document classes are initially stored in user libraries.
2. Project libraries contain project specific documents and are attached to single projects. Only the project members have reading access to this information. The project library is administered by the leader of the respective project who has read and write access.
3. Documents in the global library can be read by all SEL users. Documents of this library contain project overlapping information so that components developed for one specific project can be used in a number of different other projects. The system administrator has read and write access to the global library.

Documents and components can migrate from one library into another, e.g. to release and distribute a component or to submit a component for testing to a different software engineer. The quality of components and their descriptions that migrate to a "higher" library has to be assessed prior to migration. Quality assessment, however, is currently not directly covered by the SEL system.

3.3   The SEL as a Hypertext-system

The SEL System has been designed and implemented as a hypertext system. Component descriptions, i.e. documents, form the nodes of the hypertext network. Hyperlinks can be defined between any two documents that are related in some way. It should be emphasized that we do not restrict the type of the relationships in any respect and that the user is entirely free to decide what documents shall be linked. In general, links are defined at the instance level, i.e. between two individual documents. However, as will be seen later (Sect. 3.4) some relationships can be established independently from the particular document regarding only the document structure as defined in the corresponding document class, e.g. the "uses-used" relationship.

Links are typed, e.g. "uses-used" or "imports-imported" etc. In addition to conventional hypertext systems the SEL system also supports dynamic features (see Sect. 3.2 above). A sample hypertext document network is shown in Fig. 4.

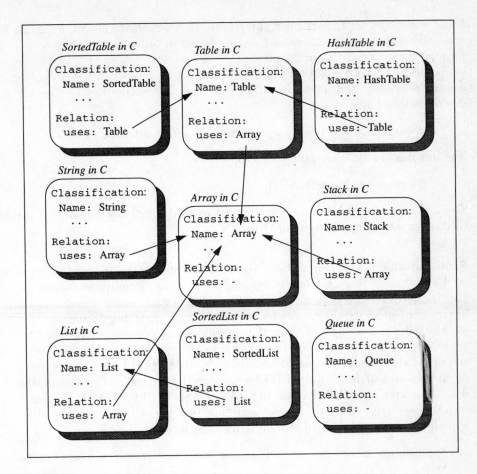

Fig. 4. Sample Hypertext Network taken from the BMW Application

3.4 Link Generation

The system supports the user in defining typed *links* between any two documents. Links that represent the same relationship R on the set of documents can be grouped. Thus links of type R materialize application specific and even user specific search heuristics that define a "R-neighbourhood" of a document. Normally, a document, and thus the component it describes, is selected whenever some user supplied selection condition is exactly matched by the component's properties. However, scanning a large library may be very costly. Links can be used to create an efficient search structure according to the specified condition.

Typed links can also be used to define *views* on a library, e.g. a view containing the documents related to a particular subproject.

Using links, the search for a document can optionally be extended to neighbouring documents[6]. In particular, this feature allows us also to relax the naming conventions that would otherwise have to obeyed in order to guide the search for a particular group of documents.

Let us first have a closer look at hyperlinks: A link consists of a *link anchor*, a *link destination*, and a *link type*. The link anchor structure can be formally described by a triple

$$(< document >, < attribute >, < text\ string\ within\ attribute\ value >).$$

The link destination corresponds to a tupel

$$(< document >, < attribute >).$$

The link type of a SEL-link can be decribed as a label defining the kind of the relation expressed by the hyperlink.

Semi-automatic link generation One of the features of the SEL system is the semi-automatic link generator. By defining a set of (pre-)conditions concerning the documents to be connected, the SEL link generator scans the document library and automatically creates hyperlinks between matching documents.

The following example explains the automatic link generation. Assume that a SEL user has created several documents, i.e. component descriptions, as instances of the document class MY_SIMPLE_DOCUMENTS. Let the documents be descriptions of implemented (procedures and) functions manipulating the data structures SORTED_TABLE, ARRAY, HASHTABLE, STACK etc. some of which are related via the "uses" attribute (see Fig. 4). The corresponding hyperlinks can be established semi-automatically as shown below.

1. Specification of the link anchor, i.e. the `document class` and `attribute` fields:
   document class := "MY_SIMPLE_DOCUMENTS"
   attribute := "uses"
2. Specification of the link destination:
   document class := "MY_SIMPLE_DOCUMENTS"
   attribute := "Name"
3. Specification of the link type, e.g.
   Link-Type := "uses-used"

The link generator is now able to create `uses-used`-hyperlinks between suitable documents belonging to the document class MY_SIMPLE_DOCUMENTS. Notice that it is not necessary to specify $< text\ string\ within\ attribute\ value >$ when automatic link generation is performed. Instead, the tool automatically determines pairs of documents one (the origin) having an attribute `RELATION.calls`

---

[6] Practical experience has shown that the search should not go beyond the nearest neighbors because otherwise the search would result in a large set of only loosely connected documents.

the other (the destination) having an attribute `CLASSIFICATION.Name` and both containing the same text string in their attribute values.

The automatic link generator is an effective tool supporting the creation of the document network. However, there may exist other relationships between documents which cannot be generated by a pure inspection of the description. Therefore the system provides additional search tools, i.e. general queries, link lists, neighbourhood search, and link pattern search.

Queries The user can define a set of search keywords which describe the desired documents. Of course, keywords can be connected by the usual connectives **and**, **or**, and **not**. The search can be extended to synonyms by a *thesaurus*. The retrieved documents are sorted according to the hit rate corresponding to the keywords. As usual in the area of information retrieval it is assumed that there is a correlation between the hit rate and the relevance of a document. Though flexible general queries suffer from some drawbacks as regards efficiency and precision.

Link list This search tool exploits results of quotation analysis. It is based on the idea that the degree of importance of a document is proportional to the number of quotations. The hyperlinks correspond to the quotations with the consequence that a document which is often defined as a link destination is of great importance with respect to the relation represented by the hyperlink type.

Assume, for example, that a SEL user intends to find descriptions of the most frequently used components. Applying the SEL link list generator to the link type **uses-used** will return a list of these descriptions.

Practical experience has shown that the link list generator complements the other search tools in a useful way.

Neighbourhood search The documents that are connected to a given document d by links of type R originating from d define the R-*neighbourhood* of d. By the neighbourhood search tool the set D of documents that form the R-neighbourhood of d can be retrieved. The search for R-related documents is easy to understand. In field tests the neighbourhood search tool turned out to be the most effective tool of the SEL system.

Link pattern search This tool supports the search for "similar" documents according to the similarity measure described in the following. Quotation analysis has shown that the similarity of two documents is strongly related to the similarity of their quotation pattern [8]. A quotation of a document d corresponds to a link that points to d. The link pattern search tool determines for a given link type and a given document a list of similar documents that is ordered according to increasing similarity values. The latter are determined by a method developed by G. Salton [8] that is known to be effective in information retrieval. A drawback of this tool is its computational complexity. It is therefore best suited for static networks because in this case the similarity values can be pre-computed and stored.

4 Implementation

The data management component of the SEL system is based on the object-oriented database system GemStone. A full fledged graphical interface has been implemented using the Smalltalk-80 language features. Currently, the system is installed on SUN IPX-Workstations with 32 MBytes main memory and runs with very reasonable performance.

5 Other Work

While various systems have been developed that support the retrieval and configuration of software components from a library the idea to utilize hypertext links to guide the navigation through a network of software components seems to be entirely new. In particular, we did not find a system that exploits techniques borrowed from information retrieval to semi-automatically generate links between documents.

Garg and Scacchi [4, 5] present a hypertext-based system that models the entire software production process. In contrast, our system concentrates on the management of *existing components*. Consequently, we had to put an emphasis on the adaptability of document descriptions and on a sophisticated semi-automatic link generation. The Museion system [2] which is also hypertext-based provides features to manage and integrate all documents produced and used throughout the software life cycle. Documents can be classified using a thesaurus and facets[7]. However, the document structure is static and there is no link generation facility.

Batory and O'Malley report on the construction of hierarchical software systems from reusable components [1]. Their approach relies on some basic assumptions such as open architecture software and interface standardization which are frequently not met by existing component libraries. Hall [6] describes a generalization of executing each component of a library with test-inputs. This technique can be viewed as complementary to automated link generation. In very large libraries, however, the user may put emphasis on the efficiency of answer generation when he or she lets the system propose a set of suitable modules. Our system is able to support him or her in this respect. The SPADE system presented in [10] is a full fledged CASE tool that manages libraries of reusable software components and their descriptors. Different from the SPADE system, the navigation support offered by our system emphasizes semi-automatic link generation based on information retrieval techniques.

---

[7] The facet scheme was first proposed by Prieto-Diaz et al.. See e.g. [7].

6 Summary

A hypertext-based tool that supports the management of large libraries of reusable software components has been presented. A flexible classification of component descriptions as well as various means to interactively retrieve components that match a given specification are provided. Some novel approaches to the semi-automatic determination of relationships between component descriptions have been described and incorporated into the system that increase both the precision and the efficiency of component retrieval. This approach can also be applied when searching for hidden relationships in existing software libraries and thus qualifies our system for re-engineering tasks. In addition, concurrent multiuser access and several levels of access privileges are supported.

The SEL system described in this paper has been developed in cooperation with software engineers of BMW, Munich, Germany, and is currently installed at the BMW facilities in Munich. First field studies indicate that it has a good acceptance and is well-suited to the every-day reusability problems that have to be solved by software engineers. One direction of future work will be the integration of code modules and testing facilities.

Of course our simple, pragmatic approach also has its limitations. For instance, type correctness and interface correctness issues have not been addressed in this paper. We are therefore looking at generalizations, like e.g. adding expressive type disciplines, and allowing various means for semantic specifications (see [3, 11]). In addition we are planning to incorporate a faceted classification scheme [7] into the SEL system as a further improvement of its search facilities.

Acknowledgement

The author is indebted to K. Raith who was the project leader at BMW of the joint project. Thanks go also to K. Avini who implemented the SEL system.

References

1. D. Batory and S. O'Malley. The design and implementation of hierachical software systems with reusable components. *ACM Transactions on Software Engineering and Methodology*, Oct. 1992.
2. M. Brorsson and I. Kruzela. Museion – a reuse support system for design of service features. In *Proc. 10th Annual International Phoenix Conference on Computers and Communications, 1991 Scottsdale, Arizona*. IEEE Computer Society Press, 1991.
3. B. Freitag, T. Margaria, and B. Steffen. A pragmatic approach to software synthesis. In *Proc. ACM SIGPLAN POPL'94 Post-Conference Workshop on Interface Definition Languages*, Portland, Oregon, Jan. 1994. (To Appear in ACM SIGPLAN Notices).
4. P. K. Garg and W. Scacchi. ISHYS - designing an intelligent software hypertext system. *IEEE Expert*, Fall 1989.

5. P. K. Garg and W. Scacchi. A hypertext system to manage software life-cycle documents. *IEEE Software*, May 1990.

6. R. J. Hall. Generalized behaviour-based retrieval. In *Proc. International Conference on Software Engineering.* IEEE Computer Society Press, 1993.

7. R. Prieto-Diaz and P. Freeman. Classifying software for reusability. *IEEE Software*, 18(1), Jan. 1987.

8. G. Salton and M. J. McGill. *Introduction to Modern Information Retrieval.* McGraw Hill, 1983.

9. J. Sametinger and A. Stritzinger. Exploratory software development with class libraries. In *Proc. 7th Joint Conference of the Austrian Computer Society, Klagenfurt, Austria*, 1992.

10. V. Seppänen, M. Heikkinen, and R. Lintulamp. SPADE – towards case tools that can guide design. In *Proc. Conference on Advanced Information Systems Engineering (CAISE '91), Trondheim, Norway*, 1991.

11. B. Steffen, T. Margaria, and B. Freitag. Module configuration by minimal model construction. Technical Report MIP-9313, Universität Passau, Passau, Germany, 1993.

An Approach to Schema Integration
Based on Transformations and Behaviour*

Christiaan Thieme and Arno Siebes

CWI, P.O. Box 94079, 1090 GB Amsterdam, The Netherlands
{ct,arno}@cwi.nl

Abstract

This article presents an approach to schema integration that combines structural aspects and behavioural aspects. The novelty of the approach is that it uses behavioural information to guide both schema restructuring and schema merging. Schema restructuring is based on schema transformations and schema merging is based on join operators.

1 Introduction

Schema integration is an important and non-trivial task in database design. It occurs when a number of different user views, developed for a new database system, or a number of existing database schemas must be integrated into a global, unified schema. As schema integration is a difficult task, methods to support the designer with this task are essential. In [6], a framework for comparing integration methods is given. The framework identifies four steps. In the first step, the preintegration step, an integration strategy is chosen and additional information on the schemas is gathered. Subsequently, the schemas are analysed and compared to find similarities/conflicts among the schemas. In the conforming step, the conflicts found in the comparison step have to be resolved. Finally, in the last step, the schemas are merged by superimposition and the resulting schema is analysed and restructured if necessary.

For our purpose, the main characteristic of an integration method is: which similarities/conflicts are detected and how are conflicts resolved? A number of integration methods use assertions among different component schemas to compare attributes and entity types. In [17], interschema assertions, names, and types are used to compare object types. In [15], schemas are merged using schema operators and assertions among entity types and attributes in different schemas. And in [13], attribute assertions (e.g., key/non-key and lower/upper bounds) are used to compare attributes and entity types. However, the assertions must be supplied by the designer and the resolution of conflicts depends heavily on the common sense of the designer. Other methods use schema transformations to resolve structural conflicts. In [9], structural transformations are defined to integrate compatible structures. In [16], a number of

---

*This research is partly funded by the Dutch Organisation for Scientific Research through NFI-grant NF74.

schema transformations (e.g., join and meet) are proposed to restructure schemas. And in [5], transformations between attributes, entities and relationships are used to resolve type conflicts. However, only the last one gives a heuristic (viz., concept likeness/unlikeness) for applying the transformations. Finally, a number of recent methods use more specific information on semantical properties of attributes and entity types to detect similarities and conflicts. In [18, 23], attribute assertions are used to define relationships between an attribute on one hand and a semantic point or a set of concepts on the other hand. Again, the assertions must be supplied by the designer. In [19], a database metadictionary is used to define a semantic domain for each attribute. And in [10], a terminological knowledge base containing information on negative and positive associations between terms and information on specialisation of terms is used to compare entity types.

This article presents a new approach to schema integration, based on schema transformations and the approach taken in [20, 21], where classes are compared by structure and by behaviour. The approach consist of two steps. First, component schemas are restructured using schema transformations, and syntactical properties of methods are used to guide the restructuring process. Subsequently, the component schemas are merged using join operators, and semantical properties of methods are used to guide the merging process. More details on the approach are given in [22]. There is, as far as the authors know, no other approach that uses methods to compare attributes. For sake of completeness, it should be mentioned that there is an approach to schema evolution that analyses methods ([8]), not to compare attributes, but to solve non-legitimate overriding of methods.

The outline of this article is as follows. In the next section, we give a brief overview and formalisation of our data model. In Section 3, we define a number of well-known type transformations and extend them to be applicable to recursive types as well. Furthermore, we show how these type transformations induce schema transformations. In Section 4, we show how methods can be used to guide schema restructuring and give a heuristic algorithm to restructure and merge schemas. In the last section, we summarise and give some directions for further research.

2 Database schemas

In this section, we introduce a subset of the database schemas found in object-oriented database languages such as Galileo [2], Goblin [12], O_2 [14], and TM/FM [4].

Informally, an object-oriented database schema is a a class hierarchy, i.e., a set of classes related by a subclass relation. A class has a name, a set of superclasses, a set of attributes, a set of constraints, and a set of update and query methods.

Definition 1 (Class hierarchies). First, five disjoint sets are postulated: a set CN of class names, a set AN of attribute names, a set MN of method names, a set L of labels, and a set $Cons$ of basic constants (i.e., 'integer', 'rational', and 'string' constants). The sets are generated by the nonterminals CN, AN, MN, L, and Cons, respectively. Class hierarchies are the sentences of the following BNF-grammar, where the plus sign ($^+$) denotes a finite, nonempty repetition, square brackets ([ ]) denote an option, and the vertical bar (|) denotes a choice:

```
Hierarchy    ::=  Class+
Class        ::=  'Class' CN [ 'Isa' CN+ ]
                  [ 'Attributes' Att+ ]
                  [ 'Constraints' Key+ ]
                  [ 'Methods' Meth+ ]
                  'Endclass'
Att          ::=  AN ':' Type
Type         ::=  BasicType | SetType | RecordType | CN
BasicType    ::=  'integer' | 'rational' | 'string'
SetType      ::=  '{' Type '}'
RecordType   ::=  '<' FieldList '>'
FieldList    ::=  Field | Field ',' FieldList
Field        ::=  L ':' Type
Key          ::=  key KeyAtt+
KeyAtt       ::=  AN | KeyAtt '.' L
Meth         ::=  MN '(' [ ParList ] ') =' AsnList |
                  MN '(' [ ParList ] →' Result ') =' AsnList |
ParList      ::=  Par | Par ',' ParList
Par          ::=  L ':' BasicType
Result       ::=  L ':' Type
AsnList      ::=  Assign | Assign ';' AsnList
Assign       ::=  Dest ':=' Source | 'insert(' Source ',' Dest ')'
Dest         ::=  L | AN | L '.' Dest | AN '.' Dest
Source       ::=  'self' | Term | Term '+' Source | Term '−' Source |
                  Term '×' Source | Term '÷' Source | 'new (' CN ')' |
                  Dest '.' MN '(' ActParList ')'
Term         ::=  Dest | Cons
ActParList   ::=  Term | Term ',' ActParList
```

□

A class hierarchy is well-defined if it satisfies four conditions. The first condition is that the **Isa** relation is acyclic, and classes have a unique name and only refer to classes in the class hierarchy. The second is that attributes have a unique name within their class and are well-typed. The third is that keys must be well-defined. The fourth is that methods have a unique name within their class and are well-typed.

2.1 Underlying types

Informally, the set of all attributes of a class consists of both the new and inherited attributes.

Definition 2 (Attributes). Let H be a class hierarchy satisfying the first condition for well-defined class hierarchies. We abbreviate every class in H to a 5-tuple (c, S, A, K, M), where c is the name of the class, S is the set of (names of) superclasses, A is the set of new attributes, K is the set of new keys, and M is the set of new methods. Now let $C = (c, S, A, K, M)$ be an abbreviated class in H. The name of C is denoted by $name(C)$ and the set of all attributes of C, denoted by $atts(C)$, is defined as:

$$atts(C) = A \cup \{a : T \mid inherits(a) \wedge$$
$$T = \sqcap\{T' \mid inherits(a, T')\} \wedge \forall a' : T' \in A[a \neq a']\}$$

where

$$inherits(a, T') = \exists C' \in H \ [name(C') \in S \wedge a : T' \in atts(C')],$$
$$inherits(a) = \exists C' \in H \ \exists a' : T' \in atts(C') \ [name(C') \in S \wedge a = a'],$$

and $\sqcap\{T_1, \cdots, T_n\}$ is the meet of a set of types [7]. Since we require that the **Isa** relation is acyclic, *atts* is well-defined. $\square$

Every class in a class hierarchy has an underlying type, which describes the structure of the class, i.e., the structure of the objects in its extensions (cf. TM/FM [4]). The underlying type of a class is an aggregation of its attributes, where recursive types [3] are used to cope with attributes that refer to classes.

Definition 3 (Underlying types). First, postulate a new type 'oid', whose extension is an enumerable set of object identifiers. Let H be a class hierarchy satisfying the first condition, C be a class in H, and c be the name of C. The underlying type of class C, denoted by $type(C)$, is defined as:

$$type(C) = \tau(c, \emptyset)$$

where

$$\tau(d, \eta) = \mu \ t_d \ . < id : oid, a_1 : \tau(T_1, \eta \cup \{d\}), \cdots, a_k : \tau(T_k, \eta \cup \{d\}) >$$
$$\quad \text{if } d \notin \eta \text{ and } \exists D \in H[name(D) = d \wedge atts(D) = \{a_1 : T_1, \cdots, a_k : T_k\}],$$
$$\tau(d, \eta) = t_d \ \text{if } d \in \eta,$$
$$\tau(B, \eta) = B \ \text{if } B \in \{\text{integer}, \text{rational}, \text{string}\},$$
$$\tau(\{U\}, \eta) = \{\tau(U, \eta)\},$$
$$\tau(< l_1 : U_1, \cdots, l_n : U_n >, \eta) = < l_1 : \tau(U_1, \eta), \cdots, l_n : \tau(U_n, \eta) >.$$

The set η contains the names of the classes for which a (recursive) type is being constructed as part of the construction of the underlying type of class C. If η contains d, then $\tau(d, \eta) = t_d$ indicates a repetition of the recursive type. $\square$

Note that the underlying type of a class depends on the hierarchy.

3 Schema transformations

In this section, we give an overview of type transformations and show how type transformations induce schema transformations.

The basic type transformations we have chosen (viz., renaming, aggregation, and objectification) are variants of type transformations in [1].

Definition 4 (Basic type transformations). Let L' be the union of L and AN and *Types* be the set of types introduced in Definition 2. Renaming is defined as a function of type $L' \to L' \to Types \to Types$:

$rename(l')(l)(B) = B$ if $B \in \{\text{oid}, \text{integer}, \text{rational}, \text{string}\}$

$rename(l')(l)(\{\tau\}) = \{\tau\}$

$rename(l')(l)(< l_1 : \tau_1, \cdots, l_n : \tau_n >) = < l_1[l' \setminus l] : \tau_1, \cdots, l_n[l' \setminus l] : \tau_n >,$

$rename(l')(l)(\mu t. < l_1 : \tau_1, \cdots, l_n : \tau_n >) = \mu t. < l_1 : \tau_1, \cdots, l_n : \tau_n >$
    if $l' = \text{id}$,

$rename(l')(l)(\mu t. < l_1 : \tau_1, \cdots, l_n : \tau_n >) = \mu t. < l_1[l' \setminus l] : \tau_1, \cdots, l_n[l' \setminus l] : \tau_n >$
    if $l' \neq \text{id}$.

Note that we do not allow renaming of id-fields.

Aggregation is defined as a function of type $\wp(L') \to L' \to Types \to Types$:

$aggregate(\{l_i, l_{i+1}, \cdots, l_j\})(l)(B) = B$ if $B \in \{\text{oid}, \text{integer}, \text{rational}, \text{string}\}$

$aggregate(\{l_i, l_{i+1}, \cdots, l_j\})(l)(\{\tau\}) = \{\tau\}$

$aggregate(\{l_i, l_{i+1}, \cdots, l_j\})(l)(< l_1 : \tau_1, \cdots, l_n : \tau_n >) = < l_1 : \tau_1, \cdots, l_n : \tau_n >$
    if $\{l_i, l_{i+1}, \cdots, l_j\} \not\subseteq \{l_1, \cdots, l_n\}$,

$aggregate(\{l_i, l_{i+1}, \cdots, l_j\})(l)(< l_1 : \tau_1, \cdots, l_n : \tau_n >) =$
    $< l_1 : \tau_1, \cdots, l :< l_i : \tau_i, \cdots, l_j : \tau_j >, \cdots, l_n : \tau_n >$
    if $\{l_i, l_{i+1}, \cdots, l_j\} \subseteq \{l_1, \cdots, l_n\}$,

$aggregate(\{l_i, l_{i+1}, \cdots, l_j\})(l)(\mu t. < l_1 : \tau_1, \cdots, l_n : \tau_n >) =$
    $\mu t. < l_1 : \tau_1, \cdots, l_n : \tau_n >$
    if $\{l_i, l_{i+1}, \cdots, l_j\} \not\subseteq \{l_1, \cdots, l_n\}$,

$aggregate(\{l_i, l_{i+1}, \cdots, l_j\})(l)(\mu t. < l_1 : \tau_1, \cdots, l_n : \tau_n >) =$
    $\mu t. < l_1 : \tau_1, \cdots, l :< l_i : \tau_i, \cdots, l_j : \tau_j >, \cdots, l_n : \tau_n >$
    if id $\notin \{l_i, l_{i+1}, \cdots, l_j\}$ and $\{l_i, l_{i+1}, \cdots, l_j\} \subseteq \{l_1, \cdots, l_n\}$,

$aggregate(\{l_i, l_{i+1}, \cdots, l_j\})(l)(\mu t. < l_1 : \tau_1, \cdots, l_n : \tau_n >) =$
    $\mu s. < l_1 : \tau_1[t \setminus s], \cdots, l : \mu t. < l_i : \tau_i[t \setminus s], \cdots, l_j : \tau_j[t \setminus s] >, \cdots, l_n : \tau_n[t \setminus s] >$
    if id $\in \{l_i, l_{i+1}, \cdots, l_j\}$ and $\{l_i, l_{i+1}, \cdots, l_j\} \subseteq \{l_1, \cdots, l_n\}$.

Objectification is defined as a function of type $Types \to Types$:

$objectify(B) = B$ if $B \in \{\text{oid}, \text{integer}, \text{rational}, \text{string}\}$

$objectify(\{\tau\}) = \{\tau\}$

$objectify(< l_1 : \tau_1, \cdots, l_n : \tau_n >) = \mu s. < \text{id} : \text{oid}, l_1 : \tau_1, \cdots, l_n : \tau_n >,$

$objectify(\mu t. < l_1 : \tau_1, \cdots, l_n : \tau_n >) = \mu t. < l_1 : \tau_1, \cdots, l_n : \tau_n >$
    if $\exists i \in \{1, \cdots, n\}[l_i = \text{id}]$,

$objectify(\mu t. < l_1 : \tau_1, \cdots, l_n : \tau_n >) = \mu t. < \text{id} : \text{oid}, l_1 : \tau_1, \cdots, l_n : \tau_n >$
    if $\forall i \in \{1, \cdots, n\}[l_i \neq \text{id}]$.

$\square$

Complex type transformations are obtained by combining basic type transformations.

Example 1. Type $\sigma = < l_1 : \mu s. < \text{id} : \text{oid}, l : \tau_1, l_2 : \tau_2 >, l_3 : \tau_3 >$ can be obtained from type $\sigma_1 = < l_1 : \tau_1, l_2 : \tau_2, l_3 : \tau_3 >$ as follows:

$\sigma_2 = rename(l_1)(l)(\sigma_1) = < l : \tau_1, l_2 : \tau_2, l_3 : \tau_3 >$

$\sigma_3 = aggregate(\{l, l_2\})(l_1)(\sigma_2) = < l_1 :< l : \tau_1, l_2 : \tau_2 >, l_3 : \tau_3 >$

$\sigma_4 = < l_1 : objectify(< l : \tau_1, l_2 : \tau_2 >), l_3 : \tau_3 > = \sigma.$

$\square$

Both the transformation for lexical attributes and the transformation for unstable subtypes from [11] can be obtained by composing one aggregate and one objectify operation.

Example 2. The following class hierarchy introduces a class Person, a class Employee, which inherits from class Person, and a class Company:

Class Person
Attributes
  name : string
  street : string
  house : integer
  city : string
Endclass

Class Employee **Isa** Person
Attributes
  employer : Company
  salary : integer
Endclass
Class Company
Attributes
  name : string
Endclass.

The underlying type of class Person is:

$\mu\ t_P.$ <id:oid, name:string, street:string, house:integer, city:string>.

The underlying type of class Person can be transformed into (by applying *aggregate* ({street,house,city}) (address)):

$\mu\ t_P.$ <id:oid, name:string, address:<street:string, house:integer, city:string>>,

which can be transformed into (by applying *objectify* to the type of address):

$\mu\ t_P.$ <id:oid, name:string,
        address:$\mu\ t_X.$ <id: oid, street:string, house:integer, city:string>>.

The composite transformation is a variant of the transformation for lexical attributes from [11]. We can redefine class Person as a class (named Person1) that refers to a new class (named X).

Class Person1
Attributes
  name : string
  address : X
Endclass

Class X
Attributes
  street : string
  house : integer
  city : string
Endclass.

The underlying type of class Employee is:

$\mu\ t_E.$ <id:oid, name:string, street:string, house:integer, city:string,
        employer:τ_C, salary:integer>,

where τ_C is the underlying type of class Company. The underlying type of class Employee can be transformed into (by applying *aggregate* ({id,name,street,house,city}) (employee)):

$\mu\ t_Y.$ <employee:$\mu\ t_E.$ <id:oid, name:string, street:string, house:integer,
        city:string>, employer:τ_C, salary:integer>,

which can be transformed into (by applying *objectify*):

$\mu\ t_Y.$ <id:oid, employee:$\mu\ t_E.$ <id:oid, name:string, street:string, house:integer,
        city:string>, employer:τ_C, salary:integer>.

The composite transformation is a variant of the transformation for unstable subtypes from [11]. We can redefine class Employee as a 'relation' (named Y) that refers to a new class (named Employee1):

Class Y
Attributes·
  employee : Employee1
  employer : Company
  salary : integer
Endclass

Class Employee1
Attributes
  name : string
  street : string
  house : integer
  city : string
Endclass.

Note that, in the original situation, an employee (an object in class Employee), does have a unique employer, whereas, in the resulting situation, an employee (an object in class Employee1) does not. Therefore, we define a key for class Y:

Class Y1
Attributes
  employee : Employee1
  employer : Company
  salary : integer
Constraints
  key employee
Endclass.

□

4 Application of schema transformations

In the previous section, we defined type transformations and showed how they induce schema transformations. In this section, we show how behaviour of methods can be used to choose among a set of schema transformations.

A class can be transformed in several ways, using different factors and different transformations.

Example 3. Let class Employee be the following class:

Class Employee
Attributes
  name : string
  dob : Date
  street : string
  house : integer
  city : string
  employer : Company
Methods
  move (s:string,h:integer,c:string) =
    street := s; house := h; city := c
Endclass

and class Address be a factor of Employee:

Class Address
Attributes
    street : string
    house : integer
    city : string
Methods
    move (s:string,h:integer,c:string) =
        street := s; house := h; city := c
Endclass.

One option to transform class Employee is to redefine Employee as a subclass of Address (factorisation by specialisation):

Class Employee1 **Isa** Address
Attributes
    name : string
    dob : Date
    employer: Company
Endclass.

Another option is to redefine Employee as a class referring to Address (factorisation by delegation):

Class Employee2
Attributes
    name : string
    dob : Date
    address: Address2
    employer: Company
Methods
    move (s:string,h:integer,c:string) =
        address := address.new_address(s,h,c)
Endclass
Class Address2
Attributes
    street : string
    house : integer
    city : string
Methods
    new_address (s:string,h:integer,c:string $\rightarrow$ l:Address2) =
        l := **new**(Address2) ; l.street := s ; l.house := h ; l.city := c
Endclass.

Note that, as an employee is not an address in the real world, it is unlikely that the first option is the right choice. The second option, where employee refers to an address (as one of its attributes) is a more reasonable choice. Now, let class Person be a factor of class Employee2:

Class Person
Attributes

```
      name : string
      dob : Date
      address : Address2
   Methods
      move (s:string,h:integer,c:string) =
         address := address.new_address(s,h,c)
   Endclass.
```

One option to transform class Employee2 is to redefine Employee2 as a subclass of Person (factorisation by specialisation):

```
   Class Employee3 Isa Person
   Attributes
      employer : Company
   Endclass.
```

Another option is to redefine Employee2 as a class referring to Person (factorisation by delegation):

```
   Class Employee4
   Attributes
      person : Person1
      employer : Company
   Methods
      move (s:string,h:integer,c:string) =
         person := person.new_person(s,h,c)
   Endclass
   Class Person1
   Attributes
      name : string
      dob : Date
      address : Address2
   Methods
      new_person (s:string,h:integer,c:string → l:Person1)
         l := new(Person1) ; l.name := name ;
         l.dob := dob ; l.address := l.address.new_address(s,h,c)
   Endclass.
```

Since the objects in class Employee2 become the objects in class Employee4, we redefine method 'move' to be applicable to objects in class Employee4. Yet another option is to redefine class Employee2 as a relation involving class Person:

```
   Class Employment
   Attributes
      employee : Person
      employer : Company
   Constraints
      key employee
   Endclass.
```

Since the objects in class Employee2 become the objects in class Person, we do not redefine method 'move', because it is already applicable to objects in class Person. Note that, as an employee is a person in the real world, it is likely that options one and three are more reasonable than option two, where an employer refers to a person (as one of its attributes). □

As we have seen, a class can be transformed in several ways, using different factors and different transformations, e.g., factorisation by specialisation, factorisation by delegation, or redefinition as a relation. But how do we choose factors and how do we choose between specialisation, delegation and redefinition as a relation? For that purpose, we introduce evidence ratios for relatedness. Weak relatedness for a set of attributes says whether the attributes are mutually related (according to the methods). Strong relatedness for a set of attributes says whether the attributes are mutually related, but not to attributes outside the set (according to the methods). Isolation for a set of attributes says whether the attributes are not related to attributes outside the set (according to the methods).

Definition 5 (Relatedness ratios). Let H be a well-defined class hierarchy, C be a class in H, c be the name of C, and M be the set of all methods of C. Furthermore, for $meth \in M$, let $atts(meth)$ consist of the names of attributes of C that occur in $meth$. Weak relatedness of a set of attributes $A \subseteq \{a \mid a : T \in atts(C)\}$ is defined as:

$$weakrel(c, A) = \frac{\mid \{meth \in M \mid atts(meth) \supseteq A\} \mid}{\mid \{meth \in M \mid atts(meth) \cap A \neq \emptyset\} \mid}.$$

Strong relatedness of a set of attributes A is defined as:

$$strongrel(c, A) = \frac{\mid \{meth \in M \mid atts(meth) = A\} \mid}{\mid \{meth \in M \mid atts(meth) \cap A \neq \emptyset\} \mid}.$$

Isolation of a set of attributes $A \subseteq \{a \mid a : T \in atts(C)\}$ is defined as:

$$isolation(c, A) = \frac{\mid \{meth \in M \mid \emptyset \neq atts(meth) \subseteq A\} \mid}{\mid \{meth \in M \mid atts(meth) \cap A \neq \emptyset\} \mid}.$$

If $\{meth \in M \mid atts(meth) \cap A \neq \emptyset\}$ is empty, then $weakrel(c, A)$ and $strongrel(c, A)$ are defined to be 0, and $isolation(c, A)$ is defined to be 1.

For a set of attributes with strong relatedness ratio 1 and any method, either all attributes occur in the method and all attributes that occur in the method are in the set, or no attribute in the set occurs in the method. In that case, the attributes are strongly related. For a set of attributes with weak relatedness ratio 0, there is no method in which all attributes occur and, hence, the attributes are not (mutually) related. And for a set of attributes with isolation ratio 1 and any method, either all attributes that occur in the method are attributes in the set or no attribute that occurs in the method is an attribute in the set. In that case, the attributes are only related within the set. □

Weak and strong relatedness can help to choose a factor. If the strong relatedness ratio of a set of attributes is high, then it is reasonable to believe that they belong together and, hence, to factorise. On the other hand, if the weak relatedness ratio is low, then it reasonable to believe that they do not belong together and, hence, not to factorise.

Example 4. Consider class Employee of Example 3. The weak and strong related-ness ratios for {street, house, city} and {name, dob} are given by:

$strongrel$(Employee, {street, house, city}) = 1

$weakrel$(Employee, {street, house, city}) = 1

$strongrel$(Employee, {name, dob}) = 0

$weakrel$(Employee, {name, dob}) = 0.

As we can see, street, house, and city are strongly related, whereas name and dob are not related.

Now, consider class Employee2 of Example 3. The weak and strong relatedness ratios for {name, dob, address} and {name, dob, employer} are given by:

$strongrel$(Employee2, {name, dob, address}) = 0

$weakrel$(Employee2, {name, dob, address}) = 0

$strongrel$(Employee2, {name, dob, employer}) = 0

$weakrel$(Employee2, {name, dob, employer}) = 0.

As we can see, in both cases the attributes are not related. □

Isolation can help to choose between specialisation and redefinition as a relation. If the isolation ratio is less than one, then specialisation is possible, but redefinition as a relation is not, since, in that case, we have to add a method to the relation that updates another relation or class.

Example 5. Consider class Employee2 of Example 3. The isolation evidence ratio for name, dob, address is given by:

$isolation$(Employee2, {name, dob, address}) = 1.

Redefinition as a relation results in a relation (Employment) that represents a simple association between a person and a company. Now, if we add a method to class Employee2 that updates attribute address and attribute employer, then we will have to add a method to Employment that creates a new person and updates attribute employee and attribute employer. Since this method is not a simple insert or update operation on Employment, Employment is no longer a relation. □

So, how do we choose factors and transformations? Factors are chosen by comparing weak evidence ratios. If the weak evidence ratio of a set of attributes is greater than some threshold, there is reason to assume that the attributes can be used as a factor. If not, there is no reason. Transformations are chosen by comparing strong evidence ratios and isolation ratios. In case the strong evidence ratio is greater than some threshold, delegation is a reasonable option, because the attributes are strongly related within the set and weakly related with other attributes. In case the isolation ratio is less than one, then specialisation is possible, but redefinition as a relation is not. Otherwise, specialisation or redefinition as a relation are both possible. It should be mentioned that, in the context of schema integration, schema transformations must be applied carefully and only if necessary. In particular, this is true for factorisation by specialisation, since a lot of new classes will be generated by this type of transformation.

The considerations for choosing factors and transformations can be used in a heuristic algorithm to support schema integration. First, the attributes of every class are partitioned in such a way that the isolation ratio of every element in the partition is one, and every class is factorised by delegation if desirable. Subsequently, for every pair of promising classes, a set of possible superclasses is computed, and both classes are factorised by specialisation or redefined as a relation if desirable.

Algorithm 1. The following algorithm is a heuristic for integrating two database schemas (resp., DBS1 and DBS2), given thresholds for strong relatedness and weak relatedness (resp., TSR and TWR):

```
integrate(DBS1,DBS2,TSR,TWR) =
    for every class C in DBS1 or DBS2
    do   for every element A in partition(C)
         do   if strongrel(c,A) ≥ TSR and 1 < |A| < |atts(C)|
              then create class C1 as the class containing A
                       and the methods that refer to A;
                       factorise C by delegation using C1;
                       mark C and C1
              elif weakrel(c,A) ≥ TWR
              then mark C
              fi
         od
    od
    for every marked C1 in DBS1
    do   for every marked C2 in DBS2
         do   if there is a superclass C of a class in joins(C1,C2) that can be used
              as a factor according to the designer
              then transform(C1,C2,C)
              else for every key a.p in keys(C1) such that a:D in atts(C1)
                       for some class D
                     do define class D1 as obtained from C1 by applying
                            the inverse of redefinition as a relation;
                            if there is a superclass C of a class in joins(D1,C2) that
                            can be used as a factor according to the designer
                            then transform(D1,C2,C)
                            fi
                     od
              fi
         od
    od;
transform(C1,C2,C) =
    begin let $\varphi_1$ be an injection from atts(C) to atts(C1) induced by $C_1 \preceq C$;
          let $\varphi_2$ be an injection from atts(C) to atts(C2) induced by $C_2 \preceq C$;
          define A1 as the attribute names in the range of $\varphi_1$;
          define A2 as the attribute names in the range of $\varphi_1$;
          if isolation(name(C1),A1) < 1 or isolation(name(C2),A2) < 1
          then factorise C1 and C2 by specialisation using C
          elif 1 < |A1| < |atts(C1)| and 1 < |A2| < |atts(C2)|
          then factorise C1 and C2 or redefine C1 and C2 as relations
                   according to the choice of the designer
          else factorise C1 and C2 by specialisation using C
```

fi
end;

where partition(C) is constructed as follows:

graph(C) has a node for every attribute name in atts(C)
graph(C) has an edge between two nodes if there is a method in the set of
    all methods of C in which both attribute names occur
partition(C) consists of sets of attribute names,
    one set for every connected subgraph of graph(C):
    two attribute names are in the same set if their nodes are connected
    two attribute names are in different sets if their nodes are not connected,

and joins(D1,D2) (i.e., the set of common superclasses of D1 and D2) and $\preceq$ (i.e., the subclass relation) are as defined in [21]. □

Note that the algorithm interacts with the designer. It should be mentioned again that the algorithm is a heuristic and should therefore be used in close interaction with the designer. The heuristic can be improved by combining the different thresholds and refining the different actions. This is the subject of future research.

5 Conclusion

In this article, we presented a new approach to schema integration based on transformations and behaviour. First, we formalised schemas using underlying types and underlying constraints. Next, we presented a number of type transformations on underlying types and used them to transform schemas. Finally, we gave a heuristic algorithm for integrating schemas. The algorithm uses schema transformations to restructure schemas and join operators to merge them and behavioural information to guide restructuring and merging. Advantages of this approach are: 1) structural aspects are integrated in a guided fashion and 2) both structural and behavioural aspects are integrated.

Further research includes 1) extension of the data model, 2) extension of the schema transformations, and 3) extension and refinement of the heuristic algorithm.

Bibliography

[1] S. Abiteboul and R. Hull. Restructuring hierarchical database objects. *Theoretical Computer Science*, 62:3–38, 1988.

[2] A. Albano, L. Cardelli, and R. Orsini. Galileo: A strongly typed, interactive conceptual language. *ACM Trans. on Database Systems*, 10(2):230–260, 1985.

[3] R. Amadio and L. Cardelli. Subtyping recursive types. In *Proc. Int. Symp. on Principles of Programming Languages*, pages 104–118, 1991.

[4] P. Apers, H. Balsters, R. de By, and C. de Vreeze. Inheritance in an object-oriented data model. Memoranda Informatica 90-77, University of Twente, Enschede, The Netherlands, 1990.

[5] C. Batini and M. Lenzerini. A methodology for data schema integration in the ER model. *IEEE Transactions on Software Engineering*, pages 650–664, November 1984.

[6] C. Batini, M. Lenzerini, and S. Navathe. A comparative analysis of methodologies for database schema integration. *ACM Computing Surveys*, 18(4):323–364, 1986.

[7] L. Cardelli. A semantics of multiple inheritance. In *Proc. Int. Symp. on Semantics of Datatypes, LNCS 173*, pages 51–67. Springer-Verlag, Berlin, 1984.

[8] E. Casais. An incremental class reorganization approach. In *European Conf. on Object-Oriented Programming*, pages 114–132, 1992.

[9] R. Elmasri and G. Wiederhold. Data model integration using the structural model. In *Proc. Int. Conf. on Management of Data*, pages 191–202, 1979.

[10] P. Fankhauser, M. Kracker, and E. Neuhold. Semantic vs. structural resemblance of classes. *ACM SIGMOD Record*, 20(4):59–63, 1991.

[11] P. Johannesson. Schema transformations as an aid in view integration. In *Proc. Int. Conf. on Advanced Information Systems Engineering, LNCS 685*, pages 71–92. Springer-Verlag, Berlin, 1993.

[12] M. Kersten. Goblin: a DBPL designed for advanced database applications. In *Proc. Int. Conf. on Database and Expert Systems Applications*, pages 345–349. Springer-Verlag, Wien, 1991.

[13] J. Larson, S. Navathe, and R. Elmasri. A theory of attribute equivalence in databases with application to schema integration. *IEEE Transactions on Software Engineering*, 15(4):449–463, 1989.

[14] C. Lécluse and P. Richard. The O_2 database programming language. In *Proc. Int. Conf. on Very Large Databases*, pages 411–422. Morgan Kaufmann, Palo Alto, CA, 1989.

[15] M. Mannino, S. Navathe, and W. Effelsberg. A rule based approach for merging generalisation hierarchies. *Information Systems*, 13(3):257–272, 1988.

[16] A. Motro and P. Buneman. Constructing superviews. In *Proc. Int. Conf. on Management of Data*, pages 56–64, 1981.

[17] S. Navathe and S.Gadgil. A methodology for view integration in logical data base design. In *Proc. Int. Conf. on Very Large Databases*, pages 142–155, 1982.

[18] A. Sheth and S. Gala. Attribute relationships: an impediment in automating schema integration. In *Proc. Workshop on Heterogeneous Database Systems*, 1989.

[19] M. Siegel and S. Madnick. A metadata approach to resolving semantic conflicts. In *Proc. International Conference on Very Large Databases*, pages 133–145, 1991.

[20] C. Thieme and A. Siebes. Schema integration in object-oriented databases. In *Proc. Int. Conf. on Advanced Information Systems Engineering, LNCS 685*, pages 54–70. Springer-Verlag, Berlin, 1993.

[21] C. Thieme and A. Siebes. Schema refinement and schema integration in object-oriented databases. In *Proc. Computing Science in The Netherlands, ISBN 90 6196 430 X*, pages 343–354. Stichting Mathematisch Centrum, 1993.

[22] C. Thieme and A. Siebes. An approach to schema integration based on transformations and behaviour. Report CS-R9403, CWI, Amsterdam, The Netherlands, 1994 (available by anonymous ftp from ftp.cwi.nl).

[23] C. Yu, W. Sun, S. Dao, and D. Keirsey. Determining relationships among attributes for interoperability of multi-database systems. In *Proc. Int. Workshop on Interoperability in Multidatabase Systems*, pages 251–257, 1991.

Deriving Transaction Specifications from Deductive Conceptual Models of Information Systems

Maria Ribera Sancho
Antoni Olivé

Facultat d'Informàtica, Universitat Politècnica de Catalunya
Pau Gargallo 5, 08028 Barcelona - Catalonia
e-mail:{riberalolivé}@lsi.upc.es

Abstract. We review the main components of a Deductive Conceptual Model (DCM) of an IS, and introduce a logic-based language for its specification.

We then present a new, formal method for the derivation of transaction specifications implied by a given DCM. The method is based on the SLDNF proof procedure, and can be implemented easily in Prolog environments.

The method requires the development of an Internal Events Model (IEM). We present such a model, point out how can it be automatically obtained and discuss its use in transaction derivation.

1 Introduction

A general trend in information systems engineering is the adoption of knowledge engineering techniques to enhance existing methodologies as well as to introduce new and more productive development paradigms, methods and supporting tools [Bub86]. This trend is based on the fact that information systems development is a knowledge intensive task [MBJ90] and, thus, it is not surprising that a lot of research has been directed toward providing knowledge-based tools to support the entire information systems development life cycle, from high-level design to low-level code generation [Fre85].

This paper describes our work on deriving transaction specifications from a Deductive Conceptual Model. Our approach uses a logic-based language for the specification of conceptual models, and applies logic-based techniques for the generation of a system design from a conceptual model.

The main originality of this work is that our language is based on the "deductive" approach to conceptual modelling, instead of the traditional, "operational" approach. Both approaches can provide a complete specification of the static and dynamic aspects of an information system, but they differ in the way the dynamic aspect is modelled.

In the operational approach, changes to the Information Base (IB), corresponding to changes in the Universe of Discourse (UoD), are defined by means of operations. The occurrence of a real-world, external event triggers the execution of an operation (transaction), which reflects the effect of the event on the IB. These effects consist usually of insertions, updates or deletions to the IB. On the other hand, operations, as well as queries and integrity constraints, usually have only access to the current state of the IB.

In the deductive approach, the IB is defined only in terms of the external events, by means of deductive rules, and queries and integrity constraints are defined as if the complete history of the IB were available. A deductive conceptual model (DCM) is a specification of an IS in the deductive approach. Examples of conceptual modelling languages using the deductive approach are DADES [Oli82] and CIAM [GKB82].

A detailed comparison of the operational and deductive approaches can be found in [BuO86, Oli86]. The main conclusions are that DCMs provide more local definitions, are easier to change and to accommodate new requirements, and provide more design freedom. However, DCMs are much more difficult to implement than operational models. The reason is that an operational model already embeds some architectural design decisions, which are not made in DCMs [Oli89].

The main design decisions required to implement an information system from a DCM are data base design and transaction design. Usually, many valid alternatives in data base design exist, and the designer must choose the alternative that he/she considers most appropriate. Complete automation of this decision is not possible, but there is a place for CASE tools that aid the designer by confirming the consistency of his/her decisions and by evaluating their impact in terms of performance.

In transaction design, the designer must decide which transactions will exist and, for each of them, when will be executed, its pre-conditions and the actions to be performed, including data base updates and output production.

Contrary to data base design, transaction design from a DCM can be completely automated. We can build a transaction for each external event, to be executed when that event occurs in the real world. Transaction pre-conditions can be determined from the integrity constraints defined in the DCM. Data base updates can be determined from an analysis of deductive rules, and output production can be determined from queries definition.

In this paper we present a new, formal method for generating transaction specifications from a DCM. We extend here the work in the ODISSEA project reported in [San92], where more details on the general framework can be found. The method is based on the use of the SLDNF proof procedure and, thus, it can be implemented easily in Prolog environments.

To our knowledge, there is no similar work to ours in the deductive approach, although there exists some similar research in the context of the operational approach. We can mention here the recent work from the DAIDA project, reported in [CKM91], where additional references to previous research can be found. DAIDA proposes a dependency-based framework for the mapping from a requirements specification into a system design. The framework is dependency-based in the sense that the mapping of parts of the requirements specification is guided by predefined allowable dependencies. At the same time, the framework is goal-oriented, in the sense that non-functional requirements are treated as possibly conflicting goals to be satisfied by the generated design.

In DAIDA, requirements specification prescribe not only the behaviour of the system, but also the environment within which it will function. Instead of this, we focus only on the system to be developed, and our specifications are executable. This allows us to automate part of the mapping from specification to design. On the other hand, we have not considered yet the role of non-functional requirements in the generation of designs.

The paper is organised as follows. Section 2 briefly introduces the main components of a DCM, including an example that is used throughout the paper. Section 3 presents the Internal Events Model (IEM), a key concept in our approach to design generation. Section 4 discusses the use of the IEM in transaction generation, and gives a formal method for deriving transaction specifications from a DCM. Finally, Section 5 summarises the results of our work and points out future research.

2 Deductive Conceptual Models

We characterise the deductive conceptual modelling approach in a first order logic framework.

Time plays a major role in this approach. Every possible information i is associated with a time point T(i), which states when the information holds. We will assume that times are always expressed in a unique time unit (such as second, day, etc.) small enough to avoid ambiguities. By life span T of an information system we mean the time interval in which the system operates. It is defined as an ordered set of consecutive time points $T=\{t_0...t_f\}$, where t_0 and t_f are the initial and final times, respectively, and where each $t \in T$ is expressed in the given time unit. We can then say that, for any information i, $T(i) \in T$.

A deductive conceptual model (DCM) of an IS consists of five sets: A set B of base predicates, a set D of derived predicates, a set IC of integrity constraints, a set Q of predefined queries and a set A of alerts. In the following, we briefly describe each of these sets. Figure 1 shows an example that will be used throughout the paper.

---

base predicates
new_person(Person,Time)
new_subject(Subject,Time)
offer(Course,Title,Subject,Time)
enroll(Person,Course,Time)
cancel(Course,Time)
derived predicates
subject(S,T) $\leftarrow$ new_subject(S,T1), T1 $\leq$ T
person(P,T) $\leftarrow$ new_person(P,T1), T1 $\leq$ T
course(C,Ti,T) $\leftarrow$ offer(C,Ti,S,T1),T1 $\leq$ T,
                 not $\exists$T2(cancel(C,T2),T2>T1, T2$\leq$ T)
subject_of_course(S,C,T) $\leftarrow$ subject(S,T), course(C,Ti,T),
                          offer(C,Ti,S,T1), T1 $\leq$ T
enrolled(P,C,T) $\leftarrow$ course(C,Ti,T), enroll(P,C,T1), T1 $\leq$ T
interested(P,S,T) $\leftarrow$ enroll(P,C,T1), T1 $\leq$ T, subject_of_course(S ,C,T1)
integrity constraints
ic1(T) $\leftarrow$ new_subject(S,T), subject(S,T-1)
ic2(T) $\leftarrow$ new_person(P,T), person(P,T-1)
ic3(C,T) $\leftarrow$ offer(C,Ti,S,T), course(C,Ti1,T1),T1<T
ic4(C,S,T) $\leftarrow$ offer(C,Ti,S,T), not subject(S,T-1)
ic5(C,T) $\leftarrow$ offer(C,Ti,S,T), offer(C,Ti1,S1,T), Ti $\neq$Ti1
ic6(C,T) $\leftarrow$ offer(C,Ti,S,T), offer(C,Ti1,S1,T), S1 $\neq$S1
ic7(T) $\leftarrow$ cancel(C,T), not $\exists$Ti(course(C,Ti,T-1))
ic8(T) $\leftarrow$ enroll(P,C,T), not person(P,T-1)
ic9(T) $\leftarrow$ enroll(P,C,T), not $\exists$Ti(course(C,Ti,T-1))
ic10(T) $\leftarrow$ enroll(P,C,T), enrolled(P,C,T-1)

Figure 1. Example of Deductive Conceptual Model

Base predicates correspond to the external event types. They are the inputs to the IS. Each fact of a base predicate, called base fact, is an occurrence of an external event. We assume, by convention, that the last term of a base fact gives the time when the event occurred and was communicated to the IS. If $p(a_1,..., a_n,t_i)$ is a base fact we say that $p(a_1,..., a_n)$ is true or holds at t_i.

In the example of figure 1 we have five base predicates: new_person, new_subject, offer, enroll and cancel. A base fact new_person(p,t) means that at time t, p becomes a person. A base fact new_subject(s,t) reports that at time t, s becomes a new subject. A base fact offer(c,ti,s,t) means that at time t, course c is offered with title ti and subject s. A base fact enroll(p,c,t) means that person p is enrolled to course c at time t. Finally, a base fact cancel(c,t) reports that course c is cancelled at time t. We take as time unit a second.

Derived predicates model the relevant types of knowledge about the Universe of Discourse. Each fact of a derived predicate, called derived fact, represents an information about the state of the UoD, at a particular time point. We also assume that the last term gives the time when the information holds. Thus, for example, a derived fact person(p,t) might mean that p is a person at time t.

Each derived predicate is defined by means of one or more deduction rules. A deduction rule of predicate p has the form $p(X_1,..., X_n,T) \leftarrow L_1,..., L_m$, where $p(X_1,..., X_n,T)$ is an atom denoting the conclusion and $L_1,..., L_m$ are literals representing conditions. Each L_j is either an atom or a negated atom. Variables in the conclusion or in the conditions are assumed to be universally quantified over the whole formula. The terms in the conclusion must be distinct variables, and the terms in the conditions must be variables or constants.

Condition predicates may be ordinary or evaluable ("built-in"). The former are base or derived predicates, while the latter are predicates, such as the comparison or arithmetic predicates, that can be evaluated without accessing a database.

We assume every rule to be allowed [GMN84], i.e. any variable that occurs in the rule has an occurrence in positive condition of an ordinary predicate. We also require every rule to be time-restricted. This means that for every positive literal q(...,T1) of a base or derived predicate q occurring in the body, the condition $L_1,..., L_m \rightarrow T1 \leq T$ must hold. This ensures that $p(X_1,..., X_n,T)$ is defined in terms of q-facts holding at time T or before.

In the example, there are six derived predicates, with their corresponding (and hopefully self-explanatory) rules. For the sake of clarity, our examples do not follow strictly the above format, but can be transformed into it using the procedure given in [LIT84].

Integrity constraints are closed first-order formulas that base and/or derived facts are required to satisfy. We deal with constraints that have the form of a denial $\leftarrow L_1,...,L_m$, with $m \geq 1$, where the L_j are literals, and variables are assumed to be universally quantified over the whole formula. More general constraints can be transformed into this form as described in [LIT84]. For the sake of uniformity, we associate to each integrity constraint an inconsistency predicate icn, with at least a time term, and thus it has the same form as the deductive rules. We call them integrity rules.

In the example of figure 1 we show ten inconsistency predicates, with their rules. To see how an inconsistency may arise, assume that base facts new_person(john,10), new_subject(maths,10), offer(c1,ti,maths,15) and enroll(john,c1,18) were received at times 10, 15 and 18, respectively. Thus, the facts that hold at time 19 are:

person(john,19), subject(maths,19), course(c1,ti,19), enrolled(john,c1,19) and interested(john,maths,19). Now, if at time 20, the IS receives offer(c1,ti,electronics,20) the inconsistency facts ic3(c1,20) and ic4(c1,electronics,20) will hold, because course(c1,ti,19) does hold and subject(electronics,19) does not hold, respectively. Therefore, the base fact offer(c1,ti,electronics,20) would be rejected.

Outputs from an IS may be requested by the users (queries) or triggered internally by the system when some condition holds (alerts). Each query is defined by a name, a number of parameters, to which the user will give values when he/she makes the query, and a body. The answer to a query is the set of values that satisfies the conditions given in the body. (In order to focus on our objective, we omit in this paper output definition and handling).

As can be observed, there is a strong similarity in form between a DCM and a deductive database. However, there are some fundamental differences between both. An explanation can be found in [Oli89]

3 The Internal Events Model

We have seen, in the previous Section, the main components of a DCM. Now, we start to describe our approach to the design and implementation of an IS from its DCM. The key concept of our approach is the Internal Events Model (IEM)[Oli89,San90]. In the following, we briefly describe the main concepts of an IEM, and show its application to the example.

3.1 Classification of predicates

Predicates defined in a DCM can be classified according to their temporal behaviour. For our purposes, the most important classification is the following. Let p be a predicate and **k** a vector of constants. Assume that fact p(**k**) holds at time T-1. What can we say about the truth of p(**k**) at time T? Three cases are possible:

a) p(**k**) will be true at time T. Then we classify p as P-*steady*.

b) p(**k**) will be false at time T. Then we classify p as P-*momentary*.

c) p(**k**) can be true or false at time T. In this case, assume that no external events happen at time T. We have tree subcases:

   c1) p(**k**) will be true at time T. Then we classify p as P-*state*.

   c2) p(**k**) will be false at time T. Then we classify p as P-*transient*.

   c3) p(**k**) can be true or false at time T, depending on the truth value of some condition that must be evaluated at time T. Then we classify p as P-*spontaneous*.

Base predicates are assumed to be P-transient. In our DCM example of figure 1, predicates "subject", "person" and "interested" are P-steady. The other derived predicates are P-state.

3.2 Internal events

The concept of internal event tries to capture, in a natural way, the notion of change in the extension of a predicate. We associate to each predicate p an insertion internal event ιp, and to each P-state or P-spontaneous derived predicate q a deletion internal event δq.

Insertion internal events are defined as follows. Let p be a P-steady, P-state or P-spontaneous predicate, then:

(1) $\forall X,T \ (\iota p(X,T) \leftrightarrow p(X,T) \wedge \neg p(X,T-1))$

If p is P-momentary or P-transient, then:

(2) $\forall X,T \; (\iota p(X,T) \leftrightarrow p(X,T))$

Observe that if p is a base predicate, ιp facts represent external events (given by the environment) corresponding to insertions of base facts. If p is a derived predicate, then ιp facts represent induced insertions of derived facts. Finally, if p is an inconsistency predicate, ιp facts correspond to violations of its integrity constraint. In this case, since we assume that the IB is consistent at time T-1, $p(X,T-1)$ is always false, and the literal $\neg p(X,T-1)$ can be removed from (1).

We similarly define *deletion internal events*. Let p be a P-state or P-spontaneous derived predicate, then:

(3) $\forall X,T \; (\delta p(X,T) \leftrightarrow p(X,T-1) \wedge \neg p(X,T))$

If p is a derived predicate, then δp facts represent induced deletions of derived facts. Note that, for inconsistency predicates, δp facts cannot happen in any transition, since $p(X,T-1)$ is always false.

Rules (1), (2) and (3) are called *internal events rules*. An internal event rule is a rule that defines the conditions upon which an internal event happens in a given transition.

For example, the rules:

$\iota course(C,Ti,T) \leftarrow \iota offer(C,Ti,S,T)$
$\delta course(C,Ti,T) \leftarrow course(C,Ti,T-1), \iota cancel(C,T)$

are an insertion and a deletion internal event rule, respectively. The first rule states that the occurrence of an $\iota offer$ fact (in this case, the insertion of an offer base fact) induces a corresponding $\iota course$ fact. The second rule states that the occurrence of a fact $\iota cancel(c)$ at time t induces a fact $\delta course(c,ti)$ at time t if course(c,ti) was true at previous time.

Internal events rules can be automatically obtained using a procedure based on a transformation of DCM rules (see [Oli89, San90] for details). These rules can be further simplified by taking into account the constraints [San93]. Part of the resulting IEM for the DCM example of figure 1 is shown in figure 2.

```
IDR.1  ιsubject(S,T) ← ιnew_subject(S,T)
IDR.2  ιperson(P,T) ← ιnew_person(P,T)
IDR.3  ιcourse(C,Ti,T) ← ιoffer(C,Ti,S,T)
IDR.4  δcourse(C,Ti,T) ← course(C,Ti,T-1), ιcancel(C,T)
IDR.5  ιsubject_of_course(S,C,T) ← ιoffer(C,Ti,S,T)
IDR.6  δsubject_of_course(S,C,T) ← subject_of_course(S,C,T-1), δcourse(C,Ti,T)
IDR.7  ιenrolled(P,C,T) ← course(C,Ti,T-1), not δcourse(C,Ti,T), ιenroll(P,C,T)
IDR.8  δenrolled(P,C,T) ← enrolled(P,C,T-1), δcourse(C,Ti,T)
IDR.9  ιinterested(P,S,T) ← ιenroll(P,C,T), subject_of_course(S,C,T-1),
                         not δsubject_of_course(S,C,T), not interested(P,S,T-1)
IDR.10 ιic6(C,T) ← ιoffer(C,Ti,S,T), ιoffer(C,Ti1,S1,T), S1 ≠S1
IDR.11 ιic8(T) ← ιenroll(P,C,T), not person(P,T-1)
IDR.12 ιic9(T) ← ιenroll(P,C,T), not ∃Ti(course(C,Ti,T-1))
IDR.13 ιic10(T) ← ιenroll(P,C,T), enrolled(P,C,T-1)
```

Figure 2. Part of the internal events model of the DCM example.

4. Deriving Base Transactions

4.1 Implementation of a DCM

Implementation of a DCM comprises two main design decisions: data base and transactions. The simplest implementation consists in storing in the data base (Extensional Data Base, EDB) only the base facts. There is a transaction (that we call Base Transaction, BT) for each base predicate. The role of each BT is to read the corresponding base fact, check the relevant integrity constraints and store the fact in the EDB. Derived facts could be computed using the DCM rules when requested, either during constraints checking or query answering. This implementation, however, would not be acceptable in practical situations from an efficiency point of view.

In general, the EDB comprises all facts explicitly stored in the data base. These facts do not need to be the base facts defined in the DCM. Indeed, it is quite usual to store in the EDB some derived facts, and not to store all base facts. Usually, there are many valid alternatives and the designer must choose in each case the most appropriate. The EDB schema is characterized by: (1) A set of base or derived predicates of the DCM to be included in the EDB (we call them *stored predicates*), and (2) for each of them, a time interval for which its facts will be stored. The Intensional Data Base, IDB, comprises all facts that can be derived from the EDB using the DCM rules.

Then, the role of each BT is to read the corresponding base fact, check the relevant integrity constraints and update the EDB (inserting and/or deleting one or more EDB-facts). In this section, we present a method for deriving the specifications of each BT. These specifications include two parts:
(1) The transaction pre-conditions, which is the set of conditions the base fact must satisfy in order to guarantee EDB integrity.
(2) The transaction updates, which are the insertions and/or deletions that must be done to the EDB.

The design and implementation of each BT will then be dependent on the particular execution environment. We will not deal with this aspect here, but we mention that it is quite straightforward to build such transactions on top of a deductive DBMS (see [San92, MSS92] for more details).

4.2 The approach

As we mentioned before, there is a BT for each base predicate defined in the DCM. We can also derive composite transactions, corresponding to the simultaneous occurrence of two or more base facts, but this extension will not be considered here.

Let $TR=\{\iota b(k,t)\}$ be the transaction corresponding to the insertion of a base fact $b(k,t)$, where k is a vector of constants denoting the transaction parameters, and t the occurrence time. We derive its effects in the following way: For each integrity constraint ic_j specified in the DCM, we check its violation by evaluating the internal event predicate ιic_j. In the same way, for each stored predicate $p(X,T)$, we derive the induced insertion (resp. deletion) of a fact $p(x,t)$ by evaluating the internal event predicate $\iota p(X,t)$ (resp. $\delta p(X,t)$). As IEM rules are defined in terms of data base predicates extensions at time t-1 or before, to evaluate internal event predicates we also need the IDB rules, which relate DCM predicates to the facts stored in the EDB.

To obtain these evaluations we use an SLDNF-based proof procedure. More precisely, let $I=[\iota/\delta]p(X,t)$ be the internal event predicate to be evaluated. We say that

TR induces I if goal $\{\leftarrow I\}$ succeeds from input set IEM $\cup$ IDB $\cup$ EDB $\cup$ TR. If every branch of the SLDNF-search space for IEM $\cup$ IDB $\cup$ EDB $\cup$ TR $\cup$ $\{\leftarrow I\}$ is a failure branch, then TR does not induce I.

Obviously, the evaluation can be completely done at execution time, when the concrete values of EDB and transaction parameters are known. However, we can do some preparatory work at compilation time, by partially evaluating IEM $\cup$ TR wrt I [LIS91]. The result of the partial evaluation is a set E of n rules $(n \geq 0)$:

$I \leftarrow C_i \qquad i = 0..n$

where C_i is a conjunction of literals such that the evaluation of $\{\leftarrow I\}$ at execution time from E $\cup$ IDB $\cup$ EDB gives the same result as the evaluation of $\{\leftarrow I\}$ from IEM $\cup$ IDB $\cup$ EDB $\cup$ TR. If n=0 then TR does not induce I. If C_i is empty then TR unconditionally induces a fact I. In this last case, if I corresponds to the insertion of an inconsistency predicate, the transaction can never happen because it violates the corresponding integrity constraint.

Applying this procedure to our example, at compilation time, assuming that the current state of all derived predicates are stored in the EDB, we have to partially evaluate, for each possible transaction, internal event predicates $\iota ic1(t)$, $\iota ic2(t)$, $\iota ic3(C,t)$, $\iota ic4(C,S,t)$, $\iota ic5(C,t)$, $\iota ic6(C,t)$, $\iota ic7(t)$, $\iota ic8(t)$, $\iota ic9(t)$, $\iota ic10(t)$, corresponding to the integrity constraints, and $\iota subject(S,t)$, $\iota person(P,t)$, $\iota course(C,Ti,t)$, $\delta course(C,Ti,t)$, $\iota subject\_of\_course(S,C,t)$, $\delta subject\_of\_course(S,C,t)$, $\iota enrolled(P,C,t)$, $\delta enrolled(P,C,t)$, and $\iota interestedf(P,S,t)$ to derive the update conditions of stored predicates.

Take, as an example, the transaction: TR=$\{\iota enroll(p,c,t)\}$, where p and c are parameters and t the occurrence time of TR. After application of our method, the set of rules obtained at compilation time will be:

$\iota ic8(t) \leftarrow$ not person(p,t-1)
$\iota ic9(t) \leftarrow$ not $\exists Ti(course(c,Ti,t-1))$
$\iota ic10(t) \leftarrow$ enrolled(p,c,t-1)
$\iota enrolled(p,c,t) \leftarrow$ course(c,Ti,t-1)
$\iota interested(p,S,t) \leftarrow$ subject_of_course(S,c,t-1), not interested(p,S,t-1)

meaning that constraint ic8 will be violated if p was not a person at previous time, constraint ic9 will be violated if c was not a course at previous time and constraint ic10 will be violated if p is already enrolled to course c. If the constraints are satisfied, the fact enrolled(p,c) must be inserted into the EDB if c was a course with title Ti at previous time, and the fact interested(p,S) must be inserted into the EDB if it was not already true, being S the previous value of subject_of_course(S,c). Note, however, that $\iota enrolled(p,c,t)$ can be unconditionally induced, instead of depending on the condition course(c,Ti,t-1), because ic9 guarantees that there exists some course(c,Ti,t-1).

4.3 Example

Before giving the formal definition of the method, we illustrate our approach with an example.

Assume that we want to derive the transaction TR=$\{\iota enroll(p,c,t)\}$ and that the current state of all derived predicates is stored in the EDB. We have first to partially evaluate IEM $\cup$ TR wrt ιicj, corresponding to the integrity constraints. Consider, for example, the partial evaluation wrt $\iota ic8(t)$. Possible sets of conditions C_i that would lead to the violation of ic8(t) are obtained by having some failed derivation of IEM $\cup$

TR ∪ {←ιic8(t)} succeed. Figure 3 shows this derivation tree, were the circled labels are references to the rules of the method, defined in section 4.4.

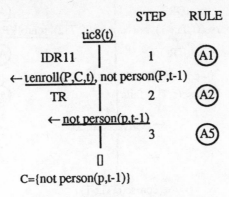

Figure 3: derivation tree for ιic8(t)

Steps 1 and 2 are SLDNF resolution steps. At step 1 rule IDR11 of the IEM acts as input clause, while at step 2 the input clause is the base fact from TR. At step 3 the selected literal not person(p,t-1) corresponds to an stored predicate and, therefore, it can not be evaluated at compilation time because it depends on the concrete value of the database at execution time. As a consequence, this literal is included in the condition set C and its evaluation is delayed until execution time.

The set of conditions obtained for ιic8(t) adds the following rule to the transaction definition:

ιic8(t) ← not person(p,t-1)

Rules for ιic1(t), ..., ιic10(t) can be similarly obtained.

We also have to derive, for each stored predicate $p(X,T)$, the set of conditions to be checked at execution time, in order to induce an insertion or a deletion of a fact corresponding to this predicate, by partially evaluating IEM ∪ TR wrt ιp(X,t) and δp(X,t). Consider, for example, the partial evaluation for ιenrolled(P,C,t). Possible sets of conditions C that would lead to the insertion of a derived fact enrolled(p,c,t) are obtained by having some failed derivation of IEM ∪ TR ∪ {←ιenrolled(P,C,t)} succeed. Figure 4 shows this derivation tree.

Step 1 is an SLDNF resolution step where rule IDR7 of the IEM acts as input clause. At step 2 the selected literal is an external event literal ιenroll(P,C,t) that can be resolved with the base fact in TR. At step 3 the selected literal is not δcourse(c,Ti,t). In order to get a successful derivation, the SLDNF-search space must fail finitely for {←δcourse(c,Ti,t)} ∪ IEM ∪ TR . The failure for δcourse(c,Ti,t) is shown in figure 5. Finally, at step 4 the selected literal course(c,Ti,t-1) corresponds to an stored predicate. Therefore, it is included in the condition set C and its evaluation delayed until execution time.

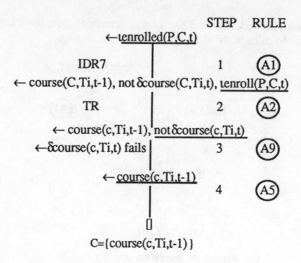

Figure 4: derivation tree for ιenrolled(P,C,t)

Figure 5 shows the failure tree for δcourse(c,Ti,t). Steps 1 and 2 are SLDNF resolution steps. At step 1 rule IDR4 of the IEM acts as input clause. At step 2, the selected literal is the external event ιcancel(c,t) which has to be resolved with facts in TR. Given that there is no fact ιcancel(c,t) in TR, the tree fails unconditionally.

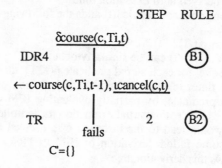

Figure 5: failure tree for δcourse(c,Ti,t)

As a consequence, the following rule will be added to the BT definition:
ιenrolled(p,c,t) ← course(c,Ti,t-1)

Rules corresponding to the insertions and deletions of the other stored predicates can be similarly obtained.

4.4 The method

This section describes, in a formal way, the method explained in sections 4.2 and 4.3. Our proposal is an adaptation of the partial evaluation procedure given in [LIS91]. The main difference consists on the treatment given to the case in which a negative and non-ground literal is selected during the SLDNF refutation. In some cases, for our particular application, the failure of such kind of literals can be guaranteed by the subsidiary derivation and, therefore, they can be evaluated at compilation time.

As we know, the transaction will be derived by partially evaluating IEM∪TR wrt internal events predicates corresponding to integrity constraints and stored predicates.

If I is the internal event predicate to be evaluated, C will be a set of conditions of I if there exists a **constructive derivation** from (I { }) to ([] C), having as input set IEM∪TR, where TR={ιb(k,t)}, being b a base predicate and k a vector of constants.

We will call:

- Non-event literal to a literal corresponding to a base, derived or inconsistency predicate.

- Accessible literal to a non-event literal corresponding to an stored predicate or to a predicate that can be deduced from stored predicates.

Constructive derivation. A constructive derivation from $(I_1 \ C_1)$ to $(I_n \ C_n)$ via a selection rule R, that selects literals not corresponding to evaluable predicates with priority, is a sequence:

$$(I_1 \ C_1) , (I_2 \ C_2),...., (I_n \ C_n)$$

such that for each $i \geq 1$, I_i has the form $\leftarrow L_1,...,L_k$, $R(I_i)=L_j$ and $(I_{i+1} \ C_{i+1})$ is obtained according to one of the following rules:

A1) If L_j is a positive internal event or transition literal, and S is the resolvent of some clause in IEM with I_i on the selected literal L_j, then $I_{i+1}=S$, and $C_{i+1}=C_i$.

A2) If L_j is a positive, external event literal $\iota p(X,t)$, and S is the resolvent of fact in TR with I_i on the literal L_j using substitution σ, then $I_{i+1}=S$, and $C_{i+1}=(C_i)\sigma$.

A3) If L_j is a negative, external event literal "not $\iota p(X,t)$", and TR can not be unified with $\iota p(X,t)$ then $I_{i+1}= \leftarrow L_1,...,L_{j-1}, L_{j+1},..., L_k$, and $C_{i+1}=C_i$.

A4) If L_j is a negative, external event literal "not $\iota p(X,t)$", and TR can be unified with $\iota p(X,t)$ using substitution $\sigma=\{X_1/k_1\}$, then $I_{i+1}= \leftarrow L_1,...,L_{j-1}, L_{j+1},...,L_k$, and $C_{i+1}=C_i \cup \{ X_1 \neq k_1 \}$.

A5) If L_j is an accessible literal then $I_{i+1}=\leftarrow L_1,...,L_{j-1},L_{j+1},...,L_k$, and $C_{i+1}=C_i \cup \{L_j\}$.

A6) If L_j is an evaluable literal then $I_{i+1}=\leftarrow L_1,...,L_{j-1}, L_{j+1},...,L_k$, and $C_{i+1}=C_i \cup \{L_j\}$.

A7) If L_j is a ground internal event or transition literal "not Q" and there exists a **consistency derivation** from $(\leftarrow Q \ \{ \ \})$ to $([] \ C')$ then

$$I_{i+1} = \leftarrow L_1,..., L_{j-1}, L_{j+1},..., L_k, \text{ and } C_{i+1} = C_i \cup C'.$$

A8) If L_j is a ground internal event or transition literal "not Q" and it does not exist a **consistency derivation** from $(\leftarrow Q \ \{ \ \})$ to $([] \ C')$ then

$$I_{i+1} = \leftarrow L_1,..., L_{j-1}, L_{j+1},..., L_k, \text{ and } C_{i+1} = C_i \cup \{L_j\}.$$

A9) If L_j is a non-ground internal event or transition literal "not Q" and there exists a **consistency derivation** from $(\leftarrow Q \ \{ \ \})$ to $([] \ \{ \ \})$ then

$$I_{i+1} = \leftarrow L_1,..., L_{j-1}, L_{j+1},..., L_k, \text{ and } C_{i+1} = C_i.$$

A10) If L_j is a non-ground internal event or transition literal "not Q" and it does not exist a **consistency derivation** from $(\leftarrow Q \ \{ \ \})$ to $([] \ \{ \ \})$ then

$$I_{i+1} = \leftarrow L_1,..., L_{j-1}, L_{j+1},..., L_k, \text{ and } C_{i+1} = C_i \cup \{L_j\}.$$

The step corresponding to rule A1) is an SLDNF resolution step. Note that we also handle transition literals, wich have not been explained in this paper (see{San90}). The step of rule A2) is also an SLDNF step, but now L_j is resolved with TR. In rule A3) not $\iota p(X,t)$ is true because $\iota p(X,t)$ can not be unified with TR.

In A4) not $\iota p(X,t)$ will be true only if $X_1 \neq k_1$. Assume, for example, that the current goal is $\leftarrow$ not $\iota enroll(P,c,t),\alpha$ and that $TR=\{\iota enroll(p,c,t)\}$. By applying A4) we get the new goal $\leftarrow P \neq p,\alpha$.

At steps A5) and A6) accessible and evaluable literals are added to the condition set C because their evaluation have to be delayed until execution time. Steps corresponding to rules A7) and A8) deal with the evaluation of ground and negative internal event or transition literals "not Q". If the failure of Q can be ensured via a consistency derivation (A7), the set of conditions is added to the condition set C. On the contrary (A8), the literal itself has to be added to the condition set C because it can not be evaluated at compilation time. Finally, steps corresponding to rules A9) and A10) perform the evaluation of non-ground and negative internal event or transition literals "not Q". If a consistency derivation ensures an unconditional failure of Q (A9), the selected literal can not fail, and thus, it can be eliminated from the goal I in order to have a failed derivation of $IEM \cup TR \cup \{\leftarrow I\}$ succeed. On the contrary (A10), the literal has to be added to the condition set C because its evaluation has to be delayed until execution time.

There are different ways in which a constructive derivation can succeed. Each one may lead to different insertion or deletion rule.

Consistency derivation. A consistency derivation from $(F_1\ C_1)$ to $(F_n\ C_n)$ via a safe selection rule R, that selects literals not corresponding to evaluable predicates with priority, is a sequence:

$$(F_1\ C_1), (F_2\ C_2),..., (F_n\ C_n)$$

such that for each $i \geq 1$, F_i has the form $\{\leftarrow L_1,..., L_k\} \cup F'_i$ and *for some* $j=1...k$, $(F_{i+1}\ C_{i+1})$ is obtained according to one of the following rules:

B1) If L_j is a positive internal event or transition literal, and S' is the set of all resolvents of clauses in IEM with $\leftarrow L_1,..., L_k$ on the literal L_j, then $F_{i+1}= S' \cup F'_i$ and $C_{i+1}=C_i$.

B2) If L_j is a positive external event literal , and TR can not be unified with L_j then $F_{i+1}=F'_i$, and $C_{i+1}=C_i$.

B3) If L_j is a ground positive external event literal $\iota p(x,t)$, and S' is the resolvent of TR with $\leftarrow L_1,..., L_k$ on the literal L_j, and $[] \notin S'$, then $F_{i+1} = S' \cup F'_i$ and $C_{i+1}=C_i$.

B4) If L_j is a ground negative external event literal "not $\iota p(x,t)$" and TR can be unified with $\iota p(x,t)$ then $F_{i+1} = F'_i$, and $C_{i+1}=C_i$.

B5) If L_j is a negative external event literal "not $\iota p(X,t)$", and TR can not be unified with $\iota p(X,t)$ then $F_{i+1} = \leftarrow L_1,..., L_{j-1}, L_{j+1},..., L_k \cup F'_i$, and $C_{i+1}=C_i$.

B6) If L_j is a ground negative internal event or transition literal "not Q" and there exists a **constructive derivation** from $(\leftarrow Q\ \{\ \})$ to $([]\ C')$ then $F_{i+1}=F'_i$, and $C_{i+1}= C_i \cup C'$.

Steps corresponding to rules B1) and B3) are SLDNF resolution steps. In case B2) and B4) the current branch fails and thus, it can be eliminated. In case B5) the selected literal can not fail, and thus, it is eliminated from the subgoal set F_i in order to make a successful SLDNF branch fail. Finally, in case B6) the current branch can be dropped if there exists a constructive derivation for the negation of the selected literal. This ensures failure for it.

5 Conclusions

We have presented the main components of a Deductive Conceptual Model (DCM). We have then discussed the main decisions involved in the design and implementation process: data base design and transaction design. Data base design can not be completely automated, although some tools to aid the designer in alternatives' generation and analysis can be built.

Once the data base has been designed, transactions can be derived automatically. Preconditions of the transactions can be determined from the integrity rules, and database updates from the deductive rules of the DCM. We have presented a formal method to derive the transactions from the DCM. The method is based on the use of the SLDNF proof procedure and can be implemented easily in Prolog.

We plan to extend our work in several directions. First, we would like to be able to simplify even more the transaction specifications. Second, we plan to consider the case of transactions consisting of multiple base facts, instead of just a single one. Finally, it might be convenient to consider the design and implementation of transactions in conventional architectures. In this sense, our current transaction must be seen as a transaction specification.

Finally, we would like to build a library of rule schemes, such that a particular DCM, and its corresponding IEM, could be developed by reusing the components of the library.

Acknowledgements

The authors wish to thank D. Costal, C. Martin, E. Mayol, J.A. Pastor, C. Quer, J. Sistac, E. Teniente and T. Urpí for their comments and suggestions on earlier drafts. This work has been supported by the CICYT PRONTIC program, project TIC 680.

References

[Bub86]   Bubenko,J.A. "Information system methodologies - A research view". In [OSV86], pp. 289-318.

[BuO86]   Bubenko,J.A.;Olivé,A. "Dynamic or temporal modelling?. An illustrative comparison". SYSLAB Working Paper No. 117, University of Stockholm, 1986.

[CKM91]   Chung,L.;Katalagarianos,P.;Marakakis,M.;Mertikas,M.;Mylopoulos,J.; Vassiliou,Y. "From information system requirements to design: A mapping framework", Information Systems, Vol.16, No.4, 1991, pp. 429-461.

[Fre85]   Frenkel,K.A. "Toward automating the software development cycle". Comm. of the ACM, Vol.28,No.6,June 1985, pp. 578-589.

[GKB82]   Gustafsson,M.;Karlsson,T.;Bubenko,J.A. "A declarative approach to conceptual information modelling". In [OSV82], pp. 93-142.

[GMN84]   Gallaire,H.;Minker,J.;Nicolas,J-M. "Logic and databases: A deductive approach". ACM Computing Surveys, Vol. 16, No. 2, June 1984, pp. 153-185.

[LlS91]   Lloyd,J.;Shepherdson,J.C. "Partial evaluation in logic programming". J. Logic Programming, 1991, No.11, pp. 217-242.

[LlT84]   Lloyd,J.W.;Topor,R.W. "Making Prolog more expressive". J. Logic Programming, 1984, No.3, pp. 225-240.

[MBJ90]   Mylopoulos,J.;Borgida,A.;Jarke,M.;Koubarakis,M. "Telos: Representing knowledge about information systems", ACM Trans. on Information Systems, Vol.8,No.4, Oct.1990, pp 325-362.

[MSS92]   Mayol,E.; Sancho,M.R.; Sistac,J. "The ODISSEA project: An environment for the development of Information Systems from Deductive Conceptual Models". Proc. Intl. Workshop on the Deductive approach to IS and DB, Roses (Catalonia), 1992, pp. 17-47.

[Oli82]   Olivé, A. "DADES: A methodology for specification and design of information systems". In [OSV82], pp. 285-334.

[Oli86]   Olivé,A. "A comparison of the operational and deductive approaches to conceptual information systems modelling". Proc. IFIP 86, North-Holland, Dublin, 1986, pp. 91-96.

[Oli89]   Olivé,A. "On the design and implementation of information systems from deductive conceptual models". Proc. of the 15th. VLDB, Amstedam, 1989, pp. 3-11.

[OSV82]   Olle,T.W.;Sol,H.G.;Verrijn-Stuart,A.A. (Eds.) "Information systems design methodologies: A comparative review". North-Holland, 1982.

[OSV86]   Olle,T.W.;Sol,H.G.;Verrijn-Stuart,A.A. (Eds.) "Information systems design methodologies: Improving the practice". North-Holland, 1986.

[San90]   Sancho,M.R. "Deriving an internal events model from a deductive conceptual model". Proc. Intl. Workshop on the Deductive approach to IS and DB, S'Agaró (Catalonia), 1990, pp. 73-92.

[San92]   Sancho,M.R. "The ODISSEA approach to the design of Information Systems from deductive conceptual models", Proc. of the IFIP World Congress, Madrid, September 1992, vol. 3, pp. 182-188.

[San93]   Sancho,M.R. "Deriving transactions from deductive conceptual models", PhD. thesis. In preparation.

Utilizing Behavioral Abstractions to Facilitate Maintenance During Class Evolution

Linda M. Keszenheimer

Northeastern University, College of Computer Science
Cullinane Hall, 360 Huntington Avenue, Boston MA, USA 02115
seiter@ccs.neu.edu

Abstract. Software maintenance can be a difficult and time consuming process. To facilitate this process, application development must produce software that is designed to continually evolve. While object oriented methodologies address some of the maintenance issues that have troubled traditional functional techniques, object oriented development must overcome the problems involved in maintaining existing object behavior when the underlying class structure evolves. Utilizing adaptable abstraction models for defining class structure and behavior can facilitate software maintenance during class evolution. This paper describes adaptive software development using the Demeter Model for defining object structure and behavior. The maintenance impact of class evolution on existing behavioral implementations is detailed.

1 Introduction

Evolution can be a difficult force to manage during the software development process. The natural tendency of application domains to change and expand can quickly turn software development into a primarily maintenance-oriented process. Object oriented programming facilitates many aspects of software development and maintenance through the features of class reuse, information hiding and delegation. However, an object oriented program is typically implemented based on a particular class structure, and it can be difficult to maintain existing behavioral implementations when the class structure evolves. Class evolution occurs often throughout the software life cycle, due to both a continual improvement in the understanding of the application domain as software development proceeds, as well as the tendency for application domains to evolve to support changing business needs. While class transformations have been studied previously, [1, 18, 19, 7, 4, 6, 14], the research has been primarily based on structural transformations and the consequences of maintaining existing object structure, not addressing the maintenance of existing object behavior.

This paper describes an adaptive software development technique for implementing applications. Since class structures tend to evolve frequently, it is desirable to implement behavior in a flexible manner that can adapt to a changing class organization. Object behavior is described using an abstraction technique called Propagation Patterns [17, 15, 10], which are specifications of class collaborations from which C++ code is generated. The ways that class structures evolve are detailed, and strategies for maintaining propagation patterns based on those transformations are given. While there exist other models for specifying inter-object behavior and patterns [3, 11, 5, 8], Propagation Patterns provide formal language support for the specification and implementation of behavior, with emphasis on supporting class evolution.

The ideas presented here are based on experience gained while using the Demeter CASE tools to implement systems for Citibank and Merrill Lynch. The systems were developed using class models that were under constant flux, requiring propagation patterns to be maintained to support the changing class structures.

1.1   Describing Class Structure with Class Dictionary Graphs

The examples presented in this paper are described using the Demeter data model for defining class structure and behavior [17]. Class structure can be represented graphically in a *Class Dictionary Graph* defined as $\Gamma = (V, \Lambda, E)$. V is a set of vertices in the graph which represent classes. E is a set of edges between vertices which represent relations among classes. Λ is a set of labels which represent the names of the relations.

The Demeter class model defines several kinds of classes, drawn as different types of vertices in the class dictionary graph. A *Construction* class denotes a concrete definition of some entity, and is drawn as a rectangular vertex. An *Alternation* class is an abstraction of the common attributes and behavior found among a group of objects, and is drawn as a hexagon. A *Repetition* class is a container class used to aggregate multiple instances of a class, and is drawn as a hexagon containing a rectangle. A *Terminal* class represents a basic data type, such as a *Number*, *Ident*, or *Real*, and is drawn as a rectangle. Construction, terminal and repetition classes are instantiable, while alternation classes are used purely for inheritance [9].

The Demeter model defines several types of relations among classes. A *Construction* edge represents the *uses* or *part-of* relation, and is drawn as a single line arrow. An *Alternation* edge represents the *isa* relation, and is drawn from superclass to subclass as a double line arrow. The inverse of the alternation relation is the inheritance relation, which is represented by an *Inheritance* edge, and is drawn from subclass to superclass as a double dashed line arrow. It is not necessary for the model to include both *inheritance* and *alternation* edges, since existence of one will imply the other in an inverse direction. Allowing the existence of both edges can simplify the visual depiction of paths in the graph.

A *Repetition* edge indicates the relation between a Repetition class and the class that it aggregates. Finally, a *Behavioral* edge indicates a relation between a source and target class which results from the source class executing a behavior which creates a relation to the target class, and is drawn as a single dashed line arrow. A model for extending the class dictionary graph to include behavior as a relation was initially presented in [16].

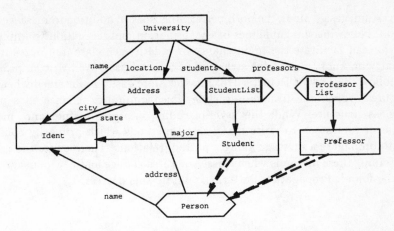

Fig. 1. A Class Dictionary Graph Describing the University Domain.

Figure 1 contains a class dictionary graph that describes the organization of classes in the university domain. The instantiable construction classes are *University*, *Address*, *Professor* and *Student*. *Person* is an alternation class. *Student* and *Professor* are the alternatives, or subclasses of *Person*, that inherit the common attributes and behavior of the *Person* class, a *name* and *home* address. *ProfessorList* and *StudentList* are repetition vertices, each representing a class that collects multiple instances of the associated class, *Professor* or *Student*. *Ident* is a terminal class, a predefined class that will instantiate identifier objects. The class dictionary graph describes only the structural relationships of the classes; behavior has not yet been added to the graph.

Given a class dictionary graph, the Demeter Tool generates C++ code to represent the organization of classes. It is easy to evolve the class structure by simply reorganizing the class dictionary graph. C++ code will be generated to correspond to the new class structure.

2 Defining Object Behavior

An object has certain responsibility and can make requests of other objects to help it accomplish a task. One task in the university domain might be to determine which professors have a long commute to work, which may be relevant in trying to schedule early morning classes. In an object oriented program, functionality is implemented by attaching responsibilities to classes, abstracting common behavior to a superclass, and using message passing protocols to disperse responsibility among many classes to accomplish a task.

It is often the case when implementing a task that it is necessary to involve several classes, each responsible for requesting some behavior of another class which may contain data relevant to the task at hand. Often behavior consists of propagating a request along a path of relations in the class dictionary graph, with certain classes along the path performing work in addition to message propagation. Following the guidelines of encapsulation and delegation to implement behavior can facilitate the maintenance of code if each class minimizes its' dependency on knowledge of the structure of other classes. Well written programs that follow the Law of Demeter [13] may be more easily maintained when class structures evolve, due to a coding style which minimizes reliance on a particular class structure. While this style of coding improves maintenance in some aspects, it forces one to write many small methods which primarily consist of code to propagate a message along a path of relations. There exists the issue of maintaining these methods when class structures change and new message paths must be found. Propagation Patterns facilitate this process.

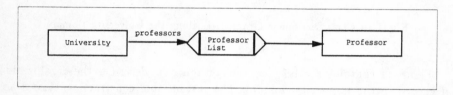

Fig. 2. Propagation Graph Describing A Path From University To Professor

For instance, to collect a list of commuting professors in a given university, the *University* class would need to request a list of commuting professors using the *professors* relation. The *professors* relation produces an instance of the *ProfessorList* class, which would iterate through each of the *Professor* objects that it aggregates. Each *Professor* class instance would be responsible for supplying behavior to provide its' *address* for comparison. The implementation of this task consists of several small methods being implemented, with reliance on the current class structure and relationships. The subgraph of the Class Dictionary Graph involved in implementing this task is shown in Figure 2. This is called the *Propagation Graph* and describes the classes and relations used in accomplishing the task.

2.1 Describing Behavior with Propagation Patterns

Code designed to propagate a message request along a path of class relations can be time consuming to produce and difficult to maintain. Certain communication paths among classes tend to be reused often, with different tasks attaching behavior to different classes along those communication paths. It is useful to define paths among classes, and augment those paths with task specific code to implement a particular behavior.

A *Propagation Pattern* [17, 15, 10] defines behavior by specifying the class collaborations which occur to implement a task, while avoiding writing traversal code that is overly dependent on the class structure. They provide a necessary level of abstraction when implementing object behavior which can facilitate class evolution. The propagation pattern to accomplish the task of determining commuting professors is shown in Figure 3. While propagation patterns have been implemented based on the Demeter class model, most of the concepts presented in this paper could easily apply to other data models.

```
*operation*  ProfessorList* commuters()
*init* (@ new ProfessorList() @)

*dir* allProfsPath = *from* University *to* Professor

*traverse* allProfsPath

*carry* Address* univAddress
 *along* allProfsPath
*at* University univAddress = (@ location @)

*wrapper* Professor *prefix*
(@
   if (univAddress->farFrom(get_address()))
      return_val->append(this);
@)
```

Fig. 3. A Propagation Pattern For Obtaining The List Of Commuting Professors.

The structure of this propagation pattern contains an interface statement with the method name *commuters* and return type *ProfessorList**. A message is sent along a path from the *University* class to the *Professor* class, with the University's *location* being transported along the path as an object that is accessible to other classes. The *Professor* class has the responsibility shown in the wrapper code which adds the current *Professor* object to the resulting list if the Professor's address is far from the University's address.

The behavior implemented by this propagation pattern effectively modifies the class structure defined in the original class dictionary graph to add a behavioral edge to the *University* class. The propagation pattern adds a new relation called *commuters* between the *University* class and the *ProfessorList* class. This new edge can now be used by other propagation patterns in defining paths.

Definition 1. The definition of a *Propagation Pattern* for a given class dictionary graph $\Gamma = (V, \Lambda, E)$ is a tuple of the form (S, M, PD, TP, CF).

- S is the *Signature* of the behavior being defined, and is of the form $(rettype, fname, init)$ where:
  - *rettype* is the return type of the behavior, $rettype \in V$
  - *fname* is the name of the behavior
  - *init* is an optional expression which initializes the result of the behavior.

The Signature S can be described in a textual form as:

```
*operation* rettype fname()  [ *init* (@ expression @) ]
```

There is a special variable named *returnval* of type *rettype*, which holds the return value of the behavior being implemented. It can be initialized using the *init* expression, and modified by any class that has the *fname* message propagated to it.

- M is a *Meta Declaration*, which is used to define constraints in the propagation pattern. While there may be several types of constraints, this paper will only describe a *Meta Graph Directive* constraint, which is used to specify a subgraph of the class dictionary graph. A Meta Graph Directive has the form $(GDName, GD)$, where $GDName$ is a variable name used to represent the graph directive GD. A propagation pattern can define several graph directives.

A Meta Graph Directive has a textual form:

```
*dir* GDName = GD
```

GD is a *Graph Directive* which specifies a subgraph of a class dictionary graph. A GD has the form (F, I, X, V, T) where:

- F is a non-empty set of vertices in the class dictionary graph specifying the starting or source vertices in the subgraph, or *from* classes.
- T is a set of vertices in the class dictionary graph specifying the ending or target vertices in the subgraph, or *to* classes.
- V is a set of vertices in the class dictionary graph specifying vertices which the subgraph must contain as intermediary vertices along the subgraph, these are the *via* classes.
- I is a set of edges in the class dictionary graph which the subgraph must include. These are the *through* edges.
- X is a set of edges in the class dictionary graph which the subgraph must exclude. These are the *bypassing* edges.

A graph directive GD has the textual form:

```
*from* class
[ *through* edge-patterns ]
[ *bypassing* edge-patterns ]
[ *via* class-set ]
[ *to* class-set ]
```

A *class-set* refers to a comma-separated list of class names, and an *edge-pattern* has one of the following textual forms:

```
-> class, label, class    (a construction or behavioral edge)
=> class, class           (an alternation edge)
<= class, class           (an inheritance edge)
~> class, class           (a repetition edge)
```

Given a class dictionary graph Γ and Graph Directive GD, the corresponding subgraph is abstracted. A vertex v or edge e is included in the subgraph if it is located along the path defined between the *from* vertices and the *to* vertices. The path must contain all vertices in the *via* clause and edges in the *through* clause, while excluding all edges given in the *bypassing* clause.

– PD is a *Propagation Directive* which specifies a *Propagation Graph*, a subgraph of a class dictionary graph which collaborates in the implementation of the behavior. A PD is defined using a graph directive.

The Propagation Directive PD can be described in a textual form as:

```
*traverse* GDName
```

GDName must be a defined meta graph directive variable.

A propagation directive will define a subgraph of the class dictionary graph, the *Propagation Graph*. Each class along the propagation graph will have a C++ member function generated that will propagate the behavior to any outgoing edges for that vertex that are in the propagation graph.

– TP is a *Transportation Pattern* which specifies how to transport objects along portions of the propagation graph. A propagation pattern can define several Transportation Patterns. Transportation allows classes along a subgraph of the propagation graph to transport information for use by other classes. A TP has the form (TT, TN, TD, TA) where:

- TT is the type of the object being transported, $TT \in V$.
- TN is the name of the object being transported.
- TD is the *Transportation Directive* which defines a *Transportation Graph*, a subgraph of the propagation graph along which the object is transported. A transportation directive is defined using a graph directive.
- TA specifies the value assignment of the transported object at a particular class along the transportation graph. It is of the form (v, e) where v specifies a vertex, and e specifies the expression that the object is being assigned in the method generated for vertex v.

The Transportation Pattern TP can be described in a textual form as :

```
*carry*
  vartype varname,
   *along* GDName
  *at* class-set
  varname = (@ expression @)
```

Transportation indicates an additional argument added to the signature of the method for each class along the Transportation Graph, which has the name and type of the transported object. This allows classes along the Transportation Graph to access or modify the transported object.

– CF is a *Code Fragment*, which has the form (t, v, cf). A propagation pattern can define many code fragments. Code fragments define behavior for class v in addition to the traversal behavior that is defined by the Propagation Graph.

- *t* specifies the type of code fragment, which is either prefix or suffix. Prefix code fragments contain behavior which should be executed before traversal behavior for the class *v*. Suffix code fragments contain behavior that should be executed after traversal behavior.
- *v* is a vertex in the propagation graph.
- *cf* is a code fragment describing the prefix or suffix behavior for vertex *v*.

Code fragments are represented in a textual form as:

```
*wrapper* class
*prefix*
(@ C++ statements @)
*suffix*
(@ C++ statements @)
```

Demeter implements the propagation pattern functionality by generating code to perform the behavior defined by the propagation pattern. For each vertex in the propagation graph, a C++ member function is created for the corresponding class that the vertex represents. The member function will contain traversal code to propagate the message along each outgoing edge contained in the propagation graph. In addition to this traversal code, any prefix or suffix code fragments that were defined for the vertex will be added into the C++ member function. The signature of the member function is extended for any class along the transportation graph to include an argument for the transported object.

A propagation pattern, as defined for a particular class dictionary graph, must satisfy several constraints in order to be considered *Legal* [17]. A propagation pattern is legal for a particular class dictionary graph if the propagation and transportation directives define valid paths in the class dictionary graph. There must exist at least one path in the class dictionary graph between the source or *from* vertices and the target or *to* vertices, including all *through* edges and *via* vertices, while avoiding any *bypassing* edges. The propagation pattern must also satisfy legality constraints involving code fragments. Each code fragment specified must be for a vertex that is defined in the propagation graph. The propagation pattern must satisfy legality constraints for the transportation pattern, which include specifying a legal transportation graph, as well as ensuring that assignments occur only at vertices defined in the graph.

3 Propagation Patterns Facilitating Class Evolution

Behavior is often implemented based on the hope of a sturdy initial class design, yet it is usually the case that the class design must continually adapt as the application domain evolves. This can be difficult to do once there exists a large body of methods which rely on a particular class structure.

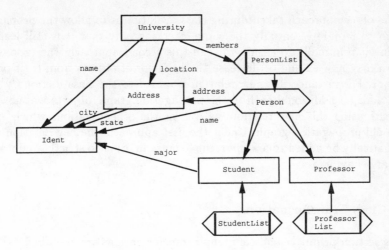

Fig. 4. A Different Class Dictionary Graph For The University Domain

Propagation patterns ease this maintenance issue by providing a more abstract manner to implement behavior than reliance on hand written C++ coding. If the class dictionary graph in Figure 4 is used instead of the original, the propagation pattern in Figure 3 does not need to be modified to maintain behavior, whereas hand-written C++ code would have to be modified to use the new class relations. Class transformations have been studied in [1, 7, 4, 6, 14], most of which discuss structural transformations, but do not address the impact of class evolution on existing behavioral implementations. In [2] the maintenance of $C++$ and CLOS code during class evolution is compared. In [12] the effects of class evolution on propagation patterns are introduced, however the model for propagation patterns and class dictionary graphs did not include behavioral edges or transportation directives. In this section, class transformations are presented, and the potential impact and maintenance requirements are detailed.

3.1 Maintaining or Extending Object Behavior

Given an existing class dictionary graph G and propagation pattern P, a transformation is applied to G which will result in a new class dictionary graph G' and may potentially require adaptation of P to remain legal.

When adapting a class structure, there are primarily two approaches one can take concerning the maintenance of existing behavior. One approach is to strictly maintain the original behavior, such that any object that can be described by both the original and the transformed class dictionary graph should behave in essentially the same manner, while excluding behavior from new objects. This approach may require the propagation pattern to be modified to define new propagation and transportation directives in an attempt to preserve the original propagation and transportation graphs, as well as ensure that the propagation pattern is still legal.

The other approach taken during class evolution is to allow the propagation pattern to remain essentially the same, checking only that it is still legal and evolving it minimally to ensure this. In this second approach, the propagation pattern may now extend or decrease the behavior of objects from their original behavior. For instance if a new relation is added to the class dictionary graph which adds an additional path to the propagation graph, objects will now communicate using this new relation, as well as the other relations which existed in the old propagation graph. Under the first approach, the new relation would automatically be added to a *bypassing* clause in order to strictly maintain the original behavior.

3.2 Class Transformations

In this section primitive and compound transformations are described, with the resulting maintenance requirements for propagation patterns detailed. Modifications which occur along a portion of the class dictionary graph that fall within the bounds defined by the propagation graph or transportation graph can automatically be maintained when the propagation pattern is regenerated.

The maintenance requirements for Primitive Class Transformations are now presented.

- Addition of a new vertex v to the existing set of vertices. This basic transformation alone, without the addition of edges which include v, will have no effect on existing propagation patterns, since there does not yet exist a path which could include it.
- Deletion of a vertex v. It is assumed that all edges which include a vertex v must first be deleted before v can be deleted. If v is used in a propagation pattern, then most issues which occur in deleting v will have already been covered during deletion of edges which utilize v. The only remaining requirement is that v not exist in a propagation or transportation directive, signature return type, or code fragment. If v is found in the signature return type, the propagation pattern is no longer legal, since the result of the propagation pattern is no longer an existent class. If v has a prefix or suffix code fragment attached to it, the propagation pattern is not legal since behavior is being defined for a nonexistent class. If v is found in a directive, it must be removed in order for the directive to be legal. Removal of v from the directive may cause it to no longer define a legal path, in which case the propagation pattern is no longer legal. This may imply that the behavior can no longer be implemented.
- Rename a vertex v to v'. Vertex v must be replaced with v' wherever v is referred to in the propagation pattern signature, propagation directive, transportation directive or code fragment. While this may require manual intervention, there is no work required when other vertices contained within the graph defined by a directive are renamed, since the code will be regenerated using the correct name.

- Addition of a new edge. To maintain the original behavior, automatically add the edge to the *bypassing* set (X) for any Graph Directive which will otherwise include the edge in its' defined subgraph. To extend or refine behavior, allow the new edge to potentially be used in the original directives to define new propagation and transportation graphs. This second approach may drastically change the behavior being defined by the propagation and transportation directives.
- Deletion of an edge. If the edge is defined in the *bypassing* set (X), remove the edge from the set to maintain a legal propagation pattern. If the edge is included in the *through* set (I), the propagation pattern will no longer be legal. The edge can be removed from (I) and another path will be used, if one exists. If deletion of the edge causes the propagation or transportation graph to become disconnected, the propagation pattern is no longer legal. If the edge is used in a code fragment, or initialization expression, the propagation pattern is no longer legal.
- Rename an edge e to e'. If the edge e is referred to in the *bypassing* or *through* sets (X, I), a code fragment or initialization expression, it must be updated to e'. Renaming of an edge which is not explicitly defined in a graph directive, but contained in a propagation or transportation graph, does not require manual maintenance since the correct code will be regenerated.

Single primitive transformations by themselves are not typically the way a class dictionary graph evolves. Experience based on transforming class dictionary graphs during application development shows that compound class transformations are often performed to a class dictionary graph and the maintenance of propagation patterns should support these higher level transformations. The maintenance requirements for compound class transformations are presented.

- Transform a construction edge to a behavioral edge. This transforms a relation from being stored (a construction edge) to being derived (a behavioral edge), and is a common transformation. From a modeling viewpoint, these two edge types should be interchangeable, since it is usually a design or performance decision to either store or calculate an attribute. This transformation should require no maintenance of the Propagation or Transportation Directives. It may be necessary to add code to handle storage issues involving the allocation and deallocation of objects, but this is dependent on garbage collection tactics [16]. Code fragments which refer to the original relation may need to be adapted to add argument parenthesis () after the label, which could be automated.
- Transform a behavioral edge to a construction edge. Opposite requirement of previous transformation.
- Abstract a relation l up the inheritance hierarchy to a superclass, indicating the deletion of a construction edge (v, l, w) and the addition of a construction edge (v', l, w), where v' is a superclass of v. This transformation occurs when a relation found in a subclass is deemed appropriate to be inherited from a superclass. If there is a subclass u of v' which did not originally have the

relation l, to maintain original behavior an inheritance edge (w, v') and an alternation edge (v', w) must be added to the *bypassing* set X. If the original edge (v, l, w) was contained in a bypassing (X) or through (I) edge directive, it must be replaced either with the new edge (v', l, w) to affect all of the subclasses which now inherit the relation, or replaced with the inheritance edge (v', v) or alternation edge (v, v') to maintain the directive. Using meta-characters for edge specifications can avoid this problem, such as specifying a *bypassing* edge as $(*, l, *)$ instead of specifying the source and target class names of the relation l.

- Distribute a construction edge down the inheritance hierarchy. Again if the edge is specified in a graph directive, the new edge(s) will have to be specified. If the edge is not specified directly, the propagation and transportation graphs will be correctly computed and the C++ code regenerated. If the relation represented by the construction edge was used in a code fragment, initialization or transportation assignment attached to the superclass, this would have to be modified to attach the code fragment or assignment to each subclass which now contains the relation.

- Replace a direct relation or edge between two vertices with a sequence of edges. This transformation often occurs when additional partitioning of objects is needed. Two objects must go through a longer sequence of objects to communicate a message. If the original edge was used in a directive, it must be replaced with enough of the new path to distinguish the new path from any other paths, potentially replacing it with the entire new path. If the old edge was not directly contained in a directive, but was contained in either the propagation or transportation graph, the new path should also be contained in the graphs, and therefore the correct code will be regenerated to utilize the new path.

- Replace a sequence of edges between two vertices with a direct edge. This transformation occurs when it is decided to simplify the object structure. The maintenance requirements are similar to the previous case.

- Generalize the domain of a relation. In this case a construction edge (v, l, w) is replaced by a construction edge (v, l, u) where u is a superclass of w. To maintain the original behavior, it is necessary to exclude any of the new objects which might have behavior propagated to them, namely the subclasses of u other than w. Therefore an alternation edge (w, w') and an inheritance edge (w', w) are added to the *bypassing* set (X) for each subclass (minus w) of u.

  If the original edge (v, l, w) was contained in a propagation or transportation directive, it must be replaced with the new generalized edge (v, l, u) for the directives to remain legal. Any code fragments which utilized the old edge should still hold correct. This maintenance effort would not be necessary if meta-characters are used in the edge specification.

- Specialize the domain of a relation. Here construction edge (v, l, w) is replaced by construction edge (v, l, u), where w is a superclass of u. The original behavior can not be maintained, since objects which received a message request given the original class dictionary graph will not be contained in the new propagation graph.

The behavior can only be refined, with substitution of the old edge for the new in any graph directives to ensure the propagation pattern is still legal.

4 Conclusion

As many of the transformations show, there may be manual effort required to maintain a propagation pattern when the class dictionary evolves. However there are many transformations that require minimal effort in comparison to maintaining hand-written C++ code. Using graph directives to specify traversal paths can greatly facilitate the maintenance of object oriented programs, which are highly reliant on class structures when implementing behavior. Defining a graph directive in a meta declaration and reusing it in many propagation directives and carry directives also facilitates maintenance since the communication paths among objects in the form of a graph directive need only be specified and maintained in one place. The benefit of propagation patterns is the ability to minimize hard-coding the class structures into C++ code, so that evolution is supported.

Propagation Patterns have been used in industry in situations where the class structure was under continuous change. The effort required to maintain existing propagation patterns was minimal as compared to maintenance of C++ code. In many cases, the graph directives were consistent with the new class structure and no change was required, the code was simply regenerated to fit the new structure.

Utilizing high-level abstractions like class dictionary graphs and propagation patterns can further expand the benefits of object oriented technology by minimizing the maintenance effort required when application domains change. The ability to support and encourage change is a necessary part of any software development model.

Acknowledgements

I would like to thank Karl Lieberherr, Greg Sullivan and Cun Xiao for providing many useful ideas about propagation patterns and modeling behavior. Cun Xiao has produced a powerful propagation pattern tool and has patiently implemented many enhancement requests.

References

1. Paul Bergstein. Object-preserving class transformations. In *Object-Oriented Programming Systems, Languages and Applications Conference, in Special Issue of SIGPLAN Notices*, pages 299–313, Phoenix, Arizona, 1991. ACM Press. SIGPLAN Notices, Vol. 26, 11 (November).
2. Paul L. Bergstein and Walter L. Hürsch. Maintaining behavioral consistency during schema evolution. pages 176–193, Kanazawa, Japan, November 1993. JSST.

338

3. Grady Booch. *Object-Oriented Design With Applications*. Benjamin/Cummings Publishing Company, Inc., 1991.

4. Eduardo Casais. An incremental class reorganization approach. In *European Conference on Object-Oriented Programming*. Springer Verlag, 1992.

5. Peter Coad. Object oriented patterns. *Communications of the ACM*, 35(9):153–159, September 1992.

6. Christine Delcourt and Roberto Zicari. The design of an integrity consistency checker (icc) for an object oriented database system. In *European Conference on Object-Oriented Programming*, pages 377–396, Geneva, Switzerland, 1991. Springer Verlag.

7. Mohammed Erradi, Gregor Bochmann, and Rachida Dssouli. A framework for dynamic evolution of object-oriented specifications. In *Proceedings of the Conference on Software Maintenance*. IEEE Computer Society, 1992.

8. Ian M. Holland. The design and representation of object-oriented components. Technical report, Northeastern University, 1993. Ph.D. thesis.

9. Walter L. Hürsch. Should Superclasses be Abstract? In *European Conference on Object-Oriented Programming*, Bologna, Italy, July 1994. Springer Verlag, Lecture Notes in Computer Science. To appear.

10. Walter L. Hürsch, Linda M. Seiter, and Cun Xiao. In any case: Demeter. *The American Programmer*, 4(10):46–56, October 1991.

11. Ralph E. Johnson. Documenting frameworks using patterns. In *Object-Oriented Programming Systems, Languages and Applications Conference, in Special Issue of SIGPLAN Notices*, Vancouver, Canada, 1992. ACM Press.

12. Linda Keszenheimer. Specifying and adapting object behavior during system evolution. In *Proceedings of the 8th International Conference on Software Maintenance*, pages 254–261. IEEE Computer Society, 1993.

13. Karl J. Lieberherr and Ian Holland. Assuring good style for object-oriented programs. *IEEE Software*, pages 38–48, September 1989.

14. Karl J. Lieberherr, Walter L. Hürsch, and Cun Xiao. Object-extending class transformations. *Formal Aspects of Computing, the International Journal of Formal Methods*, 1993. Accepted for publication, also available as Technical Report NU-CCS-91-8, Northeastern University.

15. Karl J. Lieberherr, Ignacio Silva-Lepe, and Cun Xiao. Adaptive object-oriented programming using graph-based customization. *Communications of the ACM*, May 1994. Accepted for publication.

16. Karl J. Lieberherr and Greg T. Sullivan. Procedural extensions of class dictionary graphs. Technical Report Demeter-9, Northeastern University, March 1992.

17. Karl J. Lieberherr and Cun Xiao. Object-oriented software evolution. *IEEE Software*, pages 313–343, April 1993.

18. P. Poncelet and L. Lakhal. Consistent structural updates for object database design. In *Proceedings of the Conference on Advanced Information Systems Engineering*. Springer-Verlag, 1993.

19. Christiaan Thieme and Arno Siebes. Schema integration in object-oriented databases. *Proceedings of the Conference on Advanced Information Systems Engineering*, 1993.

A PROCESS VIEW OF METHODOLOGIES

Naveen Prakash

Division of Computer Engineering, Delhi Institute of Technology
Kashmere Gate, Delhi 110006, India

email : np@dit.ernet.in

Abstract. It is argued that a methodology provides primitives using which the developer can construct the desired process. From the point of view of a process, a methodology is a passive device which only specifies a set of steps and step transition constraints. A step of a methodology can be modelled in terms of the triplet, <situation, decision, action>. A methodology is a collection of such triplets. The decisions of triplets articulate different kinds of methodology primitives like the creation, deletion, and modification of methodology-specific situations. Under this model, the development process becomes a decision making activity rooted in a methodology. The validation constraints of a methodology constrain this activity by regulating the transition from one decision to another.

I Introduction

For the last few years we have been trying to develop a model for the information system development process (Rol93a, Rol93b). In this work, we are viewing the development process as a decision making activity. Dowson(Dow87) classified development processes into three classes:
- the activity-oriented group,
- the product-oriented group,
- the decision-oriented group.
Our approach belongs to the decision-oriented group.

As argued in (Rol93a, Rol93b) we consider the process in contextual terms. A context is defined as a couple <situation, decision>. This suggests a strong coupling between the decision of a context and the situation in which this decision is taken. As a result, the process model answers the question, when is a decision taken? In addition, the model introduces the notion of macro and micro contexts. The former offer alternatives in decision-making whereas the latter cause product transformations.

It is our belief that the development process is rooted in a methodology. Because of this, the decisions and associated situations comprising a process are of two kinds
- methodology-specific,
- process-specific.
The methodology-specific aspect of a process is directly concerned with the construction of the product. As an example, consider the decision to create an entity of the ER schema. The process-specific aspect does not directly affect the product but

helps in building the process structure. An example of this is the case where the developer decides to backtrack to an earlier context of the process.

In this paper, we investigate the methodology-specific aspect and leave the process-specific aspect for another paper.

Traditionally, tools which support methodologies incorporate in them a certain technique which the developer is asked to follow. In order to make tools more responsive to developer preferences of process techniques, the need for a meta-level has been felt. These levels have been of two kinds : those that deal only with the product aspects of methodologies and those which deal with both, the product and process aspects. Smolander(Smo91) uses the Object-Property-Role-Relationship model for this meta-level. Rolland and Souveyet(Rol90) propose an object-oriented framework for this meta-level.

Chen and Nunamaker(Che89) use a semantic network to represent knowledge about process techniques used by developers. Brinkkemper(Bri90) proposes to separately model the product aspect and the process aspect of a modelling technique. For these he uses NIAM coupled with first order calculus for specifying validation rules. Wijers(Wij91) has tried to represent knowledge about development strategies and rules constraining allowable specification structures. The meta-level of Wijers is an 18-tuple consisting of a task structure, a concept structure, a set of verification rules, a set of procedures, a set of information places, a set of place labels, a set of decision rules, and of relations which relate these sets with one another. Verhoef(Ver93) uses the Predicate Set Model(PSM) of Hof(93) and LISA-D to build a formalism in which to express a methodology.

However, it seems possible to use other formalisms as well. For example, set theory(Ahi87) could also be used for modelling product aspects whereas Predicate-Transition Nets(Gen 87) and Entity Process Models(Hum 89) could be used for modeling the process aspects.

As far as we see it, the question of the meta-level is linked to the larger question of how one views a methodology. For Wijers, a methodology provides appropriate development structure by identifying useful strategies and techniques for specific problem classes. This, perhaps, explains the emphasis on the representation of knowledge about development strategies and rules constraining allowable specification structures. Brinkkemper(Bri90) looks upon a methodology as prescribing development in a hierarchy of ordered steps, which have to be performed in order to deliver the parts of a system in a proper manner.

According to us, a methodology does not identify any strategy of development. Rather, a methodology is a passive device: it provides a set of steps and step transition constraints which need to be enforced. If strategies exist then these are discovered by developers and they are enforced in practice through steps and step transitions.

To show this, we develop a methodology meta-level. This meta-level considers a methodology to be a set of triplets of the form
    <situation, decision, action>
where
- the situation is either an elementary concept of the model (an entity or a relationship of the ER model) or a more complex substance built out of these elementary concepts (a dynamic transition of Remora).

- the decision expresses the intention of the action to be taken on the situation. For example, one may want to create an entity. In this case, the decision is 'create'.
- the action specifies the manner in which the decision shall be enforced. It is a procedure which lays down the acts to be performed.

There exists a triplet corresponding to each step that can be performed in a methodology. So by analysing a step, it is possible to identify the situation, decision, and action of the triplet corresponding to it. Let there be a step S and let its corresponding triplet be T. The situation part of T corresponds to the structure that is of interest in S, the decision part captures the intention of the step, and the action part of T specifies the way in which the decsion shall be realised.

The layout of the paper is as follows. In the next section we consider the properties of a methodology. Thereafter, we highlight our view of the relationship between a product, a process, and a methodology. Then, we introduce the notion of a triplet and consider its components in detail. We deal with the manner in which situations and decisions arise and also the way in which the set of steps of a methodology can be determined. Finally, in section IV, we consider step transition and show how a methodology imposes constraints on step transitions.

II What is a Methodology

The traditional view of methodologies is that they are based on a model and consist of a number of steps which must be executed in some order. Let us consider both these aspects of methodologies in turn.

The model of a methodology provides the basic building blocks in terms of which the product is expressed. In addition there are certain constraints which must be enforced. These have been expressed in four classes of validation controls in Remora (Rol88). These controls are introduced below together with examples taken from the Remora methodology

a) conformity controls which ensure that the norms imposed on the conceptual schema by the model are met. A rule of conformity control relates different concepts of the model together. For example, given the concepts of c-event, c-object, and c-operation the following conformity rule relates these together:
Every c-event constitutes the state change of exactly one c-object and triggers at least one c-operation.   ---(1)

b) consistency controls which ensure that there are no contradictions in the description and also that it is not possible to introduce any contradictory expressions in it. For example consider
- If a c-object is modified by many operations in a given dynamic transition then all these operations must be conditionally triggered and these conditions must be pair-wise mutually exclusive.   ---(2)

c) completeness controls which ensure that the conceptual schema respects all the rules of completeness in a representation. For example the following is a completeness rule:
Every c-object modified by a described c-operation and ascertained by a described c-event must be itself described in the conceptual schema.---(3)

d) fidelity controls which ensure that the conceptual schema introduces faithfully all the phenomena sought to be represented in it. For example, a fidelity rule can ask for the identification of dynamic cycles and subsequent examination for accepting or rejecting them.

Now, let us turn to the second aspect of methodologies, that of steps. In specifying the set of steps, it is usual to explicitly specify only those steps which deal with the *creation* of the concepts of the model and in *amplifying* their properties. For example, methodologies do not have steps to retract previously created concepts, to transform, say, an entity into a relationship, or to do constraint checking. Finally, the question
  assuming that a transition is to be made, what are valid transitions?
is also left implicitly answered.

We look upon a methodology as a quadruple
        < M, MC, S, ST >
where M is the model in terms of whose concepts the IS product is to be expressed, MC is the set of model constraints, S is the set of steps that are available in the methodology, and ST is the set of step transitions. For example, we could define the ER based methodology above as having
- M, the ER model
- MC, the constraints of the ER model
- S, the set of steps as follows:
{ Define entitites, Define relationships, Define weak entities and relationships, Define keys, Define cardinalities of relationships, Define roles, Define value sets, Define attributes, Define functionality of attributes }
- ST, the step transitions, which specifies the possible step transitions. Some elements of this set are the transitions from

define entities	to	define relationships
define entities	to	define attributes
define relationships	to	define cardinalities of relationships

We show later the exact manner in which ST can be determined.

III A Methodology as a Triplet

We consider a step of a methodology to be a triplet
        < s, d, a >
where s is the situation, d is the decision and a is the action. When a step is performed, then an instance of the type, s may be created, deleted, modified, or corrected, and, additionally, it gets reflected in the product under development.

A *situation* is the element which is the object of the step being modelled. A *decision* reflects the intention of the step. It specifies the objective that the step can achieve with regard to the situation. An *action* specifies the executive action that must be performed in order to give effect to the decision. It performs a transformation on the product. Performing it changes the product and may generate new/modified instances of situations which, in turn, are subjects of steps.

As an example, consider the step, 'define subtype of an entity'. This can be represented as < entity, subtype, A >. Here, the object of the step, the situation, is 'entity'; the intention of the step, the decision, is to 'subtype' the entity; and the action, A, which enforces this decision, consists of defining the subtype structure and also of the modification of relationship structures entered into by the generic entity type. As a result of the execution of < entity, subtype, A > an instance, e of type entity, gets affected and a new situation results. This new situation can be acted upon through other steps of the methodology.

The Situation

We define a situation as follows:
A situation is either an elementary concept of the model or a more complex substance built out of these elementary concepts
The terms, concept and complex substance, used in this definition need further clarification. We need to identify what concepts and complex substances are and how do they arise. Let us consider the notion of a concept first.

It has been shown that one can develop a meta-model of the model, M, of a methodology(Rol90). Such a meta-model gives us a precise definition of what a concept is. We partition the set of concepts of M into two classes of elements, structural and definitional elements. Structural elements of M identify the structures that are permitted under it whereas the definitional elements identify the amplifications that are required to be made to define the structural elements properly.

There are two kinds of structural elements, primitive and dependent. Primitive structural elements are those which are not dependent upon other elements for their existence whereas dependent structures need other structural elements to exist. For example, the ER model can be considered to specify two structures, entity and relationship. An entity is a primitive structural element whereas the relationship is a dependent one since it is dependent on entities for its existence.

As one continues building structural elements from one another, a time comes when one is left with a set of structural components which themselves are not components of any other structure. It is possible for two or more such structural elements to be mutually dependent upon one another. Such structural elements shall be referred to as peer elements and they shall be dealt with in detail when the conformity constraints are considered. As an example of peer elements in Remora, consider the c-events and c-operations triggered by it. These are mutually dependent upon each other : it is not possible for a c-event to be defined without any c-operations. Conversely, it is not possible to have c-operations which are not associated with a c-event.

Definitional elements of a conceptual model are associated with its structural elements. Just as there are two kinds of structural elements, there are two kinds of definitional elements, primitive and dependent. Primitive definitional elements are those which do not require any other definitional element for them to be well defined. Dependent definitional elements require other definitional elements in order to be well defined. For example, with the structural elements, entity and relationship of the ER model, we have 'attribute' as a definitional element. Additionally, the properties of these attributes, whether these are mono or multi-valued, must be known. The nature of functionality of attributes is the definitional element associated with attributes. Thus, we have attributes and the nature of their functionality as the definitional elements of the ER approach. The former are dependent definitional elements whereas 'functionality' of attributes is a primitive definitional element.

Now, let us consider complex substances. A complex substance is a collection of concepts which has meaning in a methodology. A collection of concepts carries meaning if either one of the following holds

- the collection is a well defined part of the product, can be identified as such, and can be the object of a decision. As an example consider the notion of the dynamic transition of Remora.
- the collection of concepts are subjects of one or more constraints of the model. For example, consider the following consistency constraint of Remora

If the c-events triggering multiple c-operations modifying the same c-object are independent of one another or if they are chronologically dependent on one another then the triggers of these c-operations must be pairwise mutually exclusive.

Here we have two complex substances

a) c-events triggering multiple c-operations modifying the same c-object but independent of one another

b) c-events triggering multiple c-operations modifying the same c-object but chronologically dependent on one another

It must be noted that the collection of objects forming a situation is structural in nature. Further, this collection is a dependent structural substance.

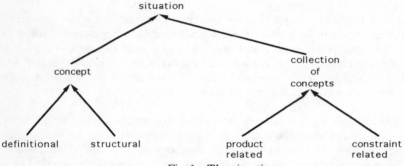

Fig 1 : The situation

The notion of a situation is illustrated in Fig. 1 We can phrase this view of the situation as follows:

A situation is
- either a structural or a definitional concept of the model
- a collection of concepts which either holds individual interest as a part/whole of the product or which is of interest in constraint enforcement.

Notice that this definition considers the entire product, that is, the product in a certain state of development, as a situation.

The Decision

The decision component of the triplet identifies the intention of a step of the methodology. Since it is an intention to create new situations in a methododlogy, we have the create class of decisions. Anything that can be created can be modified or deleted. Thus, we also have these two additional classes of decisions. Under the modification class, it is possible to group together all those decisions which cause a change in a situation that has already been defined. For example, modification could include in it, the decision sub-classes as follows:

- update : intent to update a situation. For example, update a dynamic transition by changing the trigger of an operation.
- historise : intent to keep the history of a situation. For example, keep a history of the orders delivered.
- subtype : intent to specialise a situation.
- retype : intent to change the form of a situation. For example, the change of a relationship into an attribute or the change of an relationship into an entity.

In addition, decisions related to validation controls of a methodology have to be dealt with. There are two ways of defining validation controls, depending upon the way one interprets the intention of these controls. The first of these looks upon a control as a checking device : the intention of a control is to check that a certain condition is indeed satisfied in a situation. Thus, we have a class of decisions, called check, which check the validity of a situation and whose action part returns the boolean values, TRUE or FALSE. The second way of interpreting validity controls is to look upon them as making a positive, active contribution to the situation. In this view, the intention of a control is to build a "correct" situation. Thus, we have the class of decisions, called correct, whose intention is to correct a given situation, if there are any errors in it. If not, then the intention of the decision is vacuously satisfied. The action part of the correct class of decisions returns a correct situation.

We prefer to take the second of these two options. This is because we believe that when a validity control is applied then knowledge about the correctness of the situation is desired. However, this knowledge is in a wider context : the developer desires to correct the flaws, if any, in the situation. Thus, it makes sense to accept the class of decisions, correct.

The decision classes can be organised as shown in Fig. 3. The entire set of decisions can be subdivided into the create, delete, modify, and correct classes. The modify class has under it the classes specialise, update, historise, and retype. The correctness class of decisions is subdivided into four groups, one group corresponding to each of the different kinds of validation controls. They are named according to the kind of validation control they deal with. Each class has its own instances. For example the create class has instances, create entity, create relationship etc. Similarly, the conformity class has an instance for each conformity constraint defined on the model.

Decisions may be atomic or complex. An atomic decision is one which cannot be broken up into simpler decisions. A complex decision is constructed out of other decisions which may be atomic or complex.

The designer of a methodology has the choice to define a certain decision as atomic or complex. If the exact sequence of manipulations to be performed in order to give effect to a decision, D, is pre-determined, then it is possible to define the action of D completely. In this case, D is atomic : it is implemented in its action and is not built over any other decision. On the other hand, it is possible that the exact sequence of manipulations to give effect to D is not known or that more than one alternative exists. In both these cases, the designer of the methodology may choose not to commit to any specific procedure of implementation of D. The alternative is to consider D as composed of a number of decisions A, B, C, ... such that the intention of D is realised through the intentions of its components. Then, it is clear that D is a complex decision, built out of the component decisions, A, B, C,.....

Consider an example. Let there be users who borrow books. Let it be required to specialise users into borrowers and non-borrowers. It is possible to consider this as a complex decision built out of

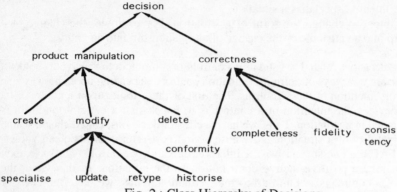

Fig. 2 : Class Hierarchy of Decisions

create entity	{create borrower}
create borrower as a subtype	{subtype borrower of user}
create entity	{create non-borrower}
create non-borrower as subtype	{subtype non-borrower of user}
define partition constraint	
between entities	{correct situation}
remove role	{remove the role user borrows}
create role	{define role borrower-borrows}

On the other hand, it is possible to treat the foregoing as an atomic decision. It can be argued that the action of specialise is the following procedure
- create entity borrower
- make it a subtype of user
- create entity non-borrower
- make it a subtype of user
- define the partition constraint between borrower and non-   borrower
- remove the role of user as borrows
- create the role borrows of borrower

This sequence of operations is frozen into the action of specialise. Consequently there is no need to consider specialise as built over other decisions : it becomes atomic.

The essential difference between a complex decision and an atomic one is that in the former, the methodology designer gives freedom to the process developer to define his/her own process. As a result, the decision is considered to be composed of a set of component ones. The developer has only to choose the particular order of these to give effect to the complex decision. In an atomic decision, on the other hand, no such freedom is given.

The Action

The action component of the triplet makes explicit the enforcement mechanism of a decision. It provides a procedure to be followed for this purpose.

To be well defined, the action must encode in it

1. Knowledge about the procedure to be followed to enforce the decision.
2. Knowledge about the part of the product that can potentially get affected.
3. Knowledge about the conditions that must be met in order for the procedure of (1) above to be carried out.

Consider property (1) above. For an atomic decision, an action can be defined provided the exact sequence of acts needed to give effect to it is known. The definition of an action is committed to by the designer of a methodology. A methodology designer leaves the definition of the action associated with a complex decision to be made by the developer. The developer is provided knowledge of the component decisions and, through the activity of decision making, selects one decision after another from among these. In this way, the action of the complex decision is determined through the actions associated with its component decisions.

It is to be noticed that development of the action of a complex decision amounts to the definition of a process. However, unlike that for an atomic decision, this process is defined by the users of a methodology.

Now, let us consider the second property above, that which relates to the part of the product affected by an action. We formalise this using the notion of an environment(Pra92).

The static environment of a structural element, E, consists of
- E itself,
- the dependent elements of E, and
- the elements which have E as their dependent element.
A situation is capable of demonstrating two kinds of dependencies
- direct structural involvement wherein it is structured out of other situations. For example, the situation, a relationship, shows direct involvement with the situation, an entity.
- peer structural involvement wherein the situation is structured out of other peer elements. For example, the dynamic transition of Remora is structured out of peer situations, c-event, c-object, and c-operation.

The effect of an action can be felt over the static environment of the situation it acts upon. The action to delete an entity, shall cause the entity to be deleted but this shall have an impact on, for example, the relationships it participates in. In this sense, the scope of an action is the static environment of the situation it acts upon.

An action has two main parts
- the condition,
- the body.
The condition part of the action specifies the pre-conditions that must hold for the body to be executed. The body specifies the procedure to be performed. If the pre-conditions do not hold then the decision is not enforceable since the body shall not be executed. A decision is considered as *effective* when the body of its action has been executed. It is said to be *ineffective* otherwise.

III.1 Defining Steps

We are now in a position to consider the manner in which steps can be represented as triplets. Steps of a methodology that create, modify, or delete situations can be represented as triplets in a straight forward manner. This has been illustrated in the foregoing with the step, create entity. However, the expression of steps dealing with validity controls is not obvious. We deal with this here.

1. Completeness Constraints

Completeness constraints can be expressed in terms of the notion of a situation introduced earlier as follows:

- Every primitive definitional element that has been been assigned values from a domain specified by the conceptual model is complete. Consider the functionality of attributes as a primitive definitional element which take values from the domain { mono-valued, multi-valued}. Then the assignment of a value from this domain defines the functionality completely.
- Every dependent definitional element is complete if all its base definitional elements are complete. Let attribute be a dependent definitional element dependent upon the primitive element, functionality. Then attribute is complete when functionality is complete.
- Every primitive structural element is complete if all its definitional elements are complete. Let there be a primitive structural element called entity which has definitional elements key and attribute respectively. Then entity is complete if key and attribute are complete.
- Every dependent structural element is complete if all its base structures are complete and if all its definitional elements are complete. Let there be a dependent structural element called relationship which is dependent upon the structural element, entity, and which has the definitional elements, cardinality, and attribute. Then relationship is complete if entity, cardinality, and attribute are all complete.
- A complex situation is complete if all its structural elements are complete. Let there be a product consisting of two entities, Employee and Department, and of a relationship, Employed, between them. This product is complete provided Employee, Department, and Employed are all complete.

The decision class relevent to the completeness constraint(see Fig. 3) is the completeness class. We define a triplet for each of the rules of completeness formulated above. The triplets corresponding to these rules are as follows:
- <primitive definitional element, complete1, action>
- <dependent definitional element, complete2, action>
- <primitive structural element, complete3, action>
- <dependent structural element, complete4, action>
- <complex situation, complete5, action>
The issue of enforcement of completeness then reduces to the selection of the appropriate triplet at an appropriate time in the development process.

2. Conformity Constraints

Conformity constraints specify constraints that must hold across peer elements. As for completeness constraint these can be represented in situational terms. For example, the constraint (1) of section II can be represented as a ternary relationship, c-ev form, between c-event, c-object, and c-operation repectively. Alternatively, it can be represented as a system of two binary relationships: the relationship, state change relating c-event and c-object, and the relationship, trigger, relating c-event and c-operation, respectively. These two possibilities are shown in Fig. 4.

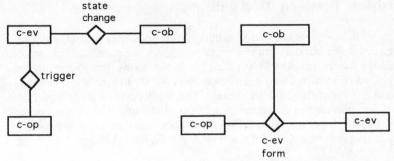

Fig. 3 : Two Forms of the Conformity Constraint

The triplet corresponding to the constraint (1) when viewed as a binary relationship is

<c-ev form, create, action>   ------(1a)

where create(c-ev form) is considered as an atomic decision.

When viewed as a system of two relationships, we have

<c-ev form, create, action>:   ------(1b)

> <state change, create1, action>
> <trigger, create2, action>

Here, create(c-ev form) is considered as a complex decision built over create1(state change) and create2(trigger).

3. Consistency Constraints

These constraints have two parts to them. The first part specifies the situation over which the property specified in the second part holds. For example in constraint 2 of section II the conditional part identifies the situation, s1, in which the property of mutually exclusive triggers must hold. The enforcement of this can be expressed as a triplet as follows

<s1, consistency, action>.   ------(2a)

It is possible to treat consistency as an atomic decision if the procedure for enforcement is contained in the action. If not, then it is a complex decision

<s1, consistency, action>.   ------(2b)

> < mut ex trigger, create, action>

where mut ex trigger is the situation, mutually exclusive trigger.

4. Fidelity Constraints

Fidelity constraints are defined to ensure that the developed product reflects the real world faithfully. The validity of these situations cannot, quite often, be determined automatically and real world knowledge is required to do so. However, a methodology highlights these special situations. As an example, consider isolated nodes of the static graph of Remora. It is not clear whether the existence of such nodes is good or bad. The developer must examine these and accept/reject them. One can represent fidelity constraints as triplets by identifying the situation whose fidelity is to be enforced. For example, the isolated node constraint can be expressed as

> < node, fidelity, action>.

IV. Transition Between Decisions

In conformity with our position that a methodology does not, in fact, impose a process on the developer but only offers a set of primitives, we postulate that any step of a methodology can be invoked at any time. In triplet terms, this means that any decision can be taken at will. Thus, a developer may decide to create a relationship before the entities participating in it are created. The application of the completeness constraint on the relationship can thereafter result in the creation of the entities. Alternatively, the developer may first create the entities and then the relationship. A methodology cannot impose either of the two strategies on the developer.

A methodology does not however, provide unlimited freedom to the developer in decision making. In a most elementary sense, there is a dependency between all decisions of the decision classes modify and delete upon the create class of decisions. Thus, nothing can be modified and/or deleted unless it has been first created. However, decisions exhibit more intricate kinds of dependency among themselves. These dependencies are on account of the constraints specified in the model.

Constraints say that after a decision has been taken some other decisions must be taken. However, when these decisions are taken is not specified. In other words, the place in the decision making activity where the choice of these decisions is made is a matter of the strategy adopted.

The foregoing notion of decision dependency can be formalised using the dependency relationship as follows

$$A \longrightarrow B$$

This says that the decision B is dependent upon the decision A. Here, B need not be distinct from A.

Decisions exhibit transitive dependency among them. Thus, if we have

> product manipulation decisions -----> correct decisions and
> correct decisions -----> product manipulation decisions

then product manipulation decisions are transitively dependent upon themselves. More informally, the creation/modification/deletion of a situation asks for decisions to manipulate the resulting situations. As an example consider the decision to create an entity class. The constraint decisions dependent upon these are

> create(entity)   -----> completeness decision
>   -----> conformity decision

Now, the completeness decision of a methodology could specify that

> complete(entity) -----> create attributes
>   -----> create key

This, by transitivity, implies that

> create(entity)   -----> create attributes
>   -----> create key

Now, let us consider the manner in which product manipulation decisions depend upon constraint decisions.

a. Dependency due to Completeness Decisions

The rules of completeness defined in section III.1 can be used to construct the dependent decisions of a decision. Consider the rule

Every dependent structural element is complete if all its base structural elements are complete and if all its definitional elements are complete.
This implies that the creation of base as well as definitional elements is dependent upon the creation of the dependent structural element.

Applying this to entities of an ER based methodology with specialisation, we have

$$\text{create(entity)} \quad -----> \text{create attributes}$$
$$-----> \text{create key}$$

If the foregoing approach to identifying dependent decisions is applied to each rule of completeness of section III.1, then we shall obtain the entire set of dependent decisions of a methodology arising out of completeness constraints.

b. Dependency due to Conformity Decisions

Dependency of product manipulation decisions on conformity decisions arises when the conformity decision is considered to be a complex decision. A determination of the dependencies of product manipulation decisions on conformity can be done by a systematic identification of all complex conformity decisions. There is a dependency of the component decisions on the conformity decision.

For example, consider (1b) above. The implied dependencies are

$$\text{create(c-ev form)} \quad -----> \text{create1(state change)}$$
$$-----> \text{create2(trigger)}$$

c. Dependency due to Consistency Decisions

In a manner similar to that for conformity decisions, a determination of the dependencies of product manipulation decisions on consistency can be done by a systematic identification of all complex consistency decisions. There is a dependency of the component decisions on the consistency decision. To see this consider (2b) above The following holds

$$\text{consistency}(s1) -----> \text{create(mut ex trigger)}$$

d. Dependency due to Fidelity Decisions

Fidelity triplets have been defined with the purpose of bringing special situations to the attention of the developer. As such, it is recognised that suppport for these in the framework of a methodology cannot be provided. The developer is expected to identify the strategies for handling these situations.

In this sense, the methodology does not identify any decisions specifically dependent on fidelity constraints

V. Conclusion

The prevalent view of methodologies is that the process of development is a part of a methodology. Instead, we have shown that a methodology provides a set of primitives. These primitives, when suitably augmented with process-specific primitives help in building the process. The exact manner in which the process is constructed is the way of working of this developer. Thus, the way of working, or the strategies actually followed in development are external to a methodology.

It has long been felt that the product and the process aspects of development are linked to each other. As we see it, the linkage lies in the fact that a triplet specifies a decision to be taken on a situation. When an entire process is built up using process and methodology primitives, then this linkage between the product and the decision gets carried over to it. The decision making activity, in so far as it causes decision selection, establishes the link between the product and the process.

References

(Ahi87) Ahituv N, A metamodel of information flow: a tool to support information systems theory, CACM, 30,9, 781-791

(Bri90) Brinkkemper S, Formalisation of information systems modelling, Ph.D. thesis, University of Nijmegen, Thesis Publishers, Amsterdam

(Che89) Chen M and Nunamaker JF, MetaPlex: An integrated environment for organisation and information systems development, Proc. tenth Int. Conf. On Info. Syst., Boston, Mass

(Dow87) Dowson M, Iteration in the software process, Proc. Ninth Intl. Conference on Software Engineering, Monterey, California.

(Gen87) Genrich H, Predicate/transition nets, in Petri Nets Central models and their properties, Brauer et al (eds.), LNCS, 1254, 207-247

(Hof93) Hofstede AHM ter and Weide Th P van der, Expressiveness in conceptual data modelling, Data and Knowledge Engineering, 10(1), 65-100

(Hum89) Humphrey WS and Kellner MI, Sotware process modelling:principles of entity process models, in Proc. eleventh Int. Conf. on software engineering, IEEE, Pittsburgh

(Pra92) Prakash N, An object oriented methodology for information systems design, in Information systems concepts:improving the understanding, Falkenberg et al(eds.), 53-86, North Holland

(Rol 88) Rolland C et al, Conception des systems d'information, Eyrolles, Paris

(Rol90) Rolland C and Souveyet C, An object-oriented framework for information systems, in Data Management, Prakash N (ed.), 280-303, Tata McGraw Hill, N. Delhi

(Rol 93a) Rolland C and Prakash N, Reusable Process Chunks, Proc. DEXA, LNCS vol720, 655-666

(Rol 93b) Rolland C and Prakash N, Modeling decisions in the requirement engineering process, Proc. CISMOD, New Delhi, 229-242

(Smo91) Smolander K et al, MetaEdit: A flexible graphical environment for methodology modelling, in Andersen R et al(eds.), Proc. CAiSE, Trondheim, LNCS vol 498, 168-193

(Ver93) Verhoef TF, Effective information modelling support, Ph.D. Thesis, Delft University of Technology, 1993

(Wij91) Wijers GM, Modelling support in information systems development, Ph.D. Thesis, Thesis Publishers, Amsterdam

Specifying Software Specification & Design Methods

Motoshi Saeki and Kuo Wenyin

Dept. of Computer Science, Tokyo Institute of Technology
Ookayama 2-12-1, Meguro-ku, Tokyo 152, Japan
E-mail : {saeki, wenyin}@cs.titech.ac.jp

Abstract. To support customizing and integrating software specification & design methods to a suitable method for designers' problem domain and environment, so-called Computer Aided Method Engineering (CAME), we need a meta model for representing the fragments of methods formally and for composing them into a method. This paper discusses a meta modelling technique by using a formal specification language Object-Z which is an object oriented version of the Z language. The logical expressions of Object-Z allows us to describe hierarchical structures and the constraints in the methods and the inheritance mechanism enables us to integrate method fragments into a new method.

1 Introduction

It is important to design software specifications effectively for developing high quality software with low cost because specification & design phases are the early step in the software development process. Many specification & design methods (shortened to methods) such as Structured Analysis & Design [5] and Object-Oriented Analysis & Design [12] have been developed to guide designers' work. However, these methods can work well only in some problem domains and/or environment, not in all, and it is very difficult to create an universal method which can work well in all the domains and/or environment. It is more feasible that the designers can select suitable methods, customize, and integrate the methods to a suitable one for their problem domains and environment.

Recently, there are some methods with multiple viewpoints to develop the large and complex software systems. For example, Shlaer's and Mellor's Object Oriented Analysis[12] can be considered as a *multi-view* method since its underlying model is the composition of three models — an information model (Entity Relationship Diagram), a state model (State Transition Diagram) and a process model (Data Flow Diagram). We know that the specifications described in several methods with the different viewpoints are more useful[4]. However, it is a problem how to integrate the specifications developed by using the different methods into a final specification. To support *multi-view specification*, we also need a mechanism for integrating the specifications written in the different methods.

One of the possible solutions for the above requirements is to use a *meta system* or *meta model* approach[1] for method modelling. The meta model is a data model or scheme for representing methods, and expresses a common conceptual structure for them. Most of the meta models which have been studied until recently are based on Entity Relationship model (shortened to ER model)[7, 14, 15]. ER model allows us to represent the methods comprehensively, but it is difficult to describe the constraints and the hierarchical structures of the methods. Most of the meta model approaches except for [2] did not deal with the constraints or the hierarchical structure. Knuth's attribute grammer approach[9] could be used to represent the hierarchical structure of products produced in the methods. However, it should include many evaluation rules called *copy rules* to specify any systems and the many occurrences of these non-essential rules allow us to construct the incomprehensible descriptions. Our technique is based on the formal specification language Object-Z[6] to specify the constraints comprehensively. Object-Z is an object oriented extension of a Z language[16] and its notation is the same as that of Z. Hierarchical structures can also be represented with *mathematical maps* or *relations* in Object-Z. Furthermore the inheritance mechanism of Object-Z allows us to integrate methods into one. Object oriented paradigm provides the reusability of method fragment descriptions for constructing new methods.

The organization of this paper is as follows. In the next section, we discuss two kinds of method modelling techniques — one is based on ER model and another is on attribute grammers. We introduce our method modelling technique based on Object-Z language in section 3. The class of data flow diagrams is also specified in our framework as an example here. Section 4 presents our meta model application — method integration. We pick up Shlaer and Mellor's OOA as an example and its description can be obtained from the four popular methods ; Data Flow Diagram, Entity Relationship Diagram, Object Communication Diagram, State Transition Diagram. The constraints for integrating these diagrams can be represented in our technique. These examples show that our modelling technique is sufficiently powerful in expression, and suitable to be a basis for Computer Aided Method Engineering.

2 Method Modelling based on ER Model and Attribute Grammer

2.1 Method Modelling based on ER model

Many studies on meta models based on ER model have been done, i.e. they used ER modeling technique to represent methods. As a simple example, let's consider the definition of data flow diagrams of Structured Analysis by using ER model. The definition has the entities for the nodes of data flow diagrams such as Processes (Bubbles) and Data Flows, and relationships between the entities for the edges or connections among the nodes, as shown in Figure 1. ER model could represent the various methods widely and easily. However, this figure does not express a *well-formed* data flow diagrams completely. In a well-formed diagram it is not permitted to directly connect the data stores to the source&sinks with data flows, but the figure 1 does not contain this constraint.

There is one more shortcoming. ER model cannot express the hierarchical structures of data flow diagrams and the constraints of the hierarchy used in

Structured Analysis. For example, a process in a data flow diagram can be hierarchically decomposed and refined to another data flow diagram. That is to say, the inside of the process is a lower-level data flow diagram. In this hierarchical structure, the inputs and outputs of the process should be equal to the external inputs and outputs of its lower-level data flow diagram.

It is difficult to represent these kinds of hierarchical structure and constraints as mentioned above by using ER model, even though ER model is such a simple vehicle to describe the methods.

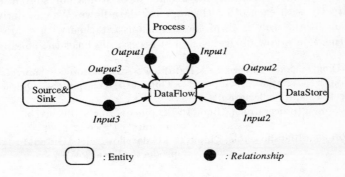

Fig. 1. A Definition of Data Flow Diagram in ER Model

2.2 Method Modelling based on Attribute Grammers

Attribute grammer approach can be an alternative to define the hierarchies and the constraints discussed before. It is an extension of context-free grammers and was proposed by Knuth to specify the formal semantics of programming languages. Attribute grammer based language was used to describe software processes[8], but unlike this, we apply an attribute grammer approach to specifying products such as data flow diagrams.

An attribute grammer consists of a set of the derivation rules associated with the evaluation rules and the conditions. The evaluation rules are used to calculate the attribute values associated with grammatical symbols in the derivation rules. The condition expresses a constraint that must be satisfied by the attribute values when the derivation rule is applied. That is to say, we cannot apply the derivation rules whose conditions do not hold.

Consider the definition of the data flow diagram in attribute grammer approach. The four entities – Process, DataStore, Source&Sink and DataFlow, and the six relationships in Figure 1 can correspond to non-terminal symbols which have the set of entity instances or relationship instances as their attributes. The first derivation rule specifies that data flow diagrams consists these ten components denoted by the non-terminal symbols. We associate a synthesized attribute "product" with the non-terminal symbols. The value of the attribute "product" is a set of the instances of the entities or relationships belonging to the

non-terminal symbols, i.e. product itself. For example," product(<Process>)"
denotes the set of instances of the processes in the data flow diagram. The conditions $Condition_1$ and $Condition_2$ express that both "Input1" and "Output1"
are the relationships between "Process" and "DataFlow". The attribute value
"process_role(<Input1>)" denotes the set of processes participating in the relationship "Input1". As you can find in the derivation rule of "Input1", this
relationship is defined as a pair of a process and a data flow which is an input
to the process. For the other relationships such as "Input2", "Input3" and so
on, we can define the similar conditions. $Condition\_3$ in the derivation rule of
<DataFlowDiagram> specifies that neither data stores nor source&sinks can
connect directly with each other through any data flows. We can derive a data
flow diagram by this rule if all of the conditions attached with it are satisfied,
i.e. well-formed data flow diagrams should necessarily meet the conditions.

<DataFlowDiagram>::= <Process> <DataFlow> <DataStore> <Source&Sink>
　　　　　<Input1> <Input2> <Input3> <Output1> <Output2> <Output3>
　　　product(<DataFlowDiagram>) ← ⋯
　　　$Condition_1$: (process_role(<Input1>) ∪ process_role(<Output1>))
　　　　　　　　　　　　　　　= product(<Process>)
　　　$Condition_2$: (dataflow_role(<Input1>) ∪ dataflow_role(<Output1>)
　　　　　　　　　　　　　　　= product(<DataFlow>)
　　　⋯
　　　$Condition_3$: (dataflow_role(<Input2>) ∪ dataflow_role(<Input3>)) ∩
　　　　　(dataflow_role(<Output2>) ∪ dataflow_role(<Output3>)) = ∅
<Process>::= ϵ
　| <process_instance> <Process>$_2$
　　　product(<Process>) ← {id(<process_instance>)} ∪ domain(<Process>$_2$)
<DataFlow>::= ⋯
　　　product(<DataFlow>) ← ⋯
⋯
<Input1>::= ϵ
　　　process_role(<Input1>) ← ∅
　　　dataflow_role(<Input1>) ← ∅
　| (<process_instance> , <dataflow_instance>) <Input1>$_2$
　　　product(<Input1>) ← { (product(<process_instance>, <dataflow_instance>) }
　　　　　　∪ product(<Input>$_2$)
　　　process_role(<Input1>)
　　　　　← { product(<process_instance>) } ∪ product_role(<Input1>$_2$)
　　　dataflow_role(<Input1>)
　　　　　← { product(<dataflow_instance> } ∪ dataflow_role(<Input1>$_2$)
<Input2>::= ⋯
⋯
<process_instance>::= <identifier>
　　　product(<process_instance>) ← Sring(<identifier>)
⋯

We can also express the hierarchical structure of the data flow diagrams by
adding the following derivation rule to the above rules.

<process_instance>::= <DataFlowDiagram>

The constraints which must be satisfied by the refined process instance <process_instance> and its lower-level data flow diagram <DataFlowDiagram> can be also specified in this attribute grammer approach. To specify them, we should add more attributes, evaluation rules, and conditions to the above grammer, and omit them on account of space.

The method model based on attribute grammers can express most of the methods and solve the problems in ER model. However, one of their shortcomings is that we need a lot evaluation rules such as value copy rules. As shown in the example of DataFlowDiagram above, we must also introduce many conditions for representing such a scheme of the data flow diagram as Figure 1. Many rules and conditions might fail down in incomprehensible descriptions of the methods.

3 Method Modelling based on Object-Z

The formal specification language Object-Z is an object oriented extension of the Z language semantically based on ZF set theory. In object oriented paradigm, the system to be specified is considered as a collection of individual objects having internal states. Object-Z defines the objects by using class concepts where the definition of their states, initial states, and the operations related to them are encapsulated. The class schema for the specification of a class may contain several kinds of schemas as well as the definitions of axioms, predicates, types, and constants. The typical class schema is be shown in the following:

$$
\begin{array}{|l}
\hline
\text{\_\_} \textit{Typical\_Class\_Schema} \text{_____} \\
\textit{InheritedClasses} \\
\quad\begin{array}{|l}
\hline
\textit{State Variable Declaration} \\
\hline
\textit{StateInvariants} \\
\hline
\end{array} \\
\quad\begin{array}{|l}
\text{\_} \textit{INIT} \text{_____} \\
\textit{InitialState} \\
\hline
\end{array} \\
\quad\begin{array}{|l}
\text{\_} \textit{OperationSchema} \text{_____} \\
\textit{Signatures (VariableDeclarations)} \\
\hline
\textit{Predicate} \\
\textit{(Pre and post condition)} \\
\hline
\end{array} \\
\quad \ldots \\
\hline
\end{array}
$$

The inherited classes are the names of the super classes whose states and operations are inherited to the class *Typical_Class_Schema*.

The aim of the methods is the navigation of designers' activities to develop specifications. The methods tell the designers what documents they should produce in a specification process, and what activities they should perform for producing the documents. So we can model the methods from two perspectives — product and activity perspectives. From the product perspective, the structures or types of the produced products (incl. hierarchical structures) and constraints on the product parts should be specified to define the method. To specify the activities in the method, we define permitted manipulations on its products and their behavioral constraints such as execution ordering. We describe a product specification of the method by a class schema in Object-Z since the instances of the produced products can be considered as objects in object oriented paradigm. The product structure and the constraints can be specified by a state schema. Operation schemas encapsulated in a class schema define the manipulations on the corresponding product, and the pre- and post-conditions of the defined operations specify the behavioral constraints on them such as possible execution order.

We begin with a simple example of the specification of the class *Product* written in Object-Z. It will be used as a super class to specify the product classes of the various methods.

```
┌─ Product ──────────────────────────────────────────────────────────┐
│  ┌──────────────────────────┐    ┌─ INIT ──────────────────────┐   │
│  │ title : Identifier       │    │ designer?, manager? : Person │   │
│  │ version : Version_Number │    ├──────────────────────────────┤   │
│  │ status : Status          │    │ version = 0                  │   │
│  │ creation_date : Date     │    │ status = 'in_progress'       │   │
│  │ last_modification_date : Date │ producer = designer?         │   │
│  │ producer : Person        │    │ responsible_person = manager?│   │
│  │ responsible_person : Person │ └──────────────────────────────┘   │
│  │ reviewers : ℙ Person     │                                       │
│  └──────────────────────────┘                                       │
│  ┌─ Notify_Completion ──────┐    ┌─ Review ────────────────────┐   │
│  │ Δ(status, creation_date) │    │ Δ(status, reviewers)         │   │
│  │ today? : Date            │    │ review_team? : ℙ Person      │   │
│  ├──────────────────────────┤    │ review_result! : Review_Report│  │
│  │ status = 'in_progress'   │    ├──────────────────────────────┤   │
│  │ status' = 'completion'   │    │ status = 'completion'        │   │
│  │ creation_date = today?   │    │ status' = 'reviewing'        │   │
│  └──────────────────────────┘    │ reviewers' = review_team?    │   │
│                                   └──────────────────────────────┘   │
│  ...                                                                 │
└─────────────────────────────────────────────────────────────────────┘
```

An object of the class *Product* has several state variables such as *title*, *version*, *status* and so on. Assume that the domains of these state variables, e.g. *Identifier*, *Date* and *Person*, would be externally defined as basic types. The operation *Notify_Completion* sets up the value of the state *creation_date* when the development of the current version of the product is completed. We must note the conventions on variables used in the operation schema. The Δ notation in the signature part declares the variables whose values may be updated by the operation. The state variables with the prime (') decoration represent the state after the operation, while the variables which are not decorated represent the state before the operation. Inputs and outputs of the operation are denoted by the variables with "?" and "!" respectively. In the schema *Notify_Completion*, 'today?' is an input to this operation and the status is also changed from 'in_progress' to 'completion' after this operation

We define the generic schema *ConnectedGraph* before the next class *DataFlow-Diagram*. This schema specifies the constraints on a special class of directed graphs whose nodes have at least one connected edge, i.e. an input edge or an output edge.

$$
\begin{array}{l}
\rule{0.3pt}{12pt}\!\!\underline{\;\;ConnectedGraph\;[Nodes,\,Edges,\,InputEdges,\,OutputEdges]\;\;}\\[4pt]
\rule{0.3pt}{28pt}\quad Nodes = (\text{ran}\,InputEdges \cup \text{ran}\,OutputEdges)\,\wedge\\
\qquad Edges = \text{dom}\,InputEdges = \text{dom}\,OutputEdges\\
\rule{0.3pt}{0pt}\underline{\hphantom{xxxxxxxxxxxxxxxxxxxxxxxxxxxxxxxxxxxxxxxxxxxxxxxxxxx}}
\end{array}
$$

Several Object-Z operators on sets and relations occur in the logical formulas of the schema. The domain and range operators, dom and ran, extract the domain and range of a relation or a function respectively, i.e. $\text{dom}\,R = \{x \mid (x,y) \in R\}$ and $\text{ran}\,R = \{y \mid (x,y) \in R\}$ where R is a relation or a function. *Nodes* and *Edges* are certain sets of nodes and edges respectively, and *InputEdges* and *OutputEdges* denote relationships between *Nodes* and *Edges*. For example, *InputEdges* expresses which nodes the edges are inputs to. Assume that these relationships are defined as finite functions *Edges* $\rightarrow\!\!\!\!\rightarrow$ *Nodes*. Thus the term "ran *InputEdges*" denotes a set of nodes to which there is at least one input edge.

We can specify a class schema for data flow diagrams and the operations on them by using *Product* and *ConnectedGraph* as shown in the next page. The class *DataFlowDiagram* incorporates all the features such as state variables, invariants, and operations of the *Product* class. For example, *DataFlowDiagram* has the state variables *title*, *status*, the operations *Notify_Completion*, *Review* and so on. In addition, the state variables or structural components of the class contain four sets (corresponding to entities in ER model) and six finite functions (corresponding to relationships in ER model), and this definition comes from Figure 1. *Process*, *DataFlow*, *DataStore*, and *Source&Sink*, which are used for defining domains of the states, are considered as basic types which are externally-given sets. The operator $\mathbb{P}$ stands for the power set. For example, the domain of the *processes* of *DataFlowDiagram* is a power set of the given set *Process*. The relationships between *DataFlow* and other entities are defined as functions because these are one-to-many relationships, i.e. each data flow has just one source and just one destination. When the development of a data flow diagram is completed, it should meet the constraint *WellFormedDataFlowDiagram* which is specified in the axiomatic definition below the state schema. It consists of two logical conjuncts — the first one specifies that processes, source&sinks, and data stores in a data flow diagram should have at least one data flow as their input or output. In addition, source&sinks and data stores can be connected only to processes through data flows. It means that there are no data flows directly between a source&sink and a data store, or data stores. The second conjunct stands for this constraint.

The *DataFlowDiagram* class has several operations on its instances. The operation *IdentifyProcesses* corresponds to the designers' activities for identifying processes and it adds a newly identified process to the state variable *processes*. The second operation *IdentifyInputs*, which corresponds to the activities for identifying an input data flow to a certain process, cannot be performed until the process has been already identified. The first logical formula on the variable "*process*? in the predicate part specifies this behavioral constraints. That is to say, this operation can be performed after at least one execution of the operation *IdentifyProcesses*. By using the predicates in operation schemas, we can specify the behavioral constraints such as execution order on the activities.

$$
\begin{array}{|l|}
\hline
\underline{\ DataFlowDiagram}\ \underline{\hspace{6cm}} \\
Product \\
\hline
\begin{array}{|l|}
\hline
processes : \mathbb{P}\ Process \\
dataflows : \mathbb{P}\ DataFlow \\
datastores : \mathbb{P}\ DataStore \\
source\&sinks : \mathbb{P}\ Source\&Sink \\
input1 : DataFlow \nrightarrow Process \\
output1 : DataFlow \nrightarrow Process \\
input2 : DataFlow \nrightarrow Source\&Sink \\
output2 : DataFlow \nrightarrow Source\&Sink \\
input3 : DataFlow \nrightarrow DataStore \\
output3 : DataFlow \nrightarrow DataStore \\
\hline
status = \text{`completion'} \Rightarrow WellFormedDataFlowDiagram \\
\hline
\end{array} \\
\hline
\end{array}
$$

WellFormedDataFlowDiagram : $\mathbb{B}$

WellFormedDataFlowDiagram =
$\quad ConnectedGraph[processes \cup source\&sinks \cup datastores,$
$\qquad input1 \cup input2 \cup input3, output1 \cup output2 \cup output3] \wedge$
$\quad (\text{dom}\ input2 \cup \text{dom}\ input3)) \cap (\text{dom}\ output2 \cup \text{dom}\ output3) = \varnothing$

$\underline{\ IdentifyProcesses}\ \underline{\hspace{6cm}}$
$\Delta(processes)$
$new\_process? : Process$

$processes' = processes \cup \{new\_process?\}$

$\underline{\ IdentifyInputs}\ \underline{\hspace{6cm}}$
$\Delta(dataflows, input1)$
$process? : Process$
$new\_dflow? : DataFlow$

$process? \in processes$
$dataflows' = dataflows \cup \{new\_dflow?\}$
$input1' = input1 \cup \{new\_dflow? \mapsto process\}$

. . .

To define hierarchical data flow diagrams, we introduce a function from processes to lower-level data flow diagrams. This function denotes what data flow diagram a process is refined to. The class of hierarchical data flow diagrams can be recursively defined by using the inheritance from the class *DataFlowDiagram*.

The class schema *HierarchicalDataFlowDiagram* has the axiomatic definition *WellFormedHierarchicalDataFlowDiagram* which defines a constraint for preserving consistency on input-output data flows between a refined process and its lower level data flow diagram. In other words, the input flows and output ones of the refined process should be equal to inputs and outputs between the lower-level data flow diagram and the external environment. In the definition of *WellFormedHierarchicalDataFlowDiagram*, you will find the operator ▷ called range restriction. It reduces a relation or function to one which has a given range, e.g. we have $input1 \rhd \{p\} = \{dfd \mapsto p \mid input1(dfd) = p\}$ where $p \in Process$, $dfd \in DataFlow$, and $input1$ is a state variable of *DataFlowDiagram* class.

$\boxed{\begin{array}{l}
\underline{HierarchicalDataFlowDiagram}\\
DataFlowDiagram\\[4pt]
\hline\\
\quad refine : Process \twoheadrightarrow HierarchicalDataFlowDiagram\\[4pt]
\hline\\
\quad status = \text{'completion'}\\
\quad\quad \Rightarrow WellFormedHierarchicalDataFlowDiagram\\[4pt]
\hline\\
\end{array}}$

$WellFormedHierarchicalDataFlowDiagram : \mathbb{B}$

$WellFormedHierarchicalDataFlowDiagram =$
  $\operatorname{dom} refine \subseteq processes \wedge$
  $\forall\, p : \operatorname{dom} refine \bullet (\operatorname{dom}(input1 \rhd \{p\})) = InputFlows(refine(p)) \wedge$
      $\operatorname{dom}(output1 \rhd \{p\})) = OutputFlows(refine(p)))$

$InputFlows : HierarchicalDataFlowDiagram \rightarrow DataFlow$

$\forall\, hdfd : HierarchicalDataFlowDiagram \bullet InputFlows(hdfd) =$
  $\operatorname{dom}(input1.hdfd \cup input2.hdfd \cup input3.hdfd)$
    $\setminus \operatorname{dom}(output1.hdfd \cup output2.hdfd \cup output3.hdfd)$

$OutputFlows : HierarchicalDataFlowDiagram \rightarrow DataFlow$

$\forall\, hdfd : HierarchicalDataFlowDiagram \bullet OutputFlows(hdfd) =$
  $\operatorname{dom}(input1.hdfd \cup input2.hdfd \cup input3.hdfd)$
    $\setminus \operatorname{dom}(output1.hdfd \cup output2.hdfd \cup output3.hdfd)$

$\underline{RefineProcesses}$
$\Delta(refine)$
$refined\_process? : Process$
$lowerdfd! : HierarchicalDataFlowDiagram$

$refined\_process? \in processes$
$refined\_process? \notin \operatorname{dom} refine$
$title.lowerdfd! = refined\_process?$
$refine' = refine \cup \{refined\_process? \mapsto lowerdfd!\}$

. . .

The functions *InputFlows* and *OutputFlows*, which are used in *WellFormed-HierarchicalDataFlowDiagram*, calculate a set of the input data flows from the external environment and a set of the output data flows to the external respectively. The term *input1.hdfd* occurring in the definitions *InputFlows* and *OutputFlows* denotes the value of the state variable *input1* of the data flow diagram *hdfd*, i.e. the relationship between processes and their input data flows in *hdfd*. The operator $\setminus$, appearing in the definitions stands for set difference, i.e. $\{a,b,c\}\setminus\{b,d\}$ is equal to $\{a,c\}$. This operator in the definition "InputFlows" calculates the data flows which are inputs to some processes, data stores or source&sinks ($\operatorname{dom}(input1 \cup input2 \cup input3)$) but which has no relation to anything as outputs ($\operatorname{dom}(output1 \cup output2 \cup output3)$).

The operation "RefineProcess" is newly added and it denotes the activities for constructing a data flow diagram (*lowerdfd!*) of a process (*refined_process?*). All of the operations defined in *DataFlowDiagram* can be applied to the instances of *HierarchicalDataFlowDiagram*.

As shown in this section, Object-Z language has powerful constructs for defining hierarchical data structures and for specifying constraints comprehensively. It can be considered as one of suitable techniques for specifying not only software specifications but also specification and design methods.

4 Method Integration – An Example

The previous section have presented the advantages of Object-Z language to use method descriptions. In this section, we will show another aspect of our technique — application to method integration. The method integration plays an important role on constructing a new method from the fragments of existing methods[10, 13, 3]. In the specification development following Shlaer and Mellor's OOA, we should have four types of the diagrams — Entity Relationship Diagram, Object Communication Diagram, State Transition Diagram and Data Flow Diagram. They are meaningfully connected to each other to express a consistent specification. This meaningful connections can be formally specified in our framework as semantic constraints for the diagrams. In this modeling, the four diagrams can be considered as the basic fragments or parts of the methods for constructing another method Shlaer and Mellor's OOA, i.e. the method can be newly obtained as the result of the integration of the four existing methods.

Entity Relationship Diagram, Object Communication Diagram, and State Transition Diagram can be defined in Object-Z language in the same way as Data Flow Diagram. Figure 2 shows graphical representations, i.e. ER Diagrams of these diagrams, and it is useful to understand the following textual representations written in Object-Z notation, which are shown in the next page.

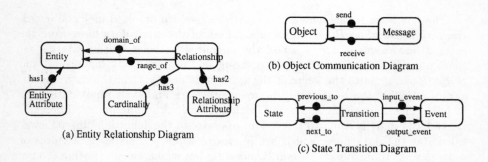

(a) Entity Relationship Diagram

(b) Object Communication Diagram

(c) State Transition Diagram

Fig. 2. ER Model Based Graphical Notation for Diagrams

```
┌─ EntityRelationshipDiagram ──────────────────────────────────────┐
│  Product                                                          │
│  ┌─────────────────────────────────────────────────────────────┐ │
│  │ entities : ℙ Entity                                          │ │
│  │ relationships : ℙ Relationship                              │ │
│  │ entity_attributes : ℙ Attribute                             │ │
│  │ relationship_attributes : ℙ Attribute                       │ │
│  │ cardinalities : ℕ × ℕ                                       │ │
│  │ domain_of : Relationship ↠ Entity                           │ │
│  │ range_of : Relationship ↠ Entity                            │ │
│  │ has1 : Attribute ↠ Entity                                   │ │
│  │ has2 : Attribute ↠ Relationship                             │ │
│  │ has3 : Relationship ↠ ℕ × ℕ                                 │ │
│  ├─────────────────────────────────────────────────────────────┤ │
│  │ status = 'completion'                                        │ │
│  │    ⇒ WellFormedEntityRelationshipDiagram                     │ │
│  └─────────────────────────────────────────────────────────────┘ │
│  ┌─────────────────────────────────────────────────────────────┐ │
│  │ WellFormedEntityRelationshipDiagram : 𝔹                      │ │
│  ├─────────────────────────────────────────────────────────────┤ │
│  │ WellFormedEntityRelationshipDiagram =                        │ │
│  │    ran domain_of ⊆ entities ∧ ran range_of ⊆ entities ∧     │ │
│  │    dom domain_of = relationships ∧ dom range_of = relationships ∧ │ │
│  │    dom has1 = entity_attributes ∧ ran has1 ⊆ entities ∧     │ │
│  │    dom has2 = relationship_attributes ∧ ran has2 ⊆ relationship_attributes ∧ │ │
│  │    dom has3 = relationships                                   │ │
│  └─────────────────────────────────────────────────────────────┘ │
│  ...                                                              │
└──────────────────────────────────────────────────────────────────┘
```

```
┌─ ObjectCommunicationDiagram ─────────────────────────────────────┐
│  Product                                                          │
│  ┌─────────────────────────────────────────────────────────────┐ │
│  │ objects : ℙ Object                                          │ │
│  │ messages : ℙ Event                                          │ │
│  │ send : Event ↠ Object                                       │ │
│  │ receive : Event ↠ Object                                    │ │
│  ├─────────────────────────────────────────────────────────────┤ │
│  │ status = 'completion' ⇒ ConnectedGraph[objects, messages, send, receive] │ │
│  └─────────────────────────────────────────────────────────────┘ │
│  ...                                                              │
└──────────────────────────────────────────────────────────────────┘
```

```
┌─ StateTransitionDiagram ─────────────────────────────────────────┐
│  Product                                                          │
│  ┌─────────────────────────────────────────────────────────────┐ │
│  │ states : ℙ State                                            │ │
│  │ transitions : ℙ Transition                                  │ │
│  │ events : ℙ Event                                            │ │
│  │ previous_to : Transition ↠ State                            │ │
│  │ next_to : Transition ↠ State                                │ │
│  │ input_event : Transition ↠ Event                            │ │
│  │ output_event : Transition ↠ Event                           │ │
│  ├─────────────────────────────────────────────────────────────┤ │
│  │ status = 'completion'                                        │ │
│  │    ⇒ ConnectedGraph[states, transitions, previous_to, next_to] ∧ │ │
│  │         transitions = dom input_event                        │ │
│  └─────────────────────────────────────────────────────────────┘ │
│  ...                                                              │
└──────────────────────────────────────────────────────────────────┘
```

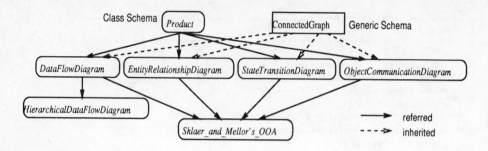

Fig. 3. Hierarchical Relationships among Schemas

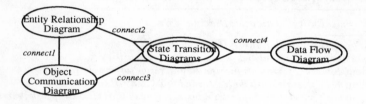

Fig. 4. Relation among Four Diagrams

To define these four diagrams, we have used the other schemas by schema reference and inheritance mechanisms. Figure 3 shows the hierarchical relationships among them. Method integration into Shlaer and Mellor's OOA will be done based on inheritance of these four diagrams.

Before defining Shlaer and Mellor's OOA, we will specify some constraints to integrate these four diagrams. Figure 4 shows the relationships among them. Connect1, connect2, connect3, and connect4 in the figure stand for mathematical constructs such as relation and functions which meaningfully connect the diagrams to each other. An entity relationship diagram is related to an object communication diagram which depicts the message flow among objects. An entity should occur as an object in the object communication diagram. For each entity occurring in an entity relationship diagram or each object in an object communication diagram, we have a state transition diagram which expresses its internal state change. Thus connect2 and connect3 have a set of functions which are from entities or objects to state transition diagrams.

$Receive^{-1}$ occurring in the schema $connection\_between\_CD\_and\_STD$ stands for the inverse map of the function $receive$. The formula in the predicate part of $connection\_between\_ERD\_and\_CD$ specifies that the entities in Entity Relationship Diagram ($erd.entities$) are the same as the objects in Communication Diagram ($cd.objects$). The second formula in $connection\_between\_CD\_and\_STD$ expresses that input messages to and output messages from an object should appear as input events and output events respectively in its state transition diagram.

```
__ connection_between_ERD_and_CD _____
connect1 : EntityRelationshipDiagram ↔ ObjectCommunicationDiagram
――――――――――――――――――――――――――――――――――――――――――――――――――――
∀ erd : dom connect1;  ∀ cd : ran connect1 • erd.entities = cd.objects
```

```
__ connection_between_ERD_and_STD _____
connect2 : EntityRelationshipDiagram ↔ (Entity ⇸ StateTransitionDiagram)
――――――――――――――――――――――――――――――――――――――――――――――――――――
∀ erd : dom connect2 • erd.entities = dom(ran connect2)
```

```
__ connection_between_CD_and_STD _____
connect3 : CommunicationDiagram ↔ (Object ⇸ StateTransitionDiagram)
――――――――――――――――――――――――――――――――――――――――――――――――――――
∀ cd : dom connect3 • cd.objects = dom(ran connect3)
∀ cd : dom connect3;  obj : dom(ran connect3);  objtostd : ran connect3
    • input_event.objtostd(obj) = receive⁻¹(cd.objects)
          ∧ output_event.objtostd(obj) = send⁻¹(cd.objects)
```

```
__ connect_between_STD_and_DFD _____
connect4 : StateTransitionDiagram ↔ (Event ⇸ DataFlowDiagram)
――――――――――――――――――――――――――――――――――――――――――――――――――――
∀ std : dom connect4 • std.output_event ⊇ dom(ran connect4)
```

Finally we can have the specification of OOA methods in the following :

```
__ Shlaer_and_Mellor's_OOA _____
DataFlowDiagram
CommunicationDiagram
EntityRelationshipDiagram
StateTransitionDiagram
―――――――――――――――――――――――――――――――――――――――――――――――――――
  connect_between_ERD_and_CD
  connect_between_ERD_and_STD
  connect_between_CD_and_STD
  connect_between_STD_and_DFD
  ――――――――――――――――――――
. . .
```

It consists of the specifications of the four diagrams and constraints for their integration, and holds the information about relationships among these diagrams in its state variables such as *connect1*, *connect2*, *connect3*, and *connect4*. Operations on *Shlaer_and_Mellor's_OOA* are inherited from the four diagram classes. For example, "IdentifyProcesses" of *DataFlowDiagram* is also an operation on *Shlaer_and_Mellor's_OOA*.

5   Conclusion

This paper has introduced another method modelling technique based on Object-Z to represent various methods for supporting specification development. It has been shown that our technique is applicable to method integration by using an example. The examples including method integration might be so simple that we could use a Z language instead of Object-Z. However, object-orientedness plays an important role on reuse of method fragments to construct new methods. Both Z and Object-Z are not executable, so we should combine our technique and other executable devices to enact the specified methods. The predicate logic underlying Z and Object-Z can provide the theoretical foundation for method integration and method synthesis. For example, we can check the consistency of the integrated method and the correctness of the integration process if the relevant methods are described in Object-Z. The logical formulas might be difficult for untrained persons to read and write. A library of method fragments, called *method base*[13, 11], are needed to specify and to integrate the methods.

References

1. A. Alderson. Meta-CASE Technology. In *Lecture Notes in Computer Science 509*, pages 81–91, 1992.
2. S. Brinkkemper. *Formalisation of Information Systems Modelling*. Thesis Publisher, 1990.
3. S. Brinkkemper. Integrating Diagrams in CASE Tools through Modelling Transparency. *Information and Software Technology*, 35(2):101–105, 1993.
4. M. Brough. Methods for CASE : a Generic Framework. In *Proc. of 4th International Conference CAiSE92, LNCS 593*, pages 525–545, 1992.
5. T. DeMarco. *Structured Analysis and System Specification*. Yourdon Press, 1978.
6. R. Duke, P. King, R. Rose, and G. Smith. The Object-Z Specification Language. Technical Report 91-1, Software Verification Center, University of Queensland, 1991.
7. A.K. Jordan and A.M. Davis. Requirements Engineering Metamodel : An Integrated View of Requirements. In *Proc. of 15th COMPSAC*, pages 472–478, 1991.
8. T. Katayama. A Hierarchical and Functional Software Process Description and its Enaction. In *Proc. of the 11th ICSE*, pages 343–352, 1989.
9. D.E. Knuth. Semantics of Context-free Languages. *Mathematical Systems Theory*, 2:127–145, 1968.
10. K. Kronlöf, editor. *Method Integration – Concepts and Case Studies*. Wiley, 1993.
11. M. Saeki, K. Iguchi, K. Wen-yin, and M. Shinohara. A Meta-Model for Representing Software Specification & Design Methods. In *Information System Development Process*, pages 149–166. North-Holland, 1993.
12. S. Shlaer and S.J. Mellor. An Object-Oriented Approach to Domain Analysis. *ACM SIGSOFT Software Engineering Notes*, 14(5):66–77, 1989.
13. K. Slooten and S. Brinkkemper. A Method Engineering Approach to Information Systems Development. In *Information System Development Process*, pages 167–186. North-Holland, 1993.
14. K. Smolander, K. Lyytinen, V.P. Tahvanainen, and P. Marttiin. MetaEdit — A Flexible Graphical Environment for Methodology Modelling. In *Proc. of 3rd International Conference CAiSE91, LNCS 498*, pages 168–193, 1991.
15. P. Sorenson, J. Tremblay, and A. McAllister. The Metaview System for Many Specification Environments. *IEEE Software*, 2(5):30–38, 1988.
16. J.M. Spivey. *The Z Notation — A Reference Manual*. Prentice Hall, 1987.

A GENERIC APPROACH TO SUPPORT
A WAY-OF-WORKING DEFINITION

Mario Moreno, Colette Rolland, Carine Souveyet

Université de Paris 1 Panthéon-Sorbonne
Centre de Recherches en Informatique
17 Rue de Tolbiac, 75013 Paris
{ moreno I rolland I souveyet }@masi.ibp.fr

Abstract. Information System Engineering has made the assumption that an Information System is supposed to capture some excerpt of the real world history and hence has concentrated on systems modelling. Very little attention has been paid to the conceptual modelling process. However the emphasis on system modelling is shifting to process modelling. The particular process modelling approach being presented in this paper advocates the definition of a way-of-working (i.e. process models) to control and guide developers. The paper introduces a classification of the various kinds of evolution of objects and presents a decision-oriented process meta model to structure ways-of-working. We also describe some guidelines, related to our classification of object evolutions, to support method engineers in the task to define a way-of-working.

1 Introduction

All recent developments in the field of Software Engineering, Databases and Information Systems seem to show that support for the various stakeholders involved in Software projects can be provided by capturing the history about the design decisions, in the early stages of the systems development life cycle, in a structured manner. Much of this knowledge which we call the process knowledge is nowadays lost in the course of engineering and maintaining such systems. In large projects, in the course of time and with changing development groups, the rationale for and context of key design decisions are confused and even lost [3]. This is particularly true in Information System Engineering which has made the assumption that an information system (IS) is supposed to capture some excerpt of the real world history and hence has concentrated on systems modelling. It is usual to view an information system as "a model of some slice of the reality of an organisation" [9] and even to regard the IS development as a problem of models construction and description. This practice provides an answer of sorts to the fundamental question : what does the information handled by an information system means? It also tends to draw the attention away from another equally fundamental question : how to define which information has to be handled by an information system?

The emphasis on product[11] i.e. the system models has hidden the importance of process i.e. the route to deliver the product. A large variety of models and especially conceptual models by which an IS can be modelled in high level terms have been developed. In contrast, very little attention has been paid to the modelling process which has the purpose of investigating the requirements of the users community and abstracting from them the conceptual specification of the IS (namely, the Requirements Engineering (RE) process).

Recent research works (see for example the special issue of the IEEE Transactions on Software Engineering on Knowledge Representation and Reasoning in Software Development, Vol. 18, Nb 6, June 1992) converge to the central idea that process modelling is as important as system modelling is. For lack of process modelling, understanding of what the development process is, what happens during it, when, why, on what it happens, by whom it is performed, is very poor.

The process semantics are not well captured, with the required level of detail, in existing process models. Consequently, the way-of-working prescribed by methodologies is badly defined, and the derived CASE-tools are efficient in recording, retrieving and manipulating system models but are almost unable to actually support the developers in performing the creative activities of model construction and transformation. Controlling and guiding developers in the progressive elaboration of a product, tracing in a structured manner the history of an IS development, keeping track of each transformation of the product, of what occurred and when in order to improve a way-of-working definition by learning is almost not possible without an adequate process modelling approach.

In the F3[1] Esprit project the need for process modelling and tracing has motivated the process stream of the project. F3 aims at defining a methodology that integrates into a coherent whole a selection of adequate techniques, all aiming at improving requirements acquisition, elicitation and validation to facilitate the construction of the IS specification. Part of our contribution within this project is to define a process modelling approach in order to be able to provide a guidance tool and a trace tool to support the developers' tasks during the RE phase.

This communication is centred on a way-of-working definition. We introduced our process modelling approach and the underlying process meta model in section 2. In section 3, we introduce some guidelines to support method engineers in the task to define ways-of-working. Finally, to centre the work presented in this paper and conclude, the architecture for CASE-Tools that we have defined to completely support our process modelling approach is introduced.

2 Way-of-working modelling

The central thesis of this paper is that a way-of-working may be partially defined by instanciation of a process meta model. In this section, such a process meta model is introduced. It has been defined for the F3 Esprit III project as an extension of the process meta model developed in the NATURE Esprit III project for the Requirements Engineering (RE) phase.

2.1 Abstraction Levels in Process modelling

We distinguish three successive abstraction levels in process modelling (see figure 1) : *process* level, *process model* level and *process meta model* level.

A *process* is an organised set of both human and computerised activities which have led to a given product definition. In Requirements Engineering, a process describes what happens during the activity of specifying an Information System by abstracting from an initial set of users' requirements. The output of a process is also called product.

---

[1]Esprit III project (n°6612) named "From Fuzzy to Formal"

A *process model* describes any process resulting from the use of a given RE methodology. i.e. it describes how things should be or could be done for the purpose of RE products prescriptive building. As a matter of fact, a process model intends to formally specify the way of working prescribed within a RE methodology.

A *process meta model* describes the generic concepts required to define process models. It brings and relates the concepts allowing to characterise any way-of-working definition.

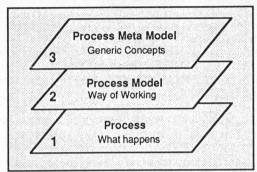

Figure 1 : Abstraction Levels in process modelling

According to this view, a process model is an instanciation of a process meta model and a process is an instanciation of a given process model which is executed. This view is similar to the theory of plans [20] from which plans can be generated (the process models) and executed (the processes).

2.2 The Process meta model

Existing process meta models can be classified into three categories [4] : activity-oriented, product-oriented and decision-oriented. The NATURE process meta model [15] is an extension of the decision-based approaches (see figure 2).

Considering the highly non-deterministic nature of the Requirements Engineering process we believe that only the decision-based approaches appear to be partially appropriate, even if they offer limited hints about when and how to decide on what. It is probably impossible to write down a realistic state-transition diagram that adequately describes what happens in requirements engineering (activity-based approaches). But relying on a pure artefact history is also insufficient (product-based approaches). Analysts react *contextually* according to the domain knowledge they acquire and react by analogy with previous situations they have been involved in. Our process modelling approach aims at capturing not only activities performed during the RE process but also why these activities are performed (the decisions) and when (the decision contexts).

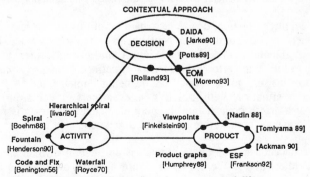

Figure 2 : State of art in process modelling

Figure 3 gives an overview of the process meta model, introducing its key concepts and their relationships (with a binary E/R based notation). This process meta model is an extension of the NATURE meta model [15] which was also an extension of the one presented in [6] and implemented in the ALECSI prototype [14].

From a theoretical point of view the process meta model defines a set of generic concepts allowing to look upon any RE process model as a network of types :

- *situation* to explain the object(s) view on which it makes sense to take a decision on. A product meta model based on a detailed description of situations is introduced in [18] ;
- *decision* to reflect a choice that a requirement engineer could take in some pre-defined situations. A decision is looked upon as an intention of object evolution ;
- *action* to implement an object evolution. It is a materialisation of the decision. Performing it, at the process level, changes the current definition of an object and may generate new situations which, in turn, are subjects to new decisions ;
- *argument* to support and object to a decision ;
- *object* to refer a product element of a particular RE methodology.

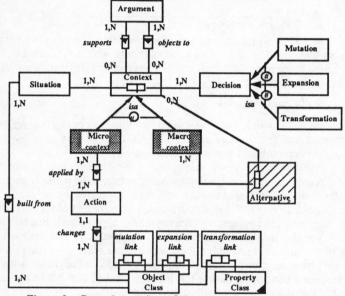

Figure 3 : General overview of the process meta model

A *context* is a couple <situation, decision> which amplifies the decision semantics by refining the "when" part of the decision. Nevertheless, the process model has to handle different levels of granularity in decision making. A *micro context* refers to a situation in which the tactic to follow to perform the decision is defined. A *macro context* refers to a strategic *decision* that has to be refined before being implemented. A macro context corresponds to a situation with possible alternatives in decision-making. The decomposition of a macro context into its more elementary contexts is represented in Figure 3 by the loop upon context through macro context and alternative.

For instance the decision to improve a product is an intention which can be achieved through several alternatives. We show, in figure 4, three alternatives related to an

Entity_type *User* : *Improve_Entity_type*, *Improve_Entity_type_in_Role* and *Add_Card*. Both first alternatives are macro contexts which are in turn refined. A terminal leaf, in a context hierarchy, means that there are no alternatives defined for it i.e. there is only one procedure to apply this decision within this situation. < {User} ; Attributise > is such an example of what we call a micro context.

In addition the process meta model recognises three types of object evolution [16], [10] : *expansion, transformation and mutation*. This classification leads to the specialisation of decisions in three groups as well as a classification of objects relationships (see figure 3) : *expansion_link, transformation_link* and *mutation_link*.

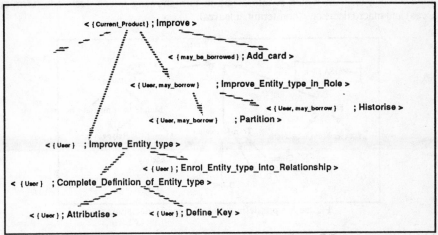

Figure 4 : Some example of contexts hierarchy in an E/R process

An *expansion* affects an expansion link between two Objects. These bi-directional links result of the structural relationships existing among the concepts of the models in use. For instance, any Entity-type may be expanded with attributes.

A *transformation* affects a transformation link between an object and a property. Such a link results of the existence of properties related to a concept. For instance, any attribute may have properties such as a name, a domain and its valuation (mono or multi).

A *mutation* occurs to an object when its type changes. This kind of link results of the mutation of concepts. For instance any relationship may be *retyped* as entity-type and further *mapped* into a relational table. By this way, an IS development may be partially viewed as a mutation process which abstracts from users requirements the conceptual specification of the information system and then converts it into an implemented system.

The mutation links are not precisely defined nowadays. We believe that they represent an important aspect of any way-of-working definition. We also believe that any way-of-working could be partially defined by a set of macro and micro contexts covering Engineering decisions on Product progressive building. In next section, we introduce an approach to facilitate this definition.

3 Way-of-working definition support

Stating that a way-of-working can be defined as a set of macro and micro contexts, we propose a generic decision hierarchy, based on the classification of object evolution (expansion, transformation and mutation), to guide a method engineer in the definition of the required set of contexts for a methodology. The examples used in this section are part of the F3 way-of-working, which has been defined with this approach, and focus on the mapping from the Enterprise model [1] to the IS model [19].

3.1 Pre-defined set of generic decisions

In the previous section we have introduced a specialisation of decisions based on a three-dimensional view of object evolution : *expansion, transformation and mutation*. We propose here to pre-define a set of generic decisions for each class. This set is introduced in figure 5, each class of which is introduced in turn showing micro decisions (terminal leaves) and macro decisions (non-terminal leaves).

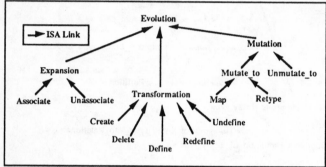

Figure 5 : pre-defined set of generic decisions

The transformation decisions affect what we call the *Inner_environment* of an Object. This environment contains the object itself and its possible properties. We have identify five types of transformation decisions : *create, delete, define, redefine* and *undefine*.
Create/delete is the decision to instanciate/remove an object. *Define* allows to associate property to an object. Notice that the related action creates a property instance and also a transformation link between both object and property. *Redefine* allows to change an existing property. Finally, *undefine* allows to delete a property previously defined. The related action deletes both the transformation link and property.

The expansion decisions express how expansions may affect what we call the *Spatial_environment* of an Object. This environment contains the objects which may be structurally and directly connected to it. We have identify two types of expansion decisions: *associate* and *unassociate*. *Associate* is the decision to structurally relate two objects. The associated action creates an expansion link between both objects which is either an inter- or an intra-model link. *Unassociate* is the pending decision to *delete* an existing expansion link.

The mutation decisions affect what we call the *Temporal_environment* of an Object. This environment allows traceability from users' requirements to implementation. The purpose of a mutation link is to relate both input and output objects of a mutation. We have identify two types of mutation decisions : *mutate_to* (which creates the link) and unmutate_to (which removes it). A creation results either from a mapping decision (an inter-model mutation) or from a retyping decision (an intra-model mutation).

3.2 Guidelines for defining the way-of-working

We show here how to use the pre-defined set of generic decisions, based on our classification of object evolution, to define a way-of-working as a set of macro and micro contexts. The approach is based on the four following steps :

(1) Identification of the classes of objects of the RE methodology,
(2) Definition of the three environments for each object class,
(3) Definition of decisions by instanciation of the generic hierarchy
     (shown in figure 5) for each object class,
(4) Refinement of macro decisions for each object class.

We exemplify the four steps with part of the F3 methodology which maps the Enterprise model [1] into the Information System (IS) model [19].

Step (1) : The IS model is an E/R like model which also describes the services provided by an entity-type. We show, in figure 6, some classes of objects such as Service or Entity-type which correspond to the concepts of same name in the IS model. We look upon a concept as a class of objects in order to be able to describe the possible evolutions of its instances i.e. their possible transformations, expansions and mutations.

For instance, we have described the association of entity-types with two objects Role and Relationship at least for three reasons : (1) a Role may have several transformations (in figure 6, we can see that the object Role has three properties : role_name, cardm and card_max), (2) a Relationship may be expanded with attributes (see, in figure 6, the expansion link between Relationship and Attribute), (3) a relationship may mutate to an Entity-type (see, in figure 7, the mutation link between Relationship and entity-type).

The Enterprise model describes the environment of Information systems. In the F3 methodology we use it to elicitate users' requirements. In this approach, an analysis of the activities related to a future information system is generally a pre-requisite to its development. In figure 7, we show the main objects which are related to activity : Actor, Event, Resource and Goal.

Step (2) : In this step, we have to define for each class of object the three environments : inner, spatial and temporal. These environments may be shown graphically as suggested in figures 6 and 7 i.e. the nodes are object classes (normal boxes) or property classes (boxes with a black corner like in the meta model), the links have three different representation according to the emphasis

The two first environments are easy to build considering the semantic of each concept. In figure 6, we can see for instance that an Entity_type may have : (a) a name in its inner_environment, (b) a key, attributes, roles and services in its spatial_environment. The inner_environments related to the objects of the Enterprise model are not shown in figure 7 for the sake of clarity. The simplified description of the spatial environment of Activity is shown in the same figure : Event, Actor, Goal and Resource.

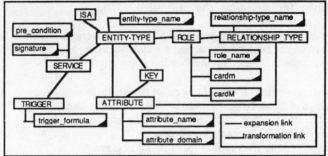

Figure 6 : Some examples of transformation and expansion links into the IS model

The temporal_environments buildings are more difficult to achieve. A method engineer must consider the semantic of concepts and the heuristics used by developers. Generally the mutations resulting from mappings or retypings relates objects, the spatial_environments of which have similarities i.e. in figure 7, we can see that an entity-type and a relationship may be both expanded with attributes. As the spatial_environment of a relationship is potentially more restricted than an entity-type one, we have defined a mutation link from relationship to entity-type and not the contrary. Of course, we could have both. The similarity between Activity and Service is more complex, yet it is easy to understand that they cover similar aspects with different languages.

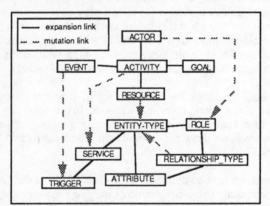

Figure 7 : Some examples of expansion and mutation links

Step (3) : In this step, the terminal leaves of the generic hierarchy are instanciated first (3.1) for each object to define a set of micro contexts i.e. the generic decisions are replaced by as many specific decisions as there are object classes and links. Then the non terminal leaves are instanciated (3.2) in turn for each object to define a set of macro contexts.

(3.1) To get micro contexts we must define : transformation decisions, expansion decisions and mutation decisions. A method engineer must have in mind that he should reuse as far as possible the decision names the Requirements engineers are familiar with. In the paper, we have tried to use decisions names which are easy to understand.

Figure 8 shows some of the transformation decisions (for the sake of clarity we show only the create and define decisions) related to the links mentioned in figure 6 : for each class there are a create and a delete decision ; for each transformation link there are a define, a redefine and an undefine decision. These decisions allow to define micro contexts related to object classes. A context rely a decision to the object(s) (i.e. the situation) on which it is applied. For instance for the entity-type object class, we have two micro contexts (with a transformation intention) :

< ( ) , Create_Entity_type > / to create an object of this class
< (Entity_type) , Define_Entity_type_name > / to create a property name

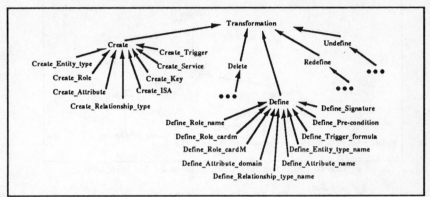

Figure 8 : Some transformation decisions in F3 RE methodology

Figure 9 shows the expansions decisions related to the links mentioned in figures 6 and 7. Specifically to each expansion link, there are an associate decision and an unassociate decision. For instance, figure 6 shows an expansion link between Entity-type and Attribute, therefore we can define two decisions : *associate_Attribute_to_Entity_type* and *unassociate_Attribute_to_Entity_type*. These decisions allow to define micro contexts too. For instance for the entity-type object class, we may define (with an expansion intention):

< (Entity_type, Attribute) , Associate_Attribute_to_Entity_type >
< (Entity_type, Role) , Associate_Role_to_Entity_type >
< (Entity_type, Service) , Associate_Service_to_Entity_type >

Figure 10 shows the mutations decisions related to the links mentioned in figure 7. Intra-model mutation links correspond to possible retypings i.e. either to improve or to correct a representation. The decision *Mutate_Relationship_to_Entity_type* belongs to this class. Inter-model mutation links, such as *Mutate_Actor_to_Role* or *Mutate_Activity_to_Service*, represent mappings from one level of modelling to another one.

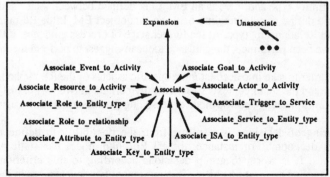

Figure 9 : Some expansion decisions in F3 RE methodology

These decisions allow to define the last sub-set of micro contexts. For instance for the relationship object class, we may define (with a mutation intention), the following micro context : < (Relationship) , Mutate_Relationship_to_Entity_type >

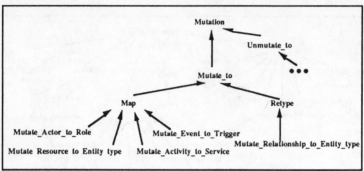

Figure 10 : Some mutation decisions in F3 RE methodology

(3.2) To get macro contexts, we take into account the non-terminal leaves of the generic decision hierarchy (see figure 5) giving new names to them in order to define specific decisions.

For instance, related to Entity-type object class, we may obtain the following hierarchy of macro contexts (which is also completed with the micro contexts defined in step (3.1) :
< (Entity_type) , Evolve_ET > / Similar to the improve decision of figure 4.

> Alt1   < (Entity_type) , Transform_ET > / alternatives shown in figure 8
> > Alt1.1   < (Entity_type) , Define_Entity_type_name >
>
> Alt2   < (Entity_type) , Expand_ET > / some of the alternatives shown in figure 9
> > Alt2.1   < (Entity_type, Attribute) , Associate_Attribute_to_Entity_type >
> > Alt2.2   < (Entity_type, Role) , Associate_Role_to_Entity_type >
> > Alt2.3   < (Entity_type, Service) , Associate_Service_to_Entity_type >
>
> Alt3   < (Entity_type) , Mutate_ET > / no alternatives shown in figure 10

In fact, the number of micro decisions and by the way the richness obtained in the F3 process model is more important than the one sketched in these lines, because we should consider that association of concepts are objects too. For instance, in the Enterprise Model (EM) all the relationships are directional links which may also carry properties such as names. As a matter of fact, we may improve the part of the way-of-working dealing with transformations and mainly with mutations. For instance, if Actor may mutate to Role, Resource to Entity-type and there is an EM_Link defined between Actor and Resource, then we could define a mutation_link between this object EM_Link_Resource_to_Role and the object Relationship_type. At the further stage of process guidance, if the two first mutations have been performed, the guidance tool can suggest to perform the third one.

Step (4) : In order to take into account more specific aspects of the RE methodologies, we propose to extend the set of contexts systematically defined in two ways : (4.1) clustering decisions, (4.2) explicating specific mode of reasoning (such as a Top-down approach).

(4.1) Clustering of decisions is resulting from the possibility to define meaningful groupings of decisions. For instance, the F3 E/R like model has static aspects and dynamics ones. It is worth to group decisions according to this criterion when the intention is to refine an existing object. This introduces two levels more in the hierarchy as showed in figure 11. For instance, if we consider the alternatives related to Expand_ET (define in step 3.2) we can separate those which are dealing with the static definition of an entity-type from those dealing with its dynamic definition :

< (Entity_type) , Expand_ET >
   < (Entity_type) , Refine_ET_definition >
      < (Entity_type) , Refine_ET_Dynamic_definition >
         < (Entity_type) , Refine_ET_with_Service_definition >
      < (Entity_type) , Refine_ET_Static_definition >
         < (Entity_type) , Refine_ET_with_Role_definition >
         < (Entity_type) , Refine_ET_with_Attribute_definition >
         < (Entity_type) , Refine_ET_with_Key_definition >
         < (Entity_type) , Refine_ET_with_Sub-type_definition >
         < (Entity_type) , Refine_ET_with_Attribute_definition >

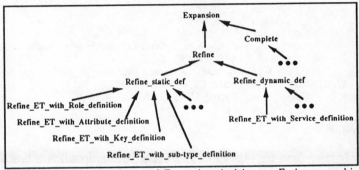

Figure 11 : Refine hierarchy of Expansion decision on Entity_type object

(4.2) Traditionally, a methodology suggests either a Top-down approach, a Bottom-up approach or mix of both. This is what we call the mode of reasoning. The point is that a mode can influence the definition of the macro contexts. Let's consider the Refine_ET_with_Attribute_definition decision (similar to the decision called *Attributise* in figure 4) mentioned in previous example. The reasoning mode used to define an Attribute can be, as it is in the F3 way-of-working, the following :

< (Entity_type) , Refine_ET_with_Attribute_definition >
Alt1   < (Entity_type) , Define_new_Attribute_of_ET >
   Alt1.1< (Entity_type) , Create_new_Attribute_of_ET >
         < ( ) , Create_Attribute_by_mutation >
           < ( ) , Create_Attribute_by_mapping >
           < ( ) , Create_Attribute_by_retyping >
         < ( ) , Create_Attribute_by_reuse >
         < ( ) , Create_Attribute_from_scratch >
           < ( ) , Create_Attribute>
         < (Entity_type, Attribute) , Associate_Attribute_to_Entity_type >
   Alt1.2< (Entity_type) , Identify_in_Current_Product_existing_Attribute_of_ET >
         < (Entity_type, Attribute) , Associate_Attribute_to_Entity_type >
Alt2   < (Entity_type) , Refine_existing_Attribute_of_ET >
   Alt2.1   < (Attribute) , Refine_Attribute_static_definition >

This last decision is similar to the Refine_ET_static_definition decision defined previously. As a matter of fact we have illustrated a Top-down approach [11] i.e. starting from the intention to Refine an Entity-type static definition we have decided to refine the static definition of one of its attributes. We can also define the reverse reasoning to get a bottom-up approach. By the way, a method engineer has a complete freedom to define the reasoning-mode he wants to allow in a given way-of-working. Let's illustrate such a bottom-up approach with the same example.

```
< (Attribute) , Refine_Attribute_Static_definition >
  < (Attribute) , Involve_Attribute_in_ET_definition >
 Alt1    < (Attribute) , Aggregate_Attribute_to_new_ET >
    Alt1.1< (Entity_type) , Create_new_ET >
              < ( ) , Create_ET_by_mutation >
                < ( ) , Create_ET_by_mapping >
                  < ( ) , Create_ET>
                  < (Resource, Entity_type) , Mutate_Resource_to_Entity_type >
                < ( ) , Create_ET_by_retyping >
                  < ( ) , Create_ET>
                  < (Relationship, Entity_type) , Mutate_Relationship_to_ET >
              < ( ) , Create_ET_by_reuse >
              < ( ) , Create_ET_from_scratch >
                < ( ) , Create_ET>
                < (Entity_type, Attribute) , Associate_Attribute_to_Entity_type >
    Alt1.2    < (Attribute) , Identify_existing_ET >
              < (Entity_type, Attribute) , Associate_Attribute_to_Entity_type >
 Alt2   < (Attribute) , Refine_existing_ET_of_Attribute >
    Alt2.1    < (Entity_type) , Refine_ET_static_definition >
```

4 Conclusion

This paper is centred on ways-of-working definition. Our proposition is based on three process modelling abstraction levels which more generally allow three complete forms of support : (1) process trace, (2) way-of-working definition and (3) process guidance. We have detailed in the paper point (2) by providing a set of guidelines for method engineers. We show in figure 12, that we can structure the process knowledge in a repository. A process meta model and some guidelines are used to define ways-of-working (as described in this paper). Then the resulting way-of-working (or process model) is used manually or not for different processes by developers. Learning from traces allow to improve the way-of-working and so the guidance support by capitalising development heuristics which are numerous in Requirement Engineering.

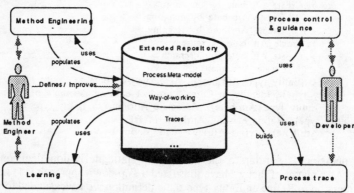

Figure 12 : Process case tools architecture

From the point of view of users, the Method Engineer knows and uses with a method engineering tool the process meta model to populate a way-of-working. Then using a learning tool, he is able to refine and complete the way-of-working by capturing Developers heuristics. The Developer uses the way-of-working definition with a process control and guidance tool or manually if he wants to apply some new decisions which could be further capitalised. He also builds the trace as the process proceeds.

This architecture is developed within two Esprit III projects in the Requirements Engineering field. The F3 project aims at tracing the process. Its guidance tool will be based on a learning facility working on RE traces. These traces relate the objects with the three kind of links introduced here (transformation, expansion, mutation links) and also keep track of objects history in terms of all the decisions which have affected its definition. Finally, the method engineering approach defined in the paper is developed in this project.

References

1. Bubenko J., Rolland C., Loucopoulos P., De Antonnellis V. : "Facilitating "Fuzzy to Formal" Requirements Modelling", Proc. of ICRE94, Colorado Springs, 1994.
2. Boehm B.W. : "A Spiral Model of Software Development"; IEEE Computer 21.
3. Curtis B., Kasner H., Iscoe N. : "A field study of the software design process for large systems"; Comm. ACM, vol. 31, 1988.
4. Dowson M. : "Iteration in the Software Process"; Proc 9th Int Conf on "Software Engineering", Monterey, CA,1988.
5. Finkelstein A., Kramer J., Goedicke M.: "ViewPoint Oriented Software Development"; Proc. Conf "Le Génie Logiciel et ses Applications", Toulouse,1990.
6. Grosz G., Rolland C. : "Using Artificial Intelligence Techniques to Formalize the Information Systems Design Process"; Proc. Int Conf "Databases and Expert Systems Applications", 1990.
7. Henderson-Sellers B., Edwards J.M.; "The Object-oriented Systems Life-Cycle"; Comm. ACM, Vol. 09, 1990.
8. Jarke M., Mylopoulos J., Schmidt J.W., Vassiliou Y.; "DAIDA - An Environment for Evolving Information Systems"; ACM Trans. on Information Systems, Vol. 10, No. 1, 1992.
9. Loucopoulos P., Zicari R.: "Conceptual Modeling, Database & Case", Wiley, 1992.
10. Moreno M., Souveyet C. : "The Evolutionary Object Model", IFIP TC8 Int. Conf. on "Information System Development Process", North Holland (pub.), 1993
11. Olle T.W., Hagelstein J., MacDonald I., Rolland C., Van Assche F., Verrijn Stuart A. : "Information Systems Methodologies : A Framework for Understanding", Addison Wesley, 1988.
12. Peugeot C., Franckson M.: "Specification of the Object and Process Modeling Language", ESF Report n° D122-OPML-1.0, 1991.
13. Potts C.: "A Generic Model for Representing Design Methods"; Proceed. 11th International Conference on Software Engineering, 1989.
14. Rolland C., Cauvet C. : "ALECSI : An Expert System for Requirements Engineering", in "Advanced Information Systems Engineering", Springer Verlag, 1991.
15. Rolland C.: "Modeling the Requirements Engineering Process", Proc. Fino-Japanese Seminar on "Conceptual Modeling", 1993.
16. Rolland C.: "Modelling the Evolution of Artifacts", Proceed. of Requirement Engineering Conference ICRE94, Colorado Springs, 1994.
17. Royce W.W.: "Managing the Development of Large Software Systems"; Proc. IEEE WESCON 08/1970.
18. Schmitt J.R.: "Product Modeling in Requirements Engineering Process Modeling", IFIP TC8 Int. Conf. on "Information Systems Development Process", North Holland (pub.), 1993
19. Sportes D. : "The Information System Model"; F3 Deliverable on T2.2, EspritIII project, n°6612, september 93.
20. Wilenski; "Planning and Understanding", Addison Wesley, 1983

Designing a User-Oriented Query Modification Facility in Object-Oriented Database Systems

K. Aberer, W. Klas, A. L. Furtado[1]

GMD-IPSI, Dolivostr. 15, 64293 Darmstadt, Germany,
E-Mail: {aberer, klas, furtado}@darmstadt.gmd.de

Abstract. The introduction of user-assisting features into database systems is discussed along two stages. The first stage involves a basic facility that can be used with standard database systems, whereas in the second stage such features are expanded in order to cope with object-oriented systems, adopting semantically richer data models. Examples involving categorization and role-specialization semantic hierarchies illustrate the discussion. A class/metaclass architecture, such as that of the VODAK database system, and an algebraic view of query processing are shown to be particularly suitable to design and implement user assistance on the database schema level.

1 Introduction

As increasingly complex databases are designed, end users may find them too difficult to use. One runs the risk to produce systems that are rich in terms of the information they contain, but that no one is able to use appropriately. The problems of accessing data in a database system are manifold: The user may not have the right conceptual understanding of what is in the database, he may not know or may not be able to use the right terminology to exactly name the constituents of a database schema (e.g., property names, class and type names), or he even may not know exactly how to express his information needs in terms of the query language offered by the database system. These problems are also well known in the framework of information retrieval and several approaches have been proposed to overcome these difficulties. An obvious solution is to interpose between user and system a module that acts as an "assistant". Such an assistant can help the user in formulating requests by means of a query statement which is then submitted to the database system, or it can modify the original query by means of abstractions or refinements, thus submitting queries which result in more information than the original query would have provided. In general, one can identify the following kinds of approaches for this problem: (1) *Interactively* support the user in formulating the query so that the submitted query be the best possible approximation to the user's information need. Then, process the query using conventional query processing techniques and return the exact result for the formulated query. The presentation of the result may be enhanced in order to make the results more understandable to the user. The whole process can be iterated in a session until the user is satisfied. (2) Take a query formulated by the user in terms of a given query language and modify the query before processing it. The modification of the query may be based on two phases: an abstraction which leads to a relaxed query, i.e., it will result in a broader answer than the original query; a refinement

[1] Visiting from the Departamento de Informatica of the Pontificia Universidade Catolica do Rio de Janeiro.

which leads to a set of more concrete queries, whose answer is better focused on the user's interests.

In [12] the problem of facilitating the access to a database system is approached by supporting the formulation of queries using fuzzy and associative knowledge about the terminology used to set up a database schema. The goal is to construct an assistant which allows to explore a database schema and to get suggestions for formulating exact queries as required by an underlying database system. This approach corresponds to the solutions of class (1). [2] presents an interesting approach for incorporating neighborhood information and associative relationships between objects to answer user requests. The approach – which is of type (2) – is based on the idea that one can use abstractions (type/class hierarchies) from the original data to broaden a request by transformations of the original query such that the relaxed query is posed against the abstractions instead of the original data. A specific operator called *nearer* subsequently allows to narrow the relaxed answer. A major drawback of this approach is that a lot of additional information is needed to build the abstractions as well as the knowledge base containing the additional information about associations. The abstractions are hard-wired into the system, and no user-oriented query processing is supported due to the lack of a user model.

In this work, where the type (2) approach is also taken, we first demonstrate how to introduce a basic user-assisting facility, which is compatible with standard databases. We then show how to gradually adapt and expand it, to achieve a more advanced assistant module, able to work on – and take full advantage of – systems providing higher level semantics and, in particular, following object orientation. Our description of the basic facility uses the experience gained with a prototype, developed as part of a larger project (NICE) [8] that investigates knowledge-based methods to create cooperative information systems. The prototype was implemented on top of an SQL relational database, using PROLOG for the rule-based algorithms. The progressive upgrading of the basic facility towards the assistant module is part of the database projects at GMD-IPSI. Prominent among the features of the VML data model [10], which underlies the VODAK database system developed at GMD-IPSI, are the notions of classes and metaclasses, and the provision made for the specification of rules for equivalence of VML-expressions. With the help of metaclasses, it is possible to represent to a large degree the general knowledge built into semantic hierarchies, such as specialization/generalization [2,13]. With the help of equivalences, it is possible to perform rule-based transformations of database queries. Moreover, classes and metaclasses have been implemented in VODAK in a way that promotes extensibility and modularity, the latter feature being indispensable for efficiently structuring large sets of rules. In spite of the fact that our project refers to a specific system, the guidelines specified are largely applicable to object-oriented database systems supporting similar features.

The text is organized as follows. Section 2 summarizes our basic approach to user-assisting query interfaces. Section 3 is a short account of properties of specialization / generalization, as e.g. supported by the VODAK data model, and illustrates the basic idea how knowledge about specialization / generalization relationships can be exploited for user assistance. Section 4 briefly introduces the basic concepts of the VODAK model language as far as needed in our discussion. Section 5 gives the approach to design and implementation of the advanced assistant module for query modification in VML. Conclusions and directions for further work are the objective of section 6.

2 Review of Basic User-Assisting Query Interfaces

Since, in general, users do not pose questions to a database system out of idle curiosity, the first objective of a user-assisting query interface should be to identify the goals and plans of the current user. A complementary objective is to keep his understanding of the system in harmony with the intentions of the designer, so that he may fully and efficiently have access to the existing information. In the following we give a short account the basic approach for a *user-oriented context-sensitive* query processing.

2.1 Forms of Assistance

To assist the user with respect to a query, the system may offer, among others, the following services [16]:
- correct the query
- complement the query, usually expanding but sometimes restricting it to a more useful scope
- provide alternatives
- offer to monitor the database and warn the user when a specified state is reached
- explain the reasons why some situation does not hold
- undo possibly wrong assumptions of the user (misconceptions)
- prevent wrong conclusions that the user may draw from an answer (misconstruals)
- make the answers more understandable

A constant danger is the possibility to become "over-cooperative". It is imperative to keep the focus on what is indeed relevant to the user's purposes. That means, that a specific user may want to get a specific kind of assistance in a situation, while another user may not want to get the same assistance in the same situation. This obviously calls for *user-oriented* assistance in contrast to general assistance which does not consider the individual needs of a user.

2.2 Rule-driven Query Modification

A usual strategy [3], which we also adopt, is to perform query modification, a device introduced with the INGRES project [15]. Query modification involves expression manipulation for which a rule-driven approach offers itself, as followed e.g. in [8]. Rules may come from different sources; they can be:general, application dependent or user dependent. Rules may be applicable at three different phases:

pre-rules: before the query is processed, in order to correct and complement the original query.

succ-post-rules: after successful processing, in order to complement the answer through additional queries.

fail-post-rules: after failed processing, in order to try alternatives; and if failure persists, to explain.

Example 1. Let us illustrate this approach by an example as reported in [8]. The format of the rules for query modification is there given in a PROLOG-like notation:

<rule_type> (<in_pattern>, <out_pattern>, <action>) ← <condition>

where the components are as stated below:

<rule_type>   one of pre-rule, succ-post-rule, fail-post-rule,

<in_pattern>   to match the original query, if the rule is applicable,

<out_pattern>	from which the new query is built,
<action>	procedure to finish the building process,
<condition>	finishes testing applicability.

To apply one rule to the original query, the algorithm first determines if the rule currently being considered is applicable. In this case it then proceeds to create the new query. To determine if the rule is applicable, it performs two steps:

(1) it checks whether the <in_pattern> matches the original query; the pattern-matching process is done through unification as defined in logic programming;

(2) it executes <condition>, which is a logical expression whose terms may check context-sensitive conditions. The characterization of context will be given later.

After these two steps, the <out_pattern> may already have been converted into the new query, although in general it will be necessary to

(3) execute <action>, which is a procedure able to access the context. ∎

2.3 Exploiting the Context of the Query

What we call "context" consists of conventional and non-conventional database components. Typical conventional components we consider the *factual database* and *data dictionary* information, like the conceptual schema, the user's external schema, and authorization and integrity constraints. The non-conventional components can include models of the application and the user, logs of user sessions, or typical users' plans.

Example 2. Let us illustrate the context-free pattern-matching process and the context-sensitive execution of rules according to the query modification approach taken in Example 1. We consider a failed query to find out if there are places on a flight from city amsterdam to city berlin by carrier klm on may.5th. Assume the existence of a fail-post-rule to ask about alternative flights. Let the original query and the two patterns in the rule be, respectively:

original query: fly(amsterdam,berlin,klm,may.5th) ?
<in_pattern>: fly(X,Y,Z,T)
<out_pattern>: fly(X,Y,W,V)

Unifying the original query with <in_pattern> binds the variables of the latter as:

X = amsterdam, Y = berlin, Z = klm, T = may.5th.

Note that consistent substitution requires that X and Y in <out_pattern> be bound to the same values. Furthermore no values were assigned to W and V, which therefore remain free variables. Now assume that <condition> can decide from the context whether a different flight would be admissible in view of the user's goals; in case this is true, the rule is indeed applicable (otherwise it would be dropped at this point). Finally, assume that <action> can find from the context whether the ticket for the original flight is endorsable, in which case it will unify V with T, so that the new query will be:

fly(amsterdam,berlin,W,may.5th) ?

Otherwise it will preserve the carrier originally indicated (by unifying W with Z) and try another date:

fly(amsterdam,berlin,klm,V) ? ∎

Algorithms realizing rule-driven query-modification are completely generic, since they do not specify the transformations. This task is deferred to the rules. One may start with just a few rules, accessing a context with few non-conventional components. For example, we feel that at least some primitive form of session log should be maintained, as a single query is not a convenient unit for cooperativeness/assistance [14]. As the context is enriched, new rules may be added to take advantage of whatever additional knowledge is available. Rules can rely on tools extracting or utilizing knowledge about the context, e.g.:

- a query-the-user module, whereby the system can directly learn about users' preferences [7];
- a plan-generation algorithm, able to construct plans as sequences of instances of operations which, as noted, are specified in a STRIPS-like style [4];
- an algorithm to extend unification to frames and to perform most specific generalization over terms and frames;
- a session manager to keep the log, and support an active environment through the creation of demons to perform monitoring tasks.

A prototype of a cooperative/assisting system, designed as outlined in this section, is fully operational [8]. An extension to the methodology is being studied for geographic databases [9]. Experience with the prototype there has demonstrated the usefulness of the basic facility.

However, more work was needed to cope with the additional problems – and opportunities – for user assistance arising from object-oriented systems based on semantically richer data models. With this purpose in mind, we chose to examine, as a significant benchmark, queries on database structures involving categorization and role-specialization semantic hierarchies.

3 Exploiting Specialization/Generalization Relationships for User Assistance

In the area of Semantic Data Modeling semantic hierarchies have long ago been borrowed from the area of Artificial Intelligence and adapted to the needs of databases [6]. In this section we briefly recall a number of basic features that have been identified with respect to specialization / generalization hierarchies and outline how these features are exploited for user assistance by query modification.

3.1 Basic constraints

A conventional way to model the application domain in a database is to start with a number of general classes of objects, to which base types are attached. If specialized classes are desired, they are derived from other classes by means of e.g. the ISA-relationship. For two classes in a ISA-relationship, their extensions are in a subset-relationship and their types are in a subtype-relationship. In [6] constraints are identified that ensure consistency of ISA relationships on classes, in particular it follows that they are hierarchical structures.

In addition to the basic constraints, other constraints may be imposed optionally, thus characterizing different kinds of ISA-hierarchies, e.g.:

(1)   be pairwise disjoint
(2)   together cover the extension of the general class
(3)   have a criterion for membership
(4)   form trees.

The first two constraints – disjointness and covering - are orthogonal to each other. Together they characterize a partition of the general class, in the sense that each general instance must correspond to an instance in exactly one specialized class. Constraint (3) means that there is a procedure to determine whether an object can be a member of a given specialized class. This procedure may either depend exclusively on intrinsic characteristics of the object, or it may depend on extrinsic criteria based on how the object is related with other objects. Constraint (4) expresses that ISA edges can be required to impose a strict hierarchy, so that the classes are structured as multi-level trees. Dropping this constraint results in a partial order structure, where a class is allowed to have more than one "parent". Constraints of the kind introduced have to be maintained by the database management system when updates are performed.

3.2 Inheritance

Another important consideration for ISA hierarchies is the inheritance of properties. In fact methods are also inherited and, for our present purposes, it is useful to note that certain methods really amount to "virtual" properties, whose values are computed by methods rather than stored in the database.

Informally speaking, the prevailing principle is that every property that is common to all specialized classes should be "factored out", i.e. moved up to the general class. Then the term "inheritance" means that, when a query asks about such properties when referring to specialized instances, the appropriate values will be found at the level of the general instance, and duly passed down. Ambiguities may arise with non strictly hierarchical ISA, when a class may specialize more than one general class having the same property. In this case a criterion must be fixed which property value should be chosen.

A situation that is, in a sense, the inverse of inheritance may occur for some properties. The value of a property of a general instance may be synthesized from properties of one or more (if overlapping is permitted) of its specialized instances. The property Revenue of Person, for example, would be calculated as the sum of salary as Employee, plus gain as Stockholder, plus other incomes that a person may receive.

3.3 Using ISA for User-Oriented Assistance – Examples

In many cases it may happen that users are not aware of all details in many possible overlapping ISA-hierarchies. In these cases the constraints on ISA-hierarchies discussed above may readily be exploited in order to properly modify the users' query. We give a number of examples which illustrate this fact.

Example 3. The examples below are expressed in natural language for readability. In each case we indicate the feature exploited (existence, etc.), the classes involved, the original query and the answer.

(1)	*feature:*	existence in another specialized class;
	classes:	Enterprise ISA Institution, Government Agency ISA Institution.
	query:	What is the address of enterprise Alpha?
	answer:	the address of government agency Alpha is Karlstr, Darmstadt.
(2)	*feature:*	location of property in specialized role;
	classes:	Employee ISA Person.
	query:	What is the salary of person John?
	answer:	as an employee, John earns 100.
(3)	*feature:*	covering;
	classes:	Emp-Level-1, ... , Emp-Level-n ISA Employee..
	query:	How many employees do not belong to any level?
	answer:	none; every employee is in a level group.

(4) *feature:* disjointness;
    classes: same as above.
    query: How many employess are in levels 4 or 5?
    answer: 15; 10 in level 4 and 5 in level 5.

(5) *feature:* overlapping;
    classes: Employee ISA Person, Shareholder ISA Person.
    query: How many employees and how many shareholders are there?
    answer: 100 employees and 15 shareholders; 5 persons are both. ∎

From the above examples it is clear that there is an potential for user-assistance with regard to semantic relationships like ISA-hierarchies. In the following we will give a detailed approach for a concrete object-oriented database management system, that supports mechanisms to define such semantic relationships in a generic manner, and then show how to adapt the system for the support of user-assistance by rule-based query modification.

4 The Extendible VODAK Database Model

In order to discuss the realization of user-oriented query modification we first summarize in this section the essential features of the VODAK database system. VODAK is an object-oriented database management system which has been implemented at GMD-IPSI [10].

4.1 The VODAK Metaclass System

In VODAK specialization/generalization relationships are realized through metaclasses. We shortly introduce the concepts of classes and metaclasses as used in VODAK [11].

Classes determine the structure and behavior of their instances. More precisely, an application class determines the *application-specific* structure and behavior of its *instances*, which represent the "real world" objects dealt with within an application program, by specifying its *instance type*; it also determines the *application-specific* structure and behavior of the application class itself, for example specific object creation and initialization methods, by specifying its *own type*.

Metaclasses are used to describe the common structure and behavior of classes and their instances which may not be known at the time a metaclass is defined. Metaclasses and application classes are treated uniformly as classes. In addition, it is possible to specify the *common* structure and behavior for the instances of the instances, the so-called *metainstances*, of a metaclass by associating an object type as *instance-instance type* to the metaclass.

The *object types* that determine the instance, instance-instance and own type of classes and metaclasses can either be defined directly within the class definition, in which case we have an *in-line type definition*, or in a separate *object type declaration*. The provision of separate object type declarations in VML is also referred to as the *dual model*, which allows a clean separation of syntactic and semantic concepts in object-oriented data base schemas. For example, the same object type declaration may be reused in different (semantically unrelated) classes.

The *interface* defined for an object is the set of methods which are defined for the object, i.e., which can be executed directly for the object. It consists of the methods specified with the *own type* of the object, if this object represents a class, and the methods specified with the *instance type* of the object's class, and the methods specified with the *instance-instance type* of the metaclass of the object's class.

In case the method is not contained in the interface defined for the object, the message handling system of VML tries to delegate the message to another object by executing the method implementation given in a **NOMETHOD** clause. This permits for example to implement different inheritance strategies.

The class system in VML is organized in four levels: the individual *object level*, the *application class level*, the *metaclass level*, and the *root level*. At the metaclass level the system administrator may define new metaclasses and, thus, enhance the modeling capabilities of the predefined kernel model. Built-in classes at the root level provide for the basic and system inherent capabilities like object creation, object deletion, and object storage.

4.2 ISA in the VODAK Data Model

Based on the need to model real-world applications we discuss two examples of ISA specialization relationships which were implemented in VODAK using the metaclass system.

(a) *Role Specialization*, wherein real world objects may appear in different roles, e.g. a person may appear in the role of a student or an employee.

(b) *Category Specialization*, where provision is made for real-world objects being categorized into disjoint sets with respect to some specific aspect, e.g. parts may be categorized into simple parts and composite parts with respect to their complexity.

In the terminology of the previous sections, role specialization is based on extrinsic criteria and permits overlapping. When declaring it, one must specify whether or not the specialization should be restricted to a single general class. An example with multiple general classes is: from the more general classes Student and Employee, define the specialized class Employed Student. Category specialization requires disjointness but not covering. The membership criterion is solely based on intrinsic characteristics.

The strategy to implement these kinds of ISA specialization takes full advantage of the Metaclass concept. At the meta level there exist metaclasses Role-Specialization-Class, General-Category-Class, and Category-Specialization-Class. For role specialization, each general class is instance of the general VML Kernel-Application-Class metaclass. Each specialized class is connected, via *rolespec* relationship edges, to the general class and is instance of the Role-Specialization-Class metaclass. A number of public methods are passed by inheritance from these metaclasses to their instances, namely the role specialization classes, as well as to their metainstances, namely the instances of the role specialization classes. These methods allow, among other tasks, to create, delete and modify role specialization classes and their instances consistently and to interrogate the structure of classes and instances, finding for example, in the case of multiple specialization, which general classes a given class specializes and which general instances correspond to a given specialized instance. Furthermore a **NOMETHOD** clause allows to specify a particular inheritance behavior for instances of the role specialization class. The body of this clause is executed whenever no appropriate method is found for the receiver object of the method.

Example 4. More specifically the (interface) definition of the metaclass Role-Specialization-Class (RoleSpec, in abbreviated form) is as follows.

```
CLASS RoleSpec METACLASS Metaclass
    INSTTYPE OBJECTTYPE      // instance type of the specialized classes (inline definition)
        PROPERTIES    roleSpecofClass: OID;
        METHODS       roleSpecof(c: OID);          // sets roleSpecofClass
                      roleofClass(): OID;          // returns OID of general class

    INSTINSTYPE OBJECTTYPE // type of the instances of the specialized classes
        PROPERTIES    roleSpecofInstance: OID;
        METHODS       roleSpecof(i; OID);          // sets roleSpecofInstance
                      roleofInstance(): OID;       //returns OID of general instance
        NOMETHOD          // inherit current method call to the object roleSpecofInstance
END;
```

An application class, e.g. Employee being a role specialization of a class Person, is then defined as follows.

```
CLASS Employee METACLASS Metaclass
    INSTTYPE OBJECTTYPE Employee_type
              // application specific type of the instances of the application class
    INIT SELF→roleSpecof(Person)
END;             // initializes this class as specialization of the class Person ■
```

For category specialization, the general classes are instances of the General-Category-Class metaclass. Each specialized class is connected by a *catspec* relationship edge to the general class and is instance of the Category-Specialization-Class metaclass. The same powerful mechanism of inheritance of public methods is provided.

5 Design and Implementation of Advanced Querying Assistance

The VODAK DBMS provides a SQL-like query language named VQL [10]. For query processing SQL style queries are translated to an internal algebraic representation, to which rule-based transformations, e.g. for the sake of query optimization are applied [1,5]. For our purposes we will adopt this algebraic approach for user-oriented query modification. After a short review of algebraic query representations in object-oriented query algebras and the available rule specifications, we will give examples, how a non-conventional context is represented and exploited within this algebraic approach.

5.1 Query Algebras and Rule Systems

For the presentation in this paper we need to introduce only two basic query algebra operators of the object-oriented query algebra that is used for the internal representation of VQL-queries in VODAK. The algebraic operators are applied to complex values built up from tuple and set type constructors over atomic domains.

The first operator is needed to select from a set C of complex values, which is for example computed as the extension of a class, a subset according to a condition

$$\mathbf{SELECT}(x: C, cond(x)) = \{ x \in C \mid cond(x) \}$$

The second operator we consider is needed to apply a function iteratively to a set of complex values.

$$\mathbf{MAP}(x: C, expr(x)) = \{ expr(x) \mid x \in C \}$$

In order to use semantic knowledge of methods for query transformation we extend the data model language by a rule specification mechanism. Rules are then given in the interface of an object type by a clause of the form

```
RULES name
    V₁: dom₁; ... ; Vₙ: domₙ; {cond(V₁,...,Vₙ): expr₁(V₁,...,Vₙ) <—> expr₂(V₁,...,Vₙ)};
```

where $V_1,...,V_n$ are the pattern variables, which stand for VML expressions of type dom_1, ... dom_n, $expr_1$ and $expr_2$ stand for (equivalent) VML expressions containing the pattern variables and *cond* stands for a Boolean VML expression containing the pattern variables.

Example 5. An example of such a rule in a person database is

   RULES family
   x : Person; {**true**: x→grandfather() <—> (x→father())→father()};

Such a rule can then be used to transform the algebraic representation of a query in the following way

   MAP(x: Person, (x→father())→father()) ⇒ **MAP**(x: Person, x→grandfather()) ∎

Including rules into object-type definitions in this way is a non-trivial enhancement of object-oriented data models towards the ADT (abstract data type) paradigm. It is not necessary that the rules provide a complete behavioral specification of the types of database objects. A fundamental point is that their declarative style makes them easier to understand and to serve for documentation purposes, for guiding the procedural development of the implemented code, and for testing its execution. The backbone for method execution is still their procedural specification. One difficult question that remains is how to maintain consistency between the declarative specification and the operational specification of a method or property. As a consequence of making rules part of the object type specification, rules can be inherited which is crucial for efficient design of rule systems.

The technique for transformation of the algebraic representation of a query by using rules specified in application schemas was implemented for VODAK in the context of query optimization. The main tool used was the Volcano optimizer generator [5]. We now show how this technique can be used for the purpose of user-assisting query modification.

5.2 Representation of Non-conventional Context in Database Schemas

The factual database and the schema (represented in the data dictionary) are already part of the context. As the assistance to the user must be tuned according to the user, characteristics of the user are represented in user models, which again take the form of classes.

Additional knowledge about the user may now be provided by specifying rules in the user model. The main idea for the implementation of query modification presented here is that the parameters given for the algebraic query operators are not taken for granted but need interpretation according to the context described. This interpretation is then provided by the rules of the user model.

Thus in a first step we produce a *context-sensitive algebraic representation* of the query. Assume the context is given by a particular user u and the query has the form

   SELECT(x: C, cond(x))

Taking the parameters not for granted means, e.g., that we are not sure whether the user u really meant class C when he specified it. Thus we replace the plain class specification C by a user-sensitive method call

   u→class_dom(C)

where the method class_domain represents the system model of how the user interprets a class specification C. The same is done for all other parameters appearing in the parameters of query operators, i.e. select and map operations are transformed to

    SELECT(x: u→class_dom(C), u→bool_expr(cond(x))),
    MAP(x: u→class_dom(C), u→int_expr(expr(x))),

provided that expr(x) evaluates to an integer value. The methods boolean_expr and integer_expr are used in the same way as class_domain to describe how the user interprets the particular expressions in the arguments.

Methods needed for transforming a query into the context-sensitive representation are given in the following object type declaration:

    OBJECTTYPE QueryContext
      INTERFACE
      METHODS   class_dom(c: **OID**): **OID**;
                     int_expr(o: **OID**, p: VML_PROP): **INT**;
                     int_equal(i: **INT**, j: **INT**): **BOOL**; ...
      RULES class_dom_rule c: **OID** {**true**: class_dom(c) <—> c};
             int_expr_rule o: **OID**, p: VML_PROP {**true**: int_expr(o,p) <—> o.p;}
             int_equal_rule i: **INT**, j: **INT** {**true**: int_equal(i,j) <—> i==j;} ...
      IMPLEMENTATION
      METHODS   class_dom(c: **OID**): **OID** {**RETURN** c };
                     int_expr(o: **OID**, p: VML_PROP) {**RETURN** o.p};
                     int_equal(i: **INT**, j: **INT**): **BOOL** { **RETURN** i==j }; ...

This object type is system-defined and is needed by a system module that will produce the context-sensitive algebraic representation of the query. Note that the implementation of the methods is simply identical to what would have been expected from the original expressions. On the basis of this type now a user class can be defined as follows:

    CLASS User
      INSTTYPE OBJECTTYPE SUBTYPEOF QueryContext
      INTERFACE
      RULES   // additional rules on class_dom, int_expr, int_equal etc.

This class makes the methods inherited from the object type QueryContext nondeterministic, by allowing different interpretations of the same expression. Otherwise the rules do not differ at all from those used, e.g. in query optimization. Concrete rules will be given in the examples of the next section.

We remark that using the object type QueryContext as indicated above is a typical example for the application of the dual model approach of VML. It can be attached to other classes like those referring to characteristics of category specialization, or application classes, in case of application-dependent rules.

5.3 Application of Nonconventional Context for Query Modification

In this section we give three typical examples of how to use the rule mechanism for query transformation.

Example 6. Assume a user u of class User in the flight database of Section 2.3 issues the following query

    SELECT f.number **FROM** f **IN** Flight **WHERE** f.price=1000

The corresponding context sensitive algebraic representation produced by the system according to the definitions given section 5.2 is as follows.

    MAP(x: **SELECT**(x: u→class_dom(Flight), u→int_equal(x.price,1000)),
                                           u→int_expr(x.number))

Assume, that the following simple user model is given

CLASS User
    INSTTYPE OBJECTTYPE SUBTYPEOF QueryContext
    INTERFACE
    RULES adapt_price
        u: User; f: Flight; p: **INT**;
        {**true**: u→int_equal(f.price,1000) <—> f.price>0.9*p **and** f.price<1.1*p};

That means that for class_dom and int_expr no rules are applicable, except the identity rules class_dom_rule and int_expr_rule, which are inherited from the system defined object type QueryContext. Applying these rules gives

    MAP(x: **SELECT**(x: Flight, u→int_equal(x.price,1000), x.number)

However, for int_equal we have an applicable rule adapt_price specified in the class User. Applying this rule results in the following modified query

    MAP(x: **SELECT**(x: Flight, x.price>900 and x.price<1100, x.number)

which eventually will be evaluated. ■

After discussing the approach of rule application in principle we come to the central examples involving ISA hierarchies. The rules relevant for these will be introduced at the same level at which the semantic relationships themselves are introduced, namely at the metaclass level.

Example 7. In Example 3, query (1), of Section 3.3, an applicable rule should express, roughly speaking: if the query refers to a class that is a category specialization, find the corresponding general class and, through it, each of the other specialized classes to be tried in the new query. In the notation described, this means that the conditional part of the rule determines if the originally indicated class orig and some other class alt are instances of the metaclass Category-Specialization-Class (CatSpec), determined by applying the method catofClass[2]. If the condition holds, then alt will replace orig in the modified query; u refers to the current user.

    RULES catgen
        u: User; orig: CatSpec, alt: CatSpec
        {orig <> alt **and** alt→catofClass() == orig→catofClass():
            u→class_dom(orig)<—>alt}

This is a rule that involves a complex condition. Hence we illustrate the whole process how the rule is applied. Let the user pose the following query:

    SELECT e.address **FROM** e **IN** Enterprise **WHERE** e.name=="Alpha"

The context-sensitive representation is then given as

    MAP(x: **SELECT**(x: u→class_dom(Enterprise), u→str_equal(x.name,"Alpha"),
                                    u→str_expr(x.address)

For the method class_domain now the rule catgen is applicable. Enterprise and Gov_agency are different category specializations of Institution. Therefore the query is transformed to

    MAP(x: **SELECT**(x: Gov_agency, u→str_equal(x.name,"Alpha"),
                                  u→str_expr(x.address)

which now produces the intended answer. Other rules can still be applied now, e.g. for relaxing the string comparison condition or enhancing the output of the query. ■

Example 8. In Example 3, query (2), of Section 3.3, which is a case of role specialization, an applicable rule expresses the following: if a query refers to p as a property

---

[2]   The method catofClass is analogous to the method roleofClass given in Example 4 in Section 4.2.

(respectively method) of a class c_gen, whereas p is a property (respectively method) of class c_spec and c_spec ISA c_gen, then make the new query refer to p of c_spec.

The conditional part of the rule finds whether there is a class c_spec that is a role of class c_gen, and whether the desired property p belongs to c_spec (rather than to c_gen, as in the original query). If the condition holds, then the new query will look for p at the level of the specialized class; o is an object identifier for an instance of class c_gen, and, again, u refers to the current user;

> **RULES** rolegen
>> u: User; c_gen: KernelApplicationClass; c_spec: RoleSpecializationClass;
>> o: **OID**; p: VML_PROP;
>> {o **IN** c_gen→allInstances() **and** p **IN** c_spec→properties() **and**
>> c_spec→roleofClass() == c_gen: u→int_expr(o,p) <—> (o→roleof()).p}

Note how in the condition part of the rule methods from the system level (allInstances), from the metaclass level (roleofClass) and from the data dicitionary level (properties) are used. Also observe that in the domain declarations the class to which o belongs is not yet determined, thus the generic type for object identifiers **OID** is used at that place. ∎

5.4 Notes on the Implementation

The features to implement user-oriented querying assistance in VODAK are rule specification in the object interface and rule-application in query processing. In the preceding sections we have described the integration of a rule-specification mechanism within the VML data model. These rule specifications will be inserted by the VML compiler into the data dictionary. VODAK uses a universal interface to the message handler which allows both the access to the database and to the data dictionary by method execution. Thus a component for performing rule application is able to access this information through this universal interface. This approach was already taken, e.g., in the query optimizer, where the *Volcano* optimizer generator [5] is used for rule-based optimization. Using the same tool for query modification suggests an interesting approach: define a cost model that relates an actual query with the relevance to the users' information needs. Alternatively a Prolog component could by used, similarly as in the NICE project.

Different developments of the VODAK prototype had been undertaken independently, particularly in the context of query processing, which were found to facilitate the implementation of the techniques described in this paper. An internal algebraic representation of VML expressions has been modelled to support the representation and manipulation of query expressions. An interface for exchanging VML expressions and messages between VODAK and the *Volcano* optimizer generator was designed. The extension of the VML data model with the rule constructs introduced in this paper completes the required set of tools.

6 Concluding Remarks

The VODAK data model has a particularly appropriate structure to accomodate user-assisting features in a natural way. Its definition in terms of metaclasses and classes has led to a modularized organization of properties and methods. This very same discipline is adopted as rules are introduced, so that they are grouped according to their degree of generality, and are inherited down or filtered away in order to take into account the needs of individual users. The architecture of the implemented VODAK database system iself was conceived to favor extensibility. We further recall that the extensions to provide (1) general-purpose rules and (2) the user-assisting algorithms, builds on our previous experience, respectively, with the rule-based tool to optimize VQL query-processing [1] and with the prototypes developed as part of project NICE [8].

Future research will be concentrated in refining the user-modelling strategies and in extending user assistance to the more advanced components of VODAK, such as: the *multimedia environment*, where template rules may be applied to guide the choice of the best medium to communicate an answer; *cooperative activities* involving several agents, where multiple user (i.e. agent) models can be simultaneously activated and used to achieve a better coordination of the users' processes; *heterogeneous database integration*, where the usual transparency paradigm for combining different schemas would be modified, by letting the original user of one of the schemas benefit from opportunities arising from richer features of the other schemas.

Acknowledgement. We would like to thank Klemens Böhm for carefully reading the paper and giving many valuable suggestions for improving the paper.

References

1. Aberer, K., Fischer, G.: Object-Oriented Query Processing: The Impact of Methods on Language, Architecture and Optimization. Technical report 763, GMD-IPSI, (1993).
2. Chu, W. W., Chen, Q.: Neighborhood and Associative Query Answering. Journal of Intelligent Information Systems, 1, 1992, 355–382 (1992).
3. Cuppens, F., Demolombe, R.: Cooperative Answering: A Methodology to Provide Intelligent Access to Databases. In: 2nd International Conference on Expert Database Systems, L. Kerschberg (ed.), Benjamin/Cummings, 621–643 (1989).
4. Fikes, R. E., Nilsson, N. J.: STRIPS: A New Approach to the Application of Theorem Proving to Problem Solving. Artificial Intelligence 2, 1971, 189–208 (1971).
5. G. Gräfe, W. J. McKenna: "The Volcano Optimizer Generator: Extensibility and Efficient Search", *Proceedings of the 9th IEEE International Conference on Data Engineering*, pp. 209–218, Vienna, Austria, April 19–23, 1993.
6. Hull, R., King, R.: Semantic Database Modeling: Survey, Applications and Research Issues. ACM Computing Surveys, 19, 3, 201–260 (1987).
7. Hammond, P., Sergot, M.: Augmented PROLOG for Expert Systems, Logic Based Systems Ltd. (1984).
8. Hemerly, A. S., Casanova, M. A., Furtado, A. L.: Cooperative behavior through Request Modification. In: Proc. 10th Conference on the Entity-Relationship Approach, 607–621 (1991).
9. Hemerly, A. S., Casanova, M. A., Furtado, A. L.: Towards Cooperativeness in Geographic Databases. In: Proc. DEXA (1993).
10. Klas, W. et al: VML – The VODAK Model Language Version 3.0. Specification Document, GMD-IPSI (1992).
11. Klas, W., Aberer, K., Neuhold, E.J.: Object-Oriented Modelling for Hypermedia Systems using the VODAK Modelling Language (VML). To appear in: A.Biliris, T.Oszu (Edt.): Object–Oriented Database Management Systems. NATO ASI Series, Springer Verlag Berlin Heidelberg, December 1993.
12. Kracker, M.: Unschafes assoziatives Begriffswissen zur Unterstützung der Formulierung von Datenbankanfragen. Dissertation, Technische Universität Wien, April 1991.
13. Neuhold, E. J., Schrefl, M.: Dynamic Derivation of Personalized Views. In: Proc. 14th VLDB Conference, 183–194 (1988).
14. Stein, A., Thiel, U.: A Conversational Model of Multimodal Interaction. Technical Report GMD-IPSI (1993).
15. Stonebraker, M. R.: Implementation of Integrity by Query Modification. In: Proc. ACM SIGMOD International Conference on Management of Data (1975).
16. Webber, B. L.: Questions, Answers and Responses: Interacting with Knowledge Base Systems. In: On Knowledge Base Management Systems, M. L. Brodie, J. Mylopoulos (eds.), Springer, (1986).

Using Visual ER Query Systems in Real World Applications

Peter Rosengren

Swedish Institute for Systems Development
Electrum 212
S - 164 40 Kista
Sweden
Telephone: #46-8-752 16 00
Fax: #46-8-752 68 00
email: peterros@sisu.se

Abstract. This paper presents experiences from using a visual ER-based query system within large organisations. The system, Hybris, has been used by end-users for retrieving information from relational databases. Hybris exploits ER-schemes, graphical querying and an integrated dictionary browser as important facilities in the user interface.

1. Introduction

Today, organisations need to make more efficient use of existing information resources. Large investments have been made in building databases and the information stored in databases represents a valuable asset. Unfortunately so far it has been difficult for end-users to access the information they need. Several reasons can be given for that - the structure of a large complex database is hard to understand and interpret, and query languages are often difficult to learn and use.

The objectives of the Hybris project have been to investigate the requirements for an end-user tool to retrieve information from large, complex corporate databases and to define and implement such a tool. The solution taken in the Hybris project was to use an ER-based approach for the graphical user interface.

The Hybris software was put into operation 1990 and have been tested and evaluated by approximately 100 users at Swedish Telecom working with a production management database and at Sweden Post with 15 users working with a market and sales support database. Also several prototype installations have been made at other sites.

The purpose of this paper is to report about our experiences from designing and evaluating a visual ER query system. The paper is organised as follows. The next chapter surveys related research on visual ER query systems. Chapter 3 gives an overview of Hybris and explains its functionality. In chapter 4 we present results of three different evaluations of Hybris. Conclusions are given in chapter 5 which also points out some important issues for future research.

2.   Related Work

Research on ER-based query interfaces started in the early eighties. Two of the first research systems to use an ER-schema as a main component in the user interface were GUIDE [23] and gql/ER [24]. Another pioneering approach for database retrieval was presented by Fogg who combined ER-models with a browsing interface [8]. The list of early contributions can be made quite long, some examples are [4, 7, 16, 18].

More recent research system make use of other data models such as the universal relation model [13] or extensions of the ER-model with specialisation, generalisation and aggregation. Examples of visual query systems exploiting extended ER-models are Candid [20], Pasta-3 [14, 15], and Super [1]. Czedjo et al also describe a query interface based on extended ER-models [6]. Visual querying and browsing interfaces for object-oriented data models have also been proposed [17, 22]. The reader is further referred to surveys of contemporary research [2, 6, 14, 21].

Although there have been many solutions suggested, as Batini et al point out, surprisingly few reports about user satisfaction have been produced [2].

3.   Lessons learned from Hybris

In this section we give an overview of Hybris and its functionality. We will also discuss various design decisions and explain how they relate to previous research system. It should be noted that it is beyond the scope of this paper to present all details about Hybris, instead we want to point out some issues that are important to consider when implementing a visual ER query system in real world applications.

The basic architecture for a visual ER query system is, as a result of extensive research, quite well understood by now. Basically, such a system requires three components - *schema browser*, user environment for *query formulation* and *database query translator* [4]. The way these three components have been implemented differs between various systems.

3.1.   Large Schema Navigation

We have learned that a large ER-schema requires good mechanisms for structuring the overall schema into different views. How to deal with views have been described by several authors. Wong and Kuo suggest a filtering approach based on *relevance ranking* [23]. However, it is not clear how to do such an objective relevance ranking since entities may be of varying importance depending on users and their tasks. Catarci and Santucci suggest two solutions - predefined *personalised schemes* that can be fetched from a library and *top-down browsing* to allow a user to view the schema at different levels of detail [4].

396

Our approach have been to design schema views together with users, where each view reflects concepts important for a well-defined task. The figure below shows the Task view at Swedish Telecom. In that view all entity classes relevant when querying about tasks are shown.

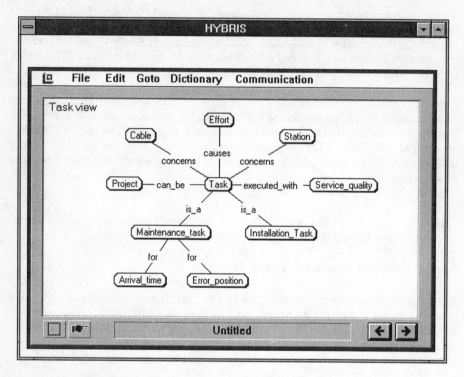

Fig. 1. A task-oriented view designed together with users.

To further simplify navigation within large schemas Hybris allows the user to type in a search string. Hybris then locates entities and attributes that match the search string and displays an appropriate view containing the entity searched for. Similar features exists in the Pasta-3 system [15] and Graqula [21].

3.2. Integrated Dictionary Browser

Our experience from evaluating Hybris is that schema browsing facilities are necessary but not enough to support a user's understanding of the database contents. The databases we have been working with so far have contained between 40 and 80 entity types which have had an average of 8-10 attributes each. In many cases there has also been multiple relationships between entity types.

To simply display the ER-schema and let the user browse through it is not enough to convey the semantics of data to the user. We therefore have designed another browsing facility - a dictionary browser where users can browse through meta data.

Figure 2 and 3 show how a user can browse through the dictionary in a hypertext fashion. The user does so by clicking on attribute names, entity names or relationship names.

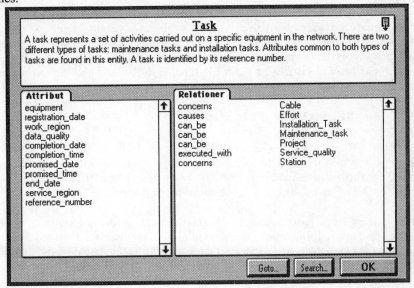

Fig. 2. The Integrated Dictionary Browser

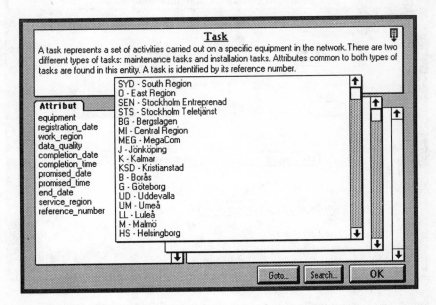

Fig. 3. The Integrated Dictionary Browser (cont.). The user has clicked on an attribute and then on the value domain for that attribute. Explanations and descriptions are shown to the user.

The dictionary browser can be accessed at anytime, during schema browsing or query formulation. A user can look at entity explanations, attribute definitions, relationship constraints etc.

The dictionary browser also solves another problem apparent in several research systems - *cognitive overload*. In order to represent as many semantic aspects as possible many systems end up with a visually too complex layout [3, 6, 20]. Our approach has been to visualise a plain ER-schema to the user and instead put extra semantic information in the dictionary browser.

3.3. Simplified Query Formulation

Most visual ER query systems imply that the user works in the following steps - the schema is browsed in order to understand the database contents, a subschema is selected for further investigations, restrictions are added for attributes belonging to relevant entities. Finally the query is submitted to the database.

Hybris differs from most research systems in that we do not separate schema browsing and query formulation. We wanted to give the user a *mental model* [9] of the schema as being the actual database. Queries are formulated by directly pointing at entities and restricting attributes in the schema. Immediate feedback is given in the ER schema. See figure 4.

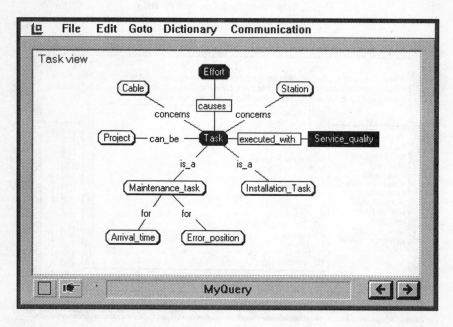

Fig. 4. Direct query feedback is given in the schema. When an entity is displayed as a rectangle it shows the user that restrictions have been added to some attribute of the entity.

This approach showed both advantages and disadvantages. The advantage were that it gave the users a straightforward and easy-to-learn model of the system. The disadvantage was that it limited the expressive power of the query language. An example is a query where an entity type plays different roles. This would require duplication of the entity directly in the schema which proved to be a difficult usability problem to solve, because it would produce clutter and confusion [21]. If we would have used two separate windows, one for schema browsing and another for query formulation this particular problem could have been solved. But then, on the other hand, the user interaction would not have been as straightforward since it would have required an extra step for the user to move items from the schema window to the query window.

One problem in real world applications is the use of cryptically numerical codes to represent attribute values. This seriously effects the ease-of-use when formulating queries. Users might very well know what they are looking for, e.g. sales in the region "Stockholm North", but if they do not know the code value for "Stockholm North" they cannot get the information.

In Hybris, we solved the problem in the same way as in GUIDE [23], by supporting value domains at the user interface level, i.e. when querying the user can select values from a list of explaining text strings, see figure 5. Hybris then automatically translates it into the correct database code.

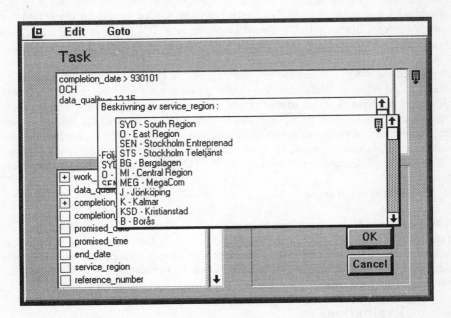

Fig. 5. The Integrated Dictionary Browser is always available. This figure shows a user that consults it for code value explanation during query formulation.

Hybris also make extensive use of value domains and value rules to ensure that a user does not enter an illegal value for the database search.

3.4. Query Translation

So far we have described how the schema browsing facilities have been implemented in Hybris and how it was extended with an integrated dictionary browser. We have also explained how query formulation works. The final component in a visual ER query system is the database query translator.

To be able to translate the visual query into SQL, Hybris uses an internal dictionary. In the dictionary the underlying database schema, the ER schema and the mapping between the ER schema and the database schema are stored. The SQL translator reads a textual description of the visual query and uses dictionary information to construct the appropriate SQL-query.

As is pointed out by Hohenstein transformations of conceptual ER-models into database schemas has been quite well investigated, but less attention has been paid to transformation of query languages [11]. If visual ER query systems are to be used in real world applications the queries formulated in the ER-tool have to be translated into SQL queries since this is the standard query language for databases.

Few published papers deal with this issue. Czedjo et al mention that they translate graphical ER-queries into SQL [6]. Hohenstein has proposed an algorithm for automatic translation of an ER-query language into SQL [11]. In both cases it is assumed that for each entity set there exists one relation in the database.

We make the same assumption but our experience has shown that this restriction needs to be relaxed. While the one-to-one assumption might be true for a newly designed database it is not true after one or two years in operation. The database structure changes due to optimisation issues but also because of new user requirements. The changes cause a denormalised database structure, for instance the entity set "Customer" might be divided into three underlying database tables - "Northern Region Customer", "Southern Region Customer" and "Other Customer".

3.5. Implementation

Two versions of Hybris have been implemented. The first one runs on Macintosh and has been built with HyperCard. The second version runs under Windows and is implemented with the tool PLUS. The query translator is written in C with the tools LEX and YACC. The database communication is implemented differently depending on specific applications.

4. Evaluations

Hybris has been evaluated in three different studies. In this chapter we will give a summary of the different studies. The first study was a usability study at Swedish Telecom that was conducted during the first three months of use [19]. The application was a production management database which was accessed to measure the quality of service offered by Swedish Telecom to their customers and to plan for future work and investments.

Prior to Hybris the users accessed the database either through predefined standard reports or through SQL for unpredictable, ad-hoc queries. However, the use of SQL at this time was limited. A study had shown Swedish Telecom that only 20 percent of the users who had been taught SQL in a 3 day course, were actually using SQL three months after the course.

Most users had very little experiences of using a graphical user interface.

The result of the Hybris evaluation was promising:

- Inexperienced users could quickly and easily get access to information needed in different situations.

- Users felt that they had access to "new" information because the overview provided by the ER-schema made them aware of new relations among data that they didn't know existed.

- Many errors in the database was discovered by users once they had the opportunity to query about their own data.

- According to users they felt a tool like Hybris would lead to increased efficiency within the organisation. They gave two reasons for that; 1) the quality of information increased since it was possible to verify the accuracy of data at the finest level of transactions, 2) they could focus their attention on their task instead of on how to handle a database query language.

- The ER-schema gave a visual view of the database which made the database less abstract and difficult to comprehend.

Sahlin concludes that Hybris gives powerful support for retrieving information and that it is especially well-suited for infrequent and novice database users [19].

The second study was a laboratory study by Karlgren and Wideroth [12]. The subjects where students at the Department of Psychology at University of Stockholm and the application used was a hospital database.

Karlgren and Wideroth showed that Hybris worked well for queries with simple logic, but that the subjects had problems when a query involved complex logical formulas, especially when the connectives AND and OR have to mixed in nested statements. The same was also noticed from use at Swedish Telecom.

This is an inherently difficult usability problem to solve since logic is difficult to master. However, there are certain things that can be done to ease the burden on the user.

The following is an example that user had many problems with. Consider the query "Efforts during April for Regions 15, 17 and 25" where the restrictions should be formulated:

```
date BETWEEN 910401, 910430
AND (region = 15 OR region = 17 OR region = 25)
```

Most users forgot the parenthesis which of course lead to an unexpected answer:

```
date BETWEEN 910401, 910430
AND region = 15 OR region = 17 OR region = 25
```

This usability problem was solved by changing the Hybris interface and allowing several values as input for a constraint:

```
date BETWEEN 910401, 910430
AND region = 15, 17, 25
```

Another improvement is suggested by Kuntz and Melchert who use indentation to show the user the different levels of nesting in a complex restriction [14].

Another problem discovered during the second study was that users were confused when they had to link entities together that were not located in the same view. This taught us the importance of having a good design methodology for ER-based query systems. The different views shown in the system have to be designed together with users and with respect to the different tasks a user may have.

A third study was done by Hogedahl and Zakizadeh for a market and sales support system at Sweden Post. Their study showed that Hybris gave the users an increased understanding of the database contents [10]. The tool also made it easier to formulate spontaneous ad-hod queries and made the users less dependent on specialist support functions, such as controllers.

5. Conclusions and further work

The main contribution of this paper is to present experiences of using a visual ER query system within large organisations. As was mentioned in chapter 2 very little has been reported on real world applications of visual ER query system.

We have also presented the Hybris system and the design decisions taken when implementing the system. Especially the integrated dictionary browser is a novel approach to supporting users understanding of the database contents.

From our experiences with Hybris we are confident that visual ER query systems are a very promising approach for increasing usability of large corporate databases. Moreover, it is an approach that has shown to be applicable in real world environments. This should encourage further research in this area.

Some important issues are:

- Improved techniques for schema visualisation. Catarci et al have started work in this area by experimenting with *iconic* interfaces [5].

- Methodology for designing visual query applications.

- Security issues, such as whether access rights should be controlled at the database level or at the ER level.

- Tools for maintaining the query system once the database structure starts to change.

We also need to study a user's overall retrieval environment. So far research have considered ER-based retrieval from structured databases. However, as part of their work, users also need to retrieve information from other sources such as a text retrieval system, a picture archive or a hypertext system.

We should also adopt an organisational perspective on visual ER-query systems not only viewing them from a single-user perspective but study which support large organisations with many users with different levels of expertise and tasks need.

6. Acknowledgements

I acknowledge the invaluable work done by my colleagues in implementing Hybris. First of all I would like to thank Stefan Paulsson without whom Hybris would never had existed. Many thanks to Jesper Lundh who worked with the Macintosh version and Peeter Kool with the Windows version. Special thanks to Ulf Wingstedt, SISU, for his encouraging support and stimulating discussions on ER subjects. The original idea for Hybris came from Björn Nilsson, SISU. Special thanks to Bertil Andersson, Swedish Telecom, for his never ending support for this work.

Finally, many thanks to all Hybris users whose enthusiasm have been the main source of inspiration for this work.

This work has been sponsored by Swedish Telecom and Sweden Post.

7. References

1. A. Audinno, Y. Dennebouy, Y. Dupont, E. Fontana, S. Spaccapietra, Z. Tari. "Super: A comprehensive approach to DBMS Visual User Interfaces", Ecole Polytechnique Fédérale, Lausanne, Switzerland.

2. C. Batini, T. Catarci, M. F. Costabile, S. Levialdi, "Visual Strategies for Querying Databases", IEEE Workshop on Visual Languages, 1991, pp 183-189.

3. D. Bryce, R. Hull, "SNAP, a Graphics-Based Schema Manager", Proceedings of the 2:th IEEE International Conference on Data Engineering, pp 151-164, 1986.

4. T. Catarci, G. Santucci, "Query by Diagram: A Graphic Query System", Proceedings of the 7:th International Conference of Entity Relationship Approach, pp 157-174, 1988.

5. T. Catarci, A. Massari, G. Santucci, "Iconic and Diagrammatic Interfaces: An Integrated Approach", IEEE Workshop on Visual Languages, 1991, pp 199-204.

6. B. Czejdo, R. Elmasri, M. Rusinkiewicz, D. Embley, "A Graphical Data Manipulation Language for an Extended Entity-Relationship Model", IEEE Computer, March 1990

7. R. Elmasri, J. Larson, "A Graphical Query Facility for ER Databases", Proceedings of the 4:th International Conference of Entity Relationship Approach, 1985.

8. D. Fogg, "Lessons from a "Living in a Database" Graphical Query Interface", Proceedings ACM Sigmod, 1984.

9. D. Genter, L. Stevens, "Mental Models", Hillsdale, New Jersey, Lawrence Erlbaum Associates.

10. H. Hogedahl, H. Zakizadeh, "PimWin - en fallstudie vid Posten", TRIAD-rapport U3, 1993, SISU, Electrum 212, 164 40 Kista, Sweden.

11. U. Hohenstein, "Automatic Transformation of an Entity-Relationship Query Language into SQL", Proceedings of the 8:th International International Conference of Entity Relationship Approach, 1989.

12. K. Karlgren, M. Wideroth, "En utvärdering av Hybris", SISU Technical Report 12.

13. H. J. Kim, H. F. Korth, A. Silberschatz, "PICASSO: A Graphical Query Language", Software - Practice and Experience, March 1988.

14. M. Kuntz, R. Melchert, "Pasta-3´s Graphical Query Language: Direct Manipulation, Cooperative Queries, Full Expressive Power", Proceedings of the 15:th International Conference on Very Large Databases, 1989.

15. M. Kuntz, R. Melchert, "Ergonomic Schema Design and Browsing with more Semantics in the Pasta-3 Interface for E-R DBMSs", Proceedings of the 8:th International Conference of Entity Relationship Approach, 1989.

16. J. Larson, J. B Wallick, "An Interface for Novice and Infrequent Database Management System Users", AFIPS Conference Proceedings, National Computer Conference, 1984.

17. M. Leong, S. Sam, D. Narasimhalu, "Towards a Visual Language for an Object-Oriented Multi-Media Database System", Visual Database Systems, T. L. Kunii (editor), Elsevier Science Publishers B. V. (North-Holland), IFIP 1989.

18. T. R Rogers, R. G. G Cattell, "Entity-Relationship Database User Interfaces", Proceedings of the 6:th International Conference of Entity Relationship Approach, 1987.

19. C. Sahlin, "Erfarenheter från användning av Hybris. - Ett multimedia hjälpmedel för navigering i Televerkets PULS databas", Försvarets Forskningsanstalt, Linköping, Sweden, report 90-5991/S. In Swedish.

20. M. Schneider, C. Trepied, "A Graphical Query Language Based on an Extended E-R Model", Proceedings of the 8:th International Conference of Entity Relationship Approach, 1989.

21. G. H. Sockut, L. M. Burns, A. Malhotra, K.-Y. Whang, "Graqula: A graphical query language for entity-relationship or relational databases", pp 171-202, Data&Knowledge Engineering, vol 11, no 2, october 1993,

22. F. Staes, L. Tarantino, A. Times, "A Graphical Query Language for Object-Oriented Databases", IEEE Workshop on Visual Languages, 1991, pp 199-204.

23. H. Wong, I. Kuo, "GUIDE: Graphical User Interface for Database Exploration", Proceedings of the 8:th International Conference on Very Large Databases, 1982.

24. Z. Q Zhang, O. Mendelzon, "A graphical query language for entity-relationship databases", Entity-Relationship Approach to Software Engineering, pp 441-448, 1983.

Category Classes: Flexible Classification and Evolution in Object-Oriented Databases

Erik Odberg*

Department of Computer Science
Norwegian Institute of Technology

Abstract

Object-oriented databases (OODBs) are believed to more naturally reflect the behavior and organization of real world objects. However, OODBs are mostly concerned about only the *static* aspects of object modeling. While real world objects typically may be *multi-perspectived* and *evolve* over time by changing classification and behavior, contemporary OODB models typically regard objects as instances of classes in such a way that classification (and thus behavior) is fixed at the time of creation.

This paper introduces the notion of an object *role* to denote a particular *perspective* of an object, corresponding to a class for which it is an instance. Roles may be dynamically added and removed from objects to reflect the way real world objects classify and evolve over time, and simultaneously change behavior. A *category class* is a special class which is associated with a *predicate*, and in this way describe *constraints* on how objects may evolve, as well as how objects may *automatically* gain and discard roles based on various criteria.

1 Introduction and Motivation

Object-oriented data models (and consequently object-oriented databases (OODBs)) are believed to better and more naturally reflecting the behavior and organization of real world phenomena, incorporating more of the real world semantics. *Objects* separate externally visible behavior from internal representation and implementation. *Classes* abstract over commonalities between objects, defining *classifications* of objects. Class *hierarchies* impose an organization of classes describing a *conceptual specialization* (i.e. that instances of one class may also be regarded as instances of more general *superclasses*) and *inheritance* of properties (i.e. that instances of one class will also contain properties as defined for superclasses)[1].

However, most object models are only concerned about the *static* aspects of modeling, and not how objects may *evolve* over time. Objects are *created* as an instance of one class, which also serves to *classify* the object according to the predefined taxonomy, and to define its properties. Once created, objects *cannot* change classification or property possession. Naturally, this does not reflect very well the way the "real world" behaves: Real-world objects ("*phenomena*") may typically have *different* appearance (exhibited behavior) in different contexts of *expectation*, and may be perceived to *classify* differently (dependent on expectation). Phenomena are often highly *dynamic*, and *evolve* over time by *changing* classification and appearance.

The remaining part of this paper describes an *extension* to the traditional notion of object-orientation which naturally reflects the behavior of the "real world". Section 2 introduces the notion of an object *role* as a particular perspective of an object, and discusses how roles may be added to and removed from objects to allow objects to evolve. Section 3 defines a *category class* as a specialization of the

---

*Detailed address: Department of Computer Science, Norwegian Institute of Technology (NTH), N-7034 Trondheim-NTH, Norway. Phone: +47 73 594484. Fax: +47 73 594466. Email: eriko@idt.unit.no

[1]The *conceptual organization* and *property reuse* dimensions of subclassing reflect the *Scandinavian* and *American* school of OO thinking, respectively.

class construct which may define *restrictions* on or *enable* certain evolutions of objects. Section 4 compares the approach with related work, while Section 5 concludes the paper and presents directions for further work.

2   Objects with Roles

The fundamental object model is "traditional" in that it adopts C++ as the primary source of influence. *Objects* are created as instances of *classes*, which have an associated collection of *properties*. Properties may be *attributes* or *methods*, defined in a way which is similar to C++, and have a *visibility* which is either *public* (accessible by external clients of the object) or *private* (only accessible to method implementations for the class). The visibility is specified by keywords public and private, with public being default (in contrast to C++). A notion of *explicit relationships* is supported to provide symmetric associations (with cardinalities) between two classes, and with special functionality for navigating over these. A class may have one or more *superclasses* (defining the class as a *subclass* of these). The subclass *inherits* the properties of the superclasses (retaining the visibility mode[2]), and may define additional properties or *redefine* inherited ones. The subclass also defines a *specialization* relationship with its superclasses, and so that instances of one class are also instances of all superclasses (transitively). Note that a class Class is the implicit superclass of all classes for which no superclass is defined; in this way a schema will consist of *one* connected class hierarchy.

2.1   Object manipulation

Persistent objects are manipulated (created, modified, deleted) through a corresponding C++ *placeholder* object. Placeholder objects are instances of C++ *persistent classes*, which are generated from the schema specification. Each persistent C++ class directly corresponds to a schema class, having the same name and properties, and providing additional functionality for persistent manipulation. Placeholders are acquired from the database by *navigation* over database relationships, by *iteration* over a set of persistent objects (possibly acquired through an *associative query*), or as a result from a *method invocation*.

Objects created as instances of persistent classes will *not* automatically persist in the database. This must be explicitly requested by invocation of a function *MakePersist*, associated with each persistent class. In this way instances of persistent classes may be *both* persistent and non-persistent, but may smoothly interact within the same application process. Object modifications are also "committed" persistently by invocation of MakePersist.

2.2   Object roles

Each class an object may be regarded an instance of will be denoted a role of this object. Each object role reflects a particular *perspective* of the object, a context of behavior which may be referenced by clients. More important, roles (i.e. class memberships) reflect characteristics of objects which may be independently gained and lost: Objects may *evolve* over time by *changing* role possession (i.e. the classification and associated properties) dynamically. Some roles may reflect *specializations* of other roles (corresponding to superclasses), however an important characteristic of the model is the ability for objects to possess roles corresponding to *sibling* classes. Between two sibling classes there is neither a subclassing relationship, nor is there a common subclass of these classes. We say that objects may contain multiple *most-specific* roles, or that objects are *multi-perspective*. This is in contrast with traditional object-oriented models where each object is an instance of *one* class

---

[2]This is the same as *public* inheritance in C++.

which is decided upon creation, and all "roles" correspond to the creation class and its superclasses. There is no ability to have object evolve or assume additional most-specific roles.

The *creation* of an object will allocate a collection of roles (for all classes the object is an instance), and simultaneously assign a unique object identifier (OID) to the new object. New roles may be added, according to the class hierarchy, and in this way "*extending*" the object downwards. *No* new OID is assigned upon role addition, it is still the *same* object. Any role(s) may also be removed from the object (without deleting the object or affecting the OID), and which will also have the impact that all roles corresponding to *subclasses* of the denoted role class are removed as well. The strong notion of identity means that no object set may contain multiple occurrences of the same object, even if different roles are regarded. Furthermore, *two* operators for checking the identity of object references are provided: Two placeholders are *object identical* if they correspond to the same (persistent) object, while placeholders are *object-role identical* if they correspond to the same object *and* role.

Figure 1 illustrates an example class hierarchy.

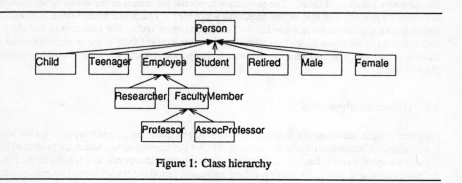

Figure 1: Class hierarchy

A *person*'s "life" is described by the way roles are gained and lost, possibly possessing many different (most-specific) roles simultaneously. Some roles may be automatically gained and lost (for instance Child and Teenager due to age), while some must be explicitly added (as for instance Student and Employee). Some roles are inherently incompatible, and may not be possessed at the same time (for instance Female and Male, or Retired and Employee). Other roles may be possessed simultaneously, as for instance a female teaching assistant which is an instance of Female, Employee and Student, and behaves in different ways in these three roles.

2.3 Object role manipulation

The introduction of the role notion have implications to the functionality provided for object manipulation.

2.3.1 Adding roles

New roles are added to persistent objects through the add operator, which is applicable to all placeholders:

```
Person *pers = ...;
Student *stud = pers add Student;
```

A role is always added as a *specialization* of some existing role, however may perfectly well be added as another *"branch"* of the object, and so that the object does not have to be an instance of a *single* most-specific class. For instance, the following example illustrates a *person* which is simultaneously also a *student* and an *employee*:

```
Employee *emp = stud add Employee;
```

It must be noted that there is *no* constraint on what is the class of the object which is the *basis* for the role addition: In principle *any* role may be added to any object, however Section 3 will show how restrictions may be imposed.

The add operator returns a pointer to a C++ placeholder object as an instance of the class corresponding to the added role. This means that the placeholders referenced by pers, stud and emp, which correspond to the *same* persistent object, need *not* be the same C++ objects[3]. Rather, they reference different *perspectives* of the same (persistent) object. Application programs must ensure, in order to avoid mutation conflicts, that objects are mutated through only *one* perspective (placeholder) at the time. That is, applications should preferably *synchronize* with the database (by invoking MakePersist) before the new role is added. The DBMS has no other means to ensure that multiple placeholders within the same process are maintained consistently wrt. mutations. Note that a role addition is not reflected persistently unless MakePersist is explicitly invoked.

If a role is added to an object which already *does* possess this role, the object is not affected by the addition. This means that an object may have only one role corresponding to each class. If a role is possessed by a persistent object, but not reflected by the actual placeholder, a *new* placeholder must be returned. This is because the result of the add operation is expected to be an instance of the added class. Consequently, for the following operation no new role is added, but another placeholder (which may be the same as for stud) is returned:

```
Student *stud2 = emp add Student;
```

It must be noted that some other approaches, notably Aspects [RS91] and Clovers [SZ89], allows for instantiating multiple roles of the *same* class. It is our position that this is *unnatural* modeling, and better reflected by the use of *relationships* between objects. Furthermore, there is an important problem wrt. *identification* of roles which reflect the same class.

A notion of a *role constructor* is provided for the initialization of new roles. Role constructors operate as ordinary constructors, but initialize *only* attributes directly associated (i.e. non-inherited) with the class of the role to be added. Zero or more role constructors may be associated with each class. If there is *no* visible role constructor defined for a particular class, this means that the class may *not* be added as a role to any existing object[4]:

```
enum {male, female} Sex;

class Person{
  char *name;
  enum Sex sex;
  int age;
  Person(char*, enum Sex, int);};

class Employee : Person {
  char *company;
  Employee(char*, char*, enum Sex, int);    // Ordinary constructor
  $Employee(char*);}                         // Role constructor
```

Similar to for object creation, role addition will thus take arguments as indicated by the role constructor:

```
Person *pers = new person(''Donald Duck'', male, 60);
Employee *emp = pers add employee (''Walt Disney Corp.'');
```

---

[3] In fact, in this case they *cannot* be, as it is not possible to have one C++ object be an instance of both Student and Employee, as there is no common subclass for these classes.
[4] As for ordinary C++ constructors, if *no* role constructor is explicitly specified, a non-argument role constructor will by default be available.

A role is always added as a *specialization* of some existing role, however may perfectly well be added as another "*branch*" of the object, and so that the object does not have to be an instance of a *single* most-specific class. For instance, the following example illustrates a *person* which is simultaneously also a *student* and an *employee*:

```
Employee *emp = stud add Employee;
```

It must be noted that there is *no* constraint on what is the class of the object which is the *basis* for the role addition: In principle *any* role may be added to any object, however Section 3 will show how restrictions may be imposed.

The add operator returns a pointer to a C++ placeholder object as an instance of the class corresponding to the added role. This means that the placeholders referenced by pers, stud and emp, which correspond to the *same* persistent object, need *not* be the same C++ objects[3]. Rather, they reference different *perspectives* of the same (persistent) object. Application programs must ensure, in order to avoid mutation conflicts, that objects are mutated through only *one* perspective (placeholder) at the time. That is, applications should preferably *synchronize* with the database (by invoking MakePersist) before the new role is added. The DBMS has no other means to ensure that multiple placeholders within the same process are maintained consistently wrt. mutations. Note that a role addition is not reflected persistently unless MakePersist is explicitly invoked.

If a role is added to an object which already *does* possess this role, the object is not affected by the addition. This means that an object may have only one role corresponding to each class. If a role is possessed by a persistent object, but not reflected by the actual placeholder, a *new* placeholder must be returned. This is because the result of the add operation is expected to be an instance of the added class. Consequently, for the following operation no new role is added, but another placeholder (which may be the same as for stud) is returned:

```
Student *stud2 = emp add Student;
```

It must be noted that some other approaches, notably Aspects [RS91] and Clovers [SZ89], allows for instantiating multiple roles of the *same* class. It is our position that this is *unnatural* modeling, and better reflected by the use of *relationships* between objects. Furthermore, there is an important problem wrt. *identification* of roles which reflect the same class.

A notion of a *role constructor* is provided for the initialization of new roles. Role constructors operate as ordinary constructors, but initialize *only* attributes directly associated (i.e. non-inherited) with the class of the role to be added. Zero or more role constructors may be associated with each class. If there is *no* visible role constructor defined for a particular class, this means that the class may *not* be added as a role to any existing object[4]:

```
enum {male, female} Sex;

class Person{
  char *name;
  enum Sex sex;
  int age;
  Person(char*, enum Sex, int);};

class Employee : Person {
  char *company;
  Employee(char*, char*, enum Sex, int);    // Ordinary constructor
  $Employee(char*);}                          // Role constructor
```

Similar to for object creation, role addition will thus take arguments as indicated by the role constructor:

```
Person *pers = new person(''Donald Duck'', male, 60);
Employee *emp = pers add employee (''Walt Disney Corp.'');
```

---

[3] In fact, in this case they *cannot* be, as it is not possible to have one C++ object be an instance of both Student and Employee, as there is no common subclass for these classes.

[4] As for ordinary C++ constructors, if *no* role constructor is explicitly specified, a non-argument role constructor will by default be available.

2.3.2 Removing roles

Roles may also be *removed* from objects, using the rem operator:

```
Employee *emp = ...;
Person *pers = emp rem Employee;
```

The rem operator removes the role corresponding to the indicated class from the object (provided it is contained), as well as all contained roles corresponding to subclasses. A pointer to the same object as an instance of the immediate *superclass* of the removed class is returned[5]. In general, this means that *another* placeholder (another C++ pointer) will be returned. MakePersist must be invoked to have the role removal to be persistently reflected. Note that it is possible to remove a role from an object even if the *placeholder* is not an instance of the corresponding persistent class, as long as the role is possessed persistently:

```
Employee *emp = ...;
Person *pers = emp rem Student;
```

A notion of a *role destructor* is provided, similarly to ordinary destructors, to "clean up" data structures when some role is removed from an object. More interestingly, if there is *no* public role destructor associated with a class, the corresponding role may not be removed from the object by any application program.

2.3.3 Reference coercion

Object references may be *coerced* to another class, in the same way as in C++. In this way the same (persistent) object may be inspected through another role and thus exhibiting itself differently. Coercions may be performed *upwards* (to a superclass, and thus restrict the set of available properties and/or change bindings for properties overridden by subclasses), *downwards* (to a subclass, and thus assuming *additional* properties), or to a *sibling* class (a class which is neither a superclass or subclass, and thus may provide a completely different set of properties). The following are some natural coercions which may originate using the class hierarchy of Figure 1:

```
Employee *emp = ...;
Person *pers = (Person*)emp;        // Upwards coercion
Professor *prof = (Professor*)emp;  // Downwards coercion
Student *stud = (Student*)emp;      // Sibling coercion
```

The coercion will return a pointer to a C++ placeholder object which is generally *different* from the original, as they reflect the same object as an instance of *different* persistent classes. Note that if the object does not *have* the role corresponding to the coercion, an exception will be raised (and the return pointer is invalid). Naturally, this may only be checked at runtime.

2.3.4 Placeholder construction

When a placeholder is constructed to reflect a persistent counterpart, it will normally be created as an instance of the persistent class corresponding to the most-specific class of the persistent object (rather than the class of the *reference*). However, according to the model of roles an object may have *multiple* most-specific classes. This cannot be expressed within C++, and thus the placeholder objects (reflecting references to persistent objects) must be created as instances of a *unique* persistent class. Different possibilities exist to decide about this class: It may the same as the class of the *reference*, but this will not work correctly in the presence of virtual functions. Rather, an object should be returned as an instance of *some* most-specific class for which the persistent object is an

---

[5] If the removed class have *multiple* immediate superclasses, the rem operator will return a pointer to an instance of the class which is the most-specific (unique) common superclass of these classes.

instance. This most-specific class may be selected arbitrarily by the system, or there may be some priority based on for instance which role was first (or last) added. Another possibility is to have application programs denote the class of the placeholder object by explicit coercion.

Virtual method invocations are bound to implementation *dynamically* (late binding), on the basis of the class of the *object* rather than the *reference* to the object. As there need not *be* a unique most-specific class of the (persistent) object, virtual binding will be based on the *placeholder* object, in this way taking advantage of C++ runtime provisions. This means that virtual binding is dependent on the strategy for placeholder object construction. Indeed, virtual binding is an *inherent* problem of the model, given the traditional interpretation. A more "natural" solution, may be to have virtual method implementations take into consideration which *subclasses* the (persistent) object is an instance of, and perform a computation based on this knowledge. In this way special *"combination methods"* may be implemented in terms of methods of multiple most-specific classes, or possibly explicitly *selecting* between these.

3   Category Classes

A **category class** is a specialization of the class construct with special abilities to *restrict* or *enable* object membership in the class through the association with a *predicate*. For *ordinary* classes, there are *no* restrictions on object creation and deletion, or role addition and removal, apart from the possible inhibition described by invisible (role) constructors or destructors. Fundamentally, any role may be added (explicitly) to any object, and any role possessed may be removed. Membership in category classes, however, depends on satisfaction of the category class predicate. For a *manual* category class, the explicit addition of the corresponding role to some object will only succeed if the predicate is satisfied at the time of addition. An *automatic* category class is different in that satisfaction of the predicate will *automatically* make the role be added to the object, however it will be *lost* if the predicate is later dis-satisfied.

In most respects category classes are similar to ordinary classes. They are organized in the same class hierarchy, and thus define *inheritance* and *substitutability* relationships with superclasses. Category classes associate with *properties* as ordinary classes, and object variables may reference instances of category classes (through the placeholder) just like instances of other classes. Category classes and ordinary classes are different variations of the *same* abstraction mechanism, with an additional ability for category classes to *restrict* or *enable* membership in powerful ways[6]. Category classes express special knowledge about phenomena evolution and classification in the domain of discourse, making the schema able to include *more* aspects of real-world semantics.

3.1   Category class definition

The general syntax of a category class definition goes as follows:

```
class catclass [:<superclasses>] [ WHEN <predicate> [ON <candclass>] ]
                       [ AND|OR]  [ IF    <predicate> [ON <candclass>] ]
       {
         // class properties
       };
```

A category class (catclass) may have one or more *superclasses*, which may be ordinary or category classes. *Manual category classes* are defined by an IF expression, for which <predicate> describes a restriction to be satisfied to permit the explicit addition (using the add operator) of the corresponding role to some object. *Automatic category classes* are defined by a WHEN expression, for which <predicate> defines the criterion for the corresponding role *automatically* to be added to some object. IF and WHEN expressions may also be *combined* (using logical operators AND or OR), as will be explained below.

---

[6] An ordinary class may thus be regarded as a manual category class with an empty (i.e. *True*) predicate.

Candidate classes

ON expressions define the *candidate class* of the particular category class. Only objects which possess the corresponding role (is an instance of the candidate class) are valid candidates for membership in the category class. Furthermore, category class predicates may only reference properties defined for the candidate class (or superclasses of this). The specification of a candidate class is optional; if *no* candidate class is defined, the immediate superclass of the category class will apply by default. If the category class has *multiple* superclasses, the lowest common superclass will be the effective candidate class. Most often, the candidate class is a *superclass* of the category class, and so that membership in the category class will reflect a *specialization* of the candidate class role. A candidate class may also be a *sibling* class of the category class, and so that a corresponding role addition may add an additional most-specific role of the object. A candidate class which is a *subclass* of the category class is meaningless.

Predicates

Category class predicates may reference *two* aspects of objects; the *properties* defined for the candidate class, and the *role possession* of the object. Both public and private attributes may be referenced as part of the predicate specification. While *clients* of objects may only access the *public* part of class definitions, category class predicates are regarded a part of the *definition* of the class and thus may reference internal representation as well. *Method-based* predicates are permitted, but must be used with care as method invocations may have undesirable *side-effects* (Cfr. for instance [Odb92]). Moreover, automatic category class predicates are (at least conceptually) *continuously* evaluated for all candidate objects, which means that side-affect methods may have arbitrary affects on objects.

Property-based predicates are specified using ordinary C++ comparison operators and boolean operators && (*and*), || (*or*) and ! (*not*), referencing the state of objects as well as *constant* values. Predicates are *evaluated* in the context of objects which are instances of the candidate class, with predicate attributes bound to the particular object. *Role-based* predicates specify requirements on the object possession of roles. Role possession is denoted through the *name* of the class, and using C++ boolean operators any predicate over role possession may be defined to *constrain* (for manual) or *enable* (for automatic) membership in the category class. Attribute- and role-based expressions may also be *combined* in the same predicate. Examples of the different kinds of predicates are shown below.

3.2 Manual category classes

Manual category classes are defined through an IF expression, giving a predicate which must satisfied to permit the explicit addition of the corresponding role to an object (which must also possess the role corresponding to the candidate class). Furthermore, for all *superclasses* of the category class, the object must either already possess the corresponding role (be a member), or addition must be permitted (i.e. predicates possibly associated must be satisfied). This means that *multiple* roles may be added in one go. If for some reason role addition is not permitted, the operation fails and an error code is set. If addition succeeds, the role is contained until the object is deleted, the role is explicitly removed, or some automatic superclass predicate is no longer satisfied (Cfr. below). However, there is no requirement that *manual* category class predicates are satisfied *after* a successful addition.

Manual category classes are most commonly used to define *constraints* on object evolution, and thus implicitly define valid patterns of migration. Addition of a particular role to some object requires that it fulfills certain characteristics in terms of state and/or that it does/does not already possess a certain combination of roles. Manual category classes generally associate with additional properties, so that new attributes are typically initialized by a role constructor.

For instance no *person* may become a *student* if not old enough:

```
class Student : Person IF age >= 17 ON Person {
    ...);
```

This predicate is attribute-based, but manual category class predicates may also be based on the possession of roles. For instance, all full or associate *professors* may be a *PhD promoter* (however does not have to), while other *faculty members* may not:

```
class PhDPromoter : FacultyMember IF Professor || AssocProfessor
    ... );
```

Note that PhDPromoter is neither a subclass nor superclass of Professor or AssocProfessor.

Manual category classes may also be defined on the basis of predicates referencing *both* attributes and role possession. For instance, to qualify for professorship you must have earned a PhD degree and have more than 25 publications, or have been employed at the university (as a *faculty member*) more than 30 years:

```
class PhD : Person { ... };

class Employee : Person {
    ...
    int employed_years;};

class Professor: FacultyMember IF (PhD && publications > 25) ||
                                   employed_years > 30 {
    ... );
```

Note that, as Professor is a *manual* category class, promotion is not guaranteed even if the predicate is satisfied[7].

3.3 Automatic category classes

Automatic category classes are defined by WHEN expressions, which define a criterion for objects to *automatically* assume the role corresponding to the category class. Logically, all objects which possess the candidate class role (i.e. is an instance of the candidate class) are (at least *conceptually*) *continuously* evaluated for possible predicate satisfaction. If the predicate is satisfied, and roles corresponding to superclasses either *are* possessed, or addition is permitted, the category class role (and possibly "missing" superclass roles) are assumed by the object. If at some time the predicate for the class, or for some automatic category superclass, is no longer satisfied the role will become *invisible*. The same applies if the candidate class role is lost. However, if the role possession is later re-enabled the *same* role (with the same state) will *reappear*; the role is *not* persistently removed. The same also applies for any *subclasses* of the automatic category class as well: Upon dis-satisfaction of an automatic category superclass predicate subclass roles will become invisible (superclass membership is a prerequisite for membership in subclasses), but will *reappear* upon predicate re-satisfaction. Note that, in contrast, for *manual* category classes predicates are *only* evaluated upon role addition, and upon role removal all roles (including for subclasses) are persistently removed.

In some cases, an object may satisfy the predicate of *multiple* automatic category classes, although membership in these may be *mutually exclusive*. In this case predicates will be *conflicting*, and membership in either may prohibit membership in others. The system will make an arbitrary choice of class membership in these cases. Note that the system is not able to detect that such a situation may possibly arise, and thus no warning may be given at schema definition time.

While any (category) class may associate with both methods and attributes, automatic category classes often tend *not* to add attributes in addition to those inherited from superclasses. The reason is that automatic category class roles are *implicitly* added, and thus only non-argument role constructors may

---

[7]Which means promotion should probably not be expected for just waiting passively for 30 years ...

be invoked for the initialization of the role. More commonly, however, automatic category classes define new *methods*, or redefine inherited ones. In this way special behavior may be associated with objects as a member of automatic category classes, and for which the association is dependent on predicate satisfaction. Automatic category classes are mostly concerned about the *membership* (extent) dimension and for which flexible specification is possible. This also reflects the typical *use* of automatic category classes, described below.

3.3.1 Using automatic category classes

Automatic category classes may be used in different ways. Typically they are used to describe one or more *partitions* of a superclass based on values for attributes of the superclass, and so that each partition class contain a *subset* of the objects in the superclass. Partition classes may be *disjoint* or *overlapping*, and may be *complete* or *non-complete* partitions. Specification of completeness and disjointness is left to the schema designer, and is dependent on the ability to define predicates which reflect the semantics of the partition. The following examples specify partition classes for Person, inherently constituting a complete and disjoint partition of Person.

```
class Child : Person WHEN age < 13 {
... };

class Teenager : Person WHEN 13 <= age < 20 {
... };

class Adult : Person WHEN  age >= 20 {
... };
```

Adding the following means that the partition is (potentially) no longer disjoint:

```
class Retired : Person WHEN age >= 67  {
... };
```

Adding the following implies there will be *multiple* partitions of Person:

```
class Male   : Person WHEN sex = male { ... };
class Female : Person WHEN sex = female { ... };
```

Automatic category classes may also be applied to define various *propagations* of class membership, on the basis of different criteria. These category classes are typically defined by *role-based* predicates, and so that possession of a special combination of roles implies automatic assumption of another role. Consider the following example:

```
class GroupLeader : Employee WHEN Professor {
... };
```

As a general rule, every *full professor* is entitled to her own group, in which the *professor* automatically becomes the *group leader*. However, the class GroupLeader is *not* a specialization of Professor: The fact that all *group leaders* are *professors* (and vice versa) is just another *role* that inherently is played by *professors*. GroupLeader and Professor are *sibling* classes in the class hierarchy; both are subclasses of Employee.

More complex propagation specifications may be defined using C++ logical operators, e.g. to define new classes as *intersections*, *unions* or *differences* between others. Due to the notion of object roles there is *no* special restrictions wrt. the placement of such classes in hierarchy[8]. For instance, a *temporary employee* is any *employee* which is not a *faculty member* or a *technical/administrative person*:

---

[8]COCOON [SS91], for instance, requires that an intersection class is a subclass and a union class a superclass of the base classes.

```
class TempEmployee : Employee WHEN !(FacultyMember || TechnAdm);
```

Property and role-based predicates may be *combined*, and so that membership in the category class is based on *both* property evaluation and role possession. This may be convenient to model *conditional* propagation. For instance, a *researcher* is automatically promoted to a *senior researcher* after ten years of employment, provided she has a *PhD* degree:

```
class Researcher : Employee { ... };

class SeniorResearcher : Researcher WHEN employed_years > 10 && PhD {
    ...};
```

Two-way propagation is useful when two classes, which are *sibling* classes, should contain the *same* objects[9]. For instance, for the *employees* at some university, all *lecturers* are *faculty members*, and vice versa:

```
class Lecturer : Employee WHEN FacultyMember OR IF ... {
    ... };

class FacultyMember : Employee WHEN Lecturer OR IF ... {
    ... };
```

Lecturer and FacultyMember are *sibling* classes in the class hierarchy, so that any *person* possessing either of these roles will also (automatically) possess the other (and generally behave in different ways in the different roles). The definition of classes Lecturer and FacultyMember also includes an IF expression, ensuring that roles corresponding to these classes may be *explicitly* added as well; otherwise there will be *no* way for any object to become a *lecturer* or *faculty member*. The combination of manual and automatic predicate expressions is elaborated upon in the next section.

3.4 Manual and automatic category classes

Category classes which are *both* manual and automatic may have membership criteria defined by a *conjunction* (AND) or *disjunction* (OR) between IF and WHEN expressions (associated with the same or different candidate classes[10]):

```
class class2 : class1 WHEN pred1 ON classX AND IF pred2 ON classY {
    ... };

class class3 : class1 WHEN pred3 ON classX OR IF pred4 ON classY {
    ... };
```

class2 is defined by *conjunction*, and the corresponding role may be assumed by an object upon *explicit* addition only, and only in the case that *both* predicates pred1 and pred2 (defined on the candidate class classX and classY, respectively) are satisfied. The role will be removed from the object by *explicit* request (using the rem operator, and irrespective of predicate evaluation), or *implicitly* if pred1 is no longer satisfied. In the latter case the role may *reappear* upon possible re-satisfaction of the predicate.

Conjunction-based category classes are most interesting in cases where the role must be *explicitly* added, although may also be *automatically* lost. For instance, only *persons* which are older than eighteen may become an *employee* (assuming this is the law for some particular work). When an *employee* retires, the *employee* role is automatically lost.

```
class Employee : Person WHEN !Retired AND IF age >= 18 {
    ... };
```

---

[9] If one class is a *subclass* of the other, propagation into the superclass will be *implicit* due to substitutability.
[10] Most frequently they associate with the same.

This is one example on the modeling of a *transition* for which the assumption of one role necessarily implies that some other (which does not reflect a superclass) must be lost. Another examples models how an *associate professor* role is revoked when promoted to a *full professor* (Professor is not a subclass of AssocProfessor):

```
class AssocProfessor WHEN !Professor AND IF True {
    ... };
```

class3 is defined by *disjunction*, and the corresponding role is added to some object *either* implicitly by the satisfaction of predicate pred3 *or* upon explicit request (provided that predicate pred4 is satisfied). *Removal* of the role from the object is dependent on the way it was added. If the role has been implicitly added (through the satisfaction of pred3) and pred3 is no longer satisfied, the role is removed from the object. If role removal is explicitly requested, the role is removed unless pred3 is satisfied. Note that it is impossible to remove explicitly a role which have been implicitly added. Furthermore, implicitly removed roles may *reappear* upon some future re-satisfaction of the pred3 predicate.

An example of a disjunction-based manual and automatic category class is the class Retired used above. In Norway, a *person* generally retires at 67, but may continue working until 70 when she *must* retire[11]:

```
class Retired : Person WHEN age >= 70 OR IF age >= 67 {
    ... };
```

3.5 Disjoint Predicates

In many cases we find that there are natural restrictions on role possession, and which are, using category classes, directly associated with each class. However, frequently we find that the restriction is more naturally associated with a complete *collection* of classes, and so that possession of a role corresponding to either of these *inhibits* the possession of others from the same collection. For instance, possession of roles corresponding to classes Child, Employee, Retired and Dead is inherently disjoint, and may be specified as follows[12]:

```
class Child : Person IF !(Employee || Retired || Dead) { ... };
class Employee : Person IF !(Child || Retired || Dead) { ... };
class Retired : Person IF !(Child || Employee || Dead) { ... };
class Dead : Person IF !(Child || Employee || Retired) { ... };
```

As a *simplified* specification of this relationship between classes, the notion of a *disjoint predicate* is introduced. Disjoint predicates specify that no object may be a member of more than *one* class in a specified collection at the same time. If an object already is an instance of *one* of the indicated classes (or a subclass of this class), it is *not* possible to add (explicitly or implicitly) any of the other classes, unless the former class is eventually removed from the object. Using disjoint predicates, the definitions above may be rewritten as:

```
disjoint(Child, Employee, Retired, Dead);
```

Disjoint predicates may range over *both* manual and automatic category classes, but most frequently apply for manual category classes as they define inherent *restrictions* on object evolution and role combination. Automatic category classes are *enabling* in nature, and thus definitions easily may *conflict* with disjoint predicates[13]. Furthermore, disjoint predicates are solely *role based*, and thus cannot reference properties of classes participating in the predicate. Disjoint predicates represent a convenient shorthand specification mechanism, however may always be rewritten in terms of equivalent restrictions directly associated with the classes involved.

---

[11] In reality, rules for retirement are more complex.
[12] Other restrictions may also be associated with these category classes, but are left out here for brevity.
[13] The class Child above may, however, typically be an automatic category class.

4 Comparison

The notion of an object role is not new, and various approaches to providing more support for multi-perspectived objects and flexible object evolution have been described i literature. In most traditional object models a multi-perspectived nature of objects may only be described through *multiple inheritance*, defining special "*intersection classes*". However, these classes are *constructed* abstractions which need not reflect any natural abstraction from the real world. Furthermore, a *single* behavioral context is imposed, when multiple independent contexts are more natural, and there is a possibility for a *combinatorial explosion* of intersection classes to model all possible combinations. McAllester [MZ86] introduce a notion of *boolean classes* to alleviate this problem. Clovers [SZ89] is particularly concerned about the ability for objects to possess multiple independent perspectives, how these may be added, and how they are independently referenced. However, while new roles (or leaves in the "*clover*") may be added, they cannot be removed. Consequently, Clovers may hardly be regarded to properly support evolving objects. OORASS [RAB+92] is more concerned about the role as the fundamental concept, describing patterns of communication between roles and how instances of different types may play one role.

Other approaches are more concerned about the flexible classification of objects through predicate (over object state) satisfaction. In this way objects may implicitly evolve, on the basis of *intensional* descriptions. Many approaches to OODB *views* have been proposed, for which objects may assume membership in *virtual* classes based on the satisfaction of a *selection* predicate. However, virtual (view) classes often cannot be managed in the same way as ordinary classes. COCOON [SS91] is one example, and will be described below. ECR [EWH85] provides flexible capabilities to define how instances of a class may be specialized into subclasses, and how these may define disjoint/non-disjoint and complete/non-complete partitions of a superclass. [Cha93] presents a notion of *predicate classes*, which are similar to ordinary classes, but membership may only be assumed automatically by predicate satisfaction. Special restrictions on class membership combination may be imposed[14]. Predicate classes are similar to our automatic category classes, however are mostly concerned about the possibility for state-specific object *specializations* for dispatching purposes (and assumption of additional attributes).

Some approaches are concerned about object evolution on explicit (*extensional*) request. Aspects [RS91] allows for arbitrary addition and removal of special "*aspects*" (chunks of state and behavior) to existing objects. Multiple aspects may be added to objects, which thus may behave in a multi-perspectived manner. The aspect definition is regarded as an *extension* to some ordinary class, but will *not* inherit strictly from this class. This means that aspects do *not* integrate properly with the ordinary class hierarchy, with the possible implication that an *employee* aspect addition to a *person* may no longer be acceptable as a *person*. Iris [FBC+87] also allows for arbitrary addition and removal of types dynamically, however there is only *one* context of behavior, and thus no notion of role. [Zdo90] allows for roles to be added and removed, providing special abilities to specify that some roles are *not* removable ("essential type"), and that some roles may only be acquired upon creation ("exclusionary type"). Based on these, other restrictions on evolution may be specified, although in an awkward and unnatural way. [Ara89] defines *conversions* (change class) and *enhancements* (add class) to objects through special functions associated with the source class of the migration, and which define *all* valid migration patterns of objects.

Finally, [Vel93, SS91] provide abilities for *both* implicit and explicit evolution (classification) of objects. [Vel93] allows object to be specialized/generalized (to a subclass/superclass) upon the occurrence of an *event* (a method invocation), provided that an associated *assertion* is satisfied. As both these are *optional*, a transition may be completely *implicit* (no event), or *explicit* (no assertion). *Life cycles* (sequences of valid event occurrences) may be defined to *restrict* valid patterns of evolution. To model the fact that instances of *different* classes may play the same role, a transition to one class may originate from *different* source classes. However, in this way the destination class (denoted a *phase*) will behave *differently* from ordinary classes wrt. inheritance and

---

[14]These restrictions are motivated by the need to ensure that some objects may *not* be a member of multiple, most-specific classes when a binding conflict may occur.

substitutability. That is, the notion of a phase is a (partially) *different* abstraction mechanism from the class. COCOON [SS91, SLT91] describes an OODB *view* mechanism which distinguishes type (interface) and class (collection of objects with the same type). These are organized in different (but often correlating) hierarchies for property inheritance and subsetting, respectively. *Classes* may be associated with a *predicate* (over the state), stating *necessary* (corresponding to our *manual*) or *necessary and sufficient* (corresponding to our *automatic*, and reflecting a select query) conditions on membership. In this way objects may dynamically evolve (by gaining/losing class membership) implicitly or upon explicit request, which may also imply the assumption of more type. However, these types are *virtual* (i.e. *derived* from other types), and thus objects *cannot* assume new state. COCOON also provides special set-theoretic operators for the definition of view classes, with special rules for how these are to be placed in the class hierarchy). No arbitrary *propagation* of membership into *sibling* classes are, however, possible. Furthermore, no *combination* of manual and automatic specifications (which was found to be very useful in Section 3.4) may be given. COCOON is primarily a *view* approach, and thus more concerned about how virtual classes and types are to be located in the class/type hierarchies, and how they map onto base classes/types.

5 Conclusions, Contributions and Further Work

A notion of an *object role*, describing a perspective of an object as an instance of a particular class, has been presented. Roles may dynamically be added or removed from objects, according to how real-world objects evolve and exhibit themselves through multiple perspectives. *Category classes* describe *constraints* on valid evolution patterns and combination of roles, as well as defining how the possession of a role may be automatically *enabled*. Finally, category classes constitute a powerful vehicle for *conceptual modeling*, with flexible means for object classification. While the model has been presented in a *database* context, the important aspects have more general applicability as a powerful *modeling* framework or part of a programming language.

The major contributions of the approach relate to the way *flexible classification*, *object evolution* and the *multi-perspectived nature* of objects are smoothly integrated within an object model based on C++. This is achieved by *retaining* the same abstraction mechanism (the class) as the basis for classification and addition/removal of roles. In this way the importance of the class hierarchy as an organization of real-world knowledge (conceptual specialization and property inheritance) is not affected by the added modeling power. The approach *integrates* multiple classification mechanisms: *Class-based* classification is defined by ordinary classes, and *set-based* classification may be defined *extensionally* (by manual category classes) and *intensionally* (by automatic category classes). Membership in different classes may be regarded *independently*, as different *perspectives* of the same object. A particularly useful provision is the ability to *propagate* objects (possibly conditionally) into other classes, i.e. acquiring new roles on the basis of some particular (combination of) role(s) possessed. The approach allows objects to *evolve* over time with special facilities to *restrict* and *enable* object evolution based on *both* the state and role possession of the object. In this way objects may explicitly and implicitly gain and lose roles and properties dynamically, *without* compromising the class hierarchy as the conceptual organization of real-world knowledge.

A prototype OODB, incorporating the notions of object role and category classes, is being implemented to demonstrate the applicability of the ideas. Preliminary results are promising. However, the primary focus of our work is within the area of *schema versioning*, and how different schema versions may contain different versions of the same class. [Odb94] will show how the evolutionary and multi-perspectived nature of *objects* have many traits which are similar to the evolutionary and multi-perspectived nature of *classes*, and how many principles of management are the same.

Acknowledgments   Svein Erik Bratsberg and Reidar Conradi are acknowledged for comments and discussions.

References

[Ara89]   Constantin Arapis. Type Conversion and Enhancement in Object-Oriented Systems. In *D. Tsichritzis: Object Oriented Development*, pages 191–205. Centre Universitaire d'Informatique, Université de Genève, July 1989.

[Cha93]   Craig Chambers. Predicate Classes. In *ECOOP '93. European Conference on Object-Oriented Programming, Kaiserslautern, Germany*, July 1993.

[EWH85]   R. Elmasri, J. Weeldreyer, and A. Hevner. The Category Concept: An Extension to the Entity-Relationship Model. *International Journal of Data & Knowledge Engineering*, 1, May 1985.

[FBC+87] D.H. Fishman, D. Beech, H.P. Cate, E.C. Chow, T. Conners, J.W. Davis, N. Derrett, C.G. Hoch, W. Kent, P. Lyngbaek, B. Mahbod, M.A. Neimat, T.A. Ryan, and M.C. Shan. Iris: An Object-oriented Database Management System. *ACM Transactions on Database Systems*, January 1987. Also in [ZM90].

[MZ86]   David McAllester and Ramin Zabih. Boolean Classes. In *Proceedings of the Conference on Object-Oriented Systems, Languages and Applications (OOPSLA), Portland, Oregon, USA*, pages 417–423, September 1986.

[Odb92]   Erik Odberg. What "What" is and isn't: On Query Languages for Object-Oriented Databases. Or: Closing the Gap - Again. In *TOOLS USA '92 (Technology of Object-Oriented Languages and Systems), Santa Barbara, California, USA*, August 1992.

[Odb94]   Erik Odberg. *MultiPerspectives: Object Evolution and Schema Modification Management in Object-Oriented Databases*. PhD thesis, Department of Computer Science, Norwegian Institute of Technology, 1994. In preparation.

[RAB+92] Trygve Reenskaug, Egil P. Andersen, Arne Jørgen Berre, Anne Hurlen, Anton Landmark, Odd Arild Lehne, Else Nordhagen, Eirik Næss-Ulseth, Gro Oftedal, Anne Lise Skaar, and Pål Stenslet. OORASS: Seamless Support for the Creation and Maintenance of Object-Oriented Systems. *Journal of Object-Oriented Programming*, 5(6):27–41, October 1992.

[RS91]   Joel Richardson and Peter Schwarz. Aspects: Extending Objects to Support Multiple, Independent Roles. In *Proceedings of ACM/SIGMOD (Management of Data), Denver, Colorado*, pages 298–307, 1991.

[SLT91]   Marc H. Scholl, Christian Laasch, and Markus Tresch. Updatable Views in Object-Oriented Databases. In *Proceedings of the Second International Conference on Deductive and Object-Oriented Databases (DOOD91), Munich, Germany, December 16-18, 1991*, pages 189–207, December 1991.

[SS91]   Marc H. Scholl and H.-J. Schek. Supporting Views in Object-Oriented Databases. *IEEE Data Engineering Bulletin*, 14(2), June 1991.

[SZ89]   Lynn Andrea Stein and Stan Zdonik. Clovers: The Dynamic Behavior of Types and Instances. Technical report, Brown University, Department of Computer Science, November 1989. Technical Report No. CS-89-42.

[Vel93]   Amandio de Jesus C. Vaz Velho. From Entity-Relationship Models to Role-Attribute Models. In *Proceedings of the 12th International Conference on the Entity-Relationship Approach, Arlington, Texas*, December 1993.

[Zdo90]   Stanley B. Zdonik. Object-Oriented Type Evolution. In *François Bancilhon and Peter Buneman (Eds.): Advances in Database Programming Languages*, chapter 16, pages 277–288. Addison-Wesley, 1990.

[ZM90]   Stanley B. Zdonik and David Maier, editors. *Readings in Object-Oriented Database Systems*. The Morgan Kaufman series in Data Management Systems. Morgan Kaufman, 1990. ISBN 0-55860-000-0. ISSN 1046-1698.

Springer-Verlag
and the Environment

We at Springer-Verlag firmly believe that an international science publisher has a special obligation to the environment, and our corporate policies consistently reflect this conviction.

We also expect our business partners – paper mills, printers, packaging manufacturers, etc. – to commit themselves to using environmentally friendly materials and production processes.

The paper in this book is made from low- or no-chlorine pulp and is acid free, in conformance with international standards for paper permanency.

Lecture Notes in Computer Science

For information about Vols. 1–735
please contact your bookseller or Springer-Verlag